W9-CTG-370

Windows Millennium Edition:
The Complete Reference

John R. Levine, Margaret Levine Young,
Doug Muder, Alison Barrows, and Rima Regas

Osborne/**McGraw-Hill**

Berkeley   New York   St. Louis   San Francisco
Auckland   Bogotá   Hamburg   London   Madrid
Mexico City   Milan   Montreal   New Delhi   Panama City
Paris   São Paulo   Singapore   Sydney
Tokyo   Toronto

Osborne/**McGraw-Hill**
2600 Tenth Street
Berkeley, California 94710
U.S.A.

For information on translations or book distributors outside the U.S.A., or to arrange bulk purchase discounts for sales promotions, premiums, or fund-raisers, please contact Osborne/**McGraw-Hill** at the above address.

Windows Millennium Edition: The Complete Reference

Copyright © 2001 by The McGraw-Hill Companies. All rights reserved. Printed in the United States of America. Except as permitted under the Copyright Act of 1976, no part of this publication may be reproduced or distributed in any form or by any means, or stored in a database or retrieval system, without the prior written permission of the publisher, with the exception that the program listings may be entered, stored, and executed in a computer system, but they may not be reproduced for publication.

1234567890 CUS CUS 01987654321

Book p/n 0-07-212750-3 and CD p/n 0-07-212749-X
parts of
ISBN 0-07-212751-1

Publisher
Brandon A. Nordin

Vice President & Associate Publisher
Scott Rogers

Acquisitions Editor
Megg Bonar

Project Editors
Jenn Tust
Elisabeth Manini

Acquisitions Coordinator
Cindy Wathen

Technical Editor
Diane Poremsky

Copy Editors
Marcia Baker
Paul Medoff

Proofreader
Linda Medoff

Indexer
Valerie Robbins

Computer Designers
Jean Butterfield
Lauren McCarthy
Kelly Stanton-Scott

Illustrator
Michael Mueller

Series Design
Peter F. Hancik

This book was composed with Corel VENTURA™ Publisher.

Information has been obtained by Osborne/**McGraw-Hill** from sources believed to be reliable. However, because of the possibility of human or mechanical error by our sources, Osborne/**McGraw-Hill**, or others, Osborne/**McGraw-Hill** does not guarantee the accuracy, adequacy, or completeness of any information and is not responsible for any errors or omissions or the results obtained from use of such information.

Windows Millennium Edition:
The Complete Reference

About the Authors

John R. Levine is the author of two dozen books, ranging from *Linkers and Loaders* to *The Internet For Dummies*. He also runs online newsgroups and mailing lists, hosts a hundred Web sites, and consults on programming language and Internet topics. He lives in the tiny village of Trumansburg, New York, where, in his spare time, he's the water and sewer commissioner. John is also active in the anti-spam movement, is a board member of CAUCE (Coalition Against Unsolicited Commercial E-mail), and runs the **abuse.net** Web site.

Margaret Levine Young is the coauthor of over two dozen books with various coauthors, including *The Internet For Dummies, Internet: The Complete Reference, Millennium Edition*, and *Poor Richard's Building Online Communities*. She holds a B.A. in Computer Science from Yale University and helps run the Unitarian Universalist Association's online communities.

Doug Muder is a semiretired mathematician who has contributed to a number of books about computers and the Internet, including *Internet: The Complete Reference* and *Dragon Naturally Speaking For Dummies*. He is the author of numerous research papers in geometry and information theory and dabbles in various forms of nontechnical writing. (Check out his fiction and essays at **http://www.gurus.com/dougdeb**.) Doug lives in Nashua, New Hampshire with his wife, Deborah Bodeau, whom he met while getting his Ph.D. in mathematics from the University of Chicago.

Alison Barrows has authored or coauthored books on Windows, the Internet, Microsoft Access, and other topics. In addition to writing books, Alison writes and edits technical documentation and training material. She holds a B.A. in International Relations from Wellesley College and an M.P.P. from Harvard University. In real life she hangs out with her baby, Parker, aspires to compete in Agility with her Portuguese Water Dog, and tries to carve out some time to practice yoga. Alison lives with her family in central Massachusetts.

Rima Regas is a writer and technical editor based in the Washington, DC area. Her background is in operating systems, multiplatform networking, and hardware management.

About the Technical Editor

Diane Poremsky is a consultant who specializes in Microsoft Windows, Outlook, and Office training and development. She is a Microsoft Outlook MVP (Most Valuable Professional) in recognition for her technical support of Microsoft Outlook. She is a technical editor for a number of computer books and is a columnist, author, and technical reviewer for *Exchange and Outlook* magazine. Diane currently resides in East Tennessee with her family.

Contents

Part II

Managing Your Disk

Part III

Configuring Windows for Your Computer

Part V

Networking with Windows Me

Part VI

Windows Housekeeping

Part VII

Behind the Scenes: Windows Me Internals

Acknowledgments

The authors would like to thank the following people for valuable assistance in writing this book: Megg Bonar, Cindy Wathen, Ross Doll, Betsy Manini, Jenn Tust, and Scott Rogers at Osborne/McGraw-Hill; Marcia Baker and Paul Medoff, copy editors; Linda Medoff, proofreader; Diane Poremsky, technical editor; Matt Ronn, Kathy Ivens, Marti Lucich, Tom Laemmel, Buz Brodin, John M. Goodman, Jordan Young, and Tyler Regas for technical information. We also thank our families and friends for putting up with us during the seemingly endless process of updating such a long book.

Introduction

Windows Millennium Edition (or Windows Me) is an update (possibly the last) to Microsoft's best-selling desktop Windows system, Windows 98. Its heritage includes Windows 95, Windows 3.1, Windows 3.0, 2.1, 2.0, all the way back to Windows 1.0 in the mid-1980s. As you might expect of a system with such a long and distinguished lineage, Windows Me has an enormous variety of functions and features, including graphics, networks, disk management, e-mail, word processing, DOS compatibility, sound and video, the Internet and World Wide Web, and multiuser games. This book helps you to make sense of the world of Windows, finding your way through all the new and sometimes confusing options, and to make the best use of the facilities that Windows offers.

If you're wondering why we say Windows Me might be the last version of desktop Windows, we say that because Microsoft claims that all its future systems will be built around versions of Windows 2000, the successor to NT.

Who Is This Book For?

This book is for everyone who uses Windows Me, and especially for people who use it to do their day-to-day computing. You might already have Windows Me installed on your computer, or you might be considering upgrading a Windows 98, Windows 95, or Windows 3.1 system to Windows Me. You might have a lot of experience with other computer systems, or Windows Me may be your first exposure to computing.

Your computer might be the only one in your home or office or one of many on a local area network (LAN). You probably have a modem or network card, although Windows works perfectly well without either.

If your computer is attached to a large network, we don't expect you to be the network manager, but if you're in a small office with two or three computers, we tell you how to set up a small, usable, Windows network. If you have a modem, we discuss in considerable detail what's involved in getting connected to the Internet, because Windows Me includes all the software you need to use the Internet.

What's in This Book?

Near the end of this Introduction, you'll find a section titled "New Features in Windows Me," an overview of Windows Me's features, which highlights changes and additions made since Windows 98.

Part I: Working in Windows Me

Part I covers the basics of using Windows. We recommend that everyone at least skim this section, because even users familiar with Windows 98 or 95 will want to learn about the new features offered by Windows Me.

Chapter 1 starts with the basics of working in Windows: using the mouse and managing your windows. Chapters 2 and 3 explain how to run and install programs beyond those included with Windows. Chapter 4 discusses Windows' simple but useful text and word processing programs, and Chapter 5 describes the other accessory programs, such as the Address Book and Calculator. Chapter 6 covers the extensive Help system, both for Windows and application programs. Chapter 7 looks at the many ways to move and share information between and among programs.

Part II: Managing Your Disks

All the information in your computer is stored in disk files and folders. Part II helps you control your files, folders, and disks.

Chapters 8 and 9 cover day-to-day file and folder operations, including how to use Windows Explorer to manage your files. Chapter 10 discusses disk setup, both removable disks and new hard disks that you may add to your computer.

Part III: Configuring Windows for Your Computer

Windows Me is extremely (some would say excessively) configurable. Part III tells you what items you can configure and makes suggestions for the most effective way to set up your computer.

Chapter 11 covers the *Start menu*, the gateway to the features of Windows. Chapter 12 details the *desktop*, the icons and other items that reside on your screen. Chapter 13 explains your keyboard and mouse (yes, lots of options exist just for the mouse), and Chapter 14 tells you how to add and set up additional hardware on your computer. Chapter 15 covers printing, including setting up printers and installing fonts. Chapters 16 and 17 examine Windows' extensive sound and video multimedia facilities, including the powerful new Windows Media Player and Windows Movie Maker. Chapter 18 highlights the special features that are useful to laptop computer users. Chapter 19 covers the accessibility features that make Windows more usable for people who may have difficulty using conventional keyboards and mice, seeing the screen, or hearing sounds.

Part IV: Windows Me on the Internet

Windows offers a complete set of Internet access features, from making telephone or network connections to e-mail and the World Wide Web.

Chapter 20 explains the intricacies of setting up a modem to work with Windows, and Chapter 21 tells you how to use that modem to create and set up an account with an Internet service provider or online service. Chapter 22 describes Outlook Express, the program that handles your e-mail. Chapters 23 and 24 cover Internet Explorer and Microsoft's World Wide Web browser, as well as Netscape Navigator, another popular browser. Chapter 25 examines online chatting and conferencing with MSN Messenger and NetMeeting, and Chapter 26 discusses the other Internet applications that come with Windows.

Part V: Networking with Windows Me

Windows Me has extensive built-in networking features. You can set up your Windows machine as a client in a large network, as a server in a small network, or as both.

Chapter 27 introduces local area networks, including key concepts such as client-server and peer-to-peer networking. Chapter 28 walks you through the process of creating a small network of Windows Me systems (the network can include Windows 98, 95, and 3.11 systems, too). Chapter 29 tells you how to share printers and disk drives among your networked computers. Chapter 30 explains how to use Internet Connection Sharing to share one Internet account and modem among all the computers on a LAN. Chapter 31 covers the limited network security features that Windows provides.

Part VI: Windows Housekeeping

Windows is sufficiently complex that it needs some regular maintenance and adjustment. Chapter 32 tells you how to keep your disk working well and how to use the facilities that Windows provides to check and repair disk problems, including the new System Restore program. Chapter 33 explains how to tune your computer for maximum performance, and Chapter 34 reviews the process of troubleshooting hardware and software problems. Chapter 35 describes the other Windows resources available on the Internet and elsewhere, including Automatic Updates, which can identify and install updated or corrected Windows components.

Part VII: Behind the Scenes: Windows Me Internals

Part VII covers a variety of advanced Windows topics. Chapter 36 describes the configuration and control files that Windows uses, and Chapter 37 describes the Registry, the central database of program information that is central to Windows' operation. Chapter 38 covers DOS compatibility and the facilities that Windows provides to run even the oldest DOS programs. The final chapter, Chapter 39, concludes with the Windows Scripting Host, a sophisticated system to automate frequently performed tasks.

Appendixes, Glossary, and Instructions for Installing the Book's CD-ROM

Appendix A describes how to install Windows Me as an upgrade to a Windows 98 or 95 system or from scratch on a blank hard disk. Appendix B describes the Microsoft Backup program that comes on the Windows Me CD-ROM. The Glossary explains all the terminology you need to know to understand Windows Me. At the very back of this book, you'll find a page of instructions for how to install the accompanying CD-ROM. (For more information on this book's CD-ROM, see "About This Book's CD-ROM" later in this Introduction.)

Conventions Used in This Book

This book uses several icons to highlight special advice:

A handy way to make Windows Me work better for you.

An observation that gives insight into the way that Windows Me and other programs work.

Something to watch out for, so you don't have to learn the hard way.

When we refer you to related material, we tell you the name of the section that contains the information we think you'll want to read. If the section is in the same chapter you are reading, we don't mention a chapter number. If you find yourself skipping around the book, consider reading the text on the screen using the CD-ROM (see the next section).

When you see instructions to choose commands from a menu, we separate the part of the command by vertical bars (|). For example, "choose File | Open" means to choose File from the menu bar and then choose Open from the File menu that appears. If the command begins with "Start |," then click the Start button on the Taskbar as the first step. See "Giving Commands" in Chapter 2 for the details of how to give commands.

About This Book's CD-ROM

The CD-ROM in the back of this book contains the entire text of the book as a set of several hundred interlinked Web pages that you can display with Internet Explorer or Netscape Navigator. Our goal is for the Web pages on the CD-ROM to be your reference and tutorial companion as you use your Windows Me system.

For instance, as you read in Chapter 32 about disk management and you want to know more about how to protect your files and recover from faults and crashes, you can click a link on the CD's Chapter 32 coverage to jump to that material. The CD makes it easy to follow links from topic to topic until you get the information you need—without flipping to the back of the book to consult the index.

Wherever the book says "See Chapter so-and-so," the CD-ROM has a link that you can follow with a single click. In the printed book, we refer you to related information using, "see Chapter 18" or referring to other sections in the current chapter. The CD-ROM version of the book has been coded—using Web-style hyperlinks—to provide references to related topics. When you read the book on CD, you can click links to jump directly to the section of the book that contains the related information.

We've also added other useful links both within the book and to external resources on the World Wide Web. For example, if Microsoft's Web site has more information about a topic, we provide you with a clickable link to the page you want. We also provide Internet addresses for companies that provide Windows-compatible products and information. The book also has its own Web site (at **http://net.gurus.com/winmetcr**) where you'll find the latest Windows Me information we think you'll find useful.

The key to the CD-ROM version of the book is the electronic Glossary page that you'll find one click away from the CD's opening screen. The Glossary provides an alphabetical list of Windows-related and Internet-related terms, each linking to the section of the book that introduces that concept. To learn about a topic, find the term in the glossary and follow the link into the text.

A page of instructions at the very back of this book describes how to install and use the CD-ROM.

Talk to Us

We love to hear from our readers. Drop us an e-mail note at **winmetcr@gurus.com** to tell us how you liked the book or just to test your e-mail skills. Our mail robot will answer right away, and the authors will read your message when time permits (usually within a week or two.)

Also visit our Web site at **http://net.gurus.com/winmetcr** for updates and corrections to this book.

New Features in Windows Me

Windows Me is very similar to Windows 98—we think they could have called it Windows 98 Third Edition. But it does include many small improvements, concentrating on the home and small business user:

- **AutoUpdate** If you enable this feature, Windows updates itself automatically over the Internet from Microsoft's Web site (see Chapter 35).

- **Hibernation** Supports this feature of some PCs that enables the computer to shut down completely while preserving what you were doing at the time (see Chapter 18).

- **Internet Connection Sharing (ICS)** Actually introduced with Windows 98 Second Edition, enables one computer on a LAN to share Internet access with other computers on the LAN (see Chapter 30).

- **Internet-based games** Games that you play with other people over the Internet, including Voice Chat, so you can talk to them (see Chapter 5).

- **Windows Movie Maker** New program for creating and editing audio and video files (see Chapter 17).

- **System Files Protection** Prevents accidental deletion or overwriting of Windows system files (see Chapter 32). This feature is part of what Microsoft calls *PC Health*—features that help keep your system running smoothly.

- **System Restore** Enables you to return your Windows and application program files to a preset state, for fixing mysterious system glitches (see Chapter 32). System Restore is part of the PC Health system, which is supposed to improve Windows' reliability.

- **Windows Media Player 7** Updated program for viewing and organizing audio and video files, including MP3 files and tracks from audio CDs (see Chapter 16).

Windows Me also removed some programs that came with Windows 98. Windows Me doesn't come with FrontPage Express (an HTML editor for creating Web pages), Microsoft Chat (an Internet Relay Chat program for chatting over the Internet), or Active Movie (which has been replaced by Movie Maker and Windows Media Player 7). Microsoft Backup no longer installs as a Windows component, but you can still install it from the Windows Me CD-ROM (see Appendix B).

The Complete Reference

Windows Me

Part I

Working in Windows Me

Windows
Me

Chapter 1

The Basics of
Windows Me

3

Windows is the most widely run computer program in the world, and *Windows Me* (short for *Millennium Edition*) is the latest version of Windows. Most of the software written for personal computers—indeed, most of the software written for any computer—is written for computers running Windows.

This chapter explains what Windows Me is and explains the objects you see on the Windows screen—the desktop, icons, the Taskbar, the Start menu, and windows. It also explains the Control Panel, a collection of programs that enable you to control how Windows and your computer work. Many Control Panel programs run *wizards*, special programs that step you through the process of creating or configuring an object on your computer. Properties are another way of choosing settings for the objects in your computer. This chapter also describes how to start Windows Me, shut it down, and suspend Windows' operation when you're not using your computer.

What Is Windows Me?

Windows Me is the latest desktop version of Microsoft's Windows series of programs. It's an *operating system*, a program that manages your entire computer system, including its screen, keyboard, disk drives, memory, and central processor. Windows also provides a *graphical user interface*, or *GUI*, which enables you to control your computer by using a mouse, windows, and icons. You can also use the keyboard to give commands; this book describes both methods.

You can upgrade to Windows Me from Windows 98, which Windows Me closely resembles, from Windows 95 or 3.1, or from any version of DOS. You can also buy a computer with Windows Me preinstalled. Once Windows Me is installed, you can run Windows-compatible *application programs* (programs for getting real-world work done).

Windows Me comes with a lot of other programs, including utilities that help with hard-disk housekeeping, Internet connection software (Dial-Up Networking), an e-mail program (Outlook Express), a Web browser (Internet Explorer), a simple word processing program (WordPad), and dozens of other programs.

Windows Me Versus Windows 2000

What's the difference between Windows Me and Windows 2000? Windows Me is an upgrade to Windows 98 (and Windows 98, Second Edition), while Windows 2000 is the upgrade to Windows NT. Microsoft designed Windows Me for home and small business users, while Windows 2000 is for use in larger organizations, where they will be connected to large LANs. Windows 2000 also contains extra security, networking, and server features. The Microsoft Web site contains details about Windows 2000 at **http://www.microsoft.com/windows2000**.

What Hardware Do You Need?

Windows Me requires the following computer hardware:

- A Pentium, Pentium Pro, Pentium II, or compatible CPU running at a speed of at least 150 Mhz.

- At least 32MB of RAM memory (although your system will run slowly with less than 64MB).

- A hard disk with at least 500MB free, depending on which options you choose to install. (You may need more for temporary files.)

- A CD-ROM drive from which to install Windows and other software.

- A screen, keyboard, and mouse or other pointing device.

- If you plan to listen to sounds played by Windows and other programs, you need a sound board and speakers attached to your computer. See Chapter 16, section "Configuring Windows to Work with Sound."

- If you plan to use your computer to connect to the Internet, you need a dial-up modem and a regular phone line, an ISDN modem and an ISDN line, a DSL modem and a DSL line, a cable modem and cable connection, or a *local area network* (*LAN*) connection (see Chapter 27).

What Appears on the Screen?

Like previous versions of Windows, Windows Me uses windows to display information on your screen, icons to provide pictorial buttons for you to click, and a Taskbar, a "mission control" center for your computer. All of these objects appear on your Windows desktop—your screen.

Welcome to Windows Me!

To see a tour of Windows Me, choose Start | Programs | Accessories | Entertainment | Windows Millennium Edition Preview (that is, click the Start button in the lower-left corner of the screen, click Programs on the menu that appears, click Accessories on the drop-down menu that appears, click Entertainment, and finally, click Windows Millennium Edition Preview). You see a window with information about some of the new features of Windows Me.

For other information about Windows, use its online help system (see Chapter 6).

What Is the Desktop?

Windows uses your screen as a *desktop*, a work area on which you see your programs. The desktop, shown in Figure 1-1, can contain windows, icons, and the Taskbar. You can think of the icons, windows, and Web pages that appear on your screen as "sitting" on your metaphorical desktop, like the papers and folders on your real desktop. Chapter 2 explains what windows are and how to use them.

What Is the Active Desktop?

Microsoft is eager to combine Internet features into Windows, and Windows Me (like Windows 98) enables you to display one or more Web pages right on your desktop.

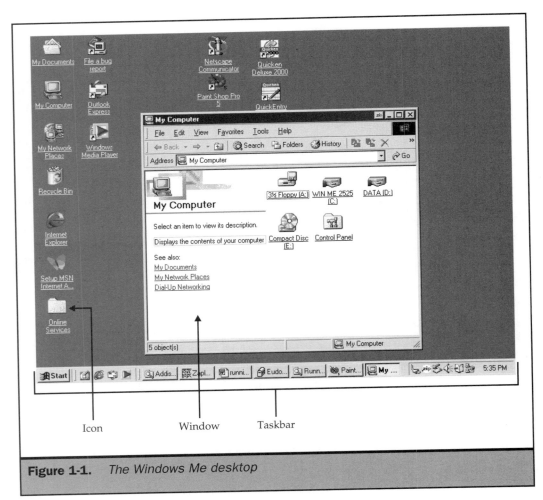

Icon   Window   Taskbar

Figure 1-1.   *The Windows Me desktop*

Before you can choose which Web pages to display, you turn on Windows' Active Desktop feature. Then you tell Windows which Web pages to display, where on the desktop to display them, and how often to update them from the Internet (see Chapter 12, section "Activating Your Desktop").

What Is an Icon?

An *icon* is a little picture on your screen. When you click the icon, double-click the icon, or select the icon with the keyboard and press ENTER, something happens. Windows uses icons to represent programs, files, and commands.

Throughout this book, the instructions tell you what icons you can expect to see, what happens when you click them, and when to use them.

 Many programs provide labels for their icons. Icon labels may appear just below the icon, or they may appear in a little box when you rest the mouse pointer on the icon for a moment.

You can choose how the icons on your Windows desktop and in Folder windows work when you click them—they can run when you double-click them (like Windows 95 and earlier versions of Windows) or click them once (like a Web page). See the section "Choosing Between Single-Click and Double-Click" later in this chapter for how to control how Windows icons behave.

Icons on your desktop that include a little back arrow in a little white box in the lower-left corner of the icon are *shortcuts* and represent files or programs on your computer. You can create your own shortcut icons (see Chapter 9, section "What Is a Shortcut?").

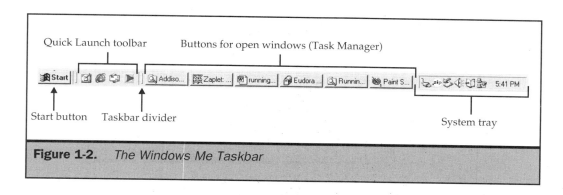

Figure 1-2.   *The Windows Me Taskbar*

What Is the Taskbar?

The *Taskbar* is a row of buttons and icons that usually appears along the bottom of the screen, as in Figure 1-2. You can configure Windows to display the Taskbar along the top or side of your screen (see Chapter 11, section "Moving the Taskbar"). You can also tell Windows to hide the Taskbar when you aren't using it.

The Taskbar has several parts:

- The Start button is usually at the left end of the Taskbar.
- The Task Manager contains buttons for each window that is open on the desktop.
- The toolbar area can contain one or more toolbars (sets of buttons).
- The system tray contains icons for some Windows programs and folders, including the system clock.

What Is the Start Menu?

When you click the Start button on the Taskbar, the *Start menu* appears. The Start menu lists commands and additional menus that list most or all of the programs that you can run on your computer. You can use the Start menu to run almost any program installed on your computer.

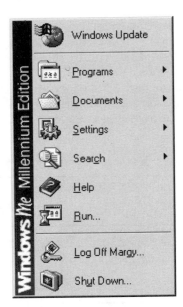

The Start menu usually includes the Windows Update, Programs, Documents, Settings, Search, Help, Run, and Shut Down commands. Other commands may also appear on the menu. For example, if you install Microsoft Office, its installation

WORKING
IN WINDOWS ME

program adds two commands to the top of the Start menu: New Office Document and Open Office Document. You can customize which programs appear on the Start menu and how they are arranged (see Chapter 11, section "Reorganizing the Start Menu").

In this book, we indicate commands on the Start menu and its submenus like this: "Choose Start | Help" means you should click the Start button and then choose the Help command from the menu that appears.

What Is the Task Manager?

The *Task Manager* is the part of the Taskbar that shows one or more buttons for each program running. If a program displays more than one window, more than one button may appear. Each Task Manager button displays the icon for the program and as much of the program name as can fit. Some programs display other information on the Task Manager button; for example, Notepad displays the name of the text file open in the Notepad window.

Click a window's button to select that window, that is, make that window active (see Chapter 2, section "Switching Programs"). You can also right-click a button to see the *system menu*, a menu of commands you can give regarding that window, including opening and closing the window (see Chapter 2, section "What Is the System Menu?").

What Are the Icons in the System Tray?

The *system tray* (or *systray*), shown here, appears at the right end of the Taskbar and contains the system clock along with a group of tiny icons.

Some programs add icons to the system tray. Windows usually displays these icons:

■ **Volume**   Click this icon to control the volume of your computer's speakers, if any (see Chapter 16, section "Controlling the Volume and Balance"). Click the desktop to close the little window that appears. Double-click the icon to set the volume and balance of the speakers when they are used to play sounds from various sources.

■ **System Clock**   The system clock shows the current time according to your computer's internal clock (see Chapter 13, section "Setting the Current Date and Time"). When you move the mouse pointer to the clock, after a moment, the current date also appears.

To find out the name of an icon, move the mouse pointer to the icon, without clicking. In a moment, the icon's label appears. Some icons display information rather than a label (for example, the Power Management icon that appears on the system tray of most laptops displays how much charge is left in the laptop's battery.) To change the settings for the program that displays the icon, or to exit the program, double-click or right-click the icon and choose a command from the menu that appears.

What Is the Mouse Pointer?

The *mouse pointer* indicates which part of the screen will be affected when you click your mouse's buttons. As you move the mouse, trackball, or other pointing device, the mouse pointer moves, too (see Chapter 13, section "Configuring Your Mouse"). A separate indicator, the *cursor*, which usually appears as a blinking vertical line, shows where text you type will appear.

How Do You Configure Windows and Other Programs?

To use Windows effectively, you need to configure it to work with your computer's hardware and with your other programs. When configuring Windows, you encounter these concepts:

- Properties, which are settings for many different objects in your computer's hardware and software.

- The Control Panel, which enables you to see and change many properties and other settings.

- Wizards, which are programs that help automate the processes of installing hardware, installing software, and configuring software.

What Are Properties?

Every object in Windows—the hardware components of your computer, software programs, files, and icons—has *properties*, the settings that affect how that object works. For example, a file might have properties such as a filename, size, and the date the file was last modified.

You can see the properties of most objects by right-clicking the object and choosing Properties from the menu that appears. Windows displays a Properties dialog box and may let you change some of the settings, depending on the type of object. Figure 1-3 shows the properties of an icon on the desktop.

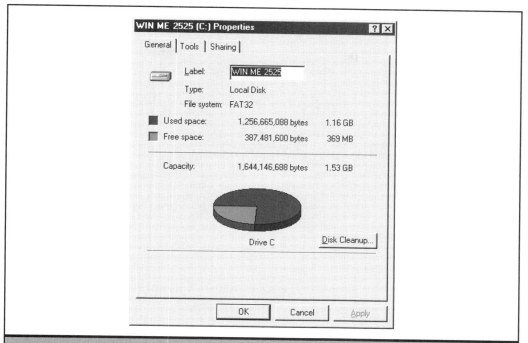

Figure 1-3.   *A Properties dialog box displays the properties of an object and may enable you to edit them.*

What Is the Control Panel?

The *Control Panel*, shown in Figure 1-4, is a window that displays icons for a number of programs that enable you to control your computer, Windows, and the software you have installed. These programs help you see and change the properties of many parts of Windows Me.

To see the Control Panel, choose Start I Settings I Control Panel. Windows displays only the most commonly used icons. To see all the Control Panel icons, click the underlined words "View All Control Panel Options" on the left side of the window. The icons in the Control Panel window may include these programs, depending on what Windows components and other software you have installed:

■ **Accessibility Options**   The Accessibility Properties dialog box enables you to configure Windows Me's keyboard, sound, display, mouse, and other options for people with disabilities (see Chapter 19). This icon appears only if you installed Accessibility options when you installed Windows.

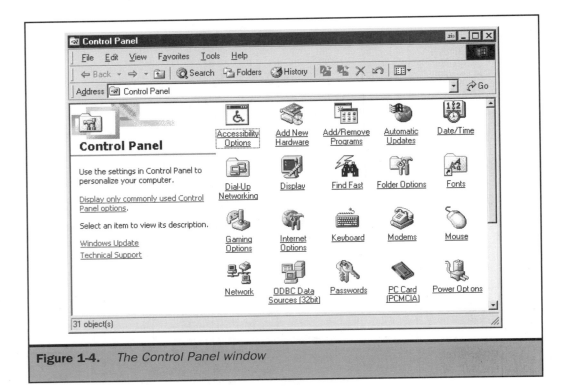

Figure 1-4.   *The Control Panel window*

- **Add New Hardware**   The Add New Hardware Wizard configures Windows when you add new hardware to your computer system (see Chapter 14).

- **Add/Remove Programs**   The Add/Remove Programs Properties dialog box helps you install new programs or uninstall programs you no longer use (see Chapter 3).

- **Automatic Updates**   The Automatic Updates dialog box enables you to specify whether you want Windows and other programs to update themselves automatically by downloading new software from the Internet (see Chapter 35).

- **Date/Time**   The Date/Time Properties dialog box enables you to set the date, time, and time zone where you are located (see Chapter 13).

- **Dial-Up Networking**   The Dial-Up Networking folder contains your dial-up Internet connections and helps you configure Windows to connect to the Internet (see Chapter 21).

- **Display**   The Display Properties dialog box controls the appearance, resolution, screen saver, and other settings for your display (see Chapter 12).

- **Folder Options**   The Folder Options dialog box enables you to choose how your Windows desktop and folder windows work (see Chapter 8).

■ **Fonts**   The Fonts window enables you to install new screen and printer fonts (see Chapter 15).

■ **Gaming Options**   The Gaming Options dialog box enables you to install games (see Chapter 14).

■ **Internet Options**   The Internet Properties dialog box contains settings for your Web browser and Internet connection (see Chapter 20).

■ **Keyboard**   The Keyboard Properties dialog box contains settings that control your keyboard and the cursor (see Chapter 13).

■ **Modems**   The Modems Properties dialog box contains settings for how your modem works and helps you diagnose problems (see Chapter 20).

■ **Mouse**   The Mouse Properties dialog box enables you both to define the buttons on your mouse and to choose how fast you need to double-click, what your mouse pointer looks like onscreen, and whether moving the mouse leaves a trail (see Chapter 13).

■ **Network**   The Network dialog box contains settings you use when configuring a LAN (see Chapter 27). It also contains settings for connecting to the Internet (see Chapter 21).

■ **Passwords**   The Passwords Properties dialog box enables you to set a password for using Windows on your computer, user profiles if more than one person will use the computer, and other security settings (see Chapter 31).

■ **PC card (PCMCIA)**   On laptops and other computers with PC card slots, the PC card (PCMCIA) Properties dialog box enables you to configure your PC cards (see Chapter 18).

■ **Power Options**   The Power Options Properties dialog box contains controls to set when Windows Me automatically turns off your monitor, hard disks, and other computer components to save electricity (see Chapter 14). Laptops have additional power use options that Window Me can handle (see Chapter 18, section "Managing Your Computer's Power").

■ **Printers**   The Printers dialog box includes icons for each printer to which you have access, as well as an icon for adding a new printer (see Chapter 15).

■ **Regional Settings**   The Regional Setting Properties dialog box enables you to tell Windows Me the time zone, currency, number format, and date format you prefer to use (see Chapter 13). Not all programs follow the settings you choose, but many do.

■ **Scanners and Cameras**   The Scanners and Cameras folder window displays the graphics hardware you have installed and helps you install new scanners and cameras (see Chapter 16).

■ **Scheduled Tasks**   The Scheduled Tasks folder window displays the programs scheduled to run automatically and enables you to add to or change the schedule (see Chapter 2).

- **Sounds and Multimedia**   The Sounds and Multimedia dialog box enables you to assign a sound to each Windows event or events in other programs (see Chapter 16). For example, you can set your computer to play a fanfare when your e-mail program receives new messages.

- **System**   The System Properties dialog box enables you to use the Device Manager to change advanced settings for each hardware component of your computer (see Chapter 14). You can also optimize the performance of your computer (see Chapter 33).

- **Taskbar and Start Menu**   The Taskbar and Start Menu Properties dialog box enables you to customize these desktop features (see Chapter 11).

- **Telephony**   The Dialing Properties dialog box contains settings that control how Windows Me dials the phone using your modem (see Chapter 20).

- **Users**   The Enable Multi-User Settings Wizard helps you set up user names and passwords so your computer can be used by more than one person (see Chapter 31). Each person's user name can store that person's desktop settings.

You may see additional icons if you have installed additional hardware or software on your computer.

What Is a Wizard?

Windows, like many other Microsoft programs, includes many *wizards*, programs that step you through the process of creating or configuring something. For example, the Internet Connection Wizard leads you through the many steps required to set up a Dial-Up Networking connection to an *Internet service provider* (*ISP*) (see Chapter 21).

Wizards include instructions for each step, telling you what information you must provide and making suggestions regarding what choices to make. Most wizards display window after window of information and questions, with Back, Next, and Cancel buttons at the bottom of each window. Fill out the information requested by the wizard and click the Next button to continue. If you need to return to a previous wizard window, click the Back button. To exit the wizard, click the Cancel button. The wizard's last screen usually displays a Finish button because there's no "next" screen to see.

Starting Up Windows Me

On most systems, Windows starts automatically when you turn on the computer. You see whatever messages your computer displays on startup, followed by the Windows Me *splash screen* (logo). If your computer is on a LAN or is set up for multiple users, you also see a logon screen (see Chapter 27). Type your user name, press TAB to move the cursor to the Password box, type your password, and then press ENTER.

If your computer system has been suspended, Windows hasn't been shut down; instead, it is "sleeping." To start up where you left off, just resume operation of your computer, which usually is accomplished by moving the mouse, pressing a key (such as the SHIFT key), or opening the cover of a laptop.

Shutting Down Windows Me

When you need to turn off the computer, you must shut down Windows first. Shutting down Windows allows it to close all its files and do other housekeeping tasks before terminating.

To shut down Windows, choose Start | Shut Down, click the desktop and press ALT-F4, or press CTRL-ESC and choose Shut Down). You see the Shut Down Windows dialog box, shown in the following illustration. Your Shut Down Windows dialog box may contain different options if your computer has a Suspend mode.

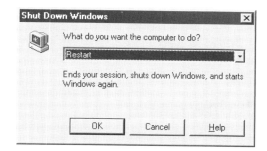

Set the What Do You Want The Computer To Do box to Shut Down and click OK. Windows displays a message when you can safely turn off the computer. Don't turn off the computer until you see this message. Computers with advanced power management shut off automatically.

When Can You Turn Off the Computer?

We recommend you *do not* turn off the computer when have finished using it. Windows likes to perform housekeeping tasks when you aren't using the computer, so leaving it on, even when you're not working, is a good idea. You can schedule programs to run at specified times—see Chapter 2, section "Running Programs on a Schedule Using Task Scheduler"—for example, you can schedule Windows to collect your e-mail at 7:00 every morning.

Many computers power down the screen, hard disk, and fan after a set time of inactivity. The computer itself, however, is still running. If your screen doesn't power off automatically, you should turn off your screen when you aren't using the computer. Computer screens use the lion's share of the electricity consumed by the computer.

Setting Windows to Shut Down by Itself

Windows includes *OnNow*, technology that allows Windows to power down the computer when nothing is happening and to power back up when the computer is needed again, if the computer's hardware permits. To use OnNow, choose Start | Settings | Control Panel, and then run the Power Options program (see Chapter 18, section "Managing Your Computer's Power").

Suspending Windows Me

Some computers have a *Suspend mode, Hibernate mode,* or *Standby mode* in which the computer remains on, but the disk drives, fan, and screen turn off. If your computer has such a mode, a Standby option appears on the Shut Down Windows dialog box. To switch your computer to suspend mode, choose Start | Suspend.

To wake up a computer that has partially powered itself down, move the mouse around without clicking or press the SHIFT key a few times.

Restarting Windows Me

Many programs require that you restart Windows after installing the program to ensure that the program's components are correctly loaded. To restart Windows, save all the files you are working on, exit your programs and choose Start | Shut Down. Choose Restart on the Shut Down Windows dialog box and click OK. Windows exits and reloads.

Restarting Windows every day or so isn't a bad idea. Windows' housekeeping isn't perfect, and it loses track of some system resources over time. Restarting Windows ensures the maximum system resources are available for your use (see Chapter 33, section "How Can You Monitor System Usage?").

Choosing Between Single-Click and Double-Click

You can choose how icons on the Windows desktop and in Folder windows behave. Your choices are

- **Single-click** (Web style) To select the icon without running or opening it, move your mouse pointer to the icon without clicking. To run or open the icon, click it once. Icon labels appear underlined (like Web page links).

- **Double-click** (Classic Windows style) To select the icon, click it once. To run or open the icon, click it twice. Icon labels are not underlined.

Follow these steps to choose between single- and double-click:

1. If the My Computer icon on the desktop has an underline, click it once; otherwise, double-click it. You see the My Computer window.

2. Choose Tools | Folder Options from the menu (that is, choose Tools and then choose Folder Options from the Tools menu that appears). You see the Folder Options dialog box, as shown in Figure 1-5.

Tip   *Whether you use single-click or double-click, you can right-click icons to see a shortcut menu of commands you can perform on the icon (see Chapter 2).*

3. If the General tab isn't selected, click it.

4. In the Click Items As Follows box, click Single-click or Double-click. If you choose Single-click, choose whether you want icon titles to be underlined all the time or only when your mouse pointer is on the icon.

5. Click OK.

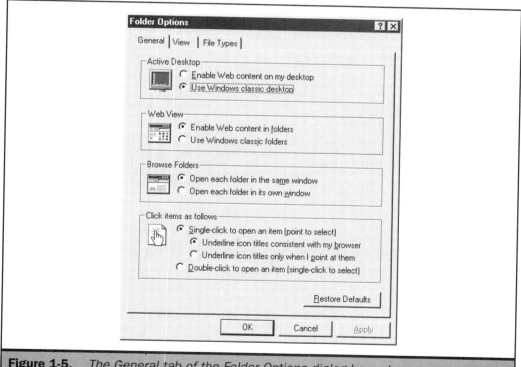

Figure 1-5.   *The General tab of the Folder Options dialog box, where you can specify how Windows icons work*

In the rest of this book, we indicate command choices from the menu bar like this: "Choose Tools | Folder Options," rather than saying "Choose Tools from the menu bar and then choose Folder Options from the Tools drop-down menu that appears."

Displaying Properties

To display the properties of almost anything you see on the screen in Windows, right-click the item and choose Properties from the menu that appears. You see a dialog box with a title that usually includes the word "Properties." If the object has too many properties to fit in a dialog box, tabs may run along the top of the dialog box. Click a tab to see the settings on that tab.

For example, to see the properties of the Windows desktop, right-click the desktop in a place where it is not covered by icons or windows. You see the Display Properties dialog box (see Chapter 12, section "What Are Display Properties?"). When you have finished looking at the properties shown, and possibly changed some of the properties that can be changed, click OK to save your changes or Cancel to cancel them and exit the dialog box.

The
Complete
Reference

Chapter 2

Running Programs

Running Windows Me alone doesn't get you very far. The point of Windows is to let you run programs that help you get work done. To take advantage of Windows' capability to *multitask* (do several things at the same time), this chapter explains how to run several programs at the same time and how to switch among them. Because programs display information in windows, you also learn how the windows you see on your screen work.

You can tell Windows to start programs for you, and you can control the size and location of the windows in which programs display information. Once a program is running, you can give it commands using the mouse and keyboard. This chapter also explains how to configure Windows to launch the programs you always use automatically so you're ready to work as soon as you start Windows, how to schedule programs to run at preset times, and how to define shortcut keys for quick-starting programs you use frequently.

What Are Windows and Programs?

Windows manages the keyboard, screen, disks, and programs that make up your computer. As you learn about Windows Me, you need to understand what windows and programs are, and you may run across the terms *processes* and *tasks*, which are related.

What Are Programs, Applications, Processes, and Tasks?

A *program* is a sequence of computer instructions that perform a task. Programs are stored in *program files*, which have the filename extension .exe or .com. When you run a program, your computer executes the instructions in the program file. In Windows, several programs can run at the same time. Programs are also called *software*.

Programs can do several things at once; for example, a word processing program may be able to print one document while you edit another. One program can run several *tasks* or *processes* at the same time. Windows itself runs many tasks at the same time, including tasks that monitor the hard disk, screen, and keyboard, update the onscreen clock, and run programs on a schedule, for example.

An *applications program*, or *application*, is a program that does real-world–oriented work. Word processors, spreadsheets, and databases are widely used types of applications. A *systems program* does computer-oriented work—an *operating system* like Windows itself is the most important systems program you use. Printer drivers (that control the actions of a printer) or disk scanners (that check disks for errors) are other examples of system programs. A *utility* is a small, simple, useful program (either a small applications program or a small systems program). Windows comes with many utilities, like Calculator and Notepad.

This chapter describes how to run programs. There's also a section on how to control the size and shape of the windows that programs display.

What Is the Primary Network Logon?

If your computer uses user profiles and isn't on a LAN, the Welcome To Windows dialog box appears when you start Windows, asking for your user name and password (see Chapter 31, section "What Is a User Profile?"). Once you hook your computer to a LAN, Windows logs on to the LAN when it starts up, and you see the Enter Network Password dialog box on startup. If there's a problem connecting to the LAN, Windows lets you know when it logs on.

If you don't want Windows to verify its connection to the LAN each time it starts, you can configure Windows to display the Welcome To Windows dialog box rather than the Enter Network Password dialog box. Open the Network dialog box and set the Primary Network Logon to Windows Logon. To switch back to logging in to the LAN on startup, set the Primary Network Logon box back to Client For Microsoft Networks.

What Are Windows and Dialog Boxes?

A *window* is a rectangular area on the screen that displays information from a running program. Under Windows, each program displays information in one or more windows. Some windows are divided into sections called *panes*.

A *dialog box* is a special kind of window that enables you to change settings or give commands in a program. For example, in most programs, when you give a command to open a file, you see an Open File dialog box that enables you to specify which file you want to open.

When a program displays a dialog box, you must exit the dialog box before continuing to use the program. Most dialog boxes include buttons to exit, with names like OK, Close, and Cancel.

What Do the Parts of Windows Do?

Figure 2-1 shows a program (this example shows WordPad, a simple word processor that comes with Windows) running in a window. Although what's inside the window frame changes from program to program, most windows you see in Windows include the following components:

- **System Menu button**   Displays a menu of commands you can use to move and resize your window (see "Controlling the Size and Shape of Your Windows").
- **Title bar**   Displays the title of the window and provides a way to move the window around within the screen (see "Moving a Window").

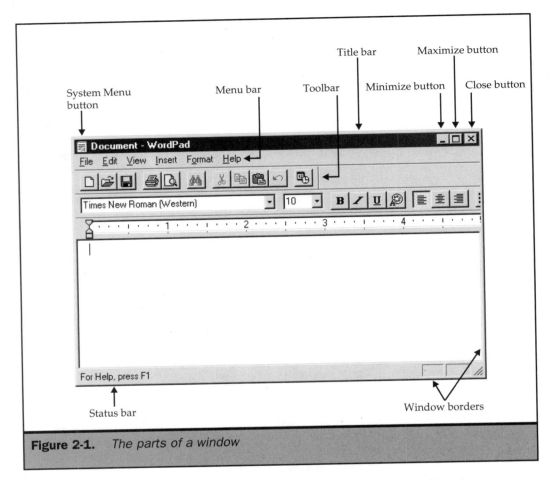

Figure 2-1.   *The parts of a window*

- **Minimize button**   Shrinks the window to an icon on the Taskbar (see "Minimizing a Window").

- **Maximize or Restore button**   When you click the Maximize button, the window expands to cover the whole screen (see "Maximizing a Window"). Once a window has been maximized, the Maximize button disappears and is replaced by the Restore button. When you click the Restore button (with two overlapping rectangles), the window shrinks to its previous size and the Maximize button reappears.

- **Close button**   Closes the window and exits the program (see "Closing Windows").

- **Menu bar**   Provides a row of menus you can use to choose commands (see "Giving Commands").

- **Toolbar**   Provides a row of buttons you can click to give commands (see "Giving Commands").

- **Status bar** Displays information about the program. Some programs enable you to give commands by clicking parts of the status bar.
- **Scroll bar** Provides a way to "pan" your window up and down, or left and right to show information that doesn't fit in the window (see "What Is a Scroll Bar?").
- **Window borders** Provide a way to drag around the edges of the window to change the size and shape of the window (see "Changing the Size and Shape of a Window").

What Sizes Can Windows Be?

A window can be in one of three states:

- *Maximized*, taking up the entire screen, with no window borders (see "Maximizing a Window").
- *Minimized*, so all that appears is the window's button on the Taskbar (see "Minimizing a Window").
- *Restored*, or *in a window*, that is, displayed with window borders (see Figure 2-1). You can change the height and width of restored windows. Most windows on your screen are restored windows (see "Restoring the Window to Its Previous Size").

You can switch among these three sizes without stopping the program that displays the window. For example, you can minimize the WordPad window shown in Figure 2-1 without interrupting the WordPad program; when you restore or maximize the WordPad window, the WordPad program picks up where you left off.

Minimize windows when you want to unclutter your desktop without exiting programs. The choice between maximizing programs and running them in windows (restored) is a matter of taste. If your screen is small or low-resolution, maximize your windows, so you can see their contents as clearly as possible. If you have a large, high-resolution screen, you can run your programs in windows so you can see several programs at the same time.

What Is the System Menu?

The *System Menu button* is a tiny icon in the upper-left corner of each window. The icon shows which program you are running (if you happen to recognize the icon). When you click the icon, you see the *System menu*, as shown here:

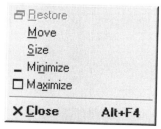

You can also display the System menu by pressing ALT-SPACEBAR or by right-clicking the title bar of the window.

The commands on the System menu do the following:

- **Restore** Resizes the window to its previous size; this command is available only when the window is maximized. This command does the same thing as the Restore button (see "Restoring the Window to Its Previous Size").

- **Move** Enables you to move the window around on your screen by using the cursor (arrow) keys. This command does the same thing as dragging the window's title bar with the mouse (see "Moving a Window"). Press ENTER to finish moving the window.

- **Size** Enables you to change the size of the window by using the cursor keys. This command does the same thing as dragging the window borders with the mouse (see "Changing the Size and Shape of a Window").

- **Minimize** Minimizes the window, shrinking it to a small icon. This command does the same thing as the Minimize button (see "Minimizing a Window").

- **Maximize** Maximizes the window to cover the whole screen. This command does the same thing as the Maximize button (see "Maximizing a Window").

- **Close** Closes the window. This command does the same thing as the Close button (see "Closing Windows").

Some applications also add their own application-specific commands to the System menu.

What Is the Menu Bar?

The *menu bar* is a row of one-word commands that appears along the top of a window, just below the title bar. When you choose a command on the menu bar, another menu, called a *drop-down menu*, usually appears (see "Choosing Commands from the Menu Bar for details").

Each drop-down menu is named after the command that displays it. For example, most programs include a File command as the first command on the toolbar. Choosing the File command displays the File menu, a list of commands that have something to do with files, such as opening, closing, or saving files (see Figure 2-2).

If your screen doesn't have room for the entire drop-down menu to appear, you see a downward-pointing triangle at the bottom of the submenu; click the arrow to see the rest of the menu. Many programs use a new feature of Windows Me that displays only the most frequently used commands or the commands you've chosen recently. At the bottom of the menu is a double-V character (a double downward-pointing arrow) that you can click to see the rest of the available commands. For example, here's a menu that displays only some of the commands available:

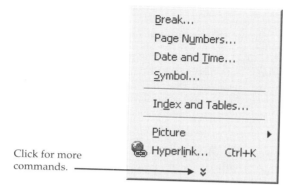

Click for more
commands.

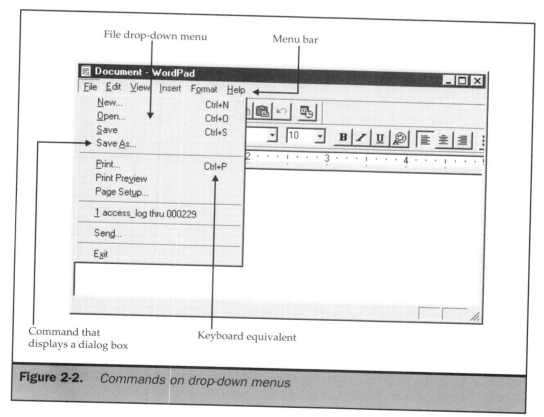

File drop-down menu

Menu bar

Command that
displays a dialog box

Keyboard equivalent

Figure 2-2.   *Commands on drop-down menus*

Other information may appear next to commands on menus:

■ Commands that have a rightward-pointing triangle to their right display another menu.

■ Commands that have an ellipsis (three dots) after them display a dialog box.

■ Some commands represent an option that can be turned on or off. A command of this type has a check mark to its left when the option is on (selected) and no check mark when the option is off (not selected). For example, a View menu might have a Status Bar command that is checked or unchecked, controlling whether the status bar is displayed. To turn an option on or off, choose the command; the check mark appears or disappears.

■ Some menus contain several options, only one of which may be selected. A large dot appears to the left of the selected option. To select an option, choose the command; the dot appears to its left.

■ For some commands, a button on the toolbar performs the command. On the drop-down menu that contains the command, the toolbar button appears to its left, just as a reminder.

■ Some commands have a keyboard shortcut. For example, many programs provide the key combination CTRL-S as a shortcut for choosing the File menu, and then the Save command. Keyboard shortcuts appear to the right of commands on drop-down menus.

In this book, instructions for choosing commands from the menu bar appear as follows: "Choose File | Open." (You give this command by clicking File on the menu bar and then clicking Open on the File menu.)

What Is a Scroll Bar?

Many programs display objects that are too large to fit in the program's window. For example, the WordPad program that comes with Windows can edit documents that are much too large to fit on the screen. Most programs provide *scroll bars*, as shown here, to enable you to choose which part of the document you want to see in the program's window.

Scroll bars may be horizontal (running along the bottom edge of a window) or vertical (running down the right edge of a window). All scroll bars have arrow buttons at each end and a sliding gray box somewhere in the scroll bar; some programs display scroll bars with additional buttons (for example, to scroll one page of a document at a time). The length of a vertical scroll bar represents the entire length of the document you are viewing, and the sliding box represents the part of the document you can currently see. For horizontal scroll bars, the width of the scroll bar represents the entire width of the document.

To change which part of the document you can see, click the arrow button at one end of the scroll bar, or click-and-drag the sliding gray box along the scroll bar.

What Is Multitasking?

The heart of Windows is its capability to *multitask*, that is, to run several programs at the same time. Some programs run several tasks at the same time; for example, many word processors can format one document for printing while you edit another.

To run more than one program at the same time, go ahead and run one program; then another; then another. The first program you run continues to run when the second program starts. Each program runs in its own window; some programs create more than one window. Each window can be minimized, maximized, or restored (see "Controlling the Size and Shape of Your Windows"). A button appears on the Taskbar for each program.

One window is always *on top*, which means it is the *active window*. The title bar of the active window is a different color than the title bars of all the other windows on your screen; in the default Windows desktop color scheme, the title bar of the active window is blue, while the other title bars are gray (see Chapter 12, in the section "What Is a Desktop Scheme?"). Where the active window overlaps with another window, the active window obscures the other window. Figure 2-3 shows several programs running at the same time; the active window is Calculator, a program that comes with Windows (see Chapter 5, section "Using Calculator").

Whatever you type on the keyboard is directed to the program in the active window. The programs in the other windows continue to run, but they don't receive input from your keyboard. To type information into a program, you switch the active window to a window displayed by that program.

Starting Programs

Windows gives you many ways to start a program, including clicking its icon on your Windows desktop, choosing it from a menu, clicking a document you want to edit or view by using the program, clicking the program's filename, and typing the program name into a Run or DOS window. The following sections describe these methods.

Starting Programs from the Desktop

If an icon for the program appears on your Windows desktop, click the icon either once or twice to run the program. If the labels under the icons on your desktop are underlined, click once. If the labels are not underlined, double-click. You can control whether you need to single-click or double-click icons to run programs by setting your Folder options (see Chapter 1, section "Choosing Between Single-Click and Double-Click").

You can change the name, graphic, and action of a desktop icon (see Chapter 12).

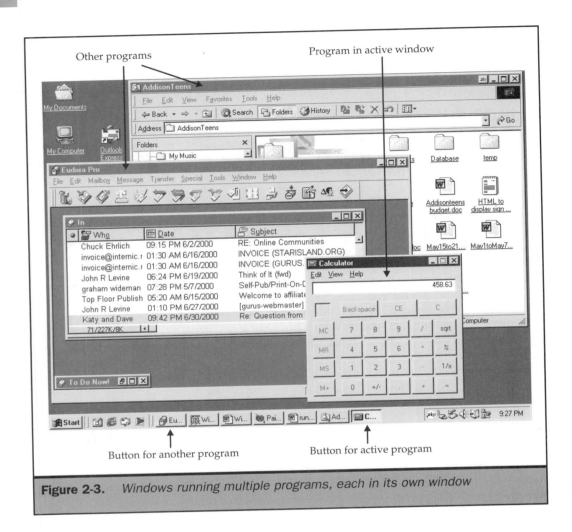

Other programs

Program in active window

Button for another program

Button for active program

Figure 2-3. *Windows running multiple programs, each in its own window*

Starting Programs from the Start Menu

Chapter 1 describes the Start menu, including the all-important Start button. To launch a program from the Start menu, click the Start button. You see the Start menu, as shown here:

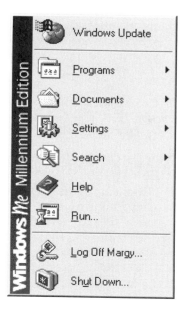

Your Start menu may have additional options, depending on which programs you have installed.

When your mouse pointer is on a menu name, a submenu appears (usually to its right). Point to menus until you see the name of the program you want to run; then click the program name. Most programs appear on the Programs menu, while a few Windows configuration programs appear on the Settings menu. Other programs appear on submenus of the Programs menu. You might need to try several menus to find the one that contains the program you want. You can always press ESC to cancel the menu you are looking at (moving your mouse pointer off the menu usually cancels the menu, too). For example, WordPad appears on the Accessories submenu of the Programs menu. To run WordPad, choose Start | Programs | Accessories | WordPad.

Windows Me has added a feature called Personalized Menus that displays only the most frequently used commands, based on your use, on the Start and Programs menus. (Microsoft Office 2000 and some other programs also include this new feature.) Less often used commands are omitted; instead, a double arrow appears at the bottom of the menu to indicate that other commands are available. If you want to choose a command you haven't used in a while, click the double arrow at the bottom of the menu, and the rest of the available commands appear.

You can rearrange the programs on your Start and Programs menus so the programs you most frequently run appear on the Programs menu rather than on a submenu (see Chapter 11, section "Reorganizing the Start Menu"). You can also create desktop icons for any programs on these menus (see Chapter 12, section "Changing Icons").

You can change the order of the items on the Start and Programs menus by dragging them up and down on the menus. If you don't intend to reorganize your menus, don't click-and-drag the commands on them!

Starting Programs Using the WINDOWS Key

You can run a program without using your mouse. If your keyboard has a WINDOWS key, press it to display the Start menu; if not, pressing CTRL-ESC does the same thing. Press the UP-ARROW and DOWN-ARROW keys to highlight a command from the Start menu and press ENTER to choose the command. The same method works for choosing commands from submenus. The RIGHT-ARROW key moves from a command to its submenu (which is usually to the right on the screen). The LEFT-ARROW and ESC keys cancel a submenu and return to the previous menu.

Starting Programs by Opening Files

Windows knows which programs you use to open which types of files. For example, it knows that files with the .doc extension are opened using Microsoft Word. Windows displays the names of files in an Explorer window. If the filenames are underlined, you single click the filename to open it. If the filenames are not underlined, you double-click the filename.

When you click or double-click a filename, you are telling Windows to run the appropriate program to handle that file (if the program isn't already running) and open the file in that program. If an icon for a file appears on your desktop, clicking or double-clicking the icon tells Windows to do the same thing.

For example, if your desktop icon labels aren't underlined and you double-click a file with the extension .mdb (a Microsoft Access database file), Windows runs Microsoft Access and opens the database file. Windows may be configured not to display extensions (the default setting is for extensions to be hidden); you can identify many types of files by their icons. To tell Windows to display full filenames, including the extensions, see the section "What Are Extensions and File Types" in Chapter 8.

If you try to open a file for which Windows doesn't know which program to run, you see the Open With dialog box, shown in Figure 2-4. Choose the program that can open the type of file you clicked; if the program doesn't appear on the list, click the Other button to find the filename of the program. If you always want to run this program when you click this type of file, leave the check mark in the Always Use This Program To Open These Files check box. Optionally, you can type a description of the

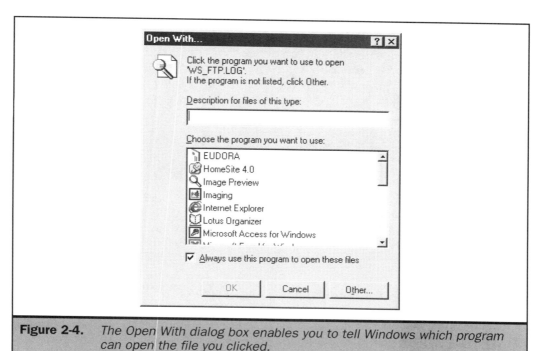

Figure 2-4.   *The Open With dialog box enables you to tell Windows which program can open the file you clicked.*

type of file in the Description box: this description appears when you select a filename and choose View | Details. Then click OK.

You can control which program runs for each type of file (see Chapter 3, section "Associating a Program with a File Extension").

If you want to open a file using a different program from the one Windows automatically runs, right-click the filename and choose Open With from the menu that appears. Windows displays the Open With dialog box shown in Figure 2-4, and you can choose the program you want to run.

Starting Programs by Clicking Program Filenames

Programs are stored in files, usually with the filename extension .exe. Windows displays the names of program files in Explorer windows. To run the program, single click or double-click the filename of the program you want to run.

For example, if you double-click the filename Mspaint.exe, Windows runs the Microsoft Paint program. You can usually guess the program name from the filename, though some filenames can be cryptic.

Starting Programs Using Shortcut Keys

If a shortcut exists for a program, you can define shortcut keys to run the program (see Chapter 9, section "What Is a Shortcut?"). *Shortcut keys* for programs are always a combination of the CTRL key, the ALT key, and one other key, which must be a letter, number, or symbol key.

To define shortcut keys for a program:

1. Right-click the shortcut that launches the program and choose Properties from the menu that appears.

2. Click the Shortcut tab on the properties dialog box for the shortcut.

3. Click in the Shortcut Key box (which usually says "None") and press the key you want to use in combination with the CTRL and ALT keys. For example, press M to specify CTRL-ALT-M as the shortcut key combination. To specify no shortcut keys, press SPACEBAR.

4. Click OK.

Once you define shortcut keys for a program, you can press the keys to run the program.

If another program uses the same combination of keys, that combination of keys no longer performs its function in the program; instead, the key combination runs the program to which you assigned the shortcut keys. However, few programs use CTRL-ALT key combinations.

Starting Programs from the Run Dialog Box

Before Windows, there was DOS, which required you to type the filename of a program and press ENTER to run the program. If you prefer this method, it still works in Windows. Choose Start | Run, and you see the Run dialog box, shown next, into which you type in the filename of the program you want to run:

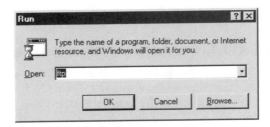

To run a program, type its full path and filename into the Open box (that is, the exact filename, including the folder that contains the file), or click Browse to locate the filename. Then press ENTER or click OK. Windows runs the program.

Depending on the program, you may need to type additional information after the filename. For example, to run the Ftp program (an Internet file transfer program that comes with Windows), type **ftp**, followed by a space and the name of a computer on the Internet (like **ftp.microsoft.com**). When you press ENTER, Windows runs the Ftp program by using the additional information you typed.

 If you've typed the filename in the Open box recently, click the downward-pointing button at the right end of the Open box and choose the filename from the list that appears.

Starting Programs from DOS

Serious DOS enthusiasts might want to see the old-fashioned DOS prompt (usually C:\>) before typing the filename of the program they want to run. To run programs from the DOS prompt, choose Start | Programs | Accessories | MS-DOS Prompt (or, you can choose Start | Run and type **command** and press ENTER). You see an MS-DOS Prompt window, a window that looks like the screen of a computer running DOS. Type the filename of the program you want to run and press ENTER.

When you have finished using the MS-DOS window, type **exit** and press ENTER, or close the window by clicking the Close button (the button with an X) in the upper-right corner of the window. You can also run DOS commands at the DOS prompt (see Chapter 38, section "Starting DOS Programs").

Controlling the Size and Shape of Your Windows

Programs display their information in windows and if you run several programs at the same time, you can end up with many windows displayed at the same time. Windows enables you to control the size and position of most windows, so you can arrange your open windows to see the information you want to view (see "What Sizes Can Windows Be?").

Moving a Window

The *title bar* is the colored bar that runs along the top of the window. To move a window, click anywhere in the title bar of the window, except for the System Menu button or the buttons at the right end of the title bar. Next, drag the window to the place you want it to appear. Release the mouse button when the window is located where you want it.

You can also use the keyboard to move a window. Press ALT-SPACEBAR to display the System menu, press **M** to choose the Move command, press the cursor keys to move the window, and then press ENTER when the window is located where you want it. You can also right-click the program's button on the Taskbar and choose Move from the menu that appears.

Minimizing a Window

A button appears on the Task Manager section of the Taskbar for each program that is running (see Chapter 1, section "What Is the Task Manager?"). To minimize a window—make a window disappear, leaving nothing but its Taskbar button—click the window's Minimize button, the leftmost of the three buttons on the right end of the title bar, or click the window's System Menu button and choose Minimize from the menu that appears.

You can also minimize a window by using the keyboard. Press ALT-SPACEBAR to display the System menu and press N to choose the Minimize command. You can also minimize a window by right-clicking the window's button on the Taskbar and choosing Minimize from the menu that appears.

Minimizing All Windows

You can minimize all the open windows on your screen by right-clicking a blank area on the Taskbar and choosing Minimize All Windows from the shortcut menu that appears. Using only the keyboard, you can press WINDOWS-M (using the WINDOWS key, which is next to the CTRL key on many keyboards). Another method is to press CTRL-ESC, and then press ESC to select the Taskbar. Then press ALT-M to minimize all windows. If the Show Desktop icon appears on your Taskbar (it's on the Quick Launch toolbar, usually right next to the Start button), you can also click this icon to minimize all your windows (see "What Is the Taskbar?" in Chapter 11 for a description of the Quick Launch toolbar).

To reverse this command, right-click a blank area on the Taskbar and choose Undo Minimize All. Or, press SHIFT-WINDOWS-M.

Maximizing a Window

To maximize a window—expand it to cover the whole screen—click the window's Maximize button, the middle button on the right end of the title bar, or, click the window's System Menu button and choose Maximize from the menu that appears. When a window is maximized, its Maximize button is replaced by the Restore button, which returns the window to the size it was before you maximized it.

If the window is currently minimized and you want to maximize it, right-click the button on the Taskbar for the window and choose Maximize from the menu that appears.

You can maximize a window by using the keyboard, too; press ALT-SPACEBAR to display the System menu and press X to choose the Maximize command. You can also maximize a window by right-clicking the window's button on the Taskbar and choosing Maximize from the menu that appears.

Restoring the Window to Its Previous Size

After you maximize a window, you can restore it—return it to its previous size. Click the window's Restore button to restore the window, or click the window's System Menu button and choose Restore from the menu that appears. The Restore button appears (as the middle button on the right end of the title bar) only when the window is maximized.

If the window is currently minimized and you want to restore it, click the button on the Taskbar for the window.

You can restore a window by using the keyboard, too; press ALT-SPACEBAR to display the System menu and press R to choose the Restore command. You can also restore a window by right-clicking the window's button on the Taskbar and choosing Restore from the menu that appears.

Arranging All Windows

If you want to see all the windows on your desktop at the same time, you can ask Windows to arrange them tastefully for you. Right-click a blank area of the Taskbar and choose one of the following commands from the menu that appears:

- **Cascade Windows**   Opens all the windows so they overlap, with their upper-left corners cascading from the upper-left corner of the screen, down and to the right.

- **Tile Windows Horizontally**   Opens all the windows with no overlap, with each window extending the full width of the screen and one window below another.

- **Tile Windows Vertically**   Opens all the windows with no overlap, with each window extending the full height of the screen and one window next to another.

If you choose one of these commands by mistake, you can undo the command by right-clicking a blank area of the Taskbar and choosing Undo Tile or Undo Cascade from the menu that appears.

Note   *If four or more windows are open, Tile Windows Horizontally and Tile Windows Vertically arrange the windows the same way—in a grid.*

Changing the Size and Shape of a Window

If a window is minimized or maximized, you can't change its size or shape. Maximized windows always take up the entire screen, and minimized windows always appear only on the Taskbar. When a program is restored (running in a window), you can change both the size and the shape (height and width) of the window by using the *window borders*.

To change a window's height or width, click the border around the window and drag it to the place where you want it. If you click along a top, side, or bottom border, you move one window border. If you click the corner of the window border, you move the borders that intersect at that corner (see Figure 2-5). When your mouse pointer is over a border, it changes to a double-pointed arrow, making it easy to tell when you can start dragging.

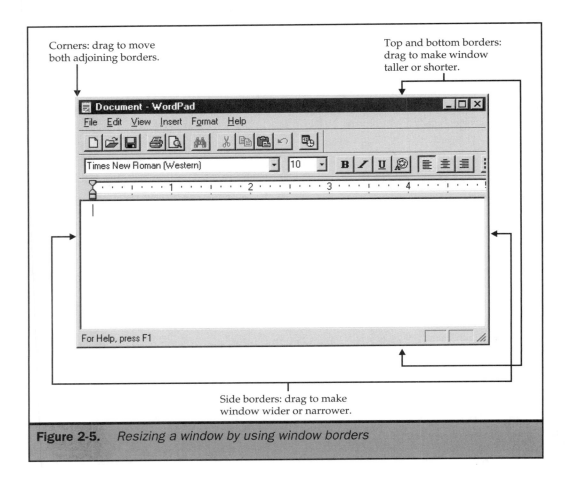

Figure 2-5.   *Resizing a window by using window borders*

You can move and resize windows by using only the keyboard, if that's your preference. To move a window, press ALT-SPACEBAR to display the System menu and press M to choose the Move command (see "What Is the System Menu?"). Press the cursor keys to move the window where you want it; then press ENTER to choose that position. To resize a window, press ALT-SPACEBAR to display the System menu and press S to choose the Size command. Next, press cursor keys to adjust the window size and press ENTER to select that size.

Closing Windows

In the upper-right corner of almost every window, you see a button with an X—the Close button. Clicking the Close button performs the same action as choosing File |

Close from the window's menu. If the program appears in only one window (the usual situation), closing the window exits from the program, the equivalent of choosing the File | Exit command.

If you'd rather use the keyboard, you can close many windows by pressing CTRL-F4. To close a window and exit the program, press ALT-F4.

If the window is minimized, you can close the window without restoring it first. Right-click the button on the Taskbar for the window and choose Close from the menu that appears.

Giving Commands

Almost every Windows program enables you to issue commands to control what the program does. For example, the WordPad program includes commands to create a new document, save the document you are working on, print the document, and exit the program (among its many other commands). Most programs provide several ways to issue commands, including choosing commands from menus and clicking icons on the toolbar.

If the program you are running enables you to view a document, spreadsheet, Web page, database, or other material, the entire item you are viewing might not fit in the program's window. Many programs also include scroll bars, which provide a way to move the material you are viewing within the program's window.

Choosing Commands from the Menu Bar

You can choose commands from the menu bar by using your mouse or the keyboard.

Using the Mouse to Choose Commands

To choose a command from the menu bar or to choose a command from any drop-down menu, click it. For example, to choose the File | Open command, click the word "File" on the menu bar and click the word "Open" on the File drop-down menu.

When a drop-down menu is being displayed, you can see a different drop-down menu by clicking a different command on the menu bar. To cancel a drop-down menu (that is, to remove it from the screen), click somewhere outside the menu.

Tip   *If you are used to a Macintosh, you can choose commands from menus the same way as you do on a Mac. Click and hold down the mouse button on the menu bar command, move the mouse down the drop-down menu to the command you want, and then release the mouse button.*

Using the Keyboard to Choose Commands

In most programs, one letter of each command in each menu is underlined. For example, most programs underline the *F* in File on the menu bar. To choose a command from the menu bar by using the keyboard, follow either of these steps:

- Hold down the ALT key while you type the underlined letter of the command you want. To choose a command from a drop-down menu, press the underlined letter for that command. For example, to choose the File | Open command, press ALT-F, and then O.

- Press and release the ALT key. The first command on the menu bar is selected and appears enclosed in a box. Press the underlined letter of the command you want. For example, to choose the File | Open command, press ALT, and then press F, and then O.

You can mix using the mouse and the keyboard to choose commands. For example, you can use the mouse to click a command on the menu bar, and then press a letter to choose a command from the drop-down menu that appears.

To cancel all the drop-down menus that appear on the screen, press the ALT key again. To back up one step, press the ESC key.

Pressing F10, in most programs, selects the first command on the menu bar (usually the File command); press ENTER to select the command and see its drop-down menu. In many programs, CTRL-O chooses the File | Open command, CTRL-S chooses File | Save, and CTRL-N chooses File | New. Other CTRL key combinations are usually shown on menus, to the right of the command name.

Finding Out More About Commands

When displaying a submenu, many programs display more information about each command as you point to the commands with your mouse. The additional information usually appears in the status bar, the gray bar along the bottom edge of the window.

Clicking Buttons on the Toolbar

Most (but not all) Windows programs display a *toolbar*, a row of small buttons with icons on them, just below the menu bar, for example,

Clicking a toolbar button issues a command, usually a command that you also could have issued from the menu bar.

WORKING IN WINDOWS ME

To find out what a toolbar button does, rest the mouse pointer on the button, but don't click. After a second, a small label appears near the button, naming or explaining the button (this label is sometimes called a *tool tip*). Some programs display toolbar buttons that contain text along with icons, for people who like words with their pictures.

 Some programs let you move the toolbar to other locations, including into a separate floating window. Try clicking a blank part of the toolbar and dragging it to another location in the program window.

Choosing Commands from Shortcut Menus

Windows and most Windows-compatible programs display special menus, called *shortcut menus*, when you click with the right mouse button. The shortcut menu displays commands appropriate to the object you clicked. For example, if you right-click a filename in an Explorer window, the shortcut menu that appears contains commands you can perform on a file, such as Open, Delete, Copy, and Rename:

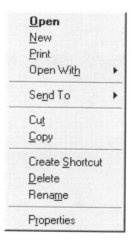

Commands on shortcut menus contain the same symbols (ellipses, triangles, and toolbar buttons) that appear on drop-down menus (see "What Is the Menu Bar?").

After you have displayed a shortcut menu, you can choose a command from the menu by clicking the command (with the left mouse button) or pressing the underlined letter in the command. To cancel a shortcut menu, click outside the menu or press the ESC key.

 You can't tell where shortcut menus will appear or what will be on them. To use shortcut menus, right-click the item you want to work with and see what appears!

You can display a shortcut menu by using only the keyboard; select the item you want to right-click and press SHIFT-F10 to display the shortcut menu. Newer keyboards include an "application key" that has the same effect as right-clicking at the cursor location. Use the UP-ARROW and DOWN-ARROW keys to select the command you want, and then press ENTER to select it, or press ESC to dismiss the menu.

Choosing Settings in Dialog Boxes

Many commands display *dialog boxes*, windows that contain settings from which you can choose (see "What Are Windows and Dialog Boxes?"). Dialog boxes (like the one shown in Figures 2-6) may also include a menu bar, a toolbar, tabs (like the ones on manila folders), graphics, and buttons that display other dialog boxes.

When a dialog box is displayed, choose the settings you want. When you have finished, click the OK or Close button to dismiss the dialog box. You can also click the Close button in the upper-right corner of the window. If you don't want to keep the changes you have made, click the Cancel button or press the ESC key. While a program

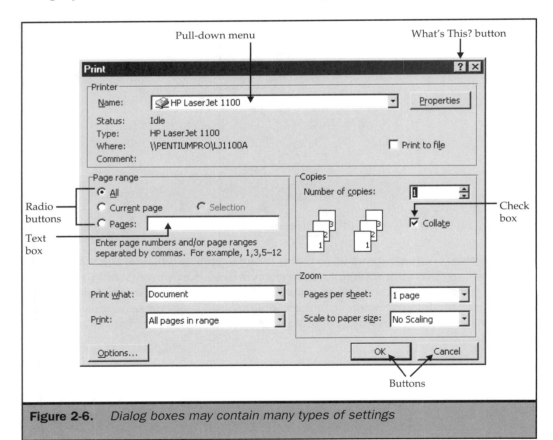

Figure 2-6. *Dialog boxes may contain many types of settings*

is displaying a dialog box, the program usually won't accept any other input until you've closed the dialog box.

 If a window has a question mark button in its upper-right corner, click it and then click the setting about which you want help. If the window doesn't have a question-mark button, click the Help button, if there is one, or press F1. Another way to obtain help is to right-click the setting you need information about and choose the What's This? command from the shortcut menu, if it appears.

Settings in Dialog Boxes

Dialog boxes contain various types of settings, and different software companies use different types of settings. The following are the most common types of settings in dialog boxes:

- **Text box** A box you can type in. To change the text in a text box, click in the box and edit the text. To replace the text with new text, select the entire contents of the box and type the new text. Some text boxes accept only numbers and have tiny up- and down-arrow buttons that you can click to increase or decrease the number in the box.

- **List box** A box that contains a list of options, one of which is selected. If the list is too long to fit in the box, a scroll bar appears along the right side of the box. To select an option from the list, click it. When a list box is selected, you can use the UP-ARROW or DOWN-ARROW keys to select an option. In many list boxes, typing a letter jumps down to the first item on the list that begins with that letter—a useful maneuver for long lists. Some list boxes include a text box just above them so you can type an entry in the text box or click an entry from the list box—your choice.

- **Check box** A box that can either be blank or contain a checkmark (or X). If the check box is blank, the setting is not selected. To select or deselect a check box, click it. When a check box is selected, you can press SPACEBAR to select or deselect it.

- **Radio button** A group of round buttons that can either be blank or contain a dot. If the button contains a dot, it is selected. Only one of the buttons can be selected at a time. To select one button in a group of radio buttons, click it. When a button in a group of radio buttons is selected, you can press cursor-motion keys on the keyboard to select the button you want.

- **Pull-down menu** A box with a downward-pointing triangle button at its right end. The box displays the currently selected setting. To choose a setting, click in the box or on the triangle button to display a menu and click an option from the menu. When a pull-down menu is selected, pressing the DOWN-ARROW key usually displays the menu of options; if it does display the menu, press DOWN-ARROW repeatedly until the option you want is highlighted and press ENTER.

- **Menu bar**   A row of commands, such as the menu bar at the top of a program window.

- **Toolbar**   A row of buttons that give commands, similar to the toolbar at the top of a program window.

- **Command button**   A box you can click to perform a command. Most dialog boxes include an OK or Close button and a Cancel button. If the label on the command button ends with an ellipsis (three dots), the button displays another dialog box. One command button on each dialog box is the default command button and has a darker border. Pressing ENTER has the same effect as clicking this button. When a command button is selected, you can press SPACEBAR to perform its command.

Except for command buttons, most settings have labels (explanatory text) to the left or right (or occasionally above) the setting.

Some dialog boxes have too many settings to fit in the window, so they contain several pages, or *tabs*, of settings. The next illustration shows a dialog box with tabs running along the top of the dialog box. When you click a tab, the rest of the dialog box changes to show the settings associated with that tab.

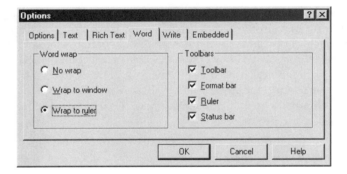

Moving Around a Dialog Box

One setting in the dialog box is selected, which means it's currently active. The selected setting is affected if you press a key on the keyboard. The selected setting is highlighted or outlined, depending on the type of setting.

Here are ways to select a setting in a dialog box:

- Click the setting you want to select.

- Press the TAB key to select another setting, usually below or to the right of the current setting. Press SHIFT-TAB to select the previous setting.

- If the setting you want to select has an underlined letter in its label, hold down the ALT key while you type that letter. For example, to select a setting labeled Save In, press ALT-I.

■ If the dialog box has tabs along the top, you can see the settings associated with another tab by clicking that tab or pressing CTRL-TAB or CTRL-SHIFT-TAB. To select a tab along the top of the dialog box, click the tab or press the ALT key and type the underlined letter in the label on the tab. Once you select a tab, you can use the LEFT-ARROW and RIGHT-ARROW keys to display the settings for each tab. The UP-ARROW and DOWN-ARROW keys move from setting to setting, too—though their action varies from dialog box to dialog box.

Open, Save As, and Browse Dialog Boxes

The Open, Save As, and Browse dialog boxes in most programs have some special settings. All three dialog boxes provide you with a way of choosing a disk drive, a folder, and a file to open, save, or run. The standard versions of these dialog boxes have a special toolbar, as shown in Figure 2-7.

Most Open, Save As, and Browse dialog boxes have the following settings:

■ **Look In or Save In pull-down menu**   The Open and Browse dialog boxes contain a Look In pull-down menu that enables you to specify the folder that contains the file you want to open. The Save As dialog box contains a similar

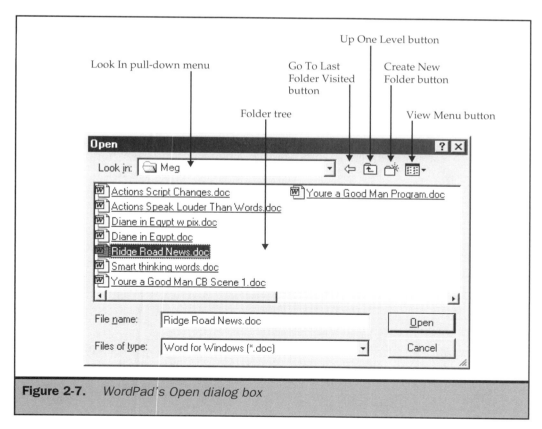

Figure 2-7.   *WordPad's Open dialog box*

Save In pull-down menu that enables you to specify the folder into which you want to save a file. Pressing F4 usually moves to this menu.

- **Folder tree**   This large list box displays the current contents of the folder you selected in the Look In or Save In pull-down menu. Press F5 to update the contents of the folder tree if you think it has changed (see Chapter 8, section "What Is the Folder Tree?").

- **Go To Last Folder Visited button**   Clicking this button goes back to the last folder you viewed.

- **Up One Level button**   Clicking this button changes which folder is named in the Look In or Save In box by moving up one level in the folder tree (to the folder's parent folder). The folder tree listing is updated, too. You can also press BACKSPACE to move up the folder tree one level.

- **Create New Folder button**   Clicking this button creates a new folder within the current folder (see Chapter 8, section "Creating Files and Folders").

- **View Menu button**   Clicking this button displays a list of the views you can choose: Large Icons, Small Icons, List, Details, and Thumbnails.

- **Files Of Type pull-down menu**   Clicking in this box displays the types of files currently displayed in the folder tree. For example, in Microsoft Word, the Files Of Type box is usually set to display only Word documents, but you can choose to see all filenames.

Switching, Exiting, and Canceling Programs

Windows enables you to run many programs at the same time, each in its own window. You can exit from one program while leaving other programs running, and you can choose which program's window is the active window—the window you are currently using.

Switching Programs

To *switch programs*—choose another window as the active window—you can

- Click in the window for the program.

- Click the button for the window on the Taskbar. If the window was minimized, clicking its button returns the window to its size before it was minimized.

- Press ALT-TAB until the window you want is active (or press ALT-SHIFT-TAB to cycle through the open windows in the reverse order).

- Press ALT-TAB and don't release the ALT key. A window appears with an icon for each program that is running, with the program in the active windows highlighted, as shown here:

The name of the highlighted window appears at the bottom of the window. To switch to a different program, keep holding down the ALT key, press TAB to move the highlight to the icon for the window you want, and then release the ALT key.

Exiting Programs

Most programs provide several ways to exit, including some or all of these:

- Choose the File | Exit command from the menu bar.
- Click the Close button in the upper-right corner of the program's window. If a program displays multiple windows, close them all.
- Press ALT-F4.
- Click the System Menu button in the upper-left corner of the program's window and choose Close from the menu that appears.
- Right-click the program's button on the Taskbar and choose Close from the menu that appears.

If you have trouble exiting from a program, you can use the Close Program dialog box, described in the next section.

Canceling Programs

When you are running several programs at the same time, you can exit a program in the usual ways (see "Exiting Programs"). For example, click the Close button for all the windows the program displays or choose File | Exit.

Another way to exit a program when multiple programs are running is to press CTRL-ALT-DEL to display the Close Program dialog box (shown in Figure 2-8). This dialog box lists all the tasks currently running, including a number you probably have never heard of. Windows itself runs a number of tasks with names like Sage and Systray. CTRL-ALT-DEL should be used only when other commands don't work because it may also stop other Windows programs from running.

To cancel a program, click the program name on the Close Program dialog box; then click the End Task button. If you were using the program to edit a file, you may lose some work.

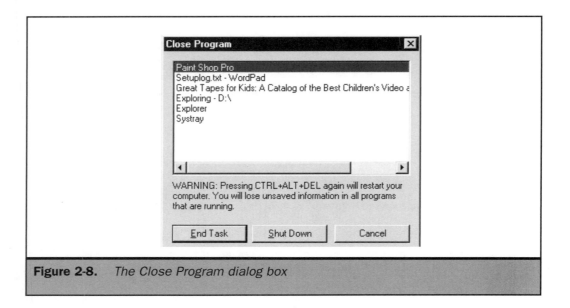

Figure 2-8.   *The Close Program dialog box*

Note *The Close Program dialog box is designed for canceling programs that have "hung"—stopped responding to the keyboard or mouse. To avoid losing unsaved work, always try exiting a program by clicking its Close button, pressing ALT-F4, or choosing File | Exit before resorting to the Close Program dialog box.*

Running Programs When Windows Starts

When Windows starts up, it looks in the C:\Windows\Start Menu\Programs\StartUp folder for shortcuts to programs (see Chapter 9, section "What Is a Shortcut?"). If any programs or shortcuts to programs are stored in this folder, Windows runs them automatically when it has finished starting up.

For example, you can use this StartUp folder to run your word processor and e-mail programs automatically each time you start Windows. Just create a shortcut in your StartUp folder (see Chapter 9, section "Making Shortcuts").

Note *The Windows Registry, which stores information about Windows and your applications, can also tell Windows to run programs automatically on startup (see Chapter 37).*

Running Programs on a Schedule Using Task Scheduler

Task Scheduler is the program Windows uses to check the files and folders on your hard disk automatically. You can also use the Task Scheduler program to run almost any program at a specified time on a regular basis. When you schedule a task, you must specify the following information:

- What program you want to run.

- How often you want to run it (daily, weekly, monthly, when your computer starts, or when you log on).

- What time you want the program to start running. For weekly and monthly schedules, you also specify what day to start the program.

When Task Scheduler is running, its icon appears in the system tray at the right end of the Taskbar.

Scheduling a Program

To tell Task Scheduler to run a program on a regular schedule, follow these steps:

1. Look at the Scheduled Tasks window by choosing Start | Programs | Accessories | System Tools | Scheduled Tasks or choose Start | Settings | Control Panel and run the Scheduled Tasks icon. You see the Scheduled Tasks window, shown in Figure 2-9.

2. Run the Add Scheduled Task item that appears in the Name column of the Scheduled Tasks window. (If it's underlined, click it once. Otherwise, double-click it.)

3. Windows runs the Add Scheduled Task Wizard, which takes you through the steps required to schedule tasks to run automatically. Follow the prompts on the screen, clicking Next to move to the next step.

4. When the Add Scheduled Task Wizard displays all the information you have specified about the program's schedule, including the name of the program and when you want it to run, click the Finish button. The program appears on a new line in the Scheduled Tasks window.

Be sure to leave your computer turned on all the time, so when the scheduled time arrives, Windows runs your program. If your computer is off (or Task Scheduler isn't running) when the time comes, the program doesn't run.

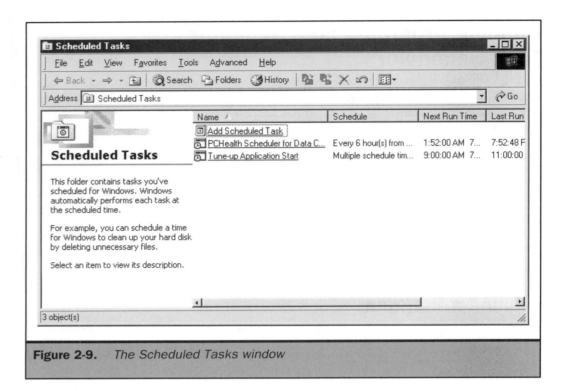

Figure 2-9.   *The Scheduled Tasks window*

> **Note**   *When you schedule a task, Windows creates a file with the extension .job in the C:\Windows\Tasks folder.*

Canceling a Scheduled Program

If you decide you no longer want Windows to run the program automatically, open the Scheduled Tasks window, select the line for the program, and click the Delete button on the toolbar. When Windows asks you to confirm that you want to delete the file for this job, click Yes.

To cancel running all scheduled programs, choose Advanced | Stop Using Task Scheduler. No scheduled programs will be run until you choose the command Advanced | Start Using Task Scheduler. You can pause the scheduler program by choosing Advanced | Pause Task Scheduler to skip running scheduled programs temporarily and choose Advanced | Continue Task Scheduler to resume. Pausing Task Scheduler is a good idea while you are installing new software, for example, so installation isn't interrupted.

Configuring a Scheduled Program

You can configure other settings for a scheduled task. Click or double-click the line for the task in the Scheduled Tasks window (or select the line and click the Properties button on the toolbar. You can also right-click the program name and choose Properties from the menu that appears). You see a dialog box with all the settings for the scheduled program (see Figure 2-10).

Click the Settings tab to tell Windows to delete the job after running it, run the program only if the computer has been idle for a specified number of minutes, stop the program if the computer is in use, or skip running the program if the computer is running on batteries. Table 2-1 lists all the settings you can specify when you schedule a program to run.

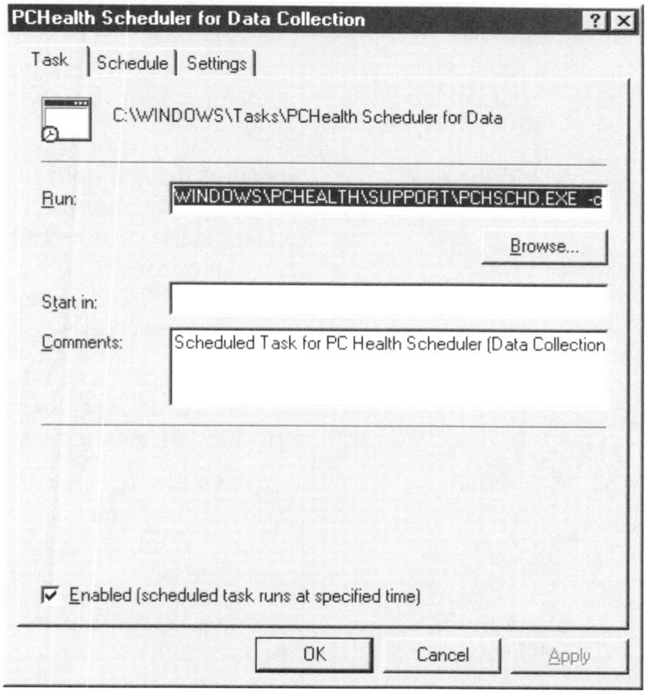

Figure 2-10. *Settings for a scheduled program*

Tab in Dialog Box	Setting	Description
Task	Run	Specifies the pathname (and optional parameters) to run the program. If the pathname includes spaces, enclose the entire pathname in double quotes.
Task	Start In	Specifies the default folder for the program's files (some programs require files other than the program file, and this setting tells the program where to look for them).
Task	Comments	Provides space for you to type comments (ignored by Windows).
Task	Enabled	Specifies that the task is scheduled. To suspend scheduling the task, clear this check box.
Schedule	Schedule Task	Specifies the frequency the task runs: daily, weekly, monthly, once, at system startup, at logon, or when idle. The rest of the settings on the Schedule tab of the dialog box depend on which frequency you choose.
Schedule	Start time	For daily, weekly, monthly, or one-time tasks, specifies the time Windows starts the program.
Schedule	Advanced	Displays the Advanced Schedule Options dialog box, shown in Figure 2-11, in which you can specify an end date or number of repetitions.
Schedule	Show multiple schedules	When this check box is selected, a box appears at the top of the Schedule tab from which you can pick from a list of the schedules you have defined.
Settings	Delete the task if it is not scheduled to run again	Specifies that Windows delete the program after running it (useful only for programs you have scheduled to run only once).

Table 2-1.   *Settings for a Scheduled Task*

Tab in Dialog Box	Setting	Description
Settings	Stop the task if it runs for xx hours xx minutes	Specifies the maximum number of hours and minutes the scheduled program can run. If the program is still running after the specified amount of time, Windows stops the program.
Settings	Only start the task if computer has been idle for at least xx minutes	Specifies that Windows should start the task only after the specified amount of time with no keyboard or mouse use.
Settings	If the computer has not been idle that long, retry for up to xx minutes	Specifies that if the computer had not been idle for long enough when Windows tried to start the program, the number of minutes during which Windows should try to run the program if the computer becomes idle.
Settings	Stop the task if computer ceases to be idle	Specifies that Windows stop the program if you begin to use the computer.
Settings	Don't start the task if computer is running on batteries	Specifies that Windows not start the task if the computer is running on batteries. Some programs, especially disk-housekeeping programs like ScanDisk, perform lots of disk access, which can run down your computer's batteries.
Settings	Stop the task if battery mode begins	Specifies that Windows stop the program if your computer switches from external power to batteries.
Settings	Wake the computer to run this task	Wakes the computer when the task is schedule to run, even if it is suspended or in sleep mode.

Table 2-1.   *Settings for a Scheduled Task* (continued)

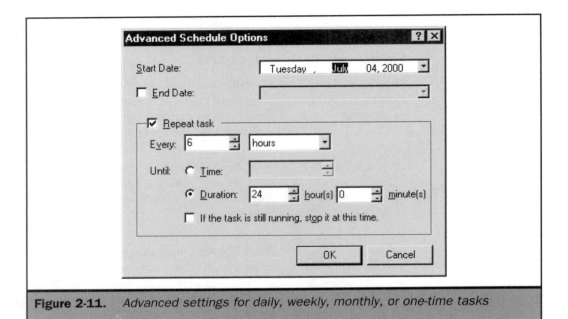

Figure 2-11. *Advanced settings for daily, weekly, monthly, or one-time tasks*

Other Scheduling Options

You can ask Task Scheduler to let you know how its scheduled programs are doing. If you want to be notified when Task Scheduler is unable to run a scheduled program, choose Advanced from the Scheduled Tasks window's menu bar and make sure a check mark appears to the left of the Notify Me Of Missed Tasks option (if no check mark appears, choose the option from the menu).

You can look at a log file of the results of scheduled programs by choosing Advanced | View Log from the Scheduled Tasks menu bar. Windows displays the log file, which is stored in text format in C:\Windows\Schedlog.txt, using Notepad. Log entries consist of several lines of text, as shown here:

```
"PCHealth Scheduler for Data Collection.job" (PCHSCHD.EXE)
      Finished 7/3/2001 1:39:35 PM
      Result: The task completed with an exit code of (0).
```

The first line describes the program, and the subsequent lines report on the outcome of running the program.

Chapter 3

Installing Programs

W indows Me comes with a number of useful programs, and many new computers come with lots more software preinstalled, but you'll want to install some programs yourself, sooner or later. For example, you might want to install some of the programs included on the Windows Me CD-ROM that may not have been installed on your system.

Or, you may want to do just the reverse—uninstall programs that you no longer use or have gone out of date. Windows comes with a built-in system for installing and uninstalling programs.

 Windows Me omits a number of programs that came with Windows 98, including FrontPage Express (a Web page editor) and Microsoft Chat (also known as Comic Chat). Microsoft Backup doesn't install as part of Windows, but you can install it separately from the Windows Me CD-ROM (see Appendix C for how to install and use Microsoft Backup). If you upgraded your system from an older version of Windows, though, these missing programs may still be installed.

What Happens During Installation and Uninstallation?

Before you can install a program, you have to get it—you have to buy or download the program. You may receive a program on a CD-ROM, as a stack of floppy disks, or as a file downloaded from the Internet. Once you have a program, you install it, usually by running an installation program to copy the program to your hard disk and configure it to run on your system.

Many programs arrive in the form of an *installation file*, or a *distribution file*, which is a file containing all the files required for a program to run, along with an installation program. You can download (copy) installation files from the Internet or other sources. If your computer is connected to a local area network (LAN), the installation file may be stored on a network disk (see Chapter 29). The files that make up the program are usually compressed to take up less space.

What Happens During Program Installation?

Most programs come with an installation program named Setup.exe or Install.exe. When you install a program, the installation program usually does the following:

- Looks for a previous version of the program on your hard disk. If it finds a previous version, the program may ask whether you want to replace the previous version.

- Creates a folder in which to store the program files. Most installation programs ask where you'd like this folder. Some installation programs also create additional folders within this folder. Windows creates a folder named Program Files, usually in C:\. We recommend you install all your programs in folders within the Program Files folder.

Note   *Microsoft and some other software vendors have the bad habit of creating programs that are installed in locations other than your Program Files folder. You can't do much about this; the additional folders may clutter up your root folder, but they don't do any harm.*

■ Copies the files onto your hard disk. If the program files are compressed, the installation program uncompresses them. Usually, the installation program copies most of the files into the program's folder, but it may also put some files into your C:\Windows, C:\Windows\System, or other folders.

■ Checks your system for the files and hardware it needs to run. For example, an Internet connection program might check for a modem.

■ Adds entries to the Windows Registry to tell Windows with which types of files the program works, in which files the program is stored, and other information about the program (see Chapter 37).

■ Adds a command for the program to your Start menu—some programs add submenus to the Start | Programs menu to contain several commands. It may also add a shortcut to your Windows desktop to make running the program easy for you. You can change the position on the Start menu of the command for the program, get rid of the command, or create a command, if the installation program doesn't make one. You can also create a shortcut icon on the desktop, if the installation program hasn't done so, or move or delete the program's shortcut (see Chapter 9, section "Making Shortcuts").

■ Asks you a series of questions to configure the program for your system. The program may ask you to type additional information, like Internet addresses, passwords, or software license numbers.

Every installation program is different, because it comes with the application program, not with Windows. If your computer is connected to a LAN or the Internet, the installation program may configure your program to connect to other computers on the network.

What Happens During Program Uninstallation?

The perfect uninstallation program exactly undoes all the actions of the program's installation program, removing all the files and folders the installation program created, and putting back everything else to where it was originally. Unfortunately, we've never seen a perfect uninstallation program, but most uninstallation programs do an acceptable job of removing most traces of a program from your system.

Which Windows Programs Might Not Be Installed?

Windows Me comes with a lot of programs and options, all of which aren't necessarily installed on your system. Many aren't necessary for Windows operation. The

following is a list of some of the optionally installed programs that come with
Windows Me:

■ Accessibility programs that make Windows and your computer more usable
for people with physical disabilities (see Chapter 19).

■ Utilities such as Compressed Folders, System Monitor, and System
Resource Meter.

■ Communications programs that include Direct Cable Communication,
HyperTerminal, Internet Connection Sharing, and Virtual Private Networking.

■ Multilanguage support for many languages, including Baltic, Central European,
and Cyrillic languages, and Greek and Turkish.

■ Games, some of which enable you to play against other people over the
Internet, and WebTV for Windows, which enables you to watch television
on your computer screen (see Chapter 17, section "Viewing TV by Using
Your Computer").

■ Decorative programs you can use to jazz up the desktop, windows, icons,
and even the mouse pointer, such as Desktop Themes and Animated Cursors
(see Chapter 12).

You can install these programs by using the Add/Remove Programs icon in the
Control Panel (see "Installing and Uninstalling Programs That Come with Windows").

Installing Programs

Windows includes a program called Add/Remove Programs that helps you find and
start the installation program for a new program. However, you can skip this step
and run the installation program yourself, if you know how. Some older DOS and
Windows 3.1 programs don't come with installation programs, and you have to
perform the actions of an installation program yourself.

Installing Programs Using the Add/Remove Programs Program

Follow these steps to use the Add/Remove Programs command to help you install
a program:

1. Choose Start | Settings | Control Panel. You see the Control Panel window.

2. Run the Add/Remove Programs program—if the icon is underlined, click it
once; if not, double-click it. You can control whether you need to single-click
or double-click icons to run programs.

WORKING IN WINDOWS ME

3. You see the Add/Remove Programs Properties dialog box, shown in Figure 3-1. If the Install/Uninstall tab isn't selected, click it. The box in the lower-half of the window lists the programs you have already installed on your system.

4. Click the Install button.

5. If you are installing a program from a floppy disk or CD-ROM, insert the disk or CD-ROM into its drive and click Next. If you are installing a program from a file on your hard disk or on a network drive, click Next. Windows looks on any floppy disk or CD-ROM in your drives for an installation program (that is, a program named Setup.exe or Install.exe). If Windows finds an installation program, skip to Step 8.

6. If Windows doesn't find an installation program, you see the Run Installation Program dialog box, shown in Figure 3-2.

7. Click the Browse button and specify the installation file you want to run in the Browse window.

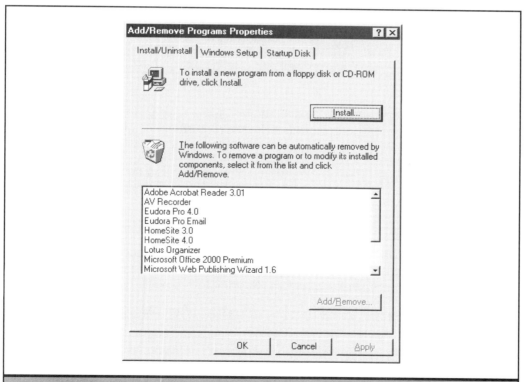

Figure 3-1. *The Install/Uninstall tab of the Add/Remove Programs Properties dialog box*

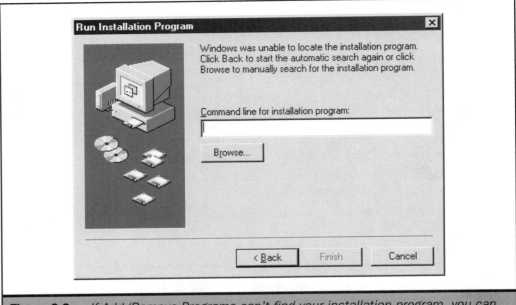

Figure 3-2.   If Add/Remove Programs can't find your installation program, you can specify where it is located.

8. When the path name of the installation program appears in the Command Line For Installation Program box, click the Finish button. The installation program runs. Follow the instructions on the screen to install the program.

Once you install a program, the program name usually (but not always) appears on the Add/Remove Programs Properties dialog box's list of programs that you can uninstall.

Running an Install or Setup Program

If you know the path name of the installation file for the program you want to install, you can run the installation program directly. Follow the instructions on the screen to install the program (see Chapter 2, section "Starting Programs").

Installing Programs Without Installation Programs

Some older programs, such as those designed to run with Windows 3.1 or DOS, don't have installation programs. Instead, the programs are delivered as a set of files. Some older programs arrive as a *ZIP* file, a file that contains compressed versions of one or more files (see Chapter 9, section "Working with Compressed Folders"). ZIP files have the extension .zip (if you can't see filename extensions in Windows, see Chapter 8, section "What Are Extensions and File Types?" to display them).

To install a program from a ZIP file, you need to install Windows Me's compressed folders feature. Follow the steps in the section "Installing and Uninstalling Programs That Come with Windows" later in this chapter to install Compressed Folders (it's in the System Tools category). Or, you can install an unzipping program such asWinZip (**http://www.winzip.com**), which comes with its own commands for unzipping (uncompressing) and installing programs from ZIP files.

To install a program that you receive as a set of files or as a ZIP file, follow these steps:

1. Open the ZIP file. In an Explorer window, it appears as a folder with a little zipper on it.

2. Look at the list of files to find files with the .exe or .com extension; these are executable programs. If one file is named Setup.exe or Install.exe, run it. Then follow the instructions on the screen. The installation program may ask you a series of questions to configure the program for your system. If one file is named Readme.txt (or some other name that suggests it contains instructions), read the contents of the file. If its extension is .txt, click or double-click the filename to see the file in WordPad.

3. Otherwise, look for an executable file with a name like the name of the program; this may be the program itself. For example, if you are installing a program called Spam Hater version 2.3, you might find a filename such as Spamhate23.exe. To run the program, click or double-click the program name. The first time you run the program, it may ask you for information with which to configure the program for your system.

Finishing Installation of a Program

After you install a program, you may still need to configure it to work with your system. Many programs come with configuration programs that run automatically, either when you install the program or when you run the program for the first time.

To make the program easier to run, you can add it to your Start menu (see Chapter 11, section "Reorganizing the Start Menu"). If the program has an installation program, the installation program may do this for you. The installation program may even put an icon on the Quick Launch toolbar (the small icons on the Taskbar you can click to run a program). If not, you can add it yourself (see Chapter 11).

You can also add a shortcut for the program to your Windows desktop. The program's installation program may have created a shortcut already. You can create shortcuts right on the desktop or in a folder (see Chapter 9, section "Making Shortcuts").

Installing and Uninstalling Programs That Come with Windows

If you want to install some of the programs that come on the Windows Me CD-ROM, follow these steps:

1. Choose Start | Settings | Control Panel. You see the Control Panel window.

2. Run Add/Remove Programs.

3. Click the Windows Setup tab. You see a list of the types of programs that come with Windows, as shown in Figure 3-3. The check box to the left of each type of program is blank (none of the programs of that type are selected), gray with a check mark (some, but not all, of the programs of that type are selected), or white with a checkmark (all the programs of that type are selected). The selections show which Windows programs have already been installed.

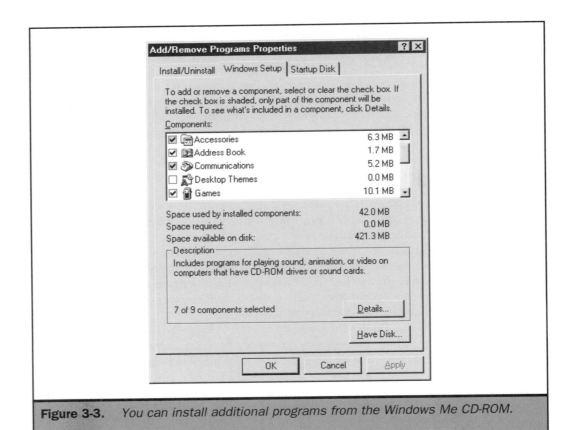

Figure 3-3.   *You can install additional programs from the Windows Me CD-ROM.*

4. To select additional programs, click the type of program to install (scroll down the Components list to see the rest of the program types). A description of the programs appears in the Description box. A few items on the Windows Setup tab of the Add/Remove Programs Properties dialog box have only one program of that type, such as WebTV for Windows. Most of the items on the list include a number of programs, and the Description box tells you the total number of programs of that type and how many are selected.

5. To select all the programs of that type, click the check box to the left of the item. To select some of the programs, click the Details button to see the list of programs of that type. Click each of the programs you want to select and click the OK button to return to the Windows Setup tab of the Add/Remove Programs Properties dialog box.

6. You can uninstall previously installed programs at the same time you install new programs. To uninstall a program, deselect it; that is, clear the check in its check box by clicking the box. Don't clear a program's check box unless you want to uninstall it.

7. After you select all the programs you want installed and deselect all the programs you don't want installed, click the OK button. Windows determines which programs you are installing and which you are uninstalling, and copies or deletes program files appropriately.

8. Depending on which programs you install, you may need to restart Windows when the installation is complete, and you may be directed to run Wizards or other configuration programs to set up the new programs.

Associating a Program with a File Extension

Many programs create, edit, or display files of a specific type. For example, the Notepad program (a text editor that comes with Windows) works with text files that usually have the filename extension .txt (the extension is the part of the filename that follows the last dot in the filename). When you open a file with the extension .txt, Windows knows to run Notepad.

The Windows Registry stores *file associations*, information about which program you use to edit each type of file. Installation programs usually store this information in the Registry, but you can, too. Chapter 37 describes how to view and edit the Registry.

Creating or Editing an Association

To associate a file type (file extension) with a program (or change the program associated with a file type), you use the File Types tab on the Folder Options dialog box.

When you select a file whose extension isn't associated with any program, Windows opens an Open With window. You can create a file association by entering a short description of the file type and selecting the appropriate application from the list. Unless you uncheck the Always Use This Program To Open This File box, Windows Explorer saves the association permanently.

To create or edit a file association, follow these steps:

1. Open a folder in a window (for example, open the My Computer icon on the desktop to display the My Computer window).

2. Choose Tools | Folder Options. You see the Folder Options dialog box.

3. Click the File Types tab, shown in Figure 3-4.

4. In the Registered File Types list, click the type of file you want to associate with a program. When you select a file type, more information about that file type appears in the File Type Details box, including the extension.

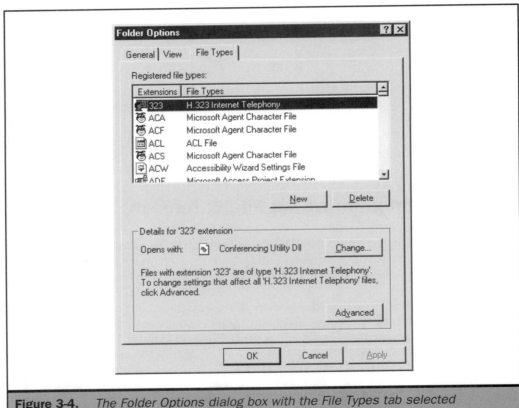

Figure 3-4.   *The Folder Options dialog box with the File Types tab selected*

5. If the file extension doesn't appear in the list of Registered Files Types, click New, type the extension, and click OK. Windows add the new type at the top of the list (not in alphabetical order, unless you close and reopen the dialog box). Select the new file type.

6. To specify the program that Windows runs to open this type of file, click Change. You see the Open With dialog box. Select the program to run or click Other to find the program file. Then click OK.

7. Close the Folder Options dialog box.

Once you tell Windows with which program to open this type of file, Windows runs the program you specified when you open a file of this type.

Three other settings appear on the Edit File Type dialog box:

- **Confirm Open After Download** Specifies to open files of this type after downloading.

- **Always Show Extension** Specifies the extension always appears after filenames of this type.

- **Browse In Same Window** Specifies if the program that opens this program is already running, you want to open the file in the existing program window, rather than opening another window.

Actions Associated with File Types

In addition to telling Windows which program to run for each file type, you can define as many *actions* for a file type as you want. For example, you can define one action that opens files of that type and another action that prints files. There are two types of actions:

- **Regular actions** These actions are listed on the shortcut menu that appears when you right-click filenames in Explorer windows. For example, when you right-click a filename with extension .txt, the Open command appears on the shortcut menu; the Open action associated with the .txt file type determines what this Open command does.

- **DDE actions** These actions define how data can be moved from one program to another using DDE (Dynamic Data Exchange, a method for programs to exchange information). DDE actions do not appear on the shortcut menu when you right-click filenames (see Chapter 7, section "What Is DDE?").

When you click the Advanced button on the File Types tab of the Folder Options dialog box, you see the Edit File Type dialog box (shown in Figure 3-5). It displays the information that the Registry knows about this file type, including the icon to use for

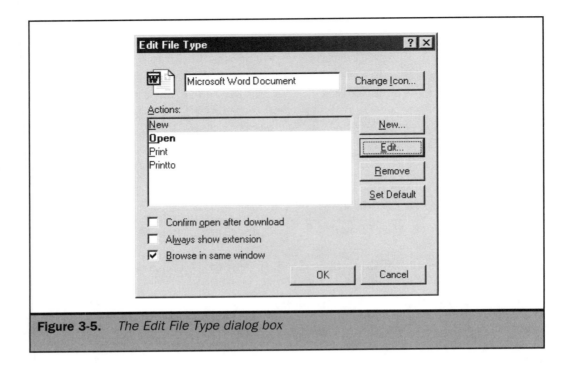

Figure 3-5.   *The Edit File Type dialog box*

files of this type and a description of the file type. The Actions box lists the tasks that Windows knows how to perform for files of this type: open, print, edit, and other actions. For each action, you can tell Windows which program to use; for example, you can use Internet Explorer to display .gif files but Paint Shop Pro to edit and print them.

> **Tip**   *This feature is useful if you use two programs with files of one file type—for example, you might use your browser to view HTML files, but your Web page editor to create and edit those files. Associate one program with the file type. Add the second program to the actions for that file type. A single- or double-click on a file of that type runs the first program. To run the second program, right-click the file and choose the program from the shortcut menu.*

To see the details of what Windows does when you choose a command like Open or Print from a shortcut menu for a type of file, choose the action from the Actions list and click the Edit button. You see the Editing Action For Type dialog box (Figure 3-6).

The Application Used To Perform Action box contains the command line Windows executes when you open files of this type. The command line usually consists of the full path name of a program, possibly followed by a space and %1. The %1 represents the name of the file you want to open; that is, this command runs the program and tells the program to open the file you double-clicked.

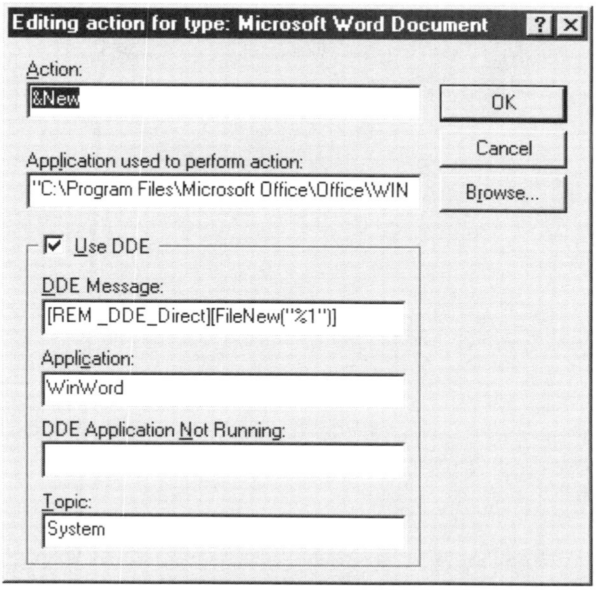

Editing action for type: Microsoft Word Document ? X

Action:
&New

OK

Cancel

Application used to perform action:

"C:\Program Files\Microsoft Office\Office\WIN

Browse...

☑ Use DDE

DDE Message:
[REM _DDE_Direct][FileNew("%1")]

Application:
WinWord

DDE Application Not Running:

Topic:
System

Figure 3-6.   *You can control which program Windows runs when you open a file of a specified type.*

If the Use DDE check box is not selected, it is a *regular* action (that is, a command that appears on the shortcut menu, which appears when you right-click a file of this type). In this case, the dialog box has only two settings:

- **Action**   Specifies the name of the action, which appears in the Edit File Type dialog box and on the shortcut menu you see when you right-click filenames of this type. You don't have to capitalize the first letter of the action: Windows capitalizes the first letter of the action name when it appears on the shortcut menu. You can choose a letter to be underlined on the shortcut menu: precede the letter with an ampersand (&). You can choose a command from the shortcut menu by typing the underlined letter.

- **Application Used To Perform Action**   Specifies the program to run to perform this action on this type of file.

If the Use DDE check box is selected, the action is a DDE action, and you see four additional settings:

- **DDE Message**   Specifies the DDE command for this action.

- **Application**   Specifies the DDE application string to start a DDE link with the program. If this box is blank, Windows runs the program specified in the Application Used To Perform Action box.

- **DDE Application Not Running**   Specifies the DDE command to use if the program (specified in the Application box) is not already running. If this box is blank, Windows sends the same command specified in the DDE Message box.

- **Topic**   Specifies the DDE topic string to start a conversation with the program. The default DDE topic string (used if this box is blank) is "System."

Uninstalling Programs

If you don't use a program, you might want to uninstall it to free up space on your hard disk. You might also want to uninstall older versions of programs before installing new versions. You can use the Add/Remove Programs program to remove some programs; some programs come with uninstall programs; and some programs require you to delete files manually.

Uninstalling Programs Using the Add/Remove Programs Program

When you want to uninstall a program, first check whether it appears on the Add/Remove Program Properties dialog box. If the program does appear in this dialog box, use Add/Remove Programs to uninstall the program, following these steps:

1. Choose Start | Settings | Control Panel. You see the Control Panel window.

2. Run Add/Remove Programs. You see the Add/Remove Programs Properties dialog box, shown in Figure 3-1. If the Install/Uninstall tab isn't selected, click it. The box in the lower-half of the window lists many of the programs you have already installed on your system.

3. In the list of installed programs, click the program you want to uninstall and click the Add/Remove button. Windows uninstalls the program, while messages appear to let you know what's happening.

If the program doesn't appear on the Add/Remove Programs Properties dialog box, you have to uninstall the program by using another way (see "Running an Uninstall Program").

  Sometimes Windows can't uninstall a program, usually because it can't find the files it needs to perform the uninstallation.

Running an Uninstall Program

Many programs come with uninstall programs, usually named Uninstall.exe or Unwise.exe. Look for an uninstall program in the same folder where the program is stored. Run the program, and then follow the directions on the screen. The uninstallation program may also be on the Start | Programs menu on the same submenu as the program.

Uninstalling Programs Without Installation Programs

What if a program doesn't appear on the Add/Remove Programs Properties dialog box and doesn't come with an uninstall program? You can delete by hand the program files and the shortcuts to the program. You might not delete every last file connected with the program, but the remaining files usually won't do any harm. Before deleting anything, check the program's documentation for instructions. Be sure to back up your hard disk before uninstalling a program by hand, in case you delete a file your system needs.

Tip

Rather than deleting a program, you might first want to move it to a new location for a few days. Make a folder named C:\Temp (or another temporary location) and move the folder containing the program files into your temporary folder. If other programs are using those files, you'll see error messages when those programs run. If no programs report errors within a week, then you know it's safe to delete the folder containing the program files.

To delete the program files, determine which folder contains them. The easiest way to find out where the program is stored is to look at the properties of a shortcut to the program (see Chapter 9, section "What Is a Shortcut?"). Right-click a shortcut to the program on your desktop, in a folder, or in the C:\Windows\Start Menu\Programs folder. Choose Properties from the menu that appears and click the Shortcut tab on the Properties dialog box for the program. The Target box contains the full path name of the executable file for the program. Click Find Target to open an Explorer window for the folder that contains the program file.

To delete the program, delete the folder that contains the program files and all the files in it (see Chapter 8, section "Deleting Files and Folders"). Then delete the shortcuts to the program so the program doesn't appear on your desktop, in any folders, on your Start menu, or in the Quick Launch section of the Taskbar.

Tip

If at all possible, use a program's uninstaller instead of just deleting all the files because the uninstaller is safer and more comprehensive. Uninstallers remove files in C:\Windows, C:\Windows\System, and other locations in which it might have installed them, as well as deleting the Registry entries for the program (see Chapter 37).

Finishing an Uninstallation

After uninstalling a program, you might see shortcuts to the program lying around on your desktop, in folders, or in your Start menu. Delete these shortcuts by right-clicking the shortcut and choosing Delete from the menu that appears or by dragging the shortcut into the Recycle Bin on the desktop.

The Complete Reference

Windows Me

Chapter 4

Working with Documents in Windows Me

Although word processing isn't glamorous, it is, and probably forever will be, one of the most popular uses for a computer. Windows Me comes with two tools for working with text documents—the first is the unsophisticated Notepad, and the second is the semi-full-featured WordPad.

Reading Text Files with Notepad

Notepad is a holdover from Windows 3.0. Back in the Windows 3.0 era, configuration information was stored in text files that regularly needed to be edited, and Notepad could edit these files. In the intervening releases of Windows, editing configuration files has become a task more often done either automatically by installation programs or manually by system administrators and hackers than by people simply trying to make their computers work the way they want.

Notepad, however, remains available in Windows Me. Using Notepad is the simplest way to edit a text file—sure, you can use a full-fledged word processor, but doing so often is more trouble than it's worth. So use Notepad to edit any *text file* (also called an *ASCII file*)—that is, files that contain only letters, numbers, and special characters that appear on the keyboard. A text file can't store formatting such as bold and italics.

Running Notepad

To run Notepad, choose Start | Programs | Accessories | Notepad. (Or, you can choose Start | Run to display the Run dialog box, and then type **notepad** and press ENTER.) Notepad looks like Figure 4-1: just a window with a menu.

The following sections offer some information about and tips on using Notepad.

Copying, Moving, and Pasting Text

You can copy or move text to or from the Windows Clipboard using the Edit | Copy, Edit | Cut, and Edit | Paste commands. See Chapter 7, section "What Is Cut-and-Paste?"

Document Settings

To change the setup of the document when you print it, choose File | Page Setup (this command isn't available if you haven't installed a printer in Windows). Use the Page Setup dialog box (shown in Figure 4-2) to change margins, page orientation, and paper size. (In the Orientation box, Portrait prints on paper in the usual way; Landscape prints sideways on the page, with the lines of text parallel to the long edge of the

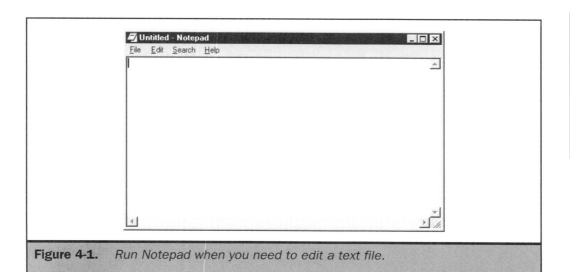

Figure 4-1.   *Run Notepad when you need to edit a text file.*

paper.) If you have more than one printer, you can select the one to use. Use the Header and Footer text boxes to add headers and footers to your documents. You can type plain text, or you can use the codes in Table 4-1.

Code	Meaning
&f	Displays the name of the file
&p	Displays the page number
&d	Displays the current date
&t	Displays the current time
&&	Displays an ampersand
&l	Left-justifies the text after this code
&c	Centers the text after this code
&r	Right-justifies the text after this code

Table 4-1.   *Header and Footer Codes in WordPad*

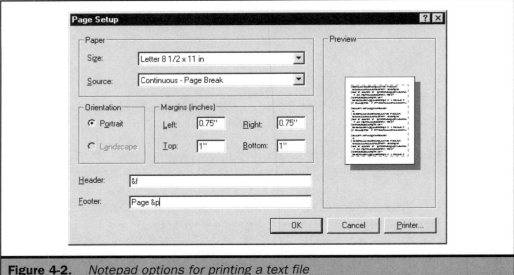

Figure 4-2. *Notepad options for printing a text file*

File Types

Choose File | Open to see the Open dialog box. Change the Files Of Type option to All Files if the file you want to open does not have the .txt extension.

Fonts

Notepad normally uses the *FixedSys* font, a fixed-pitch font, to display text files. You can change the font by choosing Edit | Set Font to display the Font dialog box and then setting the font, style, and size.

Log Files

Create a log file by typing **.LOG** in the top-left corner (the very beginning) of your Notepad file (be sure to use capital letters). Each time you run Notepad and open the file, Notepad enters the current time and date at the end of the file. You can then type an entry for that time and date.

Printing

Print the text file by choosing File | Print. Notepad prints the file with the filename at the top of each page and a page number at the bottom, unless you choose File | Page Setup and change the Header and Footer settings.

Saving Files

Save the text file you are editing by choosing File | Save. To save it with a name you specify, choose File | Save As to display the Save As dialog box.

Searching for Text

You can search for a string of text by choosing Search | Find to display the Find dialog box, and then typing the string you're looking for into the Find What text box. Click the Match Case check box if you want Notepad to find only text that matches the capitalization of the text you typed. You can also specify whether to search forward or backward in the file by clicking the Up or Down radio button. Start the search by clicking the Find Next button. To search for the same string again, press F3 or choose Search | Find Next.

Time and Date

You can insert the current time and date (according to your computer's clock) at the cursor by choosing Edit | Time/Date, or by pressing F5.

Undo

If you make a mistake, you can reverse your last edit by choosing Edit | Undo or pressing CTRL-Z.

Word Wrap

As you work with a document, you might want to turn on the *Word Wrap*, so Notepad breaks long lines of text up onto multiple lines on the screen. When Word Wrap is off, each paragraph appears as a single long line (unless it contains carriage returns). Turn on word Wrap by choosing Edit | Word Wrap. Notepad then wraps lines like a word processor wraps lines, so no line is wider than the Notepad window. Notepad's Word Wrap feature doesn't add carriage return characters to the text file when you save it and it doesn't affect the way the file appears when printed.

Files You Can Edit with Notepad

The standard file extension for text files is .txt. When you click or double-click a .txt file in Windows Explorer, Windows runs Notepad to view the files. Notepad works fine for text files up to a maximum size of about 40K. If you try to open a larger file with Notepad, Windows runs WordPad instead.

Windows associates a number of other types of files with Notepad, too, because these files contain only text and are usually small enough for Notepad to handle. These files types include

- Configuration files, such as files with the extension .ini (see Chapter 36, section "Windows Initialization Files").

- Dial-Up Networking scripts (see Chapter 21, section "Creating and Using Logon Scripts").

- Log files, with the extension .log, which many housekeeping programs create.

- Setup information files, which come with many installation programs and have the extension .inf.

Taking Advantage of Free Word Processing with WordPad

WordPad is a great little word processor if your needs are modest—and the price can't be beat! Open WordPad by choosing Start | Programs | Accessories | WordPad. (Or, you can choose Start | Run to display the Run dialog box, type **wordpad**, and press ENTER.)

Note   *WordPad is usually installed along with Windows Me. If not, install it by inserting your Windows Me CD-ROM, opening Control Panel, running Add/Remove Programs, clicking the Windows Setup tab, choosing Accessories from the Components list, clicking Details, and choosing WordPad from the list of Accessories.*

WordPad (shown in Figure 4-3) does not offer many of the advanced features that you get in Microsoft Word or Corel's WordPerfect—notably missing is a spelling checker. But WordPad does offer many of the formatting tools you need to create a spiffy letter, memo, or essay. Many of the commands and keyboard shortcuts are the same as those in Microsoft Word, which makes them easy for many people to remember. The version of WordPad that comes with Windows Me can open documents created by versions of Word up through Word 2000. And, because WordPad is a small program, it loads quickly.

Opening and Saving Files with WordPad

With WordPad, you can open and edit a document that is saved in any one of a variety of formats, including documents saved with Word 97 and 2000 (WordPad cannot preserve all of Word's formatting, however). To open a document, choose File | Open, and use the Files Of Type option on the Open dialog box to choose the type of document you want to open.

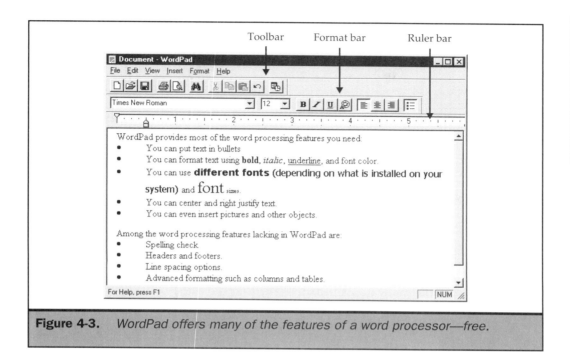

Figure 4-3.   *WordPad offers many of the features of a word processor—free.*

When you're saving a document to pass on to a friend or coworker, choose File | Save to use the existing filename or File | Save As to specify the filename. Be sure to save the document in a format that your friend's or coworker's software can open. Here's a rundown of the file formats WordPad can use to save a document:

- **Word 6.0 for Windows**   Anyone who has Microsoft Word 6.0 or later (version 6.0 was the last version for Windows 3.*x*) can read a file in this format. In addition, anyone with WordPad can read this file, even if they only use Windows 95. Word 6.0 came out quite a while ago, so any major word processing package can convert a Word 6.0 document and keep its formatting intact. Word 6.0 format is the default WordPad format and uses the extension .doc. This format preserves all the formatting WordPad can create.

- **Rich Text Format**   If Word 6.0 is not a compatible file format, chances are good that *Rich Text Format* (*.rtf*) is compatible. Formatting is preserved in .rtf files, but the files tend to be much larger than .doc files.

- **Text Document**   When you save a file in text format (with the extension .txt), you lose all formatting, but you preserve all text in the *ANSI* character set (a standard set of codes used for storing text).

- **Text Document—MS-DOS Format**   When you save a file in MS-DOS text format (also with the extension .txt), you lose all formatting, but you preserve all text in Microsoft's extended ASCII character set, which includes various accented characters and smiley faces. Use this format only if you want to use the text in a Windows or DOS application, but not if you plan to send the file to a Mac, UNIX, or other non-Microsoft system.

- **Unicode Text Document**   *Unicode* enables you to use characters from practically every language on Earth, from Latvian to Japanese. But make sure your recipient has a Unicode-compatible program before you save Unicode documents.

Formatting with WordPad

Use the options on the format bar (the row of buttons below the toolbar) to format a document in WordPad. If you don't see the format bar (or WordPad's other bars—the toolbar, ruler bar, or status bar), use the View menu to display them.

Formatting in WordPad works like this:

- Select the text you want to format, using your mouse. Or, choose Edit | Select All (or press CTRL-A) to select the entire document.

- Click the button or give the command for the type of formatting you want to apply.

The following sections describe some of the formatting options in WordPad.

Bullets

To format a paragraph with a bullet, click anywhere in the paragraph and click the Bullets button at the very end of the format bar, or choose Format | Bullet Style. To format more than one paragraph, select the paragraphs before clicking the Bullets button.

Indents

To indent a paragraph, click in the paragraph (or select several paragraphs) and choose Format | Paragraph to display the Paragraph dialog box. You can type a measurement from the left or right margin, or for the first line only. You can also specify that the paragraph is left aligned, right aligned, or centered. When you click OK, the margin indicators on the ruler bar move to show the current margins for the paragraph in which your cursor is located.

Tabs

To set tab stops, choose Format | Tabs. You see the Tabs dialog box. Set a tab stop by typing a measurement from the left margin and clicking the Set button. The tab stop appears on the list of tab stops that are set for the current position in the document.

To delete a tab stop, select it from the list and click the Clear button. When you click OK, little L-shaped tab indicators appear on the ruler bar to show the location of tab stops.

If the ruler bar is displayed (choose View | Ruler to display it), you can click a location on the ruler bar to create a tab stop there. Drag the L-shaped tab markers left or right on the ruler bar to adjust the tab stops. To delete a tab stop, drag it down off the ruler bar.

Text: Fonts, Size, and Color

To change the font, font size, or color of the selected text, click the Font or Font Size box on the format bar and choose the font or font size from the list that appears. Or, choose Format | Font to display the Font dialog box, shown in Figure 4-4. Choose the font, font size, color, and whether you want the text to be bold, italic, underlined, or struck out. If you have installed multilanguage support, you can also choose the script (alphabet). Then click OK. You can also choose settings from the Font dialog box without selecting text, before you type the text you want to format; use the Font dialog box again to turn the formatting off.

You can also format text by using keystroke combinations: CTRL-B to bold, CTRL-I to italicize, and CTRL-U to underline. You can use these keystrokes after you select text or before you type the text you want to format (press the key combination again to turn off the formatting).

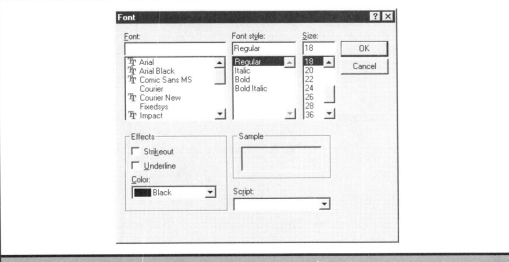

Figure 4-4. *Select the font for the selected text.*

Printing Your WordPad Document

To print your document, click the Print button, the fourth button on the toolbar, or choose File | Print, or press CTRL-P. You see the Print dialog box, in which you can select the printer, which pages to print, and the number of copies.

You may want to preview (see exactly what it will look like on paper) the document before you print it. To preview your document, click the Print Preview button, the fifth button on the toolbar, or choose File | Print Preview. The WordPad window shows approximately how the printed page will look. You can click the Zoom In button to get a closer look, click Print to begin printing, or click Close to return to the regular view of your document.

You can also format the page by choosing File | Page Setup to display the Page Setup dialog box. Use the Page Setup dialog box to change margins, paper orientation, and paper size.

WordPad Extras

WordPad has a couple of additional features you may find useful:

Copying, Moving, and Pasting Text

Use the Windows Clipboard to copy and move text within WordPad, and between WordPad and other applications. Choose Edit | Copy, click the Copy button on the toolbar, or press CTRL-C to copy selected text to the Clipboard. Choose Edit | Cut, click the Cut button on the toolbar, or press CTRL-X to move selected text to the Clipboard. Choose Edit | Paste, click the Paste button on the toolbar, or press CTRL-V to copy information from the Clipboard to the current cursor location. If you are pasting information other than text into your document, choose Edit | Paste Special to choose how the information should appear (see Chapter 7).

Date and Time

Insert the current date and time into your document by clicking the Date/Time button, the last button on the toolbar, or by choosing Insert | Date and Time. The Date and Time dialog box appears, from which you can choose the format for the date, time, or both.

Inserting Objects

Insert an object (such as a picture) into a WordPad document by

- Dragging the object into the WordPad window from Windows Explorer
- Using Insert | Object and choosing the type of object you want to insert
- Pasting an object from the Windows Clipboard

You can see the properties of an object by clicking the object and choosing Edit | Object Properties, or by pressing ALT-ENTER. If you insert a picture, you can use WordPad's simple graphic editing commands by double-clicking the picture; the annotation toolbar appears at the bottom of the WordPad window. You can also move an object in your document by clicking-and-dragging it to a new location.

Replacing Text

You can replace specific text with other text throughout your document by choosing Edit | Replace or pressing CTRL-H. You then see the Replace dialog box. In the Find What box, type the text to be replaced. In the Replace With box, type the text to be inserted. You can select the Match Whole Word Only and Match Case check boxes to tell WordPad which instances of the text to match. Click Find Next to find the next instance of the text in the Find What box, and then click Replace to replace this instance with the Replace With text. To replace all the rest of the instances in your document, click Replace All.

Searching for Text

You can search for text by using the Find button on the toolbar, which has a picture of binoculars on it, or by choosing Edit | Find or pressing CTRL-F. Use the options on the Find dialog box to find only the whole word, or to match the case of the contents of the Find What text box. To search for the same information again, press F3 or choose Edit | Find Next.

Undo

Undo your last action by clicking the Undo button, the second-to-last button on the toolbar, by choosing Edit | Undo, or by pressing CTRL-Z.

Setting WordPad's Options

You can configure WordPad by choosing View | Options to display the Options dialog box shown in Figure 4-5. Table 4-2 shows the settings for the tabs in this dialog box.

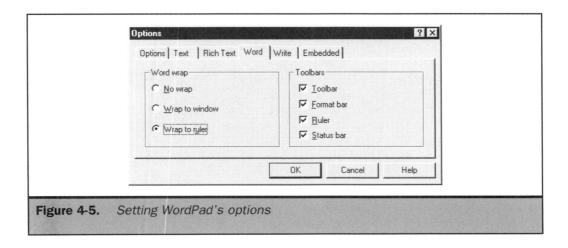

Figure 4-5.   *Setting WordPad's options*

Tab	Setting	Description
Options	Measurement units: Inches, Points, Centimeters, and Picas	Specifies how you want to see and set measurements
Options	Automatic word selection	Specifies that when you select part of a word, you want to select the whole word
Text	Word wrap: No wrap, Wrap to window, and Wrap to ruler	Specifies how to break long paragraphs into lines when you are editing normal text files
Text	Toolbars: Toolbar, Format bar, Ruler, and Status bar	Specifies which toolbars to display when you are editing normal text files
Rich Text	Word wrap: No wrap, Wrap to window, and Wrap to ruler	Specifies how to break long paragraphs into lines when you are editing .rtf files
Rich Text	Toolbars: Toolbar, Format bar, Ruler, and Status bar	Specifies which toolbars to display when you are editing .rtf files
Word	Word wrap: No wrap, Wrap to window, and Wrap to ruler	Specifies how to break long paragraphs into lines when you are editing Word documents (with extension .doc)

Table 4-2.   *Settings in WordPad's Options Dialog Box*

Tab	Setting	Description
Word	Toolbars: Toolbar, Format bar, Ruler, and Status bar	Specifies which toolbars to display when you are editing Word documents (with extension .doc)
Write	Word wrap: No wrap, Wrap to window, and Wrap to ruler	Specifies how to break long paragraphs into lines when you are editing Windows Write documents (with extension .wri)
Write	Toolbars: Toolbar, Format bar, Ruler, and Status bar	Specifies which toolbars to display when you are editing Windows Write documents (with extension .wri)
Embedded	Word wrap: No wrap, Wrap to window, and Wrap to ruler	Specifies how to break long paragraphs into lines when you are editing embedded documents
Embedded	Toolbars: Toolbar, Format bar, and Ruler	Specifies which toolbars to display when you are editing embedded documents

Table 4-2.   *Settings in WordPad's Options Dialog Box* (continued)

The Complete Reference

Chapter 5

Using Accessories

W indows Me comes with a number of useful accessories, in addition to the word processing accessories discussed in the previous chapter. Microsoft Paint and Kodak Imaging work with images. You can keep yourself amused by playing games against your computer—or against other humans over the Internet. The Phone Dialer and Calculator do exactly what their names suggest. The Character Map helps you find obscure characters to jazz up your text files and documents. And Address Book can store the e-mail addresses, mailing addresses, phone numbers, and other information about your coworkers and friends.

Working with Images

Not so many years ago, putting a picture into a text document was pretty exotic. Text was text, and pictures were pictures—newspapers and magazines might mix them together, but that was for the professionals. But now, a Web page without images is considered boring, and it's no big deal to attach photos to e-mail, or to use your computer to send an image file as a fax. Ordinary people need to have some tools for creating and working with images.

Windows Me provides two such tools: Microsoft Paint and Kodak Imaging. In general, Paint is a better drawing and drafting tool, while Imaging is designed for cropping and annotating photos.

Drawing Pictures Using Microsoft Paint

Microsoft Paint is to images what WordPad is to text documents—a simple but versatile tool for creating and editing. You can use it to make diagrams for presentations or to crop your online vacation photos; your five-year-old can use it as a coloring book, or your ten-year-old can use it to draw moustaches on the Mona Lisa.

To run Paint, choose Start | Programs | Accessories | Paint. Depending on how your file system is set up, Paint may be the default application for .bmp files or other image files. If so, Paint runs whenever you open one of these files. Figure 5-1 shows the parts of a Paint window.

Opening and Saving Files

Paint works with only one document at a time. Opening a file or creating a new one automatically closes whatever file Paint had been working on previously. Paint opens files in the following image formats: bitmap (.bmp); tagged image file or TIFF (.tif); Joint Photographic Experts Group or JPEG (.jpg); and Graphics Interchange Format or GIF (.gif). (Choose All Files in the Save dialog box to save in formats other than .bmp.) Files created or edited by Paint can be saved as bitmap files in a variety of color schemes (monochrome, 16 color, 256 color, and 24-bit color), as well as .jpg and .gif.

Selecting Objects

With the Select tool chosen (by clicking the dotted rectangle button in the Tool box), you can select objects inside the drawing area, just as you select objects inside an

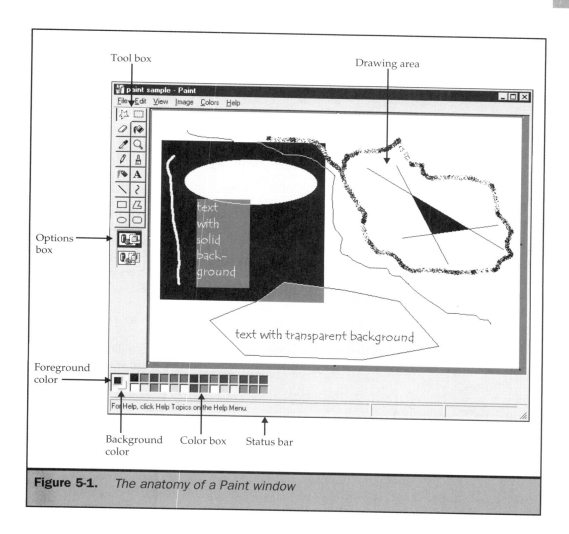

Tool box

Drawing area

Options
box

Foreground
color

Background
color

Color box

Status bar

Figure 5-1. *The anatomy of a Paint window*

Explorer window: by enclosing them in a rectangle. Move the pointer to one corner of the rectangular area that includes the objects you want to select, hold the mouse button down, move to the opposite corner of the area, and release the mouse button.

The Free-Form Select tool (the dotted star button in the Tool box) enables you to select objects and parts of objects inside a region of any shape. Drag the cursor to trace out any shape. Either close up the shape, or Paint closes it up automatically with a straight line. The enclosed region is now selected, and can be moved by dragging or copied by cutting-and-pasting—useful for creating repeated patterns.

Magnifying and Enlarging

To magnify the objects in your drawing or zoom in on a portion of the drawing area, click the Magnifier tool (the magnifying glass button in the Tool box). A rectangle appears in the drawing area; it represents the portion of the drawing that will be visible after magnification. Position the rectangle to enclose the area you want to zoom in on, and then click. The portion of the drawing that was inside the rectangle now fills the entire viewing area. To zoom back out, click the Magnifier tool again, and then click anywhere in the viewing area.

When the Magnifier tool is selected, the Options box displays four magnification levels: 1x, 2x, 6x, and 8x. The current level of magnification is highlighted. To change to another level of magnification, click that option in the Options box.

To enlarge or shrink the drawing area (the "sheet of paper"), drag its corners.

Drawing Lines and Curves

Clicking with the Line tool (the straight line button in the Tool box) nails down one end of a line; the other end moves with the cursor. When the line is where you want it, click again to fix the other end. To make a curved line, click the Curve tool (the wiggly line button in the Tool box) and begin by drawing a straight line, as you would with the Line tool. Then, click-and-drag a point on that line to make a curve. You have the option of dragging a second point to make another kink in the curve.

When the Line or Curve tools are selected, different line thicknesses appear in the Options box, just below the Tool box. Select a new thickness by clicking the line thickness you want.

When you click with the left mouse button, the Line and Curve tools draw in the foreground color. To draw lines and curves in the background color, use the right mouse button.

Drawing Freehand

Paint has four tools in the Tool box that make freehand marks as you drag them: Pencil, Brush, Spray Can, and Eraser. Pencil makes thin lines, Brush makes thick lines, and Spray Can sprays a pattern of dots. You can choose among three densities of Spray Can dot patterns by clicking the pattern you want in the Options box. As its name suggests, the Eraser erases anything in its path, replacing it with the background color.

Making Shapes

These four tools in the Tool box make shapes: Ellipse, Rectangle, Rounded Rectangle, and Polygon. The simplest shape to make is a rectangle:

1. Click the Rectangle tool (the solid—not the dotted—rectangle button).

2. Click in the drawing area where you want one corner of the rectangle located.

3. Drag to where you want the opposite corner of the rectangle located. When you release the mouse button, Paint creates the rectangle.

You use the Ellipse and Rounded Rectangle tools in a manner similar to the Rectangle tool.

The Polygon tool makes figures with any number of sides:

1. Click the Polygon tool (the L-shaped polygon button).

2. Click inside the drawing area where you want one corner of the polygon located.

3. Each click defines the next corner of the polygon. For the first side, you must click-and-drag; for subsequent sides, just click.

4. Double-click the last corner. Paint closes up the polygon automatically.

Coloring Objects

Control the colors of objects by using the Color box at the bottom of the Paint window. The two colored squares at the far left of the Color box show the current foreground and background colors, with the foreground square on top of the background square. Any object you construct using the left mouse button has the foreground color, while objects made using the right mouse button have the background color.

To choose a new foreground color, left-click the square of the new color in the Color box. To choose a new background color, right-click the square of the new color. You can match the color of any object in the drawing area by using the Pick Color tool (the eyedropper button in the Tool box). Select the tool, and then click the object whose color you want to match. Left-clicking changes the foreground color to match the object; right-clicking changes the background color to match the object.

To color within an outlined area, such as a rectangle or an ellipse, select the Fill With Color tool (the tipped paint can button), and click within the area. Right-click to fill with the background color. Using the Fill With Color tool on an area that is not outlined colors the whole "sheet of paper"—the area outside of any enclosed region.

Changing the foreground or background color does not change the color of objects already created. To change an object to the new foreground (background) color, select the Fill With Color tool and click (right-click) the object whose color you want to change. You can invert the colors in a region (that is, make a negative of the original) by selecting the region choosing Image | Invert Colors.

Adding Text

Click the Text tool (the button with the *A*), and drag across the part of your picture where you want the type to appear. Paint displays a rectangular text box for you to type in. A font selection box appears above the text box so you can select the font, size, and style of the text. The color of the text is the foreground color. Click inside the text box and type. Click outside the text box when you are done typing.

The Options box below the Tool box gives two choices for using the Text tool. The top choice makes a solid background for the text box, using the background color. The bottom choice makes a transparent background.

Flipping, Rotating, and Stretching

Commands on the Image menu flip, rotate, or stretch the entire image or the selected part of the image. Choosing Image | Flip/Rotate opens a dialog box from which you can choose to flip the image horizontally or vertically, or you can rotate it by any multiple of 90 degrees. Choosing Image | Stretch/Skew opens another dialog box from which you can stretch the image horizontally or vertically by any percentage, or slant it by any number of degrees.

Cropping Images

You can crop an image—remove unwanted material around the edges of a picture. To crop an image, use the Select tool to enclose the area of the image that you want to keep. To save the selected area as a new file, choose Edit | Copy To. Type a new filename and click Save. The original image is unaffected.

Annotating Images with Kodak Imaging

Scanners, digital cameras, clip art CDs, and the Internet give computer users access to countless images, which you can print out, insert into your documents, or display on your Web pages. Even though a picture is worth a thousand words, the impact of a picture can sometimes be improved by the addition of a few words, some highlighting, and maybe a few lines drawn on top, either straight or freehand. Kodak's Imaging for Windows is a tool for this job. You can run Imaging by choosing Start | Programs | Accessories | Imaging.

Note   *Imaging may not be not installed. If it doesn't appear on the Start | Programs | Accessories menu, you can install it from the Windows Me CD-ROM. Choose Start | Settings | Control Panel, run Add/Remove Programs, click the Windows Setup tab, choose the Accessories entry in the list of Windows Me components, click Details, and choose Imaging from the list of accessories (see Chapter 3, section "Installing and Uninstalling Programs That Come with Windows").*

Imaging has four toolbars, which are shown in Figure 5-2. Any or all of these toolbars can be made to disappear by selecting View | Toolbars and checking the appropriate boxes in the Toolbars dialog box. You can choose the standard Windows file commands (New, Open, Save, Save As, and Print) from the File menu, or by clicking the appropriate buttons on the Standard toolbar.

Note   *If you click or double-click a graphics file to run Kodak Imaging, you may run its display-only cousin instead, Kodak Preview (see "Viewing Images").*

Acquiring Images

Kodak Imaging can open files in a large number of formats: bitmap (.bmp), tagged image file or TIFF (.tif), JPEG (.jpg), GIF (.gif), Fax (.awd), PCX (.pcx), DCX (.dcx), XIF (.xif), and WIFF (.wif). If your system has a TWAIN-compliant scanner (*TWAIN* is a standard for communications between scanners and computer software), Imaging can take an image directly from the scanner. You must first select your scanner by choosing File | Select Scanner and picking the scanner from the list that appears. To scan an image, choose File | Scan New. Your scanner's driver displays its dialog box; click the Preview, Scan, or other button to scan the image, which appears in the Kodak Imaging window.

Despite what the Help files say, however, Imaging can only annotate .tif, .bmp, or .awd files, and it works best with .tif. All other files are opened in read-only mode. If you want to annotate an image file in a different format, open it in Imaging, and then save it in .tif format.

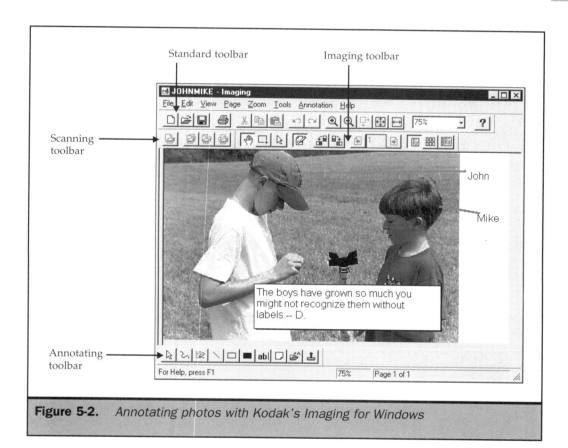

Figure 5-2.   *Annotating photos with Kodak's Imaging for Windows*

Rotating Images

At the center of the Imaging toolbar are the Rotate Left and Rotate Right buttons. Each button rotates the image 90 degrees. One button undoes the action of the other, and four clicks of either button restores the image to its original orientation.

Zooming

The Standard toolbar contains five Zoom buttons (Zoom In, Zoom Out, Zoom To Selection, Best Fit, and Fit To Width) and a Zoom display window, with a drop-down list of standard zoom percentages. Zoom In (the magnifying glass and plus (+) sign button) doubles the size of the image in all dimensions; Zoom Out (the magnifying glass and minus (-) sign button) halves the image. When a portion of the image has been selected (with the Select Image tool), Zoom To Selection expands the selected portion to fill the entire window. Best Fit fits the image to either the height or the width of the window, using whichever method results in the least unused space in the window. Fit To Width fits the image to the width of the window.

The Zoom display window shows the current zoom percentage, with 100 percent corresponding to actual size. Change the zoom by typing any number into the display, or by choosing a preset percentage from the drop-down list.

Annotating Images

Imaging has an Annotating toolbar (shown in Figure 5-3) for annotating images stored in .tif, .bmp, or .awd files. Most of the basic tools resemble those available in Paint, and they work the same way: Click the appropriate button on the toolbar; the cursor changes to represent the corresponding tool. Use the tool to annotate the image by clicking-and-dragging to define the area in which you want the annotation. Once they have been created, annotations can be selected, moved, or stretched, just like elements in a Paint image.

> **Note**
>
> *When you are annotating a .bmp or .awd image file, the annotations become permanently affixed to the image when you save the file. At that point, they can no longer be edited, moved, or deleted.*

Imaging works especially well with TIFF files. Annotated TIFF files can be saved without losing your ability to edit the annotations. You can even exit Imaging and return to edit the annotations later. To make the annotations invisible, deselect Annotation | Show Annotations. If you want to affix the annotations permanently, select Annotation | Make Annotations Permanent.

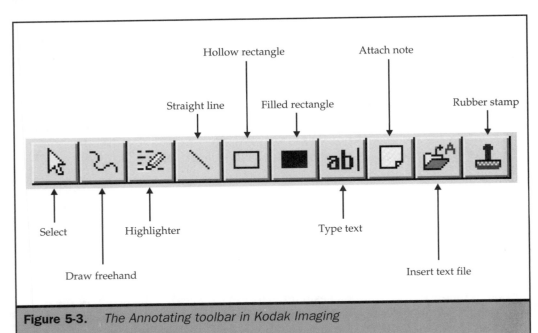

Figure 5-3.   *The Annotating toolbar in Kodak Imaging*

The Select, Freehand Line, Straight Line, and Text tools are almost identical to the corresponding Paint tools. Imaging has two rectangle tools (Hollow and Filled), whereas Paint has only one. (In Paint, Transparent and Filled are options for a single Rectangle tool.) Highlighter is a third kind of rectangle tool, one whose filling is translucent, resembling what a highlighter pen does to an image on paper.

Attach Note is a tool similar to Text. You use it by dragging a rectangle across the part of the image where you want the note to be located, and then clicking inside the rectangle and typing the note. Unlike Text, however, the attached note has a background color that obscures the original image, as if a stick-on note has been posted there. Figure 5-2 shows an attached note.

Text From File inserts an entire text file as an annotation. When you click a location in the image with the Text From File tool, an Open window appears, enabling you to choose which text file to insert. The inserted file, like text you type into a window created by the Text tool, has a transparent background, as if you are typing over the image.

Rubber stamp has four options: Approved, Draft, Received, and Rejected. Select one when you click the tool. Clicking the tool on the image "stamps" the corresponding message onto the image in that location. All the options except Draft include the date automatically, as in "Received 7/12/2000."

Changing Tool Properties

Each of the annotation tools has properties you can change. Open a tool's Properties dialog box by right-clicking the tool button and selecting Properties. The Properties dialog box of any drawing tool enables you to adjust the color and/or line width of the drawing, and the Properties dialog box of any text tool controls the font and size of the text, as well as the color of the background.

Viewing Images

You can open images for viewing alone by using the Kodak Preview program. Windows uses this program for displaying many types of graphics files. The Kodak Preview program doesn't appear on the Start or Programs menus; to run it, right-click an image file and choose Open With | Image Preview from the context menu. You see the Imaging Preview window, which looks just like the regular Imaging window, but with a simplified toolbar and no menu bar. If you want Preview to be the default viewing option, select Tools | General Options to make the General Options dialog box appear, and then click the Preview button. You can still open an image in Imaging by right-clicking its file icon and selecting Open With | Imaging.

Playing Games

Games have been an important part of the personal computer experience from the beginning. Even people who are intimidated by serious tools, such as word processors and spreadsheets, can be enticed into learning games—and the basic computer skills the games require.

Windows Me provides a variety of games:

- **Solitaire games** FreeCell, Classic Solitaire, Minesweeper, and Spider Solitaire
- **Pinball** For one to four players
- **Classic Hearts** Simulated four-player card game in which the computer plays the other three hands. If your computer is on a local area network (LAN), you can play against others.
- **MSN Gaming Zone** Internet Backgammon, Internet Checkers, Internet Hearts, Internet Reversi, and Internet Spades. In these games, you play against other people over the Internet.

You can play these games by choosing Start | Programs | Games. Once a game is running, you can look up rules and strategies on the Help menu.

Games might not be installed. If they don't appear on the Start | Programs | Games menu, you can install them from the Windows Me CD-ROM. Choose Start | Settings | Control Panel, run Add/Remove Programs, click the Windows Setup tab, and choose the Games entry in the list of Windows Me components. You can click Details to choose Classic Games (the games that came with Windows 98), Internet Games, or PLUS! Games (the games that used to come on the Microsoft Windows PLUS CD-ROM).

Using Phone Dialer

If your computer is connected to a phone line, Phone Dialer can dial calls for you. You'll need a phone connected to the same phone line with which to conduct the phone call, though. To access Phone Dialer (shown in Figure 5-4), choose Start | Programs | Accessories | Communications | Phone Dialer.

Phone Dialer might not be installed. If it doesn't appear on the Start | Programs | Accessories menu, you can install it from the Windows Me CD-ROM. Choose Start | Settings | Control Panel, run Add/Remove Programs, click the Windows Setup tab, choose the Accessories entry in the list of Windows Me components, click Details, choose Communications from the list of accessories, click Details again, and choose Phone Dialer from the list of communications programs.

Dialing the Phone

Phone Dialer works like a telephone with speed-dial buttons. Enter a phone number into the display by typing, clicking the numbered buttons, or cutting-and-pasting from a document. Dial the displayed number by clicking the Dial button.

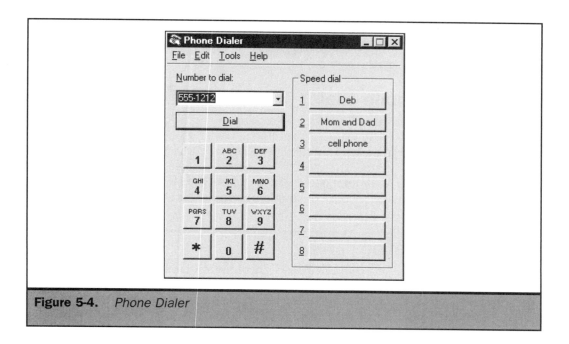

Figure 5-4. *Phone Dialer*

A list of recently dialed numbers drops down when you click the display window—redial a number by selecting it and clicking Dial. Dial any number assigned to your speed-dial buttons by clicking the button.

Storing Phone Numbers

Assign a phone number to one of the eight speed-dial buttons by clicking an unassigned button. Enter the number and a recognizable nickname into the appropriate windows of the Program Speed Dial dialog box, and then click either Save or Save and Dial. Reassign a speed-dial button by selecting Edit | Speed Dial. When the Edit Speed Dial dialog box appears, click the button you want to reassign, and type the new nickname and number in the fields at the bottom of the box. Then click Save.

Logging Your Phone Calls

Phone Dialer can keep a log of your phone calls. Choose Tools | Show Log to display the Call Log window. To tell Phone Dialer to keep a log of your calls, choose Log | Options from the Call Log window's menu bar. The Call Log Options dialog box has two check boxes: Incoming Calls and Outgoing Calls. Select the options you want, and then click OK. You can close the Call Log window by using its Close button. Reopen the window any time you want to look at the call log.

Some modems can't inform Phone Dialer about incoming calls, so the Incoming Calls option may not work. If you choose to log outgoing calls, Phone Dialer can track only those calls you dial using the program.

Configuring the Phone Dialer

If you use dialing properties to store your area code, calling cards, and other dialing information, you can use these features from Phone Dialer. Choose Tools | Dialing Properties to see or change these properties (see Chapter 20, section "Configuring Windows for Dialing Locations").

If your computer has more than one modem, choose Tools | Connect Using to choose which modem to dial. Choose the modem from the Line box, and then click OK.

Using Calculator

Windows' Calculator is really two calculators: the unintimidating Standard Calculator that does simple arithmetic, and a more complicated Scientific Calculator. To use either of them, choose Start | Programs | Accessories | Calculator. The Calculator program opens in Standard view. To use the Scientific Calculator, choose View | Scientific.

You can use the Calculator in conjunction with other programs, such as word processors, by cutting-and-pasting numbers from a document into the Calculator, doing a calculation, and then cutting-and-pasting the result back into a document (see Chapter 7, section "What Is Cut-and-Paste?"). You can also enter numbers into the calculator by clicking its buttons or by typing the numbers into the display window by using the keyboard. If you misenter a digit, click the Calculator's Back button. The CE and C buttons stand for Clear Entry and Clear, respectively.

Using the Standard Calculator

The Standard Calculator adds, subtracts, multiplies, divides, takes square roots, calculates percentages, and finds multiplicative inverses. It has a one-number memory.

Performing Arithmetic

To perform an arithmetic calculation, enter the calculation as you would type it, left to right, as in

$3 + 5 =$

To compute a percentage, make the percentage the second number in a multiplication and don't use the equal sign. For example, to figure 15 percent of 7.4, enter

$7.4 \times 15\%$

The $1/x$ button computes the multiplicative inverse of the displayed number.

Storing Numbers in Memory

The four buttons on the left side of the Standard Calculator control its memory. To store the currently displayed number in the memory, click the MS (memory store) button. An *M* appears in the box above the MC button to show the memory is in use. The memory holds only one number, so storing another number causes the calculator to forget the previously stored number. Clicking MC (memory clear) clears the memory. To recall the number stored in memory, click MR (memory recall). Clicking the M+ button adds the displayed number to the number in memory and stores the result in the memory.

 Use the memory to transfer a number from the standard to the scientific calculator or vice versa. The current display is cleared when you switch from one calculator to the other, but the memory is not cleared.

Using the Scientific Calculator

The Scientific Calculator (shown in Figure 5-5) is considerably larger, more powerful, and more complex than the Standard Calculator. Anything you can do on the Standard Calculator works exactly the same way on the Scientific Calculator, except the Scientific

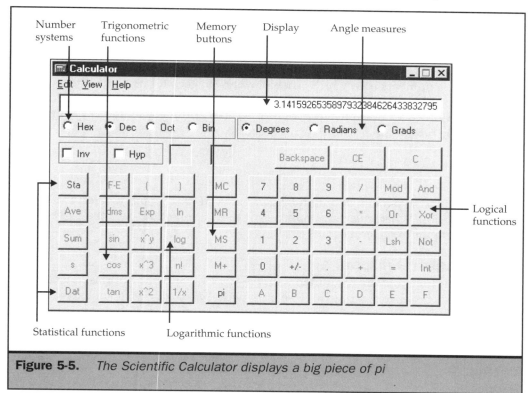

Figure 5-5. *The Scientific Calculator displays a big piece of pi*

Calculator has no % or sqrt key. (Compute square roots by clicking x^2 when the Inv box is checked.) In addition, you can perform calculations in a variety of number systems, do logical operations, use trigonometric functions, and do statistical analyses.

Why Don't All the Buttons Work?

Some buttons of the Scientific Calculator only make sense in certain situations; in other situations, they are grayed out and clicking them does nothing. For example, the A–F buttons are numbers in the hexadecimal number system, so they don't work unless the Hex radio button is selected. The hexadecimal, octal, and binary number systems are set up for whole number calculations only, so the trigonometric function buttons are grayed out when the Hex, Oct, or Bin radio buttons are selected. The statistics buttons are grayed out when no data is loaded in the statistics box.

Number Systems and Angle Measures

The Scientific Calculator can work in Dec (decimal, the default), Bin (binary), Oct (octal), or Hex (hexadecimal) number systems. Choose among number systems by using the radio buttons on the left side of the top row. When you are working in the decimal number system, you can use the radio buttons just to the right of the number-system buttons to choose among the different ways of measuring angles: degrees (the default), radians, and gradients. When using degrees, the DMS button converts a decimal number of degrees into degrees-minute-seconds form. To convert back, check the Inv box and click DMS again.

When you are working in the binary, octal, or hexadecimal number systems, the radio buttons just to the right of the number system buttons enable you to select the range of whole numbers with which you will work. (In geek terms, this is the register size.) The choices are Byte (0–255, or 8 bits), Word (16 bits), Dword (double word, or 32 bits), and Qword (quadruple word, or 64 bits). The arithmetic in these systems is modular, so in hexadecimal with Byte register size

> 2 - 3 =

yields the answer FF rather than -1.

The F-E (fixed-exponential) button toggles between fixed-point notation and scientific notation. When entering a number in scientific notation, click the Exp button before entering the exponential part.

Trigonometric Functions

Trigonometric functions are computed with the Sin, Cos, and Tan buttons. Use the Inv and Hyp check boxes to compute inverse or hyperbolic trigonometric functions. The pi button (below the memory buttons) enters the first 32 digits of π. Because trigonometric functions almost never yield whole numbers, these buttons are grayed out in any number system other than decimal.

Logarithmic Functions

The Ln and Log buttons compute natural logarithms and base-10 logarithms, respectively. The Exp button *does not* compute exponentials. (It is used for entering numbers in scientific notation.) Compute exponentials by using Ln with the Inv box checked.

Statistical Functions

To use the statistical functions of the calculator, you must first enter a list of numbers, which constitutes the data. To enter a data list:

1. Enter the first number in the calculator display.

2. Click the Sta button. The statistics buttons are activated and a statistics box opens, as shown here. The $n = 6$ line reports six entries are in the data list.

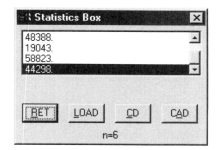

3. Click the Dat button. The number in the calculator display appears in the statistics box.

4. Enter the rest of the data, clicking Dat after each entry.

Once you enter a data list, Ave computes the average of the entries, Sum computes their sum, and S computes their standard deviation.

You can see the statistics box at any time by clicking Sta. To edit the data list, use the buttons at the bottom of the statistics box: LOAD copies the highlighted number back to the calculator display, CD deletes the highlighted number from the data list, and CAD clears the data list.

Logical Functions

When the Bin radio button is chosen, the calculator works in the binary (base-2) number system and the buttons And, Or, and Not perform the bitwise logical operations their names suggest. The Xor button does exclusive or, and Lsh does a left shift. Perform a right shift by clicking Lsh with the Inv box checked.

Other Functions

The Int button finds the integer part of a number. When Inv is checked, the Int button finds the fractional part of a number.

Compute squares and cubes with the X^2 and X^3 buttons. Compute other powers with the X^y button.

The N! button computes factorials of integers. If the displayed number has a fractional part, N! computes a gamma function.

The Mod button does modular reductions, for example:

12 Mod 5 = 2

Getting Help

In addition to the Help Topics on the Help menu, you can find out what any button on the calculator does by right-clicking it and selecting "What's This?"

Using Special Characters with Character Map

Do you need to use unusual characters, like Æ, Ö, or ®? The Character Map accessory can help you find them.

Note *Character Map might not be installed as part of the standard Windows Me installation. If it doesn't appear on the Start | Programs | Accessories | System Tools menu, you can install Character Map from the Windows Me CD-ROM. Choose Start | Settings | Control Panel, run Add/Remove Programs, click the Windows Setup tab, choose System Tools in the list of Windows Me components, click Details, and choose Character Map from the list of system tools.*

1. Open Character Map by choosing Start | Programs | Accessories | System Tools | Character Map. You see the Character Map window shown in Figure 5-6.

2. Select a font from the Font list. The characters available in this font appear in the Character Map window, arranged in a 7 × 32 grid.

3. Double-click the character you want to use; or single-click it, and then click Select. The character appears in the Characters To Copy box.

4. When you have displayed all the characters you want from this font in the Characters To Copy box, click Copy. Character Map copies the characters to the Windows Clipboard (see Chapter 7).

5. Paste the characters into a document using a command in the program you use to edit that document. (Most programs use Edit | Paste or CTRL-V to paste from the Clipboard.)

You can remove characters from the Characters To Copy box by clicking in the box and either backspacing over the characters or deleting them.

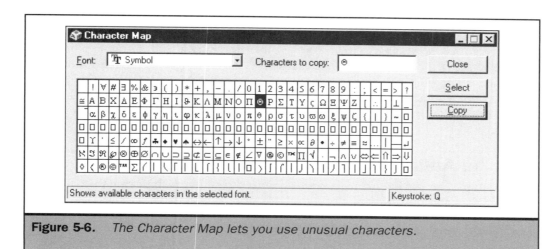

Figure 5-6.   *The Character Map lets you use unusual characters.*

Tip   *If you simply want to know what keystroke corresponds to a given character in a font, single-click the character in step 3 and look at the bottom-right corner of the Character Map window. In Figure 5-6, for example, you discover the keystroke Q in Symbol font corresponds to the Greek letter theta (Θ).*

Storing Addresses in the Address Book

One of the first things people did when personal computers were invented was to store lists of addresses on them. It makes sense—the old-fashioned little black book quickly gets filled with scratch-outs as people move, change phone numbers, or get new e-mail addresses, and you always end up wishing you had left a little more space between Sloane and Smith.

The next good idea in address management was to make the address book into a system utility so any program could access it. You shouldn't have to keep one list of addresses for your word processor, another for your e-mail program, and a third for your personal information manager. And you shouldn't have to wonder which list has the most recent phone numbers.

The Windows Address Book is still not the perfect realization of this idea, but it is a definite step in the right direction. It keeps track of nearly anything you would want to keep track of; provides a space for notes; and is accessible from Internet Explorer, Outlook Express, and NetMeeting. Unfortunately, Microsoft Exchange, Microsoft's e-mail server, has its own address book. Current versions of Word and Outlook are set up to work with Microsoft Exchange, instead of with Windows Me's Address Book (in Outlook 98 or 2000, you may be able to access your Windows Address Book contacts if Outlook is configured for Internet Mail Only).

Running Address Book

You can access Address Book either from another program—like Internet Explorer, Outlook Express, or NetMeeting—or by choosing Start | Programs | Accessories | Address Book or Start | Programs | Internet Explorer | Address Book. You see the Address Book window shown in Figure 5-7. The window lists the people you have entered into the address book with the name, e-mail address, and phone numbers for each person.

Sharing the Address Book with Other People

Several people can use the Address Book on your computer, each storing the names and addresses under a different *identity*.

Creating and Removing Identities

When you first start Address Book, one identity appears: the Main Identity (you). If you want another person to store addresses in your Address Book, create another identity by choosing File | Switch Identity, clicking the Manage Identities button to display the Manage Identities dialog box, and then clicking the New button.

To remove an identity, open the Manage Identities dialog box as before, select the identity from the list, and then click Remove.

To see the entries in an identity's part of the Address Book, click that identity in the list at the left side of the Address Book window.

Securing Your Address Book Information

If you don't want the other users of your computer to access the information in your Address Book, you can secure your identity with a password. Choose File | Switch Identity, and then click the Manage Identities button in the Switch Identities dialog box. Select your identity from the Identities list in the Manage Identities dialog box and

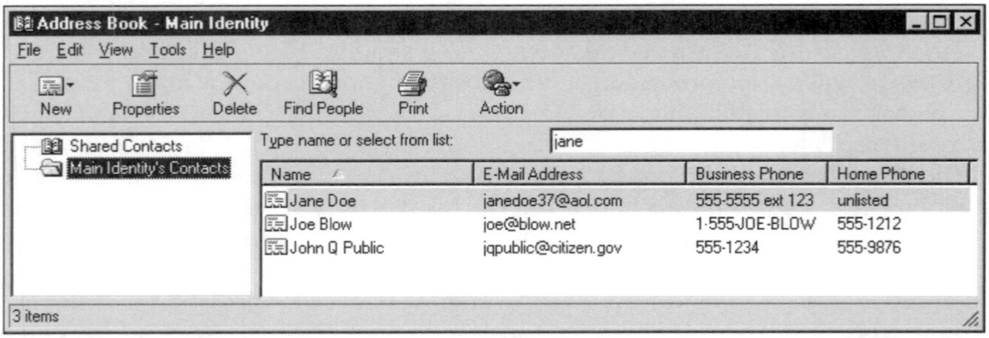

Figure 5-7.   *The contacts list in Details view*

click the Properties button. Click the Require A Password box in the Identity Properties dialog box. Choose a password and type it in the Password and Confirm Password lines of the Enter Password dialog box. Click OK or Close in all the open dialog boxes.

To change the password on your identity, follow the same instructions as in the previous paragraph until you see the Identity Properties dialog box. Click the Change Password button. Enter your old and new passwords into the Change Identity Password dialog box. Type your new password a second time in the Confirm New Password line.

 Don't confusion Address Book identities with User Profiles. Setting up Windows Me to handle multiple users doesn't give each user a unique Address Book.

Entering Information into Address Book

You can get information into Address Book in three ways: importing information from your current address book program, capturing it automatically from Outlook Express, or entering it by hand. Once you have a list of contacts in your Address Book, you can organize them into groups. To see the entries in your address book, click the Main Identity's Contacts entry on the left side of the Address Book window. The entries appear on the right side of the Address Book window.

Importing Addresses and Business Cards from Other Programs

You may already have an address book defined in another program. Address Book can import addresses from the following programs:

- Eudora Pro or Light
- LDIF-LDAP Data Interchange Format
- Microsoft Exchange Personal Address Book
- Microsoft Internet Mail for Windows 3.1
- Netscape Address Book (version 2 or 3)
- Netscape Communicator (version 4)
- vCards (virtual address cards, which can be created by exporting addresses from Microsoft Outlook)
- Text files created by any program

Selecting File | Import | Other Address Book starts an Address Book Import Tool to import address books from various types of e-mail programs. To import an address book from Outlook Express or Windows, choose File | Import | Address Book.

Virtual business cards (VCF files) can also be imported into Address Book. Select File | Import | Business Card (vCard). A Browse window opens so you can tell Address Book where your business card files are. You can also drag-and-drop vCards into the Address Book.

You can import your Windows Address Book from another computer. Look in the folder C:\Windows\Application Data\Microsoft\Address Book on the other computer to find the WAB (Windows Address Book) file that corresponds to your identity. Transfer this file to your computer, and then open Address Book and select File | Import | Address Book. When the Select Address Book File To Import From window opens, browse to find the file you want to import and click Open.

Capturing E-Mail Addresses from Outlook Express

If you use Outlook Express as your e-mail program, you can set it up to add names and e-mail addresses to Address Book automatically whenever you reply to a message.

1. Open Outlook Express, which is described in Chapter 22.
2. Select Tools | Options. The Options dialog box appears.
3. On the Send tab of the Options dialog box, check the box Automatically Put People I Reply To In My Address Book.
4. Click OK.

Entering Information by Hand

To enter a new contact into Address Book, click the New button on the toolbar and choose New Contact, or select File | New Contact from the menu bar. A blank Properties dialog box appears. Type in any information you want recorded, and leave blank any line you want. To add or change information about an existing contact, select the contact on the address list and click the Properties button. The Properties dialog box appears, as shown in Figure 5-8. Enter or edit information on any of its tabs.

To add more information to an existing contact listing, choose the contact from the contact list and click the Properties button. Enter the new information on the appropriate line and tab of the contact Properties box. Notice the Properties box has picked up a new Summary tab that you didn't see when you were entering a new contact. This tab is just for reference; each piece of information on this tab can be edited on some other tab. Any Web page listed on the Summary tab has a Go button next to it; clicking this button opens your Web browser and displays the Web page.

Address Book enables you to keep track of several e-mail addresses for a single person, with one of them specified as the default. To add a new e-mail address, type it into the E-Mail Addresses box on the Name tab of the contact Properties box. Then click the Add button. The new e-mail address appears in the list just below the E-Mail Addresses box.

To set one of a person's e-mail addresses as the default, select it from the list of e-mail addresses on the Name tab of the Properties dialog box associated with that person's name. Then click the Set As Default button.

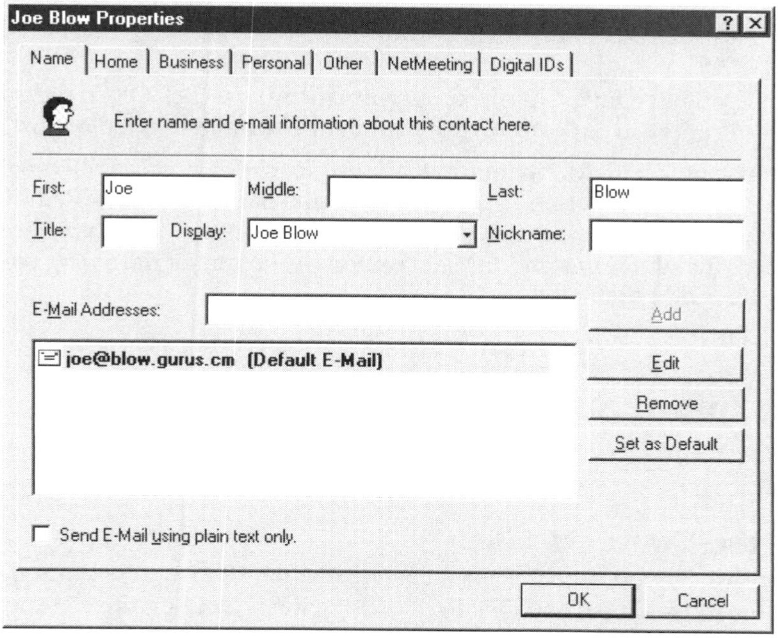

Figure 5-8. *Detailed information about a contact*

Defining Groups

Having your customers, your coworkers, and your child's piano teacher all on one big alphabetical list can be confusing. Address Book enables you to give your contact list some structure by defining groups of contacts that have something in common. An individual contact can appear in any number of groups.

To define a group:

1. Click the New button on the Address Book toolbar and choose New Group from the menu that appears. A group Properties dialog box opens.

2. Type a name for the group into the Group Name box.

3. Click the Select Members button. A Select Group Members window appears. Your contacts list is in its left pane; its right pane contains the members of the new group.

4. One by one, select names in the left pane and click the Select button to add this name to the group. You can add an entire group to the new group in the same way.

5. When you have finished selecting group members, click OK to return to the group Properties dialog box. The members you have selected are listed.

6. If you want to add new members to the group, click Select Members again. If you want to remove names from the list, select the names and click Remove. If you want to add people who aren't already in your Address Book, type the name and address into the Name and E-Mail boxes at the bottom of the dialog box, and then click the Add button.

7. Click OK.

Looking Up Information in Address Book

When you open Address Book, the first thing you see is the contacts list, as shown in Figure 5-7.

Viewing the Contacts List

Address Book offers you the same choice of views that Windows Explorer does: Large Icon, Small Icon, List, and Details. Choose among them on the View menu. The differences among Large Icon, Small Icon, and List are fairly trivial: Large Icon uses a large index card icon and lists contacts in rows, Small Icon uses a small index icon and lists contacts in rows, and List uses a small index card icon and lists contacts in columns. Details view uses small icons and presents the name, e-mail address, home phone number, and business phone number of each contact in four columns.

Sorting the Contacts List

In any of the views, you can sort contacts according to any of the information displayed. In Small Icons, Large Icons, and List views only the name is shown, so contacts can be listed according to first or last name, in ascending or descending order. Make these choices by choosing View | Sort By.

In Details view, you can list contacts according to name, e-mail address, home phone number, or business phone number. As in the Details view in Windows Explorer, click the head of any column to list contacts according to that column in ascending order. To list in descending order, click the column head a second time. To tell Address Book whether the Name column should be ordered according to first name or last name, choose View | Sort By.

Looking Up Detailed Information

Each contact has a Properties dialog box associated with it, as shown in Figure 5-8. To view the Properties dialog box for a contact, double-click the person's entry in the contact list. The entries on the NetMeeting tab refer to the conferencing server and address used with the NetMeeting program described in Chapter 25. The entries on the Digital ID tab enable you to send and receive encrypted information from the person (see Chapter 31).

Finding People

If your Address Book gets crowded, finding the address you want can be hard. To search the Address Book, click the Find People button on the toolbar. If the Address Book isn't open, you can choose Start | Search | People from the Taskbar. Either way, you see the Find People window, shown in Figure 5-9. Make sure the Look In box is set to Address Book, type in what you know about the person, and then click Find Now. Any fragment of information helps to narrow down the search. If, for example, you remember the phone number has a 456 in it somewhere, enter 456 in the Phone line of the Find People box. Or, if you recall entering "wears red ties" as a note on the Other tab of the Contact Properties box, you can find the contact by typing **wears red ties** in the Other line of the Find People box.

You can also use the Find People box to search other address directories. See the section "Using Additional Directory Services."

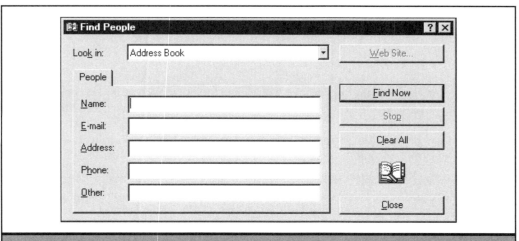

Figure 5-9. *Finding people in your Address Book or in other directory services*

Contacting People

To send e-mail to a person or group on your contacts list, select the recipient(s) from the address list, click the Action button on the toolbar, and choose Send Mail from the menu that appears; or, choose Tools | Action | Send Mail. (Choose several simultaneous recipients by holding down the CTRL key while you select them.) Your default e-mail program should start to compose a message to the person that you selected. Unfortunately, Address Book sometimes doesn't correctly read the default e-mail program you can set in the Internet Properties dialog box (see Chapter 22, section "Setting Your Mail and Newsreading Programs"). Instead, Address Book may try to run Microsoft Outlook or Microsoft Exchange to send e-mail.

To call a person from your computer via Phone Dialer, select the person from the contact list and choose Action | Dial from the toolbar (see "Using Phone Dialer"). If you have NetMeeting set up, you can select Action | Internet Call from the toolbar (see Chapter 25, section "Conferencing Using Microsoft NetMeeting").

Printing Information from Address Book

You can print information from the Address Book in three formats:

- **Memo** Prints all the information Address Book has about the selected contact(s)
- **Business Card** Prints only the information from the Business tab of the contact(s) Properties box
- **Phone List** Prints a list of phone numbers of the selected contact(s)

To print:

1. Select contacts from the contacts list. Select blocks of names by holding down the SHIFT key while you click the names. Select individuals scattered throughout the list by holding down the CTRL key. Select a group by clicking its name in the contacts list (not the group list). Select all contacts by choosing Edit | Select All. If you don't select any contacts, Address Book prints them all.
2. Click the Print button on the toolbar. A Print dialog box appears.
3. Select the Memo, Business Card, or Phone List from the Print dialog box.
4. Click OK.

To print addresses out in any other format, export them (as described in the next section) to a database or word-processing program that can print the format you want.

Exporting Names and Addresses from Address Book

You can also export names and addresses from Address Book in Microsoft Exchange Personal Address Book format, in a comma-delimited text file, or as vCards:

- **Windows Address Book Format**   Choose File | Export | Address Book, choose the folder and filename to use (with the extension .wab), and click the Save button.

- **Business Card or vCard**   Select the person whose information you want to export, and then choose File | Export | Business Card (vCard). Specify the name and folder where you want to store the business card and click Save.

- **Text File**   Choose File | Export | Other Address Book, choose Text File (Comma Separated Values) from the list that appears, and click Export. The CSV Export Wizard runs. Specify the name of the file in which you want to store the exported addresses, and then click Next. Select the information you want to include for each person, and then click Finish.

- **Microsoft Exchange Personal Address Book**   Choose File | Export | Other Address Book, choose Microsoft Exchange Personal Address Book, and click Export.

Using Additional Directory Services

When you choose Start | Search | People, you see the Find People window shown in Figure 5-9. In addition to searching Address Book entries, you can search other *directory services*—listings of names, e-mail addresses, and other information. These directory services may be public, such as the Web-based services Yahoo! People search and BigFoot (at **http://people.yahoo.com** and **http://www.bigfoot.com**, respectively). Or, they may be private, such as the employee directory for a large organization.

Windows Me comes with a number of public directory services already set up—click the Look In box in the Find People window to see a list. When you choose a directory service, the boxes in the Find People window adjust to match the types of entries the directory service can accept.

You can tell Windows about other directory services, for example, for your organization. Windows can work with any LDAP-compatible directory service. (*LDAP* stands for *Lightweight Directory Access Protocol.*) To configure Windows to work with an additional directory service, run Address Book or Outlook Express, and then choose Tools | Accounts. (In Outlook Express, described in Chapter 22, click the Directory Service tab.) You see the Internet Accounts window listing the directory services Windows Me knows about. To add a new directory service, click the Add button in the Internet Accounts window. The Internet Connection Wizard runs and asks for the information it needs to configure the new service.

To remove a directory service you no longer use, select the service in the Internet Accounts window and click the Remove button.

The Complete Reference

Chapter 6

Getting Help

Windows has always come with *online help*—helpful information stored on your computer that you can look at using a Help command. Windows Me comes with online help, too, but this help is "online" in two senses: The help system includes help files stored on your computer's hard disk, as well as a connection to online help information via the Internet. You look at the online help stored on your own computer by using the Help And Support.

To see the additional information about Windows Me offered via the Internet, you use your Web browser and your Internet connection. Chapter 21 describes how to get connected to the Internet, Chapter 23 explains how to use the Web, and Chapter 35 describes sources of information about Windows Me, including Microsoft's Windows Update and Support Online Web sites.

What Is the Help And Support Window?

The Help And Support window is a set of Web pages about Windows itself and the accessories that come with it. The pages are stored on your hard disk and are displayed by a special Internet Explorer window. Other programs you install may also come with their own online help.

Displaying Help Screens

To look at the Help And Support window (shown in Figure 6-1), choose Start | Help. The toolbar (a blue horizontal stripe across the window) shows the Back and Forward icons and the Home, Index, Assisted Support, and Tours & Tutorials commands. The left pane (left side of the window) shows a list of topics from which to choose. The right pane displays the help information you request from the left pane. The window works like a Web page—click an underlined link to see information about a topic.

When the Help And Support window first appears, you see the master list of help topics (click Home on the toolbar to return to it). Click a topic to see a more detailed list of subtopics in the left pane. When you see a topic with a question-mark icon to its left, clicking the topic displays an explanation, and steps to follow, in the right pane.

Looking Up Topics in the Help Index

When you click Index on the toolbar in the Help And Support window, the left pane displays an alphabetical index of help topics, shown in Figure 6-2. The first time you click Index, you may see the Preparing Index For First Use window, which can take several minutes to disappear.

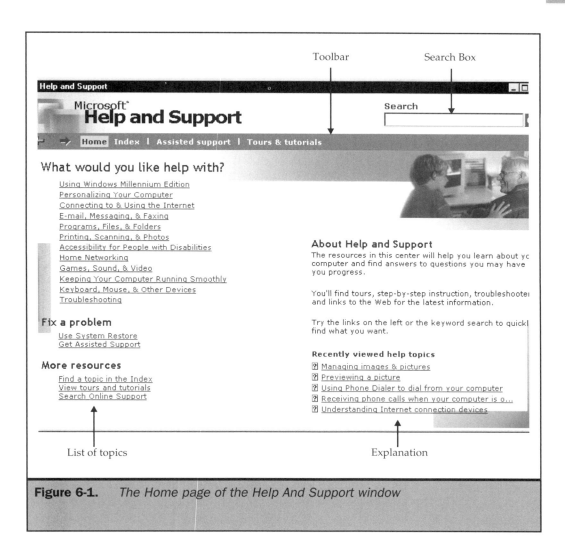

Figure 6-1.   *The Home page of the Help And Support window*

To find a topic in the index, you can scroll down it, but the list is very long. Instead, you can type a word in the box above the list. As you type the word, Windows finds the first entry in the index that begins with the letters you typed. Scroll down the list to see all the entries that start with that word.

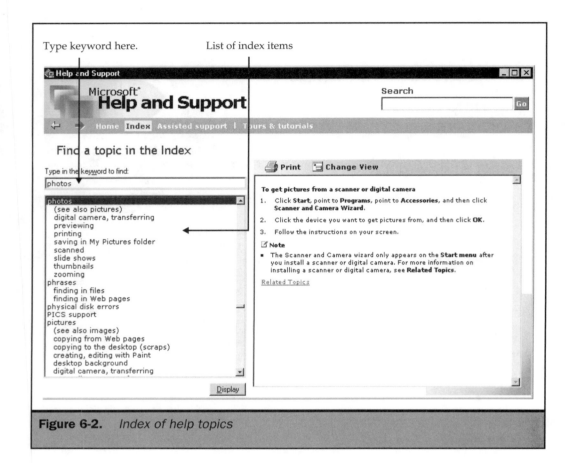

Figure 6-2.   *Index of help topics*

When you find a topic of interest, double-click the index entry. If there is only one help topic about that index entry, Windows displays it in the right pane. If more than one help topic exists, you see a Topics Found window, with a menu of topics to choose from, like this:

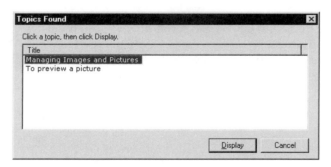

Double-click a topic, or single-click a topic and click Display. Or, use the keyboard: select a topic by using the arrow keys, and then press TAB to move to the Display button and press ENTER.

Searching for Topics

You can search for words or phrases wherever they appear in the help text, whether or not an index entry exists for that word or phrase. Click the Search box in the upper-right corner of the Help And Support window, type a word or phrase in the box, and then click the Go button. A list of topics appears in the left pane. Click a topic to display it.

We've found the index of help topics to find information more consistently than the Search box—strange but true.

Copying Help Information to Other Programs

You can use cut-and-paste to copy information from the Help And Support window to other programs. Select the part of the text in the right pane of the window that you want to copy. If you want to copy the entire help topic, right-click in the right pane and choose Select All from the menu that appears. Then right-click in the page and choose Copy from the menu that appears (or press CTRL-C). Windows copies the text to the Windows Clipboard. Now you can paste the text into a document by using the Edit | Paste command (or pressing CTRL-V) in the program you use to edit the document (see Chapter 7, section "What Is Cut-and-Paste?").

Taking Tours of Windows Features

The Help And Support window can also display tours and tutorials about Windows Me. Click Tours & Tutorials on the toolbar. You see a link list of topics about which Windows includes tours and tutorials—longer explanations that appear in a separate window, as shown in Figure 6-3. The left side of the window shows the list of pages in the tour or tutorial. Read each page, and then click the title of the next page on the list.

Getting Help from Microsoft

You can get helpful information over the Internet from Microsoft about Windows Me. Click Assisted Support on the toolbar to see a list of your options, including the support message boards on MSN Computing Central (Microsoft's technical information Web site, at **http://www.computingcentral.com**). You must be connected to the Internet to use these Internet-based resources.

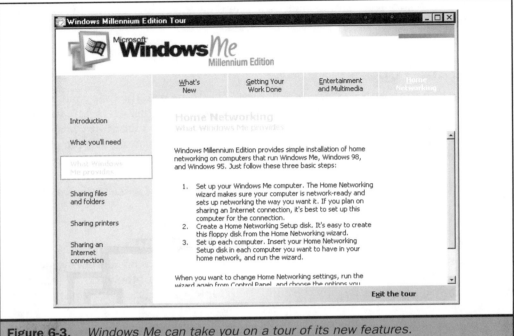

Figure 6-3.   *Windows Me can take you on a tour of its new features.*

Other Help Options

Here are other things you can do in the Help And Support window:

- Click the Back button on the toolbar to move to the previous topic you displayed, or click the Forward button to return to the next topic you displayed before clicking Back.

- If you don't want to see the left pane of the window, click the Change View icon in the right page; click the button again to display the left pane.

- To print a help topic, click the Print icon in the right pane.

- If you want to see extra help information about using the keyboard, open the Accessibility Properties dialog box, click the Keyboard tab, and select the Show Extra Keyboard Help In Programs check box (see Chapter 19, section "Making the Keyboard More Accessible").

Looking at Online Help About Other Programs

Most Windows-compatible programs have two ways of displaying Help screens:

■ Choose Help, Help | Contents, Help | Help, or Help | Topics from the menu bar.

■ Press the F1 key.

In programs designed for Windows 95, both methods run a program called Winhelp to display help screens. Windows 98 replaced Winhelp with HTML Help, which is displayed by the Hh program, and many Windows Me help files are in HTML Help format. Windows Me added the Help And Support pages about Windows itself; these pages are displayed by Internet Explorer. The Winhelp and Hh help programs are included with Windows Me (in the C:\Windows folder) for programs that use them.

Note   *The* HTML Help (Hh) *program displays* compiled help modules *with the extension .chm. The Windows 95 Winhelp program displays help files with the extension .hlp.*

Finding Out What an Onscreen Object Is

Many dialog boxes in both Windows and application programs have a small question-mark button in the upper-right corner, next to the Close button. This Help button enables you to find out what an object is. Click the question-mark Help button, and then click an item in the dialog box—an icon, button, label, or box. A small window appears with a description of the object you clicked. To dismiss the window, click anywhere in the dialog box.

Another way to display information about an item on the screen is to right-click it. If a menu appears including the What's This command, choose it. Or, select the item you want information about and press the F1 key.

Chapter 7

Copying, Moving, and Sharing Information Between Programs

Windows Me provides two methods of sharing data between different application programs (although each method has variations): You can cut or copy and then paste using the Windows Clipboard, or you can use OLE, Object Linking and Embedding. In general, cutting-and-pasting (or its variant, drag-and-drop) works well for the simpler tasks—moving text from one application to another, for instance. OLE is useful when you want all the features of one type of program to take care of an object in another program. For example, if you want to display an Excel spreadsheet in a Word document, and you want to be able to update a complicated formula and display the correct answer in the Word document, then you need to use OLE.

Which Windows Features Enable You to Share Data Among Programs and Users?

Copying or moving information from one location to another within a program is easy using the cut-and-paste commands that almost all Windows programs support. Cutting and pasting uses the Clipboard to store information temporarily. Moving or copying information between programs is also easy using the Clipboard. You can use the Clipboard Viewer to look at what's on the Clipboard. Some programs let you drag information from one location to another, too, using your mouse.

What Is Cut and Paste?

Cut and paste is a feature of Windows that enables you to select information from one file and move or copy it to another file (or to another location in the same file). Cut and paste works by storing information temporarily on the Clipboard. The following cut-and-paste techniques enable you to copy or move information within or between almost any Windows application:

- **Cut** Removes selected information from its current location and stores it (temporarily) on the Clipboard.
- **Copy** Copies selected information and makes a (temporary) copy of it on the Clipboard.
- **Paste** Copies information from the Clipboard to the location of the cursor in the active application.

To move information, you select it, cut it to the Clipboard, and then paste it in the new location. To copy information, you select it, copy it to the Clipboard, and then paste it in the new location (see "Cutting, Copying, and Pasting" later in this chapter).

What Is the Clipboard?

The easiest way to move information within an application, or from one application to another, is to use the Windows *Clipboard*, a handy little tool that works in the background, saving text, numbers, pictures, or whatever you cut or copy, and enabling you to paste that material somewhere else.

You can use the Clipboard to move or copy text, a range of spreadsheet cells, a picture, a sound, or almost any other piece of information you can create with a Windows application. The Clipboard can hold only one chunk of information at a time, so you either have to paste it somewhere else right away, or not cut or copy anything else until you've pasted the information where you want it. If you cut or copy another chunk of information, it replaces the information already on the Clipboard.

What Is the Clipboard Viewer?

The Clipboard Viewer is a program that displays the current contents of the Clipboard (see "Using the Clipboard Viewer to Look at What's on the Clipboard"). The Clipboard can contain one item at a time, and the Clipboard Viewer displays it. You can't edit what's on the Clipboard, but you can save it as a *Clipboard file*, with extension .clp, or open a clipboard file, putting the contents of that file on the Clipboard.

What Is Drag-and-Drop?

Drag-and-drop is another method of moving or copying information from one file to another or to another location in the same file. To move information from one location to another, select it with your mouse and drag it to its new location.

Not all programs support drag-and-drop. Some programs copy the information you drag, rather than move it. Some programs enable you to choose whether to move or copy the information (for example, a program may enable you to copy the information by holding down the CTRL key while dragging).

What Is OLE?

OLE (*Object Linking and Embedding*) is far more flexible and can be far more complicated than cut and paste or drag and drop. OLE enables you to use all your software applications to create an integrated document. For instance, you might want to create an annual report that includes these components:

- Text you create and format by using a word processor, such as Microsoft Word or Corel WordPerfect.

- A company logo stored in a graphics file created by Adobe Photoshop, Paint, or some other graphics application.

- Data and calculations on operating costs stored in a Microsoft Excel or Lotus 1-2-3 spreadsheet.

- Graphs and charts, which may come from your spreadsheet package or another graphics package.

These components may not reflect exactly what *you* want to do, but the point is the same—if you want to combine the output of different applications, OLE offers many advantages over the Clipboard. Why? Because, when you use OLE, the original program retains ownership of the object, and you can use the program to edit the object. For instance, if you use OLE to embed a portion of a spreadsheet in a word processing document, you can always use the spreadsheet application to edit the object. If, instead, you use the Clipboard to copy the numbers from the spreadsheet and then you paste the numbers to the word processor, they would just sit in the word processor, oblivious to their origins—you could use only the tools available in the word processor to edit the numbers. If you changed the original spreadsheet, the numbers in the word processing document wouldn't change.

In OLE, an *object* refers to a piece of information from one application that is placed in a *container file* created by another application. For example, a spreadsheet or graphic is an object when it is included in a word processing document. OLE actually is two similar methods of sharing information between applications—embedding and linking. Sticking with the previous example, *embedding* means putting the spreadsheet object in the word processing document (container file) and asking the word processor to take care of storing the object. So, although the word processor enables you to edit the spreadsheet object by using the spreadsheet application, the spreadsheet object is stored with the word processing document. *Linking*, on the other hand, allows the object to retain a close relationship with its origins—so close, in fact, if the numbers in the original spreadsheet file change, the linked spreadsheet object in the word processing document changes to match. This occurs because the word processing document doesn't really contain the object it displays—it only contains a reference to the file where the information is stored.

Whether you choose to embed or link objects, the process is similar: You create an object in one application, and then link or embed the object into another application (see "Sharing Information Using OLE").

Although using OLE to link files can be wonderfully convenient and can save you hours of revisions, it should be used judiciously. If you ever plan to move the file containing linked objects or to send it to someone, you must make sure one of the following occurs:

- The linked files also get moved or sent.
- The linked objects don't get updated. This means the host application won't go looking for the information in the linked file. To break the link, delete the object and paste in a nonlinked version instead.
- You edit the links so the host file knows where to find the source files for the linked objects.

Otherwise, your beautifully organized and time-saving document can become a complete mess. If you are going to move a document with linked objects in it, you need to know how to maintain links, a topic covered later in this chapter.

If you don't need the automatic updating you get with linked objects (for instance, if the source file isn't going to change, or if you don't want the object to reflect changes), or if you know you are going to move or send files, then stick with embedded objects—they're easier to maintain. However, embedding a large object may take more disk space than linking.

 Some applications enable you to link one file to another in a different way—by using a hyperlink (see Chapter 23, section "What Is the World Wide Web?"). A hyperlink actually takes you from one file to another, opening the application for the second file, if necessary.

What Are Scraps?

Not everyone finds scraps useful, but if you need them, they may be a lifesaver. *Scraps* are OLE objects that have been left on the desktop or in a folder. You can keep a scrap on the desktop or in the folder or, at some later point, drag it to another application. A scrap has an icon that looks like this:

Scrap icons all look the same, but their names give you a clue as to which application created them. For instance, a scrap from Word or another word processor is called a *Document scrap*, a scrap from Excel is a *Worksheet scrap*, and a scrap from Quattro Pro is a *Notebook scrap* (using the Quattro Pro terminology). Applications that support drag-and-drop can be used to create scraps. For instance, Notepad, which doesn't support drag-and-drop, cannot be used to create scraps.

To create a scrap, drag some information to the desktop or copy it to the Clipboard, and then paste it to the desktop (by right-clicking the desktop and choosing Paste). When you open a scrap on the desktop, the application that created the information opens to display it. You can drag a scrap into a different application to create an OLE object out of it.

What Is DDE?

As mentioned in Chapter 3, *DDE* stands for dynamic data exchange, and it's another way for programs to exchange information. With DDE, the programs send messages among themselves. For example, when you open a .doc file in the Windows Explorer, the program uses DDE to send a message to an already running copy of Microsoft Word, so the file opens in the current Word window, rather than starting up a second copy of Word. You can control what DDE messages your programs send, but programming is required, using macros (in programs like Microsoft Word or Excel), or using a programming language (like Visual Basic or C++)—see Chapter 3, section "Actions Associated with File Types".

Sharing Data Through the Windows Clipboard

To use the Clipboard to move or copy information within or between files or to share information between programs, you cut or copy the information from one window and paste it in another. You can also use the Clipboard Viewer to see what's on the Clipboard.

Cutting, Copying, and Pasting

You can cut, copy, and paste information by using the following methods (some methods might not work in some applications):

- **Menu** Choose the Edit menu's Cut, Copy, and Paste commands.
- **Keystrokes** Press CTRL-X to cut, CTRL-C to copy, and CTRL-V to paste.
- **Buttons** Many applications have toolbars with Cut, Copy, and Paste buttons, as shown here:

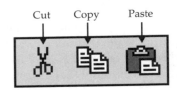

- **Mousing** Many applications provide shortcut menus that include the Cut, Copy, and Paste commands. Right-click an object to see a shortcut menu.

The Cut and Copy buttons may be disabled if you haven't selected information in the window, and the Paste button may be disabled if no information is on the Clipboard.

The following steps explain how to copy or move text from one location to another:

1. Select the information you want to copy or move.
   - You can select information by highlighting it with the mouse or by holding down the SHIFT key as you use the arrow buttons. The help system of the application you're using will contain more information regarding how to select in that application.

■ Be careful when you have information selected. Depending on the application, you can inadvertently replace the whole selection by typing a character or space or by pressing the DEL or BACKSPACE keys. Usually, a simple click deselects the information, ending the danger.

> **Tip** *If you're afraid you deleted something by mistake, press CTRL-Z to undo the change in most programs.*

2. If you want to copy the information, press CTRL-C, click the Copy button, or choose Edit | Copy. If you want to move the information, press CTRL-X, click the Cut button, or choose Edit | Cut.

3. If you are copying, you don't see any change on the screen when you give the Copy command. If you are cutting, however (which is useful if you want to move information), the selected information disappears from the screen—it is now stored on the Clipboard.

4. Move the cursor to the place you want the information to appear. This may mean changing applications by clicking a button on the Taskbar, or even opening a new application. As long as you don't cut or copy anything else or turn off the computer, the information will be available to be pasted to a new location.

5. Paste the text by pressing CTRL-V, by clicking the Paste button, or by choosing Edit | Paste. The information you cut or copy appears at the location of the cursor.

Once you cut or copy information onto the Clipboard, you can make multiple copies of it by pasting it as many times as you want.

> **Tip** *Information on the Clipboard does take up RAM, limiting the resources your computer has available to do other things. Therefore, if you cut or copy a lot of information to the Clipboard, paste it quickly. Then, cut or copy something small—one letter or word, for instance—which replaces the large chunk of information on the Clipboard and makes most of the RAM available again. Some programs clear the Clipboard. You can also use the Clipboard Viewer to delete the information on the Clipboard.*

If you use Microsoft Office 2000 you may see the Office Clipboard shown in Figure 7-1. The Office Clipboard stores up to 12 "clips" from Office applications. Rest the pointer on a clip to see its contents. You can paste any clip by clicking its icon on the Office Clipboard. The Office Clipboard opens automatically after you cut more than one selection for Office applications.

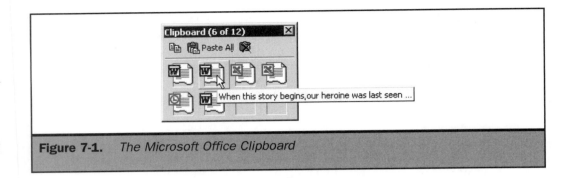

Figure 7-1.   *The Microsoft Office Clipboard*

Using the Clipboard Viewer to Look at What's on the Clipboard

You needn't take for granted that the information you want is on the Clipboard—you can actually look at it by opening the Clipboard Viewer. You may want to use the Clipboard Viewer to do the following:

■ See the information on the Clipboard.

■ Save the information.

■ Delete the information.

To open the Clipboard Viewer, choose Start | Programs | Accessories | System Tools | Clipboard Viewer, or you can open a clipboard file (with extension .clp) from Windows Explorer. The Clipboard Viewer shows the current contents of the Clipboard, which you can paste into almost any application:

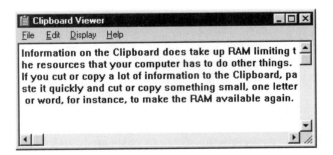

Note   *You may have to install the Clipboard Viewer (see Chapter 3, section "Installing and Uninstalling Programs That Come with Windows")—it isn't always automatically installed. Open the Control Panel, open Add/Remove Programs, click the Windows Setup tab, click System Tools from the list of components, click Details, and choose Clipboard Viewer.*

If the contents of the Clipboard Viewer look strange, they may be displayed in the wrong format. Use the Display menu to choose an appropriate display format. The display format doesn't affect the way the information on the Clipboard is saved or pasted into another application—the display format affects only the display in the Clipboard Viewer.

You can save the contents of the Clipboard by using File | Save As on the Clipboard Viewer menu. Clipboard Viewer saves the information in a clipboard file with extension .clp in the Clipboard's own format. Open a saved clipboard file by choosing File | Open. The Clipboard Viewer can open files saved in the Clipboard format only —you can give them a different extension, but the file is still in .clp format. When you open a clipboard file and the Clipboard already contains information, Clipboard Viewer asks you to confirm that you want to delete the current contents of the Clipboard.

To delete the contents of the Clipboard, choose Edit | Delete or press the DEL key. Deleting the contents of the Clipboard releases RAM for other uses.

  You can't cut-and-paste information from the Clipboard Viewer window—the information is already on the Clipboard!

Capturing Screens Using the Clipboard

Many products can take a *screen shot*, a picture of whatever is on the screen. This book is littered with screen shots that are used as figures. If you need to create a screen shot, you can use the Clipboard to create one. Use the PRINT SCREEN key that appears on your keyboard—it often is above the cursor control keys with the SCROLL LOCK and PAUSE keys. You can take two different kinds of screen shots:

- A picture of the whole screen by pressing PRINT SCREEN
- A picture of the active window by pressing ALT-PRINT SCREEN

Figure 7-2 shows a picture of a window in the Clipboard. Once the picture is on the Clipboard, you can paste it somewhere else. You may want to paste the picture into a graphics program, such as Paint (which comes with Windows), so you can save it in a graphics file format and use it later (see Chapter 5, section "Drawing Pictures Using Microsoft Paint"). Or, you might want to paste it into a file, such as a word-processing document containing an explanation of that screen or window.

Sharing Information Using OLE

To use OLE to share information, you create OLE objects, and then embed or link these objects in files (see "What Is OLE?" earlier in this chapter).

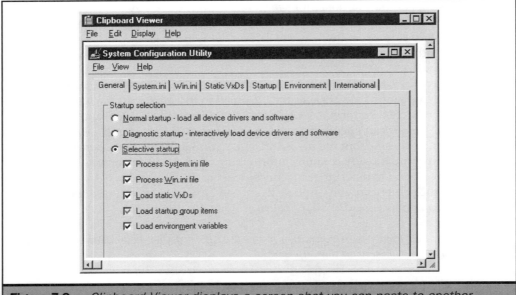

Figure 7-2.   *Clipboard Viewer displays a screen shot you can paste to another application.*

Creating Linked or Embedded Objects

The way you link or embed an object depends on the application programs you're using—the program into which you want to embed or link the object. Most programs have a menu command to create an object by using OLE, but you may have to use the online help system to find the command. In Microsoft Word, for instance, you can use Insert | Object to create an object by using OLE. The following two techniques may also work: dragging-and-dropping and using Edit | Paste Special. Neither technique is supported by all applications.

Embedding an Object by Dragging and Dropping

The easiest way to embed an object is to drag the information from one program and drop it in the other program. For this method to work, both applications must support drag-and-drop embedding. Check the documentation for the program that contains the information you want to embed. When dragging the information you want to embed, use the same technique you use to copy selected information *within* the application: Some applications require you to hold down the CTRL key while dragging the information. For instance, in Excel, you have to click-and-drag the border of the selected area to move or copy it.

Follow these steps to use drag-and-drop embedding:

1. Select the information you want to embed.

2. Use drag-and-drop to drag the selected information to the other application; use the same drag-and-drop technique you use to copy information within an application. If the second application isn't visible on the screen, you can drag the information to the application's Taskbar button—hold the mouse pointer there for a second, and the application window opens.

3. Drop the information where you want it—if the application supports OLE, you automatically create an embedded object.

You may be able to specify that the information be linked rather than embedded (the usual default when OLE drag-and-drop is supported) by holding down the SHIFT *key—try it to see whether the application you are using supports this feature.*

Linking or Embedding an Object Using Paste Special

You may want a little more control over the object than you have when you drag-and-drop it—to achieve more control over the object, use the Edit | Paste Special command found in many applications. The procedure is much like using the Clipboard to cut-and-paste, except you paste by using OLE instead, as follows:

1. Select the information you want to link or embed.

2. Press CTRL-C or CTRL-X to copy or cut the information (or use another method to copy or cut).

3. Move the cursor where you want the object to appear.

4. Choose Edit | Paste Special. You see a dialog box similar to the one shown in Figure 7-3. Choose the correct application from the choices displayed. Make sure to choose the application you want to use to edit the object—in the figure, that is Microsoft Word. If you choose another option, you won't be using OLE—instead, you will be using the Clipboard to do a simple paste of information from one application to another.

5. Choose the correct setting either to embed the object in the new file or to link the two files together. To embed the object, choose the Paste option; to link the object, choose the Paste Link option. Figure 7-3 shows the settings to embed a Microsoft Word object into a Corel Quattro Pro spreadsheet. Figure 7-4 shows the settings to link a Corel Quattro Pro spreadsheet into a Microsoft Word document. Other applications may have Paste Special dialog boxes that look different from these.

6. Change the Display As Icon setting, if necessary. If you choose to display the object as an icon, you don't see the information itself. Instead, you create a *packaged object* that shows the information it contains only when you open its icon (see "What Is OLE?" earlier in this chapter).

7. Click OK to link or embed the object. You see the object in the container file, as in Figure 7-5.

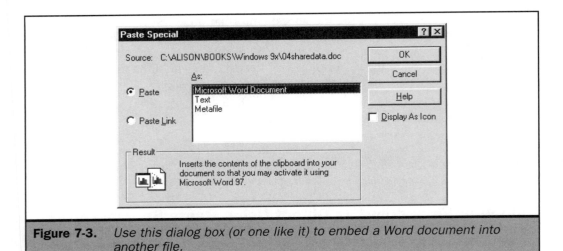

Figure 7-3. Use this dialog box (or one like it) to embed a Word document into another file.

Editing a Linked or Embedded Object

Editing a linked or embedded object is simple—in most applications, you just double-click the object. For other applications, you may need to right-click the object to display a menu with an edit option or change modes so you are in Edit mode (if you're having trouble, check the help system of the application containing the object). Once you figure out how to edit the object, the object's application opens. Next, the menu and toolbars of the window in which the object appears are replaced by the menu and toolbars of the application assigned by the registry to that file type (usually the application used to create the object). In other words, if you're editing an Excel object in a Word document, double-click the object to display Excel's menu and toolbars in

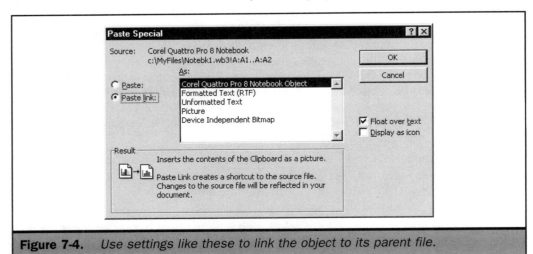

Figure 7-4. Use settings like these to link the object to its parent file.

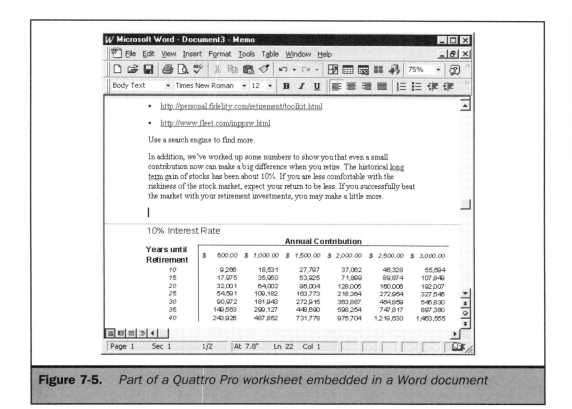

Figure 7-5. *Part of a Quattro Pro worksheet embedded in a Word document*

Word's window, as in Figure 7-6. You can edit the object by using that application's tools. When you're done, click outside the object to reinstate the regular menu and toolbars or choose File | Update or Exit. If you're asked whether you want to update the object, answer Yes.

If the object is linked, rather than embedded, you can also edit the object by editing the source file itself. If the file containing the object is also open, you may have to update it manually to see the new information in the object. Closing and opening the file containing the object may be the easiest way to update the object.

Delete an object by single-clicking it to select it—you probably see a box around it—then press the DELETE or BACKSPACE key.

Maintaining OLE Links

If you decide to use a link to put an object in a file, rather than embedding the object, you may have to do some maintenance if the linked file or the file containing the link moves to a new location. A link is usually updated each time the file containing the object is opened or printed. *Updating* means that the current information from the linked file is brought into the object.

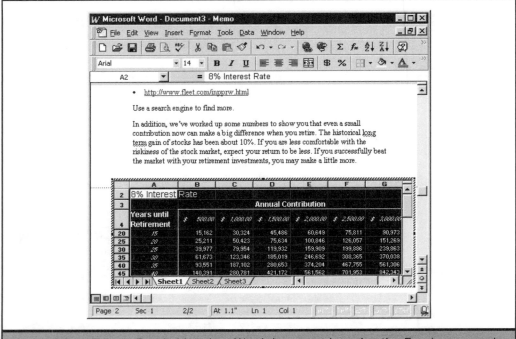

Figure 7-6. *Edit an Excel object in a Word document by using the Excel menu and toolbars that appear when you double-click the object.*

If the location of a file changes, you may need to "lock" the link so the last available information is retained, break the link so the object becomes an embedded object rather than a linked object, or edit the link so the correct path and filename are referenced. The exact commands may differ by application (check the online help), but usually there's one dialog box where all these tasks can be performed, like this one:

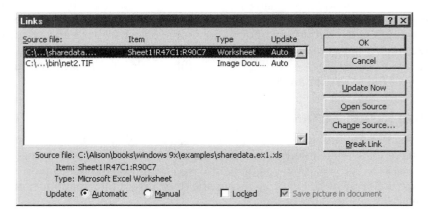

In most Microsoft applications, you can display the dialog box by choosing Edit |
Links. The following list explains how to do these three tasks in a Microsoft application.
Other applications work in a similar way, but may have different names for the dialog
box buttons and options.

- **Lock the link**   Use the Locked option on the Links dialog box to lock the
  selected link. You can select multiple links to lock by CTRL-clicking or
  SHIFT-clicking additional links. A locked link isn't updated. To check whether
  a link is locked, select the link and see whether the Locked option is checked.

- **Break the link**   Use the Break Link (or Cancel Link) button to break a link.
  When you break a link, the link disappears from the Links list and you can
  no longer use the original application to edit the object. A better choice, often,
  is to lock the link or replace the linked object with an embedded object.

- **Edit the link**   Use the Change Source button to edit the link. This enables you to
  redirect the link to a different file or to the same file stored in a different location.

Another option is to set up the file to update the links only when you tell it to do
so by specifying manual updating. The Links dialog box has an Update option that
enables you to specify automatic or manual updating. If you set this option to manual,
the links are updated only when you display the Links dialog box and click the Update
Now button.

The Complete Reference

Windows Me

Part II

Managing Your Disk

The Complete Reference

Windows
Me

Chapter 8

Using Files and Folders

135

Computers are tools for working with information—creating it, accessing it, and rearranging it. Windows stores information in files and organizes those files into folders. Everything you do with your computer involves files and folders.

This chapter describes the basic file-and-folder skills you need to operate your computer. The next chapter discusses the longer-term issues involved in managing your files efficiently. This chapter explains the anatomy of the windows in which you manipulate files and folders, and their toolbars. It tells how to use Windows Explorer to create, select, name, open, move, copy, and delete files and folders. You also learn the easiest ways to undo or recover from common mistakes.

This chapter assumes you are working with the default settings of Windows Explorer—the way Windows Explorer works before you change anything. The next chapter covers how to adjust Windows Explorer to suit your tastes and habits.

What Are Files and Folders?

Files and folders are two of the most fundamental concepts of the Windows operating system. No matter what you use your computer for, you create and organize files and folders as soon as you decide to save your work. If you have worked with any other operating system, you are probably already acquainted with the concept of a file. You probably are familiar with folders as well, though you may know them as *directories*. If you aren't already familiar with files and folders, spending a small amount of time learning their properties will serve you well.

What Is a File?

A *file* is any collection of related information that is given a name and stored on a disk so it can be retrieved when needed. A file may contain any kind of information: a program or application (WordPad, for example, is in a file called Wordpad.exe.), a document, a part of a document (such as a table or an illustration), a sound or piece of music, a segment of video, or any number of other things.

Many files are part of the Windows system itself. Windows uses files to store the information it needs to function, such as information regarding the appearance of your desktop, the kind of monitor or printer you use, the various dialog boxes and error messages, or how to display different fonts. Similarly, the applications on your computer typically have a number of auxiliary files in addition to the file containing the main program. Some of these files, for example, contain the choices you make about the program's optional settings. When you change these settings, you are not altering the program itself; you are editing some of its auxiliary files.

What Is a Folder?

Because of all the files associated with Windows and the various applications on your computer, your hard drive contains thousands of files before you begin creating files of your own. If your computer is part of a network, you may have access to millions of files. The Internet has billions of files. You would have no hope of keeping track of all those files if they weren't organized in some efficient way. In Windows (as in most other major operating systems), the fundamental device for organizing files is the folder.

Technically, a *folder* is just a special kind of file—one that contains a list of other files. The files on the list are said to be *in* the folder, and each file is allowed to be in only one folder. A folder can be either open or closed. When a folder is closed, all you see is its name and the folder icon, as shown here:

Business

When a folder is open in Windows Explorer, it has its own window, and the files contained in the folder are displayed in the window (see "What Is Windows Explorer?").

The terms "file" and "folder" were chosen to remind you of a more familiar information retrieval system—the filing cabinet. Like the folders in a filing cabinet, the Windows folders are named objects that contain other objects. For example, a Windows folder named Budget might contain four spreadsheet files for First quarter, Second quarter, Third quarter, and Fourth quarter.

What Is the Folder Tree?

The organizational power of the folder system comes from the fact that it is *hierarchical*, which means folders can contain other folders. This feature enables you to organize and keep track of a great many folders, without overstraining your memory or attention.

If Folder A is inside Folder B, Folder A is a *subfolder* of B. Any folder can contain as many subfolders as you want to put there, but each folder (like each file) is contained in only one folder. And so, a diagram showing which folders are contained in which other folders looks something like a family tree. This diagram is called the *folder tree*, or sometimes the *folder hierarchy*. Windows Help calls it the *folder list*.

Figure 8-1 shows the top levels of the folder tree as they appear in the Folders Explorer Bar. At the top of the folder tree (the founder of the Folder family, so to speak) is the desktop. Immediately under the desktop are My Computer, My Network Places, Recycle Bin, and My Briefcase, plus whatever files and folders you might have copied to the desktop. The manufacturer of your computer may also have put some files or folders on your desktop.

Underneath My Computer are icons representing all of your system's storage media: hard drives, floppy drives, CD-ROMs, and so on. (Your system configuration may differ somewhat from that pictured in Figure 8-1.) Also under My Computer is the Control Panel, the window you use for configuring your computer.

Figure 8-1.   *The upper levels of the folder tree*

 Note   *In previous versions of Windows, the folders Printers, Dial-Up Networking, and Scheduled Tasks were also immediately under My Computer. In Windows Me these folders are icons on the Control Panel.*

What Are Filenames?

To store a file and retrieve it later, Windows has to give it a *filename*. Often you are asked to invent a name for a file. Good filenames are evocative without being too cumbersome. They also have to obey some rules. Fortunately, the file-naming rules were liberalized when Windows 95 came out, and Windows Me retains these liberalized rules. You can change a filename using Windows Explorer, as well as in the Open and Save As dialog boxes of many applications.

What Filenames Are Legal?

In DOS and Windows systems prior to Windows 95, filenames could be only eight characters long, followed by a three-character extension that told the file's type—Filename.txt, for example. Inventing coherent, easily remembered filenames was an art similar to composing good vanity license plates. Even so, one frequently had to stare at files like jnsdecr.doc for some time before remembering it was John's December report.

Fortunately, Windows 95 changed all that by introducing long filenames, and Windows Me retains that advance. File and folder names can be up to 215 characters long, and can include spaces. So jnsdecr.doc can become John's December

Report.doc. Folders, likewise, can have names up to 215 characters long. These names are automatically of type "folder" and have no extension.

In addition to periods and spaces, some characters that were illegal prior to Windows 95 are now legal, including

+ , ; = [

But you still can't use a few characters in filenames

\ / : * ? " < > |

and any character you make by using the CTRL key.

What Are Extensions and File Types?

Filenames are still followed by a period and a three-letter *extension*. The extension denotes the *file type* and, among other things, tells Windows which program to use to open the file and which icon to use to represent the file. Windows handles most file-type issues invisibly. Files you create with a particular program, for example, are typically given a type associated with that program (unless you specify otherwise), and the appropriate three-letter extension is added to the name automatically.

You can do a great many things in Windows without paying any attention to file types; therefore, Windows doesn't even show you the extensions unless you ask to see them. We recommend you configure Windows to display extensions for two reasons: to help you know the complete names of your files and to help you determine the file types of files you receive from others. To see the extensions:

1. Choose Start | Settings | Control Panel. You see the Control Panel.

2. Open the Folder Options icon. The Folder Options dialog box appears.

3. Click the View tab.

4. Click the check box next to Hide File Extensions For Known File Types. If the box is checked, the extensions are hidden; if it's not checked, the extensions are shown.

5. Click OK to make the Folder Options dialog box go away, and close the Control Panel.

When you install a program, the installation program usually tells Windows the file types the program handles (see Chapter 3, section "What Happens During Program Installation?").

What Are MS-DOS Names?

In addition to its name, each file and folder in Windows has an *MS-DOS name*, an eight-or-fewer-character name that resembles its real name, but that is legal under the pre-Windows 95 file-naming rules. The MS-DOS name exists for the purpose of backward compatibility; programs written for MS-DOS or older versions of Windows might well crash if Windows hands them files with long names and previously illegal characters. So, when dealing with pre-Windows 95 application programs, Windows pretends nothing has changed and gives the application the MS-DOS name of a file rather than its real name.

For the most part, MS-DOS names are invisible in Windows, but you still may see them if you run an older application. If the file you named MySummerVacation.doc shows up later as MYSUMM~1.DOC, you'll know what happened.

What Are Addresses?

An *address* is information that tells you (and Windows) how to find something. The four kinds of addresses are

- **File addresses**   Tell you how to find files on your computer. A typical file address looks something like C:\Windows\Explorer.exe.

- **UNC (Universal Naming Convention) addresses**   Used when referring to files on some local area networks (LANs). UNC addresses are in the format *computername**drive:pathname*, where *computername* is the computer's name on the LAN, *drive* is the disk drive on that computer, and *pathname* is the file address.

- **Internet addresses**   More properly called *URLs*, specify how to find things on the Web (see Chapter 23, section "What Is a URL?"). The URL of Microsoft's home page, for example, is **http://www.microsoft.com**.

- **E-mail addresses**   Tell you how to find the e-mail boxes of the people to whom you want to write. You can comment on this book, for example, by writing to **winmetcr@gurus.com**.

The Address box in Windows Explorer handles every kind of address except e-mail addresses. Typing a file or UNC address into the Address box opens the corresponding file or folder, while typing an Internet address opens the corresponding object on the Internet (if your computer is online).

*E-mail addresses are still handled differently from the other kinds of addresses. You can send e-mail by typing **mailto:** followed (with no space) by an e-mail address into the Address box (see Chapter 22 for how to use e-mail addresses).*

File addresses, also called *paths* or *path names*, work in the following way: files and folders are stored on disks. Each disk drive has a drive letter that is its address (see Chapter 10, section "What Are Drive Letters?"). Drives A and B typically are reserved for floppy drives, and C denotes your computer's main hard drive. Subsequent letters are used for other hard drives, CD-ROMs, tape drives, removable drives, drives on other computers on your LAN (if any), and other devices. In file addresses, drive letters are always followed by a colon (:).

Each file or folder address begins with the letter of the drive on which the file or folder is stored. The *root folder*—the main or top-level folder on the disk—is designated by a backslash immediately after the drive letter and colon. (So C:\ is the root folder of drive C.) The rest of the address consists of the names of the folders on the folder tree between the given file or folder and the drive that contains it. The folder names are separated by backslashes (\).

For example, the address C:\Windows\Temp refers to a folder named Temp, inside the folder named Windows, which is stored on the C drive. If the file Junk.doc is contained in Temp, Junk.doc's address is C:\Windows\Temp\Junk.doc.

Note   *Both file address and UNC addresses use backslashes (\) to separate the pieces of the address. But URLs (for historical reasons) use slashes (/) for the same purpose.*

What Is Windows Explorer?

Windows Explorer is a versatile tool for viewing and manipulating files and folders. It appears whenever you open My Computer or any other folder on your desktop, and you can also run it by choosing Start | Programs | Accessories | Windows Explorer. The program has many features that you can display or hide, and several different views of the features it displays.

Windows Explorer is a twin of the Windows Web browser Internet Explorer (described in Chapter 23). Running either program opens an *Explorer window*. The Explorer window is extremely versatile and has many parts, which you may or may not decide to display. When all parts of the Explorer window are made visible, it looks like Figure 8-2 (in this figure, Windows is configured to single-click mode, as shown by the underlined filenames).

The window's title bar displays the name of the open folder and (optionally) the path name (the list of the folders that contain the open folder). Immediately beneath the title bar are the menu bar and the various toolbars. The working area displays icons corresponding to all the files and folders contained in the open folder. The contents of subfolders don't appear in the working area. At the bottom of the window lies the status bar, which shows the number of objects in the folder, how many objects are hidden, and the amount of space the folder takes up on its disk. To the left of the working area is the Explorer bar, which here is set to display the folder tree. Near the center of the window, on the left side of the working area, is the Web panel.

You can make the toolbars, Explorer bar, Web panel, or status bar appear or disappear (see Chapter 9, section "Configuring Windows Explorer"). When the Explorer window is stripped down to its absolute minimum, the same folder in Figure 8-2 looks like Figure 8-3.

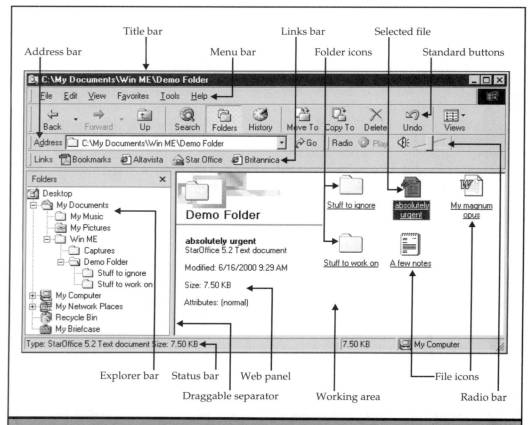

Figure 8-2. *Anatomy of Windows Explorer's Explorer window. You can choose to display as many or as few of these components as you like.*

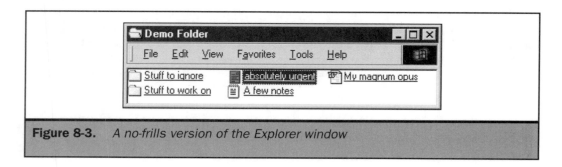

Figure 8-3. *A no-frills version of the Explorer window*

MANAGING YOUR DISK

Windows Explorer replaces the File Manager and Program Manager applications used in Windows versions 3.1 and earlier. File Manager and Program Manager are still part of Windows Me, if you want to use them, but they are no longer necessary. Most people who take time to learn Windows Explorer prefer it to the Windows 3.1 tools. If you have never used File Manager or Program Manager, we recommend you ignore them. If you have a nostalgic affection for the Windows 3.1 tools, you can find File Manager at C:\Windows\Winfile.exe, and Program Manager at C:\Windows\Progman.exe.

What Is the Address Box?

The *Address box*, which appears on the Address Bar toolbar of Windows Explorer, displays the name of the open folder. The Address box looks like this:

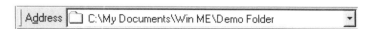

When you click the arrow at the right end of the Address box, a diagram appears. It displays the top levels of the folder tree, and allows "long-range navigation" by clicking any top-level item you want to open.

Another way to choose which folder to view is to type into the Address box the address of the file or folder you want to open. The Address box accepts file addresses, network addresses, and Web addresses (see "What Are Addresses?"). If your computer is online, you can open a Web page by typing its address into the Address box and clicking the Go button to the right of the Address box. Depending on what options you have chosen elsewhere, your computer may automatically dial up your Internet provider to open the Web page (see Chapter 21, section "Setting Additional Dial-Up Networking Options").

What Is the Standard Buttons Toolbar?

The *Standard Buttons toolbar* is an optional feature of Windows Explorer. Like most features of Windows Explorer, you can configure it to look the way you want (see Chapter 9, section "Configuring the Standard Buttons toolbar"). In the default configuration, it looks like this:

The three leftmost toolbar buttons are navigation buttons: Back, Forward, and Up. They behave like the corresponding Web-browser buttons. The Back button takes the window back to the previous folder it displayed, and the Forward button undoes Back. The Back and Forward buttons have arrows attached to them; clicking the arrow produces a drop-down list of locations to which you can go back or forward. The Up button causes the window to display the folder that contains the currently displayed folder; that is, it moves the window up the folder tree.

These buttons behave differently if you have configured Windows Explorer to open each folder in its own window (see Chapter 9, section "Opening a New Window for Each Folder").

The next three buttons—Search, Folders, and History—are three Explorer bar options. In Figure 8-2, for example, the Folders button has been clicked, and the Explorer bar displays the folder tree.

The Move To and Copy To buttons only work when a file has been selected in the working area. Clicking either one opens a new window in which you can browse for a file to move or to which you can copy the selected folder.

The Delete button moves a selected file to the Recycle Bin. The Undo button reverses your previous action, if possible. The Views button enables you to choose among several options for representing the contents of a folder (see Chapter 9, section "Changing Views"). Right-clicking anywhere in the toolbar enables you to select which toolbars are shown. This menu is the same one you see by choosing View | Toolbars.

What Is the Links Toolbar?

The *Links toolbar* is a toolbar you can fill with links to files, Web sites, or applications. When you first install Windows Me, it contains buttons that connect to various Microsoft Web sites, but you can customize it to contain whatever links you find useful (see Chapter 9, section "Configuring the Links Toolbar"). It can look like this:

In this example, the Movies button connects to a Web site listing local movies, the Weather button links to a Web site giving a local weather report, the Bookmarks button opens a file that contains a list of useful Web sites, and the Star Office button starts an application. The double arrow at the end of the toolbar indicates that additional links exist that the toolbar isn't large enough to display. Clicking the arrow displays the next link to the right, at the expense of the leftmost link.

What Is the Explorer Bar?

The left pane of a Windows Explorer window is called the *Explorer bar* (even though it's not shaped like a bar). The Explorer bar provides a variety of tools to help you find files and get a higher-level view of how your files are organized. To change what you see in the Explorer bar, select an option from the View | Explorer Bar menu or click the corresponding button on the toolbar. The choices are

- **Search**   Helps you find files or folders on your computer system, Web pages on the Internet, or people in a directory (see Chapter 9, section "Searching for Files and Folders"). You can also access the Search Explorer bar by selecting one of the options under Start | Search.

- **Favorites**   Shows you a list of favorite files, folders, and Web sites (see Chapter 11, section "Adding and Editing Favorites"). If you are online, clicking an entry for a Web site displays the site. In the default configuration, the Favorites button isn't on the toolbar, but you can always use the menu command View | Explorer Bar | Favorites.

- **History**   Displays a daily guide to whatever files or Web sites you have opened in either Windows Explorer or Internet Explorer (see Chapter 24, section "Examining History"). (The History Explorer bar doesn't keep track of the files or Web sites you open with Netscape Navigator or any other Web browser. Fortunately, Navigator has its own History file.)

- **Folders**   Displays the folder tree. (When the Explorer bar displays the folder tree, we call it the *Folders Explorer Bar*.)

You can make the Explorer bar disappear by clicking the X in the upper-right corner of the Explorer bar or by clicking the selected (pressed in) button on the toolbar. You can resize the Explorer Bar by dragging the boundary that separates it from the working area.

What Is the Status Bar?

The status bar is the bar at the very bottom of an Explorer window. It displays information about any selected object. When a file is selected, for example, the status bar shows the file's type and size. When a drive is selected, it displays the free space and capacity of the drive. When a folder is open and no object is selected, it tells you the number of objects in the folder and how many of them are hidden.

When you are connected to the Internet or another network, the right end of the status bar tells you the security zone of the open folder. If the folder is on your own computer, the My Computer icon is displayed.

What Is the Web Panel?

Windows enables you to customize the way Windows Explorer displays any particular folder (see Chapter 9, section "Customizing a Folder"). The folder can have its own special logo. Information about any selected folder can be displayed and you can even display little previews of files without opening them—a great feature if you're looking for a particular photo, for example. The place where this extra information appears in the Explorer window is called the *Web panel*. Figure 8-4 shows the My Pictures folder, which Microsoft has set up as a sample of what you can do with folder customization.

MANAGING YOUR DISK

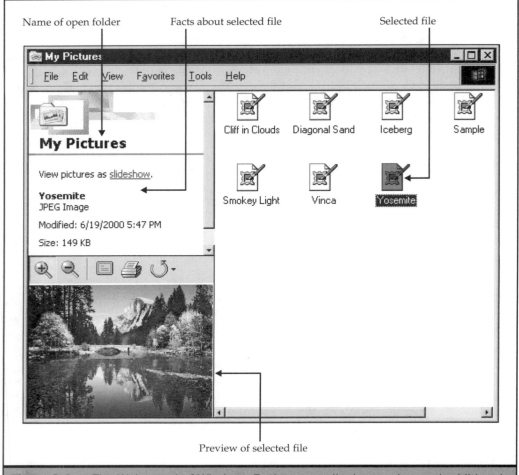

Figure 8-4. *The Web panel of Windows Explorer can display preview and additional information about files.*

What Is a Preview?

When you select an image file or HTML document in the working area of an Explorer window, a small copy of the first page of the file appears at the bottom of the Web panel. These small copies are called *previews*.

Windows doesn't know how to display previews of every type of file. If you have selected a file of a type that Windows cannot preview, the square where the preview would appear is empty. The preview also doesn't appear if the Explorer window isn't large enough. If you expect to see a preview and you don't, try enlarging the window.

Where Is the Desktop Really?

The Windows interface makes the desktop look as if it contains all hard disks, floppies, CD-ROMs, and other storage devices. But the desktop is only a virtual object, not a piece of hardware; so where is its information stored? The desktop information is stored on your computer's main hard drive, typically the one labeled C. The shortcuts, files, and folders you move to the desktop are actually stored in the folder C:\Windows\Desktop.

MANAGING YOUR DISK

Previews, in general, aren't large enough to read, though you may make out a title. The main use of a preview is to help you identify a file—to see whether it is the red picture or the blue picture, the two-column document or the one-column document.

What Is the Recycle Bin?

Files and folders deleted from your hard drives don't go away completely, at least not right away—they live on inside the *Recycle Bin*. From there, they can either be restored to the folder they were in before you deleted them or moved from the Recycle Bin to any other folder via cut-and-paste or drag-and-drop.

The Recycle Bin icon lives on the desktop and looks like a wastebasket. When you open the icon, Windows Explorer shows you the files and folders that were deleted since the Recycle Bin was last emptied.

The Recycle Bin is a hybrid object that behaves like a folder in some ways, but not in others. Like a folder, it contains objects, and you can move objects in to and out of the Recycle Bin, just as you do with any other folder. Unlike a folder, even an unusual folder like the desktop, the Recycle Bin is not contained on a single drive. Instead, each of your computer's hard drives maintains its own *Recycled folder*, and the contents of all the Recycled folders are visible whenever you open any of them.

Folders that have been sent to the Recycle Bin aren't considered part of the folder tree: they don't appear in the Folders Explorer bar, and they can't be opened. If you want to examine the contents of a folder in the Recycle Bin, you first must move the folder to another location. Likewise, files in the Recycle Bin cannot be opened, edited, or worked on otherwise.

The intention of the designers is clear: the Recycle Bin is not to be used as a workspace. Instead, it is a last-chance repository. You can put things in the Recycle Bin or take things out—that's all.

Working with the Recycle Bin under the default settings is covered in this chapter (see "Retrieving Files and Folders from the Recycle Bin"). Reconfiguring the Recycle Bin settings is covered in the next chapter (see Chapter 9, section "Managing the Recycle Bin").

Working with Windows Explorer

When you open the My Computer icon on the desktop, Windows Explorer opens an Explorer window, as in Figure 8-2. Any folder you open from the desktop creates a new Explorer window. You can also run Windows Explorer by choosing Start | Programs | Accessories | Windows Explorer. Or, you can put a shortcut to Windows Explorer somewhere more convenient, such as the top of the Start menu or on the desktop.

Every aspect of the Explorer window has numerous optional configurations, which are covered in the next chapter. This chapter describes how to do basic file and folder operations under the default configuration. If your computer works differently, someone has probably changed Windows Explorer's settings. If you want, you can change them back as follows:

1. Start Windows Explorer either by opening a folder on the desktop or by selecting Start | Programs | Accessories | Windows Explorer. An Explorer window opens.
2. Select Tools | Folder Options from the menu bar. The Folder Options dialog box appears.
3. Click the Restore Defaults button in the Folder Options dialog box.
4. Click OK.

Navigating the Folder Tree

Windows Explorer enables you to view the contents of any folder on your system. The process of changing your view from one folder to another is referred to as *navigating*. The Explorer window provides you with navigation tools that you will recognize if you have used a Web browser: You can go up or down in the folder tree and back or forth along the path you have taken. In addition, you can jump to any folder near the top of the folder tree by clicking its icon on the list that drops down from the Address box on the toolbar. You can also find a folder in the Folders Explorer bar and click its icon there to display its contents in the working area.

If you like to use the keyboard, you can use the UP ARROW and DOWN ARROW keys to move up and down the list of folders, or you can move to a folder by typing its first letter. After you select a folder, press the plus (+) key to expand the folder (display its subfolders) or the minus (–) key to collapse it.

Viewing the Folder Tree with the Folders Explorer Bar

The Folders Explorer bar is a map of the folder tree. You can expand or contract this map to whatever level of detail you find most convenient. Figure 8-5 reproduces the Explorer bar from Figure 8-2. At the top of the tree, displayed flush with the left edge of the window, is the Desktop icon. The dotted lines from the Desktop icon to

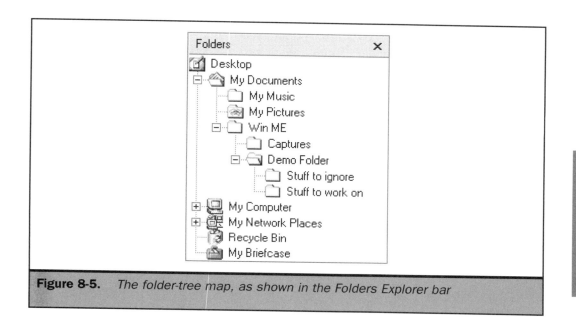

Figure 8-5.   *The folder-tree map, as shown in the Folders Explorer bar*

the other objects show those objects are contained in the desktop. Each layer of the folder tree is indented a little further to the right of the Desktop icon, showing what is contained in what.

Folders that can be expanded (in other words, folders whose subfolders are not shown) have boxes next to them containing small plus signs, called *plus boxes*. In Figure 8-5, you can expand the folders My Computer and My Network Places. Clicking the plus box next to a folder expands the tree to include that folder's subfolders. The box remains, but now contains a minus sign to denote the folder has been expanded. Clicking the *minus box* contracts the folder again. When a folder is expanded, it is connected to each of its subfolders by an additional dotted line. If any of the subfolders are expandable, new plus boxes appear next to them. Any portion of the folder tree can be expanded as much or as little as you like. In Figure 8-5, the folders My Documents, Win Me, and Demo Folder have been expanded.

The plus boxes enable you to look at the overall structure of your files without losing sight of the folder whose contents are displayed in the working area. Opening a new folder in the working area automatically expands the folder tree in the Folders Explorer bar to show you the new folder. If you use the plus boxes in the Explorer bar to contract a folder that contains the currently open folder, that folder is closed and the working area changes to display the contents of the folder you just contracted.

When the folder tree expands beyond the limits of the left pane, scroll bars appear. If you want to see the full width of the folder tree, drag the border between the right and left panes to the right.

Navigating by Using the Address Box

The Address box on the Toolbar displays the name of the folder whose contents appear in the working area. An abbreviated folder-tree diagram drops down from the Address box. It shows only the top layers of the folder tree, together with the folders between the open folder and the drive that contains it. You can use this diagram to jump to a new location in the folder tree by clicking any of the icons shown.

Going Up and Down the Folder Tree

Under the default settings, the Up button on the toolbar (or the equivalent View | Go To | Up One Level command) "moves" the window up one level of indentation in the folder tree. The window then shows the contents of the folder containing the previously viewed folder. For example, if a window displays the contents of the C:\Windows folder and you then click the Up button, a window displays the contents of the C drive. Click Up again, and you see the contents of My Computer. Wherever you begin, if you click Up often enough, you reach the desktop.

To move the window one step down the folder tree, open a subfolder of the currently open folder.

Going Back and Forth on the Folder Tree

Under the default settings, the Forward and Back buttons on the toolbar (or the equivalent commands View | Go To | Forward and View | Go To | Back) move the window back and forth among the previously displayed folders. The Back button returns to the previous open folder. Clicking the Back button again returns to the folder before that, and so on. The Forward button undoes the Back button: Clicking Back, and then clicking Forward leaves you where you started. Until you have clicked Back, there is no place to go forward to, so the Forward button is grayed out. Similarly, once you have returned to the first folder you opened, the Back button is grayed out.

Lists of folders to which you can go back or forward drop down when you click the arrows next to the Back and Forward buttons. Jump to any folder on the list by clicking its name.

Jumping to Somewhere Else Entirely

The arrow at the right end of the Address box pulls down a diagram showing the path that connects the open folder to the desktop, as well as the layers of the folder tree immediately under the desktop and My Computer. Open any of these folders by clicking its name in the list.

Jumping is particularly easy when you display the Folders Explorer bar (choose View | Explorer Bar | Folders). Just find the folder you want to view on the folder-tree map and click it.

Making and Working with Files and Folders

The basic file and folder operations—creating, selecting, naming, and opening—are relatively unchanged from earlier versions of Windows.

Creating Files and Folders

New folders and files of certain types can be created on the desktop or in Windows Explorer. On the desktop, right-click any empty area and choose New on the shortcut menu. In Windows Explorer, choose File | New. In either case, a submenu appears that lists the new objects you can create: folders, shortcuts, and a variety of types of files. Select an element of this list, and Windows creates the appropriate object. You can also create shortcuts by using this method (see Chapter 9).

You can create files of types other than the types listed from within application programs.

Selecting Files and Folders

Files and folders are represented on the desktop and in Windows Explorer by icons, with the name of the file or folder printed underneath its icon. A *file icon* is a rectangle that looks like a piece of paper. The rectangle bears the design of the default program that opens the file. Icons of Word, Notepad, and Star Office documents appear in Figure 8-2. A *folder icon* looks like a manila folder. A compressed folder icon looks like a folder icon with a zipper on it.

Under the default settings, you select a file or folder by clicking its icon, and you open it by double-clicking. If you don't like all this clicking (or you're afraid of getting repetitive stress syndrome), you can adjust Windows Explorer so resting the cursor on an icon selects the corresponding object, and single-clicking opens the object (see Chapter 9, section "Replacing Double Clicks with Single Clicks").

To select more than one object, select the first object, and then press the CTRL key while you select others. (If you don't press CTRL, selecting one object deselects all the others.)

If the objects you want to select are close together, move the cursor to an empty spot nearby, hold down the left mouse button, and drag the cursor. A rectangle forms, and any object inside the rectangle is selected. When you release the mouse button, the rectangle disappears, but the objects it contained continue to be selected. You can get the same effect by using the SHIFT key instead of dragging the mouse: Select an object, and then hold down the SHIFT key and select another object. All objects in an imaginary rectangle containing the two selected objects are also selected.

More complicated patterns of objects can be selected by combining the two methods:

1. Drag out a rectangle that contains most of the objects you want to select (and perhaps some others). That is, click in one corner of an imaginary rectangle,

hold down the mouse button, and drag the mouse pointer to the opposite corner of the rectangle.

2. Release the mouse button and press CTRL.

3. While pressing CTRL, deselect unwanted objects (if any) by clicking them.

4. Keep pressing CTRL, and select any additional objects you want by clicking them.

To select all the items in a folder, open it in a Folder or Windows Explorer window and choose Edit | Select All from the menu bar or press CTRL-A on the keyboard. To select all but a few objects in a folder, choose Select All, and then hold down CTRL while you deselect those few objects.

You can also use the keyboard to select multiple files. Hold down the SHIFT key while pressing the UP ARROW or DOWN ARROW key to select all the files from the first to the last. To select files that aren't listed together, select the first file, hold down the CTRL key, press the UP ARROW or DOWN ARROW key to move to the next file you want to select, and press SPACEBAR to select it. Continue holding down the CTRL key, moving, and pressing SPACEBAR until you select all the files you want.

If you want to select most of the files in a folder, select all the items you don't want to include. Then choose Edit | Invert Selection to deselect the selected items and to select the deselected ones.

Naming and Renaming Files and Folders

Newly created folders and files are given default names, such as New Folder and New Microsoft Word Document. To rename a file or folder, right-click its icon and choose Rename from the shortcut menu. A box appears around the current name, and the entire name is selected. Type the new name in the box and press ENTER.

You can also rename by selecting an object and then clicking the name next to the icon. Again, a box appears around the current name and you proceed as before. Be sure to pause slightly between the click that selects the object and the click that selects its name—otherwise, you double-click and open the object.

If the new name is only a minor change from the old one, edit the old name instead of typing the new one. Click inside the name box at the place where you want to begin typing or deleting.

Changing a File's Extension

Changing a file's three-letter extension changes its file type. Don't do this unless you know what you're doing. If you assign the file a type that Windows doesn't recognize, it won't know how to open the file. If you assign the file a type Windows does recognize, whenever you open the file, Windows uses the application associated with that file type. Unless you prepare the file in such a way that is appropriate for that application, the opening fails. (Consider, for example, the Paint program trying to open an audio file.)

When you are renaming a file, be sure you know whether Windows is hiding the file extensions (see "What Are Extensions and File Types?"). If file extensions are hidden, you can't change them when you rename a file. If they aren't hidden, you can make changes. When you rename a file whose extension is not hidden, you must include the extension in your renaming or else the file type is lost. Conversely, if you type in a file extension when the extension is hidden, you wind up with a double extension, like report.doc.doc.

If you change a file's extension (and, thus, its file type), Windows gives you a warning that the file may become unusable and asks you to confirm your decision. This feature, although annoying, may save you from making an occasional mistake.

Opening Files and Folders

Under the default settings, you can open any object in an Explorer window or on the desktop by double-clicking its icon. (You can change the settings of Windows Explorer so only a single-click is required; see Chapter 9, section "Replacing Double-Clicks with Single-Clicks"). If the object is a folder, its contents are displayed in an Explorer window. If the object is a file of a recognized file type, Windows opens it with the application associated with that file type.

If you open a file in an Explorer window and Windows doesn't recognize its file type, or if that file type has no associated application, an Open With box appears, asking you to identify an application to use in opening the file.

At times, you might want to open a file with an application other than the one associated with its file type. For example, Windows associates HTML files with a Web browser (Internet Explorer by default); but if you want to edit an HTML file, you need to open it with a Web page editor application. You can do this in at least two ways:

- If both the file icon and the application icon (or shortcuts to either) are visible on your screen, drag-and-drop the file icon onto the application icon. If you do this frequently with a particular application, put its icon on the Links bar (see Chapter 9, section "Configuring the Links Toolbar"). Or, you could create a shortcut to the application on the desktop (see Chapter 9, section "Making Shortcuts").

- If the application is open, choose File | Open from its menu bar. The Open window appears and enables you to indicate which file to open.

- In Windows Explorer, right-click the file icon and select Open With from the shortcut menu. Choose the application from the Open With dialog box.

Rearranging Files and Folders

The quest for the perfect system of file organization is endless—you frequently need to move or copy files and folders to somewhere other than where they were originally created. You can rearrange your files and folders by using the following:

- Buttons on the Standard Buttons toolbar
- Commands from the menus
- Drag-and-drop techniques

The commands corresponding to the buttons on the Standard Buttons toolbar are also on the menus, the only difference being how the commands are issued, not what they do. This section first examines the toolbar and menu commands and then the drag-and-drop techniques.

Moving and Copying Files and Folders

You can use buttons on the Standard Buttons toolbar to move a file, a folder, or a collection of files and folders from one folder to another. In the default configuration, the relevant buttons are Move To and Copy To. Both buttons are labeled with icons that show a document moving into a folder. The difference between these two icons is subtle: The Move To icon has a single document, while the Copy To icon has two documents. You can see the expanded buttons with their text labels in Figure 8-2. If you aren't displaying the Standard Buttons toolbar, you can use the Edit | Move To Folder and Edit | Copy To Folder commands instead.

The Move To button is similar to cut-and-paste, and it has the effect of moving objects from a source folder to a target folder (see Chapter 7, section "What Is Cut-and-Paste?"). The Copy To procedure resembles copy-and-paste, and it leaves separate copies of the objects in the source folder and the target folder.

Where did my buttons go?

Previous versions of Windows Explorer had Cut, Copy, and Paste buttons on the Standard Buttons toolbar. If you miss these buttons, you can put them back on the toolbar (see Chapter 9, section "Configuring the Standard Buttons toolbar"). Meanwhile, you haven't lost any functionality—Cut, Copy, and Paste still appear on the Edit menu.

Moving and Copying with One Explorer Window

To move (or copy) a file or folder, follow these steps:

1. Open the source folder.

2. Select the objects to be moved (or copied) from the working area of the Explorer window.

3. Click the Move To (or Copy To) button on the toolbar. A Browse For Folder window opens, as shown in Figure 8-6.

4. Select the target folder in the Browse For Folder window. This window and its plus boxes behave just like the Folders Explorer bar.

5. Click the OK button in the Browse For Folder window.

Moving and Copying with Two Explorer Windows

If both the source and target folders are already open in their own Explorer windows, you can move and copy files and folders more easily without using the Move To or Copy To buttons. You can drag-and-drop objects from the source window to the target window, or you can do the following:

1. Select the objects to be moved (or copied) from the target folder's window.

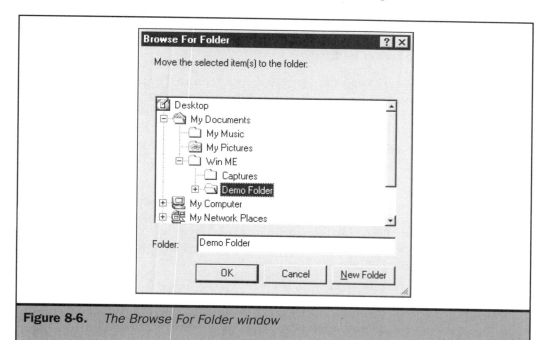

Figure 8-6.   *The Browse For Folder window*

2. Select Edit | Cut (or Edit | Copy). Ghostly images of the objects remain in their original places until the objects are pasted elsewhere. (An alternative method is to select the objects with the right mouse button and then choose Cut or Copy from the shortcut menu.)

3. Click the spot in the target folder's window where you want the objects to be placed.

4. Select Edit | Paste button, or right-click an empty spot in the Explorer window and choose Paste from the shortcut menu.

Moving and Copying with the Folders Explorer Bar

When the Folders Explorer bar is displayed, you can use the icons it displays as target folders for either the cut-and-paste techniques described in the previous section or the drag-and-drop techniques described in the next section. If you want to move or copy entire folders, you can cut or drag them from the Folders Explorer bar either into the working area or into other folders on the Explorer bar.

Dragging and Dropping Files and Folders

Drag-and-drop is often the simplest way to move or copy objects from one drive or folder to another, or between a folder and the desktop (see Chapter 7, section "What Is Drag-and-Drop?"). You can also delete objects by dragging and dropping them onto the Recycle Bin icon.

To drag-and-drop files or folders:

1. Set up window(s) so you can see both the source and the target folders (remember, the desktop itself is a kind of "window"). Our preference is to have the source folder open in the working area of an Explorer window, and the target folder visible in the Folders Explorer bar, but you can also have the source and target folders open in two separate Explorer windows.

2. Select the icons of the objects you want to drag-and-drop.

3. While holding down the left mouse button, drag the icons to the target. (You can also drag with the right mouse button. This is discussed in the following paragraphs.) If the target is an open window, drag the icons to an open space in the window. If the target is an icon in an open window, drag until the cursor rests over the icon. The target icon changes color when you have the cursor in the right place.

4. Drop by releasing the mouse button.

Drag-and-drop has one unfortunate aspect. If you experiment, you soon notice it doesn't do the same thing in all circumstances—sometimes it moves an object, sometimes it copies it, and sometimes it makes a shortcut. The reason for this behavior is the programmers at Microsoft have gone a bit overboard in trying to be helpful. Windows is doing what it guesses you intend to do, based on the file type of the objects being dragged, the locations of the source and target folders, and a few other things we haven't figured out. Here's what happens when you drag-and-drop:

- **Objects to the same disk**   If you drag-and-drop objects (other than programs) from one folder to another folder on the same disk, the objects are moved. They disappear from the source folder and appear in the target folder. Windows reasons that you are probably just rearranging your files. (Remember, the desktop is a folder on the C drive. Anything else on the C drive is considered on the same disk as the desktop.)

- **Objects to a different disk**   If you drag-and-drop objects (other than programs) from one folder to another folder on a different disk, the objects are copied. Separate copies exist in both the source and target folders. The rationale is you are probably making a backup copy on another disk or making a copy to give someone else.

- **Programs**   If you drag-and-drop a program, it may behave like any other object but, for some programs, Windows makes a shortcut in the target folder and leaves the program file where it was in the source folder. We haven't come up with a firm rule describing this, although, In general, the more complex the program, the more likely it is that dragging and dropping it will create a shortcut. So, for example, you'll get a shortcut if you drag-and-drop Windows Media Player, but not Calculator.

Windows at least tells you what it's going to do with the objects you drop. When the object icons are in a droppable position, a tiny + appears next to them if they're going to be copied, while a tiny curved arrow (the same arrow that appears on shortcut icons) appears if a shortcut is going to be created. If nothing appears, the files are going to be moved.

Tip   *If you want to use drag-and-drop, but you neither want to memorize how it works nor trust Windows to guess your intentions, drag with the right mouse button rather than the left mouse button. When you drop in the target folder, select the action you intended from the shortcut menu.*

You can also control drag-and-drop behavior by using the keyboard: If you left-drag with the SHIFT key pressed, the objects are moved when you drop them. Left-dragging with the CTRL key pressed copies the objects when you drop them. You can easily remember this by noting Copy and CTRL both begin with C, or you are "shifting" a file from one location to another.

Using the Send To Menu

Send To is a menu found on the File menu of Explorer windows and on the shortcut menu when you right-click a file or folder. The Send To menu enables you to copy files to preselected locations quickly and easily. To use Send To for this purpose:

1. Open a folder that contains files you want to copy.

2. Select the files and folders to copy (see "Selecting Files and Folders").

3. Choose File | Send To from the menu bar, or right-click the item(s) you selected and choose Send To from the shortcut menu. Either way, a menu of possible destinations appears. The Windows installation program creates a default Send To menu that varies according to the resources available to your computer. Here is a sample Send To menu:

4. Choose a destination from the Send To menu. The files are copied to the destination.

Send To is useful only if you want to move files to a destination that is on its menu. To add a new destination to the Send To menu, create a shortcut to that folder or disk in the folder C:\Windows\SendTo (see Chapter 9, section "Making Shortcuts").

To delete an item from the Send To menu, delete the corresponding shortcut from C:\Windows\SendTo.

Deleting Files and Folders

To delete a file, folder, or collection of files and folders in a single Explorer window:

1. Select the objects to be deleted.

2. Either click the Delete button on the toolbar, choose File | Delete from the menu bar, right-click the object and select Delete from the shortcut menu, or press the DELETE key on the keyboard. A dialog box appears that asks whether you

really want to send the objects to the Recycle Bin (if they are deleted from your computer's hard drive) or delete the objects (if they are on a removable disk).

3. Click Yes in the dialog box.

Under the default settings, objects deleted from your computer's hard drives go to the Recycle Bin, from which they can be recovered. You can reset your preferences so objects are deleted immediately and don't go to the Recycle Bin (see Chapter 9, section "Streamlining the Deletion Process"). Objects deleted from floppy drives or other removable disks don't go to the Recycle Bin, although they may be recoverable by other means (see "Retrieving Files with Third-Party Tools"). For this reason, be especially cautious when deleting objects from floppies or other removable disks.

You can delete files or folders directly, without sending them to the Recycle Bin, if you are certain you won't change your mind. To delete a file or folder irrevocably, select it and then press SHIFT-DELETE.

Fixing Your Mistakes

Even the most experienced computer user occasionally clicks the mouse, and then stares at the screen in horror, asking, "What did I just do?" Fortunately, the horror needn't be lasting—Windows provides tools for recovering from many common errors.

Windows Me contains a powerful new tool for fixing your mistakes, System Restore, which is described in section "Returning Your System to a Predefined State with System Restore" in Chapter 34. Using System Restore, you can return your computer's hardware/software configuration to the way it was on some previous date—when it presumably worked better than it does now.

Reversing Your Last Action Using the Undo Button

Toolbars make it easy to do what you want to do, but they also make it easy to do what you don't want to do. Be grateful that the Standard Buttons toolbar in Windows Explorer has an Undo button—the button with the counterclockwise arrow on it (see Figure 8-2). If you delete something you want to keep, or cut-and-paste the wrong file, click Undo and you can pretend the mistake never happened.

Clicking Undo multiple times steps you back through your recent actions. You can also choose Edit | Undo from the menu bar of an Explorer window. The keyboard equivalent is CTRL-Z.

Retrieving Files and Folders from the Recycle Bin

If you change your mind about deleting a file or folder and it's too late to use the Undo button, you can still retrieve it from the Recycle Bin—if it was deleted from a hard drive and you haven't emptied the Recycle Bin in the meantime.

Emptying and configuring the Recycle Bin is discussed in the next chapter (see Chapter 9, section "Managing the Recycle Bin").

Opening the Recycle Bin

The easiest place to find the Recycle Bin is on the desktop, where its icon looks like a wastebasket. You can also find the Recycle Bin on the folder tree directly under the desktop, below your computer's disk drive and other devices.

Searching the Recycle Bin

If you know exactly what file or folder you are looking for, any view will do. But if the Recycle Bin is crowded and you need to do some real detective work to determine which objects you want to retrieve, the Details view (shown in Figure 8-7) is best. Choose View | Details from the menu bar. The working area becomes a list with columns showing the following:

■ The name and icon of the file or folder

■ The address of the folder from which the object was deleted

■ The date and time the object was deleted

■ The file type

■ The size

Clicking the column header sorts the list according to that column's attribute. For example, if you know the date when you deleted the file, click the Date Deleted header

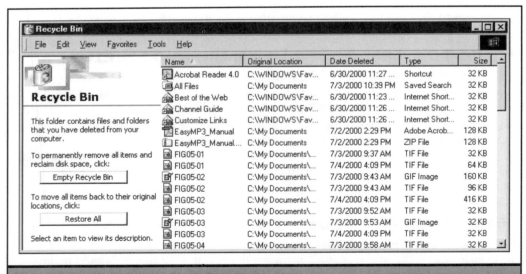

Figure 8-7.   *The Recycle Bin in Details view*

to put the objects in the order in which they were deleted. All objects deleted on the same date you deleted the file appear together. If you remember the name of the file, but know you deleted several versions of it, clicking the Name header arranges the list alphabetically by name. All the versions appear next to each other, and you can easily see which is the most recent version.

Recovering Objects from the Recycle Bin

The simplest way to recover an object from the Recycle Bin is to follow these steps:

1. Open the Recycle Bin.
2. Select the object (or collection of objects) you want to recover.
3. Choose File | Restore from the menu bar.

You can also right-click the item you want to recover and then choose Restore from the shortcut menu.

The object returns to the folder it was deleted from—the address given in the Original Location column of the Details view. If the object is a folder, all its contents return with it. You can use Restore even if the object was deleted from a folder that no longer exists. A folder of the appropriate name is then created to contain the restored object. You can restore everything in the Recycle Bin to its original location by clicking the Restore All button on the Web panel of the Recycle Bin.

To recover an object, but to put it in a new place, you can either cut-and-paste from the Recycle Bin to the new location, or do the following:

1. Open the Recycle Bin.
2. Expand the folder tree in the Folders Explorer bar so the target folder icon is visible.
3. In the working area, select the object(s) you want to recover.
4. Drag-and-drop to the target folder on the Explorer bar.

Retrieving Files with Third-Party Tools

When a file or folder is emptied from the Recycle Bin, Windows doesn't immediately do anything rash like overwrite the corresponding disk space with zeroes. Windows simply removes the file from its file allocation table, so the disk space the file occupied is no longer reserved (see Chapter 10, section "What Is a File System?"). If that disk space is needed for something else, Windows writes over it but, until then, the information stays on the disk. (Think of a restaurant with a lazy busboy; the tables don't get cleared until more customers come.)

A number of applications have been written to recover this information and reassemble the file, but none are part of Windows Me. Two of the best known are Norton Utilities by Symantec (on the Internet at **http://www.symantec.com**) and McAfee Utilities (at **http://www.mcafee.com**).

The Complete Reference

Windows Me

Chapter 9

Managing Files and Folders

The previous chapter explained what you need to know to start working with files and folders: creating and deleting them, opening them, seeing what's in them, naming them, and moving them from one place to another. This chapter discusses issues that may not come up immediately as you work with files and folders, but that you should know about if you are going to have a long-term relationship with your computer.

To a beginner, having a lot of choices is more of a burden than a convenience; but as users become more familiar with their computers, they develop their own ideas about how things should work. For this reason, Windows has default settings that cause the system to work automatically in the way the designers believe is simplest for beginners. A large number of Windows' behaviors are reconfigurable, however, so more advanced users can make their own choices.

The longer you work with your computer, the more files you create. At some point, putting them all in a folder called Jane's Files, or splitting them into two folders called Work and Home, is no longer adequate. You need to come up with a system that organizes your files into smaller, coherently related piles. Discussing organizational systems goes beyond the scope of this book, but you should know about one valuable organizational tool: the shortcut. Shortcuts enable you to access the same file or application from many different points in the folder tree, without the disadvantages that come with having several copies of the same file.

You should also know about compressed folders, which save the same files in a smaller amount of disk space, at the cost of some functionality.

Even the best-organized people occasionally forget where they put something, so you need to know how to use the Windows Search Explorer bar.

Being able to retrieve deleted files from the Recycle Bin (described in the previous chapter) is a convenience; but, in time, the bin becomes crowded with long-forgotten files that take up disk space for no purpose. You need to know how to manage the Recycle Bin so it continues to be useful without unduly burdening your hard drive.

Finally, files and folders have properties. The Properties dialog box for a file or folder contains much useful information and lets you make certain choices regarding the object's properties and attributes (see Chapter 1, section "What Are Properties?").

What Is a Shortcut?

Technically, a *shortcut* is a file with a .lnk extension. Less technically, a shortcut is a placeholder in your filing system. A shortcut has a definite position on the folder tree, but it points to a file or folder that is somewhere else on the folder tree.

The purpose of a shortcut is to allow an object to be, for most purposes, in two places at once. For example, you usually should leave a program file inside the folder where it was installed, so you don't mess up any of the relationships between it and its associated files. At the same time, you might want the program to be on the desktop, so you can conveniently open files by dragging them to the program's icon. Solution:

leave the program file where it is, but make a shortcut pointing to it, and place the shortcut on the desktop. When you drag a file to the shortcut icon, Windows opens the file with the corresponding program.

Maintaining multiple copies of documents on your system is both wasteful of disk space and potentially confusing—when one copy gets updated, you could easily forget to update the others. And yet, files often belong in many different places in a filing system. If, for example, Paul writes the office's fourth-quarter report, the document may belong simultaneously in the Paul's Memos folder and in the Quarterly Reports folder. Putting the document itself in Quarterly Reports and a shortcut to it in Paul's Memos solves the problem, without creating multiple copies of the document. Clicking the shortcut icon opens the associated document, just as if you had clicked the icon of the document itself.

You can recognize a shortcut icon by the curving arrow that appears in its lower-left corner. A shortcut icon otherwise looks just like the icon of the object it points to, a document, folder, or application. A shortcut can be on your desktop or in a folder. It looks like this:

Susan's
Address Label

You can create, delete, move, copy, and rename shortcuts from Explorer windows, just as you would any other kind of file (see "Working with Shortcuts").

Note *Windows also has things called "shortcut keys" and "shortcut menus," which have nothing to do with shortcuts (see Chapter 2).*

What Are Properties of Files and Folders?

Like almost everything else in Windows, files and folders have *properties*—information about a file or folder you can access and, perhaps, change without opening the file or folder.

To view this information and make changes, select the file or folder in Windows Explorer, and then choose File | Properties, or right-click the file or folder and select Properties from the shortcut menu.) The Properties dialog box appears, with the General tab selected (see Figure 9-1).

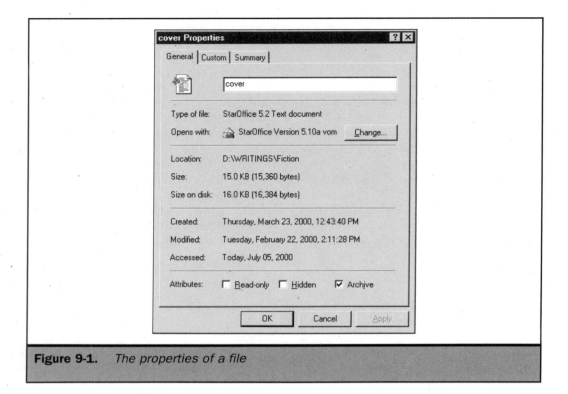

Figure 9-1.   *The properties of a file*

The General tab of a file's Properties dialog box displays the file's:

- Name and icon
- File type (see Chapter 8, section "What Are Extensions and File Types?")
- The default application that opens files of this type
- Location in the folder tree (see Chapter 8, section "What Is the Folder Tree?")
- Size (including both the actual size of the file and the slightly larger amount of disk space allocated to the file)
- Date and time of creation, most recent modification, and most recent access
- Attributes (see the next section)

Depending on a file's type, it may have additional tabs of properties, which you can access by clicking them individually. The properties of Word files (with the file extension .doc), for example, include a Summary tab and a Custom tab. The Summary tab provides room for the author of a file to give keywords and a short summary of the document. The Custom tab provides a place for the kind of information that offices used to rubber stamp onto paper documents: control number, date received, and so on.

Because a folder is technically a special kind of file, the General tab of its properties contains much of the same information: icon, name, type (File Folder), location, size (the number of bytes taken up by the folder and all its contents, including the contents of subfolders), date created, and attributes. The General tab has one additional item: Contains, which reports the number of files and folders contained in the folder and all its subfolders.

If your computer is on a local area network, folders also have a Sharing tab, with information about whether the folder (and the files and folders it contains) are shared on the network (see Chapter 29, section "Sharing Disk Drives and Folders on a LAN").

Tip *To find the total size of a group of files and folders, select them all, and then right-click anywhere in the selected filenames. Choose Properties from the shortcut menu. Windows displays the total number of files and folders, as well as their combined size. Note: You can't select multiple folders in the folder tree—display the list of files and folders in the working area of the Explorer window.*

What Are Attributes?

The *attributes* of a file or folder include these settings, which can be selected or unselected for each file or folder:

- **Read-only**   You can read and even edit this file or folder; but when you try to save your changes, Windows reminds you this is a read-only file, and asks you to save your new version as a different file. If you try to delete a read-only file or folder, Windows reminds you it's read-only, but deletes it if you insist.

- **Hidden**   A file or folder that doesn't usually appear in Explorer windows, but can be made visible if you want to see it (see "What Are Hidden Files and Folders?").

- **Archive**   This setting may mean the file or folder has been changed since the last time it was backed up, depending on which backup program you use. Windows Me comes with Microsoft Backup (see Appendix B).

The attributes of a file or folder appear at the bottom of the General tab of the Properties dialog box.

What Are Compressed Folders?

Compressed folders are folders whose contents are stored in such a way as to conserve disk space. The amount of disk space you can save by storing a file in a compressed folder varies depending upon the kind of file it is. A Word document of 100K, for example, might only take up 40K in a compressed folder, while an Acrobat document of 100K might still take up 80K in a compressed folder.

Unlike an ordinary folder, a compressed folder is actually a file—in this case, a ZIP file (with the extension .zip). All the files in the compressed folder are actually stored in the ZIP file. Compressed folders are "virtual folders"—files that masquerade as folders in Windows Explorer. Most other programs see compressed folders as single files, though, and can't read or write the files contained in compressed folders.

You may have worked with ZIP files under previous versions of Windows by using a third-party utility like WinZip or ZipMagic. Windows Me is the first version of Windows that allows Windows Explorer to work directly with compressed folders. The icon representing a compressed folder is a folder icon with a zipper on it.

You pay a price for compression: files in compressed folders are harder to work with. They take longer to open than an identical uncompressed file, and most applications can't open them directly. If you open a document by single- or double-clicking its filename in an Explorer window, Windows makes an uncompressed copy of the file and runs the associated program; however, the copy usually has a meaningless name (a temporary filename created by Windows), and it may be opened as read-only. Most applications can't save files in compressed folders. If you want to edit the document and save your changes, you must give the file a new name and save it in an ordinary folder. You can move the file into the compressed folder later, using Windows Explorer.

Given their virtues and vices, compressed folders are best for archiving information that you don't access or change often. Compressed folders are also useful for sharing information with other people; being smaller than normal folders, they take less time to transmit and occupy less disk space. Large files that you download from the Internet are frequently in .zip format. The recipients can only read the files if they have Windows Me or a third-party utility like WinZip. If you want ZIP files to look like folders in Explorer windows, including opening and saving directly from ZIP files (compressed folders), get ZipMagic (**http://www.ontrack.com/software**), which combines the power of WinZip and the convenience of Windows compressed folders.

A more detailed description of the techniques for working with compressed folders is given later in this chapter (see "Working with Compressed Folders").

Note	*The Compressed Folders utility may not be installed. To test, right-click an empty spot on the desktop and see if New	Compressed Folder appears on the shortcut menu. If not, you can install it from the Windows Me CD-ROM. Choose Start	Settings	Control Panel, run Add/Remove Programs, click the Windows Setup tab, choose the System Tools entry in the list of Windows Me components, click Details, and then choose Compressed Folders from the list of system tools.*

What Are Encrypted Folders?

Compressed folders can also be encrypted (stored in a secret code). You can attach a password to the folder so no one can open any of the files in the folder without knowing the password.

What Are Hidden Files and Folders?

Windows contains a number of files a beginner might find confusing and that you don't want to delete or change accidentally. As a safety feature, these files are *hidden*, which means, by default, they don't show up in Windows Explorer and can't be opened, deleted, or moved in Windows Explorer unless you choose to make them visible. For example, the folder C:\Windows\Spool keeps track of technical information regarding your printers—stuff you mostly don't want to mess with. But if you open My Computer, the C disk, and then the Windows folder—you won't find it. If you want to see C:\Windows\Spool (and all the other hidden files and folders), follow these steps:

1. Choose Tools | Folder Options from the menu bar of any Explorer window. The Folder Options dialog box appears. (You can also open Folder Options from the Control Panel.)

2. Click the View tab in the Folder Options dialog box. The Hidden Files section contains two radio buttons: Do Not Show Hidden Files And Folders and Show Hidden Files And Folders.

3. Click the Show Hidden Files And Folders radio button.

4. Click OK.

When hidden files and folders are shown, their icons appear as ghostly images. To hide them again, repeat the preceding procedure, but select the Do Not Show Hidden Files and Folders radio button in step 3.

Hidden files and folders usually don't play a significant role in the everyday life of the average computer user. For that reason, we recommend you leave them hidden whenever you are not working with one. This policy minimizes the chances you will alter or delete something important by accident.

Nonhidden files and folders contained in a hidden folder have an in-between status: they retain their original attributes and show up in Explorer windows if you move them to a nonhidden folder. But they are hidden in practice as long as they stay inside the hidden folder, because the path that connects them to the top of the folder tree includes a hidden link.

Caution   *A hidden file or folder shouldn't be considered secure. The Search command finds hidden files and folders (see "Searching for Files and Folders"). In fact, anyone who finds your file by using this command can open it directly from the Search window, without knowing you intended it to be hidden. Also, you can see from the preceding discussion that viewing hidden files is not difficult. If other people use your computer and you don't want them to find particular files, you should either encrypt those files or move them to a floppy disk you keep hidden in a more conventional way (see Chapter 31 for a description of Windows' limited security features).*

MANAGING YOUR DISK

You can hide a file or folder by following this procedure:

1. Select the file or folder.

2. Click the Properties button on the toolbar, or right-click the file or folder and choose Properties from the shortcut menu. The Properties dialog box appears.

3. If it is not already selected, click the General tab. Near the bottom of the General tab is a list of attributes, one of which is Hidden.

4. Click the check box next to Hidden. A check appears in that box.

5. Click OK to make the Properties dialog box disappear.

To unhide the file, repeat the same steps, but uncheck the Hidden check box.

Configuring Windows Explorer

You can configure many facets of Explorer windows to your own taste. Some of the basic choices were described in the previous chapter. At the simplest level, you can resize and move the windows themselves just like any other windows. You can choose which Explorer bar (if any) to display by clicking a toolbar button or using the View | Explorer Bar menu. You can display or hide the Standard Buttons, Address Bar, Links, or Radio toolbars by using the View | Toolbars menu, and the Status Bar by checking or unchecking View | Status Bar. (If you are wondering what any of these objects are, see the previous chapter.)

You can also make more complex changes in Windows Explorer's behavior, the information it displays, and how that information is presented.

In addition to the changes in the look and behavior of Windows Explorer in general, you can add features to individual folders that will show up whenever you open them. You can define a background wallpaper for a folder, create a comment that will appear in the Web Panel whenever the file is selected, or create a hypertext template document that opens automatically when the folder is opened, giving the folder all the capabilities of a Web page (see "Customizing a Folder," later in this chapter).

Changing Windows Explorer's Behavior

The Explorer windows of Windows Me are descended from two parents: the folder windows of Windows 95 (which were copied from the Macintosh and Windows 3.1's File Manager) and the browser windows of Internet Explorer (which were copied from Netscape Navigator). The default settings of the Explorer window borrow a little from each parent. If you don't like this compromise, you can make your own choices from the Folder Options dialog box, shown in Figure 9-2. To open this dialog box, choose Tools | Folder Options from the menu of Windows Explorer, or open the Control Panel and choose Folder Options there.

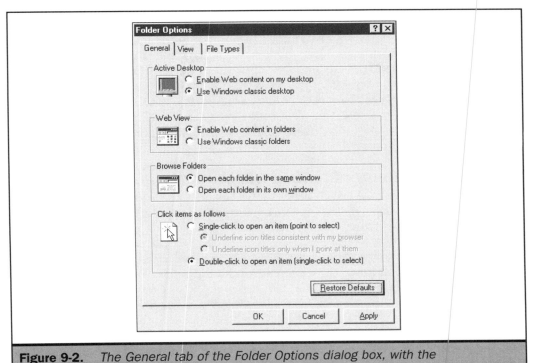

Figure 9-2.   *The General tab of the Folder Options dialog box, with the default settings*

MANAGING YOUR DISK

If, after experimenting with new settings, you decide the designers of Windows Me had it right after all, you can return to the Folder Options dialog box and click the Restore Defaults button.

Opening a New Window for Each Folder

The default setting of Windows Explorer is for a window to "navigate" up and down the folder tree, like a Web browser. When you open a subfolder of the currently displayed folder, the contents of the currently displayed folder vanish from the working area and are replaced by the contents of the subfolder. However, you still have the option of choosing the original Windows 95 behavior: the new folder can open in a new window, leaving the old window unchanged. If you do, the Windows Explorer's Forward and Back buttons stop working.

The new behaviors only apply to windows you create by opening folders on the desktop, however, or opening folders displayed in windows that already have this behavior. If you start Windows Explorer by choosing it from the Programs menu, for example, it behaves in the default (that is, the Web browser) way.

Replacing Double Clicks with Single Clicks

Under the default settings, a single mouse click selects a file or folder, and a double click opens it. If all that clicking gets to be too much, you can change the settings so a file or folder is selected when the mouse pointer hovers over it and is opened by a single click, as in Web browsers.

To make the change, choose Tools | Folder Options to open the Folder Options dialog box, shown in Figure 9-2. Then click the Single-Click To Open An Item radio button. To change back, click the Double-Click To Open An Item radio button in the Folder Options dialog box.

Disabling Web Content in Explorer Windows

Under the default settings, the Web panel shows Details-view information about a selected folder—no matter what view you are currently displaying. Certain folders in Windows Me (like My Pictures) come with special content that appears in the Web panel like previews, links, wallpaper, and anything else you can put on a Web page.

This functionality comes with a price, however: the Web panel takes up space, complicated web content can slow performance, and the behind-the-scenes workings of the Web panel can create mysterious error messages. If you get Web-customized folders from other people, you need to consider the possibility that ActiveX controls in the customization may be introducing viruses or doing other things you can't see.

To disable the Web panel in all your Explorer windows, choose Tools | Options to open the Folder Options dialog box, and then click the Use Windows Classic Folders radio button. To reenable the Web panel, click the Enable Web Content In Folders radio button in the Folder Options dialog box.

Changing the Toolbar Buttons

In addition to making the toolbars appear and disappear, as described in the previous chapter, you can choose which buttons you want to have appear on the Standard Buttons or Links toolbars.

Configuring the Standard Buttons toolbar

The 11 Standard Buttons discussed in the previous chapter are not the only ones you could have on your toolbar. In fact, you can choose from a total of 23 buttons, and you can display any collection of them in any order you want. This rearranging takes place in the Customize Toolbar dialog box, shown in Figure 9-3. To open this dialog box, select View | Toolbars | Customize, or right-click the toolbar itself and choose Customize from the shortcut menu.

The Customize Toolbar dialog box is well designed. The buttons you are currently displaying are listed in the Current Toolbar Buttons (right-hand) window, and the ones you are not displaying are in the Available Toolbar Buttons (left-hand) window. To add a button, select it in the left-hand window and click the Add button. To remove a button, select it in the right-hand window and click the Remove button.

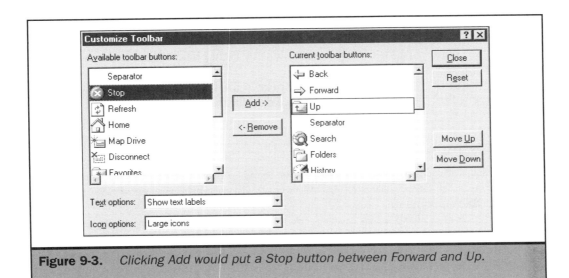

Figure 9-3. *Clicking Add would put a Stop button between Forward and Up.*

You can change the order of the buttons you display as follows: select a button in the right-hand window, and then click the Move Up or Move Down buttons. The top-to-bottom order of the buttons in the Current Toolbar Buttons window is the left-to-right order of the buttons on the Standard Buttons toolbar. Group buttons together by inserting a Separator. You can have as many Separators on your toolbar as you like; the Separator is the only item in the left-hand window that doesn't vanish when you move it to the right-hand window.

The amount of space the buttons take up on the toolbar is determined by the size of the button's icon and the text label. You can change either of these with the two drop-down lists at the bottom of the Customize Toolbar dialog box. The combination No Text Labels and Small Icons enables you to put a lot of small buttons on the toolbar, while Show Text Labels/Large Icons gives you a few big buttons.

Configuring the Links Toolbar

You can display (or hide) the Links toolbar, shown in Figure 8-2, by checking (or unchecking) View | Toolbars | Links. The Links toolbar can have its own line just above the viewing area, or it can share a line with the Address bar, the Standard Buttons toolbar, the Radio bar, or even the Menu bar. You can move it from one of these locations to another by dragging the word Links. If the Links toolbar shares a line with another toolbar, you can allocate space between the toolbars by dragging the separator bar between them. Our favorite place for the Links toolbar is just to the right of the Address bar.

The Links that Microsoft puts on the bar for you aren't very interesting. To eliminate a link button, right-click it and choose Delete from the shortcut menu. To add a new link button of your own choosing, drag any file or folder icon to the Links toolbar and drop it where you want it. The file or folder stays where it was originally, and a shortcut is put on the Links toolbar (and in the folder C:\Windows\Favorites\Links).

You can rename buttons of the Links toolbar by right-clicking them and choosing Rename from the shortcut menu.

The contents of the Links toolbar also appear in the Links folder of the Favorites menu, and another way to customize the Links toolbar is by choosing Favorites | Organize Favorites.

Changing Views

Windows Explorer can display file and folder icons in the viewing area in five different views: Large Icons, Small Icons, List, Details, and Thumbnails. You can find all these options on the View menu.

Large Icons and Small Icons are graphical views that enable you to arrange the icons in any two-dimensional pattern you like. List and Details both put the objects into a list. Details includes more information in its list and enables you to reorder the list according to various criteria. Thumbnails view displays a tiny picture of each image or HTML file.

Large Icons and Small Icons Views

Large Icons and Small Icons are both graphical ways of presenting the contents of a folder—you can drag-and-drop the files and folders in the window in any way that makes sense to you, just as you might arrange objects on a desktop, piling up some and spreading out others. The only difference between Large Icons and Small Icons (shown in Figure 9-4) is the obvious one: Large Icons (shown on the top part of the figure) gives you larger icons than Small Icons (shown on the bottom). In general, Large Icons is convenient for folders with a few files, while Small Icons works better for folders with many files.

List and Details Views

List and Details both are ways of putting the contents of a folder into a list. The difference between them is List gives only a small icon and a name for each file and subfolder. Details, as the name implies, gives a more detailed list that includes three more columns: the size of the file, its file type, and when it was last modified (see Figure 9-5). (The column headings are sometimes different for special folders. For example, My Computer's columns are Name, Type, Total Size, and Free Space.)

If you think Details view would be more informative if it had a different set of columns, right-click the bar that displays the column headings. The shortcut menu displays a list of possible column headings, with the currently displayed ones checked. Check or uncheck any you like. The changes you make apply to the current folder only, but will be remembered the next time you open that folder. You also change Details view for all folders (see "Changing How the View Settings Work").

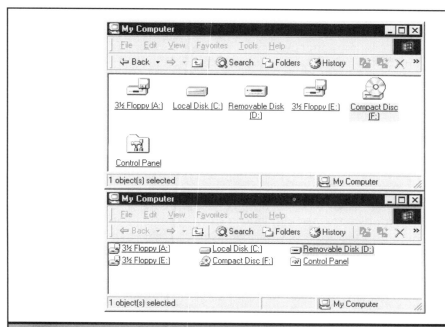

Figure 9-4.   *Two views of My Computer: with large icons (top) and small icons (bottom)*

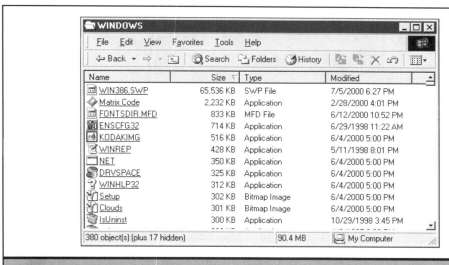

Figure 9-5.   *In Details view, you can sort by clicking any column head.*

Details view also enables you to sort the list of files and subfolders according to any column by clicking its column head. Clicking Name sorts the contents, putting them in alphabetical order. Clicking a column head twice sorts the contents in reverse order. For example, clicking the Size head once sorts from the smallest file to the largest, and clicking Size twice re-sorts from the largest file to the smallest. In Figure 9-5, clicking the column head Size twice has sorted the contents of the Windows folder by file size, largest to smallest.

You can adjust the width of the columns in a Details view by dragging-and-dropping the lines between the adjacent column heads. You can switch the order of the columns by dragging-and-dropping the column heads.

Thumbnails View

If a file icon is a little picture that is supposed to tell you something about the file, and if the file itself contains a picture, then why not let a miniature version of the picture be the file icon? That's the idea behind Thumbnails view, shown in Figure 9-6. Graphics files and HTML files are denoted by miniatures of themselves, and all other files are denoted by squares surrounding their usual file icons. If the HTML documents are text, their thumbnails are way too small to read, but at least you can tell whether this is the two-column document or the one-column document.

Figure 9-6.   *Thumbnails view shows you miniature versions of your graphics files and HTML documents.*

Changing How the View Settings Work

By default, each folder has its own view settings. If you choose a new view from the View menu, you change the view for the currently displayed folder only. Windows remembers the new view the next time you open that folder, but all other folders are unchanged. But another method enables you to change the view for all folders in one fell swoop.

Defining One View for All Folders

If you decide you like Details or Thumbnails (or some other) view and want to use it for all your folders, you can. Here's how:

1. Configure a folder the way you want all the folders to appear.

2. With that folder open, select Tools | Folder Options. The Folder Options dialog box appears (shown in Figure 9-2).

3. Click the View tab of the Folder Options dialog box. Near the top of this tab is the Folder Views box. Inside this box is the Like Current Folder button. Click it.

4. A confirmation box appears, asking you whether you really mean to change the default view settings. Click Yes.

5. Click OK to close the Folder Options dialog box.

If you want to reset all folders back to the default settings, follow the previous instructions, except in step 4, click the Restore Defaults button.

 If you add (or remove) columns of the Details view and apply the technique just given, you can make those same columns appear (or disappear) for all folders.

Defining One View for a Window

You may also decide you want the view settings to belong to the window, not to the folder. In other words, when you switch to, say, Small Icons view, you want every folder you open from that window to come up in Small Icons view until you change to something else. To change window settings:

1. Select Tools | Folder Options in Windows Explorer. The Folder Options dialog box appears (shown in Figure 9-2).

2. Click the View tab of the Folder Options dialog box. The lower portion of the tab is the Advanced Settings box.

3. In the Advanced Settings box, find the line Remember Each Folder's View Settings. Uncheck the box next to this line.

4. Click OK.

MANAGING YOUR DISK

To restore the default behavior, repeat the process, but check the box in step 3.

One thing you can't do is have Windows Explorer behave in different ways for different folders, say, open with a single click in one folder and open with a double click in another. Whatever decisions you make on the General tab of the Folder Options dialog box are applied automatically to all Explorer windows.

Changing View Settings

The stray odds and ends of how Explorer windows look and behave are controlled from the View tab of the Folder Options dialog box. From this tab you can tell Windows

- Whether to display hidden files
- Whether to display file extensions

(If you would rather see file extensions, see the section "What Are Extensions and File Types?" for how to display them.)

You can make your experience of Windows Explorer a little more comfortable by setting its options the way you like them. To open the View tab of the Folder Options dialog box, choose Tools | Folder Options from the Windows Explorer menu bar, and then click the View tab. The View tab contains the Advanced Settings window, which is a long list of check boxes, most of which are self-explanatory. For example, the Show My Documents On The Desktop check box controls whether the My Documents folder appears on the desktop.

If you decide whatever you changed on the View tab was a bad idea, but you can't remember exactly what it was, go to the View tab and click the Restore Defaults button.

Sorting and Arranging the Contents of a Folder

Windows Explorer can sort the icons in an Explorer window automatically according to any column that appears in Details view. For most folders this means the icons can be sorted by name (alphabetically), by file type, by size (from smallest to largest), and by date (earliest to most recent). Even if you aren't in Details view, you can access the same choices via a shortcut menu or on the View | Arrange Icons menu. Adding a column to Details view adds the same choice to the View | Arrange Icons menu.

In any of these sortings, folders are listed before files. Thus, in Figure 9-7, the B Folder and the C Folder come before the A File. In Large Icons and Small Icons views, the contents of the folder are sorted in rows. The first element in the order is located in the window's upper-left corner, the second is to its right, and so on. In List and Details views, the contents are sorted in a list, starting at the top of the window.

In Details view, sorting is particularly easy: click the column header to sort according to that column. Click it again to sort in reverse order (in which folders automatically go to the end of the list). Only Details view allows this reverse sorting. The column by which the list is sorted displays a small arrowhead that points up for an ordinary sort and down for a reverse sort.

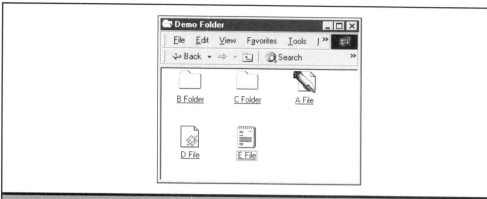

Figure 9-7.   *A folder's contents sorted by name*

In Large Icons or Small Icons views, you can also arrange icons manually, by dragging them. Figure 9-8 shows a folder whose contents have been arranged manually—notice the irregular spacing and the overlapping icons. Metaphorically, manual arrangement is more like sorting stacks of paper on a table than sorting items in a filing cabinet. The effect can be similar to having subfolders: you can put work files on the right half of the window and home files on the left, instead of having Work and Home subfolders. Files that all relate to the same project can be grouped together in the

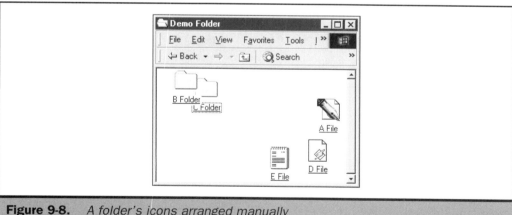

Figure 9-8.   *A folder's icons arranged manually*

Explorer window, instead of having their own subfolder. If, at some point, you decide you want everything in tidy rows again, choose View | Arrange Icons | Auto Arrange.

 If you overlap an icon too closely with a folder icon, Windows will think you want to put the corresponding object inside the folder.

Customizing a Folder

Windows gives you considerable power over the appearance of a folder in an Explorer window. You can select any image file to appear in the background whenever the folder is displayed. You can add comments that appear in the Web panel whenever the folder is selected or opened. You can add links to the Web panel. You can choose an HTML template to give the entire window a different look; and, if you can write HTML, you can edit one of Windows' provided templates to produce virtually any effect you could put on a Web page.

 The changes you make with the Customize This Folder Wizard apply only to the folder that is open when you invoke the Wizard. You can't apply them to all folders.

Giving a Folder a Background Picture

One of the most tempting ways to waste time with a computer is to experiment until you find the absolutely perfect combination of pattern and color for the desktop (see Chapter 12). Windows has multiplied this temptation tenfold (or more) by enabling you to customize the background of each folder independently. For example, you could give a folder a sky-and-clouds background like this:

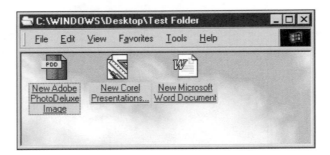

We can't think of any compelling reason to give a folder its own background picture, but it is fun. Follow these steps:

1. Open the folder upon which you want to bestow a custom background.

2. Select View | Customize This Folder. You see the Customize This Folder Wizard.

3. Click Next.

4. Make sure the Customize radio button is selected, and then check the Modify Background Picture And Filename Appearance box. Uncheck any of the other check boxes.

5. Click Next. The next page of the Wizard gives you a list of image files Windows knows. Select an image on the list and look at its preview, or click the Browse button and search for an image file somewhere else on your computer or network. Any file you select is added to the list and can be previewed.

6. When you have the right background picture, consider whether filenames will show up against this background. If not, click the Text color square in the Filename Appearance box to choose a new color for filenames, and then click the Background color square to define a small rectangle of color for the filename to be set against.

7. After you make all your choices, click Next. The Wizard shows you its completion screen. Click Finish.

Giving a Folder a Web Panel Comment

You can use the Web panel to describe folders, tell people what to do with them, or provide easy links to related folders or Web pages. Microsoft has done this with My Computer and various other folders; you can do the same with the folders you create. Here's how:

1. Open the folder.

2. Select View | Customize This Folder. The Customize This Folder Wizard opens.

3. Click Next.

4. Click the Customize radio button and check the Add Folder Comment check box. If you don't want to do any other customization simultaneously, make sure the other check boxes are unchecked. Click Next when you're done.

5. Type your comment into the Folder Comment box. You can type text or HTML commands. To create Figure 9-9, we typed **Remember to throw these files away when you're done with them**. Click Next when you are done.

6. Click Finish.

Selecting an HTML Template for a Folder

The HTML template of a folder is what gives the Web panel its distinctive look. Windows provides several basic templates and enables you to edit them (if you can write HTML). To change a folder's HTML template:

1. Open the folder.

2. Select View | Customize This Folder. The Customize This Folder Wizard opens.

3. Click Next.

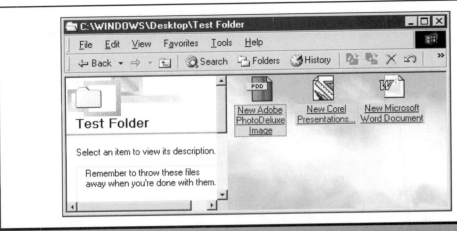

Figure 9-9.   *You can add comments to the Web panel of your folders.*

4. Make sure the Customize radio button is selected and the Choose Or Edit An HTML Template For This Folder check box is checked. Then click Next.

5. Make a selection from the Choose A Template window. A small preview appears in the window immediately to the right. Your choices are Standard (the default), Classic (with no Web panel), Simple (like Figure 9-10), and Image Preview (like Figure 8-4).

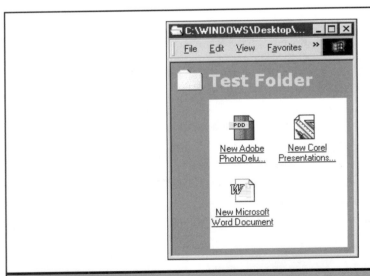

Figure 9-10.   *The Simple HTML template for a folder*

6. If you want one of the four standard templates, click Next and skip to step 8. But if you can write HTML and want to add some bells and whistles of your own to the template, check the I Want To Edit This Template check box, and then Click Next.

7. A Notepad window opens with the HTML code for the template file. Edit this to your heart's content, save your changes, and then exit the Notepad window.

8. Click the Finish button of the Customize This Folder Wizard.

Removing Folder Customization

If you decide you want to undo the customizations you gave a folder, do this:

1. Open the folder.

2. Select View | Customize This Folder. You see the Customize This Folder Wizard.

3. Select the Remove Customization radio button and click Next.

4. Check one or more of the following check boxes: Restore Default Folder Template, Remove Background Picture, Restore Filename Appearance, and Remove Folder Comment. Click Next when you are done.

5. A screen repeats the choices you made on the previous screen. If that isn't what you thought you chose, click Back; otherwise, click Finish.

Working with Shortcuts

Sometimes you want a file to be in two places at once: the place where it really belongs and on the desktop where you can easily get to it. Sometimes your filing system has two logical places to put the same file. Shortcuts enable you to deal with these situations, without the disadvantages that come from having two independent copies of the same file.

Making Shortcuts

Shortcuts are created when you:

- Drag-and-drop certain applications to a new folder or to the desktop.

- Hold down the right mouse button while you drag any object to a new location, and then select Create Shortcut(s) Here from the menu that appears when you drop the object.

- Invoke the Create Shortcut Wizard either by selecting File | New | Shortcut in an Explorer window or by right-clicking an open space on the desktop or in an Explorer window and selecting New | Shortcut from the shortcut menu.

In the first two cases, the original file or folder stays in its old location, and a shortcut to that file or folder is created in the drop location. In the third case, the shortcut is created in the folder from which the Create Shortcut Wizard was invoked.

Windows makes shortcuts automatically in certain circumstances. When you add a Web page to your list of Favorites, for example, a shortcut is created and put in the folder C:\Windows\Favorites. Dragging an application icon onto the Start button produces a shortcut in C:\Windows\Start Menu.

We find drag-and-drop techniques are the easiest way to create shortcuts. But if you prefer, you can use the Create Shortcut Wizard as follows:

1. Open the destination folder, the one in which you want to create the shortcut. If you want the shortcut to be on the desktop, make sure part of the desktop is visible on your screen.

2. Choose File | New | Shortcut in the destination folder's window. Or, if the desktop is the destination, right-click an empty place and select New | Shortcut. Either of these techniques launches the Create Shortcut Wizard.

3. If you know the address of the file or folder to which you want to create a shortcut (the target), you can type it into the Command Line box on the Wizard's first page. If you have the address written in another file, you can cut-and-paste it into the Command Line box by using CTRL-V to paste. If you use the Command Line box, skip to step 7. (If you are creating a shortcut to a folder, entering an address in the Command Line box is the only technique that works. Clicking the Browse button doesn't help.)

4. Click the Browse button. A Browse dialog box appears (see Chapter 2, section "Open, Save As, and Browse Dialog Boxes").

5. Use the Browse dialog box to find the target file. If you don't see the file you want (and it isn't a program), change the Files Of Type box to All Files.

6. Select the target file or folder, and then click the Open button. The Browse dialog box disappears. The first page of the Create Shortcut Wizard now contains the target's address.

7. Click Next. The second page of the Create Shortcut Wizard appears.

   If you don't like the suggested name for the shortcut (usually the same as the original object), type a new one in the Select A Name For The Shortcut line.

8. Click Finish.

Shortcuts can also point to Web pages on the Internet. These shortcuts have file names that end with the extension *.url*, and they also can be created by the Create Shortcut Wizard. The procedure is the same, except in step 3, you type the page's Internet address or URL (see Chapter 8, section "What Are Addresses?").

Using Shortcuts

For almost all purposes, a shortcut to a file or folder behaves just like the target file or folder. Opening the shortcut, dragging-and-dropping the shortcut, or dragging-and-dropping something onto the shortcut produces the same result as performing the same action with the target file or folder.

The most convenient place to put shortcuts is on the desktop. Documents you are currently working on can reside in the appropriate place in your filing system, yet a shortcut on the desktop can make them instantly available. Programs you use frequently can remain in the folders they were installed into, yet be accessible with a single click. For programs you use frequently, you can add an icon to the Quick Launch toolbar on the Taskbar (see Chapter 11, section "Editing the Quick Launch Toolbar").

When you frequently use two different applications with a particular file type, set up the file type to open automatically with one application and put a shortcut to the other application on the desktop. For example, HTML documents usually open automatically within your Web browser (usually Internet Explorer), which enables you to read, but not edit, them. If you also have a shortcut to a Web editor program on your desktop, you can edit an HTML document by dragging it onto the shortcut icon.

Working with Compressed Folders

Everyone who has packed a suitcase knows the basic idea of a compressed folder—it's a trick for getting the same quantity of information to fit in a smaller space on a disk. Under previous versions of Windows, you had to have a third-party application like WinZip or ZipMagic to work with compressed folders (which everyone who doesn't work for Microsoft calls ZIP files). And, in many ways, these applications are still more useful and convenient than the Compressed Folders utility in Windows Explorer. If you are going to work with ZIP files every day, you probably want to acquire ZipMagic, WinZip, or some similar program; but, for occasional use, the Compressed Folders utility in Windows Explorer works just fine.

Creating a Compressed Folder

To create a compressed folder on the desktop, right-click an empty space and choose New | Compressed Folder from the shortcut menu. To create a compressed folder inside another folder, open the folder and choose File | New | Compressed folder.

Either of these techniques creates a compressed folder called New Compressed Folder.zip (or just New Compressed Folder if Explorer is set to hide file extensions). You may rename it as you would any other folder, though (as usual) you probably don't want to change the file extension.

To create a compressed folder with a specific file or files already inside it, select the files you want to include, right-click one of the selected files, and then choose Send To | Compressed Folder from the shortcut menu. The selected files remain unchanged, and a copy of them is created inside the compressed folder. The name and location of the folder is the same as the file you right-clicked. The name of the new compressed folder is the same as the name as the last of the selected files.

Working with Files in a Compressed Folder

To add a file to a compressed folder, drag the file onto the folder's icon or into its open window, and then drop it. The file remains in its original location and a copy is created inside the compressed folder. To move the file without leaving the original behind, drag-and-drop it with the right mouse button, and then choose Move Here from the shortcut menu.

You can open a file in a compressed folder by double-clicking it, but the file usually lacks its full functionality. Windows uncompresses the file into a temporary location, and then runs the program that handles the file. In Word, for example, compressed files can be read but not changed. To regain functionality, you need to *extract* the file. The extracting process creates an uncompressed copy of the file outside the compressed folder.

To extract a file from a compressed folder, drag it from the compressed folder and drop it onto the desktop or into an uncompressed folder. One copy of the file is left behind in the compressed folder and a new, uncompressed copy appears in the new location. To extract the file without leaving a copy in the compressed folder, drag-and-drop with the right mouse button and choose Move Here from the shortcut menu.

To extract all the files in a compressed folder at once, select File | Extract All from the menu if the file is open, or right-click the folder's icon and choose Extract All from the shortcut menu. The Extract Wizard guides you in selecting a destination folder for the extracted files.

In many respects, the compressed folder and its files behave just as other folders and files. You can arrange and view the files within the folder in the usual ways, for example. However, Microsoft didn't completely integrate compressed folders into its filing system. Here is a short list of things Microsoft might want to fix:

- Compressed folders don't appear on the Folder Explorer bar.
- Compressed folders don't show up in Browse windows. So, for example, you can't save a Word document into a compressed folder by choosing File | Save As from the Word menu bar.
- Files in compressed folders don't show up in a Search.
- You can't customize a compressed folder.
- The columns in Details view are different for a compressed folder because there is more to know about a compressed file: the size of the compressed file, the size of the extracted file, the ratio between the sizes, whether the file is encrypted, and the method of compression.

■ You can't drag-and-drop or cut-and-paste a file from one compressed folder to another unless one of the folders contains the other.

Encrypting and Decrypting Compressed Folders

You can attach a password to a compressed folder so Windows will ask for the password before opening or extracting any of the files in the folder. This technique encrypts the entire folder. If you want to encrypt some of the files in a compressed folder, but not other files, create a new compressed folder, move the files you want to encrypt to the new folder, and encrypt that folder. The password scheme used in compressed folders can be broken by a determined attacker and isn't a substitute for a serious encryption program, but it's quite adequate to deter casual snooping.

To encrypt a compressed folder, right-click its icon and select Encrypt from the shortcut menu. Or, you can open the folder and select File | Encrypt. When the Encrypt dialog box appears, type a password into the Password box, and then retype the same password into the Confirm Password box. (This retyping is to make sure you didn't mistype the password the first time, thereby creating a password that even you don't know.) Click OK to make the dialog box go away and close the folder (if it was open). The folder is encrypted.

Anyone can open an encrypted folder and look at the list of files. Windows doesn't ask for a password until you try to open or extract one of the files. In Details view, someone could learn the sizes and dates of the files without knowing the password. If you want even this information to be secret, put your files in another folder inside an encrypted folder. Then the password of the outer folder is required to open the inner folder.

Opening and extracting files from encrypted compressed folders works exactly the same as opening and extracting files from ordinary compressed folders, except you have to type the password into the Password dialog box.

To decrypt an encrypted folder, so a password is no longer needed to access its files, right-click the folder's icon and select Decrypt from the shortcut menu, and then type the password into the Password dialog box.

Searching for Files and Folders

Even with a well-organized file system, you can occasionally forget where you put a file or even what the file's exact name is. Fortunately, Windows provides a Search command that takes care of this situation. By using Search, you can find a file:

■ By name or part of a name

■ By date created, modified, or last accessed

■ By file type

■ By size

- By a string of text contained in the file
- By some combination of all the previous points

All these searches follow the same basic pattern.

Starting a Search

Here's how you begin a file or folder search:

1. Select Start | Search | For Files Or Folders. Or, click the Search button in an Explorer window. Either way, you get an Explorer window with the Search Explorer bar, as in Figure 9-11.

2. Type the information about the files or folders you want to find into the blanks provided in the Explorer bar. Fill in as many or as few of the lines as you want.

3. Click Search Now to start searching for all files or folders that fit the description you've given. The magnifying glass icon moves in circles while the search continues. As matching files and folders are found, they appear in the viewing area. The number of objects found is shown in the Status bar.

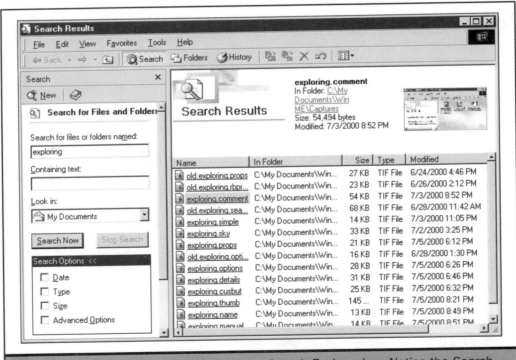

Figure 9-11. *An Explorer window with the Search Explorer bar. Notice the Search button on the toolbar is pressed.*

4. If you aren't satisfied with the files and folders Find locates, change the information you entered and search again.

When the search is done, the viewing area displays the files or folders that meet your criteria. From this window you can

- Open any of the files or folders listed.

- Copy, cut, move, or drag-and-drop any of the files or folders to the desktop or some other window.

- Sort the files or folders. If you have set the view to Details (the default, if you opened Search from the Start menu), you can sort by Name, Address, Size, and File Type by clicking the corresponding column header.

Searching by Name

The simplest kind of search is when you know the name of the file, but can't remember where it is located. Type the name of the file into the Search For Files Or Folders Named box of the Search Explorer bar, and then click Search Now.

If you know only part of the name of a file, type that part into the box. When you click Search Now, the viewing area displays all the files and folders whose names include that text string. (Even if you type in the full name, Find treats it as a substring, and returns all the files and folders whose names contain that text string.) For example, searching for "June" might yield the files june95.doc, Next June.txt, and 97june quarterly report.wks, plus the folders June's Recipes and Juneau Alaska.

If you don't remember much about the name of the file ("It had an *A* in it somewhere"), the resulting list of files and folders is likely to be daunting. You can make your search more specific by combining it with other criteria, or by using case sensitivity, and wildcards, described in the next two sections.

Case Sensitivity

In the preceding "June" example, the search for "June" was not case sensitive—the capital *J* was not taken into account, which is why june95.doc and 97june quarterly report.wks appeared on the list. If you want your capital letters to be matched only to other capital letters, do the following:

1. If it isn't already displayed (as it is in Figure 9-11, click the phrase Search Options to display the Search Options box.

2. Click the Advanced Options check box in the Search Options box in the Search Explorer bar.

3. Click the Case Sensitive check box.

Case sensitivity also applies to text searches (see "Searching for Text Strings").

Wildcards

The asterisk (*) and question mark (?) characters play a special role in filename searches. Neither is allowed to be part of a filename, so when you type them into the Search For Files And Folders Named line of the Search Explorer bar, Windows knows you intend for it to do something special with them. The asterisk and question mark are called *wildcards* because (like wildcards in poker) they can stand for any other character.

The question mark stands for any single character, so you can use it when you either don't know or don't want to specify a character in a filename. If, for example, you can't remember whether a file is named Letter to Tim or Letter to Tom, type **Letter to T?m** into the Search For Files And Folders Named line—either Tim or Tom will match T?m. Similarly, you can find both Annual Report 98 and Annual Report 99, by using "Annual Report 9?" in your search.

An asterisk stands for any string of characters. Typing **Letter to T*m** into the Named line would not only find Letter to Tim and Letter to Tom, but also Letter to Travel Management Team.

Searching for Text Strings

The Search process can also search for text strings within documents. This makes for a much more time-consuming search than that for any of the other criteria, because Search has to look inside the files themselves, rather than just at the files' properties. For this reason, you should avoid using this feature if other criteria are already enough to narrow the search. But text-string searching may be exactly what you need. For example, you could generate a list of all the letters you've written to your mother by searching for the phrase "Dear Mom."

To add a text string to your search, type it into the Containing Text line of the Search Explorer bar. Unfortunately, this technique works for contiguous phrases only. Unlike online search engines, you can't search for a series of keywords, such as "Mom" and "Christmas."

To make Windows pay attention to the capitalization in your Search, make sure the Case Sensitive box is checked on the Search Explorer bar.

Looking in the Right Place

If you know where the desired files or folders are located in the folder tree, search only that portion of the tree. That search doesn't take so long and yields fewer false "finds." The Look In pull-down list provides a number of possible limitations to the search, for example, searching only one particular drive rather than all of them. To be even more specific, click Browse on the Look In pull-down list and a Browse For Folder window opens. In this window, select a folder to search and click OK; only that folder and its subfolders are searched. Another way to tell Windows where to search is by right-clicking the folder you want to search and choosing Search from the menu that appears.

By default, the Look In box is set to the folder that was open when you pushed the Search toolbar button, or (if you opened Search from the Start menu) the C drive.

Using Search Options

Clicking the Search Options link in the Search Explorer bar displays the Search Options box, shown in Figure 9-11 just below the Search Now button. The four check boxes (Date, Type, Size, and Advanced Options) each expands the box further when checked. The fully expanded Search Options box is shown in Figure 9-12.

 You can use as many different criteria as you want to narrow your search.

Searching by Date

The Date section of the Search Options box, pictured in Figure 9-12, enables you to input information about when the file or folder was created, modified, or last accessed. If you're thinking "I just looked at the file last week," you can enter that information here, and cut down the search considerably.

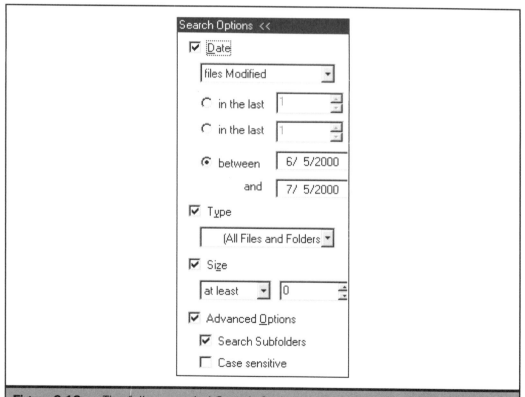

Figure 9-12.   *The fully expanded Search Options box in the Search Explorer bar*

MANAGING YOUR DISK

To specify date information:

1. Make sure the Search Options box is displayed in the Search Explorer bar. If not, click the link Search Options under the Search Now button.

2. Click the Date check box in the Search Options box.

3. Choose Files Modified, Files Created, or Files Last Accessed from the drop-down menu.

4. If you want to specify a range of dates (as in "I worked on this last summer"), click the Between radio button, and specify dates, either by typing them into the boxes in month/day/year format, or by clicking entries on the drop-down calendars. (To change months on the calendars, click the arrows in the upper-left and upper-right corners.)

5. If you want to specify a time period from some time in the past through the present, click either the In The Last *xxx* Months or the In The Last *xxx* Days radio buttons. Then enter a number in the corresponding box.

6. If you are done entering Search information, click the Search Now button.

If all you know about a file is that you accessed it recently, you might do better to look on the History Explorer bar or the Start | Documents menu.

Searching by Type

If you know, for example, that the file you want is a Word document, you can limit the search to files with a .doc extension. Click the Type check box in the Search Options box on the Search Explorer bar. Then choose a file type from the drop-down list that appears.

Searching by Size

If you know the file for which you're looking is several megabytes, don't waste time searching all those 50K files or vice versa. You can search large files only or small files only, but you can't search between two sizes. To specify a file size:

1. Make sure the Search Options box is displayed in the Search Explorer bar. If not, click the link Search Options under the Search Now button.

2. Click the Size check box.

3. Choose either At Least or At Most from the drop-down list that has appeared.

4. Type a number into the KB box to specify a limiting size.

Saving and Retrieving a Search

After performing a search, you can save the search parameters by selecting File | Save Search. The list of files found with that search is not saved. The parameters are saved in a *Saved Search* file (with extension .fnd). To perform the search in the future, open the

Saved Search file and click the Search Now button. Once a search has been saved, you can even share it with other people in the same ways you would share any other file—by copying it to a floppy, or attaching it to e-mail.

Managing the Recycle Bin

Files and folders sent to the Recycle Bin may disappear from the folder tree, but Windows still stores them on your hard drive and keeps track of them. Eventually, one of four things happens:

- You eliminate things in the Recycle Bin, either by emptying it or by deleting some of the files and folders there.

- You retrieve files from the Recycle Bin and put them in some other folder (see Chapter 8, section "Recovering Objects from the Recycle Bin").

- The Recycle Bin gets full.

- You turn off the Recycle Bin so deleted files aren't put there anymore.

This section covers all these possibilities except the second one, which was covered in the previous chapter. In addition, this section tells you how to streamline the deleting process, if you want to do so.

Like most other things in Windows, the Recycle Bin has properties. To display them, right-click the Recycle Bin icon on the desktop, and choose Properties from the shortcut menu. The Properties dialog box for the Recycle Bin is displayed, as in Figure 9-13. The Properties dialog box contains a Global tab, plus a tab for each hard drive on your system.

Emptying the Recycle Bin

Deleting old files serves two purposes: it clears useless files away so you don't confuse them with useful files, and it reclaims the disk space they occupy. The first purpose is served by deleting a file—once it's in the Recycle Bin, you aren't going to open it or work on it by mistake. But a file in the Recycle Bin still takes up disk space: The space isn't reclaimed until the Recycle Bin is emptied.

To empty the Recycle Bin:

1. Right-click the Recycle Bin icon on the desktop.

2. Choose Empty Recycle Bin from the shortcut menu. A dialog box asks you to confirm your choice.

3. Click Yes.

To purge selected files or folders from the Recycle Bin without completely emptying it, open the Recycle Bin folder and delete the files in the usual way (see

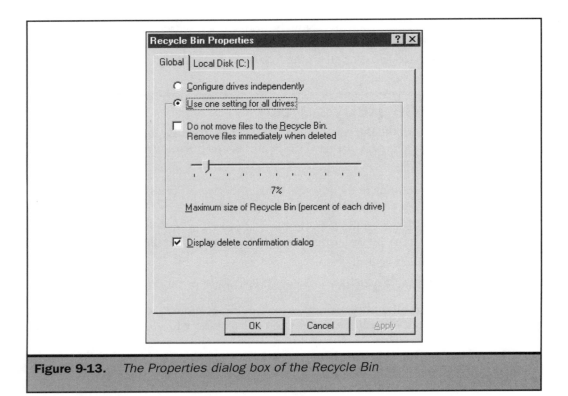

Figure 9-13.   *The Properties dialog box of the Recycle Bin*

Chapter 8, section "Deleting Files and Folders"). Objects deleted from an ordinary folder on a hard drive are sent to the Recycle Bin, but objects deleted from the Recycle Bin are really deleted.

To purge only those objects that have been in the Recycle Bin a long time:

1. Open the Recycle Bin.

2. If the window is not already in Details view, choose View | Details.

3. Click the Date Deleted header to put the objects in order of date.

4. Use the enclosing-rectangle method to select all the objects deleted prior to a certain date (see Chapter 8, section "Selecting Files and Folders").

5. Click the Delete button on the toolbar, or press the DELETE key on the keyboard.

6. When the dialog box appears, asking whether you really want to delete these objects, click Yes.

Resizing the Recycle Bin

By default, the maximum size of the Recycle Bin on any hard drive is 10 percent of the size of the drive itself. For example, a 10GB hard drive has a maximum Recycle Bin size of 1GB—a lot of space to use up for files you've decided to delete. If you delete an object that would cause the Recycle Bin to exceed that size, Windows warns you with an error message.

Having a maximum size for the Recycle Bin forces you not to clutter your hard drive with useless, deleted files, and 10 percent is as good a maximum size as any. But you may decide either to raise this limit (because you don't want to empty the Recycle Bin right now) or lower it (because disk space is getting tight or you have a large hard disk), either of which you can do by following this procedure:

1. Right-click the Recycle Bin icon on the desktop, and choose Properties from the shortcut menu. You see the Properties dialog box of the Recycle Bin (Figure 9-13).

2. The Properties dialog box contains a Global tab, plus a tab for each hard drive on your system. If you want to change the maximum size setting for all the hard drives at once, set the new maximum size of the Recycle Bin (as a percentage of total drive space) by moving the slider on the Global tab. Then click OK. Skip the remaining steps.

3. If you want to reset the maximum Recycle Bin size for only a single drive, leaving the others the same, select the Configure Drives Independently radio button on the Global tab.

4. Click the tab for the drive you want to change.

5. Set the slider on that tab.

6. Click OK.

Streamlining the Deletion Process

Many times, we've been thankful that Windows makes it so hard to eliminate a file on a hard drive. Four different actions are usually necessary: deleting the file in the first place, confirming the deletion in a dialog box, emptying the Recycle Bin (or deleting the file from the Recycle Bin), and then confirming *that* decision in a dialog box. But even though this process can occasionally be a life-saver, it can also be tedious (particularly if you are trying to get rid of sensitive files that you don't want hanging around in the Recycle Bin).

Even deleting a file from the Recycle Bin doesn't destroy the information right away. Windows makes the file's disk space available for reassignment, but doesn't immediately write over that disk space. People with the proper tools could still read the file. To prevent this, you need software that is not part of Windows.

Deleting Selected Files or Folders

If you want certain files and folders gone *right now*, with no shilly-shallying about confirmation dialog boxes, Recycle Bins, or Undo buttons, hold down the SHIFT key while you drag the files and folders onto the Recycle Bin icon. (Of course, you should be *very sure* you want the files and folders gone, and that you haven't dragged along any extra objects by accident.) Holding down the SHIFT key while you click the Delete button (or press the DELETE key) is almost as quick: you have to click Yes in a confirmation dialog box; but the objects are deleted for real, not just sent to the Recycle Bin. Either method puts the deleted files or folders beyond the power of the Undo button.

Eliminating Confirmation Dialog Boxes

To eliminate the confirmation dialog box when you send something to the Recycle Bin:

1. Right-click the Recycle Bin icon on the desktop, and choose Properties from the menu. Or, select the Recycle Bin in a Folder or Windows Explorer window and click the Properties button on the toolbar. You see the Properties dialog box of the Recycle Bin (Figure 9-13).

2. From the Global tab of the Properties dialog box, uncheck the box labeled Display Delete Confirmation Dialog Box.

3. Click OK.

Even after carrying out the preceding procedure, deleting something from the Recycle Bin (that is, getting rid of it for good) still requires a confirmation. If you decide later that you've made the deletion process too easy, you can reinstitute Delete Confirmation Dialog Boxes by repeating the preceding procedure, but checking the box in step 3.

Turning Off the Recycle Bin

If you want to stop sending deleted files to the Recycle Bin:

1. Right-click the Recycle Bin icon on the desktop, and choose Properties from the shortcut menu. You see the Properties dialog box of the Recycle Bin (Figure 9-12).

2. On the Global tab of the Properties dialog box (or on the tab corresponding to the particular drive whose Recycle Bin you are turning off, if the Configure Drives Independently option is chosen on the Global tab), check the box labeled Do Not Move Files To The Recycle Bin. Remove Files Immediately When Deleted.

3. Click OK.

After you complete this procedure, files you delete from your hard drive are gone, just as are files deleted from floppy drives. Files that were already in the Recycle Bin, however, remain there until you empty the Recycle Bin, delete them, restore them, or move them to another folder.

You can turn the Recycle Bin back on by following the same procedure, but unchecking the box in step 3.

If you turn off the Recycle Bin, don't forget you did. The Recycle Bin remains off until you turn it on again. A more prudent choice might be to make your Recycle bin smaller, but to leave it on.

Chapter 10

Formatting and Partitioning Disks

Before Windows Me can use a hard disk or removable disk (including floppy disks), the disk must be prepared for use. Hard disks have to be *partitioned*, divided into one or more logical sections, using the Fdisk program. Both hard disks and removable disks must be formatted with a *file system*, the information that keeps track of which files are stored where on the disk. Windows supports two file systems, FAT16 (the file system used in DOS and Windows 95) and FAT32 (file system introduced with Windows 95 OSR2 and used in Windows 98). Unless you have a small hard disk (smaller than 500MB), consider converting to FAT32.

On computers with Windows preinstalled, the hard disk has already been partitioned (usually into a single large partition) and formatted, but if you install an additional hard disk or replace the original hard disk, you have to partition and format the new disk. Some disks (both hard disks and removable disks) come preformatted and some don't. Whether or not a disk is preformatted, you can reformat it to remove any existing files and make it a "clean" empty disk.

Each disk drive, including floppy disk and CD drives, has a drive letter assigned by Windows, but you can change these letters, or assign drive letters to folders, if you must. You can also check how much free space is on any disk and look at the properties of a disk.

This chapter describes how to partition and format hard disks, decide whether to use FAT32 (and convert to FAT32 if you decide to use it), assign drive letters to disk drives, check for free space, and control the way in which Windows uses CD-ROMs. It also covers how to format and copy floppy disks.

| Note | *For information on dividing your hard disk into separate partitions for Windows Me and other operating systems, see "Creating Dual-Boot Installations" in Appendix A.* |

What Are Partitions, File Systems, FAT32, and Drive Letters?

Partitions and files systems determine how and where Windows stores information on your disk. Drive letters determine how to refer to the disks on your computer.

What Is a Partition?

A *partition* is a section of a hard disk. Every hard disk must be partitioned before Windows can use it. Normally, a disk is set up as a single large partition spanning the entire disk but, in some circumstances, using more than one partition makes sense. When you partition a disk, you allocate a fixed amount of space to each partition.

Each partition on a disk is marked with an operating system type. For historical reasons, the types for Windows partitions are *Primary DOS partition* and *Extended DOS partition*. If you run more than one operating system on your computer, such as Windows Me and Linux or OS/2, you can create a partition for each operating system and then start the computer from either of the partitions, depending on which operating system you want to use. Unfortunately, you can't easily use multiple partitions to switch between Windows Me and earlier versions of DOS or Windows because they all start from the Primary DOS partition. (Partition Magic, a program you can purchase separately, enables you to install more than one version of Windows (see "Installing Multiple Versions of Windows with Partition Magic").

What Is a File System?

A *file system* is the information that keeps track of which files and folders are stored where on the disk, and what disk space is free. The Windows file system includes a *FAT*, or *File Allocation Table*, which stores information about each *sector*, or physical block of storage space, on the disk.

Windows Me supports two different file system types: the older FAT16 (with a File Allocation Table that can store 16-bit entries) and the newer FAT32 (which stores 32-bit entries). It doesn't support *NTFS*, the format used by Windows 2000 and Windows NT.

Installing Multiple Versions of Windows with Partition Magic

Partition Magic is a program from PowerQuest Corp. (**http://www.powerquest.com/partitionmagic**) that allows one hard disk to include more than one Primary DOS partition. Each Primary DOS partition can contain a different version of Windows—for example, you can have a partition for Windows 95, one for Windows 98, and one for Windows Me. Partition Magic enables you to switch among the Primary DOS partitions, using one and hiding the rest.

We like to use Partition Magic to set up three partitions: one Primary DOS partition (which appears as drive C) for Windows Me, one Extended DOS partition (drive D) for data, and an extra, hidden Primary DOS partition for a duplicate copy of Windows Me. We use drive C for Windows and programs, and we use drive D for data—all documents, spreadsheets, e-mail, and other files we create or edit. The hidden partition is a copy of drive C, made right after we install all the programs we usually use. Over the months, our working Windows partition (drive C) slowly fills up with junk, and Windows slows down and becomes less reliable. When Windows starts hanging, crashing, or acting funny, we copy the hidden partition to drive C using Partition Magic, so we have a new, clean copy of Windows and our programs, without affecting our data.

Another way to keep a clean copy of your Windows partition is by using Drive Image (more information is available at **http://www.powerquest.com/driveimage**). Drive Image can make a copy of an entire partition onto a Zip disk, Jaz disk, or writable CD-ROM.

What Are the FAT16 and FAT32 File Systems?

FAT16 dates back to DOS 3.0, while *FAT32* was introduced with the OSR2 update to Windows 95. Each partition on a hard disk and each removable disk must be formatted with either a FAT16 or FAT32 file system, but it's possible (and often desirable) to have some disks with one format and some with the other format on the same system.

FAT32 is designed for large partitions and disks, larger than 500MB, and offers no significant benefits when used on smaller disks. Because Windows Me takes up over 500MB, most disks on Windows Me systems use FAT 32. FAT32 offers these advantages on large disks:

- **Nearly unlimited partition sizes**   A single FAT16 partition can be no larger than 2GB, while a FAT32 partition can be thousands of gigabytes, larger than any single disk likely to be available in the near future.

- **More efficient use of space**   FAT32 allocates disk space in 2K chunks, while FAT16 on a large disk allocates space in 32K chunks, wasting a lot of space on small files.

FAT16 offers these advantages on smaller disks:

- **Backward compatibility**   Disks can be read and written by earlier versions of DOS and Windows, back to DOS 3.0 and Windows 2.0.

- **Improved speed**   Older DOS and 16-bit Windows programs can access FAT16 file systems slightly faster than FAT32. (Native 32-bit Windows programs access FAT16 and FAT32 equally fast.)

Disks and partitions less than 500MB have to be FAT16. Partitions larger than 2GB have to be FAT32. Partitions between 500MB and 2GB can be either FAT16 or FAT32, but should be FAT32, unless you expect to use the disk with an older version of DOS or Windows. The only other reason to use FAT16 is if you need to access the disk from an older version of Windows that doesn't support FAT16.

Why Divide Your Hard Disk into Partitions?

Most often, you allocate all the space on a hard disk to the Primary DOS partition, which Windows treats as a single logical disk drive using a single drive letter (drive C for the first hard disk). You can also allocate some of the space to the Primary DOS partition and some to an Extended DOS partition, which can, in turn, be subdivided into multiple logical disks.

FAT16 partitions are limited to 2GB. FAT32 removes the size limit for the foreseeable future but, in some cases, it still makes sense to have more than one DOS partition.

■ If you want a disk to be usable from earlier versions of Windows and DOS, you need to make a FAT16 partition that is less than 2GB.

■ In some cases, it's useful to have a separate partition to use as a scratch area that you can quickly reformat to wipe out its contents and start fresh.

■ We recommend creating a separate partition for your data—all your documents, spreadsheets, databases, and other files. You should back up your data partition regularly (see Appendix B). You needn't back up your programs as often because you can restore them from your program CDs.

Don't slice your disk into too many partitions—we rarely use more than three or four. Unlike folders, when you create a partition, you must decide in advance how much disk space to devote to that partition. You are bound to run out of space in one partition while you still have plenty of space in another.

What Are Drive Letters?

Every partition, logical drive, and removable disk available to Windows has a *drive letter*. Drive A is the floppy disk drive, and drive B is reserved for a second floppy disk. Hard disk partitions are assigned letters in order. Drive C is the Primary DOS partition on your first hard disk. If logical drives are in an Extended DOS partition, they are assigned letters next. If you have more than one hard disk, the partitions on those disks are assigned letters next. Finally, each removable disk, such as a CD-ROM or Zip disk, is assigned a letter, with the order of the letters being arbitrary. Any remaining letters can be used for network drives.

On a typical system, the floppy disk is A, the hard disk is C, and the CD-ROM is D.

Although this isn't recommended, you can add your own drive letters to the ones Windows assigns to each drive, using the DOS SUBST command to assign letters to folders (see "Choosing Your Own Drive Letters").

What Are the Properties of Disk Drives, Partitions, and Logical Drives?

Windows stores a set of properties for each installed disk drive. To see the Properties dialog box for a disk drive, choose Start | Settings | Control Panel, open the System icon, click the Device Manager tab, and click View Devices By Type. Double-click the Disk Drives icon to see the list. Click a drive and click the Properties button.

The Properties dialog box for a disk drive includes three tabs—General, Settings, and Driver, as shown in Figure 10-1. Table 10-1 lists the properties of a disk drive.

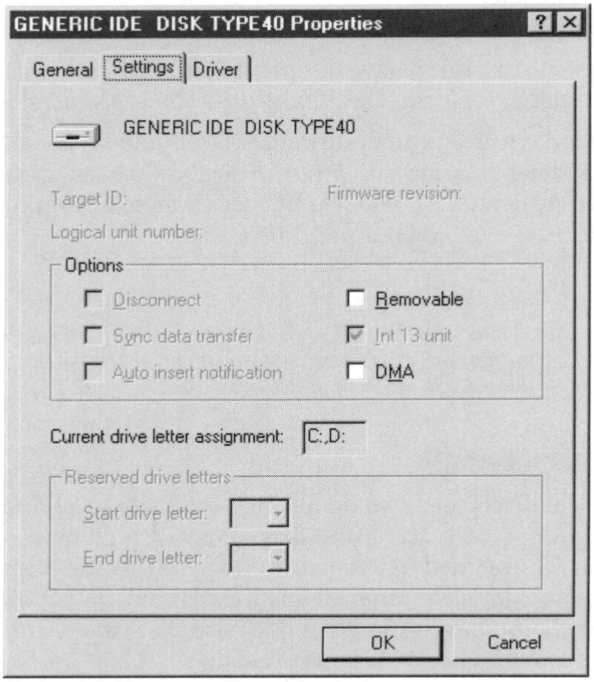

Figure 10-1. *Properties dialog box for a disk drive*

Tab	Setting	Description
General	Device type	Set to Disk Drives by Windows.
General	Manufacturer	Specifies the manufacturer of the disk drive, if known.
General	Hardware version	Specifies the version number of the disk drive hardware, if known.
General	Device status	Shows the current status of the disk drive.

Table 10-1. *Properties of a Disk Drive*

MANAGING YOUR DISK

Tab	Setting	Description
Settings	Target ID	For SCSI disks, the SCSI device number (see Chapter 14, section "SCSI Device Numbers").
Settings	Firmware revision	For SCSI disks, specifies the version number of the firmware on the disk.
Settings	Logical unit number	For SCSI disks, always zero (used for tape and CD changers).
Settings	Disconnect	For SCSI disks, whether the disk can continue working while the SCSI controller manages a different device. This setting is usually selected.
Settings	Sync data transfer	For SCSI disks, whether the disk can handle fast synchronous data transfer. This setting should be selected for all disks except CD-ROMs unless the disk is acting unreliable.
Settings	Auto insert notification	For CD-ROM drives, specifies that the drive notify Windows when you insert a CD.
Settings	Removable	Specifies whether you can remove the disk from this drive. For example, floppy disks, Zip disks, CD-ROMs, and Jaz disks are removable disks, while hard disks are not.
Settings	Int 13 unit	Specifies that this disk drive is compatible with the antiquated real-mode BIOS calls for disk access (almost all disks are). If the disk is compatible, you can't change this setting.
Settings	DMA	Specifies that this disk drive uses Direct Memory Access to communicate with the computer (see Chapter 14, section "DMA Channels").

Table 10-1.   *Properties Of A Disk Drive* (continued)

Tab	Setting	Description
Settings	Current drive letter assignment	Specifies the drive letter assigned to this disk drive. If the disk has more than one partition, more than one drive letter may appear.
Settings	Start drive letter/End drive letter	Specifies the starting and ending letters for the range of drive letters that can be used for the partitions on partitioned removable disks.
Driver	Provider/Date/Digital Signer	Specifies the source and date of the driver used for this disk drive. Many drivers come with Windows Me.
Driver	Update Driver	Runs the Update Device Driver Wizard to look for a more recent driver for your disk drive. The Wizard can look on the Windows CD (or floppies) or can connect to the Internet to look for a driver.

Table 10-1.   *Properties of a Disk Drive* (continued)

Each item on your system with a drive letter—each hard disk, floppy disk, removable disk, and logical drive—also has properties. You can display these properties from a Windows Explorer window (for example, open the My Computer icon on the desktop), right-click the drive, and choose Properties from the menu that appears. You see the Properties dialog box shown in Figure 10-2. Table 10-2 lists the settings on the General and Tools tabs. The Tools tab doesn't appear for disks you can't write on, such as CD-ROM drives. If you use a local area network (LAN), the Sharing tab appears (see Chapter 29, section "Sharing Your Disk Drives and Folders with Others"). If you have installed a hard-disk housekeeping program like Norton Utilities, additional tabs may appear.

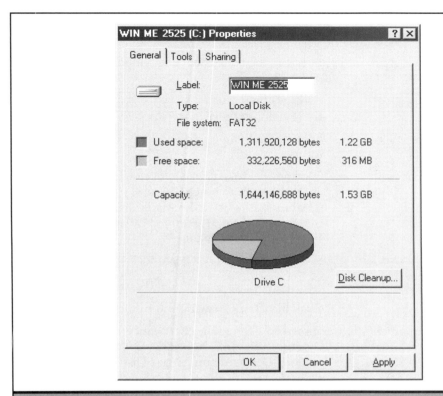

Figure 10-2. *Properties of a disk, partition, or logical disk*

Tab	Setting	Description
General	Label	Specifies the name of the disk, which you can edit.
General	Type	Specifies whether this disk is a *local disk* (disk connected to your own computer), *network disk* (hard disk connected to a computer you can access over a network), floppy disk, CD-ROM drive, *RAM drive* (memory that simulates a disk drive), or removable disk drive.

Table 10-2. *The General And Tools Tabs Settings for My Computer's Properties Dialog Box*

Tab	Setting	Description
General	File system	Specifies the file system used on the disk: FAT or FAT32.
General	Used space	Specifies how much disk space is occupied by files (including files in the Recycle Bin).
General	Free space	Specifies how much disk space is available for use.
General	Capacity	Specifies the total capacity of the disk drive; a pie chart shows how much is in use. Click the Disk Cleanup button to look for and delete unneeded files (see Chapter 32, section "Deleting Temporary Files Using Disk Cleanup").
Tools	Error-checking status	Shows how long it has been since you ran ScanDisk on this disk drive (see Chapter 32, section "Testing Your Disk Structure with ScanDisk"). Click the Check Now button to run ScanDisk.
Tools	Defragmentation status	Shows how long it has been since you ran Disk Defragmenter on this disk drive (see Chapter 32, section "Defragmenting Your Disk"). Click the Defragment Now button to run Disk Defragmenter.

Table 10-2.   *The General And Tools Tabs Settings for My Computer's Properties Dialog Box* (continued)

Partitioning a Disk with the Fdisk Program

When you buy a new computer or hard disk, you receive it ready for use—already partitioned and formatted. If you are adding new unformatted, unpartitioned disk drives, or if you want to create a computer system that can run one of several operating systems—such as switching between Windows Me and UNIX or Linux—you may need to partition a disk yourself. However, Fdisk destroys the data in the areas of the disk it partitions, so be sure to make a backup copy of all the information on your disk before running Fdisk (see Appendix B for how to back up your hard disk).

To partition a hard disk, you use the Fdisk program, a DOS-mode program that has survived nearly unchanged from the early 1980s. To start Fdisk, select Run | Start, type **fdisk**, and then press ENTER.

If your disk is larger than 500MB, Fdisk first asks whether you want to use FAT32. Press Y, unless you need to use FAT16 (unlikely). If you have more than one physical hard disk, Fdisk asks on which disk you want to work. You then see the main Fdisk screen, as Figure 10-3 shows.

To create a new partition for Windows, select 1. Fdisk "knows" what combinations of partitions are valid, suggests creating a new Primary DOS partition if none exists, and, otherwise, (rarely) suggests an Extended (or Extended DOS) partition. Fdisk then suggests allocating all available space on the disk to the partition, which usually is the right thing to do, unless you want to reserve space for other partitions or deliberately limit the size of a partition. Note that the Extended partition can be subpartitioned into logical drives. Thus, if you have an 8GB disk and want four 2MB partitions, for example, you should assign 2GB to the Primary DOS partition and the remaining 6GB to the Extended partition. After creating each partition, press ESC to return to the main Fdisk menu.

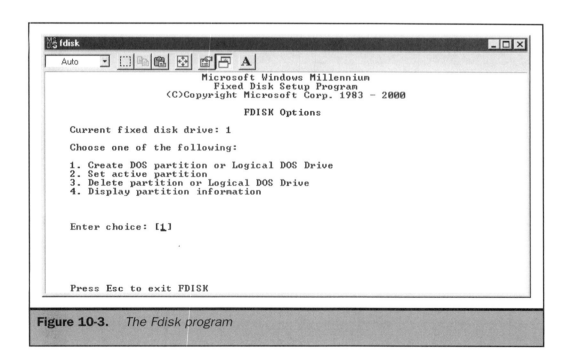

Figure 10-3.   *The Fdisk program*

MANAGING YOUR DISK

If you create an Extended partition, you have to create logical drives in that partition. In the main Fdisk menu, press 1 and then press 3 to create logical drives. Again, Fdisk suggests creating a single large logical drive, which is usually the best idea, unless you need more than one logical disk or you need smaller partitions for compatibility with earlier versions of DOS and Windows. Continuing with the preceding example, to create three 2GB logical drives, tell Windows to create a 2GB logical drive and then return to the logical-drive creation screen two more times to create the other two drives. (Because of rounding, the last drive may be a little more or less than 2GB. That's normal and creates no problems.)

After you create your partitions, press 4 on the main Fdisk menu to look at a list of the partitions. Figure 10-4 shows the arrangement on one of our computers, which we use for both UNIX and Windows. There's a 1.7GB non-DOS partition for UNIX, a 1.5GB Primary DOS partition for Windows Me, and a 599MB Extended DOS partition for data. Press Y to see the logical drives in the Extended DOS partition (not shown here, but it's a single large drive). When running Windows Me, the non-DOS partition is hidden, the Primary DOS partition is C, and the data partition is D.

Press ESC at the main Fdisk menu to exit. If you created new partitions or logical drives, Fdisk reboots your computer so Windows notices what you've done.

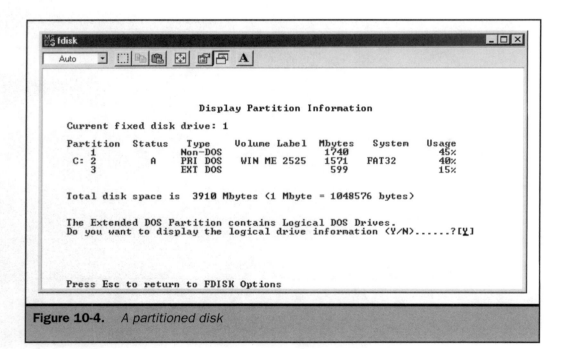

Figure 10-4. *A partitioned disk*

Selecting the Active Partition

If you partition your disk among multiple operating systems, one of the partitions is the *active partition*, the partition from which your computer starts. If you run Windows only, the Primary DOS partition is always active.

To switch to another operating system in a different partition, run Fdisk, press 2 to change the active partition, set that system's partition as active, and then reboot. To return to having Windows start when you reboot the computer, use the other system's equivalent of Fdisk to make the Primary DOS partition active and then reboot.

If you switch systems frequently, you probably want to install a *boot manager* program, which enables you to select which partition to start from each time you restart your computer. Nearly every operating system other than Windows provides a boot manager. You can also buy Boot Magic from PowerQuest Corp. at **http://www.powerquest.com/bootmagic**.

Repartitioning a Disk

Repartitioning a disk is unpleasant at best. First, back up all the useful data in the partitions you want to change. Then run Fdisk and select 2 to delete partitions or logical drives. Fdisk is reluctant to delete them because files in those partitions are lost, so you must confirm about six times that you really want to do so. (This is not a bad idea; Fdisk's skepticism has saved us from some serious mistakes.) If you want to delete the Extended DOS partition, you first have to delete all the logical drives in the partition.

Once the old partitions or logical drives are deleted, you create new ones, as previously described, and then reload the backed up data.

Third-party disk utilities, such as Partition Magic, make this process safer and easier and permit a few kinds of changes without backing up and reloading everything. Utilities like Drive Image make it easy to create a copy of a partition so you can reload it later. If you plan to use multiple partitions, we recommend you look into third-party partitioning programs (see "Installing Multiple Versions of Windows with Partition Magic" in this chapter).

Choosing Your Own Drive Letters

Whenever possible, we recommend you use the drive letters Windows assigns (see "What Are Drive Letters?"). If you can't use the letters Windows assigns by default (for example, you are using an antiquated program that expects files to be on certain drives), you have two options: change the letters in Windows or use the DOS SUBST command to create new letters.

Changing Your Drive Letters

In some cases, you can persuade Windows to assign different drive letters to your drives. The process is lengthy, but straightforward:

1. Choose Start | Settings | Control Panel.

2. In the Control Panel window, open the System icon.

3. Click the Device Manager tab and click the View Devices By Type radio button.

4. One of the icons in the window is labeled Disk Drives. If it's not already showing a list of your drives, double-click the Disk Drives icon to get the list.

5. In that list, select the drive whose letter(s) you want to change and click the Properties button at the bottom of the window. This opens the Properties dialog box for your disk.

6. In the Properties dialog box, click the Settings tab (see Figure 10-1). You see Current Drive Letter Assignment with a box listing the current drive letter(s).

7. If the box is white, you can enter new drive letters to take effect the next time you reboot. If the box is gray, as it is more often than not, you can't immediately change the letters for this disk because the software driver for your disk doesn't support it. However, you can set the Reserved drive letters at the bottom of the window to give a range of letters from which you'd like the system to select the disk's drive letter.

8. Either way, click OK when you're done.

Assigning Drive Letters to Folders

You can use the DOS SUBST command to assign new drive letters that correspond to folders on existing disks. Open an MS-DOS window and type the SUBST command in the following format (press ENTER after typing the command):

SUBST N: C:\MYAPP

This command makes the drive letter N a synonym for the folder C:\Myapp. You can use any unused drive letter and the address (pathname) of any folder. The new substituted drive letter is available immediately. If the path of your folder uses long names, then in the SUBST command, you have to use the MS-DOS name equivalent, as shown by the DOS DIR command (see Chapter 8, section "What Are MS-DOS Names?").

To disconnect a SUBSTed drive letter, type the following:

SUBST N: /D

If you use a SUBSTed drive on a regular basis, put the SUBST command in your Autoexec.bat file so it's available every time you start Windows (see Chapter 36, section "The Autoexec.bat File").

Formatting a Disk

Every disk, including hard disks and floppies, must be formatted before you can use it. Formatting a disk writes the file system, the low-level structure information needed to track where files and folders will be located on the disk (see "What Is a File System?"). When you buy a new computer, the hard disk is almost always formatted at the factory. Generally, you need to format disks only when you want to clean off a floppy disk or other removable disk (like a Zip or Jaz disk) for reuse.

Formatting a disk—hard disk or removable—deletes all the information from the disk so proceed with care!

Formatting a Hard Disk

Before formatting your hard disk (or one partition on a hard disk), be sure you make a backup copy of any files you want to keep (see Appendix B for how to use Microsoft Backup). To format a hard disk, follow these steps:

1. Run Windows Explorer and display the drive you want to format.

2. Right-click the icon for the drive and choose Format in the menu that pops up. You see the Format dialog box, shown in Figure 10-5. Almost none of the fields in the window, except for the volume label, apply to hard disks.

3. Type a drive label in the Label box (if the box is blank or if you want to change the existing label) and click the Start button in the Format dialog box.

4. If the drive contains files or folders, Windows asks whether you really want to reformat the disk because existing files will be lost. Assuming you want to format the disk, choose Yes to do so. Formatting can take several minutes—the process involves reading the entire disk to check for bad spots.

You can't format the disk from which you are running Windows; Windows displays an error message saying the disk contains files Windows is using. You can't format a CD-ROM either.

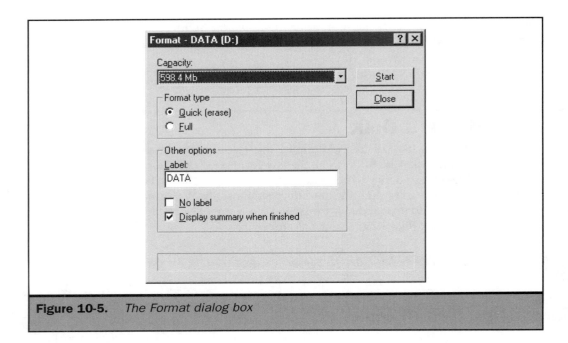

Figure 10-5.   *The Format dialog box*

Formatting a Removable Disk

Formatting a removable disk (like a floppy disk, Zip disk, or Jaz disk) is like formatting a hard disk, except more format options are available. If you only want to erase the files on a previously formatted disk without rechecking for bad spots, select Quick Format or Quick (Erase) on the Format dialog box. Then click the Start button in the Format dialog box.

When you format a disk, Windows may report bad sectors on the disk. Windows marks the sectors as unusable, to prevent programs from trying to write information there. If a floppy disk has any bad sectors, throw it away and use a new one—floppy disks are too cheap for you to fool around with the possibility of losing data.

To copy a floppy disk (that is, to copy all the information from one floppy to another while erasing the previous contents of the disk you are copying into), right-click the floppy disk in an Explorer window and choose Copy Disk from the shortcut menu that appears. Click Start and follow the prompts to insert first the original disk and then the disk onto which you want to copy.

*If you copy floppy disks often, create an icon on your desktop for the Copy Disk command. Right-click a blank space on the desktop and choose New | Shortcut from the shortcut menu that appears. In the Command Line box on the Create Shortcut dialog box that appears, type **diskcopy a: a:** (the DOS command that copies a floppy). Click Next. In the Select A Name For The Shortcut, type a name like **Copy Floppy**. Choose an icon and click Finish.*

Checking Free Space

You can easily see how much free space is available on any drive. Run Windows Explorer and select the drive. If the Web panel is displayed in the Explorer window, it shows the total size of the disk, along with the used and free space. If the Web panel doesn't appear, right-click the drive and select Properties from the menu that appears. You see a Properties dialog box with a pie chart like the one in Figure 10-2 (if the General tab isn't selected, click it).

Click the Disk Cleanup button to look for and delete unneeded files (see Chapter 32, section "Deleting Temporary Files Using Disk Cleanup").

Converting FAT16 to FAT32 Partitions

If you have an existing hard disk partition larger than 500MB that uses the older FAT16 file system, you can convert it (in place) to FAT32. (That is, you can convert the information in the partition from one format to the other without having to copy it to a temporary location during the conversion.) Conversion is a one-way process, so, remember, once you convert it, you can't use the disk with older versions of Windows and DOS.

If you do want to convert, run the FAT32 converter. Choose Start | Programs | Accessories | System Tools | FAT32 Converter. The Converter guides you through the process of conversion, telling you which drives you can convert, doing the conversion on a selected drive, and rebooting when done.

If you regret having done the conversion (unlikely), you have to repartition: back up the data, delete the partition, re-create a FAT16 partition, and reload the data (see "Repartitioning a Disk"). Or, some third-party programs, such as Partition Magic, can do a reverse FAT32-to-FAT16 conversion (for information about Partition Magic, see the Web page at **http://www.powerquest.com/partitionmagic**).

MANAGING YOUR DISK

Using CD-ROMs and Audio CDs

Because CD-ROMs and audio CDs are prerecorded at the factory, no preparation is needed to use them. Just stick them in the drive, and Windows recognizes them. If a CD-ROM contains an AutoRun program (that is, a file named Autorun.inf in the root folder of the CD-ROM, containing instructions for what program to run), Windows runs it. On audio CDs, Windows runs the Windows Media Player application automatically, turning your computer into a CD player. This is useful if you like background music while you work (see Chapter 16, section "Playing Audio CDs").

If you don't want the AutoRun program on a CD-ROM to run, or you don't want Windows to start playing an audio CD, open the drive, insert the disk, and hold down the SHIFT *key while closing the drive—keep the* SHIFT *key down until you are sure no program has started.*

You can turn off Windows' AutoRun feature, so CD-ROM programs don't run and audio CDs don't play automatically:

1. Choose Start | Settings | Control Panel. In the Control Panel, open the System icon and click the Device Manager tab.

2. Click the View Devices By Type radio button, click the plus sign next to CDROM, click the CD-ROM drive, and then click Properties. You see the Properties dialog box for your CD-ROM drive.

3. Click the Settings tab and click the Auto Insert Notification check box until it doesn't contain a check mark.

4. Click the OK button on both dialog boxes.

The Complete Reference

Windows Me

Part III

Configuring Windows for Your Computer

The
Complete
Reference

Windows
Me

Chapter 11

Setting Up Your Start Menu and Taskbar

Windows 95 introduced the Start menu and the Taskbar, and most people use them constantly. The Start menu is usually the first method you learn how to use to start programs (see Chapter 2, section "Starting Programs from the Start Menu"). For programs you run often, you might create shortcuts on your desktop to avoid having to use the Start menu (see Chapter 9, section "Using Shortcuts"). But chances are good you continue to use the Start menu—at least for programs you don't use often because cluttering up the desktop with shortcuts you hardly ever use isn't worth it. And a new Windows Me Start menu feature enables you to find Start menu commands quickly that you use frequently, hiding less often used commands.

The Start menu can contain so many submenus and commands that you can lose programs in it. Luckily, you can search the Start menu for the program you want. To make the Start menu easier to use, you might want to reorganize it, putting frequently used programs on the Programs menu and demoting other programs to submenus. You can also choose to display a Favorites menu and add or reorganize the items on it. Windows Me has added features that make the Start menu easier to edit than it used to be.

The Task Manager section of the Taskbar shows you which programs you're already running. You can customize the Taskbar, too. The Taskbar normally appears at the bottom of the screen, but you can move it, expand it, shrink it, or even make it disappear. You can also include toolbars on the Taskbar—you can display any number or none at all of the four predefined toolbars, display toolbars on the desktop, and even define your own toolbars.

What Is the Start Menu?

The *Start menu* appears when you click the Start button on the Taskbar. These items are usually on the Start menu:

- **Windows Update**   Connects to Microsoft's Web site to find out about, download, and install updates to Windows (see Chapter 35, section "Updating Your Computer with Windows Update"). Choose this command if you want to see whether Microsoft has issued new updates to Windows that are available for download.

- **Programs**   Displays the *Programs menu*, a menu of programs you can run. This menu is defined by the contents of the C:\Windows\Start Menu\Programs folder, which you can change (see "Reorganizing the Start Menu"). Choose the Programs menu when you want to run a program.

- **Documents**   Displays the *Documents menu*, a list of the documents that you have opened recently. To open one of the documents, choose it from the list. Windows runs the program that handles that type of file and opens the document in that program. You might find that a recently used file does not appear on the Documents menu—that's because not all applications update the

Documents menu. The My Documents and My Pictures folders appear on the Documents menu too, allowing you to easily open one of those folders.

■ **Settings** Displays a menu of commands you can use to control how Windows, your desktop, and your printers work. The Control Panel command helps you install software and change your Windows settings (see Chapter 1, section "What Is the Control Panel?"). The Printers command helps you see the status of your printers (see Chapter 15). The Taskbar And Start Menu command helps you customize the Taskbar and the commands that appear on the Start menu (see "Editing the Start Menu"). Windows, applications, or utility programs may add other commands to the Settings menu. You can add some commands and submenus to the Settings menu yourself (see "Adding and Deleting Other Commands and Submenus from the Start, Documents, and Settings Menus").

■ **Search** Displays a menu of the types of things Windows can help you find. The For Files Or Folders command searches your disks for files and folders (see Chapter 9, section "Searching for Files and Folders"). The On The Internet command runs your Web browser to search the Internet for information (see Chapter 24, section "Finding What You Want on the Web"). The People command searches for people's addresses by using your own Windows Address Book or various Internet address search pages (see Chapter 5, section "Storing Addresses in the Address Book"). Applications or utility programs may also add other commands to the Search menu.

■ **Help** Displays online help (see Chapter 6).

■ **Run** Enables you to run a program by typing the name of the file that contains it (see Chapter 2, section "Starting Programs from the Run Dialog Box").

■ **Log Off** If your computer is on a local area network (LAN), this command appears, enabling you to log off from one user name and to log on as another. This command also appears if your computer has user profiles to enable people to store their own settings when they share the computer (see Chapter 27).

■ **Shut Down** Displays the Shut Down Windows dialog box. On the dialog box, choose Shut Down if you are ready to turn off your computer. Choose Restart to restart your computer. Choose Standby to put Windows in a power-conserving Stand by mode. You may see other Shut Down options, such as Suspend or Hibernate, if you have turned them on and if your computer supports them.

You can add other commands to the Start menu, including the Favorites submenu. You can also add commands to the Settings submenu—see the section "Adding and Deleting Other Commands and Submenus from the Start, Documents, and Settings Menus" later in this chapter.

CONFIGURING WINDOWS FOR YOUR COMPUTER

What Is the Programs Menu?

The Programs menu, which you display by choosing Start | Programs, shows a list of the programs you can run. This is the most commonly used part of the Start menu, and it's the part you can customize to the greatest extent. The Start and Programs menus are hierarchical, that is, you can add menus and submenus to them. The Start menu includes the Program command, which displays the Programs menu. The Programs menu can contain commands that, in turn, display other menus and submenus.

Figure 11-1 shows a Start menu, the Programs menu that appears when you choose Programs from the Start menu, and the Games menu that appears when you choose Games from the Programs menu.

A new feature of Windows Me is *Personalized Menus*, which displays only those commands on the Start menu you have recently used. To see the rest of the available commands, select the double arrow that appears at the bottom of the menu or wait a

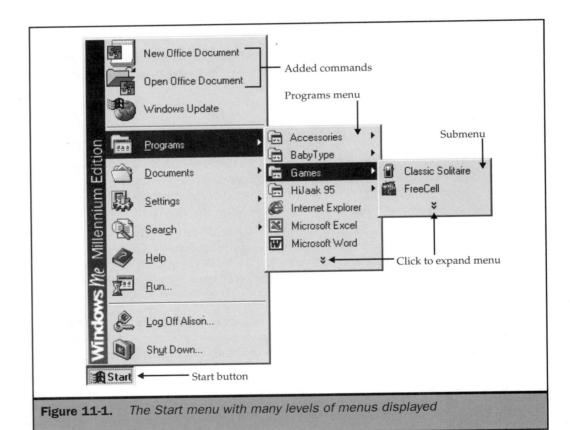

Figure 11-1. *The Start menu with many levels of menus displayed*

few seconds until they appear automatically. The commands displayed change, based on what you use and what you don't use. If you don't like this feature, you can turn it off. Figure 11-1 shows the Start menu personalized for one Windows user. Figure 11-2 shows the same menu expanded to show all commands.

When you install new programs, the installation program is likely to add a folder or item to the Start menu or (more likely) to the Programs menu. You may prefer to put these new items in a submenu of the Programs menu or perhaps eliminate them from the Start menu completely. The Start menu in Figure 11-1 has been customized with the addition of two choices: New Office Document and Open Office Document (the Microsoft Office installation program adds them). You can control what appears on the Programs menu (and its submenus) by editing the contents of the C:\Windows\Start Menu\Programs folder.

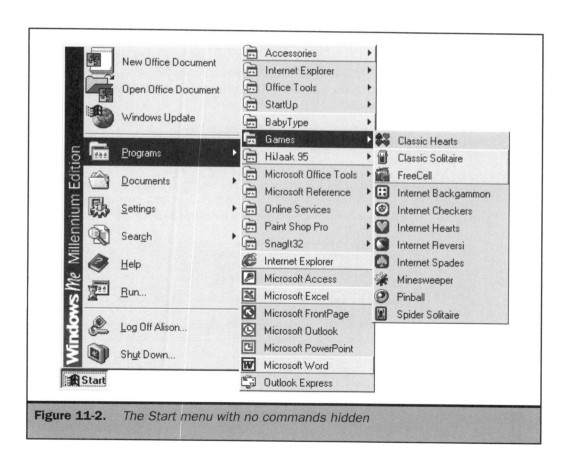

Figure 11-2.   *The Start menu with no commands hidden*

What Can Appear on the Taskbar?

The *Taskbar* is a row of buttons and icons that usually appears at the bottom of the Windows desktop. The Taskbar has four parts: the Start button, the toolbar(s), the Task Manager (with a button for each open window on the desktop), and the system tray. You can customize your Taskbar by moving it, changing its size, and changing what appears on it.

Four Taskbar toolbars come with Windows (actually, with Internet Explorer 5, which is included with Windows):

- **Quick Launch toolbar**   Usually contains four buttons, as shown from left to right in the following illustration: Show Desktop (minimizes all open windows to reveal the desktop), Launch Internet Explorer Browser, Launch Outlook Express, and Windows Media Player. You can change which buttons appear on this toolbar (see "Editing the Quick Launch Toolbar").

- **Address toolbar**   Contains a text box where you can type a URL to open a Web page or a file pathname to open a file. A drop-down list contains recently used URLs and pathnames.

- **Links toolbar**   Displays a button for each of the Web pages Microsoft would like you to visit (you can remove Microsoft's and add your own favorite sites). This toolbar also appears in Internet Explorer. Click a button to open the Web page.

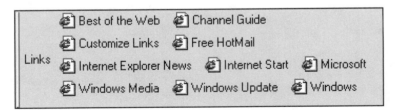

- **Desktop toolbar**   Displays a button for each icon on the desktop.

Windows usually displays the Quick Launch toolbar on the Taskbar immediately to the right of the Start button. You can remove that toolbar from the Taskbar or move it onto the desktop. You can also display other toolbars on the Taskbar or on the desktop (see "Adding and Removing Toolbars from the Taskbar").

Searching the Start Menu

If you can't find the program you want in the Start menu, you can search the menu to find what you're looking for by using the Search Results window (see Chapter 9, section "Searching for Files and Folders"). Follow these steps:

1. Right-click the Start button and choose Search from the shortcut menu that appears. You see the Search Results window, shown in Figure 11-3.

2. Type the name of the program you're looking for in the Search For Files Or Folders Named box. Notice the contents of the Look In text box are the C:\Windows\Start Menu folder, where the shortcuts used to create the Start menu are stored.

3. Click the Search Now button.

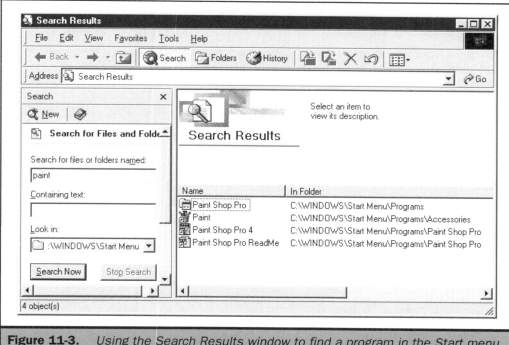

Figure 11-3.   *Using the Search Results window to find a program in the Start menu*

The files that match the text you typed are displayed in the Explorer window. Notice that the full pathname is displayed—this information can be used to find the item in the Start menu, or you can click or double-click the item in the Search Results list. If you can't see the full path, increase the width of the In Folder column by clicking and dragging its right border to the right.

Figure 11-3 shows the Search Results dialog box with the settings used to find programs with "paint" in their names. Windows found four menus or commands: the Paint Shop Pro folder in the Programs menu, the Paint program in the Accessories menu, and Paint Shop Pro 4 and the Paint Shop Pro ReadMe file in the Paint Shop Pro folder. The folder location translates to its menu command; for instance, the shortcut for Paint is in C:\Windows\Start Menu\Programs\Accessories, which means the corresponding command is Start | Programs Accessories | Paint.

Editing the Start Menu

Most of the Start menu and its submenus are customizable, except for the Shut Down, Help, Search, and Settings items on the first level of the Start menu—they cannot be removed or reorganized. You can, however, add items to the first level of the Start menu and to the Settings menu, and you have total control over the Programs menu and submenus. You might want to reorganize the menus, moving your favorite commands from submenus to the Programs menu, or even the Start menu itself.

If your Program menu has lots of submenus, getting to the choice you want may take longer than you would like. If you find the Start menu is cumbersome, you might want to explore the other methods of starting programs, covered in Chapter 2.

Reorganizing the Start Menu

You can add a program to the first level of the Start menu by dragging the program's shortcut to the Start button. You organize existing shortcuts by dragging items within the Start menu itself. However, if you want to reorganize the whole Start menu, delete parts of it, rename menu items, or add submenus, you need to go a little (but only a little) further into Windows' innards. You can organize those parts of the Start menu that you are allowed to edit in four ways—you can drag-and-drop items, cut-and-paste items, use Windows Explorer on the C:\Windows\Start Menu folders, or use the Taskbar And Start Menu Properties dialog box.

Dragging-and-Dropping Start Menu Items

The easiest way to add items to the Start menu, Programs menu, and their submenus, and to reorganize items already in the menus, is to drag-and-drop the shortcuts where you want them. To add an item to the Start menu, drag the file, folder, or program (the .exe file for the program, that is) from an Explorer window and drop it on the Start button. Windows creates a new shortcut, and the new command appears in the top part of the Start menu, where New Office Document, Windows Update, and Open

Office Document appear on the Start menu displayed in Figure 11-1. To put the item further into the Start menu hierarchy, drag it to the Start button and hold it there until the Start menu appears. Then drag the item to exactly where you want it to appear (hold it on a submenu option to open the submenu). You can also drag the item once it's in the Start menu to move it to a new position.

Reorganize the Start menu by dragging menu items when the menu is open, as follows:

1. Display the Start menu by clicking the Start button.

2. Display the menu containing the item you want to move (for instance, you might need to click the Programs command to see the Microsoft Word option, which you might want to move to a submenu called Microsoft Applications).

3. Click the item you want to move and hold the mouse button down.

4. While holding the mouse button down, move the pointer in the menu. The black bar shows you where the item you are moving will appear. You can open submenus by highlighting them, using the same method as when you are not moving a menu item.

5. When the black bar appears in the position that you want the item to appear, release the mouse button to drop the item in its new position.

Cutting-and-Pasting Start Menu Items

When you have displayed a menu command, you can right-click it and choose cut-and-paste commands from the shortcut menu that appears. To get rid of the command, display it in the Start menu or its submenus, right-click it, and choose Delete. To move (or copy) a command from one menu to another, right-click it and choose Cut (or Copy). Then display the command that displays the submenu into which you'd like to move the command, right-click, and choose Paste.

For example, if you want to copy the Netscape Navigator command from the Start | Programs | Netscape Communicator menu into the Programs menu, display the command, right-click it, and choose Copy. Then click Start to display the Start menu, right-click the Programs command, and choose Paste.

Moving Commands and Submenus by Editing the Start Menu Folder

In our opinion, the easiest way to make a lot of changes to the Start menu is to use Windows Explorer to add, remove, move, and rename shortcuts. Windows Explorer (discussed in Chapters 8 and 9) gives you a familiar tool for editing the Start menu. You can also rename submenus and menu items and create new submenus by using this method.

The Start menu displays the shortcuts stored in the C:\Windows\Start Menu folder and its subfolders. Adding, removing, and reorganizing the Start menu is as simple as adding, deleting, and moving shortcuts within the C:\Windows\Start Menu folder and subfolders. Menu items can be renamed by renaming the shortcuts.

CONFIGURING WINDOWS FOR YOUR COMPUTER

You can display the Start Menu folder in Windows Explorer by right-clicking the Start button and choosing Open or Explore from the menu (Open displays the C:\Windows\Start Menu folder in an Explorer window; Explore displays the same window with the addition of the Folders Explorer Bar—we recommend choosing Explore). Figure 11-4 shows the Start menu folder in Windows Explorer. Notice all the customizable choices that appear on the Start menu in Figure 11-1 also appear in the Start Menu folder: the Programs folder, the New Office Document shortcut, the Open Office Document shortcut, and the Windows Update shortcut. Commands you can change (like Help and Run) don't appear.

To display the contents of the Programs menu, open the Programs folder in the Start Menu folder. The shortcuts and folders in the Programs folder are the same as the commands and submenus on the Programs menu. You can continue to explore the Start Menu folders by using the same methods you use to explore all folders on your computer.

 To edit any submenu of the Start menu, you can right-click it and choose Explorer. Want to make changes to the Accessories submenu? Choose Start | Programs, right-click Accessories, and choose Explore. You see the C:\Windows\Start Menu\Programs\Accessories folder in Windows Explorer.

Figure 11-4. *Using Windows Explorer to edit the Start menu*

Because the Start menu is stored as shortcuts within folders, it can be edited in the same way you edit folders and files:

- You can move an item from one menu group to another by dragging or cutting-and-pasting the shortcut to another folder.

- You can create a new menu group by creating a new folder: Select the folder in which the new submenu will be stored and choose File | New | Folder.

- You can rename a shortcut by selecting it and pressing F2 (or right-clicking the name and choosing Rename from the shortcut menu that appears). Windows highlights the name and shows a box around it. Type a new name, or use the cursor to edit the name. Press ENTER when you finish (or press ESC if you change your mind).

Note *Although you can edit the Start menu by changing the contents of the Start Menu folder and its subfolders, the Start Menu folder and Programs folders are more than just regular folders. For instance, you can move the Programs folder out of the C:\Windows\Start Menu folder, and you still see the Programs option on the Start menu (this can lead to complications that are hard to fix, though, so don't try it).*

Moving Start Menu Items by Using the Taskbar And Start Menu Properties Dialog Box

If you aren't comfortable using Windows Explorer to edit the Start menu, you may prefer to use the Taskbar And Start Menu Properties dialog box, which contains settings for customizing both the Start menu and the Taskbar. Display the dialog box by using one of these methods:

- Choose Start | Settings | Taskbar And Start Menu.

- Right-click an unoccupied part of the Taskbar and choose Properties from the shortcut menu.

Click the Advanced tab to display the part of the dialog box you can use to reorganize the Start menu, as in Figure 11-5, using the four buttons on the dialog box: Add, Remove, Advanced, and Re-sort.

Adding a Shortcut to the Start Menu

You can add a shortcut to the Start menu by clicking the Add button. You see the Create Shortcut dialog box, shown in Figure 11-6. This Wizard guides you through adding an item to the Start menu and its three steps ask you for the following:

- **The file to which you are creating the shortcut**   You can type the full pathname or use the Browse button to find the file in the Browse dialog box.

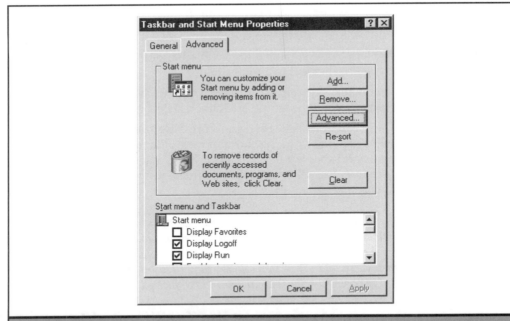

Figure 11-5.   The Advanced tab of the Taskbar And Start Menu Properties dialog box enabling you to change the choices that appear on the Start menu and its submenus.

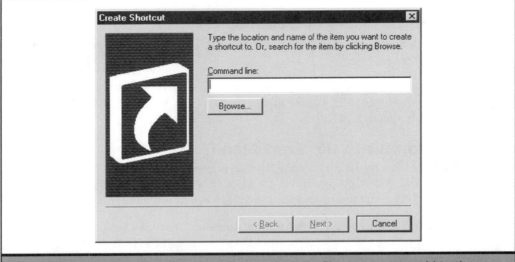

Figure 11-6.   Clicking the Browse button to find the file you want to add to the Start menu.

- **Where you want the shortcut to appear in the Start menu**   Select a folder from the folder tree or create a new folder. To create a new folder, select the folder under which the new folder will appear and click the New Folder button. The new folder can be renamed by typing a new name as soon as it is created—notice that the new folder appears highlighted with a box around it.

- **The name of the shortcut**   You can provide any name you want for the shortcut by editing the name that appears or by typing a new name.

When you click Finish, Windows adds the shortcut to the Start menu where you indicated.

Removing Items from the Start Menu

The Remove button displays the Remove Shortcuts/Folders dialog box, shown in Figure 11-7. You can remove any item in the Start menu (except those noted earlier that cannot be edited) by selecting the item and clicking the Remove button. Any folder that contains menu items or other folders appears with a plus box next to it—click the plus box to see the contents of the folder. If you remove a folder, you also remove its contents—a dialog box asks you to confirm that you want to delete the folder and its contents. A menu item that is not a folder will be deleted without any confirmation.

Removed menu items are available in the Recycle Bin, if you make a mistake and remove an item you'd rather keep (see Chapter 9, section "Managing the Recycle Bin").

CONFIGURING WINDOWS
FOR YOUR COMPUTER

Figure 11-7.   *Removing an item or subfolder from the Start menu*

Editing the Start Menu

The Advanced button displays the Start Menu folder in Windows Explorer, where you can use the file-management techniques detailed in the last section to edit the Start menu. Using the Advanced button on the Taskbar And Start Menu Properties dialog box produces a slightly different result than right-clicking the Start button and choosing Explore to edit the Start menu in Windows Explorer. The Advanced button enables you to use Windows Explorer only to edit the Start menu folders, whereas right-clicking the Start button and choosing Explorer opens a regular version of Windows Explorer you can use to display any folder on any drive.

Adding and Deleting Other Commands and Submenus from the Start, Documents, and Settings Menus

Although you can add commands at the top of the Start menu by editing the contents of the C:\Windows\Start Menu folder, this folder doesn't control the rest of the commands on the Start menu (Documents, Settings, and so forth). You can add and delete some of these commands by choosing Start | Settings | Taskbar And Start Menu to display the Taskbar And Start Menu Properties dialog box. (Another way to display this dialog box is to right-click a blank area on the Taskbar and choose Properties from the shortcut menu that appears.) This dialog box also enables you to add and delete a few commands from the Settings menu. Click the Advanced tab to display the settings shown in Figure 11-5.

At the bottom of the dialog box is the Start Menu And Taskbar list of check boxes including many (under the Start Menu heading) that add commands from the Start menu when the check box is selected:

- **Display Favorites**   The Favorites option appears on the Start menu just below the Programs command.

- **Display Logoff**   Displays the Logoff command on the Start menu just above the Shut Down command.

- **Display Run**   Displays the Run command on the main Start menu just below the Help command.

These check boxes control which submenus appear under the Settings menu:

- **Expand Control Panel**   Displays a submenu containing all Control Panel options when you choose Start | Settings | Control Panel.

- **Expand Dial-Up Networking**   Displays a submenu containing all your Dial-Up Networking options (including your Dial-Up Networking connections) when you choose Start | Settings | Dial-Up Networking (see Chapter 21, section "What Is Dial-Up Networking?").

- **Expand Printers**   Displays a submenu containing the contents of the Printers folder when you choose Start | Settings | Printers.

These check boxes control which submenus appear under the Documents menu:

- **Expand My Documents**   Displays a submenu containing the contents of the My Documents folder when you choose Start | Documents | My Documents.

- **Expand My Pictures**   Displays a submenu containing the contents of the My Pictures folder when you choose Start | Documents | My Pictures.

Changing Start Menu Properties

In addition to changing the items that appear on the Start menu and the order in which they appear, you can customize the Start menu in other ways. Choose Start | Settings | Taskbar And Start Menu to display the Taskbar And Start Menu Properties dialog box, shown in Figure 11-8.

On the General tab of the Taskbar and Start Menu Properties dialog box, the options affecting the Start menu are as follows:

- **Show Small Icons in Start Menu**   By default large icons are displayed in the Start menu. Turn on the Small Icons option to make the first level of the Start menu take up less room on the screen.

- **Use Personalized Menus**   Displays only those commands you have used recently. Turn off this option if you want to see all commands all the time.

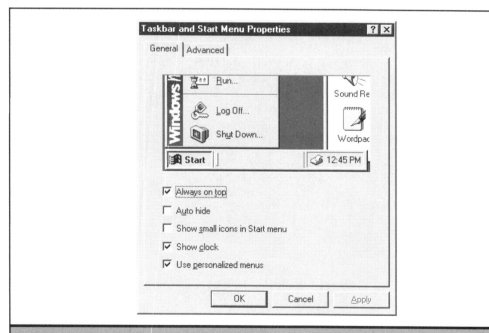

Figure 11-8.   *Changing the properties of the Start menu*

CONFIGURING WINDOWS
FOR YOUR COMPUTER

The Advanced tab of the Taskbar And Start Menu Properties dialog box has two sections. The Start menu section at the top gives you a third method of editing the Start menu, which is covered a little later in this chapter.

 To delete the contents of the Documents menu, click the Clear button on the Advanced tab of the Taskbar And Start Menu Properties dialog box.

The Start Menu And Taskbar section at the bottom of the dialog box contains a list of check boxes. Most of the check boxes control which commands and submenus appear on the Start, Settings, and Documents menus (see "Adding and Deleting Other Commands and Submenus from the Start, Documents, and Settings Menus"). The following additional check boxes have an effect on the Start menu:

- **Enable Dragging-And-Dropping**   The Start menu can be edited by dragging-and-dropping menu commands as covered earlier in this chapter.
- **Scroll Programs**   Scrolls the contents of the Programs menu up and down when the list is too big to fit on the screen; otherwise, the Programs menu expands to more than one column.

The last two settings affect the Taskbar (see "Enabling Taskbar Changes").

Adding and Editing Favorites

The *Favorites* menu, which you display by choosing Start | Favorites, displays your most frequently used files, folders, Web pages, and programs. The menu displays the contents of the Favorites folder (C:\Windows\Favorites). Windows doesn't display the Favorites menu unless you choose to display it by selecting the Display Favorites check box on the Advanced tab of the Taskbar And Start Menu Properties dialog box (see "Adding and Deleting Other Commands and Submenus from the Start, Documents, and Settings Menus"). The Favorites menu is shown here:

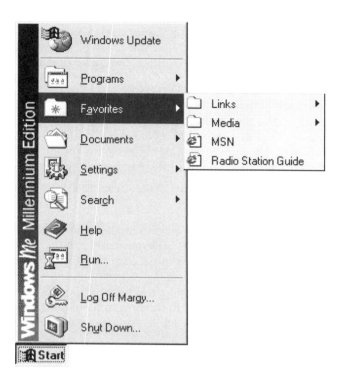

The Favorites menu is easy to access, not only from the Start menu, but also from Explorer windows and most Open and Save As dialog boxes. Most people use the Favorites folder for frequently used files, folders, and programs, but you can also store files there (just like any other folder).

Windows comes preprogrammed with some favorites. The Favorites menu can display both preprogrammed favorites and items you add. The Links and Media submenus contain Web sites selected by Microsoft.

You can easily access the shortcuts in the Favorites folder from any dialog box that has the Look In Favorites button. The Microsoft Word 97 Open dialog box (shown in Figure 11-9), like many others, has two buttons that make finding and creating Favorites easy:

■ **Look In Favorites**   Displays the contents of the C:\Windows\Favorites folder. In many applications, the Look In Favorites button is a toggle button—when the Favorites folder is displayed, the name of the button changes to Return To *previous folder*. Click it again to display the contents folder you were looking at before you displayed the contents of the Favorites folder.

■ **Add To Favorites**   Adds a shortcut to the highlighted file or folder in the Favorites folder.

To change the contents of the Favorites menu, make changes to the C:\Windows\ Favorites folder—it's the same system that reflects changes to the C:\Windows\Start Menu folder to change the contents of the Start menu. You can create new folders in the Favorites folder to create a hierarchical Favorites menu. You can also edit the Favorites menu by using the same drag-and-drop techniques used to edit the rest of the Start menu. You can drag a menu item from the Programs menu to the Favorites menu to move it. If you hold down the CTRL key while you drag, you can *copy* the item to the Favorites menu.

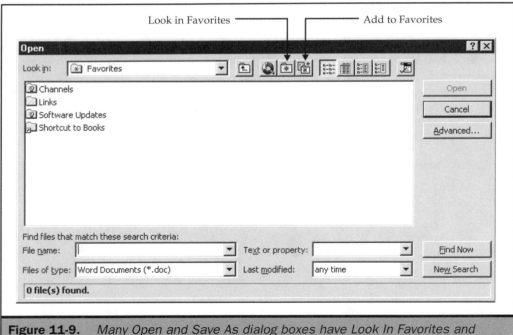

Figure 11-9.   *Many Open and Save As dialog boxes have Look In Favorites and Add To Favorites buttons.*

Customizing the Taskbar

Although many Windows users find no reason to customize the Taskbar, others do. You can move the Taskbar around the desktop, and you can control its size and whether it is visible all the time. The Taskbar is shown in Figure 11-10.

Enabling Taskbar Changes

You can disable and enable changes to the Taskbar. Some people find they drag-and-drop items from the Taskbar by accident, and they would rather have Windows prevent these changes. To disable or enable editing the Taskbar, choose Start | Settings | Taskbar And Start Menu and click the Advanced tab. You see the dialog box shown in Figure 11-8. Scroll the Start Menu And Taskbar list of check boxes all the way to the bottom to reveal the Enable Moving And Resizing check box. When this check box is not selected (it is empty), you can't edit the Taskbar, move it to another edge of the screen, or change its size. You can still change the toolbars the Taskbar displays, though.

 The Display Shortcut Menu On Right-Click check box is also at the bottom of this list of check boxes. When this check box is not selected, right-clicking an empty space on the Taskbar doesn't display a shortcut menu.

Moving the Taskbar

Move the Taskbar to any edge of the desktop by clicking-and-dragging it to the desired position. When the pointer is near an edge of the desktop, you see a gray bar showing where the Taskbar will be when you release the mouse button. You have to click an unoccupied area of the Taskbar—not the Start button, or a Task Manager program button—to drag it. An unoccupied piece of Taskbar is always at the right end of the Task Manager.

When the Taskbar appears on the left or right side of the desktop, it looks a little different, as in Figure 11-11, but it still has the same parts. The Taskbar doesn't cover icons on the desktop when it is moved—the icons shift to slightly new positions. (The exception to this "icon shifting" rule is when Auto Hide is turned on. Then the icons don't move, but the Taskbar disappears so you can see them.)

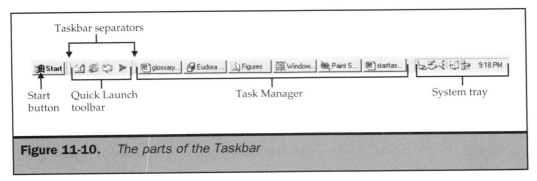

Figure 11-10.   *The parts of the Taskbar*

CONFIGURING WINDOWS FOR YOUR COMPUTER

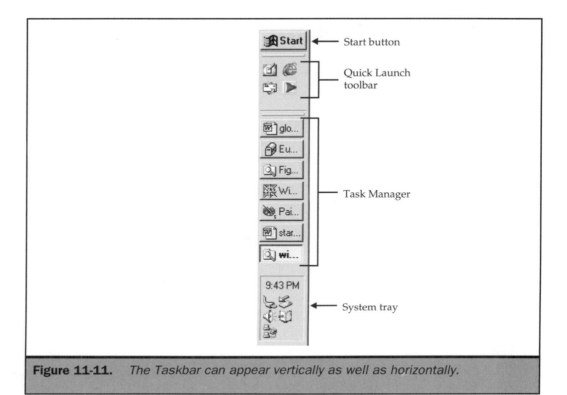

Figure 11-11.   *The Taskbar can appear vertically as well as horizontally.*

Changing the Size of the Taskbar

You can change the size of the Taskbar by clicking-and-dragging its inside edge—that is, the edge that borders the desktop. If the Taskbar appears at the bottom of the screen, then change its size by clicking and dragging its top edge. The following illustration shows a Taskbar made taller to display two rows of buttons:

A larger Taskbar displays more information on each button in the Task Manager; however, it also claims more of the screen that could be used to display other information.

You can size the Taskbar back down by clicking and dragging the inside edge back toward the edge of the screen—make sure to release the mouse button when the Taskbar is the desired size.

Decreasing the size of the Taskbar to a thin stripe along one edge of the screen is possible by using this method. If this has been done to your Taskbar, you can find the Taskbar by putting the pointer on each edge of the screen. When the pointer turns into a double-headed arrow, click-and-drag to increase the size of the Taskbar.

Changing Taskbar Properties

The General tab of the Taskbar And Start Menu Properties dialog box provides some options to change how the Taskbar works. To display the Taskbar And Start Menu Properties dialog box, choose Start | Settings | Taskbar And Start Menu, or right-click an unoccupied portion of the Taskbar and choose Properties from the shortcut menu that appears. You see the General tab of the Taskbar And Start Menu Properties dialog box, shown in Figure 11-8.

Hiding the Taskbar

You can hide the Taskbar in two different ways: by decreasing its size and by using the Auto Hide option. Changing the size of the Taskbar is covered in the previous section—click-and-drag the inside edge of the Taskbar to the screen's closest edge. The Taskbar becomes a thin gray line on one edge of the screen. The other option is to use the Auto Hide feature to hide the Taskbar. Auto Hide tries to determine when you need the Taskbar and displays the Taskbar only when you need it.

To turn on Auto Hide, display the General Options tab of the Taskbar And Start Menu Properties dialog box and click the Auto Hide option so a check appears in the box.

When Auto Hide is on, the Taskbar disappears when it isn't being used. To display it, point at the edge of the screen where it last appeared. Or, you can press CTRL-ESC or the WINDOWS key (some keyboards have a key with the Windows symbol that displays the Start menu) to display the Taskbar and open the Start menu all at the same time.

 If you can't find your Taskbar, try this: point the pointer at each edge of the screen. If Auto Hide is on, the Taskbar appears. If the Taskbar is shrunk, the pointer turns into a double-headed arrow—click and drag to increase the Taskbar's size.

Hiding the Clock on the Taskbar

You can choose to display or hide the clock that usually appears in the system tray section of the Taskbar. Display the Taskbar And Start Menu Properties dialog box, click the Taskbar Options tab, and then click the Show Clock option to clear the check from the check box.

Allowing the Taskbar to Be Covered by a Window

You can choose whether you want the Taskbar to be covered by other windows by using the Always On Top setting on the Taskbar Options tab of the Taskbar And Start Menu Properties dialog box. When the option is on, the Taskbar always appears over any other windows. When the option is off, windows may cover the Taskbar. To use the Taskbar when the Always On Top option is turned off, you can move or minimize windows until the Taskbar is visible or press CTRL-ESC or the WINDOWS key to display both the Taskbar and open the Start menu (press ESC once if you want to use only the Taskbar).

Adding Toolbars to the Taskbar

You can add toolbars to your Taskbar. Taskbar toolbars give you easy access to frequently used icons: You no longer have to minimize all open programs to display a desktop icon to open a program. Instead you can use a toolbar button. Or, you can use the toolbar button Show Desktop to minimize all open programs with one click. You can configure the Taskbar to include these toolbars, or you can display these toolbars elsewhere on your desktop. You can even edit the buttons that appear on a toolbar or create a completely new toolbar.

Adding and Removing Toolbars from the Taskbar

Use the Taskbar shortcut menu to add and remove toolbars from the Taskbar. The Taskbar shortcut menu, shown here, can be displayed by right-clicking an unoccupied part of the Taskbar (even on a full Taskbar, an unoccupied part can be found at the far right of the Task Manager).

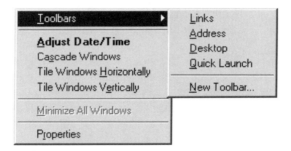

The Toolbars option on the Taskbar shortcut menu displays a menu with the four toolbars. To display a toolbar, click its name. The next time you display the shortcut menu, that toolbar has a check mark next to it. To remove a displayed toolbar, follow the same procedure, but this time click to remove the check mark.

Moving a Toolbar to the Desktop

You have the option of displaying toolbars on the desktop rather than on the Taskbar. To move a toolbar to the desktop, click-and-drag the toolbar's handle, which looks like a raised vertical bar on the left end of the toolbar.

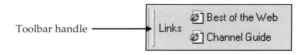

Toolbar handle

Drag-and-drop the toolbar onto the desktop. Each toolbar looks different on the desktop, but they all appear with a title bar, a Close button, and their tools, something like this:

Once the toolbar is on the desktop, you can no longer make it disappear by using the Taskbar shortcut menu—instead, you can use its Close button to get rid of it. You can move and change the size of the toolbar by using the same techniques you use on any window (see Chapter 2).

You can move a toolbar from the desktop back to the Taskbar, or to any edge of the desktop, by clicking-and-dragging the title bar—when the toolbar reaches any edge of the desktop, it changes shape to occupy the whole edge. If you move it to the edge with the Taskbar, the toolbar is integrated back into the Taskbar. If you move it to an empty edge, the toolbar takes up the whole edge of the desktop.

Controlling the Look of a Toolbar

You can control the way a toolbar works by using the Toolbar shortcut menu, shown here:

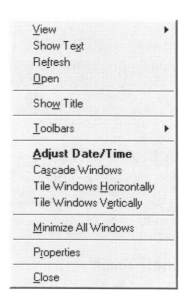

Display the Toolbar shortcut menu by right-clicking an unoccupied part of the toolbar (if you have trouble finding an unoccupied part of the toolbar, right-click the toolbar handle).

The following choices on the Toolbar shortcut menu control your toolbar (the rest of the choices that appear affect the whole Taskbar):

- **View**   Allows you to display either large or small icons. The default setting is Small.
- **Show Text**   Displays text on each button. Choose this option again to display icons with no text. Turning off this option makes a toolbar take up less space.
- **Refresh**   Refreshes the toolbar display. This is particularly useful if you create a new toolbar to display the contents of a disk or folder.
- **Open**   Displays the shortcuts that make up the toolbar in and Explorer window.
- **Show Title**   Turns off or on the display of the name of the toolbar.
- **Toolbars**   Allows you to display a new toolbar, remove an existing toolbar, or create a new toolbar. This option is the same as the Toolbars option on the Taskbar shortcut menu.
- **Close**   Removes the toolbar from the screen.

When the toolbar is attached to an edge of the desktop, but not in the Taskbar, you see two additional choices:

- **Always On Top**   The toolbar cannot be covered by a window.
- **Auto Hide**   The toolbar disappears when not in use. Move the pointer to the edge of the screen where the toolbar is located to display it.

These additional two options work the same as the Always On Top and Auto Hide options for the Taskbar (see also "Adding and Removing Toolbars").

Moving the Toolbar on the Taskbar

You can control how the Taskbar is partitioned between the Task Manager and the toolbars by dragging the divider between the two. When the Task Manager gets small, scroll buttons appear, allowing you to view all the buttons for open applications. By moving the divider all the way to the opposite end of the Taskbar, you can move the toolbar from one side of the Taskbar to the other.

Editing the Quick Launch Toolbar

You can edit the buttons on the Quick Launch toolbar in the same way that you edit the Start menu—by editing the folder that contains the shortcuts. The shortcuts for the Quick Launch toolbar are buried in the folder structure—you can find them in

C:\Windows\Application Data\Microsoft\Internet Explorer\Quick Launch. (Why does Microsoft store this information with Internet Explorer configuration data? They consider the whole desktop as a special Internet Explorer window.) You can add new shortcuts and delete the shortcuts that appear in this folder to change the buttons displayed on the Quick Launch toolbar.

You can also drag-and-drop shortcuts to the Quick Launch toolbar—convenient!

Creating a New Toolbar

In addition to the four existing toolbars, you can create your own toolbar to display the contents of a drive, folder, or Internet address. Depending on the options you choose for your new toolbar, it may look something like the one that follows, which shows the contents of a folder called Consult. The Consult folder contains three other folders and numerous files. On the toolbar, you can see the three folders—you can display the files by clicking the scroll arrow at the right end of the toolbar.

If you create a new toolbar and then click it, it's gone. To redisplay it, you need to recreate the toolbar.

Clicking a folder button opens an Explorer window for that folder; clicking a file button opens the file.

To create a new toolbar, right click the Taskbar or a toolbar and choose Toolbars | New Toolbar from the shortcut menu that appears. You see the New Toolbar dialog box, shown in Figure 11-12, which enables you to browse available drives and folders. Click the plus box next to a folder name to expand that branch of the folder tree. You can open any folder or drive available to you in Windows Explorer—these may include drives and folders on the Internet. Click New Folder to create a new folder in the highlighted folder. Select the folder you want to use to create a toolbar and click OK in the New Toolbar dialog box.

Figure 11-12.   *Selecting a drive or folder to create a toolbar with a button for each folder and file in the drive or folder*

Chapter 12

Setting Up Your Desktop

When your desktop is set up in a way that is right for you, everything flows more smoothly. Files and programs are where you expect them to be. The screen is attractive and doesn't hurt your eyes. Your wallpaper, color scheme, and screen saver are different from everyone else's, giving your computer a familiar, homey feel. You use Windows' display properties to configure your desktop and monitor. If you really want to dress up your desktop, you can change the background color or pattern, change the size, color, or font of the individual elements that make up the desktop, or install a desktop theme to give your screen an artistic look.

But Windows Me enables you to do more than just a little interior decorating. Two features create additional possibilities for your desktop. *Active Desktop* turns your desktop into a Web page, fully interactive with live content from whatever networks you have access to, including the Internet. And Windows supports multiple displays and multiple graphics adapters, greatly increasing your display options.

What Are Display Properties?

The command center for anything having to do with your monitor or desktop is the Display Properties dialog box, shown in Figure 12-1. You can access it from the Control Panel, or by right-clicking any unoccupied spot on the desktop and choosing Properties from the shortcut menu.

This Display Properties dialog box has six tabs (possibly more, if your system has any special display software). Table 12-1 lists the tabs and the purpose of each tab. You can change the settings on most of these tabs to change the way your desktop looks and acts.

Tab	What It Controls
Background	Wallpaper and background patterns
Screen Saver	Screen savers and automatic settings for turning off your monitor
Appearance	Color, size, and font of every standard type of object Windows uses
Effects	Customization of icons and visual effects
Web	Active Desktop
Settings	Size of desktop (in pixels), number of colors displayed, and monitor performance

Table 12-1.   *Display Properties Dialog Box Tabs*

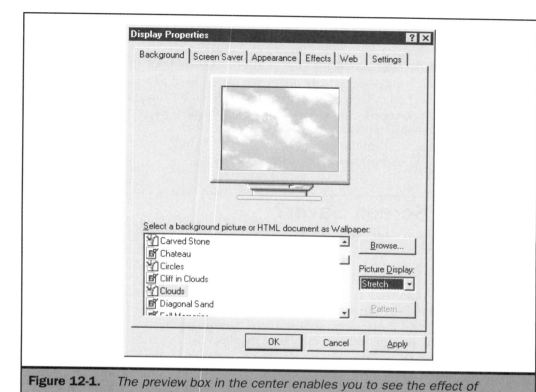

Figure 12-1.   *The preview box in the center enables you to see the effect of proposed changes before you apply them.*

What Is Active Desktop?

Active Desktop turns your desktop into a Web page. Your desktop can contain pictures, text, animation, sounds, links, weather maps, stock tickers, or anything else that can appear on a Web page. Information can be brought in automatically from the Internet or a local area network (LAN) by subscribing to the corresponding sites, or you can display HTML documents or image files from your own computer.

Some people find Active Desktop a useful way to get up-to-date information automatically; others find it little more than animated advertisements cluttering up the screen. You might want to try Active Desktop for a little while to see which camp is yours.

Microsoft maintains an online gallery of items you can add to your Active Desktop. To try Active Desktop, see "Activating Your Desktop," later in this chapter.

What Is Wallpaper?

Putting wallpaper on your desktop is a bit of a mixed metaphor—perhaps contact paper would be better. *Wallpaper* is the background pattern behind all the windows, icons, and menus on your desktop. Any image file can be used as wallpaper. The image can be centered on the screen, or it can fill the screen by being stretched or repeated as tiles. If you choose not to have wallpaper, the desktop can have either a solid background color or a two-tone repeating pattern.

To choose wallpaper from the images that ship with Windows, or any other image, (see "Wallpapering Your Desktop," later in this chapter).

What Is a Screen Saver?

If you walk away from your computer and leave the monitor on, the same image might be on your screen for hours at a time. Years ago, this would tend to "burn in" the image permanently on the screen; so people created *screen savers*—programs that kick in when the display hasn't changed in a while. A good screen saver contains some kind of moving image, so no section of the screen is consistently bright or dark.

Monitor technology eventually improved to the point that burn-in is not such a serious concern. In addition, many monitors now have an energy-saving feature that allows a monitor to turn off automatically if its display hasn't changed for some period of time (see Chapter 18, section "Managing Your Computer's Power").

But even though screen savers are no longer needed for their original purpose, many people continue to use them because they are pleasant to look at. (They also discourage random passers-by from reading the document you're working on when you step out for coffee.) Screen savers like "Mystify Your Mind" or "Curves and Colors" make attractive geometric patterns that can be soothing to watch, while others like "3D Maze" create a more active mood. In offices with multiple networked computers, the screen saver can display the computer's name, suitably colorized and animated. You can also download screen savers from the Internet, enabling you to display the latest *Harry Potter* images when you're not working. (To select and activate a screen saver, see "Setting Up a Screen Saver," later in this chapter.)

What Is a Desktop Scheme?

The ability to select any conceivable color, size, or font for every single type of object on the desktop is more power than most of us need or want. We'd like to be able to change things around every now and then, but we don't want to spend all day figuring out exactly what shade of dark green frame to put around windows with a light green background.

Windows comes with a large number of preconfigured *desktop schemes*. Making a single choice on the Appearance tab of the Display Properties dialog box simultaneously adjusts active windows, inactive windows, window backgrounds, title bars, message boxes, and all the other configurable desktop objects. It's so simple you can have one favorite desktop scheme for sunny days, another for cloudy days, and a third for nighttime—something you would never do if you had to make all the adjustments individually (for more information, see "Choosing Sizes, Colors, and Fonts of Desktop Elements," later in this chapter).

What Is a Desktop Theme?

A theme is like a scheme, only more so. A *desktop scheme* is a system of colors and fonts designed to look attractive together. A *desktop theme* takes this idea a little further, adding a screen saver, desktop background, mouse pointer, sounds, and icons all customized around a central idea.

For example, the Leonardo da Vinci theme (our favorite) has a reddish-brown color scheme and a desktop background that looks like a weathered parchment covered with Leonardo's drawings. The My Computer icon is a notebook, My Network Places is a jar of drawing tools, and the Recycle Bin is a wicker basket. The icon signifying Windows is busy changes from an hour glass to a paint brush putting blobs of color in a notebook. The screen saver includes several da Vinci sketches. The system noises are more musical than the Windows default noises.

Desktop themes are not part of the default installation of Windows and for a good reason: they hog disk space. Installing all 15 desktop themes on your system takes up 31MB on your hard drive. If you want them, you must install them from the Windows Me CD. From the Control Panel, open Add/Remove Programs, click the Windows Setup tab, and choose Desktop Themes. Check the Desktop Themes check box to install all the themes, or click the Details button to select individual themes.

Given that desktop themes add no functionality other than cuteness to your system, we forego them. If you do install desktop themes from the Windows Me CD-ROM, we recommend you play with the themes for a while, and then pick one or two favorites and uninstall the rest.

Selecting and editing desktop themes is discussed in the section "Choosing a Desktop Theme," later in this chapter.

Changing the Background

When you decorate the walls of a room, is your first choice paint or wallpaper? You have a similar choice about the background of your desktop: Do you want a solid color background or do you want to use a more complex pattern as wallpaper?

Wallpapering Your Desktop

You can cover your desktop with any image, from a straw mat to the Mona Lisa. Use either an image file of your own or one of the many wallpapers that come with Windows.

Windows doesn't automatically install all the wallpapers that come on its CD. To install the rest of the wallpaper files, open the Add/Remove Programs icon on the Control Panel, click the Windows Setup tab, choose Accessories from the list of components, click Details, and then click Desktop Wallpaper.

Selecting Wallpaper from the Wallpaper List

Select your wallpaper from the Background tab of the Display Properties dialog box, shown in Figure 12-2. The Wallpaper window of that tab lists all the available wallpapers. Click a name in this list to see the wallpaper pattern displayed on the Desktop Preview—the monitor-like graphic just above the list.

A wallpaper is only a file in an HTML or image format (with extension .bmp, .jpg, .gif, or .tif). That image has a size, which may or may not match the dimensions of your display. If the image is smaller than the display, the Display drop-down list (to the right of the Wallpaper list) gives you three choices:

- **Center** the image on the display, letting the background color of the desktop form a frame around the wallpaper. This is your best choice for photographs that are slightly smaller than the display.

- **Tile** the display with the image. This works particularly well with wallpapers such as Black Thatch or Houndstooth, which are small images designed to create intricate patterns when tiled.

- **Stretch** the image to fill the display. Photographs end up looking like fun house mirrors, but many abstract patterns stretch well.

Tile and Stretch fill the display with the wallpaper, but Center may leave a border, which you can fill with either a solid color or a pattern (see "Selecting a Background Color and Pattern").

If the wallpaper you choose is larger than your display, Center and Tile both give you a single copy of the image, with the edges of the image off the screen. If this isn't satisfactory, you can use Paint to crop the image (Chapter 5, section describes how to use Microsoft Paint), or you can redefine the dimensions of your display (see "Changing Resolution and Color Refinement").

When the preview in the Display Properties dialog box looks the way you want, click either OK (which closes the dialog box) or Apply (which doesn't).

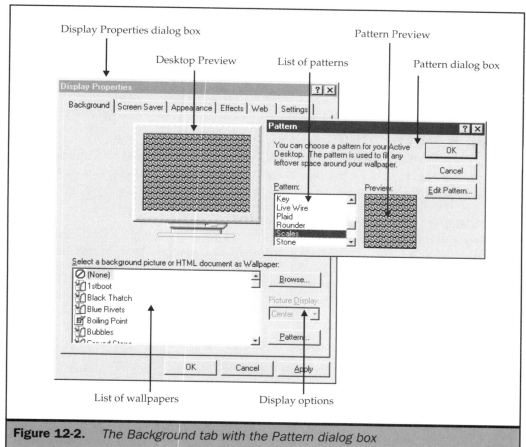

Figure 12-2. *The Background tab with the Pattern dialog box*

Windows won't let you choose a .tif, .gif, .jpg, or .htm file for your wallpaper if you haven't enabled Active Desktop. Instead, a confirmation box asks if you want to enable Active Desktop now. If you don't want to enable Active Desktop, click No and choose a .bmp file for your wallpaper.

Browsing for Wallpaper

You aren't limited to the wallpapers that come with Windows. Any image file—like a digital or scanned picture of your kids—can be used as wallpaper. To make wallpaper out of any other image file, click the Browse button on the Background tab of the Display Properties dialog box, shown in Figure 12-2. Use the Browse window that appears to find the file you want. Then click Open. The file you select should now appear in the Wallpaper list. Proceed as in the previous section.

Adding to the Wallpaper List Permanently

Browsing for wallpaper adds the selected image file to the Wallpaper list only temporarily. The next time you open the Display Properties dialog box, the browsed-for file will not be on the Wallpaper list. The Wallpaper list is actually a list of the image files in the C:\Windows folder. So, to add an image to this list permanently, move or copy its file to the C:\Windows folder.

Selecting a Background Color and Pattern

Wallpaper covers paint, so you see the background color and pattern of your desktop only if your wallpaper choice is either None or centered with the background visible around the edges.

Choosing a New Background Color

The background color of your desktop is set on the Appearance tab of the Display Properties dialog box (not on the Background tab, as you might have thought). The Appearance tab is shown in Figure 12-3.

To select a new background color:

1. Click the Appearance tab of the Display Properties dialog box.

2. Select Desktop from the Item drop-down list. The current background color is shown in the Color box to the right of the Item box.

3. Click the current background color. A palette of colors appears.

4. If one of the colors on the palette is what you want, click it. The background of the Preview window changes to the new color.

5. If you don't like any of the colors on the palette, click Other, and follow the directions in the next section, "Finding the Perfect Color."

6. Click Apply to change the desktop color or OK to change the color and make the Display Properties dialog box disappear.

You can change the colors and sizes of other elements on the desktop, too, including title bars, window borders, menus, and buttons (see "Choosing Sizes, Colors, and Fonts of Desktop Elements"). Click an object in the preview box to see the color settings for that type of object.

Finding the Perfect Color

When you start trying to change the color of the desktop, the title bars, or any of the other basic objects, Windows offers a simple palette of 16 basic colors, plus the four additional colors you have used most recently. If this isn't enough choice for you, click Other to display the Color dialog box, shown in woefully inadequate black and white in Figure 12-4.

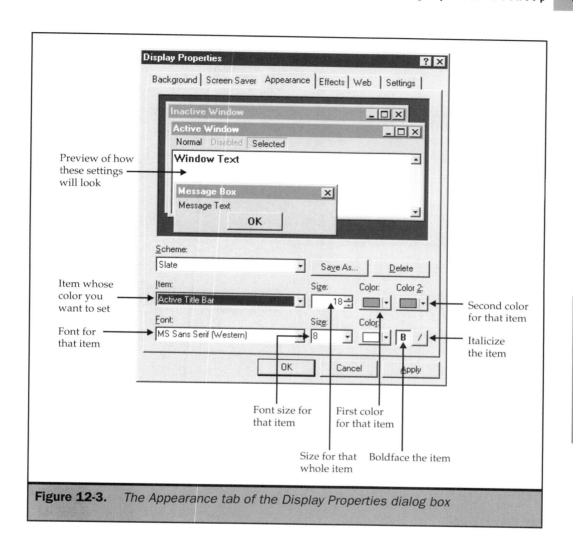

Figure 12-3.   *The Appearance tab of the Display Properties dialog box*

The number of basic colors has now tripled to 48, shown in a palette of little boxes on the left side of the Color dialog box. If the color you want is on this palette, click it, click OK, and then continue just as you would have if one of the original 16 colors had been satisfactory. But, if even the 48 colors aren't enough for you, you can use the right-hand side of the Color dialog box to get any color you want.

The currently selected color is shown in the Color I Solid box. To the right of the Color I Solid box are two different numerical systems of describing the current color: its hue, saturation, and luminescence (known as *HSV coordinates*; and its red, green,

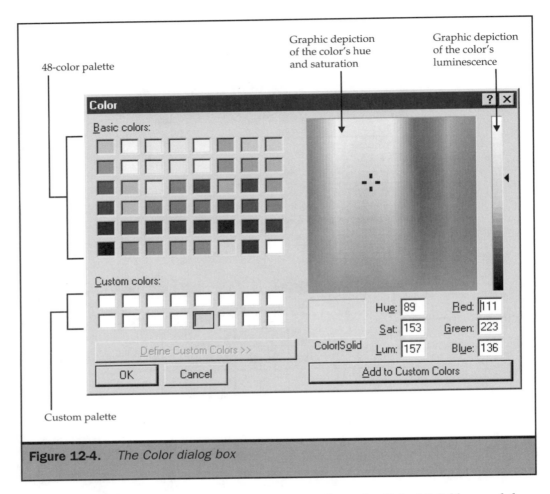

Figure 12-4.   *The Color dialog box*

and blue components (known as *RGB coordinates*). Above the Color | Solid box and the coordinates is a graphical representation of the current color's HSV coordinates. The horizontal position of the cross-hairs in the large square represents the hue, and the vertical position of the cross-hairs represents the saturation. The position of the vertical slider next to the square represents the luminescence.

Thus, the same color is represented three ways: as RGB, as HSV, and as a position of the cross-hairs and slider. You can select a new color by manipulating any of the three descriptions—move the cross-hairs and slider with the mouse, or type new numbers (from 0 to 239) into the HSV or (from 0 to 255) into the RGB coordinate boxes. However you specify the color, the other two descriptions (and the Color | Solid box) change automatically to match.

If you think you might want to use this color again in the future, click Add To Custom Colors rather than OK. The new color appears in one of the boxes in the Custom colors palette on the left side of the Color dialog box. If you like, you can define several custom colors, one at a time. Custom colors can be selected just like basic colors, by clicking them.

When you have created all the colors you want, select the one you want to use, and click OK. The color is applied and the Color dialog box vanishes.

Tip   *If your display is configured to display only 256 colors, pick only from the 48 basic colors.*

Choosing a Background Pattern

Patterns are simple 64-pixel, two-color images that interlock to give your background a textured appearance. The two colors are the background color and black. To choose or change your background pattern, follow these steps:

1. Click the Background tab of the Display Properties dialog box, which is shown (along with the Pattern dialog box) in Figure 12-2.

2. If the Pattern button is grayed out, your current wallpaper covers the entire background, making a background pattern irrelevant. The current wallpaper is probably stretched or tiled. Either choose Center from the Display list or set your wallpaper choice to None to reactivate the Pattern button.

3. Click the Pattern button. The Pattern dialog box appears, as shown in Figure 12-2.

4. Click the name of a pattern on the Pattern list to see what it looks like in the Pattern Preview window.

5. When you find a pattern you like, click OK. Then close the Display Properties dialog box.

Editing a Background Pattern

When none of the listed patterns is exactly what you want, you can create a new pattern by editing an existing one. Follow the instructions from the previous section until the Pattern dialog box appears in step 4. Then follow these steps:

1. Select the pattern you want to edit by clicking its name in the drop-down list.

2. Click the Edit Pattern button. The Pattern Editor dialog box appears, as shown in Figure 12-5. The box labeled Pattern is an 8×8 grid of pixels, each of which is either black or the background color.

3. Click any pixel to change it from one color to the other. As you change the pattern, the Sample box changes to preview how the new pattern will look on your screen.

4. When you have the pattern the way you want it, type a new name into the Name line of the Edit Pattern box and click Add. Your pattern is saved under the new name.

5. Click Done. You return to the Pattern dialog box.

CONFIGURING WINDOWS FOR YOUR COMPUTER

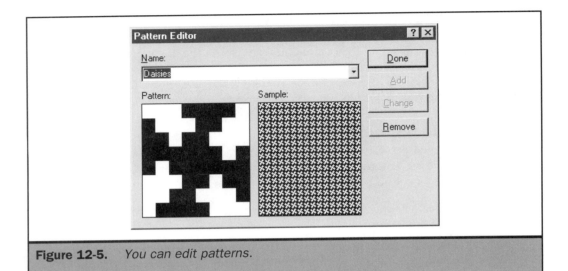

Figure 12-5.   *You can edit patterns.*

Choosing Sizes, Colors, and Fonts of Desktop Elements

You can choose much more than just the color of your background. In Windows, the color and font of almost anything is configurable—title bars, active windows, inactive windows, message boxes, you name it. You can make all these choices one by one, choose a scheme preselected by Microsoft's desktop decorators, or start with one of Microsoft's schemes and redefine one or two things.

The locus of all this power is the Appearance tab of the Display Properties dialog box, shown in Figure 12-3.

Selecting a Predefined Desktop Scheme

To select a desktop scheme (a group of preselected settings), click the scheme's name on the Scheme list of the Appearance tab of the Display Properties dialog box. The Preview window changes immediately to show you how the various components are displayed in this desktop scheme. Previewing a scheme by itself changes nothing, so feel free to check out as many schemes as you want. When you find one you like, click either Apply or OK to change your display settings to match the scheme.

Editing the Sizes, Colors, and Fonts of Desktop Elements

You can change the size, color, or font of elements individually. For example, you can make the Minimize, Maximize, and Close buttons larger or smaller, or change the color of the text on window title bars. To edit any of the screen elements that make up a desktop scheme, perform the following steps.

1. Click its name on the Scheme list of the Appearance tab of the Display Properties dialog box. To change the settings for the way the desktop looks now, skip this step.

2. Select an item to alter from the Item list (or click it in the Preview window). The Font, Size, or Color boxes become active to show what is configurable about this item. For example, when Desktop is the selected item, only the background color is configurable, so only the Color box is active. When Active Title Bar is selected, by contrast, you can select two colors and a size for the bar, as well as the size, color, font, and style of the text on the bar.

3. Using the rest of the boxes to the right of and below the Item box, change the way that item looks. (See the various settings you can use in Figure 12-3.)

4. When you alter anything in a desktop scheme, the scheme name vanishes from the Scheme window, indicating the altered desktop scheme hasn't been given a name and saved. To save your new scheme, click Save As and choose a name for it. You may give it the same name as the desktop scheme you altered (displacing that scheme in the Scheme list), or you can give it a new name. Using a new name is safer, in case you ever want to restore the previous color scheme.

5. To apply your changes, click Apply. To apply your changes and exit the Display Properties dialog box, click OK. To forget about the changes you made, click Cancel.

Choosing a Desktop Theme

A desktop theme not only provides a system of colors and fonts, but also offers sounds, icons, mouse pointers, a desktop background, and a screen saver as well (see "What Is a Desktop Theme?").

Desktop themes aren't part of the default installation of Windows, but adding them from the Windows Me CD-ROM is simple. Choose Start | Settings | Control Panel, run the Add | Remove Programs icon, click the Windows Setup tab, choose Desktop Themes from the list of components, and click OK. If desktop themes have been installed on your computer, a Desktop Themes icon appears on your Control Panel.

Selecting a Desktop Theme

To select a desktop theme:

1. Select Start | Settings | Control Panel. The Control Panel appears. If Desktop Themes is installed on your computer, you see a Desktop Themes icon.

2. Open the Desktop Themes icon in the Control Panel. The Desktop Themes dialog box opens, as shown in Figure 12-6.

3. Select the name of a theme from the Theme drop-down list. A preview of the theme appears in the Preview window below the Theme list. The theme's desktop background is the background of the Preview window. The colors and

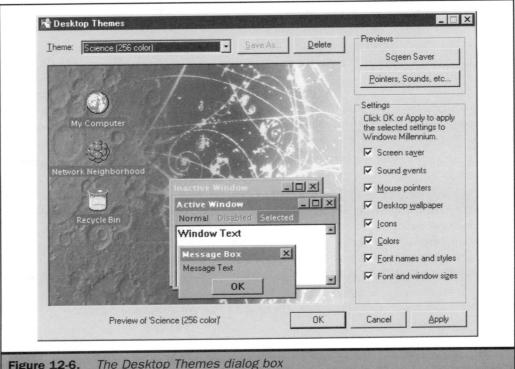

Figure 12-6. The Desktop Themes dialog box

fonts of various kinds of windows and message boxes are shown in the lower right of the Preview window. The scheme's custom icons are displayed on the left side of the Preview screen.

4. To preview the screen saver, click the Screen Saver button in the upper-right corner of the dialog box. To end the preview of the screen saver, move the mouse.

5. To preview the other aspects of the theme, click the Pointers, Sounds, Etc. button. The Preview (theme name) dialog box appears. The box has three tabs: Pointers, Sounds, and Visuals. Each tab contains a list of custom items. To preview a pointer or visual, click its name on the list and look at the preview window in the lower portion of the Preview dialog box. To try out a sound, click its name in the list and then click the arrow in the lower portion of the dialog box. Click Close to make the Preview Current Window Settings dialog box disappear.

6. When you are convinced you want to use a particular theme, examine the Settings portion of the Desktop Themes dialog box. Uncheck any of the boxes you don't want to apply. For example, if you like everything about a scheme except its sounds, uncheck the Sound Events box and leave the other Settings boxes checked.

7. Click OK. The Desktop Themes dialog box disappears and Windows applies the theme to your desktop.

If you decide you don't like the theme you've applied, return to the Desktop Themes dialog box and choose either the Windows Millennium or Windows Default theme.

Editing a Desktop Theme

The Desktop Themes dialog box doesn't let you edit a theme directly. However, you can edit any of the aspects of the theme (sounds, color scheme, icons, screen saver, background, and other elements) in the usual ways. When you have everything the way you want it, open Desktop Themes from the Control Panel. Select Current Windows Settings from the drop-down Theme list, and then click Save As to give your custom theme a name. Ever after, that theme will appear on the Theme list.

Finding New Themes

You aren't limited to the desktop themes Windows provides. You can download new themes from the Internet, often free. Check out C I NET's Web site at **http://www.download.com** in the Utilities department.

Setting Up a Screen Saver

When you aren't working on your computer, a screen saver can display something far more engaging and attractive than your desktop or your unfinished documents. To choose a screen saver:

1. Click the Screen Saver tab of the Display Properties dialog box, shown in Figure 12-7.

2. Select a screen saver from the drop-down list. The previewer shows you a miniaturized version of what the screen saver displays. Or, you can click the Preview button and see a full-size preview. Move the mouse or click a key to make the full-size preview stop.

3. When you find a screen saver you like, click either the Apply or OK button.

While you have the Screen Saver tab selected, you can make a number of choices about how your screen saver functions:

■ **Change the settings** by clicking the Settings button. Each screen saver has its own list of settings; some let you change a handful of parameters, while some have an entire screen full of choices for you to make. In general, the settings of your screen saver control how fast the screen saver cycles, the colors it uses, the thickness of the lines it draws, and so forth.

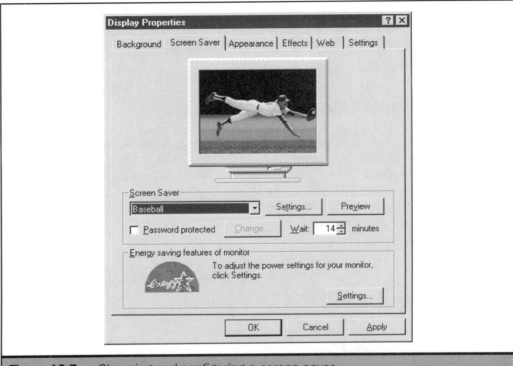

Figure 12-7.   *Choosing and configuring a screen saver*

■ **Change the wait time** for your screen saver by entering a new number of minutes into the Wait box. The *wait time* is the length of time your system must be inactive before the screen saver starts up. Windows waits this long for keyboard or mouse input before starting the screen saver.

■ **Add a password** to your screen saver by checking the Password Protected box. Remove password protection by unchecking the box. Change your password by clicking the Change button. If you have never established a screen saver password before, click Change to choose one.

Note   *Windows considers your screen saver password different from your login password. Changing one password doesn't automatically change the other.*

Windows comes with a choice of several screen savers, but that's just the beginning. Additional screen savers are available over the Internet, most of them free. You can begin your search at C|NET's Web site at **http://www.download.com**, which lists screen savers in the "utilities" department. Or, look at the Web site of your favorite TV show or movie to see whether there's a promotional screen saver. (Our current favorite is the raining–green-letters pattern from the movie *The Matrix*.)

To install a new screen saver, put the corresponding file of type screen saver (.scr) into the C:\Windows\System folder. The next time you look at the Screen Saver tab of the Display Properties dialog box, the new screen saver is on the drop-down list.

 Some screen savers use more system resources than others. Some use DirectX to create cool displays, but can take lots of room (over 1MB) on your disk.

Changing Display Settings

Windows gives you control over the dimensions of your desktop (in pixels, naturally, because the number of inches on your monitor is fixed), the color resolution of your display, the size of the standard fonts and icons, and many other properties. Most of this power resides on the Settings tab of the Display Properties dialog box, shown in Figure 12-8.

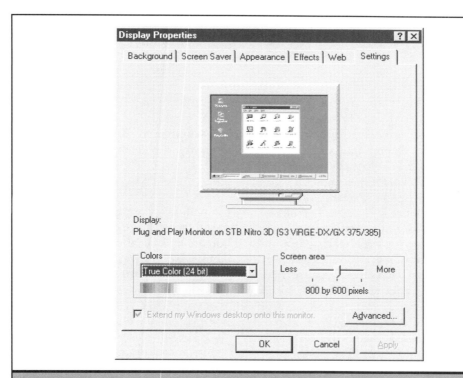

Figure 12-8.   *The Settings tab of the Display Properties dialog box*

Changing Resolution and Color Refinement

Resolution is controlled by the Screen Area slider on the Settings tab of the Display Properties dialog box. Your current desktop's dimensions (in *pixels*, or colored dots on the screen) are stated under the slider. Naturally, the size of your monitor doesn't change; so when you increase the number of pixels on your desktop, each pixel gets correspondingly smaller, increasing resolution. Icons and fonts shrink as well. As you increase desktop area, you may want to increase font and icon size to compensate (see "Changing Font Size"). The range of resolutions depends on what type of monitor you use. For a 14-inch monitor, your choices may range only from 640 × 480 to 800 × 600. For a 17-inch monitor, you can increase the resolution up to 1,024 × 768. Larger monitors support even higher resolutions, up to 1,600 × 1,200.

If you have a monitor larger than a basic 14 inches, consider increasing your screen resolution settings—you'll be able to see a lot more information on your screen. Here are our recommendations for screen resolution based on your monitor size (that is, the size of the CRT tube that can display an image, measured diagonally):

Screen Size	Maximum Usable Resolution
14 inches	640 × 480
15 inches	800 × 600
17 inches	1,024 × 768
19 to 21 inches	1,280 × 1,024 or 1,600 × 1,200

The Settings tab also controls the number of colors you display. The Colors drop-down list gives you choices that also depend on the quality of your monitor: your choices may include 16 colors, 256 colors, high color (16-bit, or 65,536 colors), 24-bit true color (16 million colors), and 32-bit true color (even more colors). Below the list is a color bar showing the spectrum under the selected color palette.

The choice to be made is a speed versus beauty tradeoff. Displaying fewer colors or pixels is less work for your computer and may help it run faster. More colors and pixels provide a richer viewing experience, particularly if you are looking at photographs—using 16-bit color or higher produces much-improved image quality. Colors and pixels also trade off against each other, because increasing either one uses more of the portion of RAM your system devotes to the display. Windows accounts for this automatically; if you increase the desktop area beyond the capabilities of your RAM, it decreases the color palette to compensate. Likewise, if you increase the color palette beyond what your RAM can handle, Windows decreases the desktop size.

Change the desktop area by moving the slider. Change the color palette by making a new choice from the drop-down list. Apply your changes by clicking the Apply button.

A few programs don't work properly with the new color palette until you restart your computer. In general, we recommend restarting your computer to be completely safe; but if you change the color palette frequently, this can get to be a nuisance. You may want to experiment to see whether the software you use has any problems when you don't restart after a color change. You can set up Windows to restart automatically when you change the color palette, ask you whether to restart, or not restart (see "Other Monitor Settings").

If you change your screen resolution or color palette often, you can add a Display Properties icon to your system tray. On the Settings tab of the Display Properties dialog box, click the Advanced button. On the General tab of the new dialog box that appears, click the Show Settings Icon On Task Bar check box. When you click OK, a Display Properties icon appears in the system tray on your Taskbar. Click the icon once to see a menu of screen resolutions and color palettes.

Changing Color Profiles

Subtle differences occur in the ways different monitor and printer drivers represent a color palette. These representation schemes are called *color profiles*. For most purposes, the difference between color profiles doesn't matter. But if you must be sure the colors you see on your monitor are exactly the colors you will get when you print, you can set the color profiles of your monitor and printer to reflect the exact way your monitor and printer render colors. Matching colors is especially important if you plan to edit and print photos.

Windows comes with profiles for many popular monitors, and a default profile called the *sRGB Color Space Profile* that matches most monitors reasonably well. Unless you are a graphic artist, you probably won't notice the difference between the default profile and a perfectly tuned one. We recommend 99 percent of users leave their color profiles alone.

To change the color profile of your monitor, click the Settings tab of the Display Properties dialog box and click the Advanced button. In the new window that opens, click the Color Management tab. Any profiles you have previously used are listed in the large window, with the current default profile in the box above the large window. To change to a new default color profile, select a new profile from the list and click the Set As Default button. To add a profile to the list, click the Add button and select from all the color profiles of which Windows is aware. To remove a profile from the list, select it and click the Remove button.

As on all the other tabs of the Display Properties dialog box, no changes are actually made until you click Apply or OK.

Changing Font Size

If the print in a book is too small to read, you can address the situation in two fundamentally different ways: get a large-type book or use a magnifying glass. Similarly, the fonts on your screen can be made larger or smaller in two fundamentally different ways: by changing point size or by changing the *magnification*. These two methods of changing fonts differ in two major ways:

- Changing point size is more specific—you can enlarge or shrink the text of title bars or menu bars, for example, and leave everything else alone. Changing font magnification changes the appearance of all fonts.

- Changing magnification affects the size of all screen elements.

 For higher magnification for the vision impaired, see Chapter 19.

Changing Point Size

The point size of the fonts used in any particular document is changed from within the applications that edit the document. The size of the fonts Windows uses in menus, title bars, and so forth, is controlled from the Appearance tab of the Display Properties dialog box. Click a text item in the Preview window, and then enter a larger number into the Size box next to the Font box.

Changing Magnification

Font magnification is controlled by displaying the Settings tab of the Display Properties dialog box, shown in Figure 12-8, and then clicking the Advanced button. You see a dialog box that displays settings that your display driver lets you change. For most display drivers, these settings include font size. A drop-down list gives you three choices: Small Fonts (defined as "normal" or 100 percent magnification), Large Fonts (125 percent magnification), and Other. Choosing Other opens a new dialog box, Custom Font Size. From this dialog box, you can type in whatever size you want, or change the size by using the ruler as a slider.

However you do it, click OK to return to the display driver's dialog box, where your chosen size is displayed under the Font Size box. If you like it, click Apply. If Windows doesn't restart your computer automatically, restart it yourself.

 Be careful choosing very large font magnifications. Changing the size of fonts changes the size of everything that contains text—like the Display Properties dialog box, for example. If you choose 200% font magnification and only have an 800-by-600 desktop, the Display Properties dialog box gets so large that the Apply button goes off the bottom of the screen.

Changing Icons

You can change the size or arrangement of the icons on your desktop. You can even define new icons for the various types of desktop objects.

Changing Icon Size

The Use Large Icons check box on the Effects tab of the Display Properties dialog box controls whether you use regular icons (32 points) or large icons (48 points). Icon size is also controllable from the Appearance tab (see Figure 12-3); but rather than choosing Large or Small, you can insert any point size between 16 and 72. Just choose Icon from the drop-down Item list, and then type a number into the Size box. (The next row of check boxes controls the font and size of the labels underneath your icons.) In either case, you have made an across-the-board change; you can't have some large icons and some small ones.

Arranging Icons on the Desktop

You can arrange your desktop icons manually by dragging-and-dropping them. If your system is set up for single-click opening, however, you may open the corresponding objects by mistake when you try to drag-and-drop icons. If you're having this problem, use right-click drag-and-drop. Select Move Here from the shortcut menu that appears when you drop the icon.

Arrange your desktop icons automatically by right-clicking any open spot on the desktop and choosing Arrange Icons from the shortcut menu. Windows arranges the icons in columns, starting on the left side of the desktop. The Arrange Icons menu gives you the option of arranging by name, type, size, or date. Make sure you really want the icons arranged in columns, however, because there is no "undo" selection on the Arrange Icons menu.

The final option on the Arrange Icons menu is Auto Arrange. If Auto Arrange is checked, the icons are arranged in rows and columns, and any new item is automatically ushered to the next open spot in the pattern. Auto Arrange prevents you from arranging your icons manually; any icon is whisked to the appropriate row or column as soon as you set it down.

You can control the spacing between icons in this automatic arrangement, as follows:

1. Click the Appearance tab of the Display Properties dialog box.
2. From the drop-down Item list, choose Icon Spacing (Horizontal) or Icon Spacing (Vertical).
3. Type a number (of points) into the Size box. Larger numbers create bigger spaces.
4. Click OK.

Changing the icon spacing affects the icon arrangement of Explorer windows, as well as the desktop.

Assigning New Icons

You can choose new icons for any of the standard desktop objects. Open the Effects tab of the Display Properties dialog box and find the type of icon you want to change in the Desktop Icons list. Just click an object from the list and select Change Icon, and then choose a new icon from the list, or browse for an icon file anywhere on your system. To change back, select the item again and click the Default Icon button. Having your own system of icons makes your computer substantially harder to use, so we recommend that you leave the default icons alone. To change all the standard Windows icons, you can use a desktop theme (see "What Is a Desktop Theme?" earlier in this chapter).

Deleting Desktop Icons

Most items on your desktop represent some kind of file or folder, and you can move or delete them just as you would move or delete any file or folder (see Chapter 8, section "Rearranging Files and Folders"). My Computer, My Network Places, and Recycle Bin, however, represent capabilities of your system, and Windows will not let you delete them.

Activating Your Desktop

Active Desktop lets your desktop do anything a Web page can do: contain pictures, text, links to other Web pages, sound, animation, or 3-D effects.

Central to Microsoft's vision of the Active Desktop is *push technology*—desktop items that are "subscribed" to information sources on the Internet. With push technology, information comes to your desktop continuously or on a schedule rather than because you looked for it and requested it. For example, the desktop in Figure 12-9 contains an ESPN sports scoreboard, a stock ticker from Microsoft Investor, a local weather forecast from Weather.com, and a headline ticker from the *New York Times.*

Active Desktop was introduced with great fanfare as part of Windows 98 and Internet Explorer 4; but, in general, users have been underwhelmed. The beauty of

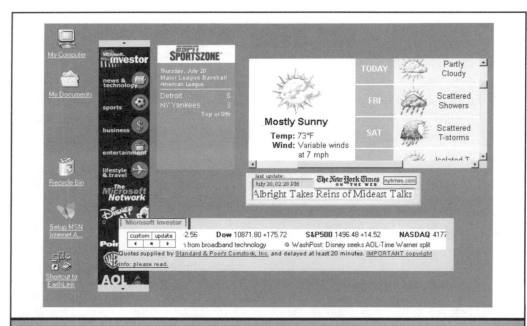

Figure 12-9.   *Your desktop can become a virtual newsroom.*

the Internet (as opposed to, say, television) is that it's a *pull* medium—you get the information you ask for when you ask for it. Also, desktop objects that move or flash can be distracting when you're trying to write e-mail to your girlfriend or a memo for your boss. You have to minimize your other windows to see the desktop. Many Active Desktop objects can use a lot of system resources and slow down your other programs. And, if you connect to the Internet by a dial-up modem, it's a little unnerving to have your computer suddenly make a phone call on its own to get the latest headlines.

At present, however, it's the more mundane features of Active Desktop that are the most attractive. Active Desktop enables you to use any image or HTML file as wallpaper, for example, rather than just .bmp files. The most striking of the wallpapers included with Windows Me require you to turn on Active Desktop, and some manufacturers include even more creative active backgrounds. The Sony Vaio, for example, comes with an ocean-view wallpaper that changes the position of the Sun (and its reflection off the water) every three hours.

Adding an Active Desktop Item

To add an item to your Active Desktop, follow these steps:

1. Right-click an empty spot on the desktop and select Active Desktop | New Desktop Item from the shortcut menu. The New Active Desktop Item Wizard opens.

2. The first screen of the Wizard gives you three ways to identify your new item. You can click the Browse button to look through your files to find an HTML document of an image file, type a URL into the Location box, or click the Visit Gallery button to visit Microsoft's online collection of desktop items. (That's where we found the stock ticker, sports scoreboard, and headline ticker in Figure 12-9.) Naturally, you can only visit the gallery if you are online.

3. When you have told the Wizard what item to add, you see the Add Item To Active Desktop dialog box. Click the Customize button to choose how often the item will be updated. Some items have their own recommended schedule, but you can always choose to have the item updated only when you request it (by choosing Synchronize from the Active Desktop menu) or on a schedule you create. Make your choice by clicking the appropriate radio button.

4. If you choose not to create a new schedule, you can now skip to step 6. If you are creating a new schedule, click Next. Set up your schedule by choosing a number of days and a time for the update to happen.

5. Decide whether you want the computer to connect to the Internet automatically at the chosen time and select the appropriate check box.

6. Click Finish. You return to the Add Item To Active Desktop dialog box. Click OK.

Updating Your Active Desktop Items

To update your Active Desktop items, right-click an empty spot on the desktop, and select Synchronize from the Active Desktop menu. When you synchronize an item, it checks the Web for any new information. For example, if a headline ticker is one of the items on your Active Desktop, it updates itself by checking the Web for new headlines.

Arranging and Removing Active Desktop Items

When you select an Active Desktop item, a bar appears above it. You can use this bar as you use a title bar to drag the window wherever you want. Click the X on that bar to close the window and make the item inactive. Restore it by right-clicking an empty spot on the desktop and selecting the item from the Active Desktop menu. Resize a window by dragging a corner. If you never want to see the item again, go to the Web tab of the Display Properties dialog box, shown in Figure 12-10. Select the item in the list of Active Desktop items and click the Delete button.

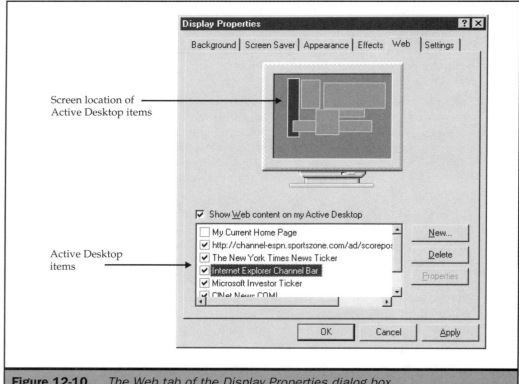

Figure 12-10.   *The Web tab of the Display Properties dialog box*

Turning Active Desktop On and Off

You can get rid of all the active items on your desktop by turning off Active Desktop. By doing this, you reserve the possibility of turning Active Desktop back on again and having everything just as it was. To turn Active Desktop on or off, right-click any empty spot on the desktop and select Active Desktop | Show Web Content from the shortcut menu. This is a toggle-switch: When it is checked, Active Desktop is on; and when it isn't checked, Active Desktop is off. Follow the same steps to turn Active Desktop back on again.

Equivalently, the Web tab of the Display Properties dialog box has a Show Web Content On My Active Desktop check box. If this box is not selected, all the stock tickers, headline-scrolling teletypes, weather maps, and so forth, vanish from your desktop. Restore them again by checking the box.

Getting Along with Your Monitor(s)

Windows can detect and install a driver for a plug-and-play monitor with little effort on your part (see Chapter 14, section "How Do You Add Hardware to a Windows Computer?"). Moreover, this monitor makes a variety of choices automatically, without you even needing to know a choice had to be made. In addition, many recent monitors comply with Energy Star power-saving standards, enabling you to choose to have Windows turn off the monitor if you have been inactive for a sufficiently long time. If you have two or more monitors hooked up to your computer, your desktop can stretch across all of them, and each can have its own settings.

Using Multiple Displays

Windows can handle two screens on a single system, displaying a single desktop that spans both screens. A pair of 15-inch monitors have considerably more screen area than a single 17-inch monitor and can be a cost-effective alternative to a single larger screen. (Similarly, a pair of 17-inch monitors provide more area than a 20-inch monitor, at a far lower cost.)

Configuring a second screen is straightforward once you install the new hardware (you need two display adapters, as well as two screens). Open the Settings tab of the Display Properties window, which now looks like Figure 12-11 if two display adapters are installed.

To configure the second display:

1. Click the picture of monitor number two to highlight it. Windows may display a box about extending the Windows desktop over two monitors. Click Yes and OK.

2. Drag the two pictures of monitors so they agree with the physical arrangement of your two screens.

CONFIGURING WINDOWS
FOR YOUR COMPUTER

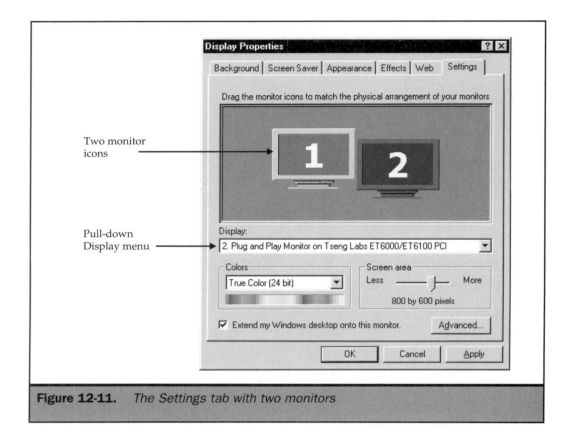

Two monitor
icons

Pull-down
Display menu

Figure 12-11. *The Settings tab with two monitors*

3. Configure the second display. If possible, configure the two displays to have the same number of colors and the same screen area, to avoid confusion when you move a window from one screen to another.

4. Click OK.

Windows configures the new display.

Once configured, the second display becomes part of the Windows desktop, and you can drag windows back and forth between the two displays. You can even have a single window that spans both screens, which can be convenient for looking at spreadsheets with wide rows. If you want to change the color depth or resolution of one of the monitors, click the monitor on the Settings tab of the Display Properties dialog box, and then change the settings.

Other Monitor Settings

Depending on the capabilities of your monitor, some other configuration settings are available. When you click the Advanced button on the Settings tab of the Display Properties window, you see a dialog box with a title based on the type of monitor you use. Settings may include

- **Show Settings Icon On Task Bar**   Displays a Display Properties icon in the system tray on the Taskbar, from which you can choose screen resolution and color palette.

- **After I Change Color Settings**   Determines what Windows does after you change the screen resolution or color palette on the Settings tab of the Display Properties dialog box. You can choose for Windows to restart automatically or for Windows to ask you first.

- **Monitor Is Energy Star Compliant**   Specifies this monitor can power down automatically after a period of inactivity.

- **Automatically Detect Plug & Play Monitors**   Specifies that Windows automatically detects which monitor driver to use. If this detection process causes your monitor to flash, deselect this option.

- **Reset Display On Suspend/Resume**   Specifies Windows reset the display once you resume using a computer (usually a laptop) that has been in standby mode.

- **Hardware Acceleration**   Specifies how fast Windows updates your screen.

- **Color Management**   Specifies the color profiles you have defined.

CONFIGURING WINDOWS
FOR YOUR COMPUTER

Chapter 13

Configuring Your Keyboard and Mouse

Windows Me, like all operating systems, sits between the programs you run and the computer you run them on. Whenever a program accepts input from the keyboard, mouse, or a game controller, or sends output to the screen or printer, Windows gets involved. As a result, when you configure Windows to work with your keyboard, mouse, or game controller, the settings you choose affect all the programs you run. You can choose the keyboard layout you want to use and set the sensitivity of the mouse.

Windows has a built-in calendar all programs can use. It knows the current date and time (usually displayed at the right end of the Taskbar), and understands time zones, U.S. daylight saving time, and leap years. You can set the date, time, and the time zone in which you are located, so the Windows calendar will be accurate.

Different countries use different currencies and formats for writing numbers, monetary amounts, dates, and times. Amazingly, Windows has regional settings that let it know about the formats used in most countries in the world (at least most of the countries where people are likely to use computers). By telling Windows which country you live in, you can cause Windows and most programs to use the date, time, and numeric formats with which you are comfortable.

You can change most of these settings by using the Keyboard, Mouse, and Regional Settings icons in the Control Panel (see Chapter 1, section "What Is the Control Panel?"). If you have installed a game controller or joystick, you can also check or change its settings.

Configuring Your Keyboard

For the keyboard, you can control the keyboard layout and how keys repeat. (You can also control how fast the cursor blinks, which is not actually a characteristic of the keyboard.)

What Are Keyboard Settings?

These settings shown in the following table, which appear on the Speed tab of the Keyboard Properties dialog box (shown in Figure 13-1), control how your keyboard works.

Setting	Description
Repeat delay	Delay between starting to hold down a key and when the key begins repeating
Repeat rate	How fast the key repeats once it starts repeating
Cursor blink rate	How fast the cursor blinks

You can also control which language layout the keyboard uses. Different languages use different letters and assign the letters to different locations on the keyboard. If you

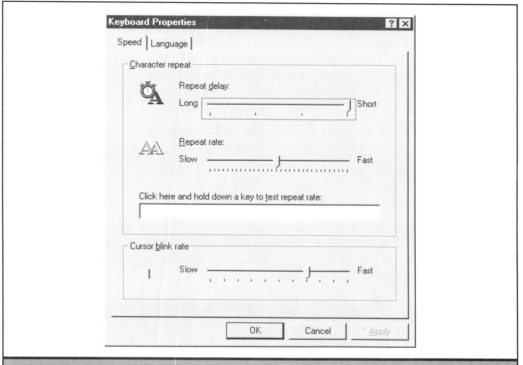

Figure 13-1. *The Keyboard Properties dialog box contains settings for the keyboard and the cursor.*

use more than one language, you can choose a key combination that switches between two keyboard layouts.

For some languages, Windows offers a selection of *keyboard layouts*, which define the physical organization of the keys on the keyboard. For example, if you choose U.S. English as your language, you can choose among layouts that include the standard 101-key layout, the Dvorak keyboard, and even the left-handed Dvorak keyboard.

To see or change the settings of your keyboard, choose Start | Settings | Control Panel. In the Control Panel window, open the Keyboard program (click the icon once or twice, depending on whether your desktop is configured for single- or double-click (see Chapter 1, section "Choosing Between Single-Click and Double-Click"). You see the Keyboard Properties dialog box shown in Figure 13-1.

Tip *Additional keyboard settings are available if you have trouble using the keyboard (see Chapter 19, section "Making the Keyboard More Accessible").*

Setting the Repeat Delay, Repeat Rate, and Cursor Blink Rate

Move the sliders on the Speed tab of the Keyboard Properties dialog box to set the repeat delay, repeat rate, or cursor blink rate. You can test how your keys repeat by clicking in the text box and holding down a key.

Installing Language and Keyboard Layouts

To choose which language and keyboard layout to use, click the Language tab of the Keyboard Properties dialog box (see Figure 13-2). To install additional layouts, click the Add button. When the Add Language dialog box appears, select a language from the drop-down list. If you have never installed this keyboard layout on this system, you may have to insert the Windows Me CD-ROM. To delete a language layout you no longer plan to use, click that language, and then click the Delete button.

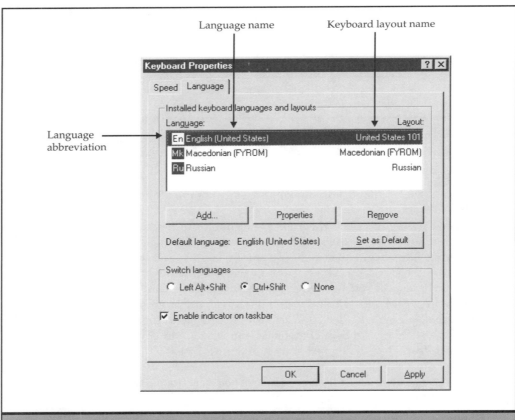

Figure 13-2.   *You can switch among several language layouts.*

If you install more than one language, you can choose one language to be the default for Windows; click that language, and then click the Set As Default button. Each language on the list has a two-letter abbreviation. When this keyboard layout is in use, the abbreviation appears on the system tray on the Taskbar.

 If you don't want the language abbreviation to appear on the system tray, click the Enable Indicator On Taskbar box to clear the check mark.

You can also set a key combination for switching among keyboard layouts. Your options are LEFT ALT-SHIFT (that is, the left-hand ALT key plus the SHIFT key), CTRL-SHIFT, or none. Another way to switch among the installed keyboard layouts is to click the language abbreviation on the Taskbar, and then choose a language from the menu that appears.

Choosing a Keyboard Layout

Even if you don't use a second language, you can use the Language tab of the Keyboard Properties dialog box to change your keyboard layout. You choose among a number of predefined layouts, including the standard 101-key layout and the Dvorak layout. In the Keyboard Properties dialog box, click the Language tab, click the language you use, and then click the Properties button. On the Language Properties dialog box that appears, choose a keyboard layout from the drop-down list. Click Apply or OK to activate your change.

Configuring Your Mouse

You can control what the mouse looks like, what its buttons do, and how fast the mouse pointer (the screen object that moves when you move the mouse) moves. You can define the shape of the mouse pointer, but not the cursor (the blinking element that shows where what you type will be inserted).

What Settings Control the Mouse?

The settings in the following table, which appear in the Mouse Properties dialog box, control how your mouse or trackball works.

Setting	Description
Button configuration	Right-handed (the default), in which the left button is for normal clicking-and-dragging and the right button is for displaying shortcut menus; or left-handed, in which the buttons' functions are reversed.

Setting	Description
Double-click speed	Time between double-clicks. If Windows frequently doesn't recognize your double-clicks, set this speed slower.
Pointer speed	How fast the mouse pointer moves when you move the mouse.
Pointer trail	Whether the mouse pointer leaves a shadowy trail behind it as it moves, and how long the trail should be. If you have trouble finding the mouse pointer, try giving it a trail.

You can also choose the shape the mouse pointer assumes when used for pointing, when Windows is busy (the hourglass), when you are typing, when selecting text, when clicking a Web link, when dragging window borders, and other functions. If you choose shapes other than the Windows default shapes, you can save the set of shapes you like to use as a *pointer scheme*. Windows comes with more than a dozen predefined pointer schemes from which you can choose. Here are some pointers from the 3-D Pointers scheme:

To see or change your mouse settings, choose Start | Settings | Control Panel. In the Control Panel window, open the Mouse program. You see the Mouse Properties dialog box, shown in Figure 13-3. (The dialog box may have other tabs, added by your mouse driver software.)

Additional mouse settings are available if you have trouble using your mouse (see Chapter 19, section "Setting Mouse Accessibility Options"). You might also consider installing a trackball or other pointing device.

Defining the Mouse Buttons

Normally, you click or double-click the left mouse button to select, open, or run items on the screen. You click the right mouse button to display the shortcut menu of commands about the item you clicked (see Chapter 2, section "Choosing Commands from Shortcut Menus"). Some programs use the right mouse button for other purposes.

If you are left-handed, you can reverse the meanings of the two buttons. In the Mouse Properties dialog box, click the Buttons tab, and click Left-handed. To switch back to the normal meanings, click Right-handed.

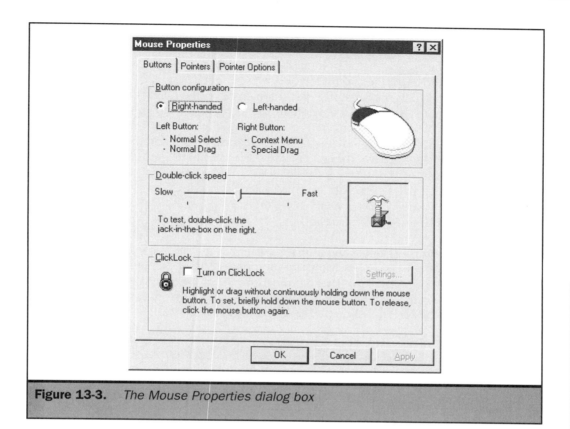

Figure 13-3.   *The Mouse Properties dialog box*

Defining Your Double-Click Speed

Windows defines a double-click as two clicks within a specified time period, with no mouse motion during that period. You can set the time period Windows uses. If you have trouble clicking fast enough for Windows to realize you want to double-click, make this time period longer. On the other hand, if you find two single clicks often get interpreted as a double-click, increase the double-click speed.

In the Mouse Properties dialog box, click the Buttons tab, and drag the Double-Click Speed slider to adjust the time period. To test the setting, double-click in the Test Area box. If you can make the jack-in-the-box come out or go back in, Windows is recognizing your double-clicks.

Configuring the Appearance of the Mouse Pointer

The mouse pointer changes shape depending on the context. For example, it appears as an arrow when you are selecting items, or as an *I* when you are editing text. You can choose the shape your mouse pointer assumes. In the Mouse Properties dialog box, click the Pointers tab to display a list of the current pointer shapes (see Figure 13-4). To choose a different set of pointer shapes (mouse pointer scheme), click in the Scheme box and choose one from the list. The list of pointer shapes shows the scheme you selected.

You can mix-and-match to assemble your own pointer scheme. Click an item in the Customize box, and then click the Browse button. Look in the folder C:\Windows\ Cursors for the cursors Windows knows. This folder contains two types of cursors: regular cursors (with the extension .cur) and animated cursors (with the extension .ani). If you want to go back to the default cursor, click an item, and then click the Use Default button. When you have things the way you want them, click the Save As button and give your new pointer scheme a name.

 Installing a Desktop Theme is another way to change all your pointers (see Chapter 12, section "Choosing a Desktop Theme").

You can also control whether the mouse pointer has a "trail" as it moves, making the pointer easier to see. Trails are useful on laptops and other displays that redraw the screen slowly. To turn the pointer trail on or off and to set the length of the trail, click the Pointer Options tab. Click the Show Pointer Trails check box to turn the trail on or off, and drag the Pointer Trail slider to the length you want.

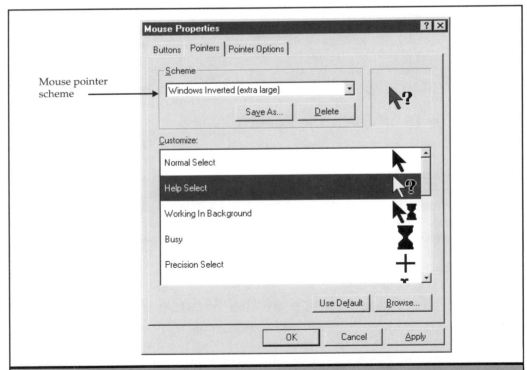

Figure 13-4. *Windows comes with predefined mouse pointer schemes.*

For animated cursors to work, your display must use at least 256 colors (to find out, choose Start | Settings | Control Panel, open the Display icon, and click the Settings tab) and your disk access must be 32-bit (choose Start | Settings | Control Panel, open the System icon, click the Performance tab).

To see how the new pointer scheme or pointer trails look, click the Apply button.

Setting the Mouse Speed

You can adjust how far the mouse pointer moves when you move the mouse. For example, if you move the mouse in a small area of your desk, you can adjust Windows to make the mouse very sensitive, so moving the mouse one inch (2.5 cm) moves the pointer halfway across the screen. If you have shaky hands, you can make the mouse less sensitive, so small motions of the mouse result in small motions of the pointer.

On the Mouse Properties dialog box, click the Motion tab and drag the Pointer Speed slider to adjust the mouse speed. To try out the new setting, click the Apply button.

If your mouse or trackball is unresponsive, it may require a low-tech solution like cleaning. Pop the ball out and look for accumulations of dust on the contacts.

Configuring Your Game Controller

Game controllers and *joysticks*—devices that enable you to play arcade-style games on your computer—come in many sizes and shapes. Windows includes drivers for many game controllers (see Chapter 14, section "What Are Drivers?").

To install a game controller, follow the instructions that come with it. Usually, you just shut down Windows, turn off the computer, plug the game controller or joystick into the game port on your computer, and turn on your computer again. Windows should recognize the new device and install it. Have the floppy disk or CD-ROM that came with the game controller handy, and insert it when Windows is looking for the driver.

To find out whether Windows has recognized your game controller or to change the settings for a game controller, choose Start | Settings | Control Panel. In the Control Panel window, run the Gaming Options program. You see the Gaming Options dialog box, shown in Figure 13-5.

If no devices are listed, Windows didn't recognize your game controller. Click the Add button in the Game Controllers dialog box to see the Add Game Controller dialog box, shown in Figure 13-6.

To specify the manufacturer and modem of your game controller, click the Add Other button, choose the manufacturer from the list, and then choose the device from the list. If your game controller came with a floppy disk or CD-ROM, click the Have Disk button and follow the instructions for installing the driver from the disk. Otherwise, choose the type of game controller you have (the number of buttons and axes the joystick can move) from the list in the Add Game Controller dialog box, and then click OK. Now the game controller appears on the list in the Gaming Options dialog box.

CONFIGURING WINDOWS FOR YOUR COMPUTER

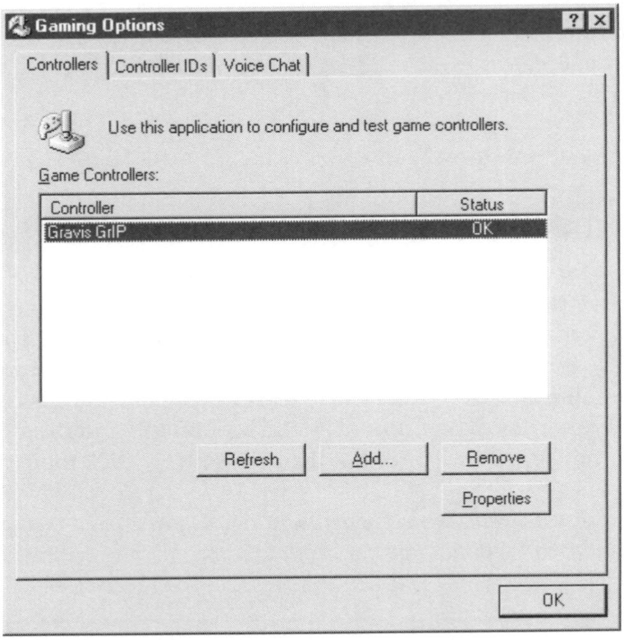

Figure 13-5. *The Gaming Options dialog box with a game controller installed*

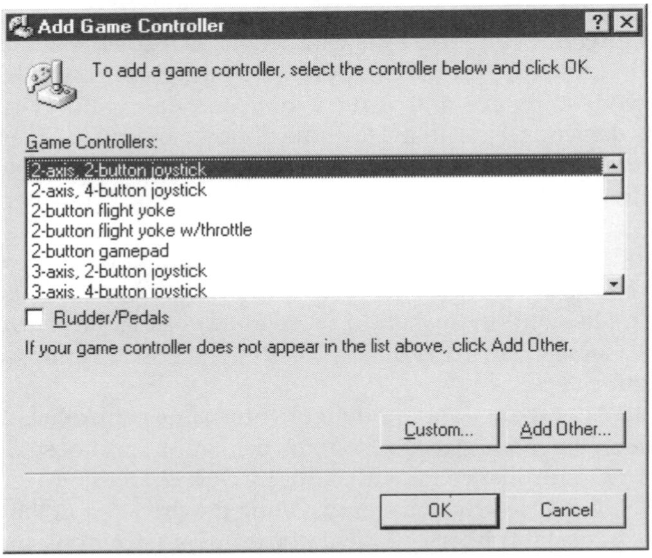

Figure 13-6. *Adding a game controller*

Displaying and Changing Game Controller Settings

To see the settings for your game controller, select it from the list in the Gaming Options dialog box and click Properties. You see the Game Controller Properties dialog box, shown in Figure 13-7.

One computer can have several game controllers attached. Each controller has an ID number, starting with 1. You can see and change the controller ID numbers by clicking the Advanced tab in the Games Controllers dialog box.

Testing Your Game Controller

To test your game controller, select it from the list in the Game Controllers dialog box, click Properties, and click the Test tab in the Game Controller Properties dialog box (see Figure 13-7). Move the joystick or yoke and see whether the cross-hairs in the Axes box move. Click the buttons on the game controller and see whether the button indicators light up. If not, calibrate the game controller by clicking the Settings tab, clicking the Calibrate button, and following the instructions.

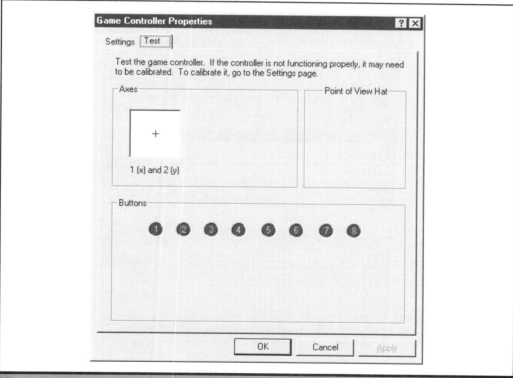

Figure 13-7.   *You can calibrate and test your game controller from the Game Controller Properties dialog box.*

Windows' Regional Settings

Windows comes with predefined regional settings for most of the countries in the world. *Regional settings* affect the format of numbers, currency, dates, and times. For example, if you choose the regional settings for Germany, Windows knows to display numbers with dots between the thousands and a comma as the decimal point, to use deutsche marks as the currency, and to display dates with the day preceding the month.

 The International tab in the System Configuration Utility window enables you to select keyboard drivers for other languages (see Chapter 36, section "Changing Your International Settings").

To see or change your regional settings, choose Start | Settings | Control Panel. In the Control Panel window, open Regional Settings. You see the Regional Settings Properties dialog box, shown in Figure 13-8.

Telling Windows Where You Live

Windows has predefined sets of regional settings, so you needn't select numeric, currency, date, and time formats separately. Click the Regional Settings tab in the

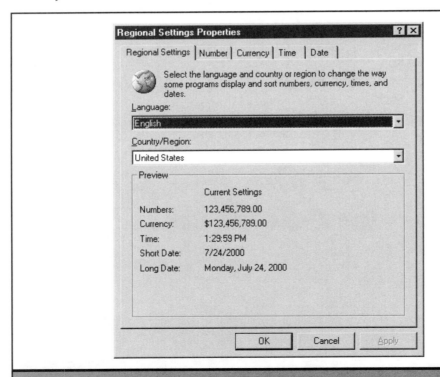

Figure 13-8. *The Regional Settings Properties dialog box*

Regional Settings Properties dialog box, and choose the language you speak and the country where you live.

Setting Number, Currency, Time, and Date Formats

After telling Windows which language you speak and where you live, you can see and change the individual settings that control how Windows displays numbers, currency, times, and dates. Click the Number, Currency, Time, and Date tabs in the Regional Settings Properties dialog box to see or change these settings.

Numbers

The following table shows the settings on the Number tab of the Regional Settings Properties dialog box that tell Windows how you write numbers.

Setting	Description
Decimal symbol	Which character appears as the decimal point, separating the whole from the fractional portion of numbers. (In the U.S., this is a dot.)
No. of digits after decimal	How many digits usually appear to the right of the decimal symbol.
Digit grouping symbol	Which character appears to group digits into groups in large numbers. (In the U.S., this is a comma.)
No. of digits in group	For large numbers, the number of digits in a group between digit grouping symbols. (In the U.S., this is three.)
Negative sign symbol	Which character indicates negative numbers. (In the U.S., this is the minus sign –.)
Negative number format	Where the negative sign symbol appears. (In the U.S., the negative sign symbol appears to the left of the number.)
Display leading zeroes	For numbers between –1 and 1, whether to display a zero before the decimal symbol. (In the U.S., a zero is displayed; for example, 0.4.)
Measurement system	Whether you use the U.S. or metric system of measurements.
List separator	Which character to use to separate items in lists, for entering lists in Windows text boxes. (The Windows default for the U.S. is a comma.)

CONFIGURING WINDOWS
FOR YOUR COMPUTER

Currency

The following settings on the Currency tab of the Regional Settings Properties dialog box control how Windows displays currency (money).

Setting	Description
Currency symbol	Symbol that indicates which currency is in use for amounts of money. (In the U.S., this is $.)
Position of currency symbol	Where the currency symbol appears with respect to the number. In the list of options for this setting, a special symbol represents the currency symbol. (In the U.S., the currency symbol appears to the left of the amount.)
Negative number format	How Windows formats negative amounts of money. (In the U.S., accountants usually enclose negative amounts of money in parentheses.)
Decimal symbol	Which character appears as the decimal point in amounts of money, separating the whole from the fractional portion of numbers. (In the U.S., this is a period.)
No. of digits after decimal	How many digits appear to the right of the decimal symbol in amounts of money. (In the U.S., this is two, so dollars and cents are displayed.)
Digit grouping symbol	Which character appears to group digits into groups in large amounts of money. (In the U.S., this is a comma.)
Number of digits in group	For large amounts of money, the number of digits in a group between digit grouping symbols. (In the U.S., this is three.)

Time Formats

This table shows your options for displaying the time (the settings are on the Time tab of the Regional Settings Properties dialog box).

Setting	Description
Time style	Format for displaying times. In the sample, *h* represents the hour, *hh* the hour with leading zeros, *H* the hour using the 24-hour clock, *HH* the hour using the 24-hour clock and leading zeros, *mm* the minutes, *ss* the seconds, and *tt* the AM/PM symbol. (In the U.S., the format is *h:mm:ss tt*, for example, 2:45:03 PM.)
Time separator	Which character separates the hours, minutes, and seconds. (In the U.S., this is :.)
AM symbol	Which characters or symbols indicate times before noon. (In the U.S., the default is AM.)
PM symbol	Which characters or symbols indicate times after noon. (In the U.S., the default is PM.)

Date Formats

The following table shows your options for displaying the date (the settings are on the Date tab of the Regional Settings Properties dialog box).

Calendar type	Which calendar your computer uses (usually the Gregorian Calendar and not editable).
When a two digit year is entered, interpret as a year between *xxx* and *xxx*	How two-digit years are converted to four-digit years (usually 1930 to 2029). Changing the end year also changes the beginning year.
Short date style	Short format for displaying dates. In the sample, *M* represents the month number with no leading zeros, *MM* the month number with leading zeros displayed, *MMM* the three-letter abbreviation for the month name, *d* the day with no leading zeros, *dd* the day with leading zeros displayed, *yy* the two-digit year, and *yyyy* the four-digit year. (In the U.S., this is *M/d/yyyy*, for example, 12/25/2000.)
Date separator	Which character separates the month, day, and year. (In the U.S., this is /.)
Long date style	Long format for displaying dates. In the sample, *dddd* represents the name of the day of the week, *MMMM* the name of the month, *dd* the day number, and *yyyy* the four-digit year.

Setting the Current Date and Time

Windows is good at keeping its clock and calendar correct. It knows about U.S. daylight saving time and leap years. But, depending on where you live and the accuracy of your computer's internal clock, you may occasionally need to reset Windows' clock or calendar.

To display the Date/Time Properties dialog box, shown in Figure 13-9, double-click the time on the Taskbar (usually displayed at the right end of the Taskbar). Or, you can choose Start | Settings | Control Panel. In the Control Panel window, open Date/Time.

To set the date or time:

- **Year** Click the year, and then type a new year or click the up and down arrow buttons to move the year forward or backward.

- **Month** Click the month and choose the correct month from the list that appears.

- **Day** Click the day number on the calendar.

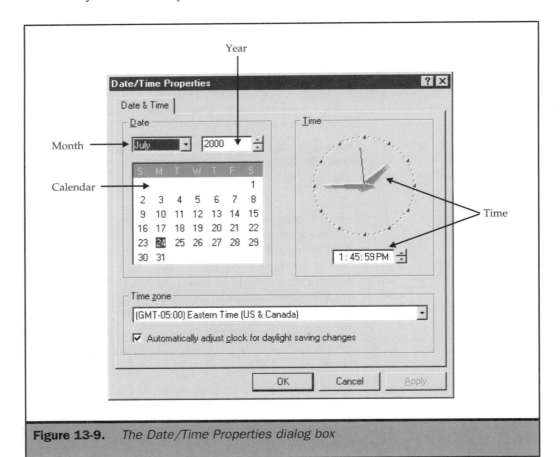

Figure 13-9. *The Date/Time Properties dialog box*

■ **Hour, minute, or second**   Click the hour, minute, or second section of the digital clock, and then type a new value or click the up or down arrows.

■ **AM or PM**   Click the AM or PM at the right end of the time, and then type the new value. Or, click the up or down arrow to the right of the time.

■ **Time zone**   Click the box that shows the time zone and choose a new time zone. If you want Windows to adjust the clock an hour for daylight saving time in the spring and fall, click the Automatically Adjust Clock For Daylight Saving Changes check box at the bottom of the window, so a check appears in the box.

Chapter 14

Adding and Removing Hardware

Windows Me lets you add new hardware to your computer relatively easily, but you still have a lot of details to get right. This chapter describes the general steps for installing hardware, the types of hardware you may want to install, how to configure Windows to work with new hardware (including modems), troubleshooting hardware, and adding memory.

How Do You Add Hardware to a Windows Computer?

Most Windows computers let you add extra hardware to extend your computer's capabilities. Some hardware fits inside your computer; some plugs into existing connectors on the back of the computer; and some requires adding a card inside your computer, into which you plug external equipment. After you add the device, you need to configure Windows to use your new hardware.

Adding hardware is a three-step process:

1. Set any switches and jumpers on the new equipment as needed.
2. Turn off and unplug the computer, open it up, install internal cards if needed, put the computer back together, and plug in external equipment.
3. Turn on the computer and tell Windows about the new equipment.

 Before adding new hardware, make a backup of your important files, in case you can't restart your computer (see Appendix B).

What Types of Hardware Can You Install?

IBM-compatible computers, having evolved for over 15 years, offer far too many ways to attach new kinds of equipment. The details of PC hardware are beyond the scope of this book, but this section describes the basics of PC hardware that you need to know to get a recalcitrant Windows driver installed, including older types of PC components, in case you are upgrading an older computer. See Chapter 10 for more information about configuring hard disks.

Integrated Versus Separate Peripherals

The original IBM Personal Computer contained nothing built into the computer beyond the *central processing unit* (*CPU*), memory, and keyboard. Everything else, including screens, floppy disk drives, hard disk drives, printers, modems, and serial ports, was provided by separate extra-cost add-in cards. (Hardware you add to your computer, other than processors and memory, is called a *peripheral*.) Over the years, manufacturers have found that, as the functions of the computer were combined into fewer and fewer chips, it became cheaper to build the most common peripherals into the computer's *motherboard* or *system board*, the printed circuit board that carries the CPU and memory. Modern computers typically include a parallel port, one or two serial ports, two *PS/2* ports, two *Universal Serial Bus* (*USB*) ports, controllers for up to two floppy disk drives and four IDE devices (typically hard drives, CD-ROM drives, CD-R drives, or DVD drives), a 56K modem, and sound and video adapters on the motherboard. Windows usually can't tell whether these items are built in or on separate cards, so Windows treats them all as though they are separate peripherals.

Connectors

The back of your PC is bristling with connectors for various sorts of devices (see Figure 14-1). If your computer has internal *expansion slots* (slots into which you insert an adapter card), each card in an expansion slot may have a connector or two, as well. Connectors to which you connect cables are also called *ports*. Most likely, the user's manual for your computer has a similar picture showing and labeling the connectors on your computer.

CONFIGURING WINDOWS
FOR YOUR COMPUTER

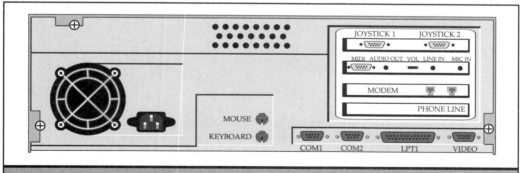

Figure 14-1.   *Connectors on the back of your computer*

Serial (Com) Ports

Most PCs have one or two *serial ports* or *com ports*, which are D-shaped connectors
with 9 or 25 pins (sometimes referred to as *DB-9* and *DB-25*):

Most commonly, you plug an external modem into a serial port, but serial ports are
also used for serial mice; computer-to-computer cabling for "poor man's networking";
and, occasionally (but rarely), for printers.

Telephone Plugs

If your computer has an *internal modem*, it installs inside your computer. If you have
an *external modem*, it is a separate box that connects to one of your computer's serial or
USB ports, as well as getting power from a wall plug. Either way, your modem has one
or two *RJ-11* telephone plugs that are identical to the plugs on the back of a U.S.
telephone.

If there are two plugs, one is for the incoming phone line plugged into the wall,
and the other is for a phone that shares the line with the modem. (The advantage to
plugging the phone in via the modem is that, while the modem is online, the phone
is disconnected, so you won't mess up your modem call if you pick up the phone by
mistake.)

Parallel Ports

Most PCs have a *parallel port*, a D-shaped socket with holes for 25 pins. Parallel ports
are used for printers, and sometimes for other devices, such as removable disk drives
(such as ZIP drives).

    *The 25-pin serial port is mechanically identical to the parallel port, except that the serial
port is "male" and the parallel port is "female." Despite the similar connectors, you
can't plug a device intended for one port into the other port.*

PS/2 (Keyboard/Mouse Ports)

All PCs have a connector for the keyboard and nearly all PCs have a connector for a
mouse. There are two kinds of keyboard connectors: the older, larger AT connector
(rarely found on computers new enough to run Windows Me) and the newer, smaller
PS/2 connector. (These types of round connectors are also called *DIN connectors*, for
the German standard-setting agency that named them.)

The mouse port is identical to the PS/2 keyboard port. You can plug a keyboard with an AT connector into a PS/2 keyboard port, or vice versa, using an inexpensive adapter plug. On computers with identical PS/2 and keyboard connectors, it's not supposed to matter which one you plug into which port, although on a few computers, it does matter nonetheless.

A few older computers use a 9-pin connector for the mouse and provide a 9–pin-to-round-mouse connector adapter. Although the 9-pin connector is physically identical to a serial port, it's electrically different. Since these older computers generally aren't powerful enough to run Windows Me, you probably won't run into them.

VGA Ports

VGA and Super VGA screens use a 15-pin (*DB-15*) connector that is similar in size to the 9-pin serial connector.

All VGA and Super VGA screens made in recent years use the same plug and are compatible with all screen controllers, at least at lower resolutions such as 640×480 (that is, 640 pixels, or dots, across the screen and 480 pixels vertically). Almost all can also display 800×600, and many can display higher resolutions like $1,024 \times 768$ or $1,280 \times 1,024$. The video display adapters that are built into new computers can support lots of colors beyond the original 256 colors (also known as 8-bit color); most can display 16-bit High Color, 24-bit True Color, and 32-bit True Color.

Multiple Displays

Windows can support more than one display (screen or monitor), continuing the Windows desktop from one display to the next. You need a video display adapter for each display (see Chapter 12, section "Using Multiple Displays").

Universal Serial Bus (USB)

The *Universal Serial Bus* (*USB*) is a new connector for which Microsoft introduced full support in Windows 98. It is intended to be a faster and simpler replacement for serial and parallel ports, as well as for low- to moderate-speed devices such as modems, printers, sound cards, and backup tapes. Few older computers come with USB ports.

The USB uses a small rectangular connector. Unlike most other connection schemes, USB lets you connect a *USB hub* to your USB port, so you can have a desk full of USB devices, even though your computer has only a single USB connector. Also remarkable is the fact that you can *hot swap* USB devices—you don't have to turn off the computer, plug in the device, and restart the computer; just plug the device in and turn it on.

Audio Jacks

Multimedia PCs have connectors for speakers or headphones, and sometimes a microphone. The speaker connector is a standard 1/8-inch stereo mini-audio jack. The microphone connector is usually also a mini-audio jack, so you have to be careful not to confuse the two. (Otherwise, your sound may play sdrawkcab. Well, not really.)

If your computer doesn't have speaker connectors, you can add an internal sound board. Many CD-ROM drives have headphone jacks so you can listen to audio CDs, even if your computer has no speakers.

PC Cards

Laptop computers usually have one or two *PC card* slots (also known as *PCMCIA* slots). A few desktop computers have them, too. These take credit-card–sized adapter cards of many varieties, including modems, networks, and disk and tape controllers. PC cards, unlike other adapter cards, can be added to, and removed from, your computer while it's running. To add a PC card, press it firmly into the slot until it seats. To remove a PC card, press the button next to the PC card to eject the card slightly and then pull out the card.

Before removing a PC card, you should first tell Windows, so that it can stop sending data to, or receiving data from, the card. To see the status of your PC cards, choose Start | Settings | Control Panel and run the PC Card (PCMCIA) icon (see "Installing PC Cards," later in this chapter).

FireWire

Some systems also supply *FireWire* ports, also known as *IEEE 1394* or Sony *i.Link*. They are typically used for digital video cameras, hard disk drives, and high-speed printers. FireWire was first developed by Apple for its computers, but is now available on many Windows-compatible PCs, too. FireWire cables are limited to about 15 feet long. FireWire, like USB, is also capable of being connected and disconnected without having to power down the computer host (that is, it allows hot swapping devices). Co-founder Steve Jobs gave a dramatic demonstration of this capability at the MacWorld convention in 1998 by booting a PowerMac from a FireWire drive, and removing the cable in the middle of the boot process and plugging it back in some three minutes later to allow the boot to complete. FireWire is efficient, self-powered, flexible, and very fast.

Internal Adapter Cards

If you add a device to your computer that can't be plugged into one of the existing connectors on your computer, you have to add an *adapter card* that plugs into a slot inside the computer.

As the PC has evolved over the past 15 years, the slots into which you can plug adapter cards have evolved as well.

ISA and EISA Cards

The original IBM PC and PC/AT defined what now are known as *Industry Standard Architecture* (*ISA*) slots, into which you plug ISA cards. An ISA slot has a two-part connector. The oldest 8-bit cards plug into the front part only, while newer (post-1983) 16-bit cards plug into both parts. Most ISA cards are configured manually; that is, you have to set the hardware parameters for the card by flipping little switches on the card or by plugging and unplugging little jumpers on the card. This manual configuration is, by far, the most tedious and error-prone part of hardware installation, and usually requires considerable manual trial and error to make it work.

Fortunately, most newer computers don't have ISA slots. PC manufacturers introduced *EISA* (*Enhanced* or *Extended ISA*) cards, an improved version of ISA slots that have now been superseded by the even newer PCI cards.

PCI Cards

PCI (*Personal Computer Interface*) slots are a modern replacement for ISA, and accept PCI cards. They are better than ISA in every way—smaller, faster, cheaper to manufacture, more reliable, and much easier to set up. A PCI connector is about half the size of an ISA connector, due to a much more advanced design. Whenever possible, use PCI cards rather than any other kind in your PC, because they're a lot easier to set up and they work better.

Other Kinds of Cards

Most computers have a few specialized slots and connectors for specific devices. There are usually four small slots for memory, and a connector or two for IDE or EIDE expansion disks (see "IDE and SCSI Devices"). Your computer's manual should list the available slots and connectors.

Hardware Parameters

Every card in your PC needs a variety of hardware parameters to be set, so that the CPU can communicate with the card reliably and without interfering with other cards. With the newer kinds of connections, such as PCI and USB, most—if not all—of these parameters are set automatically; but older ISA cards and some PCI cards require manual tweaking.

To see a list of your computer's hardware, choose Start | Settings | Control Panel, run the System icon, select the Device Manager tab, click the first entry (Computer), and click the Properties button. You see the Computer Properties dialog box, shown in Figure 14-2. You can click the radio buttons at the top of the dialog box to see a listing of the interrupts (IRQs), I/O addresses, DMA channels, or memory addresses.

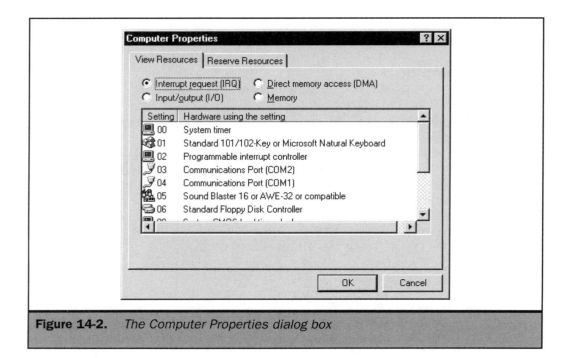

Figure 14-2.   *The Computer Properties dialog box*

    Keep a logbook for your computer, listing all the cards installed in your computer and the hardware parameters you've set on them. This makes troubleshooting a lot easier.

I/O Address

Every device attached to a PC has at least one *I/O address*, a hexadecimal number that the CPU uses to communicate with the device. All I/O addresses on a given computer must be unique; address "collisions" are the most common reason that a new I/O device doesn't work.

Devices on the motherboard have I/O addresses that either are permanently assigned or can be changed in the setup menus built into your motherboard (see the documentation that came with your computer). Devices on ISA cards have addresses that generally can be changed by moving jumpers on the card, while PCI cards have addresses that are set by software when you start your computer.

All traditional PC devices have well-known fixed addresses. These include up to four serial ports, a parallel port, floppy and hard disk controllers, and internal devices such as the clock and keyboard controller. Other add-in devices have more-or-less fixed addresses, depending on how popular the device is and how long it's been around. PCI cards automatically get unique addresses, but ISA cards often need jumpers to be reset.

See the troubleshooting section later in this chapter for advice on getting I/O addresses unscrambled.

 AGP, the Advanced Graphics Port technology from Intel, is a derivative of PCI. AGP video cards appear in the hardware list as device 1 of PCI Bus 0. This is normal, despite the name AGP.

Interrupts

The PC architecture provides 15 *interrupts*, channels that a device can use to alert the CPU that the device needs attention. The interrupts are numbered 0, 1, and 3 through 15. (For historical reasons, interrupt 2 isn't available, and the few devices that used interrupt 2 on early PCs use interrupt 9 instead.) PCI devices all can, and usually do, share a single interrupt, but nearly every ISA device that uses an interrupt needs a separate unique interrupt number. Motherboard devices use interrupts 0 and 1; built-in serial ports usually use 3 and 4; the floppy disk uses 6; the parallel port uses 7; the clock uses 8; a built-in mouse uses 12; the floating-point unit uses 13 (even if you don't do any floating-point calculations); and the hard disk controller uses 15—leaving 5, 9, 10, 11, and 14 for other devices. Assigning interrupts correctly on ISA cards is one of the most troublesome and error-prone parts of hardware configuration. A few ISA cards can have their interrupt number set in software, in which case Windows sets the interrupt automatically; but most have jumpers you have to change. Fortunately, only a few ISA cards are still available commercially; but, otherwise, everything else is PCI based.

DMA Channels

DMA, which stands for *Direct Memory Access*, is a motherboard facility used by a few medium-speed devices. There are six DMA channels, of which the floppy disk always takes DMA 2. Some sound cards need a DMA channel, usually DMA 1.

Memory Addresses

Each byte of memory in your computer has a unique *memory address*. A few devices, notably screen controllers and some network cards, use a shared memory region to transfer data between the CPU and the device. Those devices need a range of memory addresses for their shared memory. Screen cards generally use the ranges (expressed in hexadecimal numbers, or hex) 0xA0000 through 0xAFFFF, 0xB0000 through 0xBFFFF, and sometimes 0xC0000 through 0xCFFFF. The range from the end of the screen controller's memory to about 0xE0000 is available for other devices. Some ISA cards have their memory addresses set in software, in which case Windows sets the addresses automatically; but others have jumpers you have to change. PCI (and AGP) cards always have their addresses set in software.

IDE and SCSI Devices

IDE and SCSI disk controllers present an extra challenge, because you can attach more than one device to a single controller. See Chapter 10 for more information about configuring hard disks.

IDE Device Numbers

IDE (which stands for *Integrated Drive Electronics*) disk controllers support up to two devices, the first of which is usually a hard disk, and the second of which can be either a hard disk or a CD-ROM drive. The controller has two connectors into which drive cables are plugged, and which device is which depends on which connector each is plugged into. The first device is called the *primary* device, and the second the *secondary* device.

Most motherboards contain two IDE controllers, each of which can have a primary and secondary device, for a system total of four devices.

SCSI Device Numbers

Each *SCSI* (*Small Computer Systems Interface*) controller can connect up to 7 devices for older controllers, or 15 devices for more recent controllers. To identify devices attached to one SCSI controller, each device has a device number from 0 to 7, or 15.

The SCSI controller itself has a device number, usually the highest possible number—7 or 15. The first disk is invariably device 0, but other numbers can be assigned arbitrarily, as long as each device has a separate number. A few devices have subunits, such as tape or CD-ROM jukebox drives that can contain several different tapes or disks.

The Many Flavors of SCSI

Since SCSI has evolved over the years to support bigger and faster devices, several varieties have appeared: regular, wide, fast/wide, and ultra. The differences are mostly invisible to Windows, so your main concern is that your devices are compatible with the controller. If their cables use compatible connectors, the devices are almost certainly compatible.

On PCs there are also internal and external SCSI devices, depending on whether the device is housed inside the PC or in a separate cabinet. An external device is merely an internal device installed in a separate cabinet. The important difference is that internal and external SCSI cables are different: internal cables are ribbon cables and external cables are thick round cables with a variety of connectors. Again, as long as the connectors match, the devices should be compatible.

 Due to some extremely bad planning in the early 1980s, older external SCSI devices use connectors that are physically identical to the DB-25 and Centronics connectors used on modems and printers on parallel and serial ports. Even if they fit physically, don't try connecting a SCSI device to a non-SCSI controller, or vice versa, because it won't work, and you may well cause expensive damage to the electronics.

Memory (RAM)

Memory, or *RAM* (*random access memory*), is the temporary storage your computer uses for the programs that you are running and the files you currently have open. Most PCs have four special memory slots, and usually the computer is shipped with one or two of the four slots already containing memory. Memory comes in many different sizes, speeds, and types, so you must ensure that the memory you add is compatible with your particular computer (see the section "Adding Memory," later in this chapter). Memory chips are extremely sensitive to static electricity, so be sure to understand and follow the procedures needed to avoid static damage. (Some memory ships with an anti-static wrist strap and instructions on how to use it.)

What Are Drivers?

Many hardware devices—whether they come as part of your computer or are added later—require a *driver* or *device driver*, a program that translates between your operating system (Windows) and the hardware. For example, a printer driver translates printing requests from Windows (and through it, your applications) to commands that your printer can understand.

Windows comes with standard drivers for a wide range of monitors, printers, modems, and other devices. When you buy hardware, you usually receive a floppy disk or CD-ROM that contains the driver for the device, which you need to install during the configuring process to get the device to work with Windows. For some devices, Windows already has a driver on the Windows Me CD, so you never need to insert the driver disk.

Configuring Windows for New Hardware

In most cases, Windows 98 could identify and configure new hardware automatically. Windows Me does an even more reliable job of automatic configuration, because it shares a technical heritage in this respect with Windows 2000. *Universal Plug and Play* helps Windows Me automatically detect and configure itself for a wider range of hardware devices.

Follow these steps to install new hardware and configure Windows to use it (see the next section if you are installing a PC card):

1. Shut down your computer, turn it off, unplug it, and install your new hardware. This can involve opening up the computer and installing a card, inserting a card into a PC card slot, or just plugging a new external device into a SCSI adapter or USB plug. Follow the directions that come with the new hardware.

2. Turn on the device (if external), and turn on and start up your computer. PCI and SCSI devices usually have a BIOS setup routine that you have to enter when you

turn on the computer and run one time to do low-level configuration of your new device.

3. If you're lucky, Windows notices the new device as it starts and automatically configures it for you.

4. If you're less lucky, Windows just starts up. Run the Add New Hardware Wizard, described in the next section.

5. If you're unlucky, Windows doesn't start at all, or starts up in Safe Mode, and you have to figure out what's wrong (see "Booting in Safe Mode").

Installing PC Cards

You can install most PC cards without turning off your computer. For example, if you have a PC card from your digital camera with memory containing the photos you have taken, you can stick the PC card into the PC card slot of your computer at any time. Windows notices the new device within a few seconds, and you can begin using it.

To see the status of your PC cards, choose Start | Settings | Control Panel, and run the PC Card (PCMCIA) icon (click or double-click the icon, depending on how Windows is configured (see Chapter 1, section "Choosing Between Single-Click and Double-Click"). You see the PC Card (PCMCIA) Properties dialog box shown in Figure 14-3. The dialog box lists your PC cards.

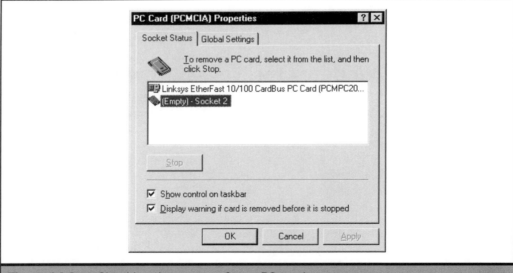

Figure 14-3. *Checking the status of your PC cards*

Using the Add New Hardware Wizard

Windows' Add New Hardware Wizard does a good job handling the details of installing new device drivers. After you've installed a new device, if Windows doesn't detect it, run the Wizard by following these steps.

1. Choose Start | Control Panel and run the Add New Hardware icon. The Add New Hardware Wizard starts. The first thing the Wizard does is search for new *Plug and Play* devices, devices that can communicate with Windows to provide their own configuration information. Even if you know you don't have any new Plug and Play devices, you have to wait while Windows checks for them. If the Wizard finds new devices (or old but unused devices), it shows you a list, as in Figure 14-4. (The list in Figure 14-4 includes unused motherboard IDE disk and PS/2 mouse devices, because the computer in this example has a SCSI disk controller and a serial port mouse.)

2. If one of the devices in the list is the one you want to install, check Yes, click the correct device, and then click Next.

3. If Windows didn't find your new device, click No and Next to proceed to the next screen, in which Windows offers to search for non-Plug and Play devices.

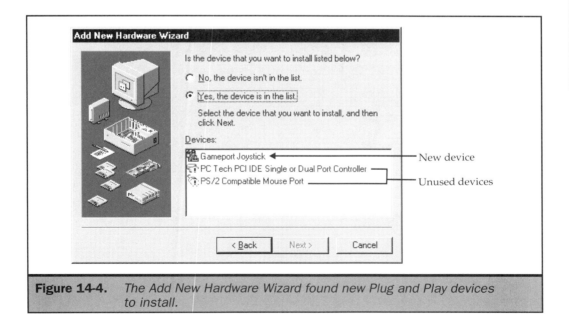

Figure 14-4.   *The Add New Hardware Wizard found new Plug and Play devices to install.*

Searching for non-Plug and Play is slower and riskier than searching for Plug and Play, and it sometimes crashes the computer. If you know what you just installed, you can click No and select the driver yourself. If you click Yes, Windows attempts to find any new devices, which takes a while. When it finishes, click the Details button to see a list of what it found (Figure 14-5).

4. If you click No and Next, you see a list of hardware types (Figure 14-6).

5. Pick your hardware type from the list and click Next to see a list of manufacturers and models (Figure 14-7). It's often difficult to guess what category a device falls into, so you might have to pick one category, look there, and then click Back and try another category or two before you find your device.

6. Choose the manufacturer and the model of your device. If your device came with a driver on a floppy disk and you want to use that driver, click Have Disk and tell Windows which drive contains the disk, which usually is drive A.

Windows contains up-to-date drivers for an enormous number of devices. If you have a driver disk, check the dates of the files on the disk. If they're older than mid-1999 and Windows has a driver for your device, the standard Windows driver is probably better than the one on the disk. You can also check the manufacturer's Web site for the latest drive.

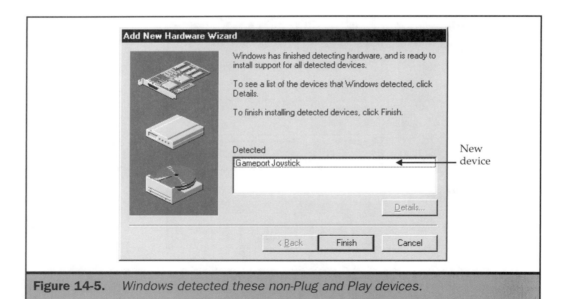

Figure 14-5.   *Windows detected these non-Plug and Play devices.*

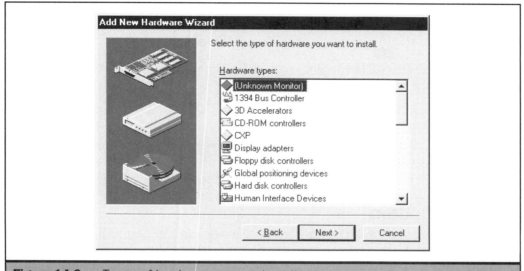

Figure 14-6.   *Types of hardware you can install*

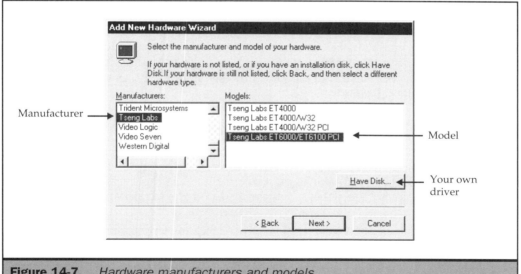

Figure 14-7.   *Hardware manufacturers and models*

7. Click Next, and Windows finishes installing your device. You might have to insert your Windows Me CD-ROM if the device needs drivers that haven't been used before, and you may have to reboot Windows.

At this point, unless Windows has reported a configuration problem, your device should be ready to use.

Windows Me ships with fewer device drivers than Windows 98 did. If you install Windows Me from scratch (rather than upgrading from Windows 98), you may be missing drivers you need. (Upgrading leaves the Windows 98 drivers in place.) If a driver is missing, use the disk that came with the device for which Windows Me has no driver, or check the device manufacturer's Web site for a downloadable driver.

Installing a Modem

When Windows detects that you have installed a new modem, it runs the Install New Modem Wizard. This Wizard also runs when you open the Modems icon in the Control Panel if Windows isn't configured to use your modem.

The Wizard asks whether the modem is a PC card (PCMCIA) modem (that can pop in or out of a laptop) or another type of modem (an internal modem that mounts permanently inside the computer or an external modem that connects to the computer by a serial cable). The Install New Modem Wizard may call the Add New Hardware Wizard described in the preceding section to find the modem, or you can choose the modem manufacturer and model from a menu.

Once Windows has installed the driver for your modem, it asks for the country and area code in which you are located, any digits you need to dial to get an outside line, and whether your telephone system uses tone or pulse dialing. Windows stores this information in your default dialing location (see Chapter 20, section "Configuring Windows for Dialing Locations").

Removing PC Cards and Unplugging Other Devices

You can remove PC cards and a few other types of hardware from your computer without turning off the computer—*hot swapping*. Before you remove the device, though, you should tell Windows that you are going to do so.

Before removing a PC card, display the PC Card (PCMCIA) Properties dialog box, click the card, and click the Stop button.

To unplug any device that can be hot-swapped, click the Unplug Or Eject Hardware icon on the system tray, shown here:

Windows displays a menu of your hot-swappable devices, including most PC cards. Choose one. You can also right-click the Unplug Or Eject Hardware icon and choose Unplug Or Display Hardware from the one-item menu that appears. You see the Unplug Or Eject Hardware dialog box, shown in Figure 14-8. Select the card or other device and click Stop.

If a device doesn't appear in the Unplug Or Eject Hardware dialog box, don't disconnect it without shutting down Windows and turning off your computer.

Troubleshooting Your Hardware Configuration

In a perfect world, every device installation would work the first time. In the real world, something goes wrong about one time in three, and you have to fix it. The most common problem is that an I/O device address or interrupt used by the new device conflicts with an older one (see the earlier section "Hardware Parameters").

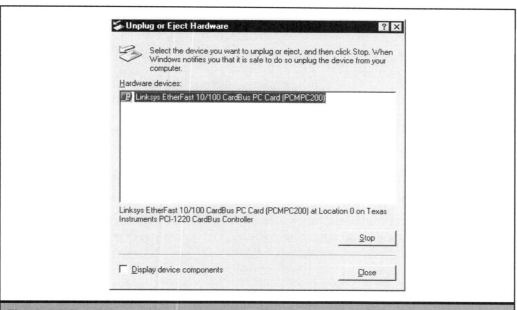

Figure 14-8.   *Removing PC Cards and other devices that can be hot-swapped*

Windows Installation Glitch

Windows' installation files are stored in a compressed format in *CAB* or *cabinet files* (with extension .cab) on your Windows Me CD-ROM. Windows usually copies these CAB files to your hard disk, in the C:\Windows\Options\Install folder. These files include many standard hardware drivers.

Sometimes, Windows can't find the component file that it is trying to install. When this happens, Windows says that it can't find the file where it is looking (usually C:\Windows\System), and asks for another location where the file might be. You need to find which CAB file Windows needs and tell it where to look for it.

To find the missing file, click the Details button in the dialog box that appears and find the name of the CAB file that contains the file that Windows is looking for. Then search your hard disk (or your Windows Me CD-ROM) for this CAB by choosing Start | Search | For Files And Folders. For example, if Windows is looking for a file named Winsock.dll that is supposed to be in Net4.cab, search your hard disk or the CD for files with the filename *.cab. Then tell Windows to look in that folder for the CAB file.

In the worst case, Windows doesn't boot at all after you add your new device. If you installed an ISA or EISA card, this invariably means that the settings on the card conflict with an existing device. Turn off the computer, take out the new device, turn on the computer, and reboot. Use the Device Manger to see what addresses and interrupts are currently in use, and use the card's documentation to find out how to change jumpers to addresses and interrupts that are available (see the upcoming section "Using the Device Manager"). Then reinstall the card and try again. If you can't tell what the conflicts are, boot the computer in Safe Mode.

Booting in Safe Mode

Safe Mode provides minimal Windows functions by disabling all devices except the keyboard, screen, and disk. If you are in Windows and would like to restart in Safe Mode, restart the computer normally, but hold the CTRL key throughout the shutdown sequence. To cold boot (turn on your computer) into Safe Mode, start your computer normally, but watch the screen carefully. As soon as you see the Starting Windows message, press F8 repeatedly. You should see a menu of startup options, one of which is Safe Mode. (Other options include Safe Mode With Network Support, which you can use if you're 100 percent sure that the problem isn't a network device, nor any other device that might be conflicting with the hardware resources used by a network device.) See "Startup Modes" in Chapter 34 for more information on starting Windows in other modes.

Note *Windows Me no longer contains a real, bootable version of DOS. It has been replaced by a DOS virtual machine (see Chapter 38).*

Once you've booted in Safe Mode, you can use the Device Manager and other Windows facilities to figure out what's wrong. To leave Safe Mode, reboot the computer normally.

Using the Device Manager

The *Device Manager* lists all the devices that make up your computer and lets you see and modify their configuration. If the Add New Hardware Wizard detects a device conflict, it starts the Device Manager automatically. To start it yourself, open the System icon in the Control Panel, and click the Device Manager tab, as shown in Figure 14-9. You can view devices by type or by connection; by connection is usually better for driver debugging, since it displays each connected device separately. If hardware is having trouble, Windows displays the devices listed by type, with the type of the problematic device

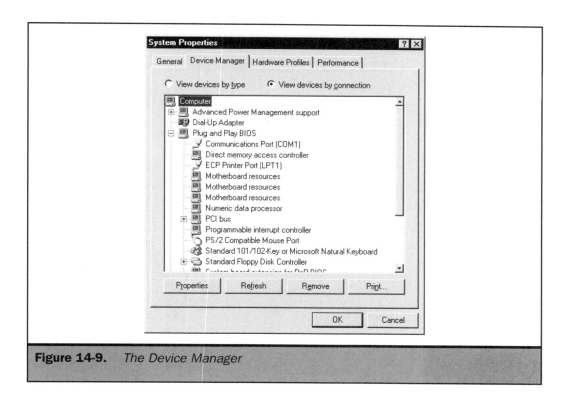

Figure 14-9. *The Device Manager*

expanded. (On most computers, the majority of devices are under the Plug and Play BIOS, so click its expansion button to see the Plug and Play devices.)

To deal with a configuration problem, follow these steps:

1. Display the Device Manager by choosing Start | Settings | Control Panel, opening the System icon, and clicking the Device Manager tab.

2. To see a particular device, click that device, and click the Properties button and then the Resource tab. If a device has resource conflicts, Windows displays them, as in Figure 14-10. In this case, the conflict is the interrupt number.

3. To resolve a conflict, uncheck Use Automatic Settings (if it's checked), click the conflicting resource, and click Change Setting. Windows lets you adjust the resource used, telling you at each step what conflicts still exist.

4. Once you've found a setting with no conflicts, write it down on a piece of paper and click OK. Windows will offer to shut down the computer to let you adjust the device to agree with the setting you just changed.

5. Do so, turn off the computer, change the jumpers as needed, reinstall the card, and restart Windows.

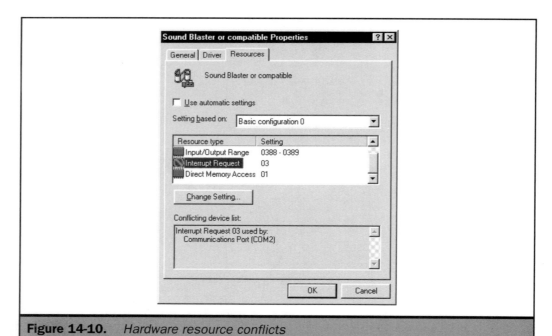

Figure 14-10. *Hardware resource conflicts*

Adding Memory

Adding memory is simple because no drivers are required. To add memory, follow these steps:

1. Shut down Windows, turn off and unplug the computer, open up the computer, and add the memory to available memory slots.

Caution   *Either use an antistatic wrist band (or a wire clipped to your metal wristwatch and the grounded metal frame); or, at the very least, touch a piece of the metal frame of the case to discharge static electricity before handling any of the delicate RAM, to prevent static shocks from damaging the RAM chips. You can even plug the computer back in while you are installing the memory chips, so that the third prong of the AC outlet connects your computer chassis to ground.*

2. Unplug the computer if you plugged it back in, close it up, plug it back in, and start it up. Most PCs do an internal memory test, notice that the amount of memory has changed, and complain before Windows starts.

3. If your computer complains, enter the computer's low-level configuration setup (also called *BIOS setup* or *CMOS setup*), and adjust the configured amount of memory to reflect the total now installed. Then reboot. When Windows starts, it automatically takes advantage of all memory installed in your computer.

Chapter 15

Setting Up Printers and Fonts

Windows Me has a sophisticated and powerful printer management system. Setting up your printers can be painful; but once they're configured, you can quickly and easily print from your programs by using any local or network printer accessible to your computer and be confident that your printouts will look the way you want.

After your printer is installed, you can manage your print jobs, holding or canceling documents you print. You can change the printer configuration, including settings such as paper size and default fonts. If you run into printer trouble, you can use the Print Troubleshooter to find the problem.

Windows handles the fonts that appear on the screen and on your printed pages. Windows itself comes with fonts, as do many application programs, and you can buy and install additional fonts.

How Does Windows Handle Printers?

Each printer installed on your system has an entry in the Windows *Printers folder*. When you print something from an application, a Windows *printer driver* (printer control program) for the current printer formats the material for that particular printer. As far as printer limitations permit, documents look the same no matter what printer they're printed on.

You can have several printers defined on your system. They may be different physical printers or different modes on the same printer. For example, a few printers handle both Hewlett-Packard's PCL printer control language and the Adobe PostScript language. You can have two printer drivers installed, one for PCL and one for PostScript. If your printer can print on both sides of the paper, you can have two drivers installed, one for single-sided printing and one for double-sided printing. To see the installed printers, open your Printers folder by choosing Start | Settings | Printers.

You can print on a *local printer* (a printer that is connected directly to your computer) or to a *network printer* (a printer that your computer can access over a local area network). Once you have configured Windows to use either a local or network printer, printing works exactly the same for either type.

At any particular moment, one of the printers is marked as the *default printer*. Anything you print goes to the default printer unless you specifically tell your program to use a different printer. In the Printers folder, you can make any of your printers the default.

Windows also provides *spooling*, a service that stores document data on disk until the printer can accept it. When you print a document from an application, the information to be printed (the *print job*) is stored temporarily in the *queue* (storage for print jobs) until it can be printed. If you print a long document to a slow printer, spooling lets you continue working with your application while the printer works in the background. (Many years ago, "spool" stood for Simultaneous Peripheral Operation On-Line, but nobody remembers that anymore.)

Note *Windows also treats a fax modem as a kind of printer. Windows Me doesn't come with a built-in fax facility, but you can install a third-party fax program, like WinFax PRO (**http://www.symantec.com/winfax**), which includes a fax printer driver. Many modems also come with fax programs. Another possibility is to use an Internet-based fax service, like eFax.com (**http://www.efax.com**) or JFAX.COM (**http://www.jfax.com**).*

What Are Fonts?

Modern computer screens and printers can display text in a variety of *typefaces* and sizes, as illustrated here:

> This is a sample of a 12-point Times, a proportionally spaced
> This is a sample of a 12-point Arial, another proportional
> This is a sample of 12-point Courier, a
> This is a very small 6-point type.
> This is a rather large 18-point type.

In *fixed-pitch* typefaces, all the characters are the same width, like on a typewriter. In *proportionally spaced* typefaces, different characters are different widths. (The relative widths vary from one typeface to another.) Most typefaces are available in different sizes, with the sizes measured in printer's points, 1/72 inch. The most common sizes are 10-point and12-point, roughly corresponding to sizes of elite and pica typewriter type. Fonts are often provided in several variations, such as normal, bold, italic, and bold-italic.

Typographers refer to the collection of all the characters in a typeface of a given size and variation as a *font*. For example, Arial italic 12-point is a font, although in the computer field, the terms *font* and *typeface* (or face) are often (incorrectly) used interchangeably.

Windows comes with a small but adequate set of fonts, but many programs and printer drivers include fonts of their own. Once a font is installed, any program can use it, no matter where the font came from. Thus, a typical Windows installation may have 50 to 100 fonts available. Entire books have been written on typeface design and usage, so we won't attempt to say anything about the topic other than to note that documents that use many different typefaces are usually harder to read than those that use only one or two.

 In additional to fonts that contain letters and numbers, Windows comes with several fonts of special characters. You can use the Character Map program to look at them and add them to your documents (see Chapter 5, section "Using Special Characters with Character Map").

What Is TrueType?

Computer printers and screens print and display characters by printing or displaying patterns of black-and-white (or colored) dots. The size of the dots depends on the resolution of the device, ranging from 72 to 100 dots per inch on screens, to 300, 600, or even 1,200 dots-per-inch on laser printers. In early versions of Windows, each typeface was provided as a *bitmap* (dot picture) of the actual black-and-white dots for each character, with separate bitmaps for each size. The bitmaps were available only in a small variety of sizes, such as Courier 10-, 12-, and 18-point.

This scheme does not produce very good-looking documents, because the dot resolution of printers is rarely the same as that for a screen. In the process of printing, Windows had to rescale each character's bitmap to the printer's resolution, producing odd-looking characters with unattractive jagged corners. Even worse, if you used a font in a size other than one of the sizes provided, the system had to do a second level of rescaling, producing even worse-looking characters.

TrueType solves both of these problems by storing each typeface not as a set of bitmaps, but essentially as a set of formulas the system can use to *render* (draw) each character at any desired size and resolution. This means that TrueType fonts look consistent on all devices, and that you can use them in any size.

 Use only TrueType fonts in documents that you plan to print, to make your documents look their best.

How Do Printers Handle Fonts?

Older printers had one or two fonts built in, and when you printed a document, those were the fonts you got. Modern printers can print any image that the resolution of the printer prints, so they can print all the fonts that are installed on your system.

Printers handle fonts in three different ways. Most printers have a reasonable set of built-in, general-purpose fonts, and some can accept font cartridges with added fonts. If you use fonts other than the built-in ones, then on lower performance printers, Windows reverts to printing graphics, in effect turning your document into a full-page bitmap image that Windows can send (slowly) to the printer. Some printers, notably laser printers that use the PostScript and PCL5 printer control languages, can handle downloaded fonts, so Windows can send the printer all the fonts that a particular document needs.

To speed up printing, Windows uses *font substitution*, using built-in printer fonts where possible for similar TrueType fonts. For example, Microsoft's Arial font is nearly identical to the Helvetica font found in PostScript printers, so when Windows prints Arial text, it tells the printer to use Helvetica instead. This process of font substitution normally works without trouble, although occasionally—on clone printers—the built-in fonts aren't exactly what Windows expects and the results can look a little off. (You can tell Windows to turn off font substitution if you suspect that's a problem.)

Adding and Deleting Printers

Windows has almost entirely automated the process of adding a new printer. Whether you are installing a new printer attached to your computer (a local printer) or configuring Windows to use a printer on your local area network, you use the Add Printer Wizard. Windows can find network printers by itself, without any action on your part.

Viewing the Printers Folder

The Printers folder contains an icon for each printer that Windows knows about, along with an icon for the Add Printer program. To see the Printers folder, use one of these methods:

- Choose Start | Settings | Printers. (Your Windows installation may be configured so that the Printers command displays another menu; see the note at the end of this section.)

- Open the My Computer window and open the Printers icon there. Click or double-click the icon, depending on how Windows is configured (see Chapter 1, section "Choosing Between Single-Click and Double-Click").

- Choose Start | Settings | Control Panel, and run the Printers icon in the Control Panel window.

Windows Me has an improved Start menu that lets you choose printers right off the Start menu. To turn on the cascading menu, choose Start | Settings | Taskbar And Start Menu. You see the Taskbar And Start Menu Properties dialog box (see Chapter 11, section "Moving Start Menu Items by Using the Taskbar And Start Menu Properties

Dialog Box"). Select the Advanced tab, and at the bottom of the dialog box you see the Start Menu And Taskbar list of check box options:

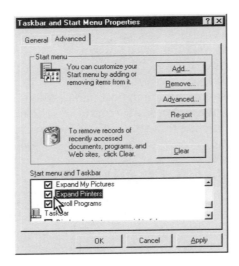

Under the Start Menu heading is the Expand Printers option. Click it to place a check in the box and click OK to save your changes and close the dialog box. Now when you choose Start | Settings | Printers, the entries in the Printers folder appear in the menu. If you use the Expand Printers option, you never see the Printers window—instead, you choose printers right from the Start menu.

Adding a New Local Printer

Be sure your printer is connected to your PC and is turned on. If the printer came with floppy disks or a CD-ROM, have them in hand, because they probably contain printer drivers for Windows to install. Follow these steps:

1. Open the Printers folder as explained in the preceding section. You see the Printers window, which displays an icon for every printer on your system. (If you use the Expand Printers option, choose Start | Settings | Printers | Add Printers and skip to step 3.)

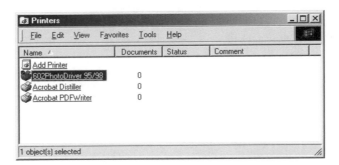

2. Run the Add Printer program. The Add Printer Wizard walks you through the process of adding a new printer.

3. The Wizard asks whether you're adding a local or network printer. Then it asks what kind of printer you're installing, showing the list of printers for which it has drivers:

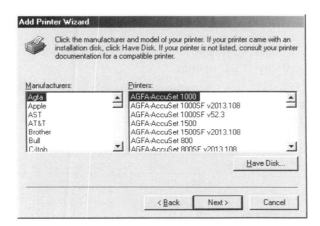

4. Windows has drivers for a huge variety of printers, so your printer will most likely be in the list. Some printers have more than one driver—for example, separate PCL and PostScript drivers for printers that can handle both, in which case you can choose any of the drivers for your printer. If your printer doesn't appear in the list, you probably can use the driver for another similar printer. Most PCL printers are similar to one of the HP LaserJet series, and most PostScript printers are similar to one of the Apple LaserWriters. If your printer comes with a diskette containing a printer driver, or you know there's a printer driver available on a network to which you are connected, you can click Have Disk and enter the location of the driver.

Tip   *If you have a disk, but your printer appears in the Windows list, use the Windows driver, unless your disk is dated 1999 or later. Older disks contain less up-to-date drivers than the ones that come with Windows. If your printer isn't listed, check the printer manufacturer's Web site for up-to-date drivers that you can download and install.*

5. The Wizard asks which port your printer is attached to. Select the appropriate port, usually LPT1.

6. The Wizard asks whether you want to change the name you use for this printer (which you probably don't), and whether to use this printer as the default printer. (You can later change the default at any time if you want.)

7. Finally, the Wizard asks whether it should print a test page. At this point, Windows installs the printer driver. Be sure the Windows CD-ROM is in the drive, unless you specified a printer driver located somewhere else.

Windows prints a test page with a Windows logo and a description of the printer. If the test page prints and looks correct, your printer is installed.

Adding a New Network Printer

Installing a new printer on a local area network is very similar to installing a new local printer.

1. Open the Add Printer icon, as previously described, to start the Add Printer Wizard, but click Network printer instead. The Wizard asks for the network path or queue name of the printer.

2. If you know the path, type it in. A network path usually looks like *computername**printername*, for example, \\pentiumpro\hplj1100. Otherwise, click the Browse button to see a map of your network, like this one:

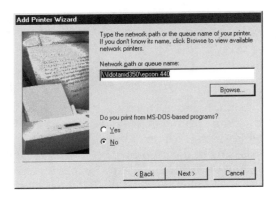

3. In this map, if the printer doesn't appear, double-click the computer to which the printer is connected to display the printers on that computer, select the printer you want to use, and then click OK.

4. You also have to specify whether you plan to print from MS-DOS programs to the network printer. MS-DOS provides no standard technique for programs to print via a network, so Windows can "capture" output sent to one of the standard printer ports and redirect it to the network printer. If you don't plan to print from MS-DOS programs, there's no need to capture a port, so click No. You can later change which ports are or are not captured (see the upcoming section "Configuring Printers").

5. To arrange to capture a printer port, click Yes where the Add Printer Wizard asks whether you print from MS-DOS programs and click Capture Printer Port on the window that follows. Windows asks you to select the printer port to capture. Choose LPT1, unless there is a local printer on that port, in which case you should choose an unused port and click OK.

6. Windows then asks you to choose a printer driver. From this point on, installing a network printer is exactly the same as installing a local printer, as described in the previous section. See Chapter 29 for more information on sharing resources (including printers) on a network.

Deleting a Printer

If you want to remove an installed printer, just drag the printer's icon from the Printer window into the Recycle Bin, or right-click the printer's icon and choose Delete from the menu that appears. If you use the Expand Printers option, choose Start | Settings | Printers, right-click the printer on the menu, and choose Delete.

Troubleshooting Your Printer

Microsoft provides a troubleshooting feature for getting printers to work correctly. Follow these steps:

1. Choose Start | Help to display the Help and Support window (see Chapter 6).

2. Click the Home button and click the Troubleshooting entry in the list of topics. Click the Hardware & System Device Problems link, then the Hardware Memory & Others link, and finally the Printing Troubleshooter link. The Printing Troubleshooter appears in the right pane of the Help And Support window.

3. The Printing Troubleshooter asks you questions about your printer problem, so that it can identify the problem; and then it makes suggestions to fix the most common printer problems, such as no printing at all, slow or garbled printing, and distorted graphics. Click the radio button that describes your problem and click the Next button to find out what Windows recommends. With luck, your problem is one that the Troubleshooter addresses.

Configuring Printers

After you install your printer or printers, you configure the driver to match your printer's setup. Some simple printers have little or no setup, while laser printers have a variety of hardware and software options.

To configure a printer, open the Printers folder by choosing Start | Settings | Printers. Right-click the printer of interest and select Properties from the menu that appears. (If you use the Expand Printers option, choose Start | Settings | Printers, right-click the printer on the menu, and choose Properties. You see the Properties dialog box for the printer, as shown in Figure 15-1. Some of the properties are the same for all printers, while others are printer specific.

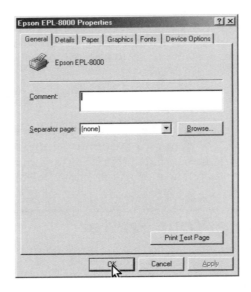

The settings for the printer are organized into groups, which you can display by clicking the appropriate tab along the top of the window. Commonly used tabs include the following:

- **General** Comments about the printer and a button to print a test page.

- **Details** Select the network connection or printer port, start or end MS-DOS port capture, and change spooler settings.

- **Color Management** For color printers, select how color profiles work (making printed colors match screen colors).

- **Paper** Change the size of paper the printer is using, handle options such as double-sided, portrait, or landscape print orientation, and the number of copies of each page to print.

- **Graphics** Change the dots-per-inch resolution of printed graphics (higher looks better, but prints slower), dithering, half-toning, and screening (techniques used to approximate shades of gray on black-and-white printers).

- **Fonts** Change which font cartridges are in use, control font substitution, control whether TrueType fonts are downloaded to the printer as fonts or graphics (can be useful to work around flaky print position problems).

- **Device Options or Setup** Change what optional equipment the printer has, such as extra memory, envelope feeders, and other paper-handling equipment, and change among various print-quality modes on ink-jet printers.

- **PostScript** On PostScript-compatible printers, select PostScript suboptions, to control whether PostScript header information is sent with each print job (important on printers shared with other computers) or only once per session.

- **Sharing**   If your computer is on a local area network and this printer is physically connected to your computer, change whether other people on the network can share this printer (see Chapter 29).
- **Services**   Some printer drivers include procedures for maintenance, like cleaning print cartridges or aligning print heads.

After you have the properties for your printer set to your liking, you'll find that you seldom need to change the properties.

Tip   *If you find that you frequently switch between two different sets of properties, such as single- and double-sided printing, install the printer twice, and configure one installation for single-sided and one for double-sided printing. Windows lets you configure single- versus double-sided printing on a dialog box, but switching "printers" is a lot easier.*

Table 15-1 lists the settings that appear in most printer Properties dialog boxes; some printers have different options or display these options on different tabs of the dialog box. For information on the Sharing tab of the printer Properties dialog box, see Chapter 29.

CONFIGURING WINDOWS FOR YOUR COMPUTER

Tab	Setting	Description
General	Comment	Allows you to type a description of the printer; the command appears when others on a network connect to the printer.
General	Separator page	Specifies whether Windows prints a *separator page* between print jobs, which can be useful for network printers. Click Browse to specify what to print on the separator page.
Details	Print to the following port	Specifies how a local printer is connected to the computer. Click Add Port to specify the address of a network printer or to add a new type of port. Click Delete Port to delete a port from the list.
Details	Print using the following driver	Specifies the printer driver. Click New Driver to choose a different printer driver.

Table 15-1.   *Printer Properties*

Tab	Setting	Description
Details	Capture Printer Port	Displays the Capture Printer Port dialog box, which allows you to assign a network printer to receive all output that applications try to send to a printer port.
Details	End Capture	Cancels the network printer connection you create using the Capture Printer Port button.
Details	Not selected: *xxx* seconds	Specifies how many seconds Windows waits before reporting that a printer is offline.
Details	Transmission retry: *xxx* seconds	Specifies how many seconds Windows waits before reporting a printer error.
Details	Spool Settings	Displays the Spool Settings dialog box, which allows you to control whether Windows stores waiting print jobs by using the spooler, the format in which print jobs are stored, and when Windows starts printing information from the spooler.
Details	Port Settings	Displays the Configure Port dialog box, which allows you to configure the port to which the printer is connected.
Paper	Copies	Specifies the number of copies of the job to print.
Paper	Orientation	Specifies whether to print using *portrait orientation* (lines of print are parallel to the short side of the paper) or *landscape orientation* (lines of print are parallel to the long side of the paper).
Paper	Paper Size	Specifies the size of paper to print on. Your options depend on the printer's capabilities.

Table 15-1.   *Printer Properties* (continued)

Managing Printer Activity

If you have a local printer that only you use now and then, you'll find that it hardly needs any management at all. When you print something from one of your programs, the printer prints it. But if you share a network printer or you use your printer heavily and spool multiple print jobs to it, some printer management is necessary.

Managing Print Jobs

Each printer has a window, like the one shown next, that shows the activity for that printer. The printer control window lists the print jobs waiting to be printed and the one that is currently printing. Open the Printers folder by choosing Start | Settings | Printers and then open the printer's icon in the Printers window. (If you use the Expand Printers option, choose the Printer from the Printers menu.)

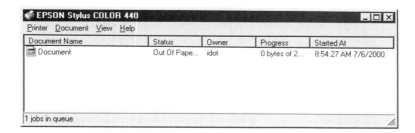

You can pause and resume printing by choosing Printer | Pause Printing from the menu. To pause or delete a particular print job, highlight the job and choose Document | Pause Printing or Document | Cancel Printing. To get rid of everything waiting for that printer, choose Printer | Purge Print Documents. To change the order in which jobs are printed, you can drag print jobs up or down the list.

Setting the Default Printer

In the Printers window (or the Start | Settings | Printers menu, if you use the Expand Printers option) the current default printer is identified with a tiny check mark in the corner of its icon. You can make any printer the default printer by opening the printer's control window and choosing Printer | Set As Default.

Printing to a File

Sometimes you want to send printer output to a file, either to print later, or to transport on floppy disk to a printer not connected to your computer. To do so, open the Printers window and open the Add Printer icon (or choose Start | Settings | Printers | Add Printer) to install the printer you want to use as a local printer, choose the type of printer to which you will print the document later, and choose FILE as the port to which it is attached.

Whenever a program prints to that printer, Windows pops up a dialog box asking you to specify which file to use.

You can temporarily arrange to print documents for one of your installed printers to a file by opening the printer's Properties dialog box, clicking the Details tab, and choosing FILE: as the port. When you're done, change the port back to the actual port or network connection.

Installing and Using Fonts

Windows provides a straightforward way to install and use fonts. To see which fonts you have installed, open the folder C:\Windows\Fonts in Windows Explorer:

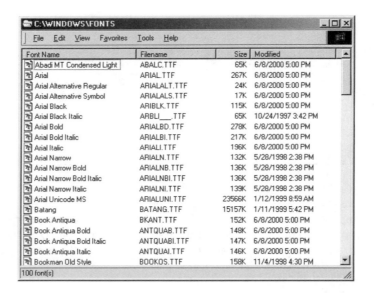

TrueType fonts have a TT icon, older fonts have an A icon. You can open any font to see a description and samples of the font in a variety of sizes. If you have a lot of fonts installed, choose View | Hide Variations to omit the icons for fonts that are bold or italic versions of other fonts.

    Windows can handle up to 1,000 fonts, but to avoid slowing down your applications, don't install more than 200.

Installing Fonts

To install new fonts from a floppy disk or network, follow these steps:

1. View the C:\Windows\Fonts folder in Windows Explorer.

2. Choose File | Install New Font, and the Add Fonts dialog box appears:

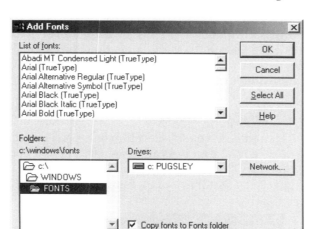

3. In the Drives and Folders boxes, select the drive and folder in which the files are located for the new font or fonts. Click the Network button if the font files are on a network drive that is not mapped to a drive letter on your computer. Windows displays the fonts it finds.

4. In the List Of Fonts box, select the font(s) you want to install.

5. Normally, Windows copies the font files into its font folder (C:\Windows\Fonts). If you are installing fonts from a networked folder, you can uncheck Copy Fonts To Fonts Folder to use the fonts where they are located, which saves space in exchange for some loss in speed.

6. Click OK, and Windows installs the fonts you want.

 Alternatively, you can just drag font files from the install disk or folder to the C:\Windows\Fonts folder.

Deleting Fonts

To delete a font or fonts, display the C:\Windows\Fonts folder in Windows Explorer. Then select the fonts you want to get rid of and choose File | Delete. However, don't delete a font unless you are sure that none of the programs on your system use it. To be safe, move the fonts to a temporary folder for a few days to see if any programs display error messages when they try to use them. If no errors appear, then delete the fonts.

Finding Similar Fonts

Windows offers an occasionally useful "font similarity" feature that lets you look for fonts that are similar to a particular font. When viewing your list of fonts, choose View | List Fonts By Similarity and choose the target font at the top of the Fonts window. The font similarity feature depends on special information in the font files, so older fonts without this information aren't ranked for similarity.

Choosing Fonts in Documents

Most windows applications allow you to select the fonts used in documents and screen displays. When you select a font, the application usually opens a Font dialog box, like the one shown next. Some applications, such as Microsoft Word and Microsoft PowerPoint, use fonts so often that they have a font selection button on the toolbar.

Either way, you select a font in three steps: the name of the font (really the name of the typeface), the style (regular, bold, italic), and the point size. TrueType fonts are available in any size and style, and are identified by the TT logo before the font name. OpenType fonts (a new type of font that is just beginning to become available) are identified by an O logo. Older fonts are available in only a few fixed sizes and styles. You can force Windows to use an older font in any size or style, but the results invariably look bad.

Chapter 16

Working with Sound and Graphics

Windows Me contains better support for multimedia devices—hardware that enables your computer to record and play sounds, and show and take photos and video. In addition to better built-in drivers for multimedia devices, Windows comes with two programs that let you record or play multimedia files or disks, Sound Recorder and the new Windows Media Player 7. This chapter provides an introduction to multimedia file formats, with instructions for using the graphics and sound programs that come with Windows Me. Chapter 17 describes Windows' video features. Chapter 14 describes how to install hardware, including multimedia hardware; this chapter explains how to configure and use these devices.

What Is Multimedia?

Multimedia is information other than plain text. Multimedia includes pictures (graphics), sound (audio), and movies (video). Multimedia information—pictures, sounds, and video—is captured and digitized by *input devices* to get the information into your computer. For example, to get a picture into your computer, you can scan it or transfer it from a digital camera. Your computer stores multimedia information in a variety of standard file formats. You can display or play multimedia information on *output devices*. For example, to play a sound file, you need speakers or headphones. In some cases, your computer needs special hardware to connect to the output device. For example, to connect a speaker to a PC, you need a sound card (which comes standard with most new computers). Table 16-1 shows input devices, output devices, and some standard file formats for the major types of multimedia.

What Is MIDI?

A specialized type of audio data is called *MIDI* (Musical Instrument Digital Interface), a format for transmitting and storing musical notes. MIDI devices are musical instruments that have digital inputs and outputs and can transmit, store, and play music using the MIDI language. For example, if you connect a MIDI keyboard to your computer, you can view the music you play on the MIDI keyboard on your computer screen and hear it on your speakers. Data from MIDI devices is stored in MIDI files. Windows includes software that can "play" MIDI files; that is, software that can translate the musical notes in the files into sound that can be played through speakers or headphones.

See the section "Working with MIDI," later in this chapter, for how to record and play MIDI files.

Medium	Input Device	Output Device	File Extensions for Popular File Formats
Graphics	Scanner, digital camera, paint program	Printer, screen display	.bmp, .pcx, .gif, .jpg, and .tif
Audio	Microphone, MIDI keyboard, synthesizers, line input	Speakers, headphones	.wav, .mp3, .m3u, .asx, .wax, and .wvx
Streaming audio	Same as regular audio	Speakers, headphones	.ram, .ra (for RealAudio files), .asf, and .asx (for Active Streaming Format files)
Video	Digital video camera, virtual reality software	Screen display, speakers, headphones	.avi, .mpg, .qt (for QuickTime files), and .wmv
MIDI	MIDI-compatible instrument	MIDI-compatible instrument, speakers, headphones	.mid, .midi, or .rmi
Streaming video	Generated from regular video	Display, speakers, headphones	.rv (for RealVideo files), .asf, and .asx (for Active Streaming Format files)

Table 16-1. *Multimedia Devices and File Formats*

CONFIGURING WINDOWS
FOR YOUR COMPUTER

What Are Streaming Audio and Video?

Streaming audio and *streaming video* are audio and video files stored in a format for use over the Internet. When you play a streaming audio or video file over the Internet, your computer starts playing the file after downloading only the beginning of the file and then continues to play the file as it downloads (optimally downloading stays a step ahead of the player). To play streaming audio or video files from the Internet, run Windows Media Player (see "Playing Sound Files with Windows Media Player," later in the chapter). The last version of Windows came with NetShow, a program for playing streaming audio and video, but Windows Me's version of Media Player handles streaming files.

Displaying and Playing Multimedia Files

Many applications, particularly games, have built-in graphics, sounds, and video features. Those programs automatically take advantage of any devices you have, once those devices are configured into your system.

Multimedia information is stored in multimedia files in a variety of formats, as you saw in Table 16-1. To see the properties of any multimedia file, right-click the filename in Windows Explorer and choose Properties from the menu that appears. You see the Properties dialog box like the one shown in Figure 16-1.

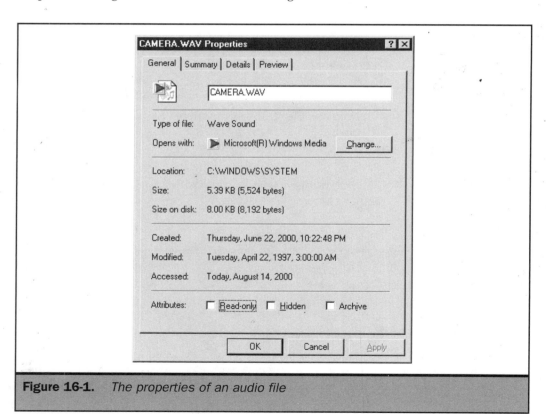

Figure 16-1.   *The properties of an audio file*

The information on the General tab parallels that provided for almost any file: type, size, and attributes. Click the Details tab to see more specific information about the contents of the file, such as its copyright holder, length, and format. If a Preview tab appears, click it to play the file. Windows runs the program that is associated with that file type, if any:

- **Media Player**   Plays a wide variety of multimedia files (see "Playing Sound Files with Windows Media Player").

- **Sound Recorder**   Plays audio files (see "Playing and Recording WAV Sound Files with Sound Recorder").

- **Kodak Imaging**   Displays graphics files (see Chapter 5, section "Annotating Images with Kodak Imaging"). Your browser or graphics editing program may have associated itself with many graphics files formats and may run to preview graphics files.

If you upgraded from Windows 98, you can also use the ActiveMovie program to play MIDI and video files and the NetShow program to play streaming files from the Internet. The rest of this chapter describes how to create and view (or play) graphics and sound files (including MIDI files). The next chapter describes how to create and play video files.

Working with Multimedia Devices

For your computer to use a multimedia input or output device, Windows has to know about the device. Information about how to send and receive information from devices is stored in drivers. When you buy a scanner, camera, or other multimedia device, a floppy disk or CD-ROM is often included with the package containing the drivers Windows needs to work with the device. Windows comes with drivers for many standard devices, including many screen displays and sound cards.

Displaying the Status of Your Multimedia Devices

To see all the multimedia devices installed on your system, as well as game controllers and joysticks, choose Start | Settings | Control Panel and open the Sounds And Multimedia icon to display the Sounds And Multimedia Properties dialog box. Click the Devices tab to see the dialog box shown in Figure 16-2 (see Chapter 13, section "Configuring Your Game Controller").

This list is organized by type. If there are devices of a specified type, a plus box appears to the left of the type; click the plus box to see a list of devices of that type. To see or change the settings for some devices, you can click the category of device (for example, Audio Devices for a microphone), click the device, and then click the Properties button. Many of the devices are software only, notably the audio and video

Figure 16-2.   *The Devices tab in the Sounds And Multimedia Properties dialog box displaying audio and video devices by type*

codecs (compressing and decompressing schemes) that determine the scheme used to encode sounds in audio and video files (see Chapter 17, section "What Is Video Data?").

Figure 16-3 shows the Properties dialog box for a sound board. The Properties dialog box for a device shows the status of the device. The settings you see depend on the driver for that device, but most Properties dialog boxes (whether the device handles graphics, audio, or video) contain the following settings and buttons:

- **Use *xxx* On This Device**   The exact name of this setting depends on the device (for example, for an sound board, it's called Use Audio features On This Device). This allows programs to use the device. This setting is usually selected.

- **Do Not Use *xxx* On This Device**   Does not allow programs to use this device. Although the driver for this device remains on your hard disk, Windows does not load it into memory. If you are not using an installed device, this option lets you free up the memory that its driver would take up. You might also want to choose this setting if you think that the driver for this device is causing a conflict with another device.

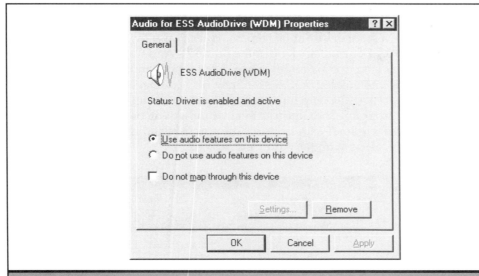

Figure 16-3.   *The properties of a sound board*

■ **Do Not Map Through This Device**   Does not allow programs to route information via this device. Windows loads the driver for this device, but programs can't use it unless they specifically request this device.

■ **Settings button**   Displays additional settings for this device, if any exist. If there are no other settings, this button may be gray and unclickable.

■ **Remove button**   Deletes the driver for this device from your hard disk. Choose this setting if you have removed a multimedia device from your system but its device driver still loads.

■ **Apply button**   Saves all the changes made to the settings in this dialog box, but doesn't close the dialog box. OK saves and closes, and Cancel closes without saving.

Working with Graphics

A *scanner* digitizes pictures or other visual information for storage in your computer. A *digital camera* does the same thing, using a camera lens instead of the flat glass panel on a scanner. Your scanner or digital camera should come with drivers that allow it to work with Windows. (Windows 95–compatible drivers should work fine.) To view pictures, you use your monitor or printer.

Configuring a Scanner or Digital Camera

To install or configure a scanner or digital camera, you can use the Scanners And Cameras window. In the Control Panel, open the Scanners And Cameras icon. If the Scanners And Cameras icon doesn't appear (it may not if no scanner or digital camera is installed), you can see the dialog box by searching for "scanner" in Windows Help And Support and displaying the help information about installing scanners; the text contains a link to the program. The Control Panel window switches to displaying the Scanners And Cameras window, with icons for the scanners and cameras that Windows has detected, along with the Add Device icon:

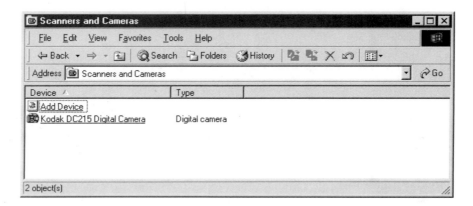

If your scanner or digital camera doesn't appear in the list of installed devices, click the Add Device button to run the Scanner And Camera Installation Wizard. Unless you are installing one of a short list of devices for which Windows has drivers, you'll need the floppy disk or CD-ROM that came with the device. Click the Have Disk button to tell the Wizard to find the device driver on the floppy disk or CD-ROM that you've inserted. After installing the drivers, the Wizard may suggest that you restart Windows so that the new drivers can take effect.

You can test your scanner or digital camera by clicking its entry in the Scanners And Cameras window, clicking the Properties button, and then clicking the Test Scanner Or Camera button.

Note *Even after you install your scanner or digital camera and it works fine, the Scanners And Cameras icon may not appear in the Control Panel. If you open the Scanners And Cameras window, your scanner or camera may not appear in the list of installed devices, either. The device may appear, however, in your System Properties dialog box: Open the System icon in the Control Panel, click the Device Manager tab, and look down the list of all installed devices (see Chapter 14, section "Using the Device Manager").*

Scanning, Editing, and Printing Digitized Pictures

Most scanners are compatible with TWAIN (a standard scanner interface), which means that most graphics programs can accept data from them. For example, you can use the Kodak Imaging program that comes with Windows to receive, edit, and store a scanned image from the scanner (see Chapter 5, section "Annotating Images with Kodak Imaging"). Microsoft Paint can display, edit, and print graphics files (see Chapter 5, section "Drawing Pictures Using Microsoft Paint"). For more advanced editing, as well as for converting files to different graphics formats, we recommend Paint Shop Pro, a shareware program you can download from the Internet (from **http://www.jasc.com/psp.html**). Other graphics editing and conversion programs are available from the Consummate Winsock Applications Web page at **http://www.stroud.com**.

Linking Your Scanner or Digital Camera to a Program

In addition to graphics programs, some other types of programs accept digital graphic information directly from a scanner or camera. For example, a database program may accept a digital picture of a person for storage in a personnel database. If both your scanner or camera and your program support this feature, you can tell Windows to run a program whenever you scan an image or take a digital picture. Follow these steps:

1. Display the Scanners And Cameras window (see earlier section, "Configuring a Scanner or Digital Camera").

2. Click the device and then the Properties button to display the Properties dialog box for that scanner or camera, as shown in Figure 16-4. Click the Events tab. (If the Events tab does not appear, your scanner or digital camera does not support linking to programs.)

3. In the list of events to which the camera or scanner can respond, click an event.

4. In the Start This Program box, click the name of the program that will receive the image from the scanner or camera. Only programs that can accept digital images appear on the list.

5. Click OK.

Alternatively, your scanner or camera may come with TWAIN software that adds an Acquire command to your graphics editor (for example, the Paint Shop Pro program gains a File | Import | TWAIN | Acquire command after you install a scanner driver). You can give this command to bring information from the scanner or camera into the program.

CONFIGURING WINDOWS
FOR YOUR COMPUTER

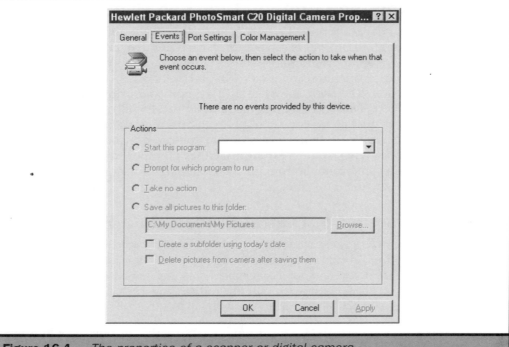

Figure 16-4.   *The properties of a scanner or digital camera*

Configuring Windows to Work with Sound

Most new computers come with a *sound board,* an adapter board inside the computer that lets you connect a microphone and either speakers or headphones to your computer for audio input and output. Many programs use sound to alert you to events, like the lovely musical snippets that you may hear when Windows starts or shuts down. You need sound capabilities to participate in Internet phone and voice chats and to listen to sound clips on the Web.

Windows plays sounds when certain events occur. You can associate a sound with a new event, or change which sounds Windows plays as described in the next few sections of this chapter. You can also play and record sounds by using the Sound Recorder or Media Player programs and play an audio CD in your CD-ROM by using the CD Player program. If you plan to use MIDI devices, see the section "Working with MIDI," later in this chapter.

You can configure how and when Windows records and plays sounds in the Sounds And Multimedia dialog box, which you display by opening the Sounds And

Multimedia icon in the Control Panel. The Sounds And Multimedia Properties dialog box has tabs for configuring when Windows plays sounds and which drivers Windows uses when playing and recording sound and displaying the properties of all your audio and video devices.

Choosing and Configuring Audio Input and Output Drivers

When you install Windows or sound equipment, Windows usually configures itself automatically to use the proper sound drivers. If you need to tell Windows which sound drivers to use or choose settings for your audio devices, including voice, follow these steps:

1. Choose Start | Settings | Control Panel and open the Sounds And Multimedia icon. You see the Sounds And Multimedia Properties dialog box.
2. Click the Audio tab if it's not already selected, shown in Figure 16-5.

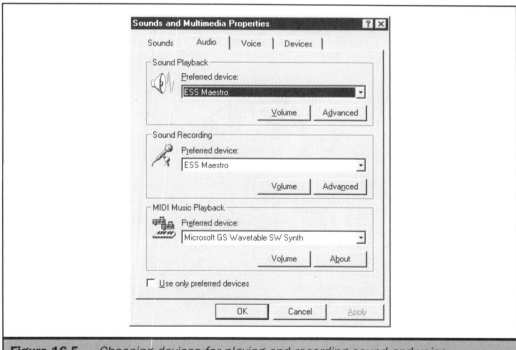

Figure 16-5.   *Choosing devices for playing and recording sound and voice*

3. Choose the driver used to play sounds by selecting the device from the list of available devices in the Sound Playback section.

4. Tell Windows more about your speakers or headphones by clicking the Advanced button in the Sound Playback section of the dialog box. You see the Advanced Audio Properties dialog box, shown in Figure 16-6.

5. Click the Speakers tab if it's not already selected. Click the Speaker Setup box and choose your computer's arrangement of speakers or headphones.

6. To set the amount of computing power your computer devotes to playing audio, click the Performance tab. Then set the Audio Playback Hardware Acceleration slider and Sample Rate Conversion Quality slider. Click OK.

7. To control the volume of your speakers or headphones, click the Volume button in the Sound Playback section of the Sounds And Multimedia Properties dialog box (see the next section "Controlling the Volume and Balance"). Close the Volume Control window when you've adjusted the volume.

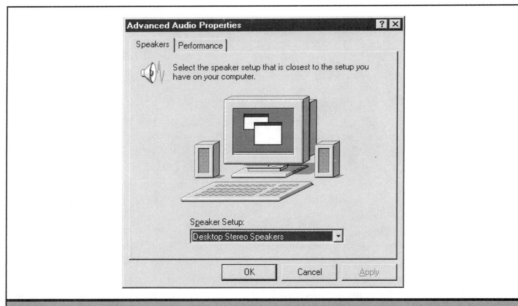

Figure 16-6. *The Advanced Audio Properties dialog box, for setting the properties of your speakers or headphones*

8. Choose the driver used to record sounds by clicking in the Preferred Device box in the Sound Recording section of the Sounds And Multimedia Properties dialog box and choosing a driver from the list that appears.

9. To set the amount of computing power your computer devotes to recording audio, click the Advanced button in the Sound Recording section. Then set the Audio Recording Hardware Acceleration slider and Sample Rate Conversion Quality slider. Click OK.

10. To control the volume when recording, click the Volume button in the Sound Recording section. You see the Recording Control window (see "Playing and Recording Sound Files," later in the chaper). Close the window when you've set the recording volume.

11. If you use voice applications (for example, to dictate into a voice-recognition system like Dragon Naturally Speaking, or to talk to other people over the Internet), click the Voice tab on the dialog box. You see sections for Voice Playback and Voice Capture, which you can set as described in steps 3–10.

12. You can control whether the Volume icon appears in the system tray on the Taskbar. Click the Sounds tab in the Sounds And Multimedia Properties dialog box and select or deselect the Show Volume Control On The Taskbar check box.

13. Click OK to exit the Sounds And Multimedia Properties dialog box and save your changes.

Tip   *If you have trouble getting sounds to play, try the Windows Sound Troubleshooter (see Chapter 34, section "Diagnosing Problems Using Troubleshooters").*

Controlling the Volume and Balance

You can control the volume and balance of the sound that comes out of your computer's speakers or headphones and goes into your microphones. You can also choose to mute (suppress) the sound for any audio device. You use the Volume icon (the little yellow loudspeaker icon) in the system tray on your Taskbar.

Note   *If the icon doesn't appear, choose Start | Settings | Control Panel, open the Sounds And Multimedia icon, click the Sounds tab (if it's not already selected), and click the Show Volume Control On The Taskbar check box until a check appears. Then click OK.*

Adjusting the Volume and Balance

To adjust the volume of your speakers, click the Volume icon on the Taskbar once; you see a Volume slider and a Mute check box:

Drag the Volume slider up for louder volume or down for softer volume. Select the Mute check box to suppress audio output. Click outside the window to make it disappear.

To adjust the volume and balance of any audio device, double-click the Volume icon. You see the Volume Control window:

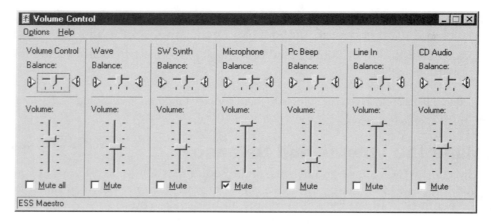

Another way to display this window is by clicking any of the Volume buttons on either the Audio or Voice tab of the Sounds and Multimedia Properties dialog box.

The Volume Control window can display a volume, balance, and mute setting for each audio input and output device on your computer. To choose which audio devices are included in the window, choose Options | Properties from its menu bar to display the Properties dialog box shown in Figure 16-7. Click the Playback setting to include audio output devices, the Recording setting to include audio input devices, or the Other setting to include other audio devices; the only other audio device is Voice Commands, which allows you to use software that interprets your voice input as

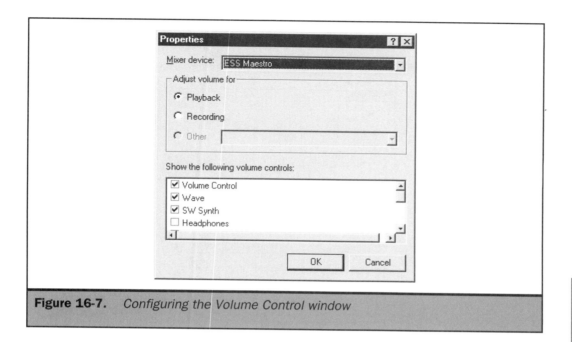

Figure 16-7.   *Configuring the Volume Control window*

commands to control programs. You can also click check boxes for individual audio devices in the Show The Following Volume Controls list. Leave the Mixer Device setting alone—it's usually a feature of your audio card. Then click OK to return to the Volume Control dialog box.

When you display volume controls for playback devices, the window is called Volume Control; and when you display recording devices, it's called Recording Control.

 If your speakers or headphones have a physical volume control knob, it's generally simpler and better to leave the Windows volume set fairly high, sending a strong signal through the wires, and just turn the knob to change the volume.

Choosing What Sounds Windows Makes

Windows comes with an array of sounds that it makes when certain *events* (Windows operations) occur. When you start Windows, for example, a rich, welcoming sound occurs; but you might prefer the sound of a friend yelling "Hello!" You can control which sounds Windows plays when specified events occur by opening the Sounds And Multimedia icon in the Control Panel. You see the Sounds tab of the Sounds And Multimedia Properties dialog box, shown in Figure 16-8.

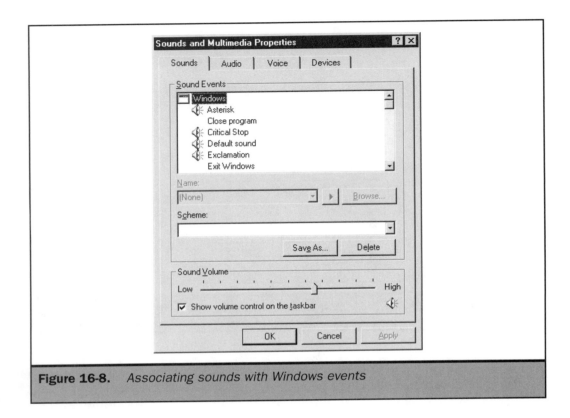

Figure 16-8. *Associating sounds with Windows events*

The Sounds Events box lists all the events that you can associate with a sound, including events that happen in Windows and other programs that use sound. Select an event, click in the Name box, and then choose a sound stored in a WAV (with extension .wav) file on your computer. To test out the sound, click the right-pointing triangle button to the right of the Name box. If an event in the Sound Events box has no yellow speaker icon to its left, no sound is currently assigned to the event.

The list of sounds in the Name box is the list of WAV files in the C:\Windows\Media folder. You can use WAV files that are stored in any folder on your computer; click the Browse button to choose a file. You can also test sounds in the Open dialog box that you see when you click the Browse button. Select any sound that appears in the window and click the Play button at the bottom of the dialog box—the sound plays. If the sound is too long, click the black square to stop it. To assign no sound to an event, choose (None) from the Name list.

You can save the set of sound associations and name the set as a *sound scheme*. Windows comes with a Windows Default sound scheme, which associates sounds with many events, and a No Sounds sound scheme, in which no sounds are associated with events. You can create your own sound schemes, too; associate the sounds you want to hear with the events that you want to prompt those sounds and click Save As.

Some PC Cards (add-on cards used in laptop computers) use drivers that generate sounds. To turn them off, open the PC Card Properties icon in the Control Panel, click the Global Settings tab, and then click Disable PC Card Sound Effects to uncheck its check box. If the PC Card Wizard runs, follow the Wizard's instructions, and try again.

Windows also comes with a set of sound schemes that are not automatically installed when you install Windows; to install them, open the Control Panel, open Add/Remove Programs, click the Windows Setup tab, choose Multimedia, click Details, and then choose Multimedia Sound Schemes from the list of Multimedia components. These sound schemes include jungle sounds, musical snippets, and robot-like sounds. The desktop themes that you can install from the Windows Me CD-ROM also include sound schemes (see Chapter 12, section "Choosing a Desktop Theme").

The Windows Default scheme is just plain sounds, but the others are more interesting. If you like lots of audio reaction, Robotz is your scheme. If you want sound but would rather it be unobtrusive, try the Utopia scheme. The Musica and Jungle schemes are between those extremes.

Playing and Recording Sound Files

Windows comes with several programs for recording and playing sound files:

- **Sound Recorder**   For recording, editing, and playing WAV files
- **Windows Media Player**   For playing WAV files
- **CD Player**   For playing audio CDs

The following sections describe how to use these programs. To play streaming audio files from the Internet, run RealPlayer or Windows Media Player (see Chapter 17, section "Playing Streaming Video Files from the Internet").

Playing and Recording WAV Sound Files with Sound Recorder

To play or record WAV files (with the extension .wav), you can use the built-in Sound Recorder program. Run it by choosing Start | Programs | Accessories | Entertainment | Sound Recorder. You see the Sound Recorder window, shown in Figure 16-9.

CONFIGURING WINDOWS FOR YOUR COMPUTER

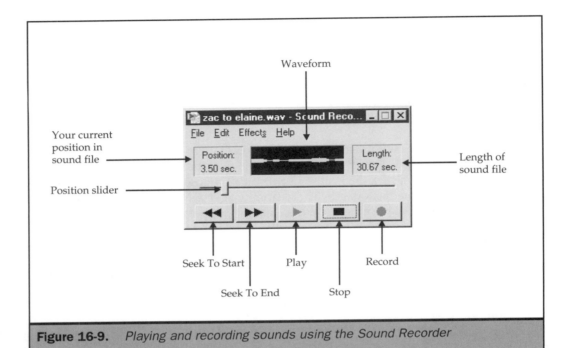

Figure 16-9.   *Playing and recording sounds using the Sound Recorder*

Playing Sounds

To play a sound file, choose File | Open, choose the filename, and click Open. Sound
Recorder opens the file, displays the filename on the title bar, the waveform of the first
part of the sound file, and the length of the sound in seconds. Next, click the Play button.
You can use the Stop button to stop playback.

The Position slider tracks your current position in the sound—it's similar to your
cursor in the file. To change your current position, drag the Position slider left or right to
move forward or backward in the sound file. For example, to hear the second half of the
sound, drag the Position slider to the middle and then click the Play button.

To discover other interesting ways that you can play back a sound (like slow or
backward), see the section "Editing Sounds," later in this chapter.

Note   *Some sound files come with information about who created the sound; choose File |
Properties to see the properties of the file.*

Windows comes with lots of sounds in WAV files; some are in your
C:\Windows\Media folder, and others are on the Windows Me CD-ROM, in
the \Cdsample\Sounds folder. To play these sounds, you can also use Media
Player (see "Playing Sound Files with Windows Media Player").

Recording Sounds

If your computer has a microphone, you can record sounds and store them in WAV
files. Follow these steps:

1. Choose File | New to begin a new sound file. If you are editing a sound file and
   haven't saved your changes, Sound Recorder asks whether you want to save
   them now.

2. Arrange the microphone so that you are ready to record.

3. Click the Record button in the Sound Recorder window.

4. Start the sound you want to record (for example, start talking).

5. When the sound you want to record has finished, click the Stop button.

6. Play back the sound by clicking the Play button.

7. Edit the sound as necessary (see the next section, "Editing Sounds").

8. If you want to save your recording, choose File | Save As, type a filename,
   and click Save.

If a file is already open in Sound Recorder when you record a sound, the recorded
sound records over part of the existing sound or is added to the end of the existing sound,
depending on the location of the Position slider. To add on to the end of a sound, move
the Position slider to the right end (or click the Seek To End button) and then record. To
replace part of any existing sound, move the Position slider to the beginning of the sound
you want to record over and record.

Editing Sounds

Once you've opened or recorded a sound file, you can fool around with it in the
following ways:

- **Copy**   To copy the entire sound to the Windows Clipboard so that you can
  paste it later, choose Edit | Copy or press CTRL-C.

- **Insert**   To insert another sound file into your existing sound, move the
  Position slider to the point at which you want to insert the file, choose Edit |
  Insert File, and choose the filename. To insert a copy from the Windows
  Clipboard, choose Edit | Paste Insert or press CTRL-V.

- **Mix**   To mix another sound file with your existing sound, move the Position slider to the point at which you want to mix the other sound, choose Edit | Mix With File and choose the filename. To mix a sound from the Windows Clipboard, choose Edit | Paste Mix. Sound Recorder mixes the two sounds together so you hear both at the same time. For example, you can record your voice several times and then mix the sounds together to sound like a crowd.

- **Cut**   You can omit parts of the sound, from the beginning of the sound to your current position or from your current position to the end of the sound. Move the Position slider to the point before or after which you want to delete and then choose Edit | Delete Before Current Position or Edit | Delete After Current Position. Click OK to confirm that you want to delete part of the sound.

- **Speed up or slow down**   To speed up the sound, choose Effects | Increase Speed. Sound Recorder plays the sound in half the time, raising the pitch at the same time. To slow down the sound, choose Effects | Decreases Speed; the sound plays in twice the time at a lower pitch.

- **Change volume**   To make the sound 25 percent louder, choose Effects | Increase Volume. To make the sound softer, choose Effects | Decrease Volume.

- **Add special effects**   To play the sound backward, choose Effects | Reverse. To add an echo, choose Effects | Add Echo.

Note   *You can't edit a sound if it is stored in compressed format. You can tell that a sound is stored in a compressed format, because no green waveform appears in the Sound Recorder window.*

Editing a sound changes the sound in memory but doesn't affect the sound file; to save your changes, choose File | Save or File | Save As. Until you save a sound, you can choose File | Revert to return to the previously saved version of the sound.

Converting Sounds to Other Formats

WAV files can use one of many different standard audio formats. Different formats offer trade-offs between audio fidelity and disk space, and are designed for different kinds of sounds, such as music or voice. You can also change the attributes of the sound, such as the sampling speed in Hertz (Hz), the number of bits used to store each sample, and whether the sound is stereo or mono. Some formats are considered to be compressed; if you convert a sound to a compressed format, you can't edit the sound in Sound Recorder.

To change the format of your WAV file, choose File | Properties to display the Properties dialog box for the file, shown in Figure 16-10. The top half of the dialog box shows information about the sound, including its format. In Figure 16-10, the format is PCM, the format that Sound Recorder uses when recording sounds from your microphone.

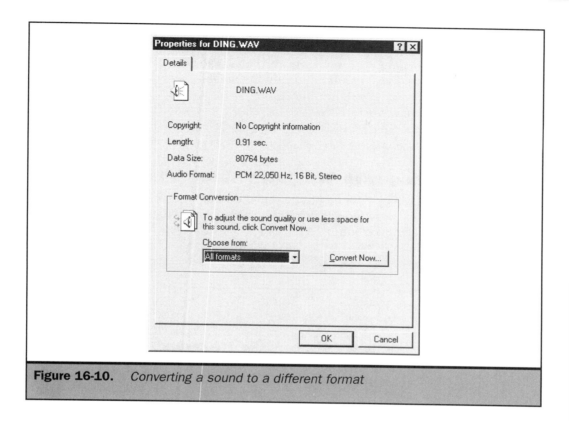

Figure 16-10. *Converting a sound to a different format*

The Format Conversion section of the Properties dialog box for a WAV file enables you to convert the sound to a different format; however, all the available formats are still stored as WAV files. Click the Convert Now button to see the Sound Selection dialog box, shown here:

You can choose the format and the attributes you want to use by clicking in the Format and Attributes boxes and making a selection in each. The list of Attributes changes based on the Format you choose. Some widely used combinations of formats and attributes have been named to make them easier to select; click in the Name box to choose a named combination of format and attributes. Then click OK twice to convert the sound. Choose File | Save or File | Save As to save the converted sound in a file.

You can also change the format when saving a file. Choose File | Save or File | Save As and type or select the filename. Click the Change button to display the Sound Selection dialog box, and then perform the conversion as described in this section.

Playing Sound Files with Windows Media Player

Another program that can play sound files, and many other types of files, is Windows Media Player. Start Windows Media Player by choosing Start | Programs | Windows Media Player or by clicking the button on the Quick Launch toolbar that sits next to your Start button. You see the Windows Media Player window shown in Figure 16-11. When it starts, no image appears on its "video screen" (the gray box in the middle of its window).

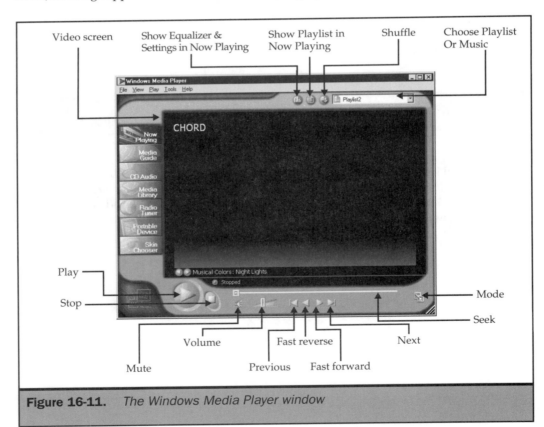

Figure 16-11. *The Windows Media Player window*

Strangely, the program doesn't update its video screen until a file is loaded, and the video screen might end up displaying bits and pieces of the windows and dialog boxes that you have displayed in that area. Don't worry—the Media Player program is fine.

To play a sound file, choose File | Open, set the Files Of Type box to Audio File, choose a WAV or other sound file, and click Open. Next, click the Play button in the lower-left corner of the Windows Media Player window to play the sound.

 See the section "Playing Video Files with Windows Media Player" in the next chapter for details about playing video files with Media Player.

The Windows Media Player Window

The program has buttons on the left, top, and bottom of the Windows Media Player window. The area in the center of the window is the "screen" on which videos and other pictures appear. You can also choose to display volume controls, playlists, and other information on the video screen.

Here is a description of the buttons that appear down the left side of the window:

 ■ **Now Playing**   Displays the currently loaded file. If the file is a video, it appears on the video screen. If an audio file is loaded, you see a visualization of the music (see the next section, "Playing Audio Files Stored on Your Computer").

 ■ **Media Guide**   Connects to the Windows Media Web site over the Internet, from which you can view video files content that is updated on a daily basis (see "Playing Streaming Audio Files from the Internet").

 ■ **CD Audio**   Plays sounds from an audio CD inserted in your CD-ROM drive (see "Playing Audio CDs").

 ■ **Media Library**   Enables you to organize your audio and video files (see "Creating and Editing Playlists").

 ■ **Radio Tuner**   Plays Internet radio stations (see "Listening to Internet Radio Stations")—that is, radio stations that are available over the Internet as streaming audio files.

 ■ **Portable Device**   Enables you to move audio files to and from a portable audio player (see "Moving Files to and from Portable Players").

 ■ **Skin Chooser**   Enables you to choose a different look (appearance and controls) for the program (see "Customizing the Windows Media Player Window").

CONFIGURING WINDOWS
FOR YOUR COMPUTER

Windows Media Player has its own Auto Update feature, which tells you when updates to the program are available from Microsoft over the Internet. When you exit Windows Media Player, a dialog box may appear offering to download and install updates. Read the information about the update and decide whether you want it.

Playing Audio Files Stored on Your Computer

To play a file on your computer (or shared drive on a LAN), choose File | Open and choose the filename. Windows Media Player can play sound files in a variety of formats, including WAV files and streaming audio files.

Click the Now Playing button to see the video that goes with the audio. If the file you are playing doesn't include video images, Windows Media Player creates them for you. As the music plays, the video screen shows *visualizations*, graphical representations of the sound. There are 46 kinds of visualizations that come with Windows Media Player—all are interesting, and some are positively mesmerizing. You can change the visualization that appears by clicking the small gray arrow buttons underneath the visualization. The name of the visualization appears to the right of the buttons. You can also surf through them all by choosing View | Visualizations from the menu, selecting the name of a group of visualizations, and choosing the specific visualization.

You can add other information to the video screen by using two buttons that always appear along the top of the Windows Media Player window:

- **Show Equalizer & Settings In Now Playing**   Displays controls along the bottom of the video screen when Now Playing is selected (see "Adjusting Volume, Graphic Equalization, and Other Sound Settings").

- **Show Playlist In Now Playing**   Displays your current playlist along the right side of the video screen.

If you have a lot of audio files stored on your computer, you can use the Media Library feature to organize your files, described in the next section.

You can remove visualizations that you never watch, change the properties of some visualizations, or add new visualizations that you download from the Internet. Choose Tools | Options from the menu and click the Visualizations tab to display a list of the available visualizations.

Organizing Your Audio Files into a Media Library

Windows Media Player includes the Media Library, a storehouse for all of your audio and video files (Figure 16-12). To organize your multimedia files (also called *tracks*, Windows Media Player can search your drives (local and shared network drives) for files. It organizes them into lists of audio files, video files, and the addresses of radio stations on the Internet. You can then organize the files into playlists, described in the next section.

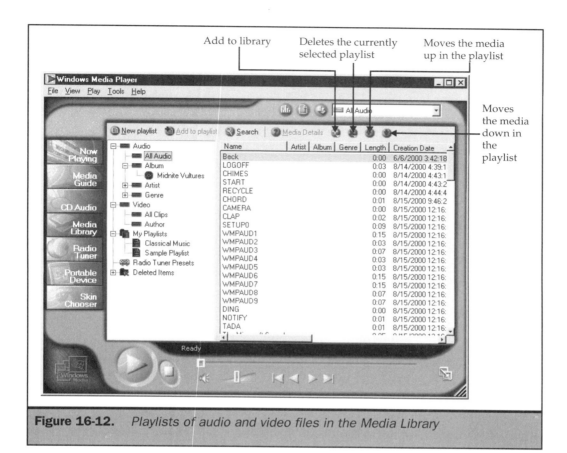

Figure 16-12.   *Playlists of audio and video files in the Media Library*

The first time you click the Media Library button, Windows Media Player offers to perform the search, or you can follow these steps at any time:

1. Choose Tools | Search Computer For Media from the menu (or press F3). You see the Search Computer For Media dialog box:

2. Specify whether to search Local Drives (disk drives on your own computer), Network Drives (shared drives on a LAN), All Drives, and a list of individual drive letters. If you select a specific drive by drive letter, you can choose a folder to start in (the program searches only that folder and its subfolders). Choose the Include WAV And MIDI Files Found In System Folders check box if you want to include the audio files that come with Windows (unlikely, if you are making a catalog of music files).

3. Click Start Search. A dialog box appears telling you the progress of the search. When it has finished, it tells you how many files it found. Click Close.

4. Click Close again to dismiss the Search Computer For Media dialog box.

Now click the Media Library button (if it's not already selected) to see all your audio and video files. The list on the left shows the categories of files, and the list on the right shows the contents of the selected category. The five major categories are Audio, Video (described in the next chapter), My Playlists (described in the next section), Radio Tuner Presets (for Internet radio stations, described in "Listening to Internet Radio Stations," later in this chapter), and Deleted Items. The Audio category lists these subcategories:

- **All Audio**   Displays all audio files in alphabetical order, no matter where they are stored.

- **Album**   Displays audio files by the album of which they are a part (if any). Windows Media Player identifies albums by information from audio CDs (see the next section) or from the MP3 ID3 tags, for MP3 format files.

- **Artist**   Displays audio files by artist. If you have songs from more than one album by a single artist, the albums appear as sub-subcategories.

- **Genre**   Displays audio files by genres and styles. Since genres and styles are primarily determined by personal taste (ever argue with someone as to whether Steely Dan is jazz, rock, or progressive?), this is an unreliable way to sort music—unless you go through each album and apply your personal touch to each album.

You can click a file to play it and the files that follow it on the list. To see more information about a file, right-click it and choose Properties from the menu that appears. If you don't want a file to appear anywhere in your Media Library, right-click it and choose Delete From Library from the shortcut menu that appears.

You can also update the information about a file. Right-click a piece of information about a file and choose Edit. Windows Media Player enables you to edit the field you clicked (this feature doesn't work on all fields). You can also make the same change to the information about a group of files (for example, change the Genre of a group of files). Select a group of files, click a field (like Artist or Genre), choose Edit Selected, edit the text, and press ENTER. Windows Media Player makes the change to all the files you selected.

Here are other things you can do when looking at your Media Library:

- **Search**   Click the Search button along the top of the video screen to search for a field by a word or phrase in its title.

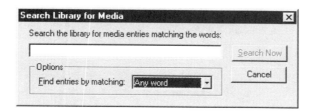

- **Media Details**   Click the Media Details button along the top of the video screen to ask Windows Media Player to get details, if any, about the selected file.

You can configure other Media Library settings. Choose Tools | Options from the menu and click the Media Library tab to set them:

- **Other Application Access Rights**   Sets the level of access other programs have to your Media Library and playlist information.
- **Internet Site Rights**   Sets the level of access that Web sites have to your Media Library and playlist information.
- **Media Files**   If you uncheck this check box, Windows Media Player asks whether you want the program to manage that media or not. This setting is only useful if you use other digital media applications like Liquid Audio.

Creating and Editing Playlists

A *playlist* is a set of audio files that you plan to play as a group. You can create a playlist, give it a name, and put audio files into it. Then you can play that group of files anytime, either in the order in which they appear on the playlist or in random (shuffled) order.

Click the Media Library button in the Windows Media Player window to see, create, and edit playlists. In the list of categories on the left side of the video screen, one category is My Playlists. Windows comes with one playlist, named Sample Playlist, containing one audio file, a rock song from Beck's "Midnight Vulture" album.

To create a new playlist, click the New Playlist button at the top of the video screen area. Type a name for the new playlist and click OK. Windows Media Player adds your new playlist to the My Playlists category.

You can add files to a playlist in several ways:

- Click the Add To Playlist button at the top left of the video screen when the Media Library button is selected. You see a menu of your playlists. Alternatively, click the unlabeled Add To Playlist button at the top right of the video screen.

You get to choose among adding a file from your computer, adding a file from the Internet, or (if you are playing a CD) adding a file from the CD.

- Right-click a file (or select a group of files and right-click them), and choose Add To Playlist from the shortcut menu that appears.
- Drag the file (or files) to the name of the playlist in the My Playlists category on the left side of the video screen when Media Library is selected.
- Click Add To Playlist.

When you add a file to a playlist, Windows Media Player doesn't copy the file to the playlist—the audio file remains where it is stored. Instead, it creates a shortcut to the file. This capability allows you to include one file in many playlists. When you delete a file from a playlist, Windows doesn't delete the audio file; it just deletes the shortcut to the file from the playlist. To delete a file from a playlist, right-click the file and choose Delete From Playlist from the shortcut menu that appears (or click the Delete Media Form Playlist Or Library button along the right top of the video screen).

You can adjust the order of the files in the playlist by dragging them up and down the list. Or, select a file and click the Moves The Media Up In The Playlist or Moves The Media Down In The Playlist buttons along the right top of the video screen. Click the Shuffle button along the top of the Windows Media Player window to play the files in random order.

You can also save your playlists in files in various formats, including the uncommon Windows Media types (with extensions .asx, .wax, and .wvx), as well as the nearly ubiquitous WinAmp format (.m3u). To export a playlist, do the following:

1. Click the Media Library button.
2. Click the My Playlists item to show your available playlists on the right.
3. Select a playlist.
4. Choose File | Export to open the Export Playlist dialog box.
5. Type a name for the file in the Save As box.
6. Add one of the file extensions to have it saved as a particular type (usually .m3u).
7. Click Save.

 To play a playlist you've heard recently, choose it from the drop-down list in the upper-right corner of the Windows Media Player window.

Playing Audio CDs

Every audio CD has a serial number that identifies the artist, album title, and the list of tracks (songs) on the CD. These serial numbers are stored in a database called the *Compact Disc Database* or *CDDB*, which is accessible over the Internet. The CDDB is a cooperative effort of the community of music lovers, entering information about their

CDs. When you insert an audio CD into your CD-ROM drive, Windows Media Player reads the number from the audio CD and sends that number to the CDDB. If the audio CD number is in the CDDB, the list of songs and artists is usually already in the CDDB, unless you have a truly obscure album. Windows Media Player downloads this information to your computer automatically. The list of tracks appears in the playlist that appears when you click the Now Playing or CD Audio button. If the CD is not in the CDDB database, then you have the option to type the titles of the tracks in yourself (do so—as a public service).

When you put an audio CD into your CD-ROM drive, the Windows Media Player program runs automatically. If AutoPlay is turned on, the music begins playing. Windows Media Player connects to the Internet and searches the CDDB for the CD's ID number. If it finds the CD's number, the CD's title appears at the top of the video screen area when you click the Now Playing button. To see a playlist, click the CD Audio button. Figure 16-13 shows the playlist for a CD of Bach's Brandenburg Concertos that isn't in the CDDB.

Figure 16-13.   *The list of tracks on an audio CD*

To play a specific track, double-click a song title, right-click a song title, and select Play; or select the song title and click the Play button at the bottom of the window. You can edit the information about a CD track the same way you edit information about the tracks in a playlist. Right-click information about the track and choose Edit from the shortcut menu that appears, or select a group of tracks, right-click the information about one track, and choose Edit Selected to make the same change to all the selected tracks. For more information about a track, right-click it and choose Properties.

You can change the order in which Windows Media Player plays the tracks on the CD. Right-click a track and choose Move Up or Move Down from the shortcut menu, or simply drag them up or down with the mouse. A gray line tracks your movement, indicating where the track will be placed when you let go. Click the Shuffle button along the top of the Windows Media Player window to play the files in random order. (The check boxes to the left of the tracks are used for selecting tracks when copying a CD; they don't affect which tracks Windows Media Player plays.)

When you are playing an audio CD, these buttons appear across the top of the video screen:

- **Copy Music**   Copies the selected tracks to the Windows Media (WMA) digital format at 128 Kbs (a format that includes most of what the human ear can discern from digital music, but is far more compact than purely raw audio data).

- **Get Names**   Checks the CDDB to see whether your CD is in the database. If there is only one match, Windows Media Player downloads the list and stores it for reuse later. If there is more than one match, you see a list of the located matches and you can select the best one. Follow the directions in the Wizard to complete the search. If the CD doesn't appear in the database, Windows Media Player asks if you would like to contribute that data to the database for others to see.

- **Album Details**   Displays a comprehensive look at the particular title you have in your CD-ROM drive, if available. You may see an album cover, a list of songs, and possibly even a review.

To see a visualization of the music, click the Now Playing button and choose a visualization (see "Playing Audio Files Stored on Your Computer," earlier in this chapter).

Windows Media Player includes several configuration settings for audio CDs. Choose Tools | Options and click the CD Audio tab to control how audio CDs play:

- **Playback Settings**   If your CD-ROM drive supports it, select Digital Playback, for a clearer sound. You can also turn on error correction, which increases the amount of RAM used to buffer the audio data.

- **Copying Settings**   You can set the quality level that you want to use when copying music from CDs to your hard disk. The higher the quality, the bigger the file. Enable or disable Personal Rights Management, which is a way of protecting the media that you copy from CD from being distributed illegally.

■ **Archive**   Click the Change button to specify the folder to which Windows Media Player stores files created by copying CDs.

Playing Streaming Audio Files from the Internet

If you know the exact URL of an audio file on the Internet, choose File | Open Location and enter the URL of the file to play it. However, it's usually easier to use the Media Guide button to help you find the file you want.

When you click the Media Guide button, the program connects to Microsoft's Windows Media site at **http://www.windowsmedia.com**. When the site loads, as shown in Figure 16-14, you can view content that is updated on a daily basis. The audio and video files on the Windows Media site usually have to do with television, movies, or music, and they often have some very neat stuff to look at or listen to.

Figure 16-14.   *The Media Guide showing broadband content*

Though the Media Guide does not have any controls for Windows Media Player itself, its interface is the Windows Media home page (also at **http://www.windowsmedia.com**). The pages have Back and Forward links in the upper-right corner of the display that allow you to move about with a modicum of the ease you get in your web browser.

If your PC connects to the Internet through a firewall, you might not be able to use Media Player's Media Guide or Radio Tuner buttons. The port numbers that Media Players uses when connecting to streaming audio material on Web sites aren't standard, and the proxy server that connects your LAN to the Internet might not be configured to handle them. Choose Tools | Options to display the Options dialog box. The Network tab controls how the program communicates over the Internet:

- **Protocols**   Defines which network access protocols the program uses to communicate with servers and (optionally) which ports to use (useful if you communicate with the Internet through a firewall).

- **Proxy Settings**   Specifies whether your PC communicate with the Internet over a LAN, using a proxy server program (see Chapter 30). The default is not to use a proxy server. If your PC connects to the Internet over a LAN, get the configuration information from your LAN administrator.

Listening to Internet Radio Stations

Many radio stations use the Internet to broadcast their signal to parts of the world that their antennas could never reach. In addition to large-scale commercial stations, hundreds of little one-, two-, and three-person operations are cropping up. Several multimillion dollar broadcasters are even hoping to find themselves at the forefront of the latest Internet craze. Window Media Player brings all of the stations that use the Windows Media streaming technology to you in the form of a searchable database.

To listen to Internet radio, click the Radio Tuner button. Windows Media Player shows the list of presets and radio stations shown in Figure 16-15. This information comes from the WindowsMedia.com Web site.

The left side of the video screen lists your preset stations (these stations also appear when you click the Media Library button in the Radio Tuner Presets category). A number of preprogrammed presets are already there, but you can remove and/or edit them. Those presets fall under the Features category. You can change categories by selecting another one from the pull-down menu that is located underneath the Presets label. At first, the only other selection is My Presets, assuming that you want to store your preset stations under a single heading. You can, however change that. Follow these instructions:

1. Click the Edit button to the right of the Presets label. A small dialog box entitled Edit Presets List—Web Page Dialog appears.

2. Click anywhere in either the Add New List or Create Local Station List fields and type a new list name. The Add button next to the field becomes active. Click it.

3. Select the list that you would like to relocate and use the Up and Down arrow buttons to move it in those directions.

4. Click the Delete button to remove any categories that you don't want.

Caution *When you delete a category that has presets in it, they are all deleted as well. Please keep this in mind, because there's no easy way to move presets from one category to another.*

5. Click Save to close the dialog box and accept the changes.

6. To add new stations to your recently created list, highlight them and click the Add button between the two panes.

You can also click the Search button located on the right end of the window to get a more advanced set of tools for finding stations. Also, take advantage of the local stations feature in the Presets edit dialog. You can even enter a ZIP code and hear what your old favorite stations are like today, if they're online.

Figure 16-15. *Tuning in to Internet radio stations*

Two configuration settings affect the quality of streaming files from the Internet. Choose Tools | Options and click the Performance tab to set them:

- **Connection Speed** You can either let Windows Media Player detect the speed at which your computer communicates with the Internet, or, if you know for sure, you can set it yourself.

- **Network Buffering** Defines how much data is stored in RAM before it actually plays. If you have trouble with getting smooth playback, click the Buffer radio button and put up to 60 seconds in the field. 30 to 45 seconds is typically good enough.

Adjusting Volume, Graphic Equalization, and Other Sound Settings

If you want to adjust how your audio files sound, click the Show Equalizer & Settings In Now Playing button at the top of the Windows Media Player window and click the Now Playing button. In the bottom part of the video screen, the equalizer and settings appear. Click the Show Equalizer & Settings In Now Playing button again to remove these tools from the screen. You can also start or stop displaying these tools by choosing View | Now Playing Tools from the menu, and choosing the tool.

Several sets of tools can appear in this area. The left arrow and right arrow buttons in the lower-left corner of the area control which tools appear. Click them to switch among these groups of tools:

- **SRS WOW Effects** Includes several special effects: TruBass, WOW Effect, SRS WOW Effect, and Speakers. TruBass adds more bass to your music the further to the right you slide it. WOW Effect adds more separation between the stereo channels. The On/Off button enables or disables all these effects. Clicking the SRS logo takes your Web browser to the SRS WOWcast.com Web site at **http://www.srswowcast.com**, in case you are interested in files that use the SES WOW technology. The Speakers button switches among Normal Speakers, Large Speakers, and Headphones.

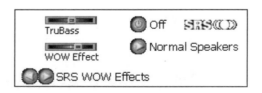

- **Graphic Equalizer** Enables you to adjust the treble and bass balance, and left and right speaker balance. The ten vertical sliders adjust the volume of the high, treble notes (at the left end) through the low, bass notes (at the right end). The On/Off button enables or disables the effects of any modifications you make to the equalizer. Turning it off means you get the sound exactly as it was recorded.

Rather than setting them individually, you can click the button below the On/Off button, which cycles through preset bass/treble settings that work for many common musical genres. The Balance slider adjusts the relative volume of left and right speakers.

- **Video Settings**   Enables you to control the color and brightness of the video images.

- **Windows Media Information**   Displays any information that the program can glean about tracks or albums you are listening to. If it's available, it even shows a picture of the album cover. When you are playing MP3 files downloaded from the Internet, no information appears.

MP3 files have their own way of identifying the file's contents to MP3 players. They are called ID3 tags, and they embed the information about artist, album, title, length, genre, track number, and notes.

- **Captions**   Displays captions, if the video includes them.

Moving Files to and from Portable Players

Portable MP3 players are quite popular, as are handheld devices that can play music, like PocketPCs. The portable digital music machines of today are as small as a nice writing instrument and can hold a few hours worth of digital music (in the case of the Sony MC-P10 Music Clip). Others can play up to 100 hours and take up no more room than a portable CD player (for example, the Creative Labs Nomad Jukebox comes with a 6GB hard disk). Whether you have a dedicated MP3 player or a handheld computer, it's easy to copy music from your PC to the portable device by using Windows Media Player. Here's how:

1. Make playlists of all the music you want to copy to your device.

2. Click the Portable Device button. The tracks on a playlist appear on the left side of the video screen, and the tracks on the portable device appear on the right side.

3. Select the files available from the left pane. Hold the SHIFT or CTRL keys to select a contiguous group or individual tracks from the available list. If no tracks appear on the left side, you do not have any playlists.

4. When you have selected all of the tracks that you want to copy and they do not exceed the storage capacity of your device, click the Copy Music button in the upper-left corner of the window.

The serial connections with which many portable music players connect to the PC are slow, but many portable music players come with USB connections that are much faster.

You can control how Windows Media Player copies files to portable players—choose Tools | Options and click the Portable Device tab of the Options dialog box to see these settings:

- **Settings**   You can set the quality of the copies to any portable devices you might have connected. Either choose yourself or let Winds Media Player choose for you.

- **Currently Supported Devices**   Click the Detail button to launch your Web browser and go to the Windows Media Web site where you can browse a list of portable music devices that Windows Media Player recognizes. This button is useful if you plan to buy a portable device—be sure to choose one that Windows Media Player can work with.

Customizing the Windows Media Player Window

When you run Windows Media Player, it appears in Full mode, with all the buttons and controls we've described so far. Another size option is Compact mode, in which the program displays two windows. The larger of the two is the video window, showing the video area:

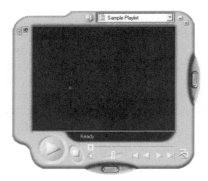

The other, tiny window displays the Mode button, which you click to return to Full mode:

Licensing Issues for Digital Music

In order to protect music transferred from audio CDs or the Internet from being copied, Microsoft has integrated some protection features that prevent you from copying *unsigned* files to a portable device. A file is *signed* if you copied the music from an audio CD using Windows Media Player. When you copy music from an audio CD, Windows Media Player assumes that the music is licensed to you to use at your discretion (as long and you don't resell it or otherwise misrepresent the media to the general public). All files that you copy are encoded in Microsoft's proprietary .wma format, so you need a device that can play them (a PocketPC, WinJam, or other digital music systems). You can also get signed music files by buying and downloading them from the Windows Media Web site.

You are fairly safe from getting improperly licensed music from unknown online sources as long as you patronize the Windows Media Web site (and maybe a few select partners). Any music purchased through the Windows Media site or from one of its partners is likely to be properly licensed.

To switch from Full mode to Compact mode, click the Mode button that appears in the lower-right corner of the Windows Media Player window.

The video area resizes itself automatically when you resize the window or open either the Equalizer & Settings or Playlist panes. You may also have both the Equalizer & Settings and Playlist panes open at the same time.

A third option for how Windows Media Player can look is *Skin mode*. WinAmp, a popular shareware MP3 player, popularized the ability to *skin* an application—that is, offer a variety of user interfaces so that you can choose among a number of window, menu, and button designs. In a complete turnaround from Microsoft's typical functional look, the company has integrated skins into the new Media Player. Full mode has only a single look; but in Skin mode, customization can run rampant.

Changing skins changes the locations of all the controls and the overall appearance of Windows Media Player, often drastically. Don't try changing the program's skins until you feel confident with the application as a whole. If you do get stuck, click the large Windows Media logo button that appears in a floating window adjacent to your newly skinned Windows Media Player.

CONFIGURING WINDOWS FOR YOUR COMPUTER

To switch to another skin:

1. If you are in Compact mode, switch to Full mode by clicking the Mode button.

2. Click the Skin Chooser button. In the video screen, you see two lists: on the left is a list of available skins and on the right is a picture of that skin (see Figure 16-16).

3. Select a skin name from the list on the left side. An image appears in the right pane showing you what the skin really looks like.

4. Click the Apply Skin at the top of the list to activate the skin and switch to Skin mode. If you want to change skins without changing modes, just leave the new skin selected and move to the tab that you want to be in.

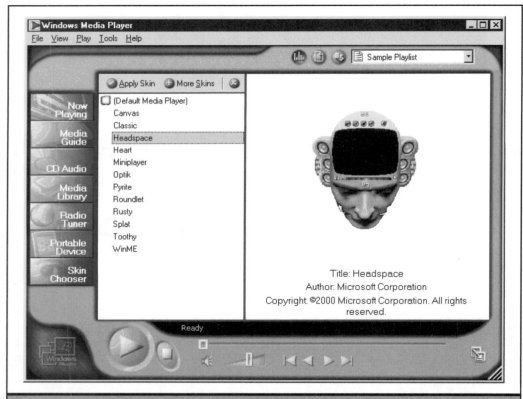

Figure 16-16. *Choosing a different skin for Windows Media Player*

You can get more skins from the Windows Media Web site at any time. Skins are stored in files with the extension .wmz in the C:\Program Files\Windows Media Player\Skins. Click the More Skins button at the top of the list and your Web browser goes to a special set of pages. When you click the picture showing the skin, Windows Media Player downloads it and asks if you would like to activate your new skin now.

Switching back from a new skin can be trickier, since the new controls may be unrecognizable. Hover your mouse over anything that looks like it might be a button until you find one with the label Return To Full Mode.

 Some skins consume lots of memory. If your computer's performance slows when you are using Windows Media Player, switch back to the default skin.

You can configure Windows Media Player by choosing Tools | Options to display the Options dialog box. The Player tab of the Options dialog box controls the program itself:

- **Auto Upgrade**   Specifies how often you want Windows Media Player to check the Microsoft Web site for upgrades. You can also enable or disable automatic codec downloads.

- **Internet Settings**   Indicate whether you want your player individually recognized and whether to get media licenses. The first option allows Web sites to store something like a media cookie on your PC.

- **Player Settings**   Specifies how Windows Media Player looks when it starts.

Specifying Which File Formats Windows Media Player Plays

You can choose which file formats Windows Media Player is configured to play. Choose Tools | Options from the menu and click the Formats tab to see a list of file formats. If you want another program to play files of a specific format, uncheck the check box for that format.

CONFIGURING WINDOWS FOR YOUR COMPUTER

Working with MIDI

MIDI devices are usually musical instruments or recording devices (see "What Is MIDI?" early in the chapter). They have digital inputs and outputs and can transmit and understand music using the MIDI language. You can connect a MIDI instrument, like a keyboard, to your PC so that you can play music on the keyboard and record and listen to the music on your PC. You need additional MIDI software to play, edit, and mix MIDI inputs.

If you have more than one MIDI instrument installed, you can configure Windows with a *MIDI scheme*, which specifies which inputs are stored on each *MIDI channel*, so that instruments can be edited separately and then mixed together later. You can use MIDI editing programs to edit and mix the MIDI inputs channel by channel.

Windows Media Player can play MIDI files. (Windows 98 came with another program, Active Movie, which you can run by choosing Start | Programs | Accessories | Entertainment | ActiveMovie Control.) This section describes how to install a MIDI device, configure Windows to use it, and play MIDI files.

Windows comes with some sample MIDI files that are not automatically installed when you install Windows. To install them, open the Control Panel, open Add/Remove Programs, click the Windows Setup tab, choose Multimedia, click Details, and choose Sample Sounds from the list of Multimedia components. Windows stores the MIDI files in the C:\Windows\Media folder in files with the .mid extension.

Installing a MIDI Device

To install a MIDI (Musical Instrument Digital Interface) device, you connect a cable from the instrument to a MIDI port on your computer's sound card. Then follow these steps:

1. Choose Start | Settings | Control Panel and open the Sounds And Multimedia icon.

2. Click the Devices tab (see Figure 16-17). Look down the list and locate the MIDI Devices and Instruments item. Select it and click the Properties button at the bottom of the list. In the MIDI Devices And Instruments Properties dialog box, click the Add New Instrument button and select the attached device from the list. If the device does not appear, check the device for proper installation and to see whether the power is on.

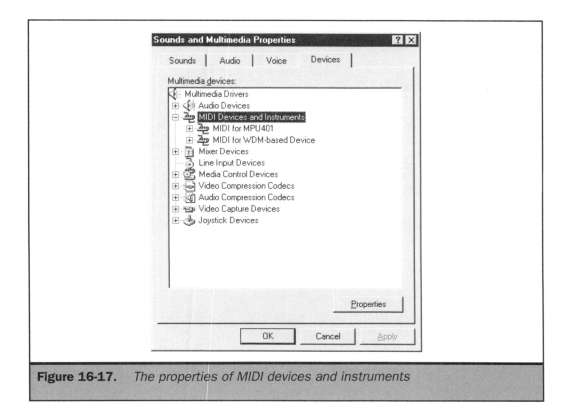

Figure 16-17.   *The properties of MIDI devices and instruments*

Playing MIDI Files with Media Player

Windows Media Player starts when you open a MIDI file. (In Windows 98, the Active Movie program—which was eliminated from Windows Me—played MIDI files.) You can also start Media Player by choosing Start | Programs | Media Player. To play a MIDI file, choose File | Open, set the Files Of Type box to MIDI File (*.mid, *.rmi, or *.midi), choose a MIDI file, and click Open. Click the Play button in the lower-left corner of the Media Player window.

Windows
Me

Chapter 17

Working with Video

It's natural for computers to handle video data—after all, when you use a computer you are already sitting in front of a video screen. Windows Me supports video, both input and output, if you add the necessary hardware to your computer. This chapter describes what formats video data is stored in, how to play video files using Windows Media Player, and how to make your own video files using the new Windows Movie Maker program. You can also use the DVD Player program to play digital video disks, and WebTV For Windows to watch broadcast television.

> **Note** *Microsoft uses the word "media" to refer to graphic, audio, and video files.*

What Is Video Data?

You can use various *video capture devices* to get video information into your computer, such as digital video cameras. See Chapter 14 for instructions on how to install video capture devices. To display video, Windows uses your screen; and to play the accompanying audio, it uses your sound board and speakers.

Because the amount of data coming from a digital video camera is so immense, your computer can't process and store it fast enough. Instead, video data is compressed on its way into the computer from the camera and is then stored in a compressed format. A very fast DSP (digital signal processor, a kind of specialized computer) chip in your video capture hardware does the actual compression. Windows Me comes with a number of *codecs*, programs for video compression and decompression, so that Windows can decompress and recompress video data when you want to display or edit it. Windows also includes *DirectX*, a feature that enhances video playback. Windows stores most video in *AVI files*, files with the filename extension .avi. Other popular formats for video files are QuickTime (.qt) and MPEG (.mpg).

To see a list of your installed video capture devices, along with a list of the available codecs, choose Start | Settings | Control Panel, open the Sounds And Multimedia icon, and click the Devices tab. You see the list of audio and video devices your computer can use (Figure 16-2 in the previous chapter). To see a list of video capture devices, click the plus box to the left of the Video Capture Devices entry. If no plus box appears, no devices are installed. To see a list of codecs that are available, click the plus box to the left of the Video Compression Codecs entry.

> **Tip** *To experiment with playing video, you can use some video clips on the Windows Me CD-ROM, in the \Cdsample\Videos folder. The video clips are all ads, but they are useful for testing.*

Playing Video Files with Windows Media Player

As described in the previous chapter, Windows Media Player is a program that can play a number of different types of multimedia files, including audio, MIDI, and video files. Windows Media Player version 7 replaces all of the disparate applications that performed its functions in previous versions of Windows. The only task it does not perform (yet) is playing DVD movies (see "Playing Video Disks with DVD Player").

To start Windows Media Player, choose Start | Programs | Windows Media Player, or click the Windows Media Player icon on the Quick Launch toolbar on the Taskbar.

 For the details on the new interface for Windows Media Player, turn to Chapter 16.

Playing Video Files from Your Hard Disk

You have several options for selecting a file to play. The easiest is for you to have Windows Media Player scan your disk drives for audio and video files of all types (see Chapter 16, section "Creating and Editing Playlists"). If you have already scanned for multimedia files, click the Media Library button, click Video in the list of categories, and click the All Clips subcategory. Windows Media Player displays all available video files. Double-click a file in the Media Library to play the file, followed by the rest of the files on the list. If the file requires a codec to tell Windows Media Player how to read its format, the program connects to the Windows Media Web site (at **http://www.windowsmedia.com**) and tries to locate the appropriate codec.

 If you access the Internet via a dial-up connection, Windows Media Player tries to connect. If you are already connected, Windows Media Player connects to the Windows Media Web site through the existing connection. You may be required to validate the installation of the new codec.

To play a video file that is not in your Media Library, choose File | Open from the Windows Media Player menu bar or press CTRL-O. In the Open dialog box that appears, type the name of a video file in the File Name box and click Open. You can also drag the video file (or any multimedia file) from the desktop or an Explorer window into the Windows Media Player window.

When you open a file, either by choosing File | Open or by using the Media Library, Windows Media Player loads the video file, switches to the Now Playing view, and displays the video in the video screen part of the Windows Media Player window. If it's not already playing, click the Play button to start the video (see Figure 17-1).

While you are playing a video file, you can also perform these actions:

■ Stop the video by clicking the Stop button.

■ View the image full-screen by pressing ALT-ENTER or by choosing View | Full Screen from the menu bar. To return from full-screen display, press ESC.

■ Move forward or backward in the file by clicking the Skip Forward, Skip Backward, Fast Forward, or Rewind buttons (the VCR-style buttons along the bottom of the window) or by dragging the Position slider.

■ Adjust the volume by clicking and dragging the Volume slider or by choosing Play | Volume from the menu bar.

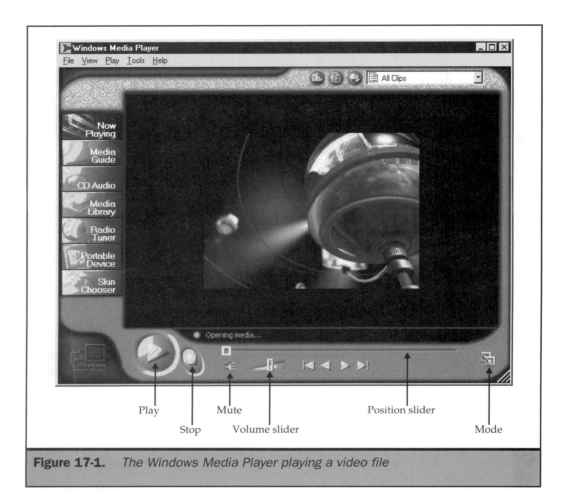

Play

Stop

Mute

Volume slider

Position slider

Mode

Figure 17-1. *The Windows Media Player playing a video file*

If you are experiencing video problems and suspect your video card, you can change your acceleration setting. Choose Tools | Options from the menu and click the Performance tab as shown in Figure 17-2. Reduce the Hardware Acceleration (that is, slide it to the left) to solve some hardware-based video problems. If you have a 400MHz machine with 128MBs of RAM or better, set the DV Settings to Large; otherwise, set it somewhere in the leftmost two-thirds of the slider.

Playing Streaming Video Files from the Internet

Video files tend to be huge because each frame of a video requires many thousands of bytes of information. Viewing video over the Internet can involve long waits for video files to arrive. The invention of streaming video improved matters: you can begin playing a streaming video file after only the first section of the file has arrived (see Chapter 16,

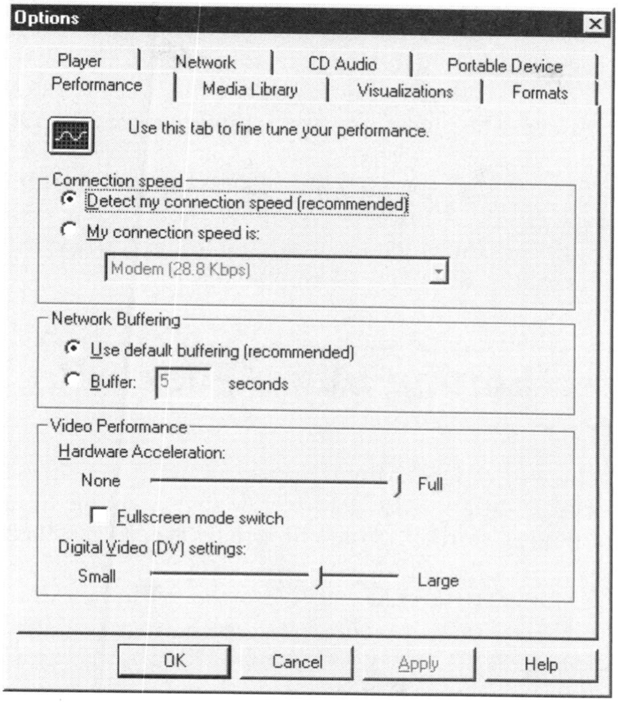

Figure 17-2.   *Windows Media Player's Options dialog box*

CONFIGURING WINDOWS
FOR YOUR COMPUTER

section "What Are Streaming Audio and Video?"). The streaming video player continues to receive later sections of the file at the same time that it is playing earlier sections. As long as the program can receive information at least as fast as it can play it, you see uninterrupted video. Streaming audio files and players work the same way.

The most popular streaming audio and video formats are RealAudio (with file extension .ra and .rm) and RealVideo (with extension .rv). You can download the RealPlayer program for free from the Real Web site at **http://www.real.com**; this program works with your Web browser to play RealAudio and RealVideo files from the Internet.

Microsoft has its own streaming video format, called *Active Streaming Format*, or *ASF*. Files in this format have the extension .asf or .asx. *ASF files* with the .asf extension contain the actual streaming video data. *ASX files* with the .asx extension contain a single line of text, with the URL of a continuously updating video newsfeed. Windows Media Player can play ASF or ASX files. Normally, Windows Media Player runs automatically when you start to download an ASF or ASX file from the Internet. You can also run Windows Media Player and then open the streaming file by choosing File | Open from the menu.

When you see a link on a Web page for an active streaming format (ASF) file or newsfeed (ASX file), click the link. Depending on how your Web browser is configured, you may see a message asking whether to open the file or save it; choose to open the file. Your browser downloads the first section of the file, runs Windows Media Player, and begins to play the file. The video may appear in your browser window or in a separate window.

You can use the Stop, Pause, and Play buttons to stop and start the video. When you are done playing the video, close the Windows Media Player window if it remains open. If you started viewing the video by clicking a link in your Web browser, the browser window is probably still open where you left it.

Creating and Editing Video Files with Windows Movie Maker

Microsoft added the new Windows Movie Maker program to help establish Windows Me's multimedia focus. Windows Movie Maker enables you to edit graphical, audio, and video files into movies, stored in video files that you can play with Windows Media Player.

Windows Movie Maker creates files called *projects*, with the extension .mswmm. Each project can contain one or more *collections*, which are lists of items to include in the movie. A collection contains *clips*, which can be video, audio, or still graphics files. Information about your collections is stored in C:\Windows\Application Data\ Microsoft\Movie Maker. Once you've created your movie, you can save it as a video file in Windows Media format with the extension .wmv.

The Windows Movie Maker Window

To open Windows Movie Maker, choose Start | Programs | Accessories | Windows Movie Maker. The Windows Movie Maker window has four areas and several toolbars, as shown in Figure 17-3:

- **Collections list**   Lists the collections in this project. One collection is selected.

- **Clips**   Shows icons for each clip in the currently selected collection. Clips can include graphics files, audio files, or video files. For graphics files, you see a small version of the file (a thumbnail). For audio files, you see a speaker icon. For video files, you see a thumbnail of a scene from the video.

- **Monitor**   Displays the current clip, if it's a graphic or video file. If the current clip is an audio file, you see a speaker icon. Below the Monitor are VCR-style buttons to play the current clip.

- **Workspace**   Displays the timeline or storyboard of your movie, as explained in the section "Composing Your Movie," later in this chapter.

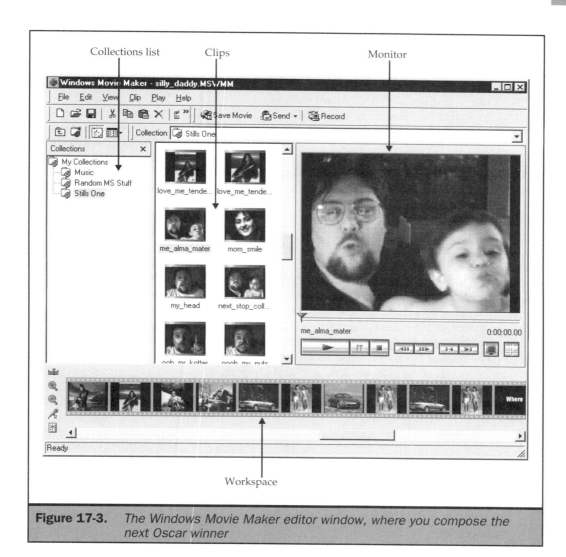

Figure 17-3. *The Windows Movie Maker editor window, where you compose the next Oscar winner*

If you've already been working on a movie, Windows Movie Maker opens the last project you opened. You can open any existing project by choosing File | Open Project from the menu or clicking the Open Project icon on the toolbar.

Importing Files

Before you can create a movie, you need to import video, audio, and graphic information with which to make the movie. Depending on where your picture, sound, and video information comes from, you need the appropriate hardware or access to a way of getting that information onto your computer. The three types of information you can import are as follows:

- **Video**   Some video equipment stores can copy your videotapes to CD-ROM, which you can then import into Windows Movie Maker. If you want to import your own video from a video camera or VCR, you need a video capture card. Both ATI (**http://www.ati.com**) and Creative Labs (**http://www.creativelabs.com**) make reasonably priced video capture cards. You can also acquire video through a FireWire port by connecting it to a digital video camera. Windows Movie Maker can import .wmv, .asf, .avi, .mpg, and other video format files.

- **Audio**   You can capture audio with your computer by running the Sound Recorder program (see Chapter 16, section "Playing and Recording WAV Sound Files with Sound Recorder"), or you can use Windows Media Player to capture music from audio CDs (see Chapter 16, section "Playing Audio CDs"). Windows Media Player can import .mp3, .asf, .wma, .wav, and other format audio files.

- **Still pictures**   You can use a digital camera or scanner to capture still pictures in graphics files (see Chapter 16, section "Working with Graphics"). You can also create drawings or titles using Microsoft Paint or another graphics editor (see Chapter 5, section "Drawing Pictures Using Microsoft Paint"). Windows Movie Maker can import .gif, .jpg, and other formats for graphics files.

Once you have graphics, audio, or video files, you can import them into Windows Movie Maker. Follow these steps:

1. Run Windows Movie Maker and open your project if it's not already open.
2. Select the collection into which you want to import the files. You can create a new collection for them by selecting the top-level collection (My Collections) and choosing File | New | Collection from the menu.
3. Choose File | Import or press CTRL-I. You see the Select The File To Import dialog box.
4. Select the file or files to import. You can select more than one file by holding the SHIFT or CTRL keys while selecting files.
5. After a potentially grueling wait, the files are added to the active collection.

Tip	*Another way to import files is to drag-and-drop them into the Windows Movie Maker window.*

After you import information into the program, Windows Movie Maker shows each clip as a little icon in the current collection. You can find out more about any clip by right-clicking it and choosing Properties from the shortcut menu that appears. To play a single clip, select it and click the Play button on the VCR-style buttons just below the Monitor (the leftmost button).

> **Tip** *When you import a video file, Windows Movie Maker automatically breaks it into clips, based on where it thinks the scenes start and end. To turn this feature off, choose View | Options and deselect the Automatically Create Clips option.*

You can organize your clips into collections by dragging the clips from one collection to another, or by using cut-and-paste (CTRL-X to cut and CTRL-V to paste).

> **Note** *If you don't have any video, just place all of your still pictures in a collection and make a slide show with still pictures and a sound track or narration.*

Composing Your Movie

The Workspace area at the bottom of the Windows Movie Maker window displays either the Storyboard or the Timeline. To create a movie out of your clips, you drag them to the Storyboard or Timeline in the order that you want them shown.

The *Storyboard* is like a book, in which each blank square is like the page of a book, and you decide what appears on each page and in what order. Find the first clip—either video or graphic file—and drag it to the first space in the Storyboard. This clip becomes the first page of your story, and the first part of your movie. Continue dragging video and graphic clips to the Storyboard in the order in which you want them to appear. You can always switch the order later. With clips, the Storyboard looks like this:

> **Tip** *To move clips around after you've placed them in the Storyboard, just drag them left or right. When a line appears between the clips where you would like to place the clip to be reordered, drop it.*

The *Timeline* gives you another view of the same movie. Display it in the Workspace area by clicking the Timeline icon at the left end of the Workspace (switch back to the Storyboard by clicking the Storyboard icon that takes the Timeline icon's place), or choose View | Timeline from the menu (View | Storyboard takes you back to the

Storyboard). The Timeline shows the timing of the clips in the movie, displaying how many seconds each clip takes:

You can add, delete, and rearrange the clips on either the Storyboard or the Timeline—the effect is the same. If you delete a clip from the Storyboard or Timeline, it disappears from the movie, but remains in the project available for reuse. If you don't think you'll use a clip after all, you can delete by selecting it in the Clips area and pressing the DEL key—this action deletes the information from the project.

Adding Sound

To provide a soundtrack, you can drag an audio clip to the Timeline (not the Storyboard). The audio clip runs along the bottom of the Timeline, showing where the audio starts and ends. You can control the balance between the sound portion of the video clips and of the audio soundtrack by choosing Edit | Audio Levels from the menu and sliding the slider between Video Track and Audio Track:

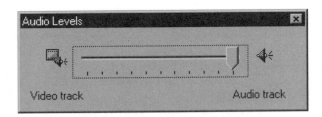

You can record a narration to go with your slide show or video. The idea is to time what you're saying with what's appearing on the screen. (Note: Your computer needs a working microphone to record the narration.) Follow these steps:

1. Choose File | Record Narration to display the Record Narration Track dialog box.

2. If you want to mute the audio track during the playback of the movie, click the check box marked Mute Video Soundtrack.

3. When you're ready, click the Record button. Be prepared—as soon as you click the Record button, Windows Movie Maker begins recording and playing the video at the same time.

4. Talk along with the movie.

5. When you've finished, click the Stop button. Windows Movie Maker prompts you to save your narration and imports it into your project.

Run through your video a few times, clicking Pause and making some notes. Then spend some time rehearsing. Don't try to be Marlin Perkins, but you'll gain appreciation if you do a well-timed job.

Previewing Your Movie

After you add the clips for your movie, you can see how it looks. Choose Play | Play Entire Storyboard/Timeline from the menu, or right-click the Storyboard or Timeline and choosing Play Entire Storyboard/Timeline from the shortcut menu that appears. You can also play a section of the movie by selecting a series of clips from the Storyboard and clicking the Play button below the Monitor. Or, select all of the clips on the Storyboard (right-click any clip and choose Select All), and then click the Play VCR button below the Monitor. The VCR-style controls look like this:

Editing Your Movie

Windows Movie Maker includes many commands for editing your movie. Here are a few neat things you can do:

- **Slide shows** If you put a graphics file in your movie, Windows Movie Maker shows it for five seconds. You can make a good-looking slide show that you can send to people through e-mail, just by adding your still photos to the Storyboard of a movie. You can change the five-second length to speed up or slow down your slide show. On the Timeline, select the clip for the still photo. A pair of triangles appears along the top of the clip, one on each end. Drag the right-hand triangle to the right to add time to the clip, or to the left to subtract time from it.

■ **Transitions**   You can create a fading transition from one video or picture to the next. Click the first clip of the pair. A pair of triangles appears along the top of the clip. Drag the right triangle into the next clip, so the clips appear to overlap:

The wider the overlap, the longer the transition will be. The resulting fade-in looks like Figure 17-4.

 Windows Movie Maker does not have integrated transition effects like all other consumer-grade video editors. You can't add special transitions other than the fade effect.

■ **Titling**   Windows Movie Maker does not have commands to create titles (as some other video edition programs do). To add titles, choose Start | Programs | Accessories | Paint to run Microsoft Paint (see Chapter 5, section "Drawing Pictures Using Microsoft Paint"). Choose Image | Attributes and change the document size to a width of 320 pixels and a height of 240 pixels. Add anything to your title page or pages that you like. A basic black background and white lettering goes well with video presentations and is easy to read. Save your document or documents using descriptive file names in a folder to import them into Windows Movie Maker.

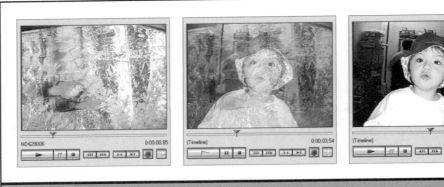

Figure 17-4.   *Overlapping two clips results in a fade-in.*

Saving Your Movie

Once your movie shines, click the Save Movie button on the toolbar or choose File |
Save Movie from the menu. You see the Save Movie dialog box shown in Figure 17-5.
The Setting box in the Playback Quality section gives you four choices for quality.
They are

- Low Quality
- Medium Quality (Recommended)
- High Quality
- Other (then choose a format in the Profile drop-down menu)

As you set the Play Quality Setting, the File Size shows how large the resulting
movie will be. The default is Medium Quality, which gives reasonable clarity and
excellent sound. A collection of photographs and music that runs 30 seconds took a
mere 791Kb of space at High Quality. It was 94Kb at Low Quality and 343Kb at
Medium Quality, all of which are reasonable sizes when sending movies via e-mail. If
you plan to make large movies with video, be aware that they can take up anywhere
from several megabytes to several hundred megabytes of disk space.

CONFIGURING WINDOWS FOR YOUR COMPUTER

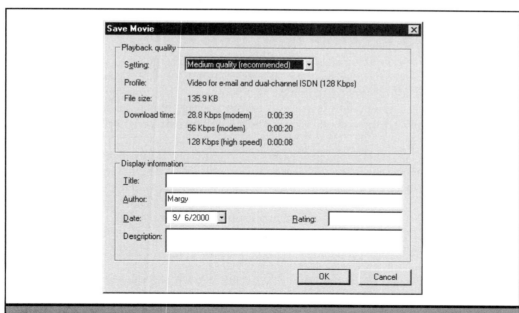

Figure 17-5.   *Saving your movie in a format that Windows Media Player can play*

Fill out the other information in the dialog box with as much or as little detail as you wish and click OK. In the Save As dialog box that appears, enter a name for the file. Windows Movie Maker saves the movie in a file with the .wmv extension.

> **Tip** *If you have a CD-R or CD-RW drive, create a CD-ROM to send your family and friends, rather than e-mail huge files.*

You can e-mail your movies or send them to your Web server directly from Windows Movie Maker. To send a movie via e-mail or the Web, click the Send button on the toolbar or choose File | Send Movie To from the menu. Select E-mail or Web Server from the menu that appears. Choose the quality for the resulting video using a dialog box that looks like the Save Movie dialog box in Figure 17-5 and fill out the other information in the dialog box. When you click OK, Windows Movie Maker asks which e-mail program to use. Select either Default E-mail Program at the top of the list or the name of the program you typically use from the items below. If you plan to send the videos using a different program another time, leave the Don't Ask Me Again item unchecked. Click OK. Your e-mail program opens and a new message appears, waiting for you to enter the addresses of those you wish to send it to.

> **Tip** *Be sure to check that your intended recipients have Windows Media Player before sending them a movie.*

Playing Video Disks with DVD Player

A *DVD (Digital Versatile Disk or Digital Video Disk)* is like a large CD—it's a digital disk that can contain video material. If you buy movies on DVDs and you have a DVD drive connected to your computer, you can play DVDs on your computer by using the DVD Player program that comes with Windows. Before you try this, make sure that your DVD drive has the appropriate decoder card and software drivers to play DVDs.

> **Caution** *You cannot play a DVD movie with just a DVD drive and a disc. You must also have a decoder, built in to the drive, on a separate card (or integrated into your systems video card), or from a software package like WinDVD. Windows comes with the program— DVD Player—but not with the decoder. The next section includes a source for decoders if your DVD drive didn't come with one. Your DVD player may have come with its own player program that you can use for playing DVDs—you don't have to use the Windows DVD Player program.*

To run DVD Player, insert the DVD in your DVD drive and then choose Start | Programs | Accessories | Entertainment | DVD Player. (If your system doesn't include a DVD player, the command doesn't appear.) If AutoRun is enabled on your system, DVD Player starts automatically when you insert a DVD into the drive.

The DVD Player interface works like a VCR (Figure 17-6). Additional controls may appear for the advanced features that a specific DVD offers: consult the DVD itself. These advanced features may play video clips, alternative edits, different endings, or the ever-popular outtakes.

Configuring Your DVD Player

If your computer has a DVD drive, you probably got it in one of two ways: preinstalled in your computer or as a third-party add-on. If the DVD drive was part of your computer system, it should have been tested and properly configured from the get-go, so no additional configuration should be needed.

If, on the other hand, you installed a third-party DVD drive, you need a decoder to read the DVD media. There are two kinds of DVD decoders: hardware and software. Hardware decoders are uncommon, as we were only able to locate a single PCI-based DVD decoder card in two hours of searching. Software decoders, however, are plentiful and inexpensive (compared to the $180–500 range we saw in hardware). WinDVD (**http://www.intervideo.com**) is the most popular package, retails for $30 and ships with various third-party DVD drives, and installs in seconds. We found it capable and easy to use, though we recommend at least a 500MHz Pentium III with

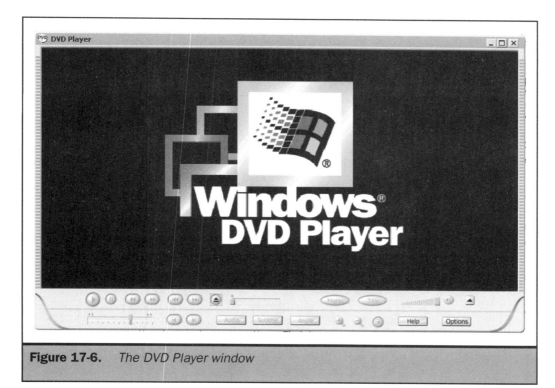

Figure 17-6. *The DVD Player window*

128MB of RAM for best playback performance. Needless to say, with such high entrance stakes, DVD on the desktop has not taken off. (Another reason, of course, is that most people prefer to watch movies on larger screens in the comfort of their living rooms, rather than on computer screens at their desks.)

Controlling Rated Movies

One feature that is popular with parents is Parental Control, which is amazingly simple and effective. The Parental Control feature uses the already existing and well-established MPAA ratings system. Each DVD movie has a lot of additional information encoded into the DVD, including the movie's rating, so the decoder software can tell a G-rated movie from an NC17-rated movie.

To control which ratings people can play on your DVD player, choose Tools | Options from the menu, and click the Parental Control tab (shown in Figure 17-7). The first time you click it, you can set a password that you need to provide any time you want to view or change the ratings. This password prevents anyone from gaining access to the configuration dialog box and modifying the limitations that you set.

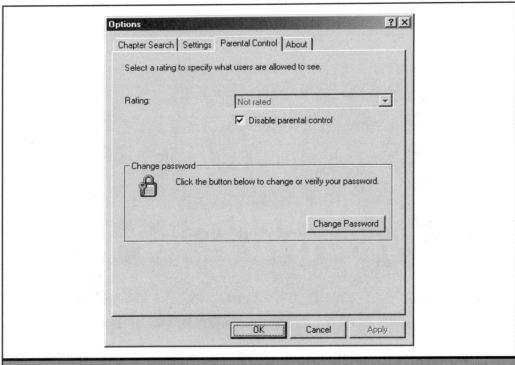

Figure 17-7. *Parental Control in DVD Player*

Note   *If you have not yet set a password, you cannot change the Rating setting.*

   To set the highest rating you want anyone to see, just select it. All ratings before it on the list will also be available. For example, to limit the available movies to PG13, PG, and G, set the Rating to PG13.

Viewing TV by Using Your Computer

Windows comes with an application called WebTV For Windows, which allows you to watch broadcast television channels on your computer screen. To use the WebTV For Windows program to watch TV, you need a TV tuner card installed in your computer. Even without a TV tuner card, you can see a program guide.

Note   *WebTV For Windows has nothing to do with WebTV. WebTV is a box you can attach to your television and phone line to convert the television into a computer capable of browsing the Web and sending and receiving e-mail. WebTV turns your television into a computer; WebTV For Windows turns your computer into a television. Actually, WebTV For Windows has one thing in common with WebTV: they are both owned by Microsoft.*

   Since, most computers don't have TV tuner cards, WebTV For Windows is not installed automatically when you install Windows. To install WebTV For Windows, open the Control Panel, open the Add/Remove Programs icon, click the Windows Setup tab, and choose WebTV For Windows from the list of components (see Chapter 3, section "Installing and Uninstalling Programs That Come with Windows"). You have to restart Windows twice in the process of configuring WebTV For Windows. Windows detects three new "hardware components" that are actually software components of WebTV For Windows: a TV Data Adapter, a codec for processing TV data, and a Closed Caption Decoder.

   To run WebTV For Windows, choose Start | Programs | Accessories | Entertainment | WebTV For Windows. The first time you run, a Wizard walks you through configuring the program. Once you see the WebTV For Windows window (Figure 17-8), which takes up the entire screen, double-click the TV Configuration channel (usually 96) to use the Wizard to change your configuration again.

   If you don't have a TV tuner card installed in your computer, you can run WebTV For Windows, but no channels appear. Even without a TV tuner card, you can display television listings in the Program Guide window. To configure WebTV For Windows to display listings, restart the configuration program by double-clicking the TV Configuration channel, and then click the GUIDE PLUS+ link. Windows connects to the Internet, asks you for your location and cable company (choose Broadcast if you don't have cable), and configures WebTV For Windows to display television listings for your area.

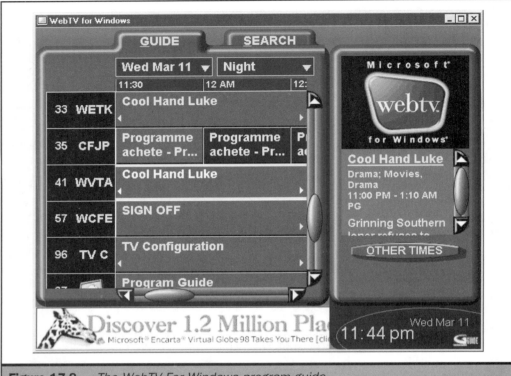

Figure 17-8.   *The WebTV For Windows program guide*

Here are some things you can do with the WebTV For Windows:

- Watch a channel by clicking a channel and clicking the Watch button.

- Display the TV Toolbar by pressing ALT or F10. Use buttons on the TV Toolbar to display the program guide (click Display) or change your selection of favorite channels (click Settings).

- Change channels by clicking one of your favorite channels on the TV Toolbar, changing the channel number on the TV Toolbar or choosing a channel from the program guide.

- Search for a program based on its title, category, actors, or movie ratings. Display the program guide and click the Search tab.

- Display the WebTV For Windows in a window (instead of full-screen) by clicking the Minimize button on the TV Toolbar. Unless you have a huge monitor, the resulting television image is too small to be useful.

- Get help by pressing F1 or by clicking Help on the TV Toolbar. WebTV For Windows displays a Help system that works like Windows Help And Support (see Chapter 6).

- Exit by clicking the Close button on the TV Toolbar.

Tip *Unless your computer came with a built-in TV tuner, a regular color television probably provides a better picture at a lower cost than a TV tuner card for your computer.*

The
Complete
Reference

Windows
Me

Chapter 18

Running Windows Me on Laptops

Many computer users use laptops—it's convenient to be able to pick up your computer, with all its data and software, and take it anywhere. But laptops have disadvantages, too, many of which are addressed by Windows Me. This chapter is full of suggestions about how to make the most of your laptop, including these suggestions:

- You can coordinate files with those on a desktop computer by using the Windows Briefcase.

- You can print a document, even when you aren't attached to a printer, by deferring printing until a printer is available.

- You can use power management to make your battery last longer.

- If you use a docking station to connect your laptop to desktop devices, you should know about docking and undocking and hardware profiles.

- You can connect to a network or another computer to use its resources when you don't have a network card by using Direct Cable Connection or Dial-Up Networking.

Coordinating Your Laptop with Your Desktop by Using the Windows Briefcase

If you use more than one computer on a regular basis, you should try the Windows Briefcase, a program that coordinates files you work on, so you always use the most current version. Windows Briefcase is especially useful if you use a laptop when you're on the road and a desktop machine in the office, but Briefcase is useful for anyone who uses several computers.

The Windows Briefcase program creates and maintains *Briefcases*, which are folders containing files and subfolders that you can move between your laptop and another computer. Your default Briefcase is called My Briefcase, but you can rename it or create additional Briefcases (see "Using Multiple Briefcases").

The easiest way to use Briefcase to coordinate files on different computers is to have the two computers connected by a network or another connection. However, you can also use Briefcase with a floppy disk, although that limits the total size of the files you can move from computer to computer.

The My Briefcase icon appears on the desktop: open the icon to see its contents. Click or double-click the My Briefcase icon depending on whether you use single-click or double-click for your desktop (see Chapter 1, section "Choosing Between Single-Click and Double-Click"). If you don't see it, you may need to install the Windows Briefcase from your Windows Me CD-ROM by using the Windows Setup program. Open Control Panel, open the Add/Remove Programs icon, click the Windows Setup tab, choose Accessories from the groups of components, click Details, and then choose Briefcase.

 If you think the Windows Briefcase is installed, but it doesn't appear on the desktop, right-click the desktop and choose New | Briefcase from the menu that appears.

The first time you open the My Briefcase window, you also see the Welcome To The Windows Briefcase window, with tips for using the program. Click Finish when you have read the tips.

Using Briefcase to Synchronize Files

The most common use of a Briefcase is for transferring files from a desktop to a laptop for use while away from the office, and then transferring the updated files back to the desktop when you return. Using Briefcase to transfer files has four steps:

1. Move files to the Briefcase. Choose only the files you will use and update while you're away from your desktop computer.

2. Copy the Briefcase to the laptop.

3. Use files from the Briefcase while you are on the road using the laptop.

4. When you are ready to work at your desktop again, tell Briefcase to synchronize the files on the two computers, so both computers contain the latest version of each file in the Briefcase.

 Briefcase uses the system time and date to synchronize files—make sure the time and date on each computer is correct.

These steps are somewhat different, depending on whether a local area network (LAN) connects the laptop and desktop computers. Without a LAN connection, you have to use a floppy disk (or disks) to move the Briefcase to the laptop. With a LAN, you can sit at the laptop and drag files from the desktop to the laptop's Briefcase.

Moving Files to the Briefcase

The first step is to find the files you want to have on the road and drag them to your Briefcase. The easiest way to do this is to select files in Windows Explorer and drag them to the Briefcase icon or window. You can do this in several steps as you select files in different folders on your hard disk. You can also right-click a file and choose Send To | My Briefcase from the shortcut menu.

You move files differently if the laptop and desktop computers are connected by a LAN—sit at the laptop and drag files from a drive located on the desktop computer to the laptop's Briefcase.

If you don't have a LAN, you need to complete a few extra steps:

1. Sit at the desktop and drag the files you need to the Briefcase icon on the desktop, or the Briefcase window if it's open.

2. Drag the Briefcase to a floppy drive or right-click the Briefcase and choose Send To | Floppy (choosing the drive where you want to move the Briefcase).

  Make sure to drag actual files to the Briefcase, not shortcuts to files.

Copying the Briefcase to the Laptop

If your desktop and laptop computers are connected by a LAN, the Briefcase with the files you need is still on the desktop computer, where it will do you no good when you leave the office. If you have a LAN, skip this section, because the Briefcase with the files you need is already on the laptop. Also skip this section if you want to use the Briefcase files from the floppy disk. However, using a floppy instead of the hard disk will slow you down noticeably if you are using large files.

To copy the Briefcase with its files to the laptop's hard drive, follow these steps:

1. Take the disk to which you copied the Briefcase, insert it in the floppy drive of the laptop, and view the contents of the drive. You see the Briefcase icon.

2. Drag the Briefcase from the floppy drive to the laptop's desktop.

  If the laptop already has an icon on the Desktop called My Briefcase, and that is the name of the Briefcase you are copying, rename the old My Briefcase, so the two don't have the same name.

Using Files in a Briefcase

While you're on the road (or just not using your desktop computer), make sure to use the files from the Briefcase. To do so, simply open the Briefcase window (My Briefcase in Figure 18-1) and double-click a file you want to use, just as you would a file in any other folder. You can use the usual Explorer window commands to control how files in the Briefcase window appear (see Chapter 9, section "Changing Views").

If you use an application's File | Open command, display the files in the Briefcase by clicking the Up One Level button in the Open dialog box until you can't go up any more levels—the Briefcase is on your computer's desktop. Open the Briefcase to see the files it contains.

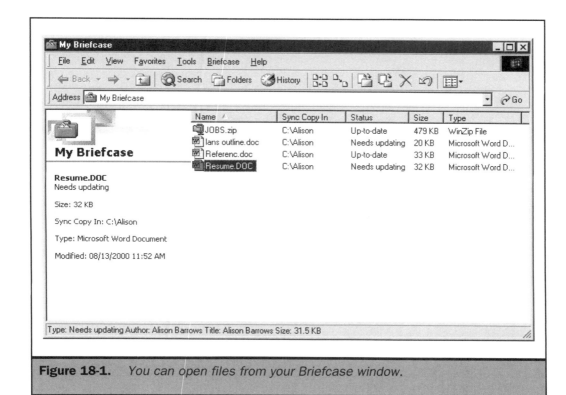

Figure 18-1. *You can open files from your Briefcase window.*

CONFIGURING WINDOWS FOR YOUR COMPUTER

When you save a file from the Briefcase, use the Save button to make sure you save it back to the Briefcase. If you don't save the file back to the Briefcase, the Briefcase won't be able to synchronize files for you.

Note *You should edit a file on only one computer before you synchronize the files with Briefcase. If you edit a particular file while you're on the road and someone at the office edits the same file, you won't be able to keep all the changes unless the program the file uses can show you what they are. Briefcase gives you the option to keep only one of the two files. However, if someone at the office edits a file you took with you in your Briefcase but you didn't edit it, you can keep the most current version of the file.*

Here are other things you can do in the Briefcase window:

■ You can see the update status of each file in the Status column in the Briefcase. You can also check the status of a file in the Briefcase by selecting it in the Briefcase window and choosing File | Properties from the menu bar, or right-click the file and choose Properties from the menu that appears. When you see the Properties dialog box for the file, click the Update Status tab (see Figure 18-2).

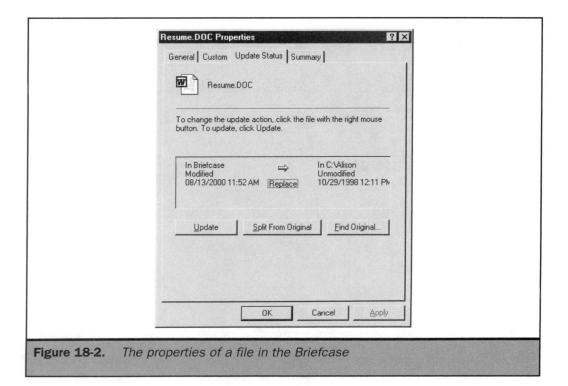

Figure 18-2. *The properties of a file in the Briefcase*

- If you drag a file from another location into the Briefcase, you can find the original copy of this file. In the Properties dialog box for the file on the Update Status tab, click the Find Original button. Windows displays the folder containing the original file in an Explorer window.

- You can sever the connection between the original file and the copy of the file in the Briefcase—for example, if the copy in the Briefcase has changed sufficiently that you also want to keep the original copy. Select the file in the Briefcase window and choose Briefcase | Split From Original from the menu bar. You can also right-click the filename, choose Properties from the menu that appears, click the Update Status tab, and then click the Split From Original button.

Synchronizing the Edited Files in a Briefcase

When you return to your desktop PC, you need to synchronize the files on your laptop and your desktop. Follow these steps to synchronize the files:

1. If you have a LAN, reestablish the connection between the two computers. If you have a docking station that supports *hot docking* (installing or removing the computer in the docking station without turning the computer off), the Briefcase may open automatically (see "Using a Docking Station"). If you don't have a LAN, move Briefcase from the laptop's desktop back to the floppy disk, take the floppy disk to the original computer, and then move the Briefcase back to the original computer's desktop.

2. Open the Briefcase window. You see the status of each file in the Status column, as shown in Figure 18-1. (Choose View | Details if this column doesn't appear.) A file's status can be one of the following three:

   - **Orphan**   The file exists only in the Briefcase and not on the source computer (in this example, the desktop computer is the source computer).

   - **Up-To-Date**   The file has not changed on either computer.

   - **Needs Updating**   The file has changed on either the desktop or the laptop (or both).

3. Click the Update All button on the Briefcase toolbar. The Update My Briefcase dialog box appears, showing how each file needs to be updated, as shown in Figure 18-3. A file can be updated in one of the following ways:

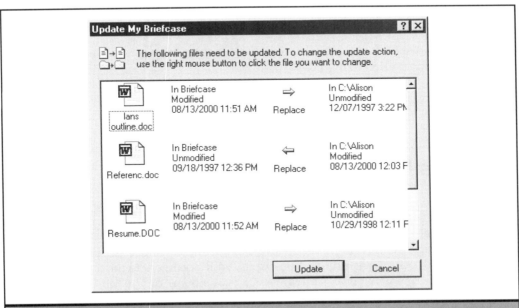

Figure 18-3.   *Briefcase tells you how files have changed and what needs to be done to synchronize the files in the briefcase with the files on the desktop computer.*

- **Replace, with an arrow pointing to the right** This is the most common action. It means the file in the Briefcase will replace the file of the same name on the desktop computer.

- **Replace, with an arrow pointing to the left** This means the file on the desktop computer is the most recent—it will replace the file of the same name in the Briefcase.

- **Skip (both changed)** This means both files (the one on the desktop and the one on the laptop) have been changed and Briefcase can't determine which file should be used. You need to determine which version of the file you want to use.

4. If you don't want a file updated as shown, right-click the file and choose a method from the shortcut menu that appears.

5. Click the Update button to update the files.

Using Multiple Briefcases

You may want to have multiple briefcases—perhaps one for each project on which you are working. Multiple briefcases enable you to take with you only the files you need. Multiple briefcases also enable you to divide your files into groups small enough to fit on to one floppy disk. Follow these steps to create additional briefcases:

1. Right-click the desktop and choose New | Briefcase from the menu that appears. An icon called New Briefcase appears on the desktop.

2. Rename the new icon to reflect the files it will contain (see Chapter 8, section "Naming and Renaming Files and Folders").

Tip *You can create a Briefcase in a folder, as well as on the desktop (in Windows Explorer, choose File | New | Briefcase).*

Deferring Printing from a Laptop

One frequent problem with traveling with a computer is you rarely have access to a printer. Even portable printers add more weight and cost to your electronic carryall than most people are willing to bear. So, instead, you survive without a printer.

You can print in several ways when you're away from home. You can connect to someone else's computer (using a network card, direct cable connection, or Dial-Up Networking) and print on its printer. You can fax your document to the nearest fax machine (assuming you have fax software and a fax modem), or you can go ahead and give the command to print the document, taking advantage of the Windows deferred printing feature.

See Chapter 15 for more information about printing from Windows.

Printing in Offline Mode

When a printer is set up but not currently attached to your computer, you can still give the command to print a document. You see a message telling you the printer isn't available and telling you the printer will be put into *offline mode*, which means files intended for the printer will, instead, be stored on your disk. When you next connect to the printer, you see a message that print jobs are waiting—you can then print or cancel the documents.

If you don't see the message asking whether you want to print, when you are reconnected to a printer, follow these steps:

1. Open the Printers folder by choosing Start | Settings | Printers.

2. Right-click the offline printer (grayed-out printers are offline). You see a check mark next to the Use Printer Offline option on the menu.

3. Choose Use Printer Offline to remove the check mark from the menu option and put the printer online. The print jobs waiting in the print queue start to print.

Printing on a Different Printer

If you want to print your queued documents using a printer other than the one you usually use, you can temporarily change the description of the printer. If the printer's drivers were included on the Windows Me CD-ROM, Windows can probably find it because Windows copies most of its files to your hard disk. If your printer's drivers aren't included with Windows (if you installed them from a CD or floppy disk that came with the printer), you might need to insert that CD or floppy when changing printer descriptions.

 If you use a wide variety of printers, you might want to install the Generic printer driver on your laptop to give you a basic printing option, no matter what kind of printer you're using.

Follow these steps to change the description of a printer temporarily:

1. Open the Printers folder by choosing Start | Settings | Printers.

2. Open the printer you printed to (the printer appears grayed-out to indicate it is offline). You see the Printer window with all your print jobs listed.

3. Right-click the printer window and choose Properties from the menu that appears. You see the Properties dialog box for the printer.

4. Click the Details tab to see the options shown in Figure 18-4.

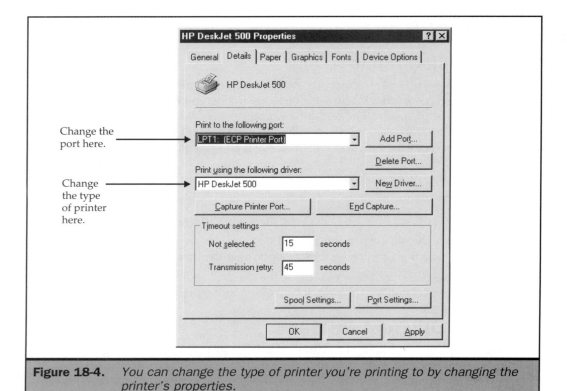

Change the port here. ▶

Change the type of printer here. ▶

Figure 18-4. *You can change the type of printer you're printing to by changing the printer's properties.*

5. If necessary, change the port in the Print To The Following Port box. If you usually print to a network printer, you definitely need to choose another port. If you print to a local printer and you've hooked the printer to the parallel port, you needn't change the port.

6. Use the Print Using The Following Driver box to choose the type of printer you have available. If the printer you have available isn't listed (because you haven't used it before), click the New Driver button to choose the kind of printer you do have.

7. Close all the dialog boxes. You may be asked for your Windows Me CD-ROM.

8. If you change the driver for the printer, you need to repeat the preceding steps to change it back when you return to the office and connect to your regular printer.

Windows uses a single driver for a variety of similar printers. If you already have a printer defined that's similar to the one you want to use, you'll probably find you can define the new printer and Windows won't need any extra files.

Managing Your Computer's Power

If you often use your laptop when it isn't plugged in, you have run into the problem of a battery that doesn't last until you've finished your work. Windows and some applications support power management, which eases this problem without actually solving it. Windows supports two power management standards: *Advanced Power Management (APM)* and *Advanced Configuration and Power Interface (ACPI)*. To take advantage of Windows' power management features, however, you must have a computer with hardware that supports one of these standards. (The computer needn't be a laptop).

> **Tip** *The most power-hungry component of your computer system is the monitor. Turning off the monitor when you won't be using it for several hours saves energy, in exchange for the relatively minor inconvenience of waiting a few seconds for it to come on again when you're ready to go back to work.*

Most laptops support *Standby mode*, in which the disks stop spinning, the screen goes blank, but the memory and CPU continue to run, using much less power than full operation. To switch to Standby mode, choose Start | Shut Down and then choose Stand By.

Many laptops also support *hibernation*, in which the laptop stores the contents of its memory in a temporary file on your hard disk and then shuts itself down completely, so it stops using power. When you reopen the laptop, click its power button, press keys, or move the mouse, and the laptop wakes up again, restoring the contents of its memory from the temporary file. If your computer supports Hibernate mode, the Power Options Properties dialog box includes a Hibernate tab. Click it and select the Enable Hibernation Support check box. The dialog box shows how much disk space will be required to store the contents of your computer's memory during hibernation, as well as the amount of free disk space currently available. When hibernation is enabled, an additional choice— Hibernate—appears when you choose Start | Shut Down.

Your computer can switch to Standby or Hibernate mode automatically after a specified number of minutes of inactivity. Power management is handled from the Power Options Properties dialog box, displayed in Figure 18-5. To display the Power Options Properties dialog box, open the Power Options icon on the Control Panel. The options displayed on your Power Options Properties dialog box depend on what type of power management your hardware supports.

> **Tip** *Many laptop manufacturers add extra power management drivers to take advantage of special power-saving features, such as running the CPU slower when the computer is working on batteries than when it's plugged in or turning off serial and parallel ports when you're not planning to use them. Consult your laptop's documentation to see whether your computer has any extra features you can enable.*

CONFIGURING WINDOWS FOR YOUR COMPUTER

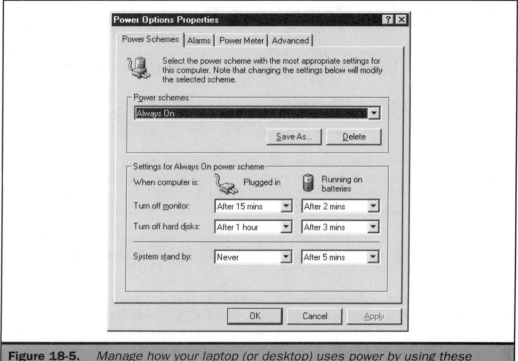

Figure 18-5.   *Manage how your laptop (or desktop) uses power by using these settings.*

You can choose a *power scheme*, which is a group of settings that define when and if Windows should turn off the power to parts of your computer, or switch to Standby or Hibernate mode. Power schemes enable you to create and use different power management profiles for use under different circumstances.

Click the Power Schemes tab in the Power Options Properties dialog box and then click the Power Schemes box (the topmost setting). Choose the power scheme that reflects the type of hardware you're using: Home/Office Desk, Portable/Laptop, or Always On. Then make changes to the rest of the settings in the dialog box. Once you choose all the power settings you want to use, you can save them as a new power scheme by clicking the Save As button, typing a new name for the power scheme, and clicking OK.

To see the status of an individual battery in your computer, click the Power Meter tab in the Power Options Properties dialog box, make sure the Show Details For Each Battery check box is selected, and click the battery icon. You can also set alarms to beep when your battery charge drops to a preset level: click the Alarms tab on the Power Options Properties dialog box to set alarms.

You can display the Power Meter in the system tray section of the Windows Taskbar. Click the Advanced tab on the Power Options Properties dialog box and click the Always Show Icon On The Taskbar check box to display a check mark. The Power Meter shows whether the computer is connected to AC power or running on batteries. Double-clicking the Power Meter on the system tray displays the Power Meter dialog box, which shows the status of your batteries.

Using a Docking Station

Docking stations enable laptop users to get around the problems of the limited resources most laptops have. A docking station gives you an easy connection to a better monitor, a real mouse and full-sized keyboard, and possibly a network. Some docking stations put additional hardware, such as a hard drive or CD-ROM drive, at your disposal. In addition to giving you access to additional resources, docking stations give you convenience—by simply clicking the laptop into the docking station, you gain access to the additional resources, rather than having to plug cables into the laptop.

Port replicators *are a kind of simple docking station that contain no resources except additional ports. A port replicator can be used to give you immediate access to a full-sized screen, keyboard, mouse, printer, and network connection, without having to plug each cable in separately. Port replicators don't have hard drives or other internal resources.*

Windows provides some features that are useful to users of docking stations:

- **Hot docking** If your hardware supports it, you can click your laptop into its docking station *without turning off the laptop* and gain access to the additional resources provided by the docking station.
- **Hardware profiles** Enables you to create profiles so your laptop works properly, whether or not it's connected to the docking station.

Docking and Undocking

If your laptop supports hot docking, you can usually undock it by choosing Start | Eject PC. Windows automatically adjusts to the change in hardware, notifying you of open files, and loading or unloading any necessary drivers. When you're ready to dock the laptop again, simply put it in the docking station. Windows again adjusts automatically to the change in hardware.

If your laptop doesn't support hot docking, you need to shut down Windows and turn the laptop off before docking or undocking. When your laptop doesn't support hot docking, you can benefit from creating two hardware profiles—one for use when connected to the docking station and one for use when the laptop is being used away from the docking station. Multiple hardware profiles can save you time. When you undock your laptop, you needn't change each hardware setting that needs to be changed; instead, you can choose the correct hardware profile when the machine boots.

Creating and Using Hardware Profiles

A *hardware profile* is a description of your computer's hardware resources. Creating multiple hardware profiles gives you an easy way to tell Windows to what hardware the computer is connected. If the laptop is attached to a network, you want to be able to use the network printer. If it's in a docking station, you want to be able to use the docking station hardware—extra drives or sound card—and you may want to change your screen resolution to take advantage of a regular monitor. Hardware profiles can save information about the available hardware and the drivers used by the hardware. You create one hardware profile for each hardware configuration you use.

Hardware profiles store information about printers, monitors, video controllers, disk controllers, keyboards, modems, sound cards, network cards, pointing devices, and ports.

Hardware profiles are useful when you have more than one way you commonly use a computer. Your computer might sometimes be connected to a network, and use shared drives and printers. At other times, your computer might be disconnected from the network without have access to the network's shared resources, or you may have a laptop you sometimes use with and sometimes use without a docking station. Hardware profiles easily enable you to load and unload the drivers needed for the resources to which your computer has access.

Creating a New Hardware Profile

The following are the steps for creating a new hardware profile. This example creates two additional profiles—one with a network card, called *Networked*, and one without the network card, called *No Network*—so three profiles exist in all. The steps are almost exactly the same, no matter what hardware you're disabling in a second profile. You can make profiles with other hardware enabled or disabled, and you may want to use different names, depending on the profiles you are creating.

Follow these steps to create new hardware profiles:

1. Configure your hardware the way you usually use your PC (for example, connected to all its hardware, including a LAN; see Chapter 14). Make sure to get all your peripherals working—printers, modems, sound cards, and extra drives. If your computer is on a LAN, configure the computer to use the network card (see Chapter 27).

2. Open the System Properties dialog box by choosing Start | Settings | Control Panel and opening the System icon.

3. Click the Hardware Profiles tab to see the options shown in Figure 18-6.

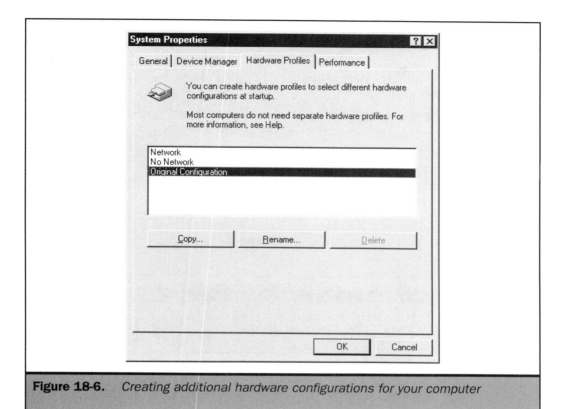

Figure 18-6.   *Creating additional hardware configurations for your computer*

4. Select the hardware profile Original Configuration.

5. Click the Copy button to display the Copy Profile dialog box.

6. Type **Networked** in the To box as the name of the profile you use when your computer is in the same configuration as you are in now (in our example, the computer is currently connected to a LAN). This configuration includes all the hardware you are using now. Click OK.

7. Click the Copy button a second time to display the Copy Profile dialog box again. Make a copy of the Original Profile for use in case something goes wrong.

8. Type a profile name in the To box, such as **Copy of Original**, and click OK. This profile remains identical to the Networked profile.

Making a copy of the Original Configuration profile is a good idea. Leave it as is, in case you have problems with the other profiles.

9. Select the Original Configuration and click the Rename button to see the Rename Profile dialog box.

10. Type **No Network** as the name of this profile and click OK. You edit this profile to disable the network card. The current profile is now called No Network.

11. Click the Device Manager tab of the System Properties dialog box to see the tab shown in Figure 18-7.

12. Expand the Network Adapters category to display the network adapter you want to disable in the No Network profile. Look for the hardware device(s) you want to disable when your computer isn't connected to the network.

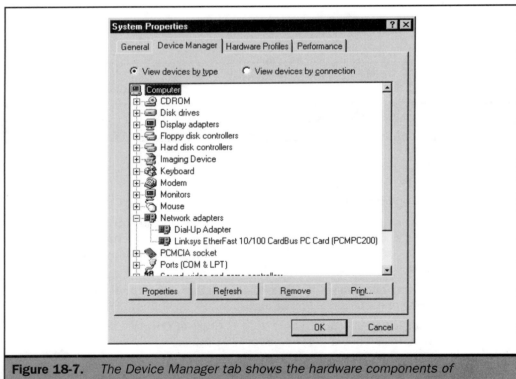

Figure 18-7.   *The Device Manager tab shows the hardware components of your computer.*

13. Select the network card and click the Properties button to see the properties for the card. The dialog box you see looks like the one displayed in Figure 18-8.

14. Select either the Disable In This Hardware Profile check box or the Remove From This Hardware Profile check box. When Disable is selected, the device appears with a red X in Device Manager, the driver is not loaded, and the hardware device is unavailable.

15. When Remove is selected, the hardware is removed from Device Manager.

16. Click OK to return to the Device Manager tab. Repeat steps 13 and 14 as necessary to disable or remove additional hardware from this profile.

17. Click OK to close the System Properties dialog box.

18. Windows asks whether you want to restart the computer. Make sure all open files in other applications are saved and click Yes.

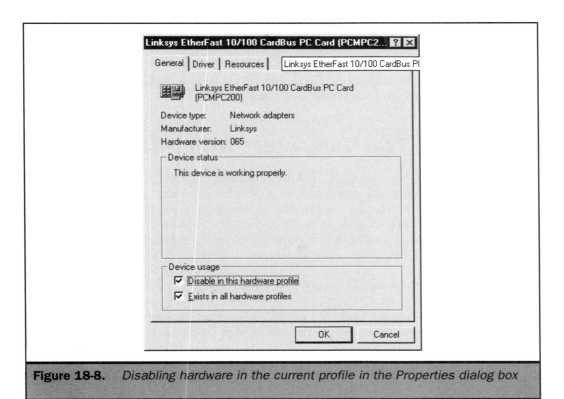

Figure 18-8.   *Disabling hardware in the current profile in the Properties dialog box*

Switching Hardware Profiles

When the computer reboots—and whenever it starts from now on—you see a menu similar to the following:

```
Windows cannot determine what configuration your computer
is in.
Select one of the following:
1. Original profile
2. Networked
3. No Network
4. None of the above
```

The menu lists the hardware profiles you created. Pick the configuration you want to use.

Modifying and Deleting Hardware Profiles

If you decide not to use a hardware profile any more, you can delete it by selecting it on the Hardware Profile tab of the System Profiles dialog box and clicking Delete.

To reenable a hardware device in a hardware profile, start the computer using the hardware profile. Then open the Add New Hardware icon in the Control Panel to add the drivers for this device to the hardware profile.

Connecting Two Computers with Direct Cable Connection

While a LAN is the best way to use resources on another computer, you may find yourself in a situation where you want to share resources, but you don't have a network card. A *direct cable connection* (or *DCC*) enables you to create a slow, but usable, network between two computers by using a cable between the serial or parallel ports of the two computers. You don't need a network card; all you need is the Windows Direct Cable Connection program.

If you need a continuous connection, you should invest in the hardware and time needed to set up a LAN (see Chapter 27)—the hardware isn't expensive, the setup isn't that onerous, and the performance and reliability are far better than a DCC. While a DCC isn't a good long-term solution to your network needs, it can be extremely useful when you need to transfer files between two computers. One particularly convenient use of a DCC is to hook up a laptop without a CD-ROM drive to a desktop machine to install new software using the desktop computer's CD-ROM drive, or to copy files to or from the laptop. A DCC can even enable you to access the network to which the host computer is attached.

When you attach two computers by using DCC, one computer is the *host computer*, the computer with the resources you want to use (usually a desktop computer). The other computer is the *guest computer*, the computer that needs to make use of the resources (such as reading from the CD-ROM drive or printing to the printer). The guest computer is frequently a laptop. A DCC is one-way: The guest computer can see and use any shared resources on the host computer, and it can access any shared network resources the host can access. However, the host computer cannot see the guest computer.

 We had trouble getting the Direct Cable Connection program to work, but other Windows users have had luck. If you can't get it working, consider a LAN.

Getting Your Cable

The only piece of hardware you need for a DCC is a cable, but you need the right kind of cable with the right kind of connectors on the ends. The cable should be called a *null-modem cable*, LapLink cable, Serial PC-to-PC File Transfer cable, or InterLink cable. Before you go shopping, check for available ports on the two computers you want to connect. You can use parallel ports, but serial ports are preferable—they are probably labeled Serial, Com1, or Com2. (Serial ports are usually used for a mouse or modem; parallel ports are usually used for a printer.)

Serial ports come in 9-pin and 25-pin varieties (see Chapter 14, section "Serial Ports"). See what you have available on the computers you want to connect and get the cable with the appropriate connectors. If you're connecting a 25-pin serial port and a 9-pin serial port, try to get a cable with a 25-pin plug on one end and a 9-pin plug on the other. If you think you may create a DCC often—and with different computers—try to find an "octopus" cable with both kinds of plugs on both ends. Also check whether pins are on the port (male), in which case you need a female plug on the cable, or whether the plug on the cable needs to have pins (male). You can buy gender changers for the plugs, if necessary.

Once you have the correct cable, you're ready to create the DCC. Follow these three steps to create the connection:

1. Connect the cable to the computers.
2. Configure the Direct Cable Connection program on the host computer.
3. Configure the Direct Cable Connection on the guest computer.

Now you are ready to use your new connection.

Connecting the Cable

The first step is to connect the cable to the computers. It's safer, but not absolutely required, to turn off both computers before connecting the cables. Note to which port the cable is attached—you need to know when you configure the Direct Cable Connection program. If you're using the parallel port, you must use the parallel port on both computers. If you're using serial ports, you can use either serial port: COM1 on one computer and COM2 on the other works fine.

When the cable is firmly connected to both ends, power up the two computers.

Networking Software Needed for Direct Cable Connection

For Direct Cable Connection to work, you must install and configure networking options first. Both computers must have the following networking components installed:

- My Network Places (see Chapter 28, section "The My Network Places Window")
- IPX/SPX-compatible Protocol (see Chapter 28, section "Installing the Protocol")
- NetBEUI Protocol (install this or IPX/SPX manually)
- Dial-Up Adapter (installed by the Direct Cable Connection Wizard)
- Client For Microsoft Networks (see Chapter 28, section "Installing the Client")
- A unique computer name
- A workgroup name in common (that is, use the same workgroup name for both computers when Windows asks you to enter one)

If you use a LAN, some of these components may already be installed and don't need to be reinstalled. The Direct Cable Connection Wizard can install the Dial-Up Adapter for you, but additional networking components must also be installed.

Configuring the Host Computer

To configure a computer as either a host or a guest, you run the Direct Cable Connection Wizard. If the command doesn't appear, you need to install it. To install this program, follow the instructions for adding a component of Windows in Chapter 3: Open the Control Panel, open the Add/Remove Programs icon, click the Windows Setup tab, choose Communications from the list of components, click Details, and then choose Direct Cable Connection.

Complete these steps on the host computer—the computer with the resources you want to access from a second computer:

1. Choose Start | Programs | Accessories | Communications | Direct Cable Connection to start the Direct Cable Connection Wizard, shown in Figure 18-9.

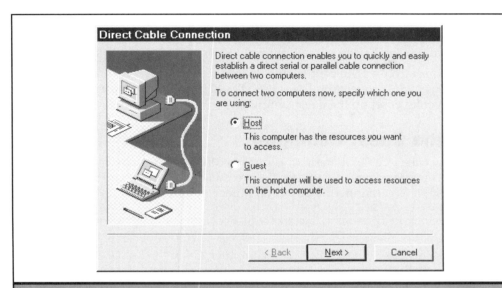

Figure 18-9.   *Once you connect the cable between the two computers, run the Direct Cable Connection Wizard.*

2. Choose Host to configure the host computer. Click Next. If Dial-Up Adapter isn't installed, the Direct Cable Connection Wizard installs it. Start again at step 1 once the adapter is installed.

3. Choose the port you are using for the cable on this computer from the list of ports. (If the port you are using doesn't appear, it may be because of interrupt [IRQ] conflicts; see Chapter 14, section "Hardware Parameters.") Click Next.

4. If the host computer isn't already configured to share resources on a network, you see the File And Print Sharing button on the next screen. Click the File And Print Sharing button to open the Network dialog box. (If you don't see this screen, skip to step 8.)

5. Click File And Print Sharing on the Network dialog box to display the File And Print Sharing dialog box.

6. Select the resources you want to share (click to display a check mark next to shared resources) and click OK.

7. Click OK to close the Network dialog box. If prompted, restart your computer, and then restart at step 1.

8. If you want to password-protect the host computer (a prudent idea), select the Use Password Protection option and click the Set Password button to set the password. A password requires the user of the guest computer to know the

password before using resources on the host computer. In the Direct Cable Connection Password dialog box, type the password twice: once in the Password box and again in the Confirm Password box. Then click OK.

9. Click Finish to complete configuring the connection. You see a dialog box with the status of the connection. The status should be "Waiting to connect" because you haven't yet set up the guest computer.

Configuring the Guest Computer

You also use the Direct Cable Connection Wizard to configure the guest computer. If the Wizard doesn't appear on your menus, see the preceding section for how to install it. Follow these steps configure the guest computer:

1. Choose Start | Programs | Accessories | Communications | Direct Cable Connection to start the Direct Cable Connection Wizard, shown in Figure 18-9.

2. Choose Guest to configure the guest computer. Click Next. If Dial-Up Adapter isn't installed, the Direct Cable Connection Wizard installs it. Start again at Step 1 once the adapter is installed.

3. Choose the port you are using for the cable on this computer from the list of ports.

4. Click Next to see the final screen and click Finish.

5. You are now ready to connect the two computers. You see a dialog box with the status of the connection. The status should be "Connecting." If the host is waiting to connect, the direct cable connection should now be working. You may see a dialog box on the guest computer asking for the Computer Name of the host computer. If you don't know the name, you can find it on the Identification tab of the Network dialog box. Display the Network dialog box by opening the Network icon in the Control Panel.

Using Direct Cable Connection

Once you have connected the first time, subsequent connections are much easier. Follow these steps to connect the two computers:

1. On the host computer, choose Start | Programs | Accessories | Communication | Direct Cable Connection to see the Direct Cable Connection dialog box, shown in Figure 18-10.

2. If Direct Cable Connection displays the wrong port in the Settings box, click the Change button to use the Direct Cable Connection Wizard to change the port to which the cable should be connected. When you finish, you again see the dialog box shown in Figure 18-10.

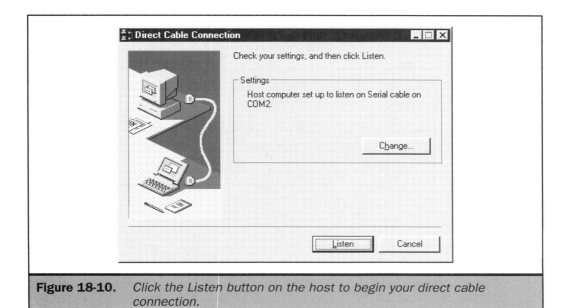

Figure 18-10. *Click the Listen button on the host to begin your direct cable connection.*

CONFIGURING WINDOWS FOR YOUR COMPUTER

3. Click the Listen button. You see a dialog box telling you that the host is waiting for a guest computer to connect. If you change your mind at this point, you can click Close to cancel the connection.

4. On the guest computer, choose Start | Programs | Accessories | Communication | Direct Cable Connection to see the Direct Cable Connection dialog box, shown in Figure 18-10. Instead of a Listen button, the dialog box on the guest computer has a Connect button.

5. Click the Connect button. You see an Explorer window containing the shared resources on the host computer. If you don't see the resource you need, you might need to change the resources property to Shared. The Direct Cable Connection dialog box on the Guest computer has a View Host button that displays this Explorer window whenever you need it.

Using the Host Computer's Resources from the Guest Computer

Remember, a direct cable connection is one-way: The guest computer can see and use any shared resources on the host computer, but the host computer cannot see the guest computer. If you need to copy files from or to the host computer, do it while you're sitting at the guest computer.

To access the shared resources on the host computer from the guest computer, click the View Host button in the Direct Cable Connection dialog box on the guest computer after the connection between the two computers has been made. You see an Explorer window showing the shared resources on the host computer (to find out how to share resources and use shared resources, see Chapter 29). You can also view shared resources by using My Network Places.

Installing Software on the Guest Computer from the Host Computer's CD-ROM Drive

One frequent use of Direct Cable Connection is to install software from a CD-ROM on to a computer that doesn't have a CD-ROM drive. After the direct cable connection is established, you can install software from a shared CD-ROM by following these steps:

1. Share the CD-ROM drive on the host.

2. Put the software CD-ROM in the drive.

3. On the guest computer, install the software according to the instructions. Usually this procedure consists of running the Install.exe or Setup.exe file on the CD-ROM. To find the installation program, you can display the My Network Places window (if you click the Up One Level button until you can't go up any more levels, you see the My Network Places icon).

4. Open the host computer's icon in the My Network Places window to see the shared drives.

5. Open the shared drive's icon and find the file you need.

6. Proceed as instructed by the software's documentation.

See Chapter 3 for more information about how to install programs.

Closing the Connection

To close Direct Cable Connection, click the Close button on the Direct Cable Connection dialog box on either computer.

Troubleshooting Direct Cable Connection

Although Direct Cable Connection should work if you follow the steps in this chapter, we have found the following useful to complete a successful direct cable connection:

- Check that the cable is securely attached to both computers.

- Check that each computer has a unique computer name and the same workgroup name (on the Identification tab of the Network dialog box).

- Check that each port used has the same settings (bits/second, data bits, parity, stop bits, flow control). Baud rate should be 115,200 to maximize the speed of transfers.

- Install an additional protocol on both computers, such as IPX/SPX-compatible Protocol or NetBEUI.

- Log in to both computers using the same username.

- If connecting using parallel ports, check that the BIOS parallel port settings are the same on both computers.

If you're setting up a direct cable connection frequently, and between the same two computers, please build yourself a LAN: It's slightly more expensive in the short run, but more reliable, easier to work with, and much faster in the long run. You can also use a LAN to share an Internet connection (see Chapter 27).

Connecting Two Computers by Using Dial-Up Networking

Dial-Up Networking is most frequently used to attach your computer to the Internet (see Chapter 21, section "What Is Dial-Up Networking?"). However, it can also be used to attach your computer to another Windows computer through a modem. For example:

- If you have a desktop computer and a laptop computer, both with modems, you can use Dial-Up Networking to call your desktop from your laptop. Your laptop can share the resources (hard disks and printers) on your desktop.

- If you have a laptop computer that is usually connected to a LAN at your office, and another computer on the LAN has a modem, you can use Dial-Up Networking when you're away from your office to call that computer from your laptop and use facilities on the LAN. Dial-Up Networking is a slow way to access a LAN's resources but, in some cases, it is exactly what you need.

The computer you call using Dial-Up Networking is called the *dial-up server*. The computer that makes the call is called the *dial-up client*. The dial-up server is usually the desktop back at the office. It has resources, such as files or a printer, that you want to use from the dial-up client computer, which is usually a laptop. Those resources must be shared. Chapter 29 discusses sharing disks and printers over a network. You cannot configure the resources for sharing from a remote location, so make sure you've shared all the necessary resources before you hit the road. You might even want to spend a day working on the laptop to discover what resources you might need to have configured for sharing while you're on the road.

When the dial-up server computer is attached to a LAN, the client computer dialing in becomes a *remote node* on the network, which means the client computer's connection to the network works exactly as it would if you were in the building and attached to the LAN. From the client computer, you can use resources on the network, and other computers on the network can see the shared resources on your computer. Of course, access from a remote node through phone lines is much slower than access from a computer that is connected to the network using cables.

Hardware and Software Needed on the Client and Server Computers

Here's a summary of what you need to connect two computers using Dial-Up Networking:

- Both the server and client computers must have a modem attached to a phone line (and, yes, you do need two different phone lines). Neither computer needs a network card. See Chapter 14 for instructions on how to configure Windows to work with your modem.

- Both computers must have Dial-Up Networking installed, as described in the next section. The following section describes how to configure Dial-Up Networking on the client computer.

- The server computer needs server software that allows it to handle incoming Dial-Up Networking calls from the client computer. Windows comes with server software called Dial-Up Server. The section "Installing and Configuring Dial-Up Server on the Server Computer," later in this chapter, describes how to install and configure Dial-Up Server.

Tip   *You needn't use the Windows Dial-Up Server to connect a remote computer to your LAN. Instead, you can use other remote server products—some only work with particular kinds of networks. For instance, Windows NT has Remote Access Server (RAS), which allows remote computers to call in. You may also want to use a remote control product that enables you to take control of a computer on a LAN when you aren't actually within a cable's reach of the LAN. Popular remote control products are ReachOut Remote and PCAnywhere.*

Installing Dial-Up Networking on Both Computers

Check whether Dial-Up Networking is installed on both the client and server computer by choosing Start | Programs | Accessories | Communications on each computer. If you don't see Dial-Up Networking on the menu that appears, you need to install it from the Windows Me CD-ROM. Open the Control Panel, open the Add/Remove Programs icon, click the Windows Setup tab, choose Communications from the list of components, click the Details button, and then choose Dial-Up Networking. You may need to restart Windows before you can configure Dial-Up Networking.

Once Dial-Up Networking is installed, you need to configure it on the client computer, as described in the next section.

Configuring Dial-Up Networking on the Client Computer

Follow these steps:

1. Open Dial-Up Networking by choosing Start | Programs | Accessories | Communications | Dial-Up Networking. You see the Dial-Up Networking window, shown in Figure 18-11.

2. Open the Make New Connection icon to start the Make New Connection Wizard, shown in Figure 18-12. (This Wizard is also described in Chapter 21.)

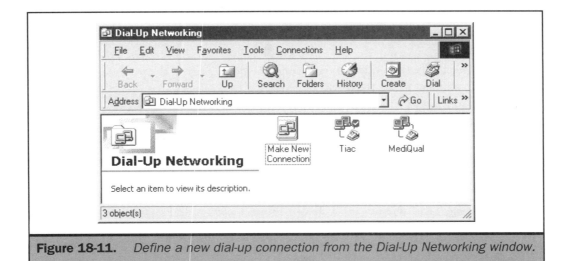

Figure 18-11.   *Define a new dial-up connection from the Dial-Up Networking window.*

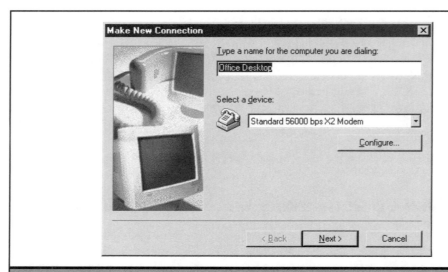

Figure 18-12. *Name your Dial-Up Networking connection and select your modem.*

3. In the first box, type a name for your connection: You can use the name of the computer you are calling or a more general name, such as the location of the network.

4. Choose your modem in the Select A Device box and click Next. The Wizard displays a window in which you enter the details about the phone number to call to connect to the network.

5. Type the Area Code and Telephone Number of the server computer's modem. If necessary, chose a Country Code from the drop-down list. Don't get fancy here with extra codes to dial an outside line or turn off call waiting—you have a chance to enter that information later.

6. Click Next and then click Finish to create a new icon in the Dial-Up Networking window.

7. Right-click the new icon and choose Properties from the menu that appears. You see the Properties dialog box for the connection.

8. Click the Networking tab to see the options shown in Figure 18-13.

9. Set the Type Of Dial-Up Server to PPP, and set the other options so the Server Types tab looks like Figure 18-13. (Enable Software Compression is selected, as are all three network protocols.)

If you plan to call more than one dial-up server, you can create additional Dial-Up Networking connections by repeating steps 2 through 9. If you need to change the phone number or modem, right-click the new icon and choose Properties from the shortcut menu.

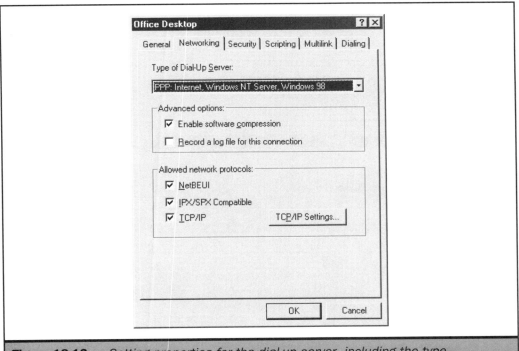

Figure 18-13.   *Setting properties for the dial-up server, including the type of connection*

Installing and Configuring Dial-Up Server on the Server Computer

To configure a computer as a dial-up server, you need to install Dial-Up Server. If it's not already installed on the server computer, install it. Open the Control Panel, open the Add/Remove Programs icon, click the Windows Setup tab, choose Communications from the list of components, click the Details button, and then choose Dial-Up Server. You may need to restart Windows.

To configure Dial-Up Server on the server computer, follow these steps:

1. Choose Start | Programs | Accessories | Communications | Dial-Up Networking to display the Dial-Up Networking window, like the one shown in Figure 18-11.

2. Choose Connections | Dial-Up Server from the window's menu bar. (If you don't see the Dial-Up Server option on the Connections menu, you haven't installed the Dial-Up Server component of Windows.) You see the Dial-Up Server dialog box, shown in Figure 18-14.

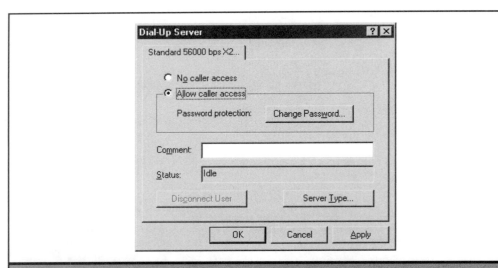

Figure 18-14.   *When you choose Allow Caller Access, you enable networking via a dial-up connection.*

3. Choose the Allow Caller Access option.

4. Click the Change Password button to display the dialog box in which you type a password for the server.

5. Type the password twice (once in each box). Protecting your computer with a password is important—otherwise, anyone with Windows can dial in and do whatever they like to your shared resources. Then click OK to return to the Dial-Up Server dialog box.

6. Click the Server Type button to see the Server Types dialog box:

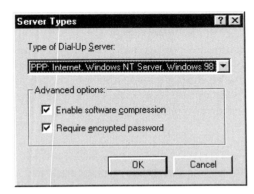

7. Select PPP as the Type Of Dial-Up Server and select both the Enable Software Compression and Require Encrypted Password check boxes on the dialog box.

8. Click OK to close all open dialog boxes.

Once you configure a computer as a dial-up server, be sure to read the section "Dial-Up Networking Security Issues" later in this chapter.

 Before you leave your server computer, make sure it picks up the phone when the remote computer calls in. Because this seemingly small glitch can totally ruin your plans to access network resources remotely, you might want to make a trial run before you go very far, following the steps in the next section.

Connecting Via Dial-Up Networking

Once you configure both the client and the server computers, you can use Dial-Up Networking to connect the two computers. If your client computer is sometimes connected to a LAN, the easiest way to initiate Dial-Up Networking is to request a

LAN resource from the client computer. When Windows cannot find the resource through a LAN, it suggests finding it by using Dial-Up Networking.

You can also establish a Dial-Up Networking connection manually by following these steps on the client computer:

1. Open the Dial-Up Networking window by choosing Start | Programs | Accessories | Communications | Dial-Up Networking.

2. Open the connection icon you created when you configured Dial-Up Networking. You see the Connect To dialog box, shown in Figure 18-15.

3. Click the Dial Properties button to display the Dialing Properties dialog box (see Chapter 20, section "Configuring Windows for Dialing Locations").

4. You can use the Dialing Properties dialog box to set properties for the different places from which you dial in. To create a new dialing profile, change all the options that need to be changed, type a new name in the I Am Dialing From box and click the New button. For instance, you may create different profiles depending on whether you're calling in from the office, home, or a hotel.

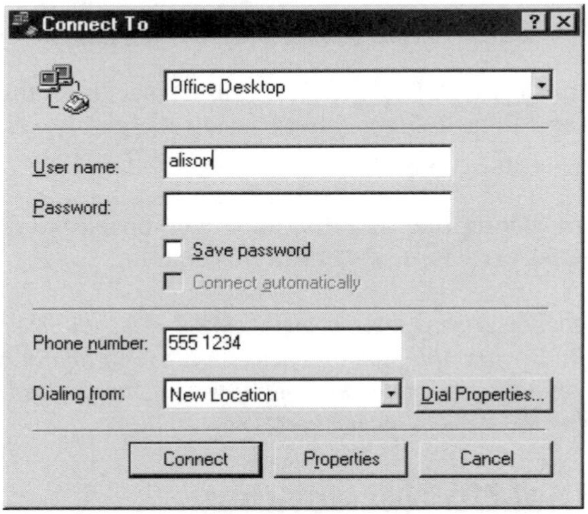

Figure 18-15.   You see the Connect To dialog box when you open your new Dial-Up Networking connection.

5. Click OK to close the Dialing Properties dialog box. Check that the correct location is chosen in the Dialing From setting on the Connect To dialog box.

6. Type the password needed to access the dial-up server in the Password box. Use the password you used in step 5 of the section "Installing and Configuring Dial-Up Server on the Server Computer," earlier in this chapter.

7. Click Connect to make the connection to the dial-up server. Establishing the connection takes a few seconds. When the connection is made, you see a dialog box telling you that you are connected.

Note   *When you want to close the connection, click the Disconnect button on the dialog box.*

Once you establish the connection, you can use My Network Places on the client computer to use resources on the dial-up server.

Dial-Up Networking Security Issues

When a computer is configured as a dial-up server, anyone with a computer and a modem can dial in to it and use its shared resources. This includes reading and destroying files on shared drives, as well as introducing viruses, so disabling Dial-Up Networking when you won't be using it is a good idea. Here's how:

1. Open the Dial-Up Networking window by choosing Start | Programs | Accessories | Communications | Dial-Up Networking.

2. Choose Connections | Dial-Up Server from the menu.

3. Click the No Caller Access option.

Repeat the same steps, but choosing Allow Caller Access, to turn Dial-Up Networking back on when you plan to use your computer as a dial-up server. Because Dial-Up Networking does you no good when it's turned off, you should take some additional measures for the times you need it enabled. Additional prudent security measures include the following:

■ Keep your modem's phone number a closely guarded secret.

■ Use passwords and change them regularly.

■ Consider using the callback feature.

■ Use a third-party security device or software.

■ Monitor network activity for abnormalities.

CONFIGURING WINDOWS FOR YOUR COMPUTER

Chapter 19

Accessibility Options

Windows Me includes a number of options to help people who have disabilities that make using a computer difficult. In some cases, people without disabilities may also find the accessibility options useful. The options include settings for your keyboard, sound, display, and mouse.

To set your accessibility options, you can use the Accessibility Wizard, described in this chapter. (You may need to install the options from your Windows Me CD-ROM first.) After you set your options, you can turn them on and off by using the Accessibility Properties dialog box or the icons that appear in the system tray on your Taskbar. Internet Explorer (Windows's Web browser) has additional accessibility options.

What Accessibility Options Are Available in Windows Me?

Windows includes the accessibility options for people who have difficulty typing, reading the screen, hearing noises the computer makes, or using a mouse.

Keyboard aids for those who have difficulty typing include

- **StickyKeys** Enables you to avoid pressing multiple keys by making keys like the CTRL, SHIFT, and ALT keys "sticky"—they stay in effect even after they have been released.

- **FilterKeys** "Filters out" repeated keystrokes. Good for typists who have trouble pressing a key once briefly.

- **ToggleKeys** Sounds a tone when the CAPS LOCK, SCROLL LOCK, and NUM LOCK keys are activated.

- **Onscreen Keyboard** Displays a keyboard on the screen that enables you to type by using your mouse.

Visual translation of sounds for those who have difficulty hearing include

- **SoundSentry** Displays a visual warning when the computer makes a sound.

- **ShowSounds** Displays a caption when the computer makes a sound.

Display options for those who have trouble reading the screen include

- **High Contrast** Uses a high-contrast color scheme and increases legibility wherever possible.

- **Magnifier** Displays a window magnifying part of the screen.

Mouse options for those who dislike or have trouble using a mouse or trackball include

- **MouseKeys** Enables you to use the numeric keypad to control the pointer.

- **SerialKey** Turns on support for alternative input devices attached to the serial port.

Do Applications Use the Windows Accessibility Settings?

Although accessibility options are built into the Windows operating system, software applications must be designed to work with them. Microsoft maintains standards, including standards for accessibility, that developers must meet to put the Designed for Windows logo on their product. The standards include support for high-contrast and enlarged displays, keyboard use with a single hand or device, adjustable timing for the user interface, and keyboard-only operation. If you need to use accessibility options with new software, make sure the software supports Windows's accessibility options before you buy. Microsoft maintains an accessibility Web site at: **http://www.microsoft.com/enable**.

Installing Accessibility Options

Most of Windows accessibility options are found on the Accessibility Properties dialog box. Choose Start | Settings | Control Panel to display the Control Panel. Then, open the dialog box by opening the Accessibility Options icon on the Control Panel. Click or double-click the Accessibility Options icon, depending on how your desktop is configured (see Chapter 1, section "Choosing Between Single-Click and Double-Click").

The Accessibility Wizard steps you through the settings for the accessibility options that make using a computer easier for you. All the accessibility options changed by the Accessibility Wizard appear on the Accessibility Properties dialog box and are covered in detail in the rest of this chapter. To run the Accessibility Wizard, choose Start | Programs | Accessories | Accessibility | Accessibility Wizard. (If Accessibility doesn't appear on the Accessories menu, click the arrow at the bottom of the Accessories menu to add the missing commands to the menu.)

Note

Although accessibility options are packaged with Windows, they may not have been installed on your computer. If you don't see the Accessibility Options icon on the Control Panel or the Accessibility command on the Accessories menu, you need to install the Accessibility Options by opening the Add/Remove Software icon on the Control Panel. Click the Windows Setup tab and choose Accessibility from the list of components.

CONFIGURING WINDOWS FOR YOUR COMPUTER

Making the Keyboard More Accessible

Most of the options to change the way the keyboard accepts input are found on the Keyboard tab of the Accessibility Properties dialog box, shown in Figure 19-1. Choose Start | Settings | Control Panel, run the Accessibility Options program, and click the Keyboard tab if it's not selected.

Other keyboard settings, including character repeat settings and language, are available on the Keyboard Properties dialog box (see Chapter 13, section "Configuring Your Keyboard"). To ask programs to display all available help information about the keyboard when you use their online help systems, select the Show Extra Keyboard Help In Programs check box on the Keyboard tab of the Accessibility Properties dialog box.

Making Your Keys Stick

If you have trouble holding down two keys at once, activate StickyKeys, so you can press the keys separately and still get the same effect. When StickyKeys is on, you can save a document (for instance) by pressing the CTRL key, and then pressing the S key—you needn't press them at the same time. Pressing a second key turns off (or unsticks) the first key. StickyKeys works only with the *modifier keys*: SHIFT, CTRL, and ALT.

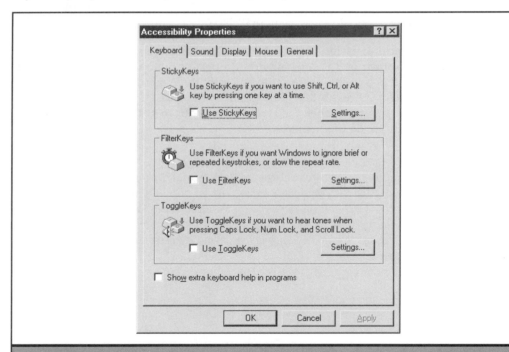

Figure 19-1.   *The Keyboard tab of the Accessibility Properties dialog box*

Tip   *The* ALT *key is sticky all the time—to choose a command from a menu bar, you can press and release the* ALT *key before you press the letter for the command.*

To turn on StickyKeys, select the Use StickyKeys check box on the Keyboard tab of the Accessibility Properties dialog box. Then, click the Settings button to define exactly how StickyKeys works. The following are the options on the Settings For StickyKeys dialog box:

- **Use Shortcut**   Use this check box to enable you to turn StickyKeys on or off by pressing SHIFT five times.

- **Press Modifier Key Twice To Lock**   Use this check box to enable you to lock on a modifier key when you press it twice. Turn off the key by pressing it once again.

- **Turn StickyKeys Off If Two Keys Are Pressed At Once**   This option does just what it says—if two keys are pressed at once, StickyKeys is turned off. To make a modifier key sticky again, StickyKeys must be turned on again by using the shortcut (if the Use Shortcut option is selected) or by displaying the Keyboard tab of the Accessibility Properties dialog box and selecting the Use StickyKeys option. This option can be annoying if you ever want to press two keys at the same time.

- **Make Sounds When Modifier Key Is Pressed**   When this option is on, you hear a beep when a modifier key is struck. This is particularly useful when the previous option is turned on—it lets you know when StickyKeys is turned off.

- **Show StickyKeys Status On Screen**   When this option is on, a small graphic appears to the left of the time in the system tray, as shown here:

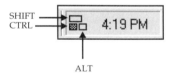

The three blocks represent the three modifier keys: SHIFT at the top, CTRL at the bottom left, and ALT at the bottom right. When a modifier key is stuck, its block is shaded on the diagram. When StickyKeys is off, the diagram is removed from the system tray.

Filtering Out Extra Keystrokes

If you have trouble typing each letter only once, you might want to turn on FilterKeys rather than spending time editing out extra keystrokes. FilterKeys can be configured to ignore repeated keystrokes repeated too quickly and to slow down the repeat rate (the rate at which a character is repeated when a key is held down).

To turn on FilterKeys, select the Use FilterKeys check box on the Keyboard tab of the Accessibility Properties dialog box. Then, click the Settings button to define exactly how FilterKeys will work. The following are the options on the Settings For FilterKeys dialog box:

- **Use Shortcut**   Use this check box to enable you to turn FilterKeys on or off by holding down the right SHIFT key for eight seconds.

- **Ignore Repeated Keystrokes**   This option is sometimes called BounceKeys—it tells Windows to ignore keys repeated without a sufficient pause. When you choose this option, click the Settings button next to it, and then define the interval within which repeated keys should be ignored. Getting the right interval is crucial to avoiding frustration, so use the Test area to type words with repeated letters to see whether the setting works for you.

- **Ignore Quick Keystrokes And Slow Down The Repeat Rate**   These options are also called RepeatKeys and SlowKeys. RepeatKeys enables you to change the way keys are repeated (see Chapter 13, section "What Are Keyboard Settings?")—normally, if you hold down a key, it repeats at a certain rate after it has been held down for a certain interval. SlowKeys enables you to filter out keys that are pressed only briefly. When SlowKeys is on, typing must be more methodical, but keys touched lightly or quickly are ignored. When you choose this option, click the Settings button next to it, and define the RepeatKeys and SlowKeys settings—whether holding down a key should cause it to repeat; if so, after what interval and at what rate should it repeat; and how long a key should be held down to register.

- **Beep When Keys Pressed Or Accepted**   When this option is on, Windows beeps when a key is pressed, and Windows beeps again when a key is accepted.

- **Show FilterKey Status On Screen**   When this option is on, a small graphic appears to the left of the time on the system tray, as shown here:

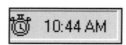

Hearing When a Toggled Key Is Pressed

ToggleKeys is the last option on the Keyboard tab of the Accessibility Properties dialog box. ToggleKeys is useful if you accidentally press keys that change the behavior of the keyboard. When ToggleKeys is turned on and CAPS LOCK, NUM LOCK, or SCROLL LOCK are toggled on or off, a tone sounds.

To turn on ToggleKeys, select the Use ToggleKeys option on the Keyboard tab of the Accessibility Properties dialog box. Click the Settings button to turn on the Use Shortcut setting, which enables you to turn on ToggleKeys by holding down the NUM LOCK key for five seconds.

 We had trouble getting ToggleKeys to work consistently.

Displaying the On-Screen Keyboard

If using the mouse or other pointing device is easier for you than typing on the keyboard, Windows can display a picture of a keyboard on the screen. You can use a mouse, joystick, pointing stick, or other pointing device to choose characters from the On-Screen Keyboard:

To display the On-Screen Keyboard, choose Start | Programs | Accessories | Accessibility | On-Screen Keyboard. The program displays an explanatory dialog box along with the On-Screen Keyboard. After reading it, click Do Not Show This Message Again and then OK to dismiss the dialog box.

You can type by choosing the keys on the On-Screen Keyboard with your mouse in one of three ways (typing modes):

- **Click To Select**   Click an on-screen key.
- **Hover To Select**   Rest the mouse pointer on the on-screen key for the specified period of time. You can choose the amount of time the mouse pointer must "hover" before the key types.

■ **Joystick Or Key To Select** Windows automatically moves the highlight from key to key on the On-Screen Keyboard, cycling endlessly across the keys. When the highlight gets to the key you want, press a key or click the mouse to select that key. You can choose how fast the highlight moves and what key or click chooses the selected key.

Choose your typing mode by choose Settings | Typing Mode from the menu bar at the top of the On-Screen Keyboard window.

The characters you "type" using the On-Screen Keyboard appear in the active window—be sure to select the window into which you want to type first. When you choose the "shft" button on the screen, it remains on until you choose the next button (for example, choose "shft" and then *a* to type a capital *A*).

You can also choose whether the keyboard appears "on top" of other windows that it overlaps (by choosing Settings | Always On Top), whether the on-screen "keys" make a sound when chosen (by choosing Settings | Use Click Sound), and what font appears on the keys of the On-Screen Keyboard (by choosing Settings | Font).

Setting Sound Accessibility Options

Windows includes options to help translate the sounds programs make for people who have difficulty hearing. The sound accessibility options don't work for all sounds, but they do work for most sounds generated by Windows and for some sounds generated by applications. The options are found on the Sound tab of the Accessibility Properties dialog box, shown in Figure 19-2. Choose Start | Settings | Control Panel, run the Accessibility Options program, and click the Sound tab.

The two sound options are SoundSentry and ShowSounds. SoundSentry tells Windows to use a flashing element on the screen to tell the user a sound has been made. Click the Settings button next to the Use SoundSentry option to choose a screen element to flash. A good idea is to use either the Flash Active Caption Bar or the Flash Active Window option—otherwise, it's impossible to determine which application caused the sound. The ShowSounds option displays a caption on the screen each time Windows (and some other programs) makes a sound.

Setting Display Accessibility Options

Windows has three features that make the screen easier to read: a high-contrast color scheme, configurable cursor appearance, and Magnifier, which can magnify part of the screen.

 Other display settings—including colors and fonts—are available on the Display Properties dialog box (see Chapter 12, section "What Are Display Properties?").

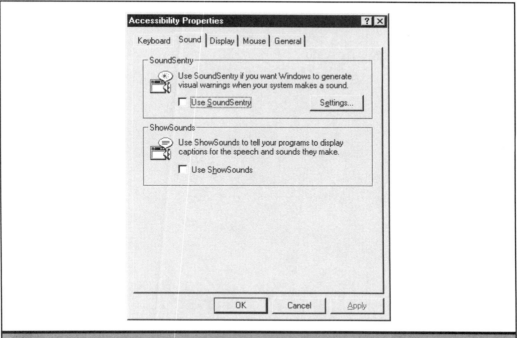

Figure 19-2. *Use the Sound tab of the Accessibility Properties dialog box to turn on the accessibility options for the hearing-impaired.*

Displaying in High Contrast

The High Contrast feature is controlled from the Display tab of the Accessibility Properties dialog box, shown in Figure 19-3. Choose Start | Settings | Control Panel, run the Accessibility Options program, and click the Display tab.

High Contrast changes the Windows color scheme and increases legibility wherever possible, often by increasing font sizes. Turn on the High Contrast feature by clicking the Use High Contrast check box and control the way High Contrast is implemented by clicking the Settings button. Also, use the Settings button to display the Use Shortcut check box. The shortcut for turning High Contrast on or off is LEFT ALT-LEFT SHIFT-PRINT SCREEN (that is, hold down the ALT and SHIFT keys that appear on the left side of the keyboard near the X and Z keys, and also press the PRINT SCREEN button).

The result of turning on High Contrast is a screen that looks like Figure 19-4 (the black-on-white color scheme is shown). Using bigger fonts results in less information fitting on the screen, so you see more scroll bars than usual. Also, the different color scheme may take some getting used to—it's a lot different than the default color scheme and can be confusing.

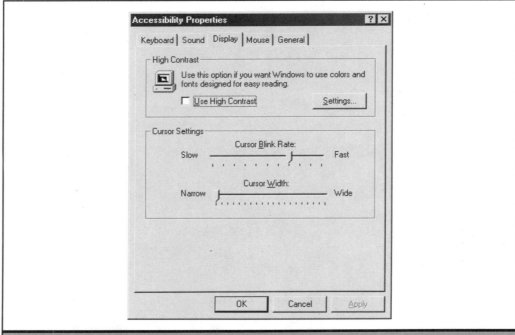

Figure 19-3.   *Turn on the High Contrast option by using the Display tab of the Accessibility Properties dialog box.*

Controlling the Cursor's Size and Blink Rate

The Display tab of the Accessibility dialog box (shown in Figure 19-3) also contains the Cursor Blink Rate and Cursor Width settings. Move the sliders to control how quickly the cursor blinks and how wide it appears on the screen.

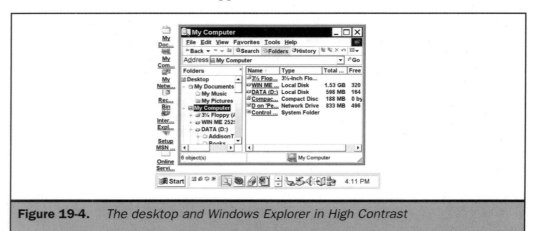

Figure 19-4.   *The desktop and Windows Explorer in High Contrast*

Magnifying the Screen

The Magnifier is an alternative to High Contrast mode—it enables you to magnify only a part of the screen at a time. Turn on Magnifier by choosing Start | Programs | Accessories | Accessibility | Magnifier. Once you give the command, you see the magnification window on your screen and the Magnifier Settings dialog box, as shown in Figure 19-5.

You can control the magnification level, which part of the screen is displayed in the magnification window, its color scheme, and its location on the screen:

■ **Magnification Level**   Use the Magnification Level setting on the Magnifier Settings dialog box. The larger the level, the more the contents of the magnification window are magnified. You can also change the magnification level without displaying the Magnifier Settings dialog box—hold down the WINDOWS key (the key with the Windows logo, if your keyboard has one), press the UP ARROW to increase magnification, and the DOWN ARROW to decrease magnification.

■ **Tracking**   The part of the screen shown in the magnification window is determined by your tracking options. You can choose to Follow Mouse Cursor, Follow Keyboard Focus, and Follow Text Editing. These three options are not mutually exclusive—if you select all three, the display in the magnification window is determined by what you are currently doing—in other words, Windows does its best to display the part of the screen you're working with in the magnification window.

CONFIGURING WINDOWS
FOR YOUR COMPUTER

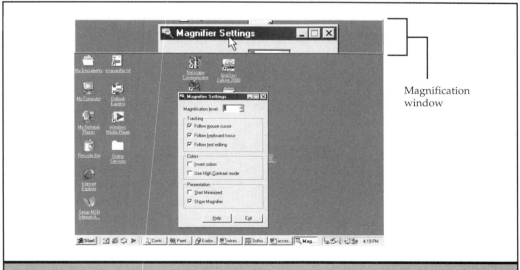

Magnification window

Figure 19-5.   *The Magnifier dialog box and the Magnification window at the top of the screen*

■ **Colors**   You have two choices for the colors you see in the magnification window—the same colors as whatever it's magnifying or inverted colors. Inverted colors may make it easier to see that the magnification window is a special part of the screen—on the other hand, inverted colors may make the display more confusing. Use the setting you prefer. The Use High Contrast Mode option changes the color scheme for the whole screen (not only the magnification windows) to the high-contrast color scheme selected on the Settings For High Contrast dialog box.

■ **Size and Location**   You can change the size of the magnification window by dragging the window border up or down. You can change the position of the window by clicking inside the window and dragging. You can "dock" the window along any edge of the desktop or put it somewhere in the middle of the screen. If the magnification window appears as a window rather than a wide border, you can control its size and position in the same way you'd change them for any window. Your ideal magnification window may be a small square near one corner of the screen. The magnification window always appears on top—it cannot be covered by another window.

When you have adjusted the settings in the Magnifier Settings dialog box, click its Minimize button to shrink it to a button on the Taskbar. Don't click Exit unless you want to stop seeing the magnification window on your screen. You can redisplay the Magnifier Settings dialog box by right-clicking the magnification window and choosing Options from the shortcut menu or by clicking its button on the Taskbar. Close the magnification window by closing the Magnifier Settings dialog box or by right-clicking the magnification window and choosing Exit.

Setting Mouse Accessibility Options

If you have difficulty using a mouse or other pointing devices, if your pointing device is broken, or if you don't like to use it, turn on MouseKeys. If you have trouble using a keyboard and mouse for input, let Windows know you use an alternative input device. Windows also includes a number of keyboard shortcuts for giving commands from the keyboard (see "Useful Keyboard Shortcuts").

Note   *Other mouse settings—including button configuration, double-click speed, and mouse pointer speed—are available on the Mouse Properties dialog box (see Chapter 13, section "Configuring Your Mouse"). See Chapter 14 for information on installing other pointing devices.*

Controlling the Pointer by Using the Number Pad

MouseKeys enables you to control the mouse pointer by using the numeric keypad on your keyboard. To turn on MouseKeys, choose Start | Settings | Control Panel, and run the Accessibility Options program to display the Accessibility Properties dialog

Useful Keyboard Shortcuts

If you prefer using the keyboard to the mouse, you may want to try the following key combinations, which many but not all programs support:

- ■ ALT-SPACEBAR Displays the system menu, from which you can choose to close, minimize, restore, maximize, or move the current window.
- ■ ALT-F4 Closes the current program.
- ■ ALT-TAB or TAB Switches to another running program. Keep pressing TAB or ALT-TAB to cycle through all the programs that are running.
- ■ CTRL-C Copies the selected information to the Clipboard.
- ■ CTRL-V Copies the current contents of the Clipboard to the current position of the cursor.
- ■ CTRL-A Selects all the information in the window.
- ■ CTRL-F4 Closes the current window. Ctrl-W performs the same task in some programs.
- ■ SHIFT-F10 Displays the shortcut menu (the same menu you would see if you right-clicked at the current position of the mouse).
- ■ ESC Cancels the current dialog box (the same as clicking the Cancel button).
- ■ ENTER Click the currently selected button.

box. Click the Mouse tab, select the Use MouseKeys check box, and click the Settings button to display the Settings For MouseKeys dialog box, shown in Figure 19-6.

The following are the options on the Settings For MouseKeys dialog box:

- ■ **Use Shortcut** Enables you to turn MouseKeys on or off by pressing LEFT ALT-LEFT SHIFT-NUM LOCK (hold down the ALT and SHIFT keys that appear on the left side of the keyboard near the X and Z keys, and also press the NUM LOCK key). When you turn MouseKeys on using the keyboard shortcut, Windows displays a little dialog box.
- ■ **Top Speed** Changes the pointer's top speed when you hold down keys to move it.
- ■ **Acceleration** Changes the speed at which the pointer accelerates when you hold down a key to move it. A faster rate of acceleration means the pointer reaches its top speed sooner.
- ■ **Hold Down Ctrl To Speed Up And Shift To Slow Down** Gives you more ways to control the speed of the mouse pointer. When this option is selected, you can hold down CTRL when you want the pointer to move in big jumps across the screen, and hold down SHIFT when you want the pointer to move in smaller-than-usual increments.

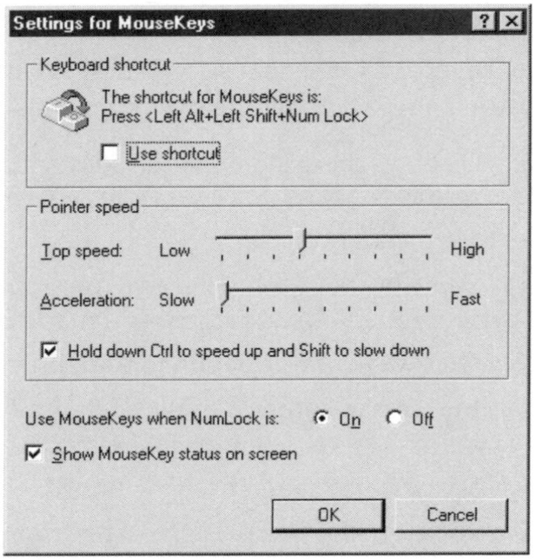

Figure 19-6. *The Settings For MouseKeys dialog box*

■ **Use MouseKeys When NumLock Is: On/Off** Determines when the number pad keys move the mouse pointer—when NUM LOCK is on or off. If you choose the Off setting, then you can enter numbers by using the number pad when NUM LOCK is on. However, you need another set of arrows to move the cursor.

■ **Show MouseKeys Status On Screen** When this option is on, a small graphic appears in the system tray to the left of the time, as shown here:

The shaded key shows which mouse key is elected—which mouse button is pressed when you press the 5 key on the numeric keypad. Switch between the mouse keys by pressing the – key.

The following list shows how to use the number pad to control the pointer when MouseKeys is on (be sure to use the keys on the numeric keys, not the equivalent keys elsewhere on your keyboard):

■ Press the arrow keys to move the pointer.

■ Press the 5 key to click whatever the pointer is on.

- Press the + key to double-click whatever the pointer is on.
- Press the 0 or INSERT key to begin dragging (the equivalent of holding down the mouse button). Move the item by pressing the arrow keys on the number pad. Drop the item (release the mouse button) by pressing the "." or DELETE key.
- Press the – key to set MouseKeys to click the right mouse button.
- Press the / key to MouseKeys to click the left mouse button.
- Press the * key to set MouseKeys to click both mouse buttons.

Configuring an Alternative Input Device

If you're using an alternative input device (something other than the keyboard and a mouse) and you want to connect that device to a serial port, turn on the Support SerialKey Devices option on the General tab of the Accessibility Properties dialog box (Shown in Figure 19-7). Use the Settings button to choose the serial port and baud rate for the device.

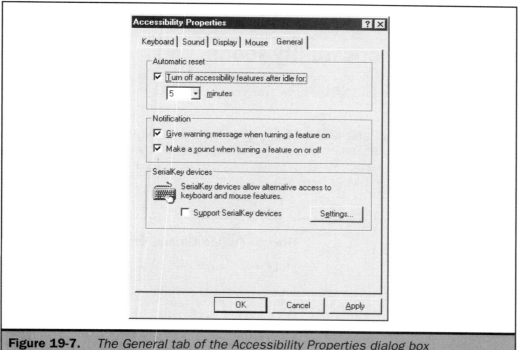

Figure 19-7.   *The General tab of the Accessibility Properties dialog box*

CONFIGURING WINDOWS
FOR YOUR COMPUTER

Turning Accessibility Options Off and On

In general, you probably want to turn on whichever accessibility options you find useful and leave them turned on, but if you share your computer, you might want the capability to turn them on and off easily. The General tab of the Accessibility Properties dialog box (shown in Figure 19-7 has some options for turning accessibility options off and on. Choose Start | Settings | Control Panel, run the Accessibility Options program, and click the General tab.

If more than one person uses the computer, you might want the accessibility options turned off when it has been idle for a certain interval. The Turn Off Accessibility Features After Idle For option on the General tab enables you to choose how long the computer must be idle before all accessibility options are turned off. If you always want accessibility options to remain on, make sure this option is not selected.

You may also want notification when accessibility options are turned on or off. The Notification options enable you to see a message when an accessibility feature is turned on and to hear a sound when an accessibility option is turned on or off.

After you activate an accessibility option and enable its shortcut by using the Accessibility Properties dialog box, you can turn the option on and off by using the keys in Table 19-1.

Using the Accessibility Icons

If you choose to display the status of your accessibility options in the system tray (StickyKeys, FilterKeys, and MouseKeys give you that option), you can do a number of things with those icons:

■ You can either double-click an icon—or right-click it and choose Adjust Settings on the shortcut menu—to change the settings for the accessibility option it represents (this works for icons in the Accessibility Status window, too, as described later in this section).

Setting	How to Toggle On and Off
FilterKeys	Hold down SHIFT for eight seconds.
High Contrast mode	Press LEFT ALT-LEFT SHIFT-PRINT SCREEN.
MouseKeys	Press LEFT ALT-LEFT SHIFT-NUM LOCK.
StickyKeys	Press SHIFT five times.
ToggleKeys	Hold down NUM LOCK for five seconds.

Table 19-1.   *Accessibility Option Shortcut Keys*

■ You can right-click the icon and choose Show Status Window to display the accessibility options in their own small window—the Accessibility Status window.

The Accessibility Status window displays icons for accessibility options, similar to the icons that can appear in the system tray, like this:

Right-click the Accessibility Status window's title bar to change how the window works. You can choose to have the window Always On Top so it won't get covered by other windows. You can also turn on small icons (small icons are about the size of the icons in the system tray); otherwise, the icons are slightly larger. You can move and size the Accessibility Status window in the same way you move and size other windows.

Making Internet Explorer Accessible

Internet Explorer has additional accessibility features you can use:

■ **Keyboard** Press TAB and SHIFT-TAB to cycle among the active parts of the Internet Explorer window, including links and buttons. The selected item is highlighted with a thin box.

■ **Display** Internet Explorer can use the font sizes and formatting you choose, even if they are different from those specified in the Web page (see Chapter 23, section "Choosing Fonts").

To choose other accessibility options, choose Tools | Internet Options on the Internet Explorer menu bar and click the Advanced tab. In the list of settings that appears, you can select or unselect these settings:

■ **Always Expand ALT Text For Images** Turn this setting on (in the Accessibility section) to display the entire ALT (alternative) text supplied on some Web pages as captions for pictures, so a screen reader can read the caption.

■ **Move System Caret With Focus/Selection Changes** Turn this on (in the Accessibility section) so the cursor moves along with the mouse pointer, and a screen reader or magnifier program can read or display the right part of the Internet Explorer window.

■ **Enable Page Transitions, Use Smooth Scrolling** Turn these off (in the Browsing section) to make screen readers and voice recognition programs work better.

- **Play Animations, Play Videos, Show Pictures**   Turn these off (in the Multimedia section) if your vision is impaired and you want to speed up Web browsing.
- **Play Sounds**   Turn this off (in the Multimedia section) if sounds are annoying or interfere with your screen reading program.
- **Print Background Colors and Images**   Turn this off (in the Printing section) for clearer printouts.

The Complete Reference

Windows Me

Part IV

Windows Me on the Internet

The Complete Reference

Windows Me

Chapter 20

Configuring Windows to Work with Your Modem

Before you connect to the Internet (or any other computer) using a modem, you must install your modem, whether you use a conventional modem and phone line, or a high-speed ISDN line, DSL line, or cable modem (see Chapter 14, section "Installing a Modem").

For users of regular dial-up modems, this chapter describes how to configure your dial-up modem, set up a dialing location for each phone line from which you dial, tell Windows how your phone company requires you to dial 1 and area codes, and configure Windows to dial using your telephone calling card. Users of ISDN phone lines, DSL lines, and cable modem services need to configure Windows to work with both these high-speed modems and adapters. Once your modem is up and running, you're ready to read Chapter 21 to choose an account with which to connect to the Internet and sign up for a new Internet account, or to set up Windows Me to connect to an existing account.

> **Note**   *If you connect to the Internet over a local area network rather than by using a modem, contact your LAN system administrator. If you are the system administrator, see Chapter 30.*

Configuring Windows to Use Your Dial-Up Modem

This section describes how to configure Windows to work with a dial-up modem that attaches to a regular phone line. Each modem is programmed to respond to a set of commands that tell it to pick up the phone, dial, and hang up, as well as a set of configuration commands. Windows needs to know exactly which make of modem you have, so it can send the appropriate commands. You can also tell Windows from which area code you usually dial, from what other locations you make calls (if you have a portable computer), and to which calling cards you want to charge your phone calls.

What Does Windows Know About Your Modem?

When you install a modem, Windows either determines what kind of modem it is or it asks you what kind it is (see Chapter 14, section "Installing a Modem"). Windows installs a modem driver that includes information about the commands that the modem understands. You can look at or change your modem configuration settings by choosing Start | Settings | Control Panel, and then running the Modems program. Click or double-click the Modems icon depending on how your desktop is configured (see Chapter 1, section "Choosing Between Single-Click and Double-Click"). (If Windows doesn't know you have a modem, the Install New Modem Wizard runs.

If your modem is external, make sure it is on, and then follow the Wizard's instructions to set up the modem.) You see the Modems Properties dialog box shown in Figure 20-1.

Select the modem from the list of installed modems on the Modems Properties dialog box, and then click the Properties button to see another Properties dialog box, shown in Figure 20-2. (The exact appearance of this dialog box depends on the modem driver.)

Table 20-1 lists the modem properties that appear on the General, Connection, and Forwarding tabs of the Properties dialog box for most modems, as well as those on the Advanced Connection Settings dialog box, which are accessible by clicking the Connection tab on the modem's Properties dialog box, and then clicking the Advanced Settings button. Except where noted, don't change the settings listed in Table 20-1 unless you are sure your modem is configured incorrectly. Most people never have to mess with these settings except in consultation with their modem manufacturer, communications software publisher, or Internet service provider.

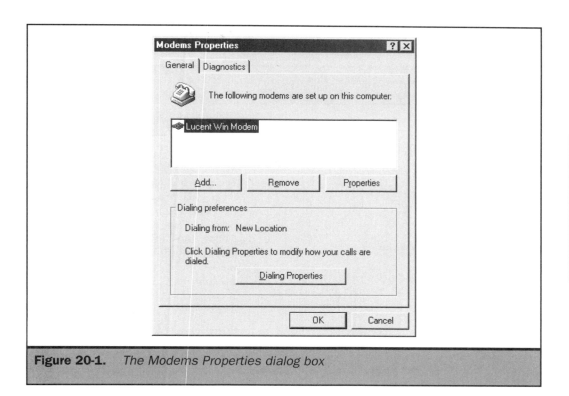

Figure 20-1. *The Modems Properties dialog box*

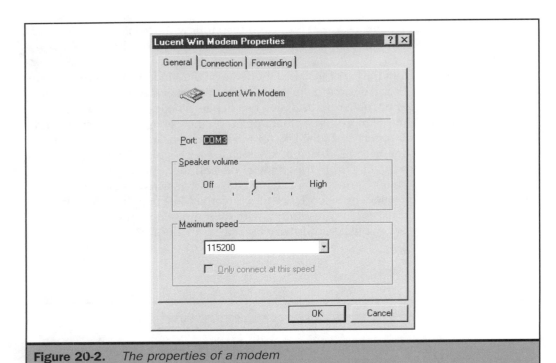

Figure 20-2. *The properties of a modem*

Dialog Box Tab	Setting	Description
General	Port	Specifies how your modem is connected to your computer. PCs have serial communications ports named COM1, COM2, COM3, and COM4 (most PCs come with only COM1 and COM2). Even if your modem is internal (installed inside the computer), it is assigned a port. If you connect your modem to a different port, update this setting.
General	Speaker volume	Specifies how loud the modem's speaker is set.

Table 20-1. *Modem Properties*

Dialog Box Tab	Setting	Description
General	Maximum speed	Specifies the maximum speed at which your modem can communicate over the cable to your computer (not over the phone to another modem), in *bps* (*bits per second*).
General	Only connect at this speed	Prevents the modem from connecting at a slower speed than the maximum speed you specified (not all modems support this option).
Connection	Data bits	Specifies the number of *data bits*, the number of bits of information included in each byte sent (must be 8 bits).
Connection	Parity	Specifies whether the modem uses *parity*, which means the modem sends an error-detection bit as the eighth bit of each byte; and, if so, which type of parity bit (must be None).
Connection	Stop bits	Specifies how many extra *stop bits* are sent after each byte (must be 1 bit).
Connection	Wait for dial tone before dialing	Specifies whether to wait for the modem to detect a dial tone before sending commands to dial; if the modem can't detect a dial tone, this should be unselected. Outside North America, many modems require this to be unselected.
Connection	Cancel the call if not connected within *xxx* secs	Specifies whether to time-out after the specified number of seconds if no connection occurs (usually selected, with a time-out period of 60 seconds).

Table 20-1.   *Modem Properties* (continued)

WINDOWS ME
ON THE INTERNET

Dialog Box Tab	Setting	Description
Connection	Disconnect a call if idle for more than *xxx* mins	Specifies whether to hang up the phone connection if no data is transmitted for a specified number of minutes (usually not selected). Choose this setting if you want to avoid leaving the phone off the hook when you remain online by accident.
Advanced Connection Settings	Use error control	Whether to use error control (usually selected). Not all modems support error control.
Advanced Connection Settings	Required to connect	Whether to allow a connection without error control (usually not selected). If selected, the modem won't connect unless error control works.
Advanced Connection Settings	Compress data	Whether to compress data before transmitting it (usually selected). Not all modems support data compression, and the modem to which it is communicating must also support it.
Advanced Connection Settings	Use cellular protocol	Whether to use the cellular protocol, which is used in cellular phones and modems. Most modems don't support the cellular protocol. Set only if your modem is connected to a cellular phone.
Advanced Connection Settings	Use flow control	Whether to use a system of *flow control* to control the flow of data between your modem and your computer. If selected, you have two options: XON/XOFF or RTS/CTS (preferred).
Advanced Connection Settings	Modulation type	Specifies the *modulation*, which is how your modem converts the digital information from your computer into analog "sound" information for transmission over the phone. Usually set to Standard.

Table 20-1. *Modem Properties* (continued)

Dialog Box Tab	Setting	Description
Advanced Connection Settings	Extra settings	Additional commands to send to your modem after Windows sends the standard initialization commands. Consult your modem's manual for a list of commands your modem understands.
Advanced Connection Settings	Append to log	Whether to store information sent to and from the modem in a log file—C:\Windows\Modemlog.txt (usually not selected). The log file is useful for troubleshooting; to see the log file, click View Log.
Forwarding	This phone line has Call Forwarding	Whether your phone line has call forwarding, which enables you to have calls forwarded to another number.

Table 20-1.   *Modem Properties* (continued)

 Note   *If you display the modem's Properties dialog box from the properties dialog box for a Dial-Up Networking connection, an Options tab appears with settings for dialing an Internet connection (see Chapter 21, section "Changing the Settings for a Dial-Up Networking Connection"). If you display it from the Device Manager, Windows displays additional modem settings.*

To see additional technical information about your modem, click the Diagnostics tab in the Modems Properties dialog box, select the port to which your modem is attached, and then click the More Info button. The More Info dialog box that appears shows a lot of information about your modem, including its response to a series of configuration commands sent by Windows and the date of its firmware (program stored on a chip inside the modem).

To communicate with your modem, Windows uses a *modem driver*, a small program that usually comes with the modem (Windows comes with modem drivers built in for many popular modems). To see which modem driver Windows uses for your modem, click the Diagnostics tab in the Modems Properties dialog box, select the modem, and then click the Driver button. Windows displays a small window showing the name, size, and date of the modem driver file.

WINDOWS ME ON THE INTERNET

Does Your Modem Use the Fastest UART?

All computers and internal modems manufactured within the last decade use a 16550A-compatible *UART* (*Universal Asynchronous Receiver/Transmitter*) chip in their serial communication ports rather than the older 8250 or 16450. This chip provides buffering in the serial port, so it can communicate more reliably at high speeds. If your modem is connected to a serial port with a 16550A UART chip, you can configure your modem to transmit faster.

To find out whether your computer's serial port uses a 16550A-compatible chip, click the Diagnostics tab in the Modems Properties dialog box, select the port to which your modem is attached, and then click the More Info button. The More Info dialog box that appears (Figure 20-3) shows the type of UART the serial port uses; 16550A-compatible UARTS have the characters "16550A" in the part number.

If your serial port does have a 16550A UART, you can configure your modem to use FIFO (first in, first out) buffers, which speed up data rates. Select the modem from the list of installed modems in the Modems Properties dialog box, and then click the Properties button. Click the Connection tab, and then the Port Settings button. You see the Advanced Port Settings dialog box for the port to which the modem is attached (Figure 20-3). Make sure a check mark appears in the Use FIFO Buffers box.

Troubleshooting Your Modem

If you have trouble getting your modem to connect, here are some things to check:

- **Make sure the right modem driver is installed.** Look on the General tab of the Modems Properties dialog box to make sure the correct modem is listed. Remove any modem drivers that are no longer installed. If the wrong modem is listed, click Add to run the Install New Modem Wizard. If your modem doesn't appear on the Wizard's lists of models, choose Standard Modem Types for the manufacturer and choose the modem speed from the list of models.

- **Make sure the modem driver is enabled.** Choose Start | Settings | Control Panel, run the System program, and click the Device Manager tab. Click View Devices By Type, and then click the plus (+) sign next to the Modems entry on the list of devices. Your modem should appear. Click it and click the Properties button (this version of the properties dialog box for the modem contains additional settings). On the General tab, make sure neither check box is selected.

- **Make sure the modem is connected to the right port.** Display the properties dialog box for the modem as described in the preceding paragraph. On the Modem or General tab, check that you see the port to which the modem is connected (see Chapter 14, section "Connectors").

- **Make sure the modem speed is right.** On the Modem or General tab in the Properties dialog box for the modem, check the Maximum Speed setting. Choosing a lower speed may solve your problem.

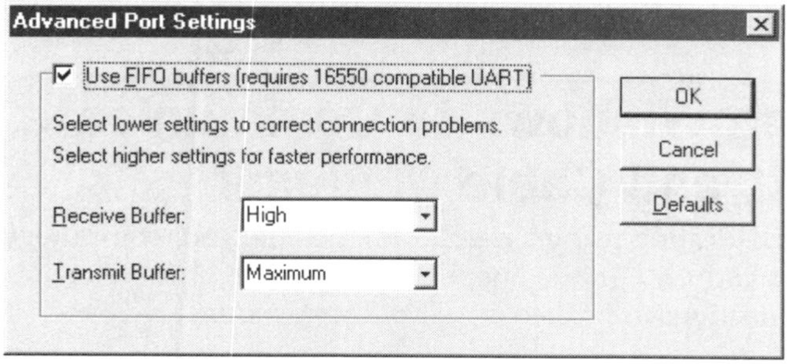

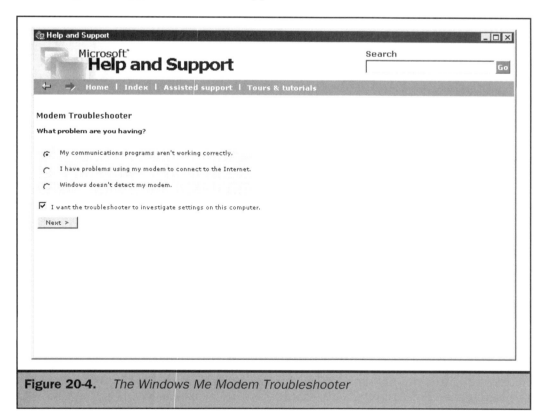

Figure 20-3.   *Advanced settings for the port to which a modem is attached*

You can also use the Windows Me Modem Troubleshooter (Figure 20-4) to help pinpoint the problem. To start the troubleshooter, click the Diagnostics tab in the Modems Properties dialog box, and then click the Help button. Follow the instructions in the Help And Support window that appears.

Figure 20-4.   *The Windows Me Modem Troubleshooter*

If you have an external modem, be sure the modem is turned on.

Configuring Windows to Communicate Using ISDN, DSL, and Cable Modems

Rather than communicating using a regular phone line, your computer can communicate much faster using an ISDN phone line, DSL phone line, or cable modem service. These higher-speed connections are called *broadband* connections.

What Is ISDN?

ISDN (Integrated Services Digital Network) is a special type of phone line. It lets your computer connect to another computer faster than with a normal phone line and enables your computer to transfer data more quickly. An ISDN line is entirely digital. With a normal phone line, your modem converts the digital information from your computer into an analog signal for transmission. At the other end, another modem converts the analog signal back into digital information. Along the way, your phone company may perform additional conversions. With an ISDN line, your digital information never has to be converted. You can use an ISDN line for both voice and data; when you are talking on the phone, your computer can communicate at the same time at 64 Kbps. When you aren't using the voice channel, you can connect at 128 Kbps (over twice the speed of a fast dial-up line).

ISDN lines are usually priced with a monthly charge that includes a base number of minutes of usage, plus a per-minute charge if you use the line for additional minutes.

You can order an ISDN line from your local telephone company, but you should call your ISP first to confirm they can also provide ISDN service. ISDN lines are more expensive than normal phone lines, and not all phone companies can provide them. Even companies that do provide ISDN lines often have trouble installing them correctly; so if your ISP can arrange to set up the line, order it through them.

You also need an *ISDN terminal adapter* (also called an *ISDN adapter, ISDN TA,* or *ISDN modem*), to connect your computer's serial port to the ISDN phone line. Better yet, get an ISDN adapter card that installs inside your computer for faster communications. Your Internet service provider (or whatever computer you are connecting to) must have ISDN phone numbers for you to connect to (see Chapter 21, section "Internet [PPP] Accounts"). Finally, you need to configure Windows to use your ISDN line; you can use the ISDN Configuration Wizard.

 *Microsoft provides information at their Web site about how to sign up for an ISDN account: go to the Web page **http://www.microsoft.com/windows/getisdn**.*

Once you have an ISDN line and terminal adapter installed, you can run the ISDN Configuration Wizard to set up your connection. Choose Start | Programs | Accessories | Communications | ISDN Configuration Wizard. The Wizard steps you through the procedure for configuring an ISDN connection.

What Is DSL?

DSL (*Digital Subscriber Line*), also called *ADSL* or *xDSL*, is a special phone line that communicates digitally, and supports simultaneous computer and voice use. There are several varieties of DSL:

- **ADSL**   Asymmetric DSL, because it downloads faster than it uploads
- **SDSL**   Symmetric DSL
- **IDSL**   ISDN emulating DSL
- **HDSL**   A modern replacement for a T1 line

ADSL, the most common type of DSL line, supports faster communication to your computer (downloading) than from your computer (uploading), which matches the way most people use the Internet. Unlike dial-up lines and ISDN lines, DSL lines stay connected all the time—there's no waiting for your computer to connect.

DSL is not available from all phone companies, but its use is growing. Prices and speeds vary. Downstream (downloading) speeds range from 384 Kbps to 8 Mbps, and upstream (uploading) speeds from 90 Kbps to 640 Kbps. You can call your local phone company for pricing and availability in your area. Better yet, call your ISP and ask them to order the DSL line for you. Some DSL lines are from third-party providers like Covad or Rhythms.

To connect your computer to a DSL line, you need a *DSL modem* and a network interface card (the DSL modem connects using the same type of adapter you use for connecting to a LAN). Order the DSL line from your ISP when you check whether they offer DSL service; your ISP can probably order the line for you from your phone company. Ask for the phone company or ISP to provide the DSL modem, too. Get a network adapter from a computer store. Your phone company may also offer an internal DSL modem that includes the network adapter. The ISP or phone company should provide the software and instructions for configuring Windows to work with the DSL modem—some phone companies don't support DSL modems purchased elsewhere. You must configure your network interface card to work with the DSL modem (see Chapter 30, section "Connecting to a Broadband Internet Account").

 Because DSL is high-speed and connects using a network adapter, it's well suited for allowing a LAN (like a group of networked computers in a home or small office) to share one Internet account (see Chapter 30).

What Is Cable Modem Service?

Some cable TV companies offer *cable Internet accounts*—cable connections to the Internet over the same cable. Not all cable companies can do so—they must have cables that support two-way transmissions. Downloading speeds can be fast, although the more people in your neighborhood who are using the cable, the slower transfers go. Uploading usually isn't as fast, but cable connections are almost always faster than dial-up lines. Call your local cable company to find out if it offers an Internet service.

A few cable companies still offer one-way cable with dial-up return—downloading occurs over the cable connection, but you use a regular phone line for uploading. This system is far less convenient than a two-way cable connection, but downloading speeds are an improvement over a regular dial-up line.

To connect your computer to the cable system, you use a *cable modem*. It connects to a network interface card (also used for connecting to a LAN) or (less commonly) to a USB port. Your cable company should supply the modem, along with the software and instructions for installing the cable modem and configuring Windows to use it. Some cable companies let you buy or lease the cable modem; consider leasing, because cable modem failure rates are reported to be high. You must configure your network interface card to work with the cable modem (see Chapter 30, section "Connecting to a Broadband Internet Account").

Configuring Windows for Dialing Locations

If you have a laptop computer, you may connect to the Internet or your online service from different locations using different phone numbers. Windows enables you to define one or more dialing locations so Windows knows from what area code you are calling and can dial numbers appropriately.

What Is a Dialing Location?

A *dialing location* defines a location from which you use your modem. Windows stores information about the area code and phone system from which you are dialing, including whether to dial extra digits to get an outside line. It also remembers whether the phone line at that location uses *call waiting*, a phone line feature that beeps when another call is coming in on the line. The call waiting beep disrupts most modem connections, so you should tell Windows to turn off call waiting before dialing the phone if you don't want your online session interrupted.

You can use dialing locations when connecting to Internet accounts via Dial-Up Networking (explained in the next chapter) or when placing voice phone calls via Phone Dialer (see Chapter 5, section "Using Phone Dialer").

Displaying Your Dialing Locations

To define or change your dialing locations, choose Start | Settings | Control Panel, run the Telephony program, and then click the My Locations tab if it's not already selected. You see the Dialing Properties dialog box, shown in Figure 20-5. (You can also display this dialog box from the Modems Properties dialog box, by clicking the Dialing Properties button on the General tab.)

The Dialing Properties dialog box also enables you to create area code rules to tell Windows when to dial 1, and calling cards to tell Windows the access number, account number, and PIN you use when charging phone calls to a calling card.

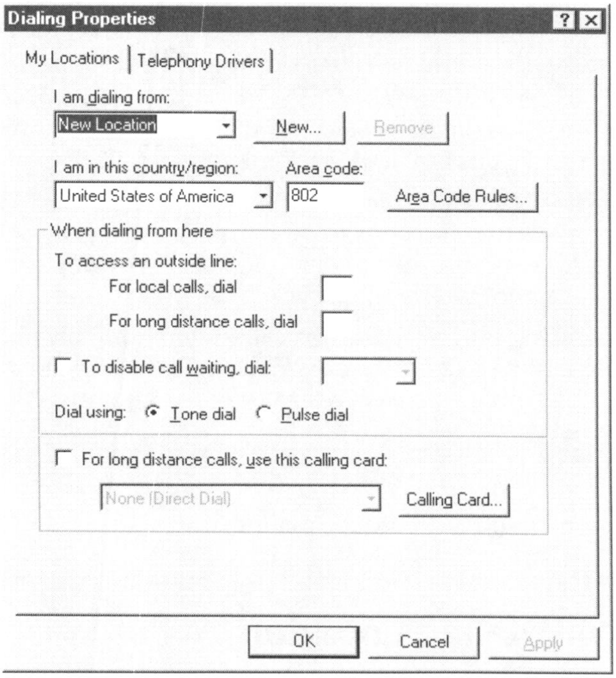

Figure 20-5.   *Creating or editing dialing locations*

Note   *The Telephony Drivers tab in the Dialing Properties dialog box displays the installed telephony drivers, which will eventually be used by Windows with software for making phone calls over the Internet.*

Creating a Dialing Location

To make a new dialing location, follow these steps:

1. Click the New button in the Dialing Properties dialog box. Windows creates a new dialing location named New Location. (If this is the first dialing location you create, you can skip this step and edit the New Location dialing location that already appears.)

2. Type a name for the dialing location in the I Am Dialing From box, choose the country from the list, and type the area code or city code from which you are dialing.

3. If you have to dial 1 and the area code for some exchanges in this area code, or if you have to dial 1 and the area code for all exchanges—even within your own area code—click the Area Code Rules button to tell Windows exactly what to dial (see the upcoming section "Setting Up Area Code Rules").

4. If you need to dial extra digits before dialing the phone number, type the digits into the For Local Calls Dial and For Long Distance Calls Dial boxes.

5. If the phone line has call waiting (that is, if incoming calls cause a beep on the phone line), select the check box to disable call waiting and select the number to disable it. (Check with your phone company if you are unsure.) If your phone doesn't accept tone dialing, click Pulse Dial.

6. If you use a calling card to charge the calls made from this phone line, select the For Long Distance Calls Use This Calling Card check box, and then click the Calling Card button to select a card (see "Configuring Windows to Use Calling Cards," earlier in the chapter).

7. Click OK.

To delete a dialing location, choose the dialing location from the list (using the I Am Dialing From box), and then click Remove.

Setting a Default Dialing Location

Before you exit from the Dialing Properties dialog box, select the dialing location you use most often, and then click OK to exit the dialog box. Windows displays this dialing location in Dial-Up Networking and Phone Dialer as the default dialing location.

When you go on a trip and arrive at your destination, create a dialing location for the phone from which your computer will be dialing. Select this dialing location before exiting the Dialing Properties dialog box to make this location the default. When you return from your trip, display the Dialing Properties dialog box again, select the dialing location for your home or office, and click OK. This resets the default to your usual dialing location.

Using Dialing Locations

Dialing locations come in handy when connecting to the Internet and when using Windows to dial voice phone calls.

■ **Internet connections** In the Dial-Up Networking dialog box, you select your dialing location by clicking the Dialing From box and choosing another location (see Chapter 21, section "What Is Dial-Up Networking?"). To make changes to the settings for a dialing location, you can click the Dial Properties button to display the Dialing Properties dialog box.

- **Voice calls** In the Phone Dialer, you select your dialing location by choosing Tools | Dialing Properties from the menu bar, and then choosing a location in the Dialing Properties dialog box (see Chapter 5, section "Using Phone Dialer").

Setting Up Area Code Rules

You can configure Windows to dial 1 and the area code automatically when necessary, but not to dial it for local calls.

What Are Area Code Rules?

In the old days, you probably had to dial 1 and the area code only for numbers outside your own area code. Now, you may have to dial 1 and the area code for some or all of the phone numbers, even within your own area code. In other areas, you dial a 1 only for calls to other area codes. You can tell Windows exactly when it has to dial what numbers, so when you type a phone number, Windows can dial the correct sequence of digits. Windows stores this information as *area code rules*.

Creating Area Code Rules

To tell Windows the dialing rules for an area code, choose Start | Settings | Control Panel, run the Telephony program, and then click the My Locations tab if it's not already selected. (Or, you can click the Dialing Properties button on the General tab of the Modems Properties dialog box.) In the I Am Dialing From box, choose the dialing location for which you want to create area code rules, and then click the Area Code Rules button. You see the Area Code Rules dialog box, shown in Figure 20-6.

If you must dial 1 and the area code for all calls (this is true for area codes that overlap another area code), click the Always Dial The Area Code (10-Digit Dialing) box.

If you have to dial 1 plus the area code for some exchanges within your area code for in-area toll calls, you can tell Windows which exchanges require the 1. For each exchange that requires a 1, click the New button in the When Calling Within My Area Code section of the dialog box, type the prefix (a three-digit exchange) in the box on the New Area Code And Prefix dialog box that appears, and then click OK. The exchange appears on the list of prefixes. To delete an exchange that doesn't require dialing 1, click the exchange on the list, and then click the Remove button.

If you don't have to dial 1 when calling certain other area codes, because you're in an area where local calls to other area codes are dialed with ten digits (notably Texas, metro Washington, D.C., and all of Maryland), you can tell Windows which area codes these include. For each area code for which you don't have to dial 1, click the New button in the When Calling To Other Area Codes section of the dialog box, type the area code in the New Area Code dialog box that appears, and then click OK. The area code appears on the list of area codes. To delete an area code that does require dialing 1, click the area code on the list, and then click the Remove button.

WINDOWS ME ON THE INTERNET

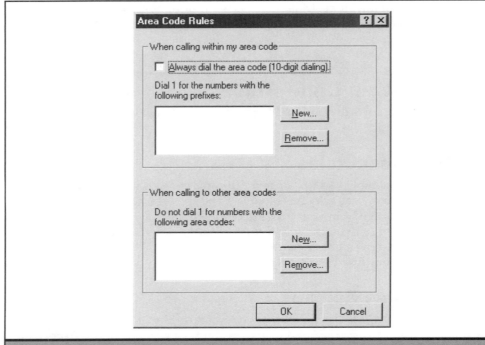

Figure 20-6. *The Area Code Rules dialog box tells Windows when to dial 1 and the area code.*

Configuring Windows to Use Calling Cards

If you use a telephone calling card to charge your phone calls, especially when you are away from your home or office, Windows can dial all the extra digits for you.

What Is a Calling Card?

A *calling card* is a telephone credit card to which you charge toll calls. To use a calling card, you dial several series of digits in addition to the phone number you want to call, usually including some digits to identify your calling card account. Windows can store information about your telephone calling cards; so when you need to connect to an Internet account via a calling card, Windows can dial the special digits for you.

Setting Up Calling Cards

To create, edit, or delete your list of calling cards, choose Start | Settings | Control Panel, run the Telephony program, click the My Locations tab if it's not already selected, and then click the Calling Card button. You see the Calling Card dialog box, shown in Figure 20-7.

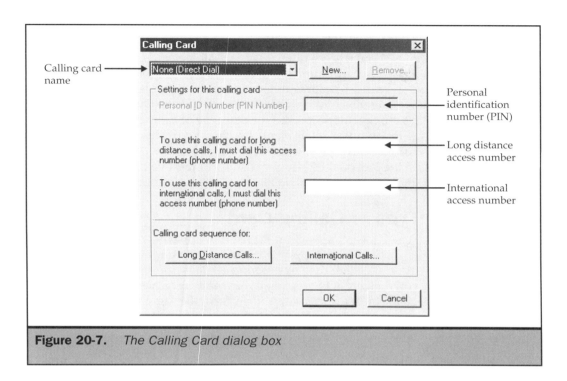

Calling card name

Personal identification number (PIN)

Long distance access number

International access number

Figure 20-7.   *The Calling Card dialog box*

Windows needs to know the following to place calls using a calling card:

■ **Personal ID Number (PIN)**   The number that identifies you to the calling card company, frequently your phone number preceded or followed by four additional digits.

■ **Long distance access number**   The digits you dial to connect to your calling card company before you dial the phone number you want to call or your calling card number. Windows doesn't let you type punctuation, such as dashes—just the digits to dial. For example, to use AT&T from most locations in the U.S., you dial 10288, followed by 0; so you would type **102880**.

■ **International access number**   The digits you dial to connect to your calling card company when you want to place an international call. For example, to dial an international call using AT&T from most locations in the U.S., you dial 10288, followed by 01; so you would type **1028801**.

■ **Calling card sequence**   The sequence of steps you follow when you place a call using the calling card, including what you dial and how long you have to wait before the next step.

Creating a Standard Calling Card

Windows already knows about dozens of widely used calling cards, including their access numbers and the sequence of numbers to dial when placing a call. To set up a calling card that Windows already knows about, choose the type of card from the list in the unnamed pull-down menu box in the upper-left corner of the Calling Card dialog box. Windows displays the default properties for that type of calling card. Only the Personal ID Number (PIN number) box is blank; you must type this number before Windows can use the calling card.

Type your PIN into the Personal ID Number (PIN Number) box, and review the rest of the settings to make sure they match the way you use your calling card.

Creating a New Type of Calling Card

If your type of calling card doesn't appear on the list that appears when you click in the unnamed pull-down menu box in the upper-left corner of the Calling Card dialog box, you can create a new type of calling card by entering all the settings for the card. First, make a note of what you dial and what you wait for when you place a call by hand. Then follow these steps to configure Windows to perform the same sequence of steps automatically:

1. Click the New button in the Calling Card dialog box, type the name of the calling card, and then click OK twice. The settings for a new calling card are blank, so you have to enter all of them.

2. Type your calling card's PIN, long distance access number, and international access number into the three boxes in the Calling Card dialog box (see Figure 20-7).

3. Click the Long Distance Calls button to display the Calling Card Sequence dialog box, shown in Figure 20-8. In this dialog box, you tell Windows the sequence of steps to follow when dialing a long distance number by using the calling card. Each step includes dialing something or switching to tone dialing. After each step, you can tell Windows to wait a specified amount of time or until it detects a tone on the phone line.

4. In the Step 1 section of the dialog box, click the Dial box and choose the number to dial by choosing it from the list that appears (see Table 20-2). For most calling cards, the number to dial in Step 1 is the calling card's access number (choose CallingCard Phone Number from the list).

5. Click the right-hand box in the Step 1 section, and then choose what Windows should do after dialing the number. You can choose to wait for a tone, wait a specified number of seconds, or not wait at all (wait for nothing).

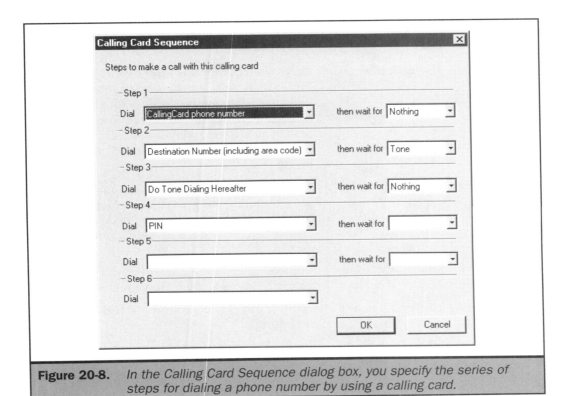

Figure 20-8. *In the Calling Card Sequence dialog box, you specify the series of steps for dialing a phone number by using a calling card.*

6. Select the settings in Step 2 and the following sections of the dialog box until you have completed the series of numbers Windows must dial to use the calling card. Refer to Table 20-2 for descriptions of the numbers you can dial. For the last step, choose Done in the right-hand box.

7. Click OK to save the sequence of steps for dialing long distance numbers.

8. Click the International Calls button. Repeat steps 4 through 7 to tell Windows the sequence of steps for dialing international calls.

 To test your calling card, run the Phone Dialer and try dialing a call.

Deleting a Calling Card

To delete a calling card, choose the calling card you no longer want to use from the Calling Card dialog box, and then click Remove.

Number to Dial	Description
CallingCard phone number	Access number for this calling card. You enter this long distance access number (used when you are specifying the steps for long distance calls) or international access number (used when you are specifying the steps for international calls) in the Calling Card dialog box.
Destination Number (without area code)	Number you want to call. This number comes from the program that is placing the call—Dial-Up Networking or Phone Dialer. This option omits the area code (rarely useful).
Destination Number (including area code)	Number you want to call. This option dials the area code (usually correct for U.S. calls).
Destination Country/Region	Country code for the country or region you are calling.
PIN	Personal Identification Number for this calling card. This PIN may be your phone number preceded or followed by some additional digits.
Specified digits	Digits that you type. If you choose this option, a Digits To Dial dialog box appears in which you type in the digits to dial, and then click OK.

Table 20-2.   *Numbers to Dial in the Calling Card Sequence Dialog Box*

Caution   *Don't delete any of the standard calling cards that come with Windows. You might want to use one again later, and losing all the specifications of that type of calling card would be a shame. To avoid using the calling card, just erase the entry for its PIN.*

Using Calling Cards

When placing calls using Phone Dialer, choose Tools | Dialing Properties to display the Dialing Properties dialog box (see Chapter 5, section "Using Phone Dialer"). Click the For Long Distance Calls, Using This Calling Card check box, and then click the Calling Card button to choose the calling card you want to use. When you click OK, Phone Dialer stores this information and dials all subsequent long distance calls with the calling card you chose.

When placing calls using Dial-Up Networking, click the Dial Location button to display the Dialing Properties dialog box, and then click the Calling Card button to choose or configure the calling card you want to use (see Chapter 21, section "What Is Dial-Up Networking?").

Chapter 21

Connecting to Internet and Online Service Accounts

O nce your modem is installed, you need to decide (or find out) what kind of account you'll be using: an Internet account, an online service, a UNIX shell account, or a bulletin board. The next step is to set up an account, if you don't already have one; Windows Me comes with sign-up software for several online services and large Internet service providers (ISPs).

If you choose an Internet account (the most popular choice), you need to configure the Internet connection programs that come with Windows—Dial-Up Networking and Dial-Up Adapter—to work with the account. Luckily, the Internet Connection Wizard makes this process relatively easy, assuming you'd rather not type a lot of Internet parameters by hand. Then you use Dial-Up Networking to connect to and disconnect from the Internet. You can configure Windows to connect automatically when you request information from the Internet. The built-in Ping, Tracert, and Netstat programs can help you test your connection. This chapter describes all these programs.

Getting connected to the Internet can be harrowing the first time, but it's worth it. Once you know how to get online, you can read Chapter 22 for how to send and receive e-mail by using Outlook Express, Chapters 23 and 24 for how to browse the World Wide Web (the Web) using Internet Explorer or Netscape Navigator, Chapter 25 for how to chat over the Internet, and Chapter 26 for how to use the other Internet programs that come with Windows.

If your computer is connected to a local area network (*LAN*), you can connect to the Internet over the LAN if another computer serves as an Internet gateway. If you have a small LAN at home or in a small organization, Windows Me comes with a program called Internet Connection Sharing that allows a computer running Windows to act as an Internet gateway for all the computers on the LAN (see Chapter 30).

This chapter describes how to choose, sign up for, test, and use an Internet PPP account from an ISP or an online service account. If you use a UNIX shell account, bulletin-board system, or other text-based system, you can connect to the Internet by using HyperTerminal, Windows's terminal program (see Chapter 26, section "Logging in to Text-Based Systems Using HyperTerminal").

 No matter what kind of account you select, if you connect to the account by phone, you can tell Windows either to dial direct or use a telephone calling card, and you can specify whether to dial the area code (see Chapter 20).

What Types of Internet Accounts Can Windows Connect To?

To connect to the Internet, you can use one of several types of accounts: Internet PPP accounts, cable Internet accounts, or online services. You might also want to consider a free Internet account (see the "Free Internet Accounts" sidebar) or an old-fashioned text-based account (see the "UNIX Shell Accounts and Bulletin Board Systems" sidebar).

Internet (PPP) Accounts

A *PPP* (*Point-to-Point Protocol*) account is an Internet account that uses the PPP communications protocol. PPP is the most popular type of Internet account because the most popular software—Internet Explorer, Netscape Navigator, Outlook Express, Eudora, and other programs—is designed to work with PPP accounts. Occasionally, you may run into a *SLIP* (Serial Line Internet Protocol) or *CSLIP* account (compressed SLIP), which are old, less-reliable protocols than PPP, but they work the same way. This book refers to PPP, CSLIP, and SLIP accounts as *Internet accounts*.

An *Internet service provider* (*ISP*) is an organization that provides Internet accounts, usually PPP accounts, but occasionally UNIX shell accounts. All ISPs provide dial-in accounts using regular phone lines, and many also provide ISDN and DSL connections.

U.S. versions of Windows come with sign-up programs for three ISPs that provide PPP accounts: AT&T WorldNet, EarthLink Internet, and Prodigy Internet. You aren't limited to using these ISPs, though—you can sign up for an account with any ISP. The most important consideration when choosing an ISP is that they provide a local number for you to dial, or ISDN or DSL accounts for higher-speed connections.

To use an Internet account, you need a PPP-, CSLIP-, or SLIP-compatible communications program, such as Windows's Dial-Up Networking program. This program dials the phone by using your modem, connects to your ISP, logs into your account by using your user name and password, and then establishes a PPP, CSLIP, or SLIP connection, so your computer is on the Internet. While connected, you can use a variety of Winsock-compatible programs to read your e-mail, browse the Web, and access other information from the Internet. When you are done, you use Dial-Up Networking to disconnect from your Internet account.

To sign up for an Internet account with one of the ISPs included with Windows or to set up your computer to use an account you already have with one of those services, see the section "Signing Up for a New Account." To connect to an existing account with another ISP over a regular phone line, you configure Dial-Up Networking by using the Windows Internet Configuration Wizard (see "Creating a Dial-Up Networking Connection Using the Internet Connection Wizard"). You can also create and edit Dial-Up Networking configurations manually (see "What Is Dial-Up Networking?"). For information on configuring Windows to connect to an ISP over a DSL link, see section "Connecting with a DSL Line or Cable Internet Account" in Chapter 30.

Cable Internet Accounts

Some cable TV companies also provide Internet accounts to which you connect using cable. The cable company provides a cable modem that connects your computer to the cable company's system. You connect the cable modem to your computer by using a network interface card (the same adapter card you use to connect your computer to a LAN—see "Buying Network Interface Cards"). You configure Windows to communicate with the Internet by configuring its TCP/IP connection (see Chapter 30, section "Connecting to a Broadband Internet Account").

Free Internet Accounts

Why pay for an Internet account if you can get one free? Several companies offer free dial-up Internet accounts, including:

- **AltaVista, at http://microav.com** AltaVista, one of the major Web search engines, also provides a free Internet access server called Free Access. It displays a window called the navigation bar whenever you are connected to your free account, include small buttons that link to advertisers. It chooses advertisers that might interest you based on the Web sites you've visited (it tracks your Internet use).

- **FreeNet, at http://www.freenet.co.uk** FreeNet uses Windows' own Dial-Up Networking software rather than requiring a proprietary connection program, and doesn't force you to display ads on your screen. FreeNet is available only in the U.K, and supports itself by getting a percentage of the cost of your local call when you connect.

- **Juno, at http://www.juno.com** Juno started as an online service, then added free advertising-supported Internet account. You use its free software to connect to your account. Juno is available only in the U.S.

- **NetZero, at http://www.netzero.com** When you sign up, you provide demographic information about yourself, including information about your hobbies and interests. You connect to your NetZero account using its proprietary connection program, which displays the "ZeroPort" window on your screen at all times, displaying advertisements targets to what NetZero knows about you. NetZero is available in the U.S. and Canada.

- **FreeDSL, at http://www.winfire.com** They offer free high-speed DSL accounts, along with the DSL phone line you need for access. You do need to buy the DSL modem, which costs about $200. (Their terms may change—check their Web site.) They offer accounts in limited geographical areas and display ads the entire time you are connected.

Some free ISPs offer only dial-up Internet connections, without e-mail accounts or Web space for your own Web pages. High-speed ISDN and DSL accounts aren't supported. Many other free ISPs are in over 49 countries—see the FreedomList at **http://www.freedomlist.com** for a list.

Cable Internet accounts have several advantages over dial-up Internet accounts:

- **Speed** Cable modems can communicate much faster than dial-up modems. Expect downloading speeds of 1 to 2 Mbps or more, and uploading speeds of between 500 Kbps and 1 Mbps.

■ **Separate line**   If you use a cable account, you don't tie up your regular phone line. If you currently pay for a separate phone line for your Internet connection, the cost of a cable Internet account won't be much more (depending on the phone and cable rates in your area).

Not all cable television companies offer Internet accounts, however, and not all towns (especially rural towns) have cable TV. The more people in your neighborhood who have cable Internet accounts, the slower your connection goes because the entire neighborhood shares the cable.

If you are interested in using a cable Internet account, contact your cable television company. If it provides Internet accounts, it can set up your account (the fee for which includes rental of a cable modem) and help you get connected. Cable Internet accounts usually cost about $40 per month. See section "Connecting with a DSL Line or Cable Internet Account" in Chapter 30 for how to configure Windows for a cable account.

Online Services

An *online service* is a commercial service that enables you to connect and access its proprietary information system. Most online services also provide an Internet connection, e-mail, the Web, and, sometimes, other Internet services. Online services usually rdequire special programs to connect to and use your account.

UNIX Shell Accounts and Bulletin Board Systems

Before the advent of PPP and SLIP accounts, most Internet accounts were text-only *UNIX shell accounts*. You run a *terminal-emulation program* (a program that pretends your PC is a computer terminal) on your PC to connect to an Internet host computer. Most Internet hosts run UNIX, a powerful but frequently confusing operating system, and you have to type UNIX commands to use a UNIX shell account. To send and receive e-mail or browse the Web, you run text-only programs, such as *Pine* (the most popular UNIX e-mail program) and *Lynx* (the most widely used UNIX Web browser). UNIX shell accounts don't let you see graphics, use a mouse, or easily store information on your own computer.

Some ISPs give you both a PPP account and a UNIX shell account; you use the PPP account for your regular Internet work, and the UNIX shell account only when you need to change your account's password.

A *bulletin board system* (*BBS*) is another type of text-based account to which you dial in directly. Like UNIX shell accounts, you usually connect to BBSs with a terminal emulator. Most bulletin board systems have moved on to the Internet, but a few are still independent, including the card-catalog systems of some small libraries.

Windows comes with a terminal-emulator program you can use to connect to UNIX shell accounts and BBSs: HyperTerminal (see Chapter 26, section "Logging in to Text-Based Systems Using HyperTerminal").

U.S. versions of Windows come with sign-up programs for two online services: *America Online (AOL)* and *Microsoft Network (MSN)*. Versions of Windows for other countries may come with signup programs for online services or ISPs with local access numbers for that country.

Some online services—including AOL and MSN—let you use some Winsock-compatible programs while you are connected to the account. For example, you can use the Internet Explorer or Netscape Navigator Web browsers with any of these accounts.

> **Tip** *You can also use Windows to connect to CompuServe and other online services, but you have to get the proprietary connection software for these services from the online service. Download the software from the service's Web site, if you haven't already received it in on a CD-ROM bound into a magazine or in a direct mail solicitation.*

To sign up for an online service, see the section "Signing Up for a New Account," later in this chapter.

What Are Dial-Up Networking, the Dial-Up Adapter, and Winsock?

To use an Internet account over a dial-up phone line, you use Dial-Up Networking and the Dial-Up Adapter to connect to the account, and Winsock software to send and receive information. To use an Internet account over a high-speed DSL line or cable connection, you use a network interface card and the same Winsock software (see Chapter 30, section "Connecting to a Broadband Internet Account").

What Is Dial-Up Networking?

You use the Dial-Up Networking program to connect to an Internet (PPP, CSLIP, or SLIP) account over a regular dial-up telephone line or an ISDN telephone line. Dial-Up Networking uses the Windows Dial-Up Adapter to communicate with Internet accounts by using TCP/IP, the communication protocol used on the Internet. You needn't use Dial-Up Networking to connect to your Internet account—you can use another compatible communications program, like Trumpet Winsock, instead—but Dial-Up Networking works well, and comes with a Wizard to set it up. We recommend you use Dial-Up Networking to make your dial-up connection, rather than risking installing outdated or incompatible connection software.

> **Note** *Dial-Up Networking provides only the communication link needed by Internet services. You use Winsock-compatible applications to read e-mail, browse the Web, and transmit and receive other information on the Internet.*

To use Dial-Up Networking, you create a *Dial-Up Networking connection*, which is an icon with all the settings required to connect to an Internet account. You can have several Dial-Up Networking connections on one computer. For example, your laptop might have one connection for the local ISP you use every day and another connection for the national ISP you use when you are away from home.

To create a new connection, connect to the Internet by using a Dial-Up Networking connection, edit the settings for an existing connection, or get rid of a connection, choose Start | Programs | Accessories | Communications | Dial-Up Networking. You see the Dial-Up Networking window, shown in Figure 21-1. (If you don't have any connections defined, Windows automatically also runs the Internet Connection Wizard.) You can also see the contents of the Dial-Up Networking window using Windows Explorer. At the bottom of the folder tree, Dial-Up Networking is listed as a subfolder of Control Panel.

What Is the Dial-Up Adapter?

The *Dial-Up Adapter* is a Windows network driver that Dial-Up Networking uses to connect to the Internet with a modem or ISDN line. To use the Dial-Up Adapter with an Internet account, you configure it to communicate via TCP/IP (see "Setting Up Dial-Up Networking Manually"). The Dial-Up Adapter can also be used with protocols other than TCP/IP, if your computer communicates with other computers that use a NetWare network.

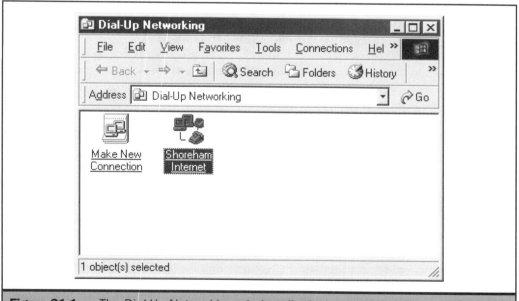

Figure 21-1.   *The Dial-Up Networking window displays your Internet connections.*

What Is TCP/IP?

TCP/IP is the acronym for Transmission Control Protocol/Internet Protocol, the way computers communicate with each other on the Internet. Both PPP and SLIP accounts use TCP/IP. Windows comes with a *TCP/IP stack*, a communications program with which programs such as Dial-Up Networking communicate with the Internet.

When you create a Dial-Up Networking connection, Windows checks whether the Dial-Up Adapter is installed. If it isn't, Windows instructs you to install it, and may prompt you to insert the Windows Me CD-ROM.

If you connect to an Internet account using a DSL or cable modem, you don't use the Dial-Up Adapter. Instead, you configure a network adapter; open the Network icon the Control Panel (see the section "Connecting with a DSL Line or Cable Internet Account" in Chapter 30 for how to configure a network adapter).

What Is Winsock?

Winsock (short for *Windows Sock*ets) is a standard way for Windows programs to work with Internet connection software. Any Winsock-compatible program can work with any Winsock-compatible connection software. Dial-Up Networking is Winsock-compatible; if you use Dial-Up Networking to connect to your Internet account, you can use almost any Winsock-compatible program with your account. Most popular Internet programs are compatible with the Winsock standard.

The key file for Winsock is named Winsock.dll. Dial-Up Networking comes with a Winsock.dll file in the C:\Windows folder. The connection software for some online services (such as America Online) also provide Winsock.dll files, so you can use Winsock-compatible software with their services.

Windows comes with a bunch of Winsock-compatible programs, including Internet Explorer (see Chapter 23) and Outlook Express (see Chapter 22). See Chapter 26 for descriptions of other Winsock programs.

Signing Up for a New Account

U.S. versions of Windows come with automated sign-up programs for two online services (America Online and The Microsoft Network) and three ISPs (AT&T WorldNet, EarthLink, and Prodigy Internet). Non-U.S. versions may come with sign-up programs for other ISPs and online services, varying country by country. To sign up for a high-speed ISDN or DSL account, contact your ISP for instructions; to open a cable Internet account, contact your cable television company.

Note *You need a credit card so the online service or ISP can bill you.*

To sign up for one of these online services or ISPs, or to set up your computer to use an existing account with one of these providers, choose Start | Programs | Online Services and choose a provider. Or, open the Online Services folder on your desktop and open the icon for the provider. Click or double-click the icon, depending on whether you have configured your Windows desktop to use single or double-click style (see Chapter 1, section "Choosing Between Single-Click and Double-Click"). Then, follow the instructions the sign-up program displays. To sign up with MSN, run the Setup MSN Internet Access icon on the desktop.

Caution *Before using your account, find out whether the number your modem will be dialing to connect to the account is a local call for you. If not, you should probably cancel the account, because the long distance charges for using the account will be many times more than the cost of the account itself. Instead, find a local ISP with a local phone number and configure Dial-Up Networking to connect to the account, or consider a free ISP (see "Free Internet Accounts").*

Signing Up for an Internet Account

Windows Me comes with signup programs for several large ISPs—in the U.S., they are AT&T WorldNet, Prodigy Internet (the Internet incarnation of Prodigy, one of the older online services), and EarthLink. AT&T WorldNet, Prodigy Internet, and EarthLink give you a standard Internet PPP account to which you can connect by using Dial-Up Networking.

To sign up for an account either with one of these ISPs or to connect to an existing account, choose Start | Programs | Online Services | and choose the ISP you prefer, or open the Online Services folder on your desktop and run the icon for the ISP. Either way, the ISP's set-up program runs; follow its instructions. The process may involve restarting Windows, so save any files you are editing and exit all other programs.

During the sign-up process, the ISP may display information about your account, including your account name, password, e-mail password, support phone numbers, and other information. Write down all the information you see! You may need it. When you are done signing up for your account, a new command may appear under Start | Programs, and then a new icon may appear on the desktop—use these to connect to your Internet account.

Tip *Consider signing up for a free ISP in addition to your regular account, for use as backup when your regular account is unavailable. If you have a laptop and use a cable modem, ISDN, or DSL account, you might also want a free dial-up Internet account for when you are away from your regular Internet connection.*

WINDOWS ME
ON THE INTERNET

Signing Up for a DSL or ISDN Account

If you want to use a high-speed Internet account, check with local and national ISPs to see which ones offer ISDN or (preferably) DSL in your area. If your ISP offers ISDN or DSL accounts, they can work with your telephone company to get the high-speed phone line installed and tell you the type of ISDN or DSL modem you need. See Chapter 30 for how to configure Windows to work with a high-speed account (which can be used to connect LANs, as well as individual PCs to the Internet).

Signing Up for a Cable Internet Account

Contact your cable television company to find out whether it offers Internet accounts. If it does, sign up to open an account. The monthly fee usually includes the rental of a cable modem. See Chapter 30 for how to configure Windows to work with a cable Internet account (which can also be used to connect LANs to the Internet).

Signing Up for America Online (AOL)

America Online, an online service geared toward individual rather than business users, requires its own proprietary connection software, also called America Online. You can't use Dial-Up Networking to connect to your AOL account, but once you are connected, you can use many Winsock-compatible programs, such as Netscape Navigator and Internet Explorer (see Chapter 23). One exception is e-mail—the only way to send and receive mail on your AOL account is to use the AOL software, not Outlook Express or any other mail program. (AOL also lets you to check your mail via the Web, using its Web site.)

AOL is available in the U.S., Canada, and the U.K., with other countries being added. The latest version of the America Online software (as of 2000) is 5.0.

To install the America Online software and either sign up for a new AOL account or connect to an existing account, choose Start | Programs | Online Services | AOL. The AOL Setup program runs; follow its instructions. You may need your Windows Me CD-ROM or floppy disks along with the following information:

- If you want to connect to an existing AOL account, you need your account name and password.

- If you are signing up for a new account, you need to choose a "screen name" (user name), which can be up to ten characters long. Because AOL already has over 9 million members, many of whom have several different screen names, all the good ones are long since taken, so be creative.

Signing Up for Microsoft Network (MSN)

Microsoft Network (MSN) is Microsoft's entrant in the world of online services. Although MSN has gained a lot of users because of the easy-to-click icon on the Windows 95, 98, and Me desktops, it's never been as highly rated as AOL or

CompuServe. Microsoft has been slowly changing MSN from an online service to a regular Internet account since the service was introduced in 1995. You use Dial-Up Networking to connect to MSN and Winsock programs to access its services.

Creating a Dial-Up Networking Connection Using the Internet Connection Wizard

To create a new Dial-Up Networking connection to a dial-up or ISDN Internet account, you can use the Internet Connection Wizard to create a Dial-Up Networking connection. The Wizard can help you sign up for a new Internet account or configure your computer to work with an existing account. The Wizard doesn't always do all the configuration needed to get your Windows system on the Internet; you may need to configure your Dial-UP Networking connection further. This Wizard does a lot more than the Make New Connection program whose icon appears in the Dial-Up Networking window; Make New Connection only creates a Dial-Up Networking connection, while the Internet Connection Wizard both creates a connection and configures it (see "Making a New Dial-Up Networking Connection").

Note *If your computer is on a LAN that uses file and printer sharing, the Internet Connection Wizard may offer to turn off file and printer sharing on the Internet connection. This is a good idea; you probably don't want to let people on the Internet have access to your files or printers! When the Wizard creates your Dial-Up Networking connection, if you don't have the Dial-Up Adapter installed, Windows offers to install it; click Yes to do so.*

You can start the Internet Connection Wizard by choosing Start | Programs | Accessories | Communications | Internet Connection Wizard. (Close all your other programs first, though, because the Wizard usually needs to restart your computer.) The Internet Connection Wizard gives you three choices (shown in Figure 21-2):

- **I Want To Sign Up For A New Internet Account**   The Wizard helps you sign up for a new Internet account and configures Dial-Up Networking to connect to it.

- **I Want To Transfer My Existing Internet Account To This Computer**   The Wizard uses its autoconfiguration feature (which not all ISPs support) to configure your computer to connect to an existing account.

- **I Want To Set Up My Internet Connection Manually**   The Wizard helps you configure Dial-Up Networking to connect to an existing account.

Note *If you want to create a new Dial-Up Networking connection without any help from a wizard, run the Make New Connection program in the Dial-Up Networking window (see "Making a New Dial-Up Networking Connection"). For more information about the Internet Connection Wizard, click the Tutorial button on its first dialog box.*

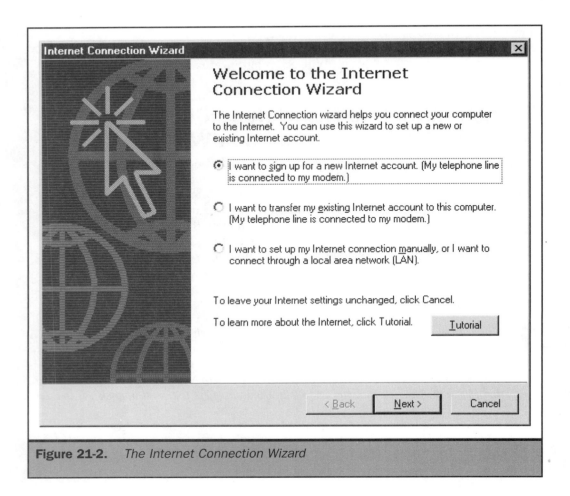

Figure 21-2. *The Internet Connection Wizard*

Creating a New Account Using the Wizard

If you choose I Want To Sign Up For A New Internet Account from the Internet Connection Wizard's first dialog box, the Wizard asks you for your phone number, and then (if you are in the U.S.) connects to the Microsoft Internet Referral server, using a toll-free number. After a delay, you see a window that lists its suggested ISPs and online services (shown in Figure 21-3). You can read about each ISP or online service by clicking its name. If you want to sign up for an account with one of these ISPs, click Next. Otherwise, click Cancel.

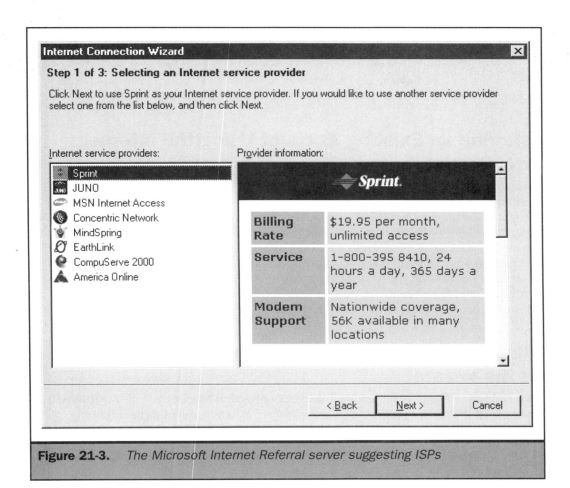

Figure 21-3.   *The Microsoft Internet Referral server suggesting ISPs*

Caution

Microsoft's list of ISPs includes only a few of the large national ones, but no local ISPs. In fact, Microsoft may choose to make a deal with one or two big ISPs and recommend only those ISPs to everyone. The ISPs listed don't necessarily have local numbers in your area, even though you told Microsoft your area code and exchange. Before you choose an ISP, look for ads in the business section of your local newspaper to see what local ISPs are available. A small, local ISP usually gives better service and support than a large one, along with having a better selection of local numbers. If you travel frequently with a laptop, consider a national ISP, or stick with a small, local ISP and use a free, national ISP when you're on the road.

If you choose to create a new account by using one of the ISPs Microsoft lists, the Wizard asks you to provide information about yourself, including a credit card to which you want to charge your account. The sign-up procedure varies by ISP. During the sign-up, be sure to write down all the information the sign-up program displays, including technical support phone numbers, account numbers, and passwords.

Transferring an Existing Account Using the Internet Referral Service

If you choose the I Want To Transfer My Existing Internet Account To This Computer from the Wizard's first dialog box and you are in the U.S., the Wizard connects to the Microsoft Internet Referral Service over the phone using a toll-free number. It downloads a list of the ISPs in your area that work with its autoconfiguration system. If the list includes your ISP, choose it and click Next. The Wizard connects to your ISP and sets up your Dial-Up Networking connection.

If your ISP isn't on the list that appears, choose My Internet Service Provider Is Not Listed and click Next. The Wizard asks you to enter the information about your Internet account, as described in the next section.

Creating a Connection to an Existing Account Using the Wizard

If you choose I Want To Set Up My Internet Connection Manually from the Internet Connection Wizard's first dialog box, the Wizard asks you to enter the following information about your Internet account:

- Whether your connection is via a LAN or a phone line. If you connect via a LAN, see Chapter 30.
- Your telephone area code and country code.
- The phone number you dial to connect to the account.
- The user name and password for the account.
- The name you want to use for the connection (this name appears under the Dial-Up Networking icon that the Wizard creates).

The Wizard also asks whether you want it to set up Outlook Express as the e-mail program to use with your account (see Chapter 22). Choose No if you want to deal with e-mail later or if you want to use an e-mail program other than Outlook Express. If you decide later to use Outlook Express, you can configure it the first time you run it.

When the Wizard is done running, it creates a Dial-Up Networking connection with an icon in the Dial-Up Networking window (shown in Figure 21-1).

When you installed Windows, you may not have installed all the program files the Internet Connection Wizard needs. If not, the Wizard may prompt you to insert your Windows Me CD-ROM so it can load the program files it needs. The Wizard may also require you to restart Windows before it can proceed.

Setting Up Dial-Up Networking Manually

You needn't use the Internet Connection Wizard to create a Dial-Up Networking connection and to configure your Windows system to use it. You can install and configure a Dial-Up Networking connection yourself. Knowing how to do this isn't a bad idea because the Internet Connection Wizard can't create every connection you might need and, occasionally, you'll want to change the details of an account the Wizard set up.

Before you make a new Dial-Up Networking connection, you need to make sure the Dial-Up Adapter is installed and configured to work with TCP/IP. The Dial-Up Adapter and TCP/IP may not have been installed when you installed Windows. If not, Windows installs it the first time you create a Dial-Up Networking connection.

Installing and Configuring the Dial-Up Adapter and TCP/IP

To check whether the Dial-Up Adapter and TCP/IP are installed or to check or change their configuration, choose Start | Settings | Control Panel and run the Network program. Or, you can right-click the My Network Places on the desktop and select Properties from the shortcut menu that appears (see Chapter 27 for more information about My Network Places). Either way, you see the Network dialog box, shown in Figure 21-4. Click the Configuration tab, if it isn't already selected.

Check whether the list of network components includes these two items:

■ Dial-Up Adapter
■ TCP/IP -> Dial-Up Adapter

If the Dial-UP Adapter doesn't appear, don't worry—Windows installs it when it notices you are using Dial-Up Networking. The second item indicates the Dial-Up Adapter is configured to communicate using TCP/IP. (The Dial-Up Adapter can also work with other network protocols, such as NetBEUI and IPX/SPX, if your computer is connected to a LAN.)

WINDOWS ME
ON THE INTERNET

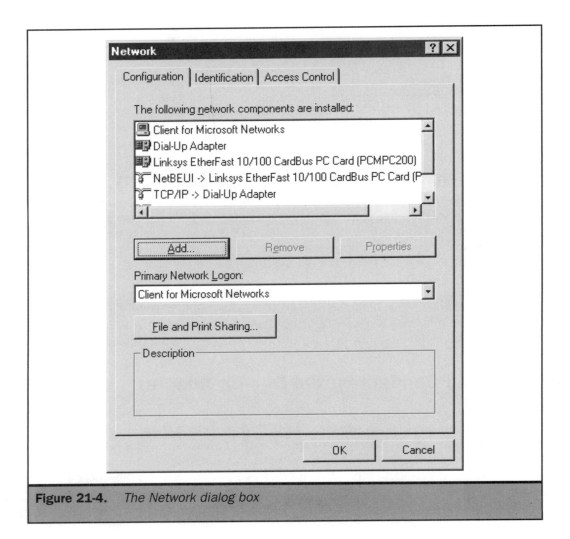

Figure 21-4. *The Network dialog box*

If the TCP/IP -> Dial-Up Adapter entry doesn't appear on your list, follow these steps:

1. In the Network dialog box, click the Add button. You see the Select Network Component Type dialog box:

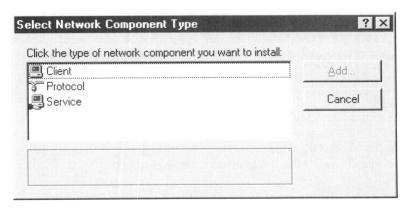

2. Select Protocol, and then click Add again. You see the Select Network Protocol dialog box, shown in Figure 21-5.

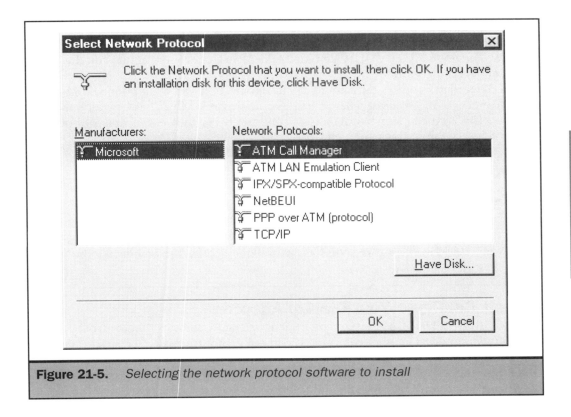

Figure 21-5. *Selecting the network protocol software to install*

3. In the list of manufacturers on the left side of the dialog box, click Microsoft (it's probably the only manufacturer that appears). The list of Microsoft's network protocols appears in the box on the right side of the dialog box.

4. Click TCP/IP in the right-hand box and then click OK to install the protocol and return to the Network dialog box.

TCP/IP -> Dial-Up Adapter now appears on the list of installed network components. Now you can use the Dial-Up Adapter with TCP/IP to communicate with the Internet. Click OK to close the Network dialog box. Windows prompts you to restart Windows for the new network settings to take effect.

   If you use networking only to dial into an Internet account and your computer is not on a LAN, you can delete all the protocols except TCP/IP. To delete NetBEUI and IPX/SPX, select the entries for them from the list of components in the Network dialog box and click Remove. Extra protocols can slow down your Windows system.

Making a New Dial-Up Networking Connection

To make a new Dial-Up Networking connection, choose Start | Programs | Accessories | Communications | Dial-Up Networking to see the Dial-Up Networking window (shown in Figure 21-1). Open the Make New Connection icon to run the Make New Connection Wizard.

The Wizard asks what you want to call the connection and what phone number to dial to connect to the account. Then it creates a new icon in your Dial-Up Networking window. This connection may not be fully configured; see the next section for how to enter the rest of the settings yourself.

Changing the Settings for a Dial-Up Networking Connection

To configure a Dial-Up Networking connection or to change an existing connection's configuration, right-click the icon for the connection in the Dial-Up Networking window and choose Properties from the menu that appears, or select the connection

Don't Configure Your Dial-Up Adapter

The TCP/IP -> Dial-Up Adapter component has many settings that control how Windows connects to other computers. You can configure these TCP/IP settings by using the Properties button on the Network dialog box, but it's better not to configure them. Instead, configure each of your Dial-Up Networking connections with the appropriate settings for the account to which it connects.

and choose File | Properties. Either way, you see the Properties dialog box for the Dial-Up Networking connection (see Figure 21-6); the name of the dialog box depends on the name you gave the connection. Table 21-1 lists the properties for a Dial-Up Networking connection. Table 21-2 lists the settings that appear on the Options tab of the modem Properties dialog box, which you see when you click the Configure button on the General tab of the Properties dialog box for the connection (these settings don't appear on the modem Properties dialog box when you display it from the Control Panel).

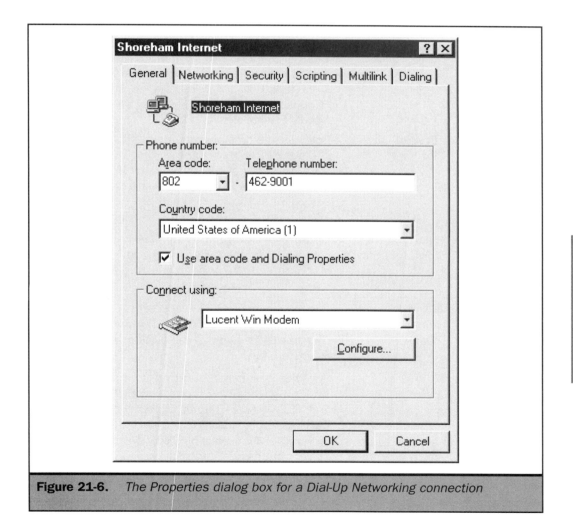

Figure 21-6.   *The Properties dialog box for a Dial-Up Networking connection*

Tab in Properties Window	Setting	Description
General	Phone number	Specifies the phone number your computer dials to connect to the account. Composed of the area code, telephone number, and country code (you choose from a list of countries).
General	Connecting using	Specifies which modem to use to connect. Click the Configure button by this setting to check or change the configuration of the modem (see Chapter 20 for how to configure your modem). You can choose *VPN* (Virtual Private Networking) if you have installed it (see Chapter 30, section "Connecting to Your Organization's LAN with Virtual Private Networking").
Networking	Type of Dial-Up Server	Specifies the type of account; all ISPs now provide PPP. Choice of SLIP, CSLIP, PPP (three standard types of accounts available from ISPs), NRN (NetWare Connect for NetWare-based LANs), or Windows for Workgroups and Windows NT 3.1 (for Windows-based LANs).
Networking	Enable software compression	Compresses information sent between this computer and the account; your Internet account must also support compression (PPP and CSLIP accounts do).
Networking	Record a log File for this connection	Log events in a text file stored in your Windows program folder (usually C:\Windows). The filename is the name of the modem, with the extension .log.
Networking	Allowed network protocols	Specifies how to communicate over the network. You can select any of these: NetBEUI, IPX/SPX, and TCP/IP (see Chapter 28, section "Installing the Protocol"). Select TCP/IP for Internet accounts and unselect NetBEUI and IPX/SPX. To set options for TCP/IP accounts, click the TCP/IP Settings button (see Table 21-3).

Table 21-1.   *Settings for a Dial-Up Networking Connection*

Tab in Properties Window	Setting	Description
Security	Authentication	Specifies the user name and password to use when you connect to the account. The Domain box is usually left blank.
Security	Connect automatically	Specifies that when you open the Dial-Up Networking connection, Windows connects automatically. Save Password must also be selected on the Dial-Up Connection dialog box when you connect manually.
Security	Log on to network	Tells Dial-Up Networking to log on to the account by using your Windows user name and password. Usually not selected for Internet accounts.
Security	Require encrypted password	Encrypts your password before sending it to your Internet account when logging on. Your Internet account must support password encryption (most don't).
Security	Require data encryption	Encrypts data to and from your ISP (we've never seen this setting used).
Scripting	Script file	Specifies the name of the file containing the logon script for this connection (see "Creating and Using Logon Scripts"). Click Edit to edit a script file or Browse to select an existing file.
Scripting	Step through script	Runs the logon script for this connection.
Scripting	Start terminal screen minimized	Minimizes the terminal window that shows the interaction between the Dial-Up Networking connection and the account while the logon script is running. During debugging, deselect this setting so you can see the terminal window.

Table 21-1. *Settings for a Dial-Up Networking Connection* (continued)

WINDOWS ME
ON THE INTERNET

Tab in Properties Window	Setting	Description
Multilink	Do not use additional devices	Specifies this connection uses only one device to connect (see "Creating Multilink Connections").
Multilink	Use additional devices	Specifies this connection uses more than one device to connect (for example, two modems and two phone lines). The large box below this setting lists the additional devices used by this connection, and the Add, Remove, and Edit buttons let you add, delete, or change devices on the list.
Dialing	This is the default Internet connection	Specifies if you have more than one Dial-Up Networking connection, this connection is the one to dial automatically. When this is selected, you can choose whether Windows dials your Internet account when an Internet program (like an e-mail program or Web browser) needs to connect.
Dialing	Redial settings	Specifies how many times Dial-Up Networking dials the connection if it can't connect (the default is 10 times) and how long to wait between attempts (the default is five seconds).
Dialing	Enable idle disconnect	Specifies Windows disconnect if the Internet connection is idle for a specified length of time (the default is 20 minutes). Windows considers the connection idle if it is used no more than the specified connection speed.
Dialing	Don't prompt before disconnecting	Specifies whether Windows asks before disconnecting an idle Internet connection.

Table 21-1.   *Settings for a Dial-Up Networking Connection* (continued)

Tab in Properties Window	Setting	Description
Dialing	Disconnect when connection may not be needed	Specifies whether Windows disconnects the Internet connection when you close the program that initiated the connection (for example, if a request from a browser caused Dial-Up Networking to log on, exiting the browser can cause Windows to disconnect).

Table 21-1.   *Settings for a Dial-Up Networking Connection* (continued)

Options Tab Setting	Description
Bring up terminal window before dialing	Displays a terminal window, before dialing, which you can use to type modem commands and see the results (see "Creating and Using Logon Scripts"). (Refer to your modem's manual for the commands it understands.)
Bring up terminal window after dialing	Displays a terminal window after dialing, which you can use to type commands as see the results.
Operator assisted or manual dial	Prompts you to dial the phone yourself, for situations where you need to speak to an operator. When you are connected, click the Connect button and hang up your phone.
Wait for credit card tone: *xxx* seconds	Specifies the number of seconds to wait for a tone when you are using a telephone credit card.
Display modem status	Displays a status window indicating the progress of your phone connection.

Table 21-2.   *Settings on the Options Tab of the Modem Properties Dialog Box*

Configuring a TCP/IP Connection

For a connection to an Internet account, you must also configure the TCP/IP protocol. On the Properties dialog box for the connection, click the Server Types tab, select TCP/IP as an allowed network protocol, and then click the TCP/IP Settings button. You see the TCP/IP Settings dialog box, shown in Figure 21-7. Table 21-3 shows the settings on this dialog box. Contact your ISP for the settings and addresses to enter.

When your computer is connected to the Internet using TCP/IP, it has its own *IP address* (IP is the acronym for Internet Protocol). An IP address is in the form of *xxx.xxx.xxx.xxx*, where each *xxx* is a number from 0 to 255. (That is, an IP address consists of four eight-bit numbers.) For example, a computer's IP address might be 204.71.16.253.

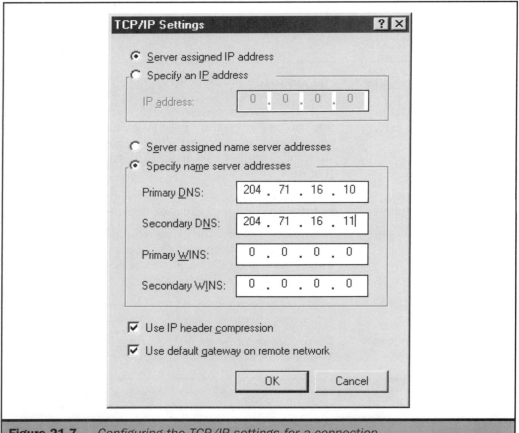

Figure 21-7. *Configuring the TCP/IP settings for a connection*

Setting	Description
Server assigned IP address	Specifies that your ISP assigns your computer an IP address when you log on (most ISP accounts do this).
Specify an IP address	Indicates that your computer has a permanently assigned IP address, which you specify in the IP Address setting.
IP address	Specifies your permanently assigned IP address.
Server assigned name server addresses	Specifies that your ISP assigns your computer domain name servers when you log on (most ISP accounts do this).
Specify name server addresses	Indicates that you have entered Primary and Secondary domain name server IP addresses in the next two settings.
Primary DNS	Specifies the IP address of your ISP's domain name server.
Secondary DNS	Specifies the IP address of another domain name server your account can use when the primary DNS doesn't respond.

Table 21-3. *TCP/IP Settings*

A few ISPs assign you a permanent IP address. If you have been assigned a permanent IP address, select Specify An IP Address on the TCP/IP Settings dialog box and then type the IP address. Most ISPs assign you a temporary IP address when you log on. If you have been assigned a temporary IP address, select Server Assigned IP Address.

In addition to IP addresses, computers on the Internet have *domain names*, alphanumeric names like **www.microsoft.com** or **net.gurus.com**. A *domain name server* or *DNS* is a computer on the Internet that translates between domain names and numeric IP addresses. Your ISP provides you at least one domain name server to do these translations. Some ISPs assign the domain name server when you log on; if so, select Server Assigned Name Server Addresses. Most ISPs give you the IP address of two domain name servers your computer can use. If so, select Specify Name Server

Addresses and enter the IP addresses in the Primary DNS and Secondary DNS settings. Some ISPs (not many) also provide *WINS* (Microsoft's Windows Internet Naming Service) servers, which provide other name lookups.

If your computer is connected to a large corporate system via a LAN or by dialing in, your connection may use WINS to manage network parameters automatically. Your computer contacts the WINS server when Windows starts up (if you connect via a LAN) or when you dial up to get its own configuration information.

Creating and Using Logon Scripts

Dial-Up Networking tries to log on to your account automatically. Most accounts follow a standard series of steps: they transmit your user name and your account's password, and then receive confirmation that you are logged in and communications can begin.

If your account uses a nonstandard dialog box for logging in, Dial-Up Networking can't log in automatically. You can automate logging in by creating a *logon script*, a text file containing a small program that tells Dial-Up Networking what prompts to wait for and what to type in response. For example, if your ISP's computer uses a nonstandard prompt to ask for your password, or requires you to type a command to begin a PPP session, you can write a script to log on for you. If your ISP uses the standard series of transmissions, you don't need a logon script. Logon scripts have the file extension .scp.

To use a logon script, follow these steps:

1. Log on manually, making notes about which prompts you see and what you must type in response to those prompts. To log in manually, you can use your Dial-Up Networking connection with a *terminal window*, which enables you to see the session and type commands to your ISP. To tell Windows to open a terminal window while connecting, click the Configure button on the General tab of the Properties dialog box for the connection to see the Properties dialog box for your modem (see Chapter 20, section "What Does Windows Know About Your Modem?"). Then, click the Options tab and select the Bring Up Terminal Window After Dialing check box. Another way to log in manually is by using HyperTerminal to connect to your ISP (see Chapter 26, section "Logging in to Text-Based Systems Using HyperTerminal").

2. Create a logon script by using a text editor, such as Notepad (see Chapter 4, section "Reading Text Files with Notepad"). Windows comes with a short manual about writing logon scripts in the file C:\Windows\Script.doc. (This file and the scripting language you use in logon scripts have remained unchanged since Windows 95.)

3. Tell Windows about the logon script by typing the filename in the File Name box on the Scripting tab of the Properties dialog box for the Dial-Up Networking connection. (See Table 21-1.)

4. Test the script, editing it with your text editor and viewing the results in a terminal window.

Dial-up Networking comes with a set of well-commented sample scripts. Customizing one of the sample scripts is usually easier than writing your own from scratch. These sample scripts are stored in C:\Program Files\Accessories with the extension .scp.

Creating Multilink Connections

Multilink enables Windows to use multiple modems and phone lines (usually two modems and two phone lines) for a single Internet connection to increase the effective connection speed (throughput). For example, you can use two 56K modems together to simulate a 108K connection to the Internet. Data flows through both modems and both phone lines for a single connection.

Your ISP must support multilink connections for you to use such a connection because the ISP's hardware and software must be able to combine the packets of information from the two phone lines into one Internet connection. Multilink connections, where they're available, usually cost more than a regular dial-up Internet account (but not as much as two separate accounts); contact your ISP for details. You also need to pay for an additional phone line.

When you create a multilink connection, you specify one device—usually a modem—on the General tab of the connection's Properties dialog box. Then you list the other device(s)—usually one other modem—on the Multilink tab. Click the Use Additional Devices setting to tell Windows this is a multilink connection and then add the additional devices. To add a device, click the Add button and, in the window that appears, select the name of the device to use (usually a second modem) and the phone number to dial. (The Add button doesn't work unless you have two modems installed.) When you finish, the device name appears in the large box in the Multilink tab of the Properties dialog box for the connection.

To change the configuration of a device, select it and click the Edit button. To remove a device from the list, select it and click Remove.

Once you set up a multilink connection, it works just like a regular Internet connection, but faster.

Setting Additional Dial-Up Networking Options

You might think all the properties of a Dial-Up Networking connection would appear on the connection's Properties dialog box (shown in Figure 21-6), but they don't. Most of the settings on the (ill-named) Internet Properties dialog box pertain to your Web browser, rather than to your Internet connection, but a few additional settings appear on its Connections tab. (This dialog box is called Internet Options when you dispaly it by choosing Tools | Internet Options from Internet Explorer.)

To display the Internet Properties dialog box, choose Start | Settings | Control Panel and run the Internet Options program. Figure 21-8 shows the Connections tab of the Internet Properties dialog box. The other tabs of this dialog box apply to using a Web browser, and are covered in Chapter 24. Most of the settings on the Connections tab control your Internet connection, however; those settings are listed in Table 21-4. The LAN Settings button displays the LAN Settings dialog box, which you use if you connect to the Internet over a LAN (see Chapter 30, section "Configuring and Using

WINDOWS ME ON THE INTERNET

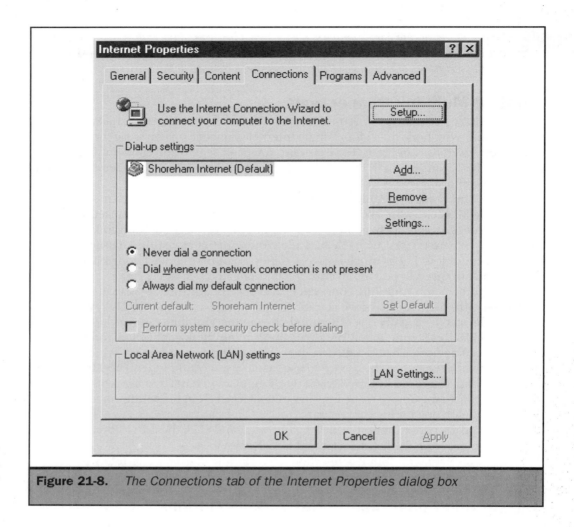

Figure 21-8.   *The Connections tab of the Internet Properties dialog box*

Internet Connection Sharing"). The Settings button displays a Setting dialog box that contains other LAN-related settings for the selected connection (see Chapter 30, section "Using Gateway Programs Other Than ICS").

Deleting a Dial-Up Networking Connection

If you don't expect to connect to a particular account in the future, delete its connection from the Dial-Up Networking window by selecting the icon for the connection and pressing the DEL key. Be sure you also delete any shortcuts to the connection.

Setting	Description
Dial-up settings	Lists your Dial-Up Networking connections, so you can enable those to use and disable those not to use.
Never dial a connection, Dial whenever a network connection is not present, and Always dial My Default connection	Specify what Windows does when a program tries to connect to the Internet (for example, an e-mail program tries to connect to a mail server, or a Web browser tries to retrieve a Web page).
Current default	Displays the name of the connection Windows will use unless you specify another connection. To change the default, select a connection from the Dial-Up Settings list and click the Set Default button.
Perform system security check before dialing	Before connecting to the Internet, checks whether your network settings might let others read or change files on your computer.

Table 21-4.   *Connection-Related Settings on the Internet Properties Dialog Box*

Other Dial-Up Networking Settings

When you display the Dial-Up Networking window (shown in Figure 21-1) by choosing Start | Settings | Dial-Up Networking, the menu bar contains a new command, Connections. Choose Connections | Settings to display the Dial-Up Networking dialog box, shown in Figure 21-9.

The dialog box contains settings that affect all Dial-Up Networking connections:

- **Show An Icon On Taskbar After Connected**   Displays the Dial-Up Networking icon on the Taskbar. This icon provides a convenient way to monitor or hang up your connection.

- **Show A Confirmation Dialog After Connected**   Deselect this check box so you don't have to see a confirmation dialog box each time you connect.

- **Disable Sending Of LAN Manager Passwords** For backward compatibility with Windows NT; specifies that passwords not be sent over the LAN in plain text (unencrypted), for better security.

- **Require Secure VPN Connections** If you use Virtual Private Networking (VPN) to connect to your organization's intranet, specifies that secure (encrypted) connections be used (see Chapter 30, section "Connecting to Your Organization's LAN with Virtual Private Networking").

- **Only Accept 128 Bit Encryption (When Required)** When connecting to secure Web servers, rejects encryption lower than 128 bits.

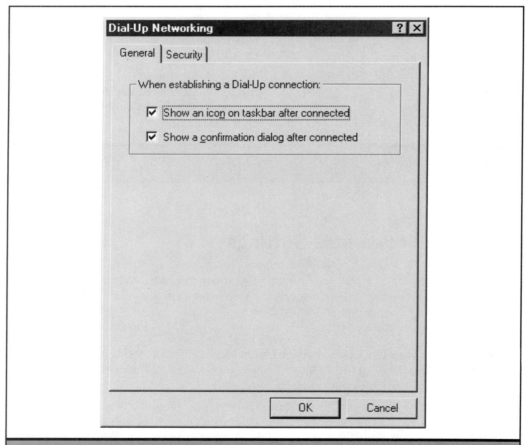

Figure 21-9. *Choose Connections / Settings from the Dial-Up Networking window to display these settings.*

Speeding Up Connecting to the Internet

Your Internet connection uses TCP/IP, not NetBEUI (Microsoft's file- and printer-sharing protocol) or IPX/SPX (Netware's protocol). You can speed up the process of connecting to your ISP by removing these protocols if your computer doesn't use them to communicate on a LAN. If your computer is *not* on a LAN, follow these steps:

1. Choose Start | Settings | Dial-Up Networking to display the Dial-Up Networking window.

2. Right-click the connection you use to connect to your ISP. Choose Properties from the shortcut menu that appears.

3. Click the Networking tab. Click the NetBEUI and IPX/SPX check boxes until they are cleared.

4. Click the Security tab. Click the Log On To Network check box until it is cleared.

5. Click OK.

6. Connect to your ISP to make sure that changing these settings doesn't prevent you from connecting. (If so, repeat the steps and reverse your changes.)

Dialing the Internet Manually

When you want to connect to an account by using Dial-Up Networking, follow these steps:

1. Choose Start | Programs | Accessories | Communications | Dial-Up Networking to display the Dial-Up Networking window (shown in Figure 21-1). Then run the connection icon. If a connection icon appears on your desktop, you can run it instead. You see the Connect To dialog box, shown in Figure 21-10.

2. If the user name, password, or phone number don't appear, fill them in. (See "Configuring Windows for Dialing Locations" in Chapter 20 for how to set up dialing locations, if you use a laptop computer in more than one location.)

3. Unless you are worried about someone else using your computer to connect to your account, select the Save Password check box so you needn't type your password each time you connect.

4. Click the Connect button. Dial-Up Networking dials your account, logs in, and starts the type of connection you set in the Type of Dial-Up Server setting in the Properties dialog box for the connection. You see a window telling you you're connected to the account (Figure 21-11).

5. Click the Close button.

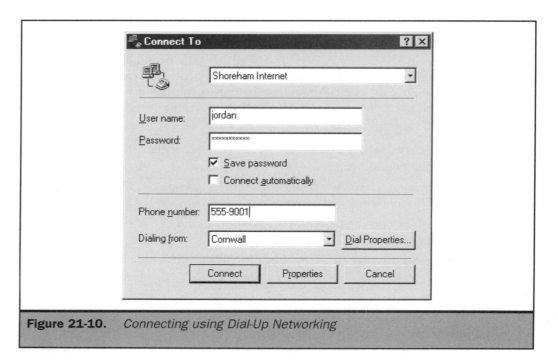

Figure 21-10. *Connecting using Dial-Up Networking*

Tip *Click the Do Not Display This Message In The Future check box, so you needn't see this confirmation dialog box each time you connect to the Internet.*

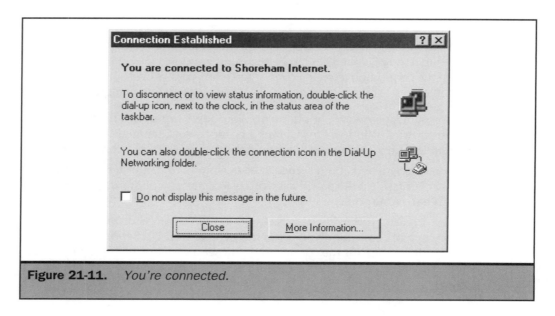

Figure 21-11. *You're connected.*

To make starting Dial-Up Networking easier, copy the icon for your connection from the Dial-Up Networking window to your desktop. Right-click the connection's icon and choose Create Shortcut from the menu that appears. Windows asks whether to put the shortcut on your desktop. Click Yes. You may also want to add the connection to your Start menu or Programs menu (see Chapter 11).

While you are connected, the Dial-Up Networking icon—two overlapping computer screens—appears in the system tray on the Taskbar. Move the mouse pointer to it (without clicking) to see how many bytes have been sent and received, as well as your connection speed. Double-click the icon to see more details.

Disconnecting from Your Account

To disconnect your Internet connection, double-click the Dial-Up Networking icon in the system tray. You see the Connected dialog box, shown here. Click Disconnect.

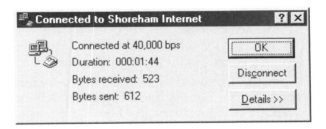

If you are connected to your Internet account and don't use it for a while (usually 20 minutes), Windows or your ISP may disconnect you automatically. You may see this dialog box asking whether you want to disconnect:

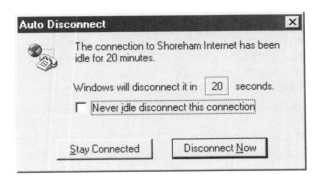

Instead, you may see a dialog box saying you have been disconnected and asking whether you want to reconnect. See the next section for how to configure Windows to connect and disconnect automatically.

Dialing the Internet Automatically

What happens if you aren't connected to the Internet and you tell your e-mail program to fetch your mail, or you ask your Web browser to display a Web page? Dial-Up Networking can dial up and connect to your Internet account automatically when you request Internet-based information.

To set Windows to connect automatically, follow these steps:

1. Choose Start | Settings | Control Panel and run the Internet Options program. Click the Connections tab on the Internet Properties dialog box and make sure the Always Dial My Default Connection setting is selected.

2. Click the Dial-Up Networking connection you want to use and then click the Set Default button to make this connection the one Windows will use.

3. Click OK to dismiss the Internet Properties dialog box.

4. Choose Start | Settings | Dial-Up Networking to display the Dial-Up Networking window (shown in Figure 21-1), right-click the same connection you chose in Step 2, and choose Properties from the shortcut menu that appears. You see the properties dialog box for the connection, as shown in Figure 21-8.

5. Click the Security tab (shown in Figure 21-12) and type your user name and password into the boxes, if they don't already appear. Select the Connect Automatically check box.

6. Click the Dialing tab (shown in Figure 21-13). Set the options to dial your default connection and tell Windows how many times to try and how long to wait between attempts (if your ISP's line is busy, for example). If you want Windows to disconnect automatically after a period of inactivity, chose the Disconnect If Idle For *xxx* Minutes check box and type the number of minutes.

7. Click OK to dismiss the properties dialog box for the connection.

When you use an Internet program and Windows detects you are asking for information from the Internet, you see the Dial-Up Connection dialog box shown in Figure 21-9. If you want Windows to remember your Internet password, select the Save

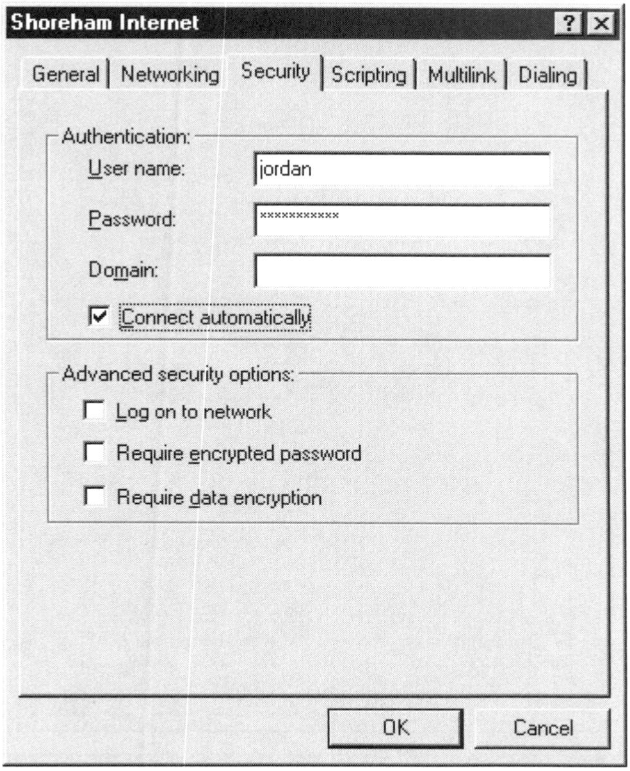

Figure 21-12. *Providing the information Windows needs to log on to your Internet account automatically.*

Password check box. If you want Windows to connect without waiting for you to click the Connect button, select the Connect Automatically check box.

The Dial-Up Connection dialog box displays messages as it dials, connects, and logs in to your Internet account using the information in the Dial-Up Settings dialog box.

Automatically dialing the Internet can be annoying, too. For example, if you are reading your e-mail offline and open a message that contains a link to the Web, you might not want your computer to dial into the Internet. If you no longer want Windows to connect automatically to the Internet, run the Internet Options program in Control Panel, click the Connections tab, and click the Never Dial A Connection option.

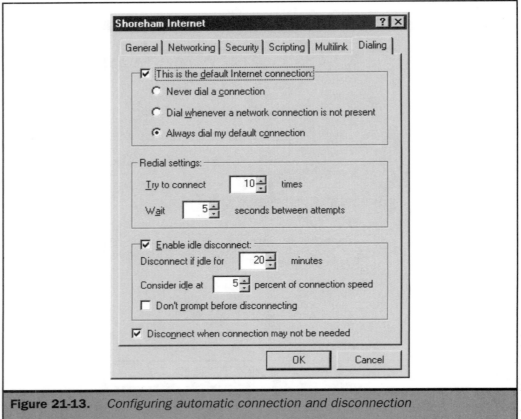

Figure 21-13. *Configuring automatic connection and disconnection*

Testing Your Connection

After dialing up a Dial-Up Networking connection, you can use Windows's Ping program to test whether packets of information can make the round trip from your computer, out over the Internet to another computer, and back to your computer. You can use the Tracert program to trace the route packets take to get from your computer to another computer, and you can use the Netstat program to find out to which computers your computer is talking.

Pinging Another Computer

Sending a small text packet on a round trip is called *pinging*, and you can use Windows's built-in Ping program to send one.

To run Ping, open a DOS window (described in Chapter 38) by choosing Start | Programs | Accessories | MS-DOS Prompt and type the Ping command as shown here.

```
ping system
```

Replace *system* with either the numeric IP address or the host name of the computer you want to ping. Choose any Internet host computer you're sure is up and running, such as your ISP's mail server. Then press ENTER.

> **Tip**   *To see a listing of all the command-line options for the Ping program, type **ping /?** at the DOS prompt.*

For example, you can ping the Yahoo! Web server (a Web search engine and directory) by typing

```
ping www.yahoo.com
```

Ping sends out four test packets (pings) and reports how long the packets take to get to Yahoo's computer and back to yours (see Figure 21-14). For each packet, you see both how long the round trip takes in milliseconds and summary information about all four packets' trips. Ping has a number of options listed in Table 21-5. Ping has other options, not listed here, useful only to network managers.

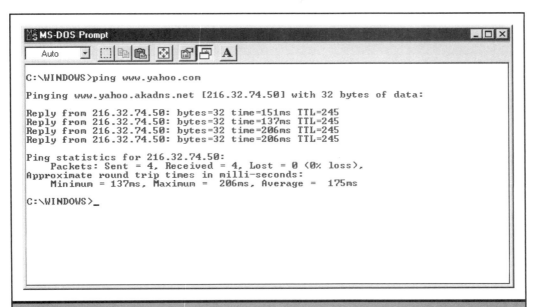

Figure 21-14.   *Ping tests your Internet connection.*

WINDOWS ME
ON THE INTERNET

Option	Description
-a	Reports numeric addresses rather than host names.
-f	Specifies that packets contain a Do Not Fragment flag, so packets aren't fragmented on route. (Useful to test very slow dial-up connections.)
-i *ttl*	Specifies the *Time To Live* for the packets (how many times the packet can be passed from one computer to another while in transit on the network).
-l *length*	Specifies the length of the packets to send. The default length is 64 bytes. The maximum length is 8192 (8K).
-n *n*	Specifies to send *n* pings. (The default is four.)
-r *n*	Specifies the outgoing and returning packets should record the first *n* hosts on the route they take, using the Return Route field; *n* is a number from 1 to 9.
-t	Specifies to continue pinging until you interrupt it. (Otherwise, it pings four times.)
-w *n*	Specifies a time-out of *n* milliseconds for each packet.

Table 21-5.   *Options for the Ping Program*

Tip   *First try Ping with a numeric IP address (for example, 216.32.74.50 for one of Yahoo!'s Web servers), to see whether packets get out to the Internet and back. Then try Ping with a host name, to see whether you successfully contact your DNS to convert the name into an IP address. If the first test works and the second doesn't, your connection isn't set up properly to contact a DNS.*

Tracing Packets over the Internet

Packets of information don't usually go directly from one computer to another computer over the Internet. Instead, they are involved in a huge game of "whisper-down-the-lane," in which packets are passed from computer to computer until they reach their destination. If your data seems to be moving slowly, you can use the *Tracert* (short for *trace route*) program to follow your packets across the Internet, from your computer to an Internet host you frequently use. The technique Tracert uses doesn't always work, so it's quite possible running Tracert to a remote computer can fail, even though the computer is working and accessible.

To run Tracert, open a DOS window by choosing Start | Programs | Accessories | MS-DOS Prompt (see Chapter 38). Then type the Tracert command:

```
tracert system
```

Replace *system* with either the numeric IP address or the Internet name of the computer to which you want to trace the route. Then press ENTER.

Tip *To see a listing of all the command-line options for the Tracert program, type **tracert** at the DOS prompt, with no address.*

For example, you can trace the route of packets from your computer to the Yahoo! Web directory at **www.yahoo.com** by typing:

```
tracert www.yahoo.com
```

You see a listing like the one in Figure 21-15, showing the route the packets took from your computer to the specified host (sometimes Tracert reports a different host name from the one you specified, which means the host has more than one name).

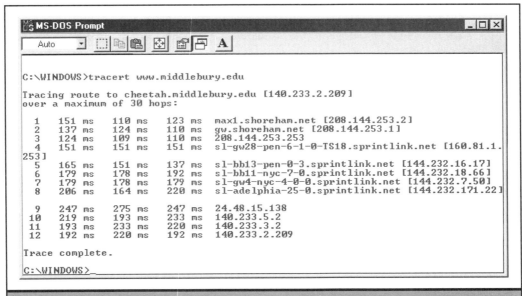

Figure 21-15. *Tracert shows the route packets take from your computer to an Internet host.*

WINDOWS ME
ON THE INTERNET

For each *hop* (stage of the route), Tracert sends out three packets and reports the time each packet took to reach that far. It also reports the name and numeric IP address of the host.

Table 21-6 shows the options you can use with the Tracert program. A few other options, not listed here, are useful only to network managers.

Displaying Internet Connections Using Netstat

Netstat is a network diagnostic program you can use for any TCP/IP connection—Internet connections or LANs. You can run Netstat to see which computers your computer is connected to over the Internet—not the ISP to which you dial in, but other Internet hosts to or from which you are transferring information.

To run Netstat, open a DOS window by choosing Start | Programs | Accessories | MS-DOS Prompt (see Chapter 38). Then type the following:

```
netstat
```

When you press ENTER, you see a listing of the Internet connections currently running. Figure 21-16 shows the computer is connected to several computers for receiving Web pages (the 80 at the end of the address signifies the port commonly used for Web page retrieval). The computer is also picking up mail from **mail.iecc.com** and **rodney.concentric.net** (signified by the pop3 at the end of the address).

Tip   *To see a listing of all the command-line options for the Netstat program, type **netstat /h** at the DOS prompt.*

Option	Description
-d	Specifies not to resolve addresses to host names, so the resulting list of hosts consists only of numeric IP addresses
-h *n*	Specifies a maximum number of *n* hops to trace before giving up
-w *n*	Specifies that the program wait *n* milliseconds for each reply before giving up

Table 21-6. *Options for the Tracert Program*

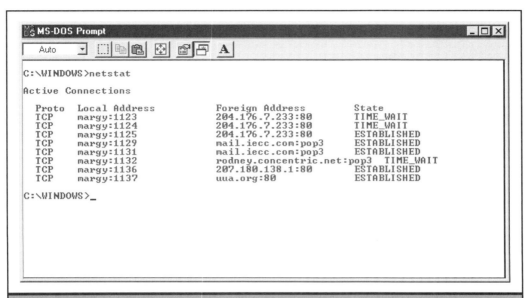

Figure 21-16. *The Netstat program lists Internet hosts you are using.*

Chapter 22

E-Mail and Newsgroups Using Outlook Express

The most popular use of the Internet is to send and receive messages from other Internet users. Windows Me comes with Outlook Express 5, Microsoft's free e-mail and newsreading program. You can also install and use any number of mail and newsreading applications, whether they are Microsoft products or not.

This chapter describes how to use Outlook Express to send and receive e-mail messages, organize the messages you decide to keep, and read and post messages to Usenet newsgroups. If you correspond with people whose software can read messages written in HTML (the language in which Web pages are written), you can compose them using Outlook Express. Whatever program you use for e-mail or newsreading, you should learn *netiquette* to avoid getting into trouble.

*If you'd like to test your e-mail program, get news about updates to this book, or just say "Hi" to the authors, send a message to **winmetcr@gurus.com** (our mail robot will send an automatic response, and we read all our messages).*

Should You Use Outlook Express?

Outlook Express has a number of advantages. It's free, already installed, and easy to use; it has a nice collection of features for handling e-mail and newsgroups; it lets you import messages and addresses from most other popular e-mail programs; and it works well with HotMail, Microsoft's free Web-based e-mail provider.

Why wouldn't you want to use Outlook Express? In a word: security. Outlook Express (along with Outlook, which is part of Microsoft Office) has increasingly been the target of e-mail viruses like the ILOVEYOU virus (see Chapter 31, section "The Story of the ILOVEYOU Worm"). Most of these viruses have been relatively harmless, but they have demonstrated vulnerabilities that more destructive viruses may use in the future.

Part of the problem is simply the popularity of Outlook and Outlook Express. The people who write viruses (like the people who write any other kind of software) want to write for the largest possible market, so they target Microsoft products. But the problem is exacerbated by Microsoft itself, which has historically taken a lax attitude toward security.

To sum up: If you are a happy user of Eudora, Netscape Messenger, or one of the other major e-mail programs, Outlook Express doesn't contain any gotta-have features that would make you want to switch. It is awfully convenient, though, and if the prospect of getting an e-mail virus doesn't keep you up at night, convenience may win the day.

*If you use Netscape Navigator as your Web browser, you may want to use its e-mail program, Netscape Messenger, which comes as part of the Netscape Communicator set of programs. See Netscape's Web site at **http://home.netscape.com/products**. Another excellent e-mail program, Eudora, is available at **http://www.eudora.com**.*

What Is E-Mail?

E-mail, short for *electronic mail*, is a way to send messages over the Internet (or a local area network or other network) to people who may not be logged in right now. (To send messages right away to people who are logged in at the same time you are, and receive answers in seconds, use an instant messaging program like MSN Messenger; for more information, see Chapter 25, section "Chatting Online Using MSN Messenger").

How Does E-Mail Work?

Oversimplifying somewhat, the process works like this:

1. Using an e-mail program, such as Outlook Express, the sender creates a message and decides who the recipients should be.

2. At a designated place at the beginning of the message, the sender lists the e-mail addresses of all the recipients. (The sender can specify a long list of recipients, but for simplicity, we'll pretend there is only one.) An *e-mail address* specifies two things: a computer on the Internet on which a recipient receives mail (called an *incoming mail server*), and the name that the incoming mail server uses to designate the mailbox of the recipient. So, for example, the e-mail address **president@whitehouse.gov** specifies the incoming mail server whitehouse.gov and a mailbox on whitehouse.gov called president.

3. The sender connects to an *outgoing mail server*, a computer connected to the Internet (usually a computer owned by the sender's Internet service provider) that runs a mail-handling program that supports *SMTP* (the Simple Mail Transfer Protocol used for Internet mail)—these servers are usually called *SMTP servers*. The message is sent from the sender's computer to the outgoing mail server.

4. From the outgoing mail server, the message is passed across the Internet to the recipient's incoming mail server.

5. The recipient's incoming mail server files the message in the recipient's *mailbox*, a file or folder containing all the messages that the recipient hasn't downloaded to her own computer yet.

6. Using an e-mail program (which need not be the same as the one the sender used to create and send the message), the recipient looks for new mail by logging in to the incoming mail server. Incoming mail servers use one of two protocols for receiving mail. Servers that use *Post Office Protocol 3* (*POP3*, or just *POP*) are called *POP servers*, and servers that use *Internet Message Access Protocol* (*IMAP*) are called *IMAP servers*. The incoming mail server uses POP or IMAP to deliver the message, along with any other messages that may have arrived since the recipient last checked, to the recipient's computer.

7. The recipient uses the e-mail program to read the message.

WINDOWS ME ON THE INTERNET

Every e-mail message consists of a *header* (lines containing the address, the return address, the date, and other information about the message) and a *body* (the text of the message).

What Is Web-Based E-Mail?

Web-based e-mail is an e-mail account that you access by visiting a Web site with your Web browser, rather than your mail program. After you identify yourself by giving a user name and a password, the Web site shows you your messages and allows you to send e-mail to other people.

Typically, Web-based e-mail is a free service offered by a Web portal like Yahoo! or Excite, a news Web site like CNN or ZDNet, or any other Web site that wants you to keep coming back. You could easily sign up for a dozen such accounts, which would cost you nothing. (We don't recommend this, though, because of the confusion you would cause yourself.)

Web-based e-mail is a great convenience if you travel a lot or regularly use more than one computer. Your files stay on the Web site's computer, rather than being scattered over all the computers you've ever used. To keep up with your e-mail in a strange place, all you need is a computer that is connected to the Internet and has a Web browser—which you can usually find in a public library or an Internet café. You can also use a Web-based e-mail account to keep your personal e-mail separate from your work e-mail, even if your only Internet connection is at work.

The disadvantages of Web-based e-mail are related to the advantages. If the provider's Web site goes down, you not only lose the ability to send and receive mail, you also temporarily lose access to all the files you have stored there. Most providers also place a limit on the amount of disk space they're willing to devote to your files. Downloading your mail to your own computer (so that you can read and respond to it offline) is typically a clumsy process. An exception is Yahoo! Mail (at **http://mail.yahoo.com**), which enables you to collect your Web-based messages using your favorite e-mail program.

What Is Hotmail?

Hotmail (at **http://www.hotmail.com**) is Microsoft's own Web-based free e-mail service. You can set up an account through the Internet Connection Wizard and access that account through a Web browser or through Outlook Express. In general, Hotmail is as good as any other Web-based e-mail service, and Outlook Express is set up to deal with it. Using Hotmail together with Outlook Express gets around many of the usual aggravations of Web-based e-mail, because your e-mail interface resides on your own computer rather than on a Web site. You can conveniently work with your downloaded mail when you are offline. However, when you are away from your usual computer, you can work with your e-mail through a Web browser and leave the messages on Hotmail's computer.

*Eudora, a powerful e-mail program you can get from **http://www.eudora.com**, can also download messages from Hotmail.*

What Are Newsgroups?

Newsgroups are another way to use your computer and the Internet to communicate with the outside world. Unlike e-mail, however, a newsgroup is a public medium. When you send a message to a newsgroup, the message is available to anyone who wants to look at it—it's as if you have tacked up a notice in a public place. You never know who—if anyone—reads your message. The Internet-based system of newsgroups is called *Usenet*.

Newsgroups are organized by topic. Since there are tens of thousands of newsgroups, topics can be very specific. When you have something to say about the topic of a newsgroup, you can use a *newsreading program*, such as Outlook Express, to compose a message (which may be many pages or only one line) and send it to your *news server*, a computer on the Internet that supports *NNTP* (Net News Transfer Protocol), which makes your article available to other news servers. People who want to read the recent contributions to this newsgroup (including your message) can use a newsreading program (not necessarily the same as yours) to download messages from their own news servers.

What Is Netiquette?

A contraction of "net etiquette," *netiquette* is the informal system of courtesies that people expect from you when you trade e-mail with them or participate in newsgroups. Much of netiquette is common sense, and has to do with not wasting people's time or resources, giving people credit when you quote them, and not forwarding messages to a wider audience than the author would want.

The purpose of most netiquette is to compensate for the peculiarities of the medium. For example, the Internet unfortunately is the ideal medium for chain letters and mass mailings. With a few easy clicks, you can forward a chain letter to 100 people, or send your get-rich-quick scheme to every newsgroup in the world. If social convention did not restrain people, such messages would choke the whole Internet. The Internet is also an ideal medium for destructive gossip. If Bill told Mary in person what John told Bill about her, she might take it with a grain of salt. But if Bill forwards John's exact e-mail message to Mary, or if a chain of 15 people forward John's message (eventually reaching Mary), a more difficult situation emerges.

A lighthearted online reference for netiquette is Brad Templeton's satirical "Emily Postnews" Web page at **http://www.templetons.com/brad/emily.html**, or check our site at **http://net.gurus.com/winmetcr**.

WINDOWS ME
ON THE INTERNET

Getting Started with Outlook Express

To begin using Outlook Express, click the Outlook Express icon on the Quick Launch toolbar or choose from Start | Program | Outlook Express. If you have never used Outlook Express before, the Internet Connection Wizard starts (see Chapter 21, section "Creating a Dial-Up Networking Connection Using the Internet Connection Wizard"). After you complete or cancel the Wizard, the Outlook Express opening screen appears, as shown in Figure 22-1.

Working with the Outlook Express Window

The Outlook Express window, shown in Figure 22-1, resembles an Explorer window. At the top is a menu bar, with a toolbar underneath it. Below the toolbar, the window is cut into three panes. The right pane contains links that you can click to do the things

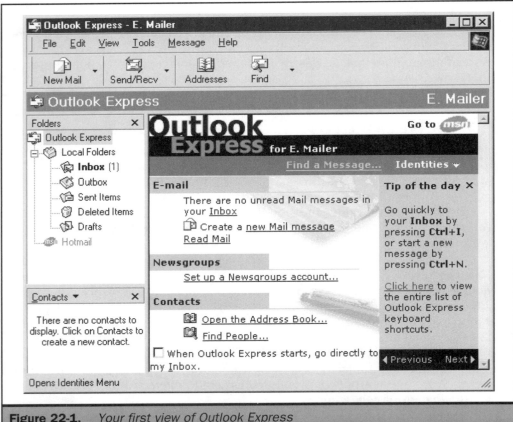

Figure 22-1.   *Your first view of Outlook Express*

that the text describes, such as set up a newsgroup account or create a new mail message. The upper-left pane is a folder list, similar to the left pane in an Explorer window. Outlook Express is at the top of the list and is highlighted, indicating that it corresponds to what is currently shown in the right pane.

The folders immediately beneath Outlook Express on the folder list are necessary parts of the mail system:

- **Inbox**   Where Outlook Express puts the incoming messages that it downloads from your incoming mail server. The messages remain there until you delete them or move them to another folder.

- **Outbox**   Contains the outgoing messages that you have completed and chosen to send, but have not yet been sent. For example, you might complete and choose to send several messages while you are offline. Those messages wait in the Outbox folder until the next time your computer is connected to your outgoing mail server.

- **Sent Items**   Contains messages that you have sent. They remain in this folder until you delete or move them.

- **Deleted Items**   Contains the messages (both incoming and outgoing) that you have deleted. Like the Recycle Bin, it is a last-chance folder that gets unwanted messages out of the way, but from which they still can be retrieved. Outlook Express can be set up to clean out the Deleted Items folder automatically, or you can delete messages from it manually (see "Saving and Deleting Messages"). Messages deleted from the Deleted Items folder are beyond Outlook Express's power to retrieve.

- **Drafts**   Contains unfinished messages that you have chosen to save and work on later. Any time you are composing a message, you can choose File | Save to save the message in the Drafts folder.

As you begin sending and receiving messages, you can set up other folders to keep track of your correspondence (see "Organizing Your Correspondence"). You don't have to do so, but if you plan to keep copies of messages, they will be easier to find if you sort them into folders by topic or by correspondent.

Setting Up Your Accounts

Before Outlook Express can send or receive mail, or allow you to interact with newsgroups, you need to tell the Internet Connection Wizard what accounts you have and how it can access them. Before you start the Wizard, make sure you have the following information handy:

- **The name you want attached to any message you send**   Do you want to be known as Johnny Public, Jonathan Q. Public, or by some nickname?

■ **Your return e-mail address** If people want to reply to your messages, where should the replies go?

■ **The name of the servers your account deals with** For a *news account* (which lets you read newsgroups), this is an NNTP server with a name like *news.serviceprovider.com*. For an e-mail account that is not Web based, you provide two names: one server for incoming mail (a POP or IMAP server) and one server for outgoing mail (an SMTP server). Your ISP should have given you this information—if you don't have it, check their Web page or call them. Outlook Express already knows the mail server names for Hotmail (a Web-based e-mail account), because Microsoft owns Hotmail. For Yahoo! Mail, enter **pop.mail.yahoo.com** for your incoming mail server and **smtp.mail.yahoo.com** for your outgoing mail server. You can't use Outlook Express to read e-mail from Web-based e-mail accounts that don't have mail servers.

■ **Your user name and password (if any) for logging in to the servers.**

Once you have assembled this information:

1. Choose Tools | Accounts. The Internet Accounts dialog box opens.
2. Click the Add button and select the type of account you want to define: mail, news, or directory service. The appropriate Internet Connection Wizard begins.
3. Insert the information the Wizard asks for.

You have to go through this process once for each account you want to establish.

Importing Messages from Other Mail Programs

If you've been using e-mail for a while, your message files are an important asset. Continuity can be an important reason to stick with whatever mail program you've been using. Outlook Express 5 lets you convert your message files from these other mail programs:

■ Previous versions of Outlook Express.

■ Eudora Pro or Light; the menu claims only to convert versions 1 through 3, but we imported messages from Eudora Pro 4.1 with no problems. Just pretend that you're importing from version 3.

■ Microsoft Exchange, Outlook, Internet Mail for Windows 3.1, or Windows Messaging.

■ Netscape Mail or Messenger (part of Netscape Communicator).

> **Note**
>
> *Migrating into a Microsoft product is easier than migrating out of it. Outlook Express' export feature only exports to other Microsoft e-mail clients. If you decide to go back to your old e-mail client later on, you'll be relying on that client's ability to import Outlook Express messages. If you plan to try Outlook Express for a few days before choosing between it and your old mail program, set Outlook Express to leave your incoming messages on your incoming mail server, and collect your mail using both programs until you make up your mind. Choose Tools | Accounts, click the Mail tab, select your e-mail account, click Properties, click the Advanced tab, and select the Leave A Copy Of Messages On Server check box.*

In Outlook Express 4, the importation program got all the messages, but sometimes messed up the dates. Microsoft seems to have fixed this bug in Outlook Express 5. Still, you should inspect your imported files for completeness before throwing away the originals, or just archive the originals somewhere.

To import messages from one of these mail applications:

1. Select File | Import | Messages from the menu.
2. Answer the questions asked by the Outlook Express Import Wizard. It needs to know from which application it is importing, and where the files are located. If your old e-mail program isn't installed, you may need to install it for the import to work (for example, if are moving your e-mail files to a new computer).

Folders of imported messages show up in the Outlook Express folder list, from which you can move them into whatever folders you like (see "Organizing Your Correspondence"). The imported folders retain their names and structure. If, for example, you import the People At Work folder from Eudora, when it arrives in Outlook Express, it should still have the subfolders Bob and Jenny, and those subfolders should contain all the messages they had in Eudora. (Subfolders don't always import correctly in our experience.)

Importing Addresses from Other Mail Programs

Outlook Express can import addresses from these programs:

- Eudora Pro or Light, versions 1 through 3
- LDIF-LDAP data interchange format
- Microsoft Exchange or Internet Mail for Windows
- Netscape Address Book or Communicator
- Text files

To import addresses from one of these mail applications:

1. If you want to import a Windows Address Book (.wab) file, select File | Import | Address Book from the menu. If you are importing addresses from another program, select File | Import | Other Address Book.

2. Answer the questions asked by the Outlook Express Import Wizard.

If all goes well, the addresses wind up in the Windows Address Book (see Chapter 5, section "Storing Addresses in the Address Book").

Setting Your Mail and Newsreading Programs

You can tell Windows which mail and newsreading programs to run with Internet Explorer; these are the programs that Internet Explorer runs when you click a mail or news link (see Chapter 23). Choose Start | Settings | Control Panel. In the Control Panel window, open the Internet Options icon. On the Programs tab in the Messaging section, the Mail and News boxes show the default programs that Internet Explorer runs; both are set to Outlook Express when you install Windows.

Choosing a Layout for the Outlook Express Window

Like Windows Explorer, the Outlook Express window provides a number of features that you can choose to display or not display. When all the pieces are made visible, you get the busy, complicated window shown in Figure 22-2.

You can make any of these pieces (other than the working area) appear or disappear as you like. Choose View | Layout to display the Window Layout Properties dialog box, check the features that you want to have in your Outlook Express window, and click OK.

We recommend displaying the folder list, toolbar, and status bar. You might also find the Contacts list useful. If you like the Views bar, you can drag it up to the right end of the menu bar.

Sending and Receiving E-Mail

After you set up one or more mail accounts, you can check your mail by clicking the Send and Receive button on the toolbar or choosing Tools | Send And Receive | Send And Receive All or pressing F5. After you have clicked Send And Receive, Outlook Express goes through the following process automatically.

1. Connects to your mail servers. If you are on a local area network, this part of the process may happen so quickly that it is almost invisible to you. If you connect to the Internet over a modem, however, and are not already online for some other reason, Outlook Express runs Dial-Up Networking to dial up your ISP and establish a connection. Once an Internet connection is established, Outlook Express contacts your mail servers over the Internet.

2. Sends all the messages in your Outbox. Messages you aren't ready to send should be stored in the Draft folder, not in the Outbox.

3. Downloads all the incoming messages from the server into your Inbox.

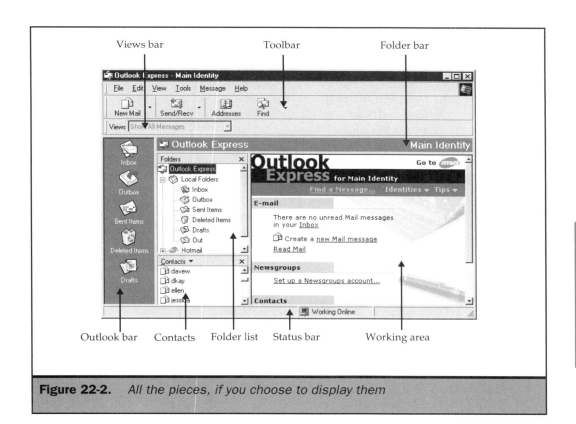

Figure 22-2.   *All the pieces, if you choose to display them*

WINDOWS ME
ON THE INTERNET

By default, the Send And Receive button sends all queued messages and checks for mail in all of the e-mail accounts it knows about. If you want to be more selective, click the down arrow next to the Send and Receive button. A menu drops down offering you the following choices:

- **Send and Receive All**   The default.
- **Receive All**   Checks for incoming mail in all known accounts, but doesn't send queued messages.
- **Send All**   Sends all queued messages, but doesn't check for incoming mail.
- **Individual Listings Of Your E-Mail Accounts**   Choosing an account sends and receives for that account only.

The same choices are available from the Tools | Send And Receive menu.

While messages are downloading, a dialog box appears. You may click the Hang Up When Finished box if you want Outlook Express to close the Internet connection when it is done.

Table 22-1 shows configuration options for sending and receiving messages. Choose Tools | Options to display the Options dialog box that shows these settings.

Tab	Setting	Description
General	Send and receive messages at startup	When you start Outlook Express, sends messages in your Outbox and downloads messages from your incoming mail server.
General	Check for new messages every *xxx* minutes	Specifies how often Outlook Express connects automatically to the mail servers to download incoming messages and upload outgoing messages.
General	If my computer is not connected at this time	Specifies what to do if your computer is not connected to the Internet when Outlook Express tries to check for new messages.

Table 22-1.   *Send/Receive Settings of the Options Dialog Box*

Tab	Setting	Description
Read	Mark message read after displaying for *xxx* seconds	Specifies that Outlook Express mark a message as read after displaying it in the preview pane.
Read	Fonts button	Enables you to set the fonts in which Outlook Express displays unformatted messages.
Receipts	Returning Read Receipts	Specifies how to process return receipts (tags attached to e-mail messages that request a receipt so that the sender knows that you've seen the message).
Send	Save copy of sent messages in the 'Sent Items' folder	Specifies that Outlook Express keep copies of your outgoing messages. You can move them from the Sent Items folder to another folder after the message is sent.
Send	Send messages immediately	Specifies that Outlook Express connect to your outgoing mail server and send messages whenever a message is in your Outbox (see "Sending Messages Automatically (or Not)").
Security	Select the Internet Explorer security zone to use	Specifies which downloaded object security zone to use when deciding whether to allow ActiveX controls and other possibly dangerous programs to run (see Chapter 31, section "Downloaded Object Security").
Connection	Ask before switching dial-up connections	If you have more than one Dial-Up Networking connection, specifies that Outlook Express ask you when one connection isn't working.
Connection	Hang up after sending and receiving	Specifies that after sending and receiving messages, Outlook Express disconnect from the Internet.

Table 22-1.   *Send/Receive Settings of the Options Dialog Box* (continued)

Receiving Mail

New mail accumulates in your Inbox, staying there until you decide to delete it or move it to another folder. To look at it, click Inbox in the folder list of the Outlook Express window. The window now has three panes, as it does when you look at any mail folder. You can drag the boundaries of these three panes to reallocate the space occupied by each. The three panes are the following:

- **The folder list view in the left pane**   The selected folder is highlighted. In Figure 22-3, Inbox is the selected folder.

- **The selected folder's message list in the upper-right pane**   Each message receives one line in the list. The line tells who is the author of the message, what the subject line says, and when the message was received (or sent, if the message is outgoing). If the author rated the message as Urgent, an exclamation point (!) appears on the left side of its entry on the list. If the message has an *attachment* (a file attached to the message), a paper clip appears to the left of its entry. The currently selected message is highlighted. Unread messages have a closed-envelope icon next to them; read messages have an open-envelope icon.

- **A preview of the selected message in the lower-right pane**   The bar at the top of the lower-right pane lists the sender and receiver of the message, together with its subject line. Below this bar is a scrollable window containing the full text of the message.

Customizing the Message List

To choose what columns are displayed in the message list, right-click the row of column headings and choose Columns from the shortcut menu. The Columns dialog box appears, listing the possible columns Outlook Express can display. Check the columns you want. You may also use this dialog box to rearrange the columns by selecting a column name and clicking the Move Up or Move Down button. You can switch the order of the columns by dragging the header left or right. You can use the Columns dialog box to fix the widths of the columns in the message list as well, but dragging the boundaries between the columns in the message list itself is simpler.

Sorting the Messages in a Folder

You can sort the messages in a folder according to any of the columns in the message list—just click the label above any of the columns. Click once to sort in ascending order, twice for descending order.

For example, clicking the From column label sorts the messages according to sender. The various senders appear in alphabetical order. Click From again to sort in reverse alphabetical order.

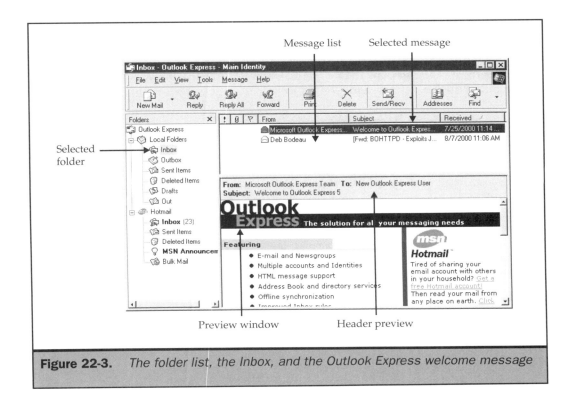

Figure 22-3.   *The folder list, the Inbox, and the Outlook Express welcome message*

Reading the Messages in a Folder

To read the messages in any folder:

1. Click the name of the folder in the folder list of the Outlook Express window. If the folder you want is not visible, it is either off the screen or contained in another folder. Use the left pane scroll bar to look up or down in the folder list. Click the plus box next to a folder's name to see the list of folders contained inside it.

2. Find the message you want to read in the message list in the upper-right pane.

3. Double-click to read the message in its own window, or single-click to read the message in the preview pane of the Outlook Express window.

Opening Attached Files

Messages with attached files are denoted with a paper clip icon in the message list of the Outlook Express window. When the message is selected, a larger paper clip icon appears in the title bar of the preview pane. When the message is opened, the attached files appear as icons just below the subject line.

Clicking the large paper clip icon produces a list of the attached files; selecting one of the files from this list opens the file. Similarly, selecting an attached-file icon from the bottom of the message window opens the file.

Caution *When an attached file opens, it uses whichever application is associated with its file type—you are no longer dealing with Outlook Express. For this reason, we recommend that you do not open unsolicited file attachments from strangers, or even from friends, unless you're sure you know what the files are. It's usually safe to read e-mail messages from strangers—they're just text, and they can't change how your system works unless they take advantage of a flaw in Outlook Express itself. However, attached files can make changes to your system. Program (.exe) files and script files (.vbs) are particularly dangerous, but other attached files can also contain viruses, depending on the file type. If you have doubts, either delete the message or save it to a disk and run a virus-checking program on it (see Chapter 31, section "What Is a Virus or Worm?").*

Composing Messages to Send

You create messages in three ways:

- **Compose a new message from scratch**   Click the New Mail button on the Outlook Express toolbar.

- **Reply to a message you have received**   Select a message from an Outlook Express folder (such as Inbox) and click either the Reply button or the Reply All button on the Outlook Express toolbar.

- **Forward a message you have received**   Select a message from an Outlook Express folder and click the Forward button on the Outlook Express toolbar.

Any of these three actions opens a message window, as shown in Figure 22-4. The message window has two main parts: a header and a body. The body is the window into which you enter the text of your message. Use it as you would use a text processor (no fancy formatting stuff). If you are composing a message from scratch, the body of the message window has nothing in it other than what you type. If you are forwarding a message, the text of the original message is included automatically. If you are replying, Outlook Express can be set up to either include or not include the original text (see "Including the Original Message in Your Reply").

Note *When you reply to a message that has an attachment, the attachment is not included in the reply (because the person presumably doesn't want another copy of the file back). When you forward a message with an attachment, the forwarded message includes the attachment.*

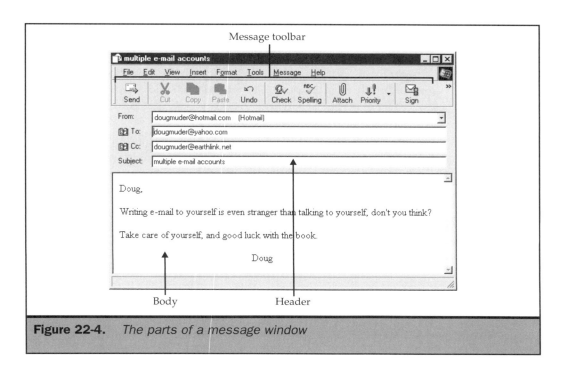

Message toolbar

Body

Header

Figure 22-4.   *The parts of a message window*

Table 22-2 shows the settings in the Options dialog box that affect composing messages. Choose Tools | Options to display the Options dialog box.

WINDOWS ME
ON THE INTERNET

Tab	Setting	Description
Receipts	Requesting Read Receipts	Specifies that your outgoing messages include requests for return receipts so you know when the person saw the message. Not all e-mail programs respond to return receipt requests.
Receipts	Secure Receipts	Specify whether your outgoing messages include a request for a secure receipt and how to respond to requests for secure receipts.

Table 22-2.   *Message Composition Settings of the Options Dialog Box*

Tab	Setting	Description
Send	Automatically put people I reply to in my Address Book	Adds entries to your Address Book for each person to whom you send a reply (see Chapter 5, section "Storing Addresses in the Address Book").
Send	Include message in reply	Specifies that replies contain the text of the original message in a quoted format (see "Including the Original Message in Your Reply").
Send	Reply to messages using the format in which they were sent	Composes replies to HTML formatted messages using HTML formatting and composes replies to plain text messages using plain text (see "Turning HTML On and Off").
Send	Mail Sending Format: HTML/Plain Text	Specifies whether your e-mail messages are sent as HTML or as plain text.
Compose	Compose Font: Mail	Specifies how unformatted messages appear on your screen when you are composing them.
Compose	Stationery: Mail	Specifies what stationery (standard formatting) your new messages will use. Rather than specifying mail stationery here, turn it on only for occasional messages (by choosing Format | Apply Stationery when composing a message).
Compose	Business Cards: Mail	Specifies that your virtual business card (vCard) be included when you compose new messages (see Chapter 5, section "Importing Addresses and Business Cards from Other Programs").

Table 22-2.   *Message Composition Settings of the Options Dialog Box* (continued)

Tab	Setting	Description
Signatures	Signatures	Enables you to create one or more *signatures*—a few lines of text that are appended to messages you send. Your signatures should contain your name and e-mail address, and should be no more than four lines long. Click New to create a signature, then type the text in the Edit Signature box.
Spelling	Always check spelling before sending	Specifies that Outlook Express automatically run its spell-checking when you send each message (this option is available only if you have the spell-checker from Microsoft Office installed). Other settings on this tab control whether it suggests correct spellings and which words to skip.
Security	Digitally sign all outgoing messages	Adds a digital signature to all messages that proves that you sent the messages. Click Advanced Settings to specify the type of digital signature.
Security	Encrypt contents and attachments for all outgoing messages	Encrypts (encodes) all outgoing messages so that they cannot be read unless the recipient has the encryption key. Click Advanced Settings to specify the type of encryption.

Table 22-2.   *Message Composition Settings of the Options Dialog Box* (continued)

Completing the Header

The header section of the message window consists of four lines:

- ■ **To**   Type the e-mail addresses of the primary recipient(s) of your message. If there is more than one recipient, separate the e-mail addresses with commas. Click the open book icon to look up addresses in the Address Book (see

Chapter 5, section "Storing Addresses in the Address Book"). This is the only line of the header that cannot be left blank (unless you enter addresses in the Cc or Bcc lines). If you generate the message window by choosing Reply, Outlook Express puts the address of the author of the original message on this line. If you use Reply All, Outlook Express lists the addresses of the author and the other primary recipients of the original message. You may add more addresses or delete some of them if you want to.

■ **Cc (Carbon Copy)** Type the e-mail addresses of secondary recipients (if any). If you opened this message window by clicking the Reply All button, Outlook Express uses the same Cc list as the original message. You may add to or delete from the list if you want to.

■ **Bcc (Blind Carbon Copy)** Type the e-mail addresses of other secondary recipients, if any. The recipients listed in the To and Cc boxes can see the list of other recipients listed in the To and Cc boxes, but not those listed in the Bcc box. If one of the To or Cc recipients replies to your message with Reply All, someone on your Bcc list will not receive the reply.

■ **Subject** Enter a word or short phrase to describe the subject of your message. The subject line helps both you and your recipients keep track of the message in your files. If you are replying to another message, Outlook Express automatically uses the original subject line, preceded by Re. If you are forwarding, Outlook Express uses the original subject line, preceded by Fw.

Including the Original Message in Your Reply

One advantage e-mail has over paper mail is that you can indicate exactly what part of an e-mail message you are responding to. To make Outlook Express automatically include the original message in any reply:

1. Select Tools | Options to open the Options dialog box.
2. Select the Send tab.
3. Check the Include Message In Reply check box and click OK.

Now whenever you click the Reply or Reply All buttons, the body of the message window contains a divider, with the original message below the divider. The text of the original message is indented, with a > at the beginning of each line.

To remove the indentation or change the indentation character:

1. Open the Send tab of the Options dialog box, as just explained.
2. If Plain Text is selected as the Mail Sending Format, click the Plain Text Settings button to open the Plain Text Settings dialog box. (If HTML is selected, see "Composing HTML Messages," later in this chapter.)

3. Unchecking the Indent The Original Text With check box at the bottom of the Plain Text Settings dialog box causes the original text to not be indented. The drop-down list next to the Indent The Original Text With check box lets you choose a different indentation character.

You can use the original text in two different ways. You can type your message at the beginning of the message window body leaving the original message at the end for reference. Or, you can edit the original message to delete all but the parts relevant to your reply, and then type your reply in parts (each immediately below the portions of the message to which you are responding), as in Figure 22-5. The second method creates the appearance of a dialog, and is especially useful if you are answering a series of questions. Given the proper context from the original message, a reply like "Yes. Yes. No. Not until Thursday" can actually make sense. (Even if you want to start a new message to a person from whom you just received a message, clicking Reply is convenient: select all of the message text and replace it with your message, and then fix the subject line.)

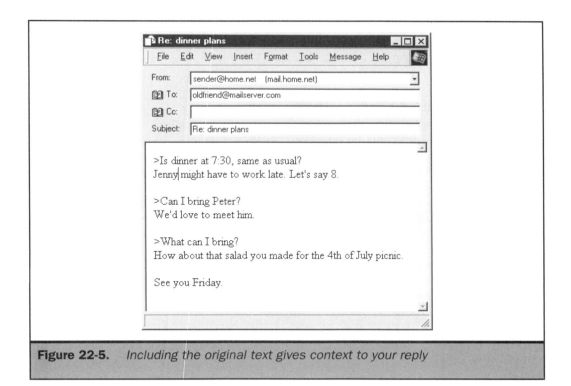

Figure 22-5.   *Including the original text gives context to your reply*

Pay attention to whether the original message is making your reply wastefully long. You probably shouldn't include an entire three-page original message in your three-word reply. If a topic goes back and forth many times, with both authors including the original message, the entire history of the correspondence is sent with each message—usually a waste. Delete the headers of the original message along with the parts of the message to which you aren't responding.

Inserting Text Files into a Message

If what you want to say is already contained in a text file, you don't have to retype the text or even cut-and-paste the text out of the file. Just follow these steps to incorporate the text into your message:

1. Move the insertion point to the place in the text of your message that you want the text file inserted.

2. Select Insert | Text From File.

3. When the Insert Text File window opens, browse to find the text file you want.

4. Click Open.

The complete text of the text file is now inserted into the spot where the insertion point is located.

Attaching a File to a Message

You can use e-mail to send more than just text. Any file—a picture, a spreadsheet, a formatted text document—can be sent along with your message as an attachment. To attach a file to a message, click the Attach button on the message window toolbar or select Insert | File Attachment. When the Insert Attachment window appears, browse to find the file you want to attach, and click OK.

When sending plain text messages, Outlook Express encodes file attachments using *MIME*, the most widely used method of attaching files to messages. Most e-mail programs, including Netscape, Eudora, and AOL's mail program, can deal with MIME attachments. But some e-mail programs can't, especially LAN e-mail programs that weren't originally designed to work with the Internet. You can switch to a different encoding method called *Uuencode*: Select Tools | Options and click the Plain Text Settings button on the Send tab of the Options dialog box. Now click the Uuencode radio button in the Plain Text Settings dialog box.

When Outlook Express is set up to send HTML messages, the situation is reversed: Uuencode is the default, and you can switch to MIME using the HTML Settings button in the Options dialog box.

Don't send attached files to people who don't have the software to read them. Ask first before sending an attachment. Everyone can read plain text files (with the extension .txt), and anyone with Internet Explorer or Netscape Navigator can display graphics files in .gif or .jpg format.

Saving and Deleting Messages

Outlook Express hangs on to the messages that you send and receive until you tell it to forget them. Messages that you receive are stored in your Inbox folder. Messages that you send wind up in your Sent Items folder. They remain there until you either delete them or move them to another folder (see "Organizing Your Correspondence").

Saving Messages

Even though Outlook Express saves your messages automatically, you need to pay attention to three issues:

- **Outlook Express folders and the messages in them are separate from the overall filing system of your computer.**   You may have a folder called Mom in Outlook Express, but no Mom folder exists on the folder tree you see in Windows Explorer. If you want a message to be a file in your computer's filing system, you have to save it as a file. Select the message in the Outlook Express message list window, and select File | Save As. Give the file a name, and it will be saved in a text file with the extension .eml.

- **Unfinished messages are lost when you close Outlook Express unless you save them.**   You don't have to start and finish a message in one sitting. If you want to put the message away and work on it later, select File | Save to save the message in your Drafts folder. If you want the unfinished message to be in an Outlook Express folder other than Drafts, save it to Drafts first, and then drag it to another folder.

- **Your mail files should be backed up as often as (perhaps more often than) any other files on your system.**   The simplest method is to back up the entire folder in which you told Outlook Express to store your messages. The default folder is called Outlook Express and lies inside the C:\Windows\Application Data\Identities*Your Identity Code*\Microsoft folder.

Deleting and Recovering Messages

Delete a message by selecting it in the message list and pressing DELETE. The message is sent to the Deleted Items folder, which functions within the Outlook Express filing system as a kind of Recycle Bin.

You can examine messages from the Deleted Items folder by opening them, and you can move them to another folder if you change your mind about deleting them. If you delete an item from the Deleted Items folder, it is gone permanently.

Outlook Express can be set up to empty the Deleted Items folder automatically when you exit the program:

1. Select Tools | Options. The Options dialog box appears.

2. Click the Maintenance tab and check Empty Messages From The 'Deleted Items' Folder On Exit.

3. Click OK.

Naturally, you can stop doing this at any time by unchecking the Empty Messages From The 'Deleted Items' Folder On Exit check box.

Sending Messages

Once you are satisfied with the message you've composed, click the Send button in its message window. The message is moved to your Outbox folder, where it stays until the next time your computer is connected to your outgoing mail server. To send the contents of your Outbox immediately, click the Send And Receive button on the Outlook Express toolbar. Outlook Express connects to your ISP and finds your outgoing mail server automatically.

Sending Messages Automatically (or Not)

If you decide it's a waste of time for messages to sit in your Outbox until you get around to clicking Send And Receive, you can tell Outlook Express to connect to your outgoing mail server automatically whenever there is a message in your Outbox:

1. Open the Options dialog box by selecting Tools | Options.

2. Select the Send tab.

3. Check the Send Messages Immediately check box.

4. Click OK.

You can undo this decision at any time by returning to the Send tab of the Options dialog box and unchecking Send Messages Immediately.

Even if Send Messages Immediately is checked, you can move a message to your Outbox without sending it immediately to your outgoing mail server by selecting File | Send Later. In particular, this is handy if you are temporarily unable to connect to the Internet—if you are on the road, for example, and your computer is not currently connected to a phone line.

Canceling Messages

As long as the message is sitting in your Outbox, you can still intercept it:

1. Select the Outbox folder from the folder list of the Outlook Express window.

2. Select the message from the Outbox message list.

3. Press DELETE or select Edit | Delete to get rid of the message completely. To put the message away to edit later, drag-and-drop the message from the upper-right pane into the Drafts folder in the folder list, or select Edit | Move To Folder and choose a folder in which to move the message. Alternatively, you can right-click the message and select Move To Folder from the shortcut menu.

Organizing Your Correspondence

A mail program is more than just a way to read and write messages, it is also a filing system. Over time, the records of your correspondence may become a valuable asset. Although you can leave all of your mail in your Inbox, it's a lot easier to find messages if you file messages by sender or topic.

Outlook Express allows you to create folders and move messages from one folder to another. It also provides an Inbox Assistant utility to allow you to perform some secretarial actions automatically.

Working with Folders

The Outlook Express filing system resembles the filing system that Windows itself uses, but the Outlook Express files and folders can't be seen by other programs (see Chapter 8)—you must use Outlook Express to manipulate them.

Creating and Deleting Folders

To create a new folder in Outlook Express:

1. Click the Local Folders icon in the folder list.

2. Select File | Folder | New Folder. The Create Folder window opens.

3. Type the name of your folder into the Folder Name line.

4. In the bottom half of the Create Folder window, select the folder into which you want to place the new folder.

5. Click OK.

To delete a folder, select it in the folder list of the Outlook Express window and select File | Folder | Delete.

WINDOWS ME
ON THE INTERNET

Moving and Copying

To move or copy a message from one folder to another:

1. Select the folder that contains the message in the folder list of the Outlook Express window. You may need to expand some folders (by clicking the plus boxes in the margin) to find it.

2. Find the message in the message list and right-click it.

3. Select either Move To Folder or Copy To Folder from the right-click menu. A window appears displaying a folder list.

4. Select the folder into which you want the message moved or copied.

5. Click OK.

You can also move a message by dragging it from the message list and dropping it onto the icon of the target folder in the folder list.

To move a folder, drag-and-drop its icon on the folder list to the location you want it to be located.

    You can move several messages or folders at the same time by holding down the CTRL *key while you select the items to move.*

Finding Messages in Your Files

A filing system isn't worth much unless you can find what you put there, when you want to retrieve it. Outlook Express gives you a search tool that lets you search for messages based on

- The sender
- The recipient
- The subject
- A word or phrase in the message body
- Whether the message has attachments
- The date received
- A folder containing the message

Begin your search by selecting Edit | Find | Message. The Find Message dialog box appears, as shown in Figure 22-6. Enter as much information as you know about the message and click Find Now. Outlook Express lists at the bottom of the window all the messages that fit the description you've given. Open any message on this list by double-clicking.

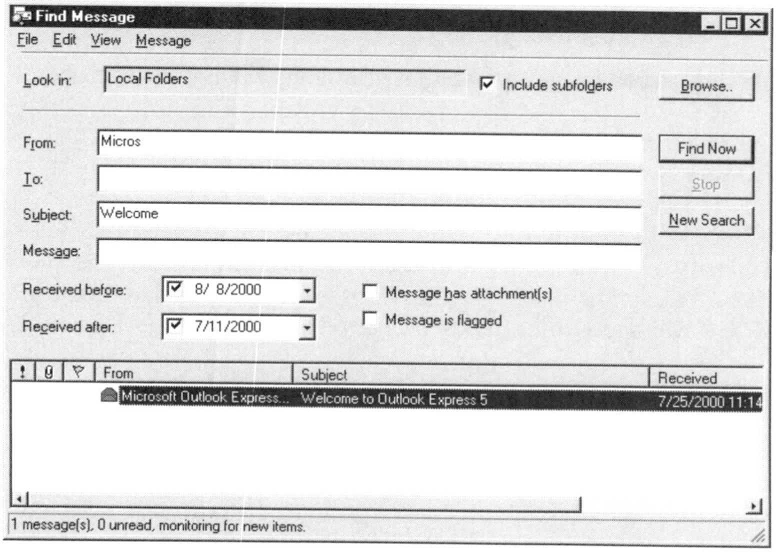

Figure 22-6.   *The Find Message dialog box*

Type any string of characters into the From, Sent To, Subject, or Message Body lines of the Find Message dialog box. This restricts your search to messages whose corresponding parts contain those character strings.

To specify the date of a message, check either the Before or After check box in the Received box. Enter a date in MM/DD/YY format into the corresponding line or click the drop-down arrow to locate the date you want on a calendar. (Change months on the calendar by clicking the left or right arrows at the top of the calendar.) You can use Before and After together to specify a range of dates, as shown in Figure 22-6.

The Look In box specifies a folder in which to search. Click the Browse button to locate a new folder to look in. The Include Subfolders check box does just what it says—if the box is checked, the search includes all the subfolders of the specified folder; if it is not checked, the subfolders are not included.

Filtering Your Mail with Message Rules

Outlook Express can do a little secretarial work to help you manage your POP e-mail messages automatically. It can do the following:

■ File messages to the appropriate folders, rather than letting them pile up in the Inbox

- Forward messages to another e-mail address
- Send a stock reply message
- Delete unwelcome messages so that you never have to look at them

An easy way to delete messages from a particular person automatically is to add his/her name to your Blocked Senders list (see "Blocking a Sender").

You tell Outlook Express to do these things by establishing *message rules* or *mail rules*, which specify a kind of message and a type of action to take when such a message arrives. To establish a message rule for your e-mail, select Tools | Message Rules | Mail. The Message Rules dialog box appears, as shown in Figure 22-7.

Note

You can't use message rules with IMAP or HTTP mail (Web-based mail) accounts.

The upper portion of the Message Rules dialog box lists the rules you have created. A rule is active if its check box is checked, so you can turn a rule on and off easily. The lower portion of the dialog box gives a description of the currently selected rule. Some parts of the description are underlined in blue; these are links to other dialog boxes that

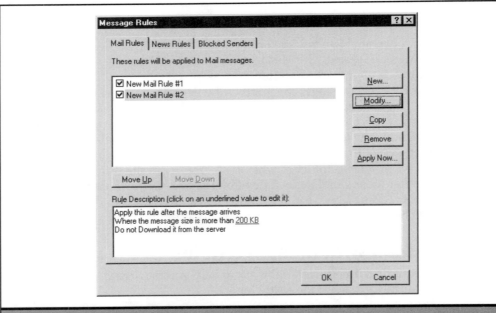

Figure 22-7. *New Rule #2, telling Outlook Express not to download new messages larger than 200 KB*

allow you to edit these particular portions of the rule. In Figure 22-7, "200 KB" is linked—clicking it opens a box in which a new file size can be chosen.

To define a new rule, click the New button in the Message Rules dialog box. This opens the New Mail Rule dialog box, shown in Figure 22-8. This box has four sections.

- **Select The Conditions For Your Rule**   Enables you to define the messages that the rule should apply to. These conditions are vague, but you specify their details in the third section.

- **Select The Actions For Your Rule**   Enables you to specify what Outlook Express should do when such messages arrive. As in the first section, these actions are also vague, but are spelled out in the third section.

- **Rule Description**   Gives a description of the rule as you have defined it so far; when more information is needed, the description contains a placeholder phrase that is linked to a dialog box for specifying the information. In Figure 22-8, for example, the phrases "contains people," "contains specific words," and "message" are all placeholders. Clicking these phrases opens additional dialog boxes that allow you to specify which people, which words, and what message.

- **Name Of The Rule**   Enables you to specify a name for your rule. Otherwise, the rule will be numbered, like New Mail Rules #1 and #2 in Figure 22-7.

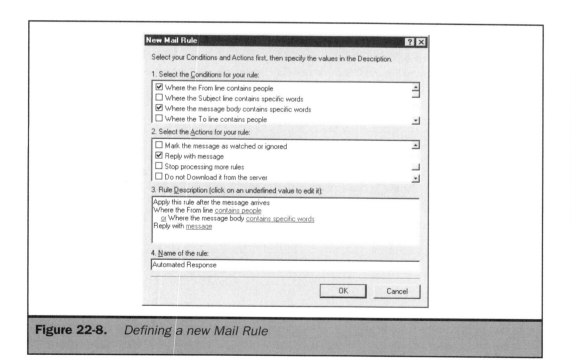

Figure 22-8.   *Defining a new Mail Rule*

Defining Conditions for Message Rules

You define conditions for your message rules by checking the appropriate boxes in the Select Conditions For Your Rule section of the New Mail Rule dialog box. As you check boxes, the text next to those boxes appears in the Rule Description section, in which you click the linked phrases to specify any additional information that the condition requires.

If you check more than one box, the conditions are connected with an "and"—in other words, all checked conditions need to be true before the action you specify is taken. You can change this "and" to an "or" by clicking an "and" in the rule description and selecting the Messages Match Any One Of The Criteria radio button. There is no way to create more complicated conditions that mix "ands" and "ors."

You can choose from 12 conditions listed in section one of the New Mail Rule dialog box:

- **For All Messages**

- **Where The From Line Contains People**, **Where the To Line Contains People**, **Where the CC Line Contains People**, and **Where The To Or CC Line Contains People**   Any of these four conditions requires you to specify which people the condition applies to. Click the phrase "contains people" in the Rule Description section to display the Select People dialog box. Add people to your list either by typing their e-mail addresses into the top line and clicking the Add button, or by clicking the Address Book button and selecting them from your address book. By default, the rule applies to a message in which any of the selected people are included in the specified line. You can require that the condition apply only if *all* of the people are included or if *none* of the people are included by clicking the Options button and choosing the appropriate radio button in the Rule Condition Options dialog box.

- **Where The Subject Line Contains Specific Words** and **Where The Message Body Contains Specific Words**   Either of these conditions requires you to specify which words or phrases the rule is looking for. Click the phrase "contains specific words" in the Rule Description section. When the Type Specific Words dialog box appears, type a word or phrase and click the Add button. If you specify more than one word or phrase, click the Options button to specify whether all words/phrases must be present or just one of them.

■ **Where the Message Is Marked As Priority**, **Where The Message Is From The Specified Account**, **Where The Message Size Is More Than Size**, **Where The Message Has An Attachment**, and **Where The Message Is Secure**   These five conditions require you to specify which priority, which account, what size, and what kind of security. Click the highlighted phrase in the Rule Description section and choose the appropriate radio button from the dialog box that appears.

Specifying Actions for Message Rules

By setting conditions in the Select The Conditions For Your Rule section of the New Mail Rule dialog box, you have picked out a particular class of messages. Now you need to tell Outlook Express what to do with those messages by filling out the Select The Actions For Your Rule section. Select actions by checking the check boxes. You may select as many actions as you like. You have 12 choices:

■ **Move It To The Specified Folder** or **Copy It To The Specified Folder**   Either of these actions requires you to specify a folder to put the message into. Click the word "specified" in the Rule Description section and choose a folder from the dialog box that appears.

■ **Forward It To People**   This action requires you to specify which people to forward the message to. Click the word "people" in the Rule Description section and enter an e-mail address into the Select People dialog box.

■ **Delete It, Flag It, Mark It As Read**, **Do Not Download It From The Server**, **Delete It From The Server**, and **Stop Processing More Rules**   These are well-described actions that require no further elaboration. No highlighted words or phrases appear in the Rule Description.

■ **Highlight It With Color**   This action requires you to choose a color. Click the word "color" in the Rule Description section and make your choice from the Select Color dialog box.

■ **Mark The Message As Watched Or Ignored**   Click "watched or ignored" in the Rule Description and choose the Watch Message or Ignore Message radio button.

■ **Reply With Message**   This action requires you to tell it which message to use as your automatic reply. Click the word "message" and identify a message file when the Open dialog box appears. (Prior to defining the rule, you should compose your reply and select File | Save As to save it as an .eml file.)

Blocking a Sender

You can't stop annoying people or organizations from writing to you, but you can have Outlook Express send their e-mail messages straight to the Deleted Items folder or refuse to display their newsgroup messages. Make this happen by adding their names to the *blocked senders list* as follows:

1. Select Tools | Message Rules | Blocked Senders List from the Outlook Express menu bar. The Message Rules dialog box appears with the Blocked Senders tab on top, as shown in Figure 22-9.

2. Click the Add button. The Add Sender dialog box appears.

3. Enter the soon-to-be-blocked sender's e-mail address in the Address field. If you want to block all messages from an entire Internet domain (the part of the address after the @), type only the domain name.

4. Choose whether to block e-mail messages, newsgroup messages, or both by clicking the appropriate radio button.

5. Click OK. The Blocked Senders list now includes the new entry, with check boxes that say whether the blocking applies to the sender's e-mail or newsgroup messages.

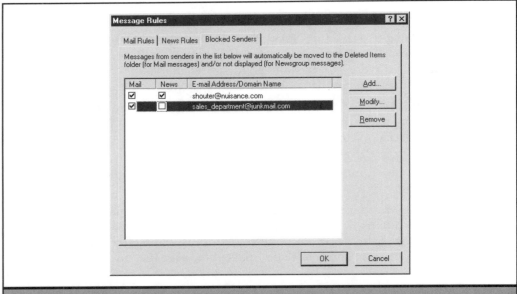

Figure 22-9.   *Blocking a few selected senders can lower your blood pressure*

Remove a sender from your Blocked Senders list by choosing Tools | Message Rules | Blocked Senders List, selecting the sender in the Message Rules dialog box, and clicking the Remove button.

Managing Your Message Rules

All your message rules are listed by name in the upper section of the Message Rules dialog box. Outlook Express only applies rules whose check boxes are checked, so you can turn rules on and off easily by checking or unchecking their boxes. When you click a rule's name, its description appears in the Rule Description section of the dialog box. You can edit any of the highlighted phrases in the rule description, or you can rewrite the rule completely by clicking the Modify button. The Edit Mail Rule dialog box appears; it behaves in the same manner as the New Rule dialog box.

To get rid of a rule completely, select its name and click Remove.

Reading and Posting to Newsgroups

Before you can read and post to newsgroups with Outlook Express, you must set up a news account (see the earlier section "Setting Up Your Accounts"). Once your account is set up, its folder appears in the folder list of the Outlook Express window, just below your mail folders. To begin using your news account, click its icon.

Note *You can read and post to newsgroups using a Web browser rather than a newsreader. The Deja.com Usenet Web site at **http://www.deja.com/usenet** gives you access to a large number of newsgroups.*

Notice that a news folder has a different icon than a mail folder, and that selecting a news folder rather than a mail folder changes the Outlook Express toolbar. Many of the news buttons resemble the mail buttons in name and function, but some do not. Left to right, the news buttons are as follows: New Post, Reply Group, Reply, Forward, Print, Stop, Send/Receive, Addresses, Find, Newsgroups, and Headers. You can choose which buttons should be on the toolbar in the same way that you can with Windows Explorer—right-click the toolbar and choose Customize from the shortcut menu.

Table 22-3 shows configuration settings that affect newsgroup reading and posting. Choose Tools | Options to display the Options dialog box that shows these settings.

Subscribing to Newsgroups

The main thing that a newsreading application does is look at the list of newsgroups to which you subscribe and then check its news server to see whether those newsgroups have any new messages. The first step, then, in learning to use Outlook Express as a newsreader is to find some interesting newsgroups and subscribe to them.

WINDOWS ME
ON THE INTERNET

Tab	Setting	Description
General	Default Messaging Programs: News Handler: Make Default button	Specifies that when you click the URL of a newsgroup, Outlook Express opens to display the newsgroup messages.
Read	Get *xxx* headers at a time	Specifies how many message headers to download when you read a newsgroup.
Read	Mark all messages as read when exiting a newsgroup	Specifies that when you are done reading a newsgroup, Outlook Express marks the unread messages as read, so that they don't show up as unread the next time you read the newsgroup.
Send	News Sending Format: HTML/Plain Text	Specifies whether your newsgroup postings are sent as HTML or as plain text (see "Turning HTML On and Off"). Always set this option to Plain Text.
Compose	Compose Font: News	Specifies how unformatted messages appear on your screen when you are composing them.
Compose	Stationery: News	Specifies what stationery (standard formatting) your news messages will use. *Never* use stationery for newsgroup messages.
Compose	Business Cards: News	Specifies that your virtual business card (vCard) be included when you compose new messages (see Chapter 5, section "Importing Addresses and Business Cards from Other Programs"). *Never* include business cards in news messages.

Table 22-3. *Configuration Settings for Newsgroup Reading and Posting*

Tab	Setting	Description
Maintenance	Delete news messages *xxx* days after being downloaded	Specifies whether old news messages are deleted automatically, and if so, after how many days. Because of the volume of messages in many newsgroups, you are unlikely to want to save all the messages you receive.

Table 22-3. *Configuration Settings for Newsgroup Reading and Posting* (continued)

Downloading the List of Available Newsgroups

The first time that you click your news account icon, Outlook Express informs you that you are not subscribed to any newsgroups, and asks whether you want to download a list of available newsgroups from your news server. Be aware that there are thousands and thousands of newsgroups on most servers, so downloading the whole list takes some time. Fortunately, you have to do this only once for each news account you establish. From time to time you will want to update this list, but updating does not take nearly as long.

Searching for Interesting Newsgroups

Once you have a list of available newsgroups, you can view it by doing the following:

1. Select a news account in the left pane of the Outlook Express window.
2. Click the Newsgroups button on the toolbar. The Newsgroups window appears, as shown in Figure 22-10.

In the early days of the Internet, you could choose the newsgroups to which you wanted to subscribe just by scanning the list of available groups. By now, the number of groups has grown so large that this is a little like wandering through the stacks of a poorly organized library. Scrolling down this list can be an entertaining way to give yourself an idea of the kinds of things that are available, but it is not an efficient way to look for interesting newsgroups.

Fortunately, the Newsgroups window gives you a few tools to aid in your search. This window has three tabs:

- **All**   Shows the complete list of newsgroups available on this server
- **Subscribed**   Lists the (much smaller) list of newsgroups to which you have chosen to subscribe
- **New**   Shows the newsgroups that your server has added since the previous time you updated the newsgroup list

Above each of these tabs is the Display Newsgroups Which Contain line. When this line is blank, a tab lists all the newsgroups appropriate to it. (That is, All lists all newsgroups.) Typing something onto this line restricts the list to newsgroups containing what you have typed. In Figure 22-10, for example, the All tab lists all newsgroups that have "x-files" somewhere in their names.

So, for example, if you want to know whether there is a newsgroup devoted to your favorite author or entertainer, go to the All tab of the Newsgroups window and type his or her last name into Display Newsgroups Which Contain. If you have already done that search last week, but want to know whether there are any new newsgroups you should look at, do the same thing with the New tab.

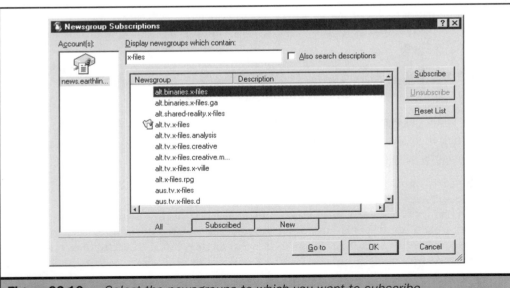

Figure 22-10.   *Select the newsgroups to which you want to subscribe*

Subscribing to a Newsgroup (or Not)

Once you have found a newsgroup you want to try out:

1. Select its name in the Newsgroups window. (In Figure 22-10, alt.binaries.x-files is selected.)

2. Click the Subscribe button.

The newsgroup is now listed on the Subscribed tab of the Newsgroups window, and a folder corresponding to the newsgroup is automatically created as a subfolder of the news account folder. Whenever the newsgroup appears in the Newsgroups window, it has a newsgroup icon next to it. For example, in Figure 22-10, alt.tv.x-files has been subscribed to.

To unsubscribe, right-click the newsgroup in the folder list and choose Unsubscribe from the shortcut menu.

You can examine a newsgroup without subscribing to it by selecting it in the Newsgroups window and clicking the Go To button rather than the Subscribe button. Outlook Express downloads the headers of recent articles on a one-time-only basis. When you stop looking at the newsgroup, Outlook Express asks whether you want to subscribe.

Reading a Newsgroup

Outlook Express displays newsgroups in a format that is similar to the way it displays mail folders: the left pane contains a folder list, the upper-right pane contains a message list for the currently selected newsgroup, and the lower-right pane previews the currently selected message. Most newsgroup messages are sufficiently short that the preview pane is all you'll really need.

Unread articles are displayed in bold in the message list, and their icon is slightly different than the icon of messages that have been read. Newsgroups containing unread messages are displayed in bold on the folder list, with the number of unread messages in parentheses next to the name.

The message list groups all the messages that reply to a particular message. A plus box appears in the margin next to the original message; when clicked, it changes to a minus sign, and the replies are displayed underneath (and slightly indented from) the original message.

Reading a Newsgroup Online

If you are online, selecting a subscribed newsgroup from the folder list causes Outlook Express to download the headers of the messages on that newsgroup. In other words,

WINDOWS ME
ON THE INTERNET

the message list window fills up automatically. The messages themselves, however, are not downloaded until you select them in the message list. (The point of this is to save both download time and disk space on your computer.) When you find an intriguing header in the message list, click it to see its text in the preview pane, or double-click it to give the message a window of its own.

Reading a Newsgroup Offline

To read a newsgroup while spending the minimum amount of time online, download the headers as in the preceding section, and then disconnect by choosing File | Work Offline. You can examine the headers of messages offline. When you find one you want, select it in the message window and then choose Tools | Mark For Offline | Download Message Later. The next time you are online and synchronize your new account, Outlook Express downloads all the marked messages, which you can then read either online or offline.

Using Message Rules to Filter a Newsgroup

Message rules for newsgroups work very much like message rules for e-mail (see "Filtering Your Mail with Message Rules"). They instruct Outlook Express to handle certain kinds of messages automatically. In particular, you can tell Outlook Express not to display messages written by particular people by adding them to your Blocked Senders list (see the earlier section "Blocking a Sender"). Applying message rules to a newsgroup also gives you a more focused list of headers and saves download time.

Conceptually, establishing a new message rule has two basic steps: you list the criteria that define a class of messages, and you tell Outlook Express what to do with the messages in that class. More precisely, you do the following steps:

1. Select Tools | Message Rules | News. The Message Rules dialog box opens with the News Rules tab on top. (If you have no other rules defined, Outlook Express may open the New News Rule dialog box as well; if so, you can skip step 2.)

2. Click the New button. The New News Rule dialog box opens.

3. Check boxes in the Select Conditions For Your Rule section of the New News Rule dialog box. These boxes correspond to criteria that describe messages. You may need to choose several of these boxes to get the exact messages you want to act on. When you check a box, the corresponding text appears in the Rule Description section of the New News Rule dialog box. Most of the criteria need some other piece of information in order to make sense. For example, Where The From Line Contains People needs you to specify *which* people the rule should apply to. In these cases, the phrase that needs to be specified appears in blue. You'll insert this extra information in step 5. (A more detailed description

of how to work with these criteria is contained in the section "Filtering Your Mail With Message Rules," earlier in this chapter.)

4. Check boxes in the Select The Actions For Your Rule section of the New News Rule dialog box. These boxes correspond to the actions you want Outlook Express to perform on the messages described in step 3. Like the Conditions in step 3, the Actions contain phrases that may require additional specification. For example, Highlight It With Color doesn't say which color should be used. You'll insert this extra information in step 5.

5. Examine the Rule Description section of the New News Rule dialog box. If any word or phrase is highlighted in blue, click it. A dialog box appears to allow you to insert the extra information needed to make the phrase specific.

6. When you have specified all the highlighted phrases in the Rule Description section, type a name into the Name Of The Rule section of the New News Rule dialog box.

7. Click OK. The Message Rules dialog box returns. Your new rule is included in the list of message rules.

8. Click OK.

Tip   *Mark all messages from yourself as watched so that you can easily spot replies to them.*

You can turn a message rule on or off by choosing Tools | Message Rules | News and checking or unchecking the rule's check box in the Message Rules dialog box. To remove a rule, select it from the list in the Message Rules dialog box and click Remove. To edit a rule, select it from the list in the Message Rules dialog box and click Modify.

Saving Messages

By default, Outlook Express saves the text of downloaded news messages only for five days after you download them. When you close Outlook Express, messages older than that are thrown away, unless you save them by selecting File | Save As. Messages are saved in files with the extension .nws. Alternatively, you can tell Outlook Express to save messages longer—choose Tools | Options, click the Maintenance tab, and set the Delete News Messages *xxx* Days After Being Downloaded setting.

Participating in a Newsgroup

Many people read a newsgroup for years and never respond to it in any way, neither writing e-mail messages to the authors of the messages they read, nor posting messages of their own. This is called *lurking*, and is a widely accepted practice. In fact, even if you do intend to post your own messages to a group eventually, we recommend that you lurk for a while first to learn the social norms of the group.

One alternative to lurking is to examine the archives of the newsgroup. Many newsgroups are archived at the Web site **http://starbase.neosoft.com/~claird/ news.lists/newsgroup_archives.html**, at Deja.com **http://www.deja.com/usenet**, or at RemarQ **http://www.remarq.com**.

Very few newsgroups tolerate posting HTML formatted messages or messages with attachments. Be sure to post messages as plain text.

Reading the FAQ

One use of a newsgroup is to ask questions about a subject in the hope that someone more experienced can answer them for you. For example, if you have just bought a gadget that is supposed to slice and dice, and you only have been able to make it slice, you might find that there is a newsgroup devoted to this product, to which you can address the question "How do I make it dice?" Unfortunately, the regular readers of this newsgroup, who are mainly interested in discussing the existential implications of slicing and dicing in this postmodern world, are probably sick to death of newbies interrupting their discussion to ask this question and are likely to make unpleasant and unhelpful suggestions.

To avoid problems like this, many newsgroups maintain a list of common answers to *Frequently Asked Questions (FAQ)*. As a courtesy to the other readers of the newsgroup, you should check whether the FAQ answers your question, before you post it to the group. Typically, the FAQ is reposted at regular intervals (usually monthly), so if you look at a month's worth of postings, you should find it. If that sounds like too much work, several Web sites maintain archives of newsgroup FAQs. One such site is the International FAQ Consortium at **http://www.faqs.org/faqs**. A search engine at this Web site will help you find the FAQ you are looking for.

Replying to Authors

Replying to the author of a newsgroup message is no different from replying to the author of a mail message. Just select the message and click the Reply button on the toolbar. Outlook Express opens a mail message window with the author's e-mail address entered automatically in the recipient list. You can create and edit this message just as you would any other mail message.

Posting a Message to a Newsgroup

To begin creating a newsgroup message, select a newsgroup from the folder list of the Outlook Express window, so that the Outlook Express News toolbar replaces the Mail toolbar. You may then create a message in any of the following three ways:

- **Composing a new message from scratch**   Click the New Post button on the Outlook Express toolbar.

- **Replying to a message**   Select a message from the message list of a newsgroup and click the Reply Group button on the toolbar. (Clicking the Reply button creates a mail message addressed to the author of the selected message and does not create a message to the newsgroup.)

- **Forwarding a message from one newsgroup to another**   Select a message from the message list of a newsgroup and click the Forward button on the toolbar.

Any of these actions creates a New Message window. Like an e-mail message window, it has a header and a body, as shown in Figure 22-11.

A news message header has three lines:

- **Newsgroups**   List the newsgroup(s) to which the message is to be posted. If you are replying to a message, Outlook Express inserts the newsgroup of the original message automatically. If you are composing a new message, Outlook Express inserts the currently selected newsgroup. If you are forwarding, this line is initially blank. To add newsgroups to the list, click the icon on the Newsgroups line of the header. The Pick Newsgroups dialog box appears. Its right pane lists the newsgroup(s) the message is currently addressed to, while its left pane lists the newsgroups you subscribe to. Clicking the button below the left pane causes the left pane to list all newsgroups, not just the ones you subscribe to. The line at the upper-left of the Pick Newsgroups window is labeled Type Name Or Select From List, which is what you do. When this line contains the name of a newsgroup you want to add to the Newsgroups To Post To list in the right pane, click the Add button. Repeat this process until the right pane lists all the newsgroups to which you want to post your message.

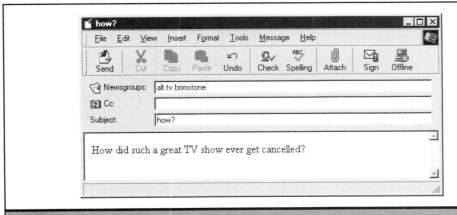

Figure 22-11.   *Creating a newsgroup message*

WINDOWS ME
ON THE INTERNET

If you change your mind about any of the newsgroups you have selected, select those newsgroups in the right pane and click the Remove button. When you are satisfied that you have just the right list of newsgroups, click OK to make the Pick Newsgroups window vanish.

Avoid cross-posting messages. Instead, choose the newsgroups most likely to be interested in your message. Under no circumstance cross-post a message to more than five newsgroups.

- **Cc**   If you want your message sent (as e-mail) to anyone, list their e-mail addresses in the Cc line of the header. Click the index card icon if you want to choose an address from the Address Book.

- **Subject**   Give your message a title. If you are replying or forwarding, the subject line is automatically the same as the original message, preceded by Re or Fwd. Short, specific subject lines are the best.

After you have completed the header of your message, type the text into the body of the New Message window and click the Post button. The message is then sent to your Outbox, where it is treated the same as your outgoing mail messages (see "Sending Messages").

Composing in HTML

Hypertext Markup Language (or *HTML*) is the language Web pages are written in. Outlook Express allows you to send HTML e-mail messages or newsgroup postings. This is a great idea, *but only if your recipients are set up to receive HTML messages*. At the moment, some e-mail programs and most newsreaders aren't equipped to receive HTML messages. If they don't have an up-to-date e-mail or newsgroup reader, your recipients will probably receive either

- A text version of your message with the HTML version as an attachment

- A text version of your message either followed or preceded by a version in raw HTML—it sort of looks like text, but includes control codes that look like gibberish to the uninitiated

At some point, HTML may take over as the dominant language for e-mail, just as it has for Web sites. But plain text is showing remarkable staying power, especially in newsgroups; so for now, we recommend using HTML *only* if you are sure that your recipient uses Outlook Express or some other e-mail program (such as Netscape Mail or Eudora Pro) that speaks HTML.

 Never post an HTML formatted message to an e-mail mailing list, since you don't know whether every subscriber to the list has a mail program that can handle HTML.

Assuming that your recipient can read HTML, though, some very cool possibilities open up. You can do the following:

■ Use different fonts, sizes, and colors of text (which can be handy when replying to a message with corrections or further information)

■ Embed pictures, charts, or other graphics in your messages

■ Include links to the World Wide Web

Turning HTML On and Off

To set up Outlook Express to compose (or stop composing) messages in HTML:

1. Select Tools | Options to open the Options dialog box.
2. Select the Send tab of the Options dialog box.
3. Choose either the Plain Text or HTML radio button in the Mail Sending Format box (for e-mail) and the News Sending Format box (for newsgroups).

 We recommend that you set your News Sending Format to Plain Text, since few newsreaders can display HTML formatting. Choose your Mail Sending Format setting based on whether most of your correspondents have e-mail programs that can display HTML formatting.

Composing HTML Messages

When Outlook Express is composing in HTML rather than plain text, the message box contains another toolbar (called the *formatting toolbar*) just below the header, as shown here:

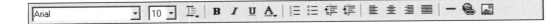

Most of the tools on the formatting toolbar are familiar if you have used a word processor. From left to right, the tools are the following:

- **Font Name**   Choose another font from the drop-down list.
- **Font Size**   Choose from the drop-down list.
- **Paragraph Style**   The drop-down list shows the choices of paragraph style.
- **Bold, Italic, Underline**
- **Font Color**   Click to see the palette.
- **Formatting Numbers**   For making numbered lists.
- **Formatting Bullets**   For making bulleted lists.
- **Decrease/Increase Indentation**
- **Align Left/Center/Right/Justify**
- **Insert Horizontal Line**   Draws a dividing line across your message.
- **Insert Hyperlink**   Links text in your message to Web addresses (see the next section, "Linking to the Web").
- **Insert Picture**   Inserts any image file into your message (see the upcoming section "Inserting Pictures").

Linking to the Web

If your message mentions a Web page, or if a Web page reference would back up the point you are making, why not link to it? If your recipients have HTML-reading e-mail programs, they'll be able to open the page with their Web browsers just by clicking the hyperlink in your message.

To insert a hyperlink into a message you are writing in HTML:

1. Select the text you want to link to the Web.

2. Click the Insert Hyperlink button on the formatting toolbar, located below the header. The Hyperlink dialog box opens.

3. Select the Web address prefix from the drop-down list of the Hyperlink dialog box.

4. Type the Web address into the URL box of the Hyperlink dialog box.

5. Click OK. The selected text should now appear in a different color from the rest of the message.

Inserting Pictures

You can insert photographs, diagrams, charts, or other image files into any message you compose in HTML.

1. Move the insertion point to the place in your message that you want the picture to be located.

2. Click the Insert Picture button on the formatting toolbar, below the header. The Picture Source dialog box appears.

3. Type the location of the image file into the Picture Source box or click the Browse button and find the file with a Browse window.

4. Type into the Alternate Text box the text that recipients will see if the picture (for whatever reason) is not displayed.

5. Choose the alignment from the drop-down list. This controls where the picture appears relative to the text.

6. Type a number into the Border Thickness box. This defines the width (in points) of a border surrounding the image.

7. Type numbers into the horizontal and vertical spacing boxes. These numbers define the width (in points) of a region of empty space surrounding the image.

8. Click OK. You see the image inserted into the message window.

If you want to change any of these decisions before you send the message, select the image in the message window and click Insert Picture on the formatting toolbar. The Picture dialog box opens with all your current choices. Change anything you want to change and click OK.

The Complete Reference

Windows
Me

Chapter 23

Browsing the World Wide Web

The World Wide Web is (with e-mail) one of the two most popular Internet services. This chapter describes the concepts behind the Web, including HTML, URLs, browsers, the default Web browser, and plug-ins. When you want to use the World Wide Web, this chapter describes how to set up your Web browser and configure it, along with how to use the various buttons and menus that your browser displays.

The next chapter describes how to configure your browser, find what you are looking for by using Web guides and search engines, and control what your Web browser can display.

Windows Me includes Internet Explorer (IE) 5.5, its popular Web browser. In this chapter and the next we describe how to use IE 5.5 and its most popular competitor, Netscape Navigator 6.

What Is the World Wide Web?

The *World Wide Web* (usually just referred to as "the Web") is a collection of millions of files stored on thousands of computers (called *Web servers*) all over the world. These files represent text documents, pictures, video, sounds, programs, interactive environments, and just about any other kind of information that has ever been recorded in computer files. It is probably the largest and most diverse collection of information ever assembled.

What unites these files is a system for linking one file to another and transmitting them across the Internet. HTML codes allow a file to contain links to related files (see "What Is HTML?"). Such a *link* (also called a *hyperlink*) contains the information necessary to locate the related file on the Internet. When you connect to the Internet and use a Web browser program, you can read, view, hear, or otherwise interact with the Web without paying attention to whether the information you are accessing is stored on a computer down the hall or on the other side of the world. A news story stored on a computer in Singapore might link you to a stock quote stored in New York, a picture stored in Frankfurt, and an audio file stored in Tokyo. The combination of the Web servers, the Internet, and your Web browser assembles this information seamlessly and presents it to you as a unified whole. This system of interlinked text, called *hypertext*, was first described in the 1960s by Ted Nelson, but it took thirty years for it to be widely used in the form of the World Wide Web, which was invented by Tim Berners-Lee at CERN, a particle physics lab in Geneva, Switzerland in 1990.

By following links, you can get from almost any Web document to almost any other Web document. For this reason, some people like to think of the entire Web as being one big document. In this view, the links just take you from one part of the document to another.

An *intranet* is an internal network that uses the same communication protocols as the Internet, but is limited to a specific group, usually the employees in one company. Some organizations create private versions of the World Wide Web on their intranets so that access to the Web pages is limited to employees of that organization.

What Is HTML?

The *Hypertext Markup Language* (*HTML*) is the universal language of the Web. It is a language for laying out pages that are capable of displaying all the diverse kinds of information that the Web contains.

This chapter and the next chapter discuss Web browsers, which are programs that read and interpret HTML.

While various software companies own and sell HTML-reading and HTML-writing programs, noone owns the language HTML itself. It is an international standard, maintained and updated by a complicated political process that so far has worked remarkably well. The World Wide Web Consortium (W3C), at **http://www.w3.org**, manages the HTML standard.

What Is a URL?

When the pieces of a document are scattered all over the world, but you want to display them seamlessly to a viewer who could be anywhere else in the world, you need a very good addressing system. Each file on the Internet has an address, called a *Uniform Resource Locator* (*URL*), also sometimes called an *Internet address* or *Web address*. For example, the URL of the ESPN Sportzone Web site is **http://espn.go.com**.The first part of a URL (the part before the first colon) specifies the *transfer protocol*, the method that a computer needs to use to access this file. Most Web pages are accessed with the *Hypertext Transfer Protocol* (*HTTP*, the language of Web communication), which is why Web addresses typically begin with http (or its secure versions, https or shttp). The http:// at the beginning of a Web page's URL is so common that it is assumed as the default protocol by modern browsers. If you simply type **espn.go.com** into the address window of Internet Explorer or Netscape Navigator, the browser fills in the **http://** for itself. In common usage, the http:// at the beginning of a URL is left out.

The rest of the address denotes the Web page, but might not tell you where its files are actually located. Whether ESPN's Web server is in Los Angeles or Bangkok is invisible from most URLs. Information about which Web server is responsible for answering requests for which URLs is contained in a huge database that the Web servers themselves are constantly updating. As users, we don't need to deal with this level of detail, and that's a good thing. The World Wide Web would be much less usable if sports fans had to learn a new set of URLs every time ESPN got a new computer.

What Are Internet Keywords?

For many years AOL users have navigated within AOL's system by typing simple keywords, rather than anything as complicated as a URL. More recently this idea has been extended to the more popular sites on the Internet. Current versions of Internet Explorer and Navigator allow you to go to a popular site like CNN by just typing **go CNN** (for Internet Explorer) or just **cnn** (for Netscape) into the Address box. Navigator lets you find a stock quote on (for example) IBM by typing **quote IBM** into the Address box or search for computer retailers by typing **buy computers**.

Unlike URLs, however, Internet keywords are not standardized. Netscape uses a keyword system that has evolved from AOL's; Internet Explorer uses MSN's keywords. Other browsers might use other systems or none at all. The more popular sites usually have the same keyword in all systems, but there are occasional discrepancies. Also, no keyword system is complete. Every page on the Web has a URL, but only a (comparative) handful have their own keywords.

What Are Web Pages and Web Sites?

A *Web page* is an HTML document that is stored on a Web server and has a URL so that it can be accessed via the Web.

A *Web site* is a collection of Web pages belonging to a particular person or organization. The *home page* is the "front door" of the site and is set up to help viewers find whatever is of interest to them on that site. The URL of the home page also serves as the URL of the Web site.

For example, the URL of Microsoft's home page is **http://microsoft.com**. From the home page, you can get to Microsoft's Web pages about Windows Me at **http://microsoft.com/WindowsMe/**. The product guide for Windows Me is at **http://microsoft.com/WindowsMe/guide/**.

What Is a Web Browser?

A *Web browser* is a program that your computer runs to communicate with Web servers on the Internet so that it can download the documents you ask for and display them. At a bare minimum, a Web browser has to be able to understand HTML and display text. In recent years, however, Internet users have come to expect a lot more. A state-of-the-art Web browser provides a full multimedia experience, complete with pictures, sound, video, and even 3-D imaging.

The most popular browsers, by far, are Microsoft Internet Explorer and Netscape Navigator. Both are state-of-the-art browsers, and the competition between them is fierce. Both are regularly upgraded, so it is worthwhile to keep an eye on the Netscape and Microsoft Web sites to see when new versions are available. Both are available over the Internet at no charge. Internet Explorer 5.5 is included with Windows Me.

What Is Internet Explorer?

Internet Explorer is the Web browser that comes with most versions of Windows Me and is available for free from the Internet (from **http://www.microsoft.com/ie/**). It is ready to go as soon as you install Windows Me and set up an Internet connection.

The Internet Explorer window that you see when you browse the Web is similar, but not identical, to the Explorer window that you see when you look at folders on your own system (see Chapter 8, section "What Is a Folder?"). Technically, both are Internet Explorer windows, but the toolbar is *context sensitive*, which means that you get different toolbar buttons, depending on what you are looking at. If you are looking at a Web page, the toolbar looks like this:

But when you look at a folder, the toolbar looks like this:

 For updates and enhancements to Internet Explorer, visit the Windows Update Web site at http://www.windowsupdate.com.

What Are Netscape Navigator and Netscape Communicator?

Netscape Navigator is the Web browser that dominated the market prior to Microsoft's aggressive push of Internet Explorer (which is the origin of the famous Microsoft antitrust trial). Netscape Communicator is Netscape's suite of Internet utilities that contains Navigator as a component.

Though no longer dominant, Navigator is a state-of-the-art browser that remains popular. Occasionally you may find Navigator already installed on a computer when you buy it (as on iMacs, for example), or you may get it free from your ISP. You can even buy it in a software store, if you want to get Netscape's printed manual. But most people get Navigator from the Netscape Web site at **http://home.netscape.com**. There is a small charge if you want Netscape to ship you the software on CD.

In addition to Navigator, Communicator also contains the following:

- **Mail**   An e-mail and newsreader comparable to Outlook Express (see Chapter 22)
- **Composer**   An HTML composing program that allows you to create Web pages (Internet Explorer doesn't include this feature).
- **Address book**   A list of e-mail addresses for Netscape Mail

 For updates and enhancements to Navigator, visit the Netscape Web site at http://home.netscape.com.

What Is the Default Web Browser?

Internet Explorer is the only Web browser that is included with Windows (though the maker of your computer may have installed Navigator or some other browser), and

WINDOWS ME ON THE INTERNET

Windows uses it to open Web pages and Internet shortcuts unless you tell it to use something else. When you install a second browser, however, you may have the option of declaring it to be the *default Web browser*, the one that Windows uses when you don't specify a particular browser. Then the new browser is invoked whenever you open a Web page, an HTML document on your local file system, an Internet shortcut, or an item on the Start | Favorites menu.

Naturally, when you open a Web page by clicking a link in a Web page that is being displayed by a Web browser, the new page opens in the same browser you are using, whether it is the default browser or not.

Your Internet shortcuts and HTML documents bear the icon of the current default Web browser. You can easily check which browser is the default by looking at these icons and then change the default browser if you prefer to use another browser as the default (see "Defining a Default Browser").

Navigator allows you to make it the default browser for some types of files but not others. For example, you can make Navigator the default for HTML files, but let Kodak Imaging or some other graphics program continue to handle JPEG files.

What Is a Browser's Home Page?

Your browser's home page (also called a *start page*) is the Web page that the browser loads when you open the browser without requesting a specific page. You can also see the browser's home page by clicking the Home button on the toolbar of either Internet Explorer or Navigator. (Don't confuse this use of "home page" with the home page of a Web site.)

A good home page for your browser is one that loads quickly (so you don't sit forever waiting for the first page to come up), it contains information you want to check regularly (like headlines in your area of interest, or a local weather forecast), and it links to a wide variety of other pages (so that you can go where you want quickly). Each browser has a default home page on its company's Web site. In general, these are not bad home pages, and many people never change them. (Microsoft and Netscape count on that; the Internet Explorer and Navigator default home pages are some of the most valuable real estate in cyberspace.) However, you can select any Web page or file that you want to be your browser's home page (see "Choosing and Customizing Your Browser's Home Page"). If you don't want to wait for a Web page to load (or don't want to get advertised at) every time you start your browser, you can set your browser to start up with a blank page—you don't *need* to have a start page.

What Are Plug-Ins?

Plug-ins are programs that are independent of your Web browser, but "plug in" to it in a seamless way, so that you might not even be aware that you are using software that is not part of Internet Explorer or Navigator. Typically, plug-ins arise when a software company develops a way to display a new type of data over the Web such as 3-D animation, for example. Rather than create a whole new browser with this additional capability, the software company writes a plug-in for Navigator or Internet Explorer. Users who want to extend the capabilities of their browser in this particular way can install the plug-in, which then operates as if it is part of the Web browser.

A number of plug-ins (such as Shockwave for animated graphics or Net2Phone for making telephone calls over the Internet) have become standard accessories for Internet Explorer or Navigator, and are installed automatically when you install the Web browser. To install other plug-ins, download them from the Internet (the Web site at **http://www.tucows.com** has a wide variety) and follow the directions that come with the plug-in (see Chapter 26, section "Downloading, Installing, and Running Other Internet Programs"). Don't worry about installing plug-ins until you run into a Web page that requires them—those Web pages usually include instructions for downloading and installing the plug-in you need.

As with any kind of software, downloading and installing a plug-in requires faith in whoever created and distributed it. A plug-in can introduce viruses into your system, modify files without your consent, or transmit data from your machine without your knowledge. Plug-ins from reputable software companies are as safe as any other kind of Internet software, but you should be cautious about downloading plug-ins from Web sites that you know nothing about.

Setting Up a Web Browser

Internet Explorer is installed automatically when you install Windows Me. If Netscape Navigator or Communicator comes with your Internet account, it might be installed automatically when you set up your account. If not, you can install Navigator or Communicator either from the CD-ROM that you get by purchasing the software in a store or by opening the file that you download from the Netscape Web site. In either case, once you start the process, a wizard guides you through the installation.

To run Internet Explorer, choose Start | Programs | Internet Explorer | Internet Explorer. To run Navigator (if it is installed), choose Start | Programs | Netscape Communicator | Netscape Navigator.

Defining a Default Browser

When you install a new browser (other than Navigator) on your system, the installation wizard usually asks whether this should be your default browser (see "What Is the Default Web Browser?"). If you click Yes, then any HTML document or Internet shortcut on your system carries the icon of the new browser, and opening that document or shortcut opens the new browser.

You can open any browser by choosing Start | Programs or by opening its icon on the desktop, whether it is the default or not. Once a browser is running, you can use it to open any Web page.

When you run a browser that is not currently the default browser, it typically asks whether you want to make it the default browser—unless you have clicked the box telling it to stop asking you that question. You can define Internet Explorer to be the default browser, even if it no longer asks. In Internet Explorer, choose View | Internet Options. When the Internet Options dialog box appears, go to the Programs tab. Click the check box labeled Internet Explorer Should Check To See Whether It Is The Default Browser.

Navigator takes a different approach to the notion of a default browser. Rather than a single yes/no choice, Navigator allows you to specify precisely what types of files you want Navigator to open by default. To make these choices follow these steps:

1. Select Edit | Preferences from the Navigator menu bar. The Preferences dialog box opens.

2. Look at the Advanced heading in the Category list. If the arrow next to Advanced is horizontal, click it to expose a list of subcategories under Advanced.

3. Select Desktop Integration from the Category list. The Desktop Integration panel takes over the right side of the dialog box.

4. In the Desktop Integration panel, click the check boxes corresponding to the types of files and shortcuts that you want Navigator to handle by default.

5. Click OK.

Defining User Profiles

Internet Explorer inherits its user profiles from Windows (see Chapter 31, section "What Is a User Profile?"). Anyone who has a Windows user name has his or her own Favorites list, History folder, and preferences in Internet Explorer.

Navigator does not inherit user profiles from Windows. If more than one person uses Navigator on your computer, and if you want each user to be able to have a Bookmarks file, a History list, and preferences that are independent of the other users, each person must define a user profile within Navigator.

 Because Navigator has its own user profiles, your Navigator user name may be different from your Windows user name, although we recommend that you make the names the same.

To set up, remove, or rename a Netscape user profile, follow these steps:

1. If Navigator is running, exit by selecting File | Exit.

2. Choose Start | Programs | Netscape 6 | Profile Manager. The Profile Manager dialog box opens.

3. To delete or rename an existing user profile, select it from the list and click the Delete Profile or Rename Profile button. If you are renaming the profile, enter the new name in the dialog box that appears.

To create a new user profile, click the Create Profile button. The Create Profile dialog box opens. Give the new profile a name and click Finish.

Setting Your Preferences

You see Internet Explorer preferences on the Internet Options dialog box (shown in Figure 23-1), which you access by opening the Internet Options icon on the Control Panel or by choosing Tools | Internet Options from Internet Explorer's menu bar. (Strangely, if you open it from the Control Panel, the dialog box is called Internet Properties, but it contains the same tabs, buttons, and settings.) From the name, and from its appearance on the Control Panel, you might expect the Internet Options dialog box to set preferences for any Web browser on your system, but it does not. You set Navigator preferences on its own Preferences dialog box (shown in Figure 23-2), which you access by selecting Edit | Preferences from Navigator's menu bar.

The Navigator Preferences dialog box has two panes. The left pane is a list of the categories of preferences. Click the horizontal arrow to the left of a category to see its subcategories. One category is highlighted, and the controls for that preference category

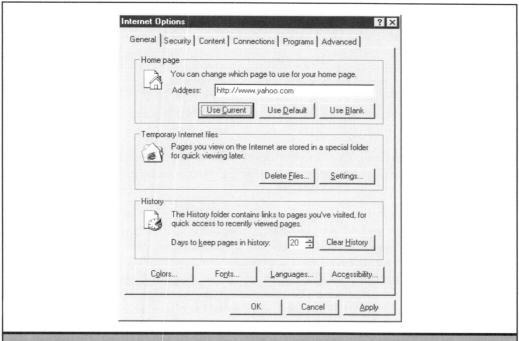

Figure 23-1. *The Internet Options dialog box is used for Internet Explorer, not Navigator.*

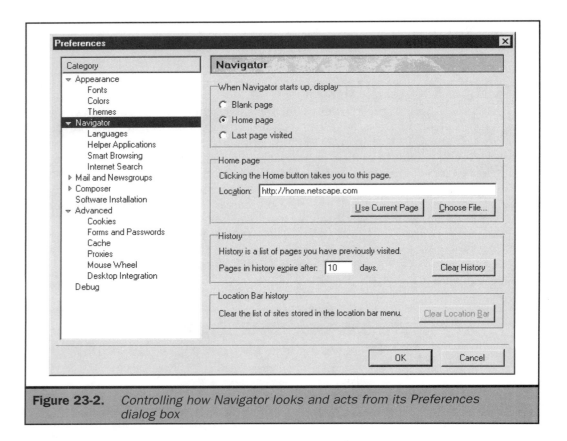

Figure 23-2.   *Controlling how Navigator looks and acts from its Preferences dialog box*

are shown in the right pane. To access any of the preference controls, click the category in the left pane and express your preferences in the right pane.

Choosing Fonts

Navigator has a very simple way to expand or shrink the size of the text on a Web page, without making any permanent changes to the way it displays text: select View | Enlarge Text Size or View | Reduce Text Size. The changed font size applies to the current session only, and is forgotten when you exit. In Internet Explorer, use the View | Text Size menu to choose font size; your choice persists until you change it.

Navigator and Internet Explorer have similar dialog boxes for making longer-lasting changes in the fonts they use to display text. Control the fonts Internet Explorer uses by clicking the Fonts button on the General tab of the Internet Options dialog box. The Fonts dialog box opens, shown in Figure 23-3. In Navigator, click Fonts in the Categories window of the Preferences dialog box.

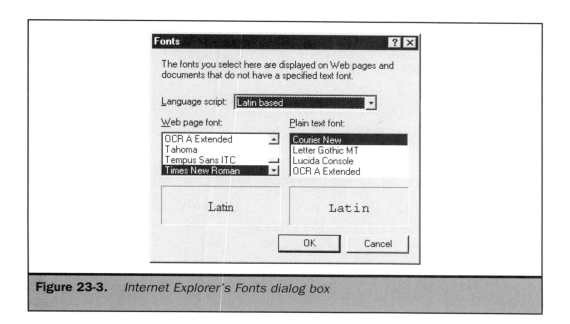

Figure 23-3.   *Internet Explorer's Fonts dialog box*

Each of these dialog boxes contains the same basic elements:

■ **A drop-down list of alphabets**   In Internet Explorer this list is labeled
Language Script and the English language script is "Latin based." In Navigator
the drop-down list is labeled Fonts For and "Western" is the choice
corresponding to English.

■ **Lists specifying the Web page (or variable-width) font and the plain text
(or fixed-width) font for the selected character set**   Change the font by
picking a new one from the list. Navigator distinguishes between serif and
sans serif fonts, with one or the other specified as the default; Internet Explorer
includes both types of font in the same list. Change the font size in Navigator
by typing a point size into the boxes next to the font names. Change the font
size in Internet Explorer by choosing from a drop-down list that goes from
smallest to largest. The default proportional font for the Western character set is
Times New Roman (12 point), and the default fixed-width font is Courier New
(10 point). Internet Explorer lists both of these default sizes as Medium.

Navigator's Fonts page also contains a set of radio buttons that let you decide
whether your font choices should override those of the Web page author, in case the
Web page specifies a font. To find these choices in Internet Explorer, click the
Accessibility button on the General tab of the Internet Options dialog box.

Choosing Colors

You can change the colors your browser uses to display text, backgrounds, and links. To change the color of the text and background in Internet Explorer, click the Colors button on the General tab of the Internet Options dialog box. In Navigator, click Colors in the Categories window of the Preferences dialog box. The two dialog boxes are almost identical.

In each case, the default is to use Windows colors—that is, the colors defined on the Appearance tab of the Display Properties dialog box (see Chapter 12, section "Changing Icons").

If you don't want to use the Windows colors, take the following steps:

1. Remove the check from the Use Windows Colors check box.
2. Click the colored button next to the Text or Background labels. A palette of colors appears.
3. Click the color you want for the Text or Background and click OK to make the palette disappear. The button next to Text or Background should now be the color you selected.
4. Click OK to close the Colors dialog box.

Changing the colors used for links is a similar process, except that you don't need to remove the check from Use Windows Colors. The Internet Explorer Colors dialog box also allows you to define a *hover color*, a color that links change to when the cursor *hovers* over them.

We suggest you leave the colors alone, except perhaps for making the background color white (if it's not white already).

Internet Explorer has other accessibility features for the visually impaired (see Chapter 19).

Changing Language Preferences

Some Web pages are available in multiple languages, and your Web browser picks the one that matches your preferences. To define or change your language preferences in Internet Explorer, click the Languages button near the bottom of the General tab of the Options dialog box to open the Language Preferences dialog box. In Navigator, open the Preferences dialog box and click Languages in the Category list. The Internet Explorer and Navigator dialog boxes are quite similar.

The purpose of each of these dialog boxes is to maintain a list of favored languages in order, with your preferred language on top. Add a language to the list by clicking the Add button and selecting a language from the list that appears. Remove a language from the Language list by selecting it and clicking the Remove button. Reorder the

Languages list by selecting a language on the list and clicking the Move Up or Move Down buttons in Internet Explorer, or the up and down arrow buttons in Navigator. When you are satisfied with the list of languages, click OK.

Internet Explorer's Language Preferences dialog box enables you to make a separate choice of language for its menus and dialog boxes. The current language is reported near the bottom of the dialog box. To change language, click the Change button and select a different language from the list that appears.

Choosing Whether to Download Images, Audio, and Video

Many Web pages have pictures or other graphics on them. These are more time-consuming to download than text, so if your connection is slow, you may decide not to bother downloading graphics. Many Web pages also have multimedia content, such as audio, video, or animation. These are even slower to download, and you can tell your browser to ignore them, too. To do this in Internet Explorer, go to the Advanced tab of the Internet Options dialog box. Scroll down until you see the Multimedia heading. Remove the check from each box next to any type of content that you want to ignore.

To control image downloading in Navigator, click Advanced on the Category list of the Preferences dialog box. If the Automatically Load Images check box is not checked, Navigator does not download the images on a Web page. If you are viewing a page whose images are not being displayed, you can display them (for this page only, without changing the policy) by selecting View | Show Images.

Choosing and Customizing Your Browser's Home Page

The home page or start page is the page that your browser looks up when you start your browser without choosing a specific page (see "What Is a Browser's Home Page?").

WINDOWS ME
ON THE INTERNET

Netscape Navigator's New Look

Navigator 6 looks rather different from previous versions of Navigator. If you prefer the old look, you can switch *themes*, which enable you to choose the look and arrangement of a program's menus and buttons from a list of predefined designs. Navigator comes with at least two themes (Modern and Classic), which control the appearance of Navigator's window. Select your favorite theme by choosing Edit | Preferences, clicking the Appearance category, clicking the Themes subcategory, choosing a theme (Classic looks like Navigator version 4.7), and clicking Switch Themes.

Customizing Internet Explorer's Home Page

Choose a new home page for Internet Explorer from the Internet Options dialog box. Choose View | Internet Options from Internet Explorer to display the Internet Options dialog box with the General tab on top (as you saw in Figure 23-1). You can type the URL of the new home page into the Home Page box on this tab, or you can click one of the following buttons:

- **Use Current**   The page currently displayed by Internet Explorer becomes the home page. (If Internet Explorer is not open, this button is grayed out.) This can be any page on the Web, or even an HTML document on your hard drive.
- **Use Default**   You get a personalizable MSN homepage at http://www.msn.com.
- **Use Blank**   The home page is blank. This is handy if you want Internet Explorer to start up as quickly as possible, and don't necessarily want to invoke your Internet connection.

The top portion of the MSN home page, shown in Figure 23-4, is the same for everyone, but you can customize the lower sections of the page to include your local weather forecast, local news, and headlines in your areas of interest, among other options. Clicking the Change Content link takes you to a questionnaire about your preferences.

Customizing Navigator's Home Page

Navigator regards the home page (which you reach by clicking the Home button on the toolbar) as different from the start page (which opens when Navigator starts up). Change either page by choosing Edit | Preferences. Then select Navigator in the Category box.

The When Navigator Starts Up Display box gives you three choices for your start page: It can be the same as the home page, a blank page, or the last page that you visited in your previous session.

Change the home page by entering a URL into the Location line or by clicking the Use Current Page button (to make the page Navigator is currently displaying the home page) or the Choose File button (if you want the home page to be a page on your system).

Choosing a Different Home Page

Lots of Web sites would like to be your home page, because they can sell advertising based on the number of viewers they get. Many allow you to customize the page to get local weather, headlines in your areas of interest, scores for your favorite teams, quotes for the stocks you own, and so on. The competition is intense, and all the competitors add features as fast as they can think of them. None of them charge a fee for this service, though they do display advertising. Some of the industry leaders are

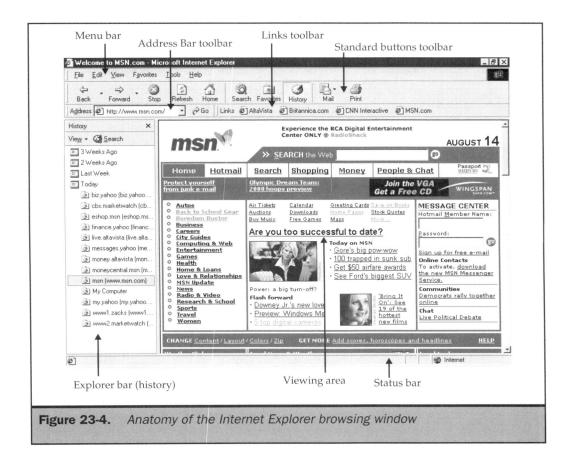

Figure 23-4.   *Anatomy of the Internet Explorer browsing window*

Yahoo! (**http://my.yahoo.com**), Excite (**http://my.excite.com**), and Altavista (**http://live.altavista.com**). A customized Yahoo! home page is shown in Figure 23-5.

If you choose a Navigator home page different from the default, you can still access the Navigator default home page by clicking the My Netscape button on the personal toolbar.

Making Your Own Start Page

Your browser's start page can be a file on your own computer. This lets you control what's on the page, and provides very fast browser startup. Often, a simple page with links to your favorite Web sites is more useful than any outside page.

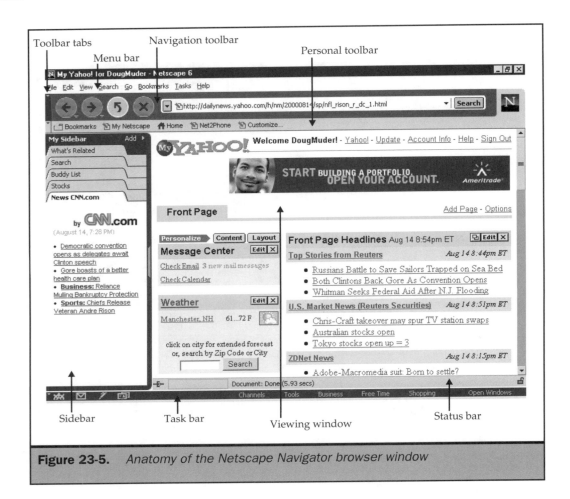

Figure 23-5. *Anatomy of the Netscape Navigator browser window*

You can create a simple Web page by using an HTML-editing application like Microsoft Word or Netscape Composer. Then, view the file containing the page in your browser and tell your browser to make that your home or start page.

If you use Netscape, your bookmarks are stored in a file called Bookmarks.htm, usually stored in C:\Program Files\Netscape\Users*yourname*. If you make that file your start page, your browser starts up displaying links to all of your bookmarks. We find this very convenient.

Working with the Browsing Window

The main window of Internet Explorer or Navigator provides you with an array of menus, buttons, labels, and information displays. Depending on what you are trying to do and how familiar you are with the workings of the browser, these elements may be either useful tools or distracting clutter. Fortunately, most of what you see can be customized, so that you can display exactly what you find worthwhile.

Configuring the Internet Explorer Browsing Window

When all of its major components are made visible, the Internet Explorer browsing window looks like Figure 23-4. These components are identical to those of Windows Explorer (see Chapter 9, section "Configuring Windows Explorer"), and can be hidden or reconfigured in the same ways. From top to bottom, it contains the following:

- **Menu bar**   Visible at all times, not configurable. You can move it to a different location in the window by clicking and dragging the handle (ridge) at its left end.

- **Standard buttons toolbar**   The same toolbar you see in Explorer windows, and you can customize its appearance for Internet Explorer in exactly the same way (see Chapter 8, section "What Is the Standard Buttons Toolbar?"). This is the toolbar we are referring to if we don't specify which toolbar we mean. It can be hidden or displayed with or without text labels. You can also choose what buttons to display. To hide this toolbar, uncheck View | Toolbars | Standard Buttons. To change the toolbar's appearance, select View | Toolbars | Customize and work with the Customize Toolbar dialog box (see Chapter 9, section "Configuring the Standard Buttons toolbar"). Drag it to another location by the handle at its left end.

- **Address Bar**   Displays the URL of the currently displayed Web page or the Windows address of the currently displayed local file. Hide the Address Bar by unchecking View | Toolbars | Address Bar. Expand or shrink the Address Bar by dragging the right boundary. Drag it to another location by the handle at its left end.

- **Links toolbar**   A row of icons that you can link to files on your computer or to Web pages (see Chapter 9, section "Configuring the Links Toolbar"). Hide Links by unchecking View | Toolbars | Links. Expand or shrink this toolbar by dragging the left boundary.

- **Explorer bar**   Displays Search, History, Favorites, or Folders in a pane at the left side of the Internet Explorer window (see Chapter 8, section "What Is the

Explorer Bar?"). Choose which of these to display from the View | Explorer Bar menu or by clicking a toolbar button. Hide these by selecting View | Explorer Bar and choosing the option that has a check mark to its left, or by clicking the X in the upper-right corner of the Explorer bar. You can drag the border between the Explorer bar and the viewing window.

■ **Viewing window** Displays Web pages. It can't be hidden, since otherwise there would be no point in running a browser. Maximize the viewing window by selecting View | Fullscreen or pressing F11. Return to the previous (unmaximized) state by selecting View | Fullscreen or pressing F11 again.

■ **Status bar** Displays a variety of useful information. When the cursor passes over a link in the viewing window, the URL of the link is displayed in the status bar. When Internet Explorer is looking for or downloading a Web page, the status bar keeps you apprised of its progress. Hide the status bar by unchecking View | Status Bar.

Configuring the Navigator Browsing Window

When all of its components are made visible, Navigator's browsing window looks like Figure 23-5. From top to bottom, it contains the following:

■ **Menu bar** Visible at all times, not configurable.

■ **Toolbar tabs** Each visible toolbar has a vertical tab on its left edge. Clicking the tab makes the toolbar disappear. The tab then turns horizontal and moves to a narrow bar just above the Viewing window, as if the toolbar has been folded up. Clicking the horizontal tab makes the toolbar reappear. The tab disappears completely if you choose the View | Hide command for that toolbar.

■ **Navigation toolbar** We usually just refer to this as the toolbar. It includes both the toolbar buttons and the address window. Hide or restore the toolbar by clicking its toolbar tab or by choosing View | Toolbars | Navigation Toolbar from the menu bar.

■ **Personal toolbar** Similar to the Links toolbar in Internet Explorer. Click an icon to go to the corresponding site. Click the Bookmarks icon to organize bookmarks. Hide or restore this toolbar with its toolbar tab or from the View | Toolbars menu.

■ **Sidebar** Similar to the Explorer bar, the Sidebar occupies the left side of the Navigator window below the toolbars and contains a number of tabs containing News headlines, your buddy list, a search panel, and so on. To add or remove tabs from the Sidebar, click the Add button at the top of the Sidebar and select commands from the menu that appears.

■ **Viewing window** Displays Web pages.

■ **Status bar**   Similar to the Status bar in Internet Explorer.

■ **Task bar**   Not to be confused with the Windows Taskbar at the bottom of the screen, the Navigator Task bar runs along the bottom of the Navigator window. Clicking an icon on the left side of the bar opens the corresponding component of Communicator. The right side of the bar is a second menu bar devoted to tools available on the Netscape Web site.

Working with Browser Toolbars

Navigator and Internet Explorer used to have very similar toolbars, but the current versions of these browsers have gone in opposite directions. The Internet Explorer 5.5 toolbar initially has ten buttons, and offers thirteen others that you could include if you so desire. Navigator 6, by contrast, has opted for simplicity in its toolbar, which has only four buttons.

Using Buttons Common to Both Browsers

The four Navigator buttons correspond to the four most commonly used buttons on Internet Explorer's toolbar: Back, Forward, Refresh, and Stop. In addition, Navigator has a Home link on its personal toolbar; it corresponds to the Home button on the Internet Explorer toolbar.

■ **Back and Forward**   Behave just like those on the Windows Explorer Standard Buttons toolbar (see Chapter 8, section "What Is the Standard Buttons Toolbar?"). Back is denoted by a left arrow and Forward by a right arrow. Back and Forward have drop-down menus that let you choose from the most recently visited Web pages. In both browsers these menus are accessed just as they would be in Windows Explorer —by clicking the arrow to the right of the button.

■ **Stop (denoted by an X)**   Active only when the browser is in the process of downloading a page from the Web; clicking it stops this process.

■ **Home (on the Personal toolbar in Navigator)**   Linked to the browser's home or start page. In both browsers Home is denoted by a house icon. To redefine the home page, see "Choosing and Customizing Your Browser's Home Page," earlier in this chapter.

■ **Refresh/Reload**   The Internet Explorer Refresh button (two curved arrows) and the Navigator Reload button (one curved arrow) do approximately the same thing—ask the server to send the most recent version of the page currently being viewed. When a page is updated on the server, the new version is not automatically sent out to anyone who might be viewing an older version. Pushing Refresh/Reload makes sure you have the latest version. Clicking Reload causes Navigator to check to see whether the server has a more recent version of the Web page you are viewing. If there is a more recent version, it is downloaded; if not, the page is reloaded from Navigator's cache. Pressing the SHIFT key while you click Reload downloads the page from the server, whether there is a new version or not.

Using the Other Default Internet Explorer Buttons

Five buttons on the default Internet Explorer toolbar don't correspond to anything on the Navigator toolbar:

- **Search, Favorites, and History**   Display the Search, Favorites, and History Explorer Bars.

- **Mail**   Opens your designated e-mail program. By default, this is Outlook Express, but if you have named another client such as Eudora on the Programs tab of the Internet Options dialog box, that program opens instead.

- **Print**   Sends the current page to the printer.

Optional Internet Explorer Toolbar Buttons

You can choose which buttons appear on Internet Explorer's Standard Buttons toolbar by right-clicking the toolbar and choosing Customize from the short-cut menu. The Customize Toolbar dialog box appears. This is the same dialog box that you use to customize the Windows Explorer toolbar (see Chapter 9, section "Changing the Toolbar Buttons").

Depending on how you use Internet Explorer, you might consider adding one of these buttons:

- **Disconnect**   Breaks your internet connection quickly and easily.

- **Edit**   Opens the current page in whatever HTML editing program is listed on the Programs tab of the Internet Options dialog box. This button is handy if you do a lot of Web page development.

- **Full Screen**   Maximizes the viewing area by stretching the Internet Explorer window to the full size of your monitor while shrinking all the other features of the Internet Explorer window. Click it again to return to the previous configuration.

- **Copy**   Moves selected text to the clipboard. This button is convenient if you frequently use quotes from Web pages in your e-mail messages or other documents.

- **Size**   Provides a drop-down menu of five font sizes. Choosing one changes the size of all the text Internet Explorer displays.

- **Related**   Produces a Related Links Explorer bar, which gives a list of Web pages that might be related to the current page. This service is hit-or-miss, and is similar to the What's Related Sidebar in Navigator.

Understanding Browser Display Conventions

On a standard Web page, text phrases that are links to other Web pages are displayed in underlined blue type. If you have recently displayed the Web page to which the text is linked, the text is displayed in maroon. When you are exploring a Web site, this feature lets you know where you've been and keeps you from going in circles. In Internet Explorer you can also define the color a link turns when the cursor is above it (the default is red). You can change these colors (see "Choosing Colors" earlier in this chapter).

When you pass the mouse pointer over a linked object (including a linked text phrase), the pointer changes from an arrow to a hand, and the URL of the Web page that the object is linked to is displayed in the status bar of the browser window (if you have the status bar enabled). Not all links on a page are obvious; a small picture, for example, might just be an illustration, or it might be linked to a larger version of the same picture. Passing the mouse pointer over an object is the easiest way to tell whether it is linked.

While files are being downloaded to your Web browser, the mouse pointer changes to an hourglass. However, it is still functional—you can push buttons or scroll the window with an hourglass pointer. Most importantly, you can use it to click the Stop button if a link is taking longer to download than you're willing to wait.

The Complete Reference

Windows Me

Chapter 24

Working with Your Browser

Your Web browser is one of the most powerful programs in your computer. Although basic browsing is extremely easy, many facilities exist to make the browsing experience faster, richer, and easier, including favorites (also called bookmarks), cookies, and various types of applets. Your browser displays various buttons and menus (many of which you can configure) in addition to the Web page you are looking at.

Once you start to browse the Web, finding what you are looking for can be hard; so this chapter describes Web guides and search engines, as well as ways to control what your Web browser can display and making Web forms more convenient. You can get more information about both Internet Explorer and Netscape Navigator from—where else?—the Web.

What Are Internet Shortcuts, Favorites, and Bookmarks?

Even though URLs are a step easier than needing to know the exact computer that contains the information you want, they are still not very easy to remember, and mistyping one can take you someplace totally unexpected. Favorites, bookmarks, and Internet shortcuts are all ways to get your computer to remember URLs so that you don't have to.

What Are Internet Shortcuts?

Shortcuts are files that you can put on your desktop (or anywhere you like) as placeholders for other files on your system (see Chapter 9, section "What Is a Shortcut?"). *Internet shortcuts* work the same way, except that they have a different file extension (.url) and point to pages on the Web rather than files on your system.

If, for example, you have an online brokerage account, you can define an Internet shortcut called My Broker.url and put its icon on your desktop (see "Creating Internet Shortcuts"). The URL is contained in the shortcut file, so you don't need to remember it. When you open the shortcut, Windows connects to your Internet account, starts your default Web browser, and displays the Web page of your broker.

What Are Favorites?

Favorites are entries in a folder of shortcuts and Internet shortcuts, accessible by choosing Start | Favorites or from the Favorites menu in Internet Explorer (see Chapter 11, section "Adding and Editing Favorites"). Choosing an entry on the Favorites menu has the same effect as opening the corresponding shortcut or Internet shortcut. Internet Explorer uses the Favorites folder to keep track of the Web sites to which you want to return.

If Favorites doesn't appear on your Start menu, you can add it as follows: Right-click an empty spot on the Taskbar to bring up the Task Bar And Start Menu Properties dialog box. Then click the Advanced tab and check the Display Favorites check box.

The location of the active Favorites folder depends on whether or not your computer has user profiles (see Chapter 31, section "What Is a User Profile?"). If the user profiles feature is off, the entries you see when you choose Start | Favorites are those stored in the folder C:\Windows\Favorites. If the user profiles feature is on, it shows the entries in C:\Windows\Profiles*your user name*\Favorites.

What Are Bookmarks?

The Bookmarks menu is Navigator's version of a Favorites menu. Clicking the Bookmarks button on Navigator's toolbar displays a menu of favorite Web pages. Choosing an entry from that menu tells Navigator to display the corresponding Web page.

Although bookmarks work like favorites, bookmarks technically are quite different. While favorites are Internet shortcut files stored in a folder called Favorites, bookmarks are lines in an HTML file of links. The location of this file is C:\Program Files\Netscape\Users*your Netscape user name*\bookmark.htm. The *user name*, in this case, is the one that you defined while installing Communicator, or created later in Navigator or another one of Communicator's components. It can be different from your Windows user name.

What Are Portals, Web Guides, and Search Engines?

Portals, Web guides, and search engines are all Web sites that help you find information and services on the Web.

A *Web guide* (or *Web directory*) is a Web site that sorts other Web sites into a system of categories and subcategories. A Web guide can help you zero in on the information you want in the same way that the Dewey decimal system helps you find the book you want in a library.

A *search engine* is a Web site that maintains an index of terms and Web pages that mention those terms. You use a search engine by submitting a list of words or phrases that you expect to be in Web pages relevant to your area of interest. The search engine returns a list of Web pages that contain those words and phrases. The engine organizes the list automatically according to certain rules that are supposed to pick out the pages most likely to be of interest; this is not a scientific process, and different search engines apply different rules that produce different lists. We recommend experimenting with a variety of search engines until you find one that you like.

A *portal* is a Web site that assembles a variety of free services and resources in hopes that you will visit the site frequently, look at their ads, and buy products through their shopping guides. Portals provide both Web guides and search engines, as well as free e-mail accounts, stock quotes, news headlines, weather reports, Web-based calendars, and other services.

Both Internet Explorer and Navigator are set up to direct you to their own respective portals, MSN (**http://www.msn.com**) and NetCenter (**http://www.netcenter.com**). Many ISPs, like AOL or EarthLink, are set up to direct subscribers to their own portal site. In any case, users can always choose a different portal. Other popular portals include Yahoo! (**http://my.yahoo.com**) and Go (**http://mypage.go.com**).

What Are Cookies?

A *cookie* is a small (at most 4K) file that a Web server can store on your machine. Its purpose is to allow a Web server to personalize a Web page, depending on whether you have been to that Web site before and what you may have told it during previous sessions. For example, when you establish an account with an online retailer or subscribe to an online magazine, you may be asked to fill out a form that includes some information about yourself and your preferences. The Web server may store that information (along with information about when you visit the site) in a cookie on your machine. When you return to that Web site in the future, the retailer's Web server can read its cookie, recall this information, and structure its Web pages accordingly.

Much has been written about whether cookies create a security or privacy hazard for you. If your Web browser is working properly, the security hazard is minimal. It is, at first glance, unsettling to think that Web servers are storing information on your hard drive without your knowledge. But cookies are not executable programs. They cannot, for example, search for and accumulate information from elsewhere on your system. They simply record information that you have already given to the Web server.

Cookies do make it easier for advertising companies to gather information about your browsing habits. For example, a company that advertises on a large number of Web sites can use cookies to keep track of where you have seen its ads before, and which ads (if any) you clicked. If this possibility bothers you, both Navigator and Internet Explorer let you control their use of cookies, including the option to disable the storage of all cookies (see "Managing Cookies").

Unfortunately, none of the Internet Explorer options for avoiding cookies is really satisfactory. Disabling all cookies blows away the utility of personalized Web sites; for example, we were unable to log on to My Yahoo! or access any other site that requires a password. You can require that Internet Explorer ask you whether to accept each cookie that a Web site offers, but you will spend more time answering questions than browsing the Web. In addition to these options, Navigator lets you accept only those cookies that get sent back to the originating server—a good compromise.

What Are Java, JavaScript, VBScript, and ActiveX?

Java is a language for sending small applications (called *applets*) over the Web, so that your computer can execute them. *JavaScript* is a language for extending HTML to embed small programs called *scripts* in Web pages. The main purpose of applets and scripts is to increase the interactivity of Web pages; rather than interacting with a distant Web server, you interact with an applet or script that the Web server runs on your machine. Java and JavaScript are also used for animation; rather than transmitting the frames of an animation over the Internet, the Web server sends an animation-constructing applet or script that runs on your computer. Typically, this process is invisible to the user—the interaction or the animation just happens, without calling your attention to how it happens.

VBScript, a language that resembles Microsoft's Visual Basic, can be used to add scripts to pages that are displayed by Internet Explorer. Anything that VBScript can do, JavaScript (which Microsoft calls JScript) can do, too—and vice versa.

ActiveX controls, like Java, are a way to embed executable programs into a Web page. Unlike Java and JavaScript, but like VBScript, ActiveX is a Microsoft system that is not used by Navigator. When Internet Explorer encounters a Web page that uses ActiveX controls, it checks to see whether that particular control is already installed; and if it is not, IE installs the control on your machine.

Some people are squeamish about the idea of a strange Web server running applications on their machine without their knowledge, and their concerns are not entirely unjustified. These programming systems have security safeguards; but from time to time, bugs are found either in the programming languages themselves or in the way that they have been implemented by a particular browser or on a particular machine. These bugs involve some security risk. You can disable all three systems (see "Managing Your Web Browser").

 ActiveX controls are considerably more dangerous than JavaScript or VBScript scripts or Java applets. Java applets and JavaScript scripts are run in a "sandbox" inside your Web browser, which limits the accidental or deliberate damage they can do, and VBScript scripts are run by an interpreter, which should limit the types of damage they can do. However, ActiveX controls are programs with full access to your computer's resources.

Netscape and Microsoft have a strong interest in reacting quickly to fix the security holes that people discover in their browsers, which is a good reason to check their Web sites (at **http://home.netscape.com** and **http://www.windowsupdate.com**) periodically to make sure that you are running the most recent versions of Navigator or Internet Explorer. See "What Security Do Web Browsers Offer?" in Chapter 31 for details about the security features of Internet Explorer and Navigator.

What Are Content Advisor and NetWatch?

Content Advisor and NetWatch are features of Internet Explorer and Navigator, respectively, that allow you to block access to Web sites that have objectionable content, such as nudity, profanity, or violence. Both work with the ratings system devised by the Recreational Software Advisory Council for the Internet (RSACi). Whoever holds the Content Advisor or NetWatch password can set the acceptable levels of the various types of (possibly) objectionable content, and the browser then refuses to display Web pages whose ratings exceed those levels unless the password is given.

The idea sounds good, but in practice it isn't working out very well, and we don't recommend that you use these applications. The problem with the RSACi system is that it relies on Webmasters to rate their own sites voluntarily, and the vast majority—from Penthouse to Billi Bear Toddler Preschool—have not done so. This situation leaves the user with a no-win choice: either you set the standards so that unrated sites are displayed (which lets your kids see almost anything) or you block all unrated sites (which lets them see practically nothing).

As things currently stand, a RSACi-based system is only practical if you have small children who only use a handful of Web sites. If those sites are unrated, you can create exceptions for them. Set up Content Advisor from the Content tab of the Internet Options dialog box. Consult the help files of your browser.

If you want some kind of automatic filter that prevents your kids (or your workers) from accessing objectionable Web sites, we consider buying software specifically for that purpose. Several commercial products filter Web sites in ways that do not rely on the cooperation of the Web sites themselves. Read reviews carefully before buying, however, because one person's definition of "objectionable" is very different from another's.

Viewing Web Pages

The main purpose of a Web browser is to display Web pages. Those pages may actually be on the Web, or they may be on your own computer.

Before you can display Web pages, though, you need to find them. The Web itself provides search engines and Web guides for finding your way around. Once you have found a Web site that you like, you need to be able to mark it so that you can go back to it easily. Internet Explorer and Navigator provide a variety of tools to help you do this—Internet shortcuts, favorites, bookmarks, history files, and lists that drop down from the Address box.

Since some content on the Web may be offensive to you, you may decide to avoid it or limit your children's access to it. To help you create and implement such a policy, Internet Explorer provides a Content Advisor that is based on a Web site rating system called *PICS* (Platform for Internet Content Selection; see the Web site **http://www.w3.org/PICS**). PICS lets you use ratings from any number of ratings bureaus; but the only bureau that Internet Explorer knows about (unless you add others) is the Recreational Software Advisory Council for the Internet (RSACi).

Finally, having found content that you want to examine at leisure or share with those who aren't connected to the Internet, you may decide to print it out. Internet Explorer and Navigator give you several options for doing this.

Opening Files on Your System

You can use either Navigator or Internet Explorer to view HTML files that are stored on your hard drive or elsewhere on your system. You can also view images stored in several different image formats, such as JPEG, GIF, or BMP:

1. Select File | Open in Internet Explorer and then click the Browse button in the dialog box that appears. In Navigator, select File | Open. In either case you see a dialog box almost identical to the Open dialog box of Windows Explorer.

2. Make sure that the Files Of Type line of the Open window contains the type of file you want to open. Web pages are of type HTM, and pictures are of type JPG, GIF, or BMP, depending on picture format. If the Files Of Type line doesn't contain the file type you want to open, choose another type from the drop-down menu. If you can't find the right type, choose All Files.

3. Browse until you find the file you want to open.

4. Select the file by clicking its name. Its name then appears in the File Name line.

5. Click Open. In Navigator, the file opens and you are done. In Internet Explorer, you are returned to the Open dialog box, with the address of the file entered. Click OK.

 Try right-clicking items on Web pages—both Internet Explorer and Navigator provide shortcut menus of useful commands.

Getting Around on the Web

You can open a Web page by using any of the following methods:

- **Entering its URL into a Web browser's Address box**   The most direct way is to type the URL, but if you have the URL in a file or a mail message, you can cut-and-paste it. The Paste command on the Edit menu may not work when the cursor is in the Address window, but you can always paste by pressing CTRL-V. Both Internet Explorer and Navigator have an auto-complete feature— the browser tries to guess what URL you are typing and finishes it for you, by guessing similar URLs that you've visited before.

- **Typing its Internet keyword into Internet Explorer or Navigator's Address box**   Many Web pages have been assigned Internet keywords that you can substitute for their URLs. So, for example, you can arrive at the home page of the University of California at Los Angeles by typing **UCLA** into the Address box. (Note: Navigator uses AOL's keyword system, while Internet Explorer uses MSN's system, so you don't always get the same results with both browsers.)

- **Selecting it from the list that drops down from the Address box**   Both Internet Explorer and Navigator remember the last 25 URLs or keywords that you have typed into the Address box.

- **Linking to it from another Web page**   The reason it's called a "web" is that pages are linked to each other in a tangled, unpredictable way. Click a link (usually underlined, blue text or icons) to see the Web page it refers to.

- **Linking to it from a mail message or newsgroup article**   If Outlook Express, MSN Messenger, or Netscape Messenger notices that a URL appears in a message, it automatically links it to the corresponding Web page (see Chapter 22). Clicking the URL opens a Web browser, which displays the Web page. If your browser can't find the page, try copying and pasting the URL into your browser and making sure it looks right (remove spaces and line breaks from the URL, for example).

- **Selecting it from History**   Both Internet Explorer and Navigator maintain records of the Web pages you have viewed in the past several days. You can display these records and return to any of the Web pages with a click (see "Examining History").

- **Selecting it from the Favorites menu or (in Navigator) from the Bookmarks list**   Accessing a Favorite from the Start | Favorite menu opens the target Web page in the default browser. Accessing a Favorite from the Internet Explorer Favorites menu opens it in Internet Explorer, no matter what the default browser is.

- **Opening an Internet shortcut**   An Internet shortcut displays the icon of the default browser. Opening it starts the default browser (even if another browser is already running), connects to the Internet, and displays the Web page to which the shortcut points.

Finding What You Want on the Web

No one designed the content of the Web—it's a collection of whatever various people and businesses have decided to put there. It also changes quickly as Web sites come and go or get reworked. Consequently, finding your way around is a bit of an art. The Web provides two main tools, Web guides and search engines, for you to work with.

Using Web Guides

Web guides take a top-down approach to finding your way on the Web. Various companies have taken on the job of trying to be the librarians of the Web and have created classification systems. They divide the Web into a list of categories, each of which is subdivided into categories, and so on. If you have a vague idea of what you want to find, you can start at the top and work your way down through the levels of categories and subcategories until you find what you want. Yahoo! (at **http://www.yahoo.com**) was one of the first Web guides.

For example, if you hear that United Airlines has a Web site that allows you to check whether the flight you are meeting has been delayed, you might start at the top of Yahoo!'s classification system and zero in on the site with the following series of clicks: Recreation | Travel | Air Travel | Airlines | United Airlines. The United Airlines listing is linked to United's Web site.

The easiest place to find a Web guide is at your portal (see "What Are Portals, Web Guides, and Search Engines?"). Most portals (like Yahoo!) started out as Web guides, and turned into portals as a way to capitalize on the traffic the Web guide brought in. However, there is an inherent conflict of interest between being a portal and being a Web guide: portals want to hold your attention as long as possible, while Web guides should send you promptly on your way. You may find that your portal's Web guide keeps directing you to its own Web sites and the Web sites of its sponsors, rather than where you want to go. If this becomes annoying, check a nonportal Web guide like Google (**http://directory.google.com**) or About.com (**http://www.about.com**).

Using Search Engines

Internet Explorer and Navigator each give you three ways to search the Web. Simple convenient searches can be done from the Address box; more complex searches using a variety of search engines are possible from the Explorer bar or Sidebar; and you can always do your searches from the Web site of whatever search engine you like.

Searching from the Address Box

The simplest way to search the Web is to type a question mark followed by a word or phrase into the Address box and then either press the ENTER key (in Internet Explorer) or click the Search button (in Navigator). By default, Internet Explorer uses the MSN search engine and Navigator uses Netscape search for Address bar searches; but in either case, you can choose a different default search engine as follows:

In Internet Explorer, click the Search button on the toolbar or choose View | Explorer Bar | Search to open the Search Explorer bar. Click the Customize button in the Search Explorer bar to open the Customize Search Settings dialog box. Now click the Autosearch Settings button in the Customize Search Settings dialog box. The Customize Autosearch Settings dialog box contains a drop-down list of search engines: AltaVista, Euroseek, Excite, Go, GoTo, Lycos, MSN, RealNames, and Yahoo!. Select one and click OK.

In Navigator, select Edit | Preferences to open the Preferences dialog box and choose the Internet Search subcategory under the Navigator category. In the right panel of the Preferences dialog box, choose a search engine from the drop-down list. Your choices are AOL, ClassifiedPlus, CompuServe, Google, ICQ, Music: Artists by Rolling Stone, Netscape, Netscape Germany, Shareware, Shop@Netscape, TechNews by CNET, Voila Germany, and WEB.DE. Click OK to make the dialog box go away.

Using Internet Explorer's Search Explorer Bar

The Search Explorer bar allows you to search not just for Web pages, but for addresses, businesses, maps, words, pictures, and newsgroups. Open the Search Explorer bar by clicking the Search button on the toolbar or choosing View | Explorer Bar | Search from the menu. Choose the kind of search you want to do by clicking the appropriate radio button at the top of the Explorer bar and enter text into the text boxes under the radio buttons. Start your search by clicking Search button on the Search Explorer bar.

To change the search engines that are used for these searches, click the Customize button on the Search Explorer bar. The Customize Search Settings dialog box appears. This dialog box is organized according to the type of search. The possible search engines for that kind of search are listed with check boxes next to their names. The checked search engines appear in a list that gives the order in which these engines are consulted. (Typically only results for the first engine in the list are displayed.) Click entries in this list and use the Move Up and Move Down buttons to rearrange the order. Remove an entry from the list by unchecking its check box.

Remove a type of search from the list of radio buttons on the Search Explorer bar by unchecking its check box on the Customize Search Settings dialog box.

To use one search engine for all your searches, click the Use One Search Engine For All Searches radio button at the top of the Customize Search Settings dialog box and click OK. The Search Explorer bar then displays a narrow version of your chosen search engine's home page.

Using Navigator's Search Sidebar

Navigator's Search sidebar allows more specific and complex searches than you can do from the Address box on the Navigation toolbar. If the Sidebar is not visible on the left side of the Navigator window, make sure that View | My Sidebar is checked and then click the narrow blue slider at the left edge of the viewing area. If the Search tab is not displayed, click the Add button at the top of the Sidebar and check Search on the menu that appears.

The Search tab has two settings: Basic and Advanced. Choose between them on the Search | My Sidebar Search Panel menu. The Basic setting accesses the Netscape Search engine, just as you would if you typed your search request into the Address box or clicked Search | Search The Web.

The Advanced setting, shown in Figure 24-1, offers more possibilities. Choose a type of search from a drop-down list at the top of the Search Sidebar: Web, Tech News, Shopping, Shareware, and Music. For each type of search, the Search Engines window lists the engines available for this kind of search. Check the check boxes in this window to choose which search engines will be used in your search. Then type keywords into the text window and click the Search button.

The results of the Search are displayed both on the Sidebar and in the main viewing area. The viewing area displays the results in a manner similar to a newsgroup reader: The top of the viewing area is a list of Web pages; select one to see a description of the page in the lower half of the viewing area. Click a link in the lower half to go to the page.

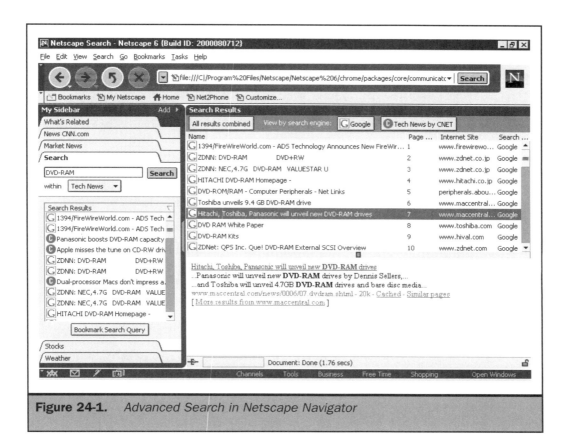

Figure 24-1.   *Advanced Search in Netscape Navigator*

To change the search engines listed for each type of search, click the Customize button near the bottom of the Search Sidebar. (This button vanishes after you do a search.) When the Customize Search dialog box appears, choose a type of search from the drop-down list in the dialog box. The search engines used for this kind of search (the ones that appear in the sidebar) are listed in the Search Engines window of the dialog box. All available search engines are listed in the All Engines window. To add an engine to the Search Engines listed, select it in the All Engines list and click Add. To remove an engine, select it in the Search Engines list and click Remove.

Using Other Search Engines

Some search engine Web sites offer more complex or specialized services. On Ask.com (**http://ask.com**), you can type a question in English, such as **What are the largest cities in the world?** The Web site's automated system does its best to find a Web page that answers your question and succeeds surprisingly often.

On AltaVista (**http://www.altavista.com** or **http://www.av.com**), you can search for resources other than just pages of text (though it does a good job searching for them, too). For example, if you type **Mona Lisa** into the Search box, AltaVista simultaneously constructs lists of results of several types, including Web pages containing the phrase "Mona Lisa," news stories mentioning "Mona Lisa," images (like the Mona Lisa painting), MP3 audio files (like the song "Mona Lisa"), and products whose names contain "Mona Lisa" (like Amazon.com selling the book *Mona Lisa Overdrive* by William Gibson).

The search engine rated highest in most surveys is Google (**http://google.com**). Google searches are quick and yet more complete than most. (No search engine has the entire Web indexed, but some search engines have more of it indexed than others.) They also contain very few dead links—Web pages that used to refer to the search terms, but no longer exist. You can do a simple Google search by typing words or phrases into the text box on Google's Web page and clicking the Google Search button. For a more advanced search (in which you can ask for pages that contain these words but not those words), click the Advanced Search link on the Google Web page. To specify that you are only looking for Web pages in a particular language, or that you don't want sexually explicit pages to appear on the results list, click the Language, Display & Filtering Options link.

Wherever you do it, the key to any good Web search is to find words and phrases that are specific to the subject you are interested in, and don't apply to a lot of other, more popular subjects. If, for example, you are looking for references to Madonna and Child imagery in Renaissance art, don't just type **Madonna and child** into a search engine—your results list will be full of references to the singer Madonna and her children. Include a term like **Renaissance** that narrows the search.

Remembering Where You've Been on the Web

Navigator and Internet Explorer provide a variety of ways to remember which Web sites you've already visited and how to get back to them. Both browsers have a Back menu that keeps track of the last few Web pages you've viewed and a drop-down list from the Address (or Location) box that shows the most recent URLs that you've typed. There's also a History feature that you can check when you find yourself saying "I know I saw that last week."

Using the Back Menu

Both Navigator and Internet Explorer have a Back button on the toolbar. These buttons each have a drop-down menu of the last several Web pages you have looked at during the current session. To access the Back menu, click the arrow on the right side of the Back button.

Using the Address List

Both Navigator and Internet Explorer have an Address box on the toolbar into which URLs can be typed. As you type a URL into the box, the browser generates a menu of URLs, based on what you have typed so far and the URLs you have visited recently. If the URL you want appears, you can save yourself some typing by choosing it from the menu.

In addition, each browser maintains a drop-down list of the last URLs that you have typed into the Address box. Internet Explorer keeps track of the 25 URLs you have typed in most recently, while Navigator lists only the URLs you have typed during this session. In either browser, you can select an entry off the drop-down list, and the browser fetches the corresponding Web page.

Examining History

Both Internet Explorer and Navigator maintain a list of Web pages that you have accessed recently. Internet Explorer stores this information in the form of Internet shortcuts that are arranged into a hierarchy of folders inside the History folder. Navigator maintains a history database that can be accessed or edited only from within Navigator. Both browsers allow you to return to a Web page with a single click.

If other people use your computer, you need to be aware of the privacy implications of having a History list. A History list is a trail that someone else can follow to see what you've been viewing on the Web. Conversely, you may use the History list to see what other people (your children, for example) have been viewing on the Web.

Both Navigator and Internet Explorer allow you to turn off the History list, or wipe clean the History list. Internet Explorer allows you (or someone else) to edit the History folder selectively, removing only the Web pages you (or they) don't want recorded.

 Clearing the History list in either Internet Explorer or Navigator does not clear the Back menu In Navigator The drop-down list under the Address box is also not cleared when you clear History. If you want to be sure to cover your tracks, exit the browser after you clear History—when it restarts, the Back menu and the Address box drop-down list is empty as well

In both Navigator and Internet Explorer, History is subject to user profiles: each user has his/her own History list, with its own settings. Navigator has its own user profiles (see Chapter 23, section "Defining User Profiles"). Internet Explorer applies the Windows user profiles (see Chapter 31, section "What Is a User Profile?").

WINDOWS ME
ON THE INTERNET

Using Internet Explorer's History Folder

Clicking the History button on the Internet Explorer toolbar or selecting View | Explorer Bar | History opens the History Explorer bar, shown here:

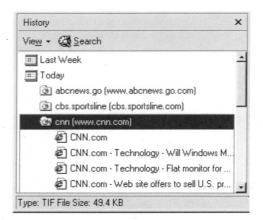

Clicking the History button again causes the History pane to disappear. The History folder is organized into subfolders—one for each day of the current week, and one for each previous week, going back 20 days. (You can use the steps listed in the following paragraphs to change the number of days History remembers.) Selecting a closed folder expands the tree to show its contents; selecting an open folder compresses the tree to hide its contents. Each day's folder contains one subfolder for each Web site visited with Internet Explorer. Inside the Web site folders are Internet shortcuts to each of the
pages viewed on that Web site.

Internet Explorer stores some Web pages on your hard drive so that it can display them quickly if you decide to come back to that page. Such a page is said to be *cached* on your drive. In the History Explorer bar, cached pages appear as solid icons all the time, while noncached pages appear as ghostly images when you are offline. Opening a cached Web page's icon when you are offline lets you view the cached copy, while you can only return to the noncached pages by going online. Selecting a shortcut displays its title and address in a tool tip window. When you are offline, a symbol having a circle with a line through it appears next to the cursor if the page is not cached. You can look up the exact time when the page was accessed by choosing Properties from the right-click shortcut menu.

Delete a shortcut or a subfolder from the History folder by selecting Delete from the right-click menu.

To change the History settings:

1. Open the Internet Options dialog box either by choosing View | Internet Options from within Internet Explorer or by opening the Internet Options icon

on the Control Panel. The dialog box opens with the General tab on top. The History box is near the bottom of the General tab.

2. If you want to delete all the entries in the History folder, click the Clear History button in the History box of the General tab.

3. If you want to change the number of days that the History folder remembers a Web page, enter a new number into the Days To Keep Pages In History box.

4. Click OK.

The History folder can also be viewed and edited in Windows Explorer. If your system is not using user profiles, there is a single History folder, C:\Windows\History (see Chapter 31, section "What Is a User Profile?"). If your system is set up for user profiles, your history folder is C:\Windows\Profiles*your user name*\History.

Using Navigator's History List

Access the Navigator History list by selecting Tasks | Tools | History from the Navigator menu bar. The History list appears in its own window, organized into three columns: page title, URL, and when the page was last visited. Double-clicking a line in the History list accesses the corresponding Web page.

Clicking a column head sorts the list according to that column; clicking it again sorts the list in descending order. Search the History list by selecting Edit | Find In History.

To change Navigator's History settings:

1. Choose Edit | Preferences. The Preferences box opens.

2. Select Navigator in the Category window.

3. If you want to delete all entries on the History list, click the Clear History button and click OK when Navigator asks you to verify the decision.

4. If you want to change the length of time that entries remain on the History list, type a number into the Pages In History Expire After *xx* Days box.

5. Click OK.

Revisiting Where You've Been with Favorites, Internet Shortcuts, and Bookmarks

When you find a Web page you like, you likely will want to look at it again sometime. Favorites, Internet shortcuts, and bookmarks allow you to return easily to a Web page without having to write down or remember the page's URL (see "What Are Internet Shortcuts, Favorites, and Bookmarks?").

Using Favorites, Internet Shortcuts, and Bookmarks

Opening an Internet shortcut causes Windows to connect to your Internet provider (if necessary), open your default Web browser, and display the Web page that the shortcut points to.

Favorites is a folder of Internet shortcuts, so choosing Start | Favorites and selecting a Web page has the same effect as opening an Internet shortcut that points to that Web page. Choosing a Web page from the Favorites menu of Internet Explorer opens the page in Internet Explorer, even if another browser is the default browser.

The Bookmarks menu is a part of Navigator. To use it, click the Bookmarks button on the Personal toolbar and select a bookmark from the menu that appears. Navigator then opens the Web page that the bookmark points to.

Adding Favorites

To add favorites in Internet Explorer:

1. Display the page you want to add in Internet Explorer.

2. Select Favorites | Add To Favorites. An Add Favorite dialog box opens, as shown here:

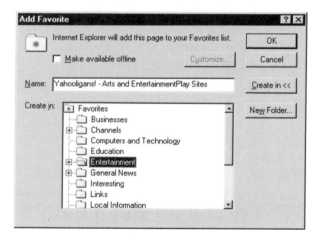

3. Select a name to appear on the Favorites menu. The dialog box suggests the name that the page's creator has given it. If some other name would do a better job of reminding you which Web page this is, type it into the Name line.

4. If you organize your Favorites menu into folders (a good idea if you have a lot of favorites), click the Create In button to choose a folder in which to put this new favorite. The dialog box enlarges to include a folder tree showing the subfolders of the Favorites folder.

5. Select a folder in which to create the new favorite. If you want to define a new folder for the favorite, select a folder in which to put the new folder and then click New Folder. The new folder appears on the folder tree.

6. Click OK to create the new favorite in the selected folder.

To add favorites in Navigator: In between the words Bookmarks and Location on the Location toolbar is a bookmark icon. This icon represents a bookmark or shortcut pointing to whatever page is currently displayed.

1. Display the page you want to add in Navigator.

2. In a separate Explorer window, display the Favorites folder. It's called C:\Windows\Favorites if you don't have personal profiles on your system, or C:\Windows\Profiles*your user name*\Favorites, if you do.

3. Switch to the Navigator window and then drag the bookmark icon into the Favorites folder. This creates the Favorites entry.

4. The new Favorites entry will be named Temp Title. To change the name to something snappier, right-click the new entry, select Rename, and change the name.

Creating Internet Shortcuts

To create shortcuts in Internet Explorer, open the page to which you want to create a shortcut and choose File | Send | Shortcut To Desktop.

To create shortcuts in Navigator, open the page to which you want to create a shortcut and drag the bookmark icon to the desktop or into an Explorer window.

You can also create shortcuts in Windows Explorer or the desktop. From Windows Explorer, choose File | New | Shortcut. From the desktop, right-click, and then choose New | Shortcut. Either way, a Create Shortcut box opens. Type the URL of the Web page into the Create Shortcut box; or, if you have copied the command line from some other document, paste it into Create Shortcut by pressing CTRL-V. Click Next. Give the shortcut a name. Click Finish.

Adding Bookmarks in Navigator

Add a bookmark in Navigator by displaying the page you want to mark and selecting Bookmarks | Add Current Page.

Organizing Favorites and Bookmarks

If you have picked out only a few Web pages, your favorites and bookmarks don't have to be well organized. But as time goes by, favorites and bookmarks accumulate like knick-knacks. It saves time to reorganize them once in a while and toss out the ones that are obsolete. Both Internet Explorer and Navigator let you create a folder system to organize your list of favorite sites.

The Favorites list is actually a folder (C:\Windows\Favorites, if you haven't established user profiles on your computer; C:\Windows\Profiles*your user name*\Favorites, if you have), and each of the entries on the Favorites list is a shortcut pointing to the URL of the corresponding Web page. Consequently, one way to organize Favorites is to use the same techniques you would use to organize any other folder in Windows Explorer. You can choose Favorites | Organize Favorites from any Explorer or Internet Explorer window. An Organize Favorites box opens. Move, rename, or delete entries on your Favorites list by selecting the entries and clicking the corresponding buttons in the Organize Favorites box.

To reorganize your Navigator bookmarks, select Bookmarks | Manage Bookmarks. The Manage Bookmarks window opens, allowing you to delete, cut, paste, and drag bookmarks. New folders and separators (which go between classes of folders) are created from the File | New menu of this window.

You can't reorganize the Imported IE Favorites folder from within Navigator. Instead, use the Organize button on the Favorites Explorer bar of an Explorer or Internet Explorer window to reorganize the Favorites folder; the changes you make are reflected on Navigator's Bookmarks | Imported IE Favorites menu.

Importing and Exporting Favorites and Bookmarks

When you install Internet Explorer on a computer that already has Navigator, the Navigator bookmarks are automatically imported to the Favorites list. Conversely, there is no need to convert the Favorites folder to Navigator bookmarks, as long as you are using both on the same computer: The Bookmarks | Imported IE Favorites menu in Navigator displays an up-to-date list of the entries in the Favorites folder.

To import bookmarks to Internet Explorer after installation, select File | Import And Export to start the Import/Export Wizard. This Wizard provides the best way to convert between Internet Explorer's Favorites (a folder of Internet shortcuts) and Navigator's bookmarks (an HTML file of links).

To import or export a bookmark file from Navigator on one computer to Navigator on another computer, follow these steps:

1. Select Bookmarks | Manage Bookmarks on the exporting copy of Navigator to open the Manage Bookmarks window.

2. Select File | Export Bookmarks from that window's menu bar. The Export Bookmark File dialog box appears. It resembles a Save dialog box in Windows Explorer.

3. Using the Export Bookmarks File window, save a copy of your Bookmarks.html file somewhere else, such as a floppy disk or the hard drive of another computer on the same network.

4. Make the copy of Bookmarks.html available to the importing computer. (For example, transfer a floppy disk from one computer to the other.)

5. From the copy of Navigator on the importing computer, open the Manage Bookmarks window in the same manner.

6. Select File | Import Bookmarks. The Import Bookmarks File dialog box appears. It resembles the Open dialog box in Windows Explorer.

7. Use the Import Bookmarks File dialog box to retrieve the copy of Bookmarks.html.

Interacting with Web Sites Automatically

Web sites that provide some personalized service typically ask you to fill out a registration form when you first establish a relationship with the site and to log in by giving a user name and password when you return to the site in the future. Filling out forms and typing in passwords are precisely the kinds of repetitive, mindless work that computers are supposed to do for us, so both Internet Explorer and Navigator both provide ways to do these small tasks automatically.

You should give some thought as to whether to let the browser remember passwords and which passwords to entrust to it. Once a browser has been allowed to remember a password for some kind of private account on a Web site, anyone who uses your computer and opens your browser can get into that account.

Whether this risk is worth taking depends on the physical security of your computer and the value of the information protected by the password. You do not, for example, want someone who steals your laptop to be able to gain access to your online bank or brokerage accounts, though you might not care if they used your subscription to the online version of *The Wall Street Journal.*

Remembering Passwords in Internet Explorer

If you want Internet Explorer to remember passwords for you, do the following:

1. Choose Tools | Internet Options to open the Internet Options dialog box.

2. Go to the Content tab.

3. Click the AutoComplete button to open the AutoComplete Settings dialog box, as shown here:

4. Check the User Names And Passwords On Forms check box. This setting means that Internet Explorer will insert the user names and passwords it has memorized into the appropriate logon forms for Web pages.

5. Check the Prompt Me To Save Passwords check box. This setting means that whenever you log in to a site whose password Internet Explorer hasn't memorized, it will ask you whether you want it to memorize that password. If Internet Explorer already knows all the passwords you want it to know, leave this box unchecked.

6. Click OK in each of the open dialog boxes.

When these settings are in place, you will encounter the following dialog box every time you enter a new password:

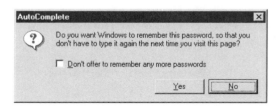

Click Yes if you want the password remembered. Checking the Don't Offer To Remember Any More Passwords check box has the same effect as unchecking the Prompt Me To Save Passwords box on the AutoComplete Settings dialog box: Internet Explorer remembers and continues to use the passwords it knows, but stops asking whether it should remember new passwords.

If you want Internet Explorer to forget all the passwords it knows (as you might if someone else is going to be using your office while you are on vacation), open the AutoComplete Settings dialog box (as in the previous steps) and click the Clear Passwords button. Unfortunately, there is no way to instruct Internet Explorer to forget one or two of your passwords but remember the others.

Using Internet Explorer's Profile Assistant

Profile Assistant is Internet Explorer's tool for filling out Web forms automatically. Rather than capturing information from Web forms directly (as Navigator does), Profile Assistant asks you to fill out a profile form like the Windows Address Book contact form. Information from this profile is used to fill out Web forms that ask for things like your address or phone number. (No information is transmitted automatically. You have an opportunity to review forms and delete or change information before submitting forms.)

To set up your profile:

1. Open the Internet Options dialog box by selecting Tools | Internet Options from the menu bar.

2. Go to the Content tab of the dialog box and click the My Profile button. The Address Book – Choose Profile dialog box appears.

3. If you already have your own information stored as an entry in your address book, click the Select An Existing Entry From The Address Book To Represent Your Profile radio button, and do just that: select an entry from the list in the dialog box. Click OK, and your profile is established.

4. If you do not want to use an existing Address Book entry to establish your profile, click the Create A New Entry In The Address Book To Represent Your Profile radio button and click OK. A Properties dialog box opens, showing a form from the Windows Address Book. Fill out as much or as little of it as you like, using the Name, Home, Business, and Personal tabs. Click OK and your profile is established.

Internet Explorer can fill in Web forms with the information from the Address Book only when the names of the boxes on the form match the pieces of information that are entered in the Address Book—items like name, ZIP code, and phone.

Remembering Forms and Passwords in Navigator

Navigator's ability to remember forms and passwords is managed from the Forms and Passwords panel of the Preferences dialog box. To open this box, select Edit | Preferences and choose Forms and Passwords in the Category list.

To have Navigator offer to remember passwords, check the Remember Passwords For Sites That Require Me To Log In check box. To have Navigator remember data that you type into Web forms, check the Save Form Data From Web Pages When Completing Forms check box. After these boxes are checked, Navigator will offer to remember new forms and/or passwords; as with Internet Explorer, you have the option of saying no on a case-by-case basis. When a Web page presents you with a logon or other form that Navigator recognizes, it fills in the stored data automatically; you can then type over it if you want to make changes.

To see what information Navigator is storing, click the View Saved Data or View Saved Passwords button. These buttons call up dialog boxes that allow you to review, change, or delete stored information. In particular, you can delete stored passwords site by site, something Internet Explorer does not allow. (Note that the Saved Passwords box lists only the Web sites and user names, not the passwords themselves.)

Managing Your Web Browser

Web browsers are intended to be simple enough for novice users. For this reason, most of what the browser does is invisible. Some choices that your browser makes for you, however, have implications for your system's use of disk space or its security—implications that more advanced users may want to consider. Internet Explorer and Navigator allow you some limited opportunities to "get under the hood" and make choices for yourself about caching Web pages, accepting cookies, and running applets in Java or ActiveX.

Managing Caches of Web Pages

Web browsers store some of the pages that you view so that they can be redisplayed quickly if you return to them. In general, this speeds up the browsing experience; but if you are running short of disk space, you may decide to limit or eliminate these caches. Navigator stores Web pages in the folder C:\Program Files\Netscape\Users*your Navigator user name*\Cache, while Internet Explorer uses C:\Windows\Temporary Internet Files or C:\Windows\Profiles*your user name*\Temporary Internet Files.

You control Internet Explorer's cache of Web pages from the General tab of the Internet Options dialog box. Delete all these Web pages by clicking the Delete Files button. To set limits on the amount of disk space that can be devoted to temporary Internet files, click the Settings button to open the Settings dialog box. Move the slider to raise or lower the percentage of your hard drive that the Temporary Internet Files folder is allowed to use. Click OK to apply your changes.

Navigator has two caches for Web pages: a small but extremely fast cache in your computer's memory (RAM), and a larger but slower one on your hard disk. To empty or change the size of either one:

1. Select Edit | Preferences to open the Preferences dialog box.

2. Expand the Advanced category by clicking the arrow next to Advanced in the Category list.

3. Select Cache in the Category list. The Cache controls appear in the right pane of the Preferences dialog box.

4. Empty either cache by clicking the corresponding Clear button.

5. Change the size of either cache by entering a new size into the Memory Cache or Disk Cache box.

6. Click OK.

Managing Cookies

Both Internet Explorer and Navigator let you control how they use cookies, though Navigator's cookie controls are far more extensive and useful (see "What Are Cookies?"). In each case, the default option is to accept all cookies (except in the Restricted Sites content zone in Internet Explorer). You also have the option to refuse all cookies or to be asked whether to accept or refuse cookies on a case-by-case basis. Navigator gives you the additional option of accepting only cookies that get sent back to the originating server.

Managing Cookies in Internet Explorer

Internet Explorer maintains a separate cookie policy for each Web content zone. To change your cookie policy, go to the Security tab of the Internet Options dialog box. Select the Web content zone whose policy you want to change (or examine) and click the Custom Level button. Scroll down until you see Cookies. The three options are presented as radio buttons: Enable, Disable, and Prompt. Click the button next to the policy you prefer and click OK.

If you choose Prompt, you face a dialog box every time a Web site wants to set a cookie—amazingly often, you will find. Each time you are offered the tempting check box In The Future Do Not Show This Warning. If you click it and then click the Yes button, you have changed your cookie policy back to Enable.

We recommend you leave Internet Explorer's default cookie policy alone. Refusing all cookies makes all the personalized services on the Web unusable; and if you choose the Prompt option, you'll spend all your Web-browsing time accepting and rejecting cookies. If you want to manage your cookies while using Internet Explorer, install a third-party cookie manager.

Internet Explorer cookies are stored as text files either in the folder C:\Windows\Cookies (if user profiles are not being used on your system) or in C:\Windows\Profiles*your user name*\Cookies. Some cookies may also be in C:\Windows\Temporary Internet Files (or one of its subfolders) or C:\Windows\Profiles*your user name*\Temporary Internet Files (or one of its subfolders).

Reading a cookie in WordPad or some other text program probably will not tell you much, though it may set your mind at ease to realize just how little information is there

(see Chapter 4, section "Taking Advantage of Free Word Processing with WordPad").
Delete cookies from your system by deleting the corresponding text files.

Setting Cookie Policy in Navigator

In Navigator, select Edit | Preferences to open the Preferences dialog box and click the
arrow next to Advanced in the Category list. This displays the subcategories under
Advanced, one of which is Cookies. Select Cookies in the Category list. The bottom
portion of the right pane controls your cookie policy. The options to accept all cookies,
accept only those that get sent back to the originating server, and disable all cookies are
given as radio buttons. Click the radio button corresponding to your chosen policy. In
addition, a check box controls whether Navigator should warn you before accepting a
cookie. The warning includes the option to refuse the cookie.

*In Navigator, we like the Accept Cookies That Get Sent Back To The Originating Server
Only choice.*

Navigator lists the cookies it is currently storing in a text file, Cookies.txt. In the
default installation, this file is in the folder C:\Program Files\Netscape\Users*your
Navigator user name*. Looking at this file in Notepad won't tell you much, though, other
than the fact that cookies are small. The better way to view your Navigator cookies is to
click the View Stored Cookies button on the Cookies panel of the Preferences dialog
box. The Cookie Manager dialog box appears, as shown in Figure 24-2. From this
dialog box, you can see what is in each cookie, remove cookies individually by
selecting them and clicking the Remove Cookie button, or toss all your cookies by
clicking the Remove All Cookies button.

Managing Cookies Site by Site in Navigator

Another way to manage cookies in Navigator is on a site-by-site basis. Navigator asks
whether to accept or reject cookies on each new Web site that you visit, but then
remembers your choice and doesn't ask you when you visit the same sites again.

To set this up, select Edit | Preferences to open the Preferences dialog box. Then
select Cookies from the Category list. Check the Warn Me Before Accepting A Cookie
check box, and click OK.

Now, whenever you go to a new Web site that wants to set a cookie, the following
dialog box appears:

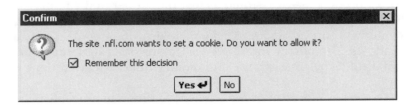

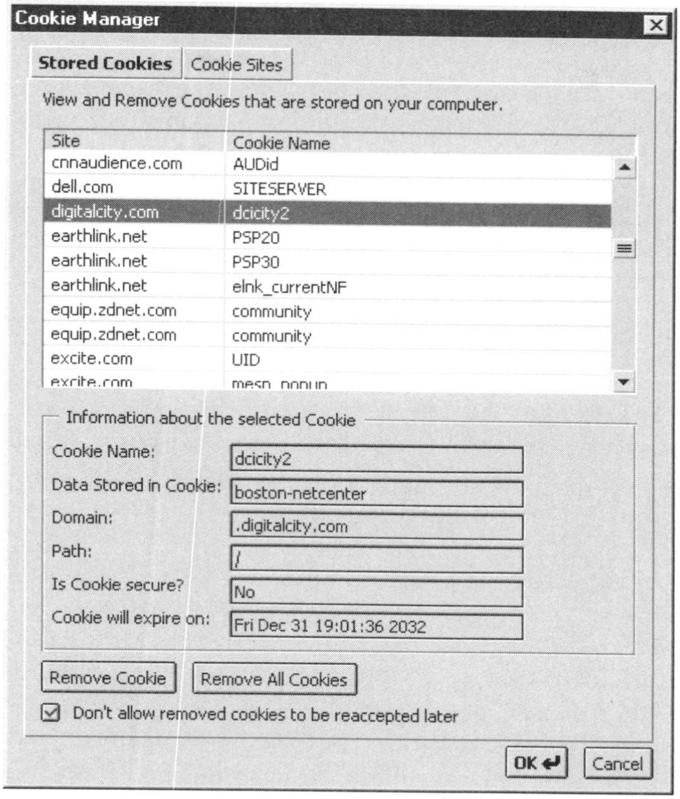

Figure 24-2. *Navigator's Cookie Manager*

Make sure that the Remember This Decision check box is checked and click Yes or No. If you change your mind, go to the Web site and choose Tasks | Privacy and Security | Cookie Manager | Allow This Site To Set Cookies or Tasks | Privacy and Security | Cookie Manager | Block This Site From Setting Cookies. To see what decisions you have made, open the Cookie Manager by choosing Tasks | Privacy and Security | Cookie Manager | View Stored Cookies. When the Cookie Manager dialog box appears, click the Cookie Sites tab.

Managing Java and JavaScript

Java and JavaScript are programming languages that are used to give some Web pages advanced features. If you want to deactivate Java and JavaScript in your Web browser, you can. In Navigator, select Edit | Preferences and click Advanced in the Categories window of the Preferences dialog box. The check boxes Enable Java and Enable JavaScript turn Java and JavaScript on or off. In Internet Explorer, open the Internet Options dialog box from the Control Panel or by choosing Tools | Internet Options and go to the Advanced tab. The check boxes Java Console Enabled, JIT Compiler For Virtual Machine Enabled, and Java Logging Enabled control Internet Explorer's use of Java.

The specific permissions granted to Java applets by Internet Explorer are controlled on the Security tab of the Internet Options dialog box and are set independently for each security zone. The default settings are Low Safety in the Trusted Sites zone and High Safety everywhere else. To examine or change these settings:

1. Open the Internet Options dialog box by selecting Tools | Internet Options from the Internet Explorer menu bar.

2. Click the Security tab of the Internet Options dialog box.

3. Select the security zone you want to examine or change.

4. Click the Custom Level button. The Security Settings dialog box opens.

5. Scroll down until you see Microsoft VM | Java permissions. The radio buttons show you what level is currently selected. Change the Java security level by choosing a different radio button.

6. Click OK to close each open dialog box.

If you want to get into the nitty-gritty of Java permissions, select the Custom radio button in step 5. Press the Java Custom Settings button that appears. A new dialog box opens, allowing you to make very specific choices about what Java applets can and cannot do. We recommend you leave these settings alone unless you know what you are doing.

Managing ActiveX Controls

We have never been big fans of ActiveX controls. They allow Web sites to have too much power over your system and are hard to monitor. If you should happen to download and install a rogue ActiveX control by mistake, it could (on its own) download and install lots more rogue ActiveX controls—which would then be permanent parts of your software environment, even when you are offline. None of this would appear the least bit suspicious to any virus-detecting software you might own, because ActiveX controls aren't viruses: They have the same status as applications that you install yourself.

Disabling ActiveX controls is one option. However, if you frequent Microsoft Web sites like MSN or MSNBC, you will be exposed to numerous temptations to turn them back on. (We finally gave in to the excellent portfolio-tracking services at MSN Moneycentral.) We suggest the following compromise: Turn off ActiveX controls everywhere but in the Trusted Sites security zone. When you find a Microsoft Web site that offers some wonderful service involving ActiveX controls, move that site into the Trusted Sites security zone. See Chapter 31 for a discussion of security zones and trusted sites.

ActiveX controls are themselves controlled by the Security tab of the Internet Options dialog box, which you open by choosing Tools | Options from the Internet Explorer menu. Each security zone has its own settings for ActiveX controls, which, under the default settings, are enabled everywhere but in the Restricted Sites zone.

ActiveX controls are stored in the folder C:\Windows\Downloaded Program Files. If you use Internet Explorer, you should check this file periodically to see what applications Internet Explorer has downloaded. Deleting files from this folder uninstalls the associated applications.

Getting Help

Access Internet Explorer Help by choosing Help | Contents And Index. The format of this window is similar to Windows Help. You can find what you want by looking through the table of contents on the Contents tab, seeing the topics listed alphabetically on the Index tab, or searching for particular terms on the Search tab. Clicking the Web Help button opens a browser window displaying the Microsoft Support Web page at **http://support.microsoft.com/directory**.

To get help in Navigator, select Help | Help Contents | Web Browsing from the Navigator menu bar. The Help Contents window is in two panels. The left panel, resembling a sidebar, is a list of major topics, while the right panel is a document window. Clicking a topic in the left panel displays the beginning of that section of the Help document in the right panel. Consult Netscape's online help and technical support by selecting Help | Netscape.com Help.

Chapter 25

Internet Conferencing with MSN Messenger and NetMeeting

W indows Me comes with two programs for chatting and conferencing over the Internet. MSN Messenger lets you instantly communicate with anyone else online who is also using MSN Messenger. Microsoft NetMeeting lets you use the Internet as a long distance phone service, including videoconferencing, typed chat, and even sharing programs over the Internet.

This chapter describes how to use these two programs. You can download other Internet chat and conferencing programs from the Internet itself; Chapter 26 tells you how.

Note   *Choose Start | Programs | Accessories | Communications to find the MSN Messenger Service and NetMeeting programs. If they don't appear, you can install them from your Windows Me CD-ROM (see Chapter 3, section "Installing and Uninstalling Programs That Come with Windows"). Open Control Panel, run the Add/Remove Programs program, click the Windows Setup tab, choose Communications from the list of components, click Details, and choose MSN Messenger Service and NetMeeting.*

Chatting Online with MSN Messenger

MSN Messenger enables you to chat with friends or coworkers who are online at the time that you want to chat. It's quicker than e-mail, and multiple people can take part in the conversation. Messenger also enables you to speak to other users and send messages to pagers.

Run MSN Messenger by choosing Start | Programs | Accessories | Communications | MSN Messenger Service. MSN Messenger may ask whether you want to download updates to the program. This chapter describes the program that ships with Windows Me, but updated versions of MSN Messenger should be similar.

Setting Up MSN Messenger

If you haven't used MSN Messenger before, you need to establish a Microsoft Passport—an ID on the MSN Messenger system. You get a Microsoft Passport by creating a Hotmail account (Microsoft's Web-based e-mail service, at **http://www.hotmail.com**) or by using your e-mail address. Follow these steps to establish a Microsoft Passport:

1. Run MSN Messenger by choosing Start | Programs | Accessories | Communications | MSN Messenger Service. The first time you run MSN Messenger, you see the first window of the Setup Wizard. The Wizard's first window has a Click For More Information button that opens a Web page about MSN Messenger.

2. Click Next. If you don't have a Hotmail account, click Get A Passport. If you have a Hotmail account, skip to step 4 (click Next to view the next window).

3. The Get A Passport button opens a browser window to the Passport registration page, in which you can create a free Hotmail account. Fill in the form and click

Sign Up. If you don't want to create a Hotmail account, you can click the Try This Instead link. Then fill in the form using your existing e-mail address, rather than a Hotmail address (you must use a real e-mail address). You must complete the whole process, which may include clicking a link sent to you in an e-mail message. When you have created a Passport, click Next to view the next window of the Messenger Setup Wizard.

4. Enter your Sign-in name and your password. Your sign-in name is the full e-mail address you used to create your Passport, in the form *name@yourhost.com*.

5. Click Finish to log on to MSN Messenger. You see the MSN Messenger Service window shown in Figure 25-1.

The MSN Messenger Service window lists your contacts—those who are online and those who are not. Of course, if you've never used MSN Messenger, you don't have any contacts (yet).

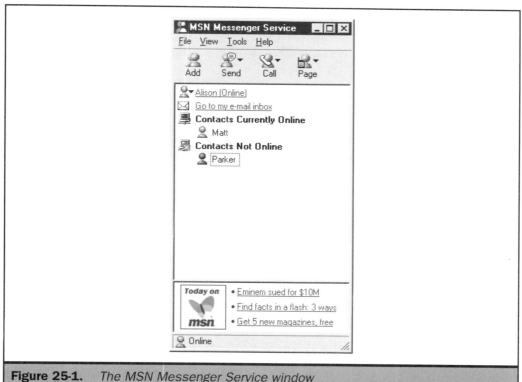

WINDOWS ME
ON THE INTERNET

Figure 25-1.   *The MSN Messenger Service window*

*The MSN Messenger Server window includes an entry showing how many new e-mail messages are in your Hotmail account (free Web-based e-mail, at **http://www. hotmail.com**). If you don't have any new messages, you see a Go To My E-mail Mailbox link; otherwise, MSN Messenger tells you how many new messages you have. To read your Hotmail messages, click the E-mail Message link: your browser starts and displays the Hotmail Web site. There's no way to configure MSN Messenger to display how many messages are in mailboxes other than your Hotmail mailbox (Microsoft owns Hotmail, and they are using Windows to promote it).*

Telling MSN Messenger About Your Contacts

Before you can begin to chat, you have to have someone to chat with. The easiest way is to ask your friends if they use MSN Messenger; and, if so, what their e-mail address is (at least, the e-mail address they use for messaging—some people use a different address to avoid getting spam at the regular e-mail address). Once you know their e-mail address, add them to your contacts by following these steps:

1. Open MSN Messenger.

2. Click Add on the toolbar. You see the Add A Contact dialog box, shown here:

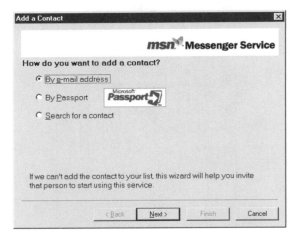

3. Choose By E-mail Address and click Next.

4. Enter the person's e-mail address and click Next.

5. MSN Messenger adds the person to your contact list if they have a Microsoft Passport. If the person does not have a Microsoft Passport, you can send them an e-mail message telling them how to get up and running with MSN Messenger.

If you think someone has a Microsoft Password but you don't know the person's e-mail address, choose Search For A Contact from the Add A Contact dialog box. Enter the information you know about the person and click Next. You see a list of people who meet your search criteria—select one and click Next. If the person has a Passport, MSN Messenger adds the person to your contacts.

Chatting with MSN Messenger

To chat with a contact who is online, click his or her name in the MSN Messenger Service window. An Instant Message window appears like the one in Figure 25-2.

To converse, type in the box at the bottom of the window and click Send or press ENTER. When another person is typing a response, you see a message to that effect on the status line (the bottom line) of the Instant Message window. If you have a sound card, microphone, and speakers, and the person you're chatting with does also, click Talk to speak with them. You can invite other contacts to join in the chat by clicking Invite. You can block the person you are talking to from contacting you by clicking Block. (If you want to unblock someone, right-click the person's name in your contact list and select Unblock.)

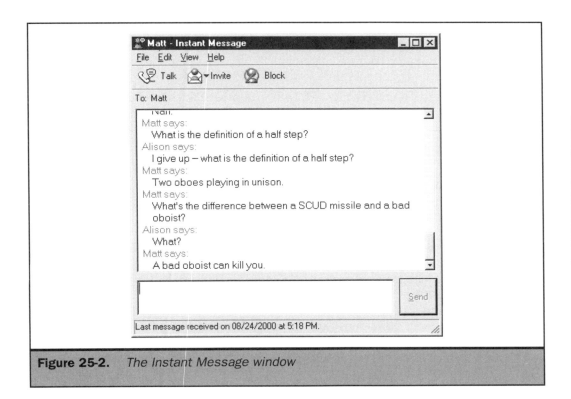

Figure 25-2.   *The Instant Message window*

Other Things You Can Do with MSN Messenger

MSN Messenger is an easy way to chat with people online using text, but you can use it in a few other ways, too:

- **Sending a file**   Right-click the name of the contact to whom you are sending the file and choose Send A File. Select the file and click Open. The contact has to accept the file for the transfer to occur.

- **Starting NetMeeting**   If you want to do more than just chat—if you want to work on a project, share an application window, or use video—you can start NetMeeting right from Messenger by choosing Invite | To Start NetMeeting from the Instant Message window (see the next section, "Conferencing with Microsoft NetMeeting").

- **Calling**   You can call anywhere in the U.S. or Canada for free if you have a sound card, microphone, and speakers. Click Call, choose Dial A Phone Number, and enter the country code (1 for the U.S.), followed by the 10-digit phone number. Click Hang Up to end the call.

- **Paging**   You can send a message to a pager if the pager is set up to receive MSN Messenger messages. Just click Page in the MSN Messenger window, select the contact, enter a call back number, and click Send.

- **Changing the way your name appears to others**   Click your own name in the list of contacts and choose Personal Settings.

- **Getting Help**   Choose Help | Help Topics to see the Help window.

Conferencing with Microsoft NetMeeting

Microsoft NetMeeting is like a specialized chat program with lots of extra features. In addition to typing messages to other people in the chat room, all participants can draw on a shared virtual whiteboard, transfer files to each other, or edit a file together. If you have microphones, speakers, and video cameras, you can even use NetMeeting for voice or videoconferences.

In order to connect to the other people with whom you want to meet, NetMeeting uses a *directory server* that stores the addresses of people who use NetMeeting. When you are logged on to a directory server, your name appears on its lists, so that anyone else can "call" you. Once you have connected to a directory server, you can call another person or several other people. You can start a new call or join an existing call.

When you're connected to one or more people, you can do the following:

- **Converse using audio**   You can speak with a contact, assuming that both callers' computers have microphones and speakers (audio is limited to two-person calls). You must have a reasonably fast Internet connection (at least a 28.8 bps modem) for acceptable audio quality.

- **Chat by typing messages**   This is very much like Instant Message in MSN Messenger.

- **Share a whiteboard**   This is useful in a conference, so that everyone can see what everyone else is drawing.

- **See the person you are calling**   You can do this if both callers' computers have video cameras (video is limited to two-person calls, too).

- **Transfer files**   This is a good way to move files from one caller to another.

- **Collectively edit a file**   A group can work together on a document such as a word processing document, graphics file, or database, so that everyone in the call can see the changes everyone else has made.

NetMeeting lets you connect only with other people who use NetMeeting: it doesn't conform to any Internet conferencing standards. For example, you can't join a meeting with people who use Internet Relay Chat (IRC), CU-SeeMe, PowWow, Internet Phone, or other online chat programs.

 This section describes NetMeeting version 3.01.

Configuring NetMeeting

To run NetMeeting, choose Start | Programs | Accessories | Communications | NetMeeting. If you haven't already configured NetMeeting, you see a series of windows that tell you about the program and ask for the following information:

- **Your name, e-mail address, location, and comments**   You have to type your name and e-mail address, as you can see next, but you can leave the rest of the information blank. In fact, we recommend that you leave everything but your name blank and type a fake e-mail address, to avoid receiving unsolicited e-mail from unscrupulous Internet users.

NetMeeting

Enter information about yourself for use with NetMeeting.
Note: You must supply your first name, last name, and E-mail address.

First name:

Last name:

E-mail address:

Location:

Comments:

< Back   Next >   Cancel

■ **Which directory server to use**   The default is Microsoft Internet Directory, shown next, which is the same directory you see when you use MSN Messenger. A number of other public directory servers are also available. You can find a list of them at the NetMeeting Zone Web site at **http://www.netmeet.net**. If your organization uses NetMeeting, you may use a private directory server. You can choose to Log On To A Directory Server When NetMeeting Starts (the alternative is to log on manually using the NetMeeting menu bar). You can also choose whether you want to be listed in the directory on the server you choose. If you choose a public server, you may prefer not to be listed, so that strangers don't contact you.

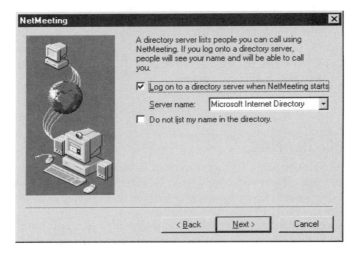

■ **Connection speed**   Choose the speed of your modem or specify that you are connected via a LAN (see Chapter 27). NetMeeting uses this information when sending audio or video data to you.

■ **Shortcuts**   If you use NetMeeting often, you might want to add a shortcut to the desktop or to the Quick Launch toolbar on your Taskbar.

NetMeeting runs the Audio Tuning Wizard to make sure that your speakers are working. When it finishes, the configuration program displays the NetMeeting window. You may want to make some other changes to your configuration by choosing Tools | Options. On the Options dialog box that appears, shown next, you can set these types of options:

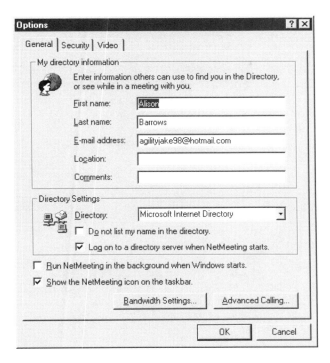

- ■ **General tab**   Make changes to the configuration information you typed when you first ran NetMeeting.
- ■ **Security tab**   Specify whether to accept incoming calls automatically, whether to make secure outgoing calls, and other security options.
- ■ **Audio tab**   Configure NetMeeting to work with your microphone and speakers.
- ■ **Video tab**   Specify the size and quality of video images to display.

Connecting to a Directory Server

When you start NetMeeting, you see the NetMeeting window, shown in Figure 25-3. From this window, you can open a meeting.

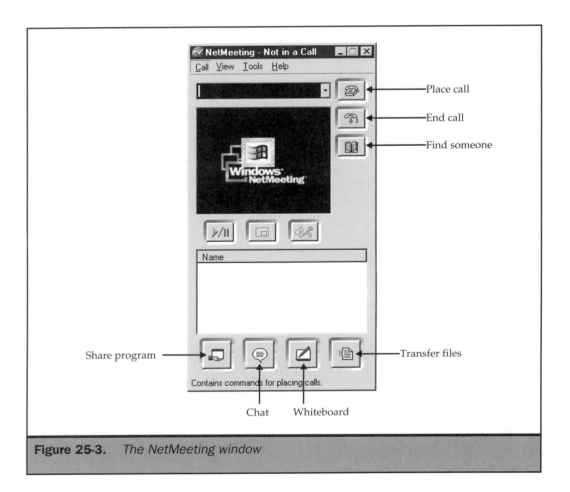

Figure 25-3. *The NetMeeting window*

You can start a meeting by clicking the Place Call button if you know the address of the person you want to talk to. However, you can also start the call by selecting the person from a directory. If you've chosen the Microsoft Internet Directory, your NetMeeting directory is the same as your MSN Messenger contact list, like the one shown in Figure 25-4.

You may want to connect to a public directory server. You can find a list of them at **http://www.netmeet.net**. However, when you are connected to a public server and your name is listed, you are likely to get unwanted calls. When you click Find Someone In A Directory when you are connected to a directory server, you see a directory of the people connected to the same server, as in Figure 25-5. The little icon to the left of each person's e-mail address shows their status. A PC icon with a blue screen and red twinkle means that the person is currently in a call, while a gray PC icon means

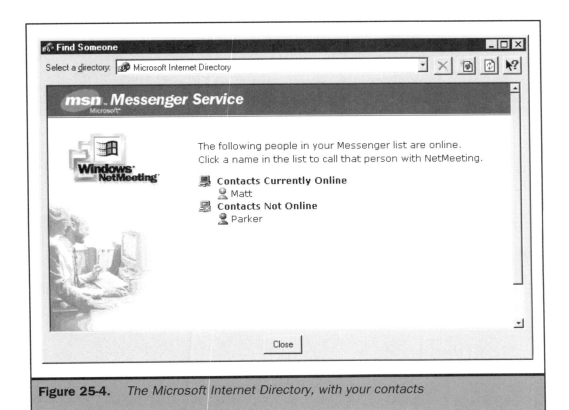

Figure 25-4.   *The Microsoft Internet Directory, with your contacts*

that the person is not in a call. A little yellow speaker icon indicates that the person can communicate via audio. A little gray camera icon means that the person can communicate via video. On the listing of people, click the column headings to sort by that column; sorting by last name or e-mail address makes finding the person you want easier.

If you want to choose a different server, click in the Select A Directory box and type the address of a different directory. However, you need to have the same directory selected in your Options dialog box as the people you want to meet with.

Making or Receiving a Call

To call someone, double-click the person's name on the directory list. If you are using Microsoft Internet Directory, then the person is contacted through MSN Messenger Service. Otherwise, NetMeeting contacts the directory server to make the connection and displays a dialog box on that person's computer screen, asking them whether they

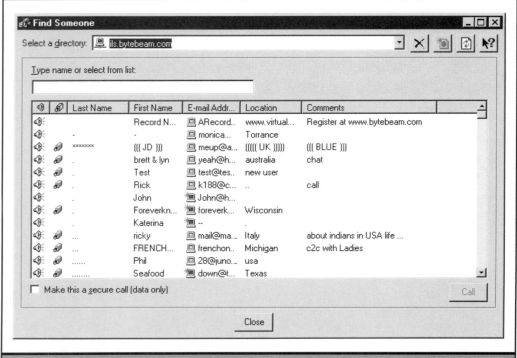

Figure 25-5.   *Clicking the Directory icon displays a listing of people connected to your directory server.*

want to connect with you. If the person accepts your call, the NetMeeting window lists the people who are in your current call, as shown in Figure 25-6.

When someone calls you, you see a dialog box asking whether you want to take the call or a message in MSN Messenger inviting you to join the meeting; click Accept in either case, if you do. You see the NetMeeting window with the callers listed.

Another way to make a call is to click the Place Call button, choose Call | New Call, or press CTRL-N. You see the New Call dialog box, as in Figure 25-7. In the Address box, type the name of the directory server to which the person is connected, followed by a slash (/) and the e-mail address of the person you want to call. If the person you are calling uses a computer with its own computer name or IP address, you can type that instead. Then click the Call button.

Once you are connected to at least one other person, click the Chat button to display a window in which you can type messages to the other people in the chat. If both of you have microphones and speakers, you can just begin talking. Speak slowly,

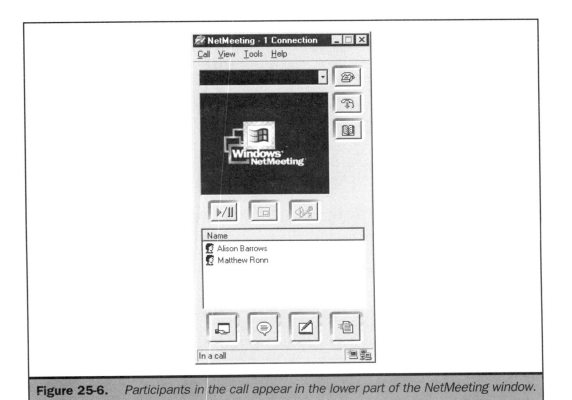

Figure 25-6.   *Participants in the call appear in the lower part of the NetMeeting window.*

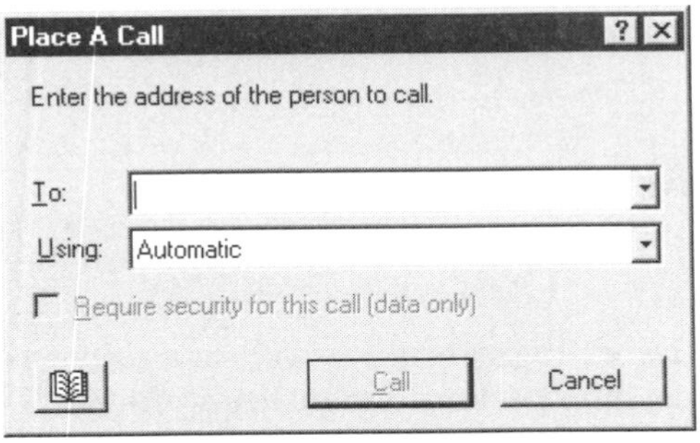

Figure 25-7.   *The Place A Call dialog box*

one at a time (as though you were using a walkie-talkie—over!). Unless you have a very fast connection, you may experience "breaking up"—the sound may be interrupted and "staticky." Keep your microphone away from the speakers, or use headphones, to avoid feedback.

If one other person in the call has a video camera connected to the computer, video of the other person appears in the NetMeeting window (see "Seeing Callers on Video").

Hanging Up

When you are done with the call, click the Hang Up button. NetMeeting maintains its connection with the directory server but disconnects from the call.

Hosting a Meeting or Joining an Existing Meeting

In addition to calls, you can communicate in *meetings*, calls that are scheduled in advance. Hosting a meeting allows you to define some properties for the meeting. To host a meeting, let everyone invited to the meeting know when the meeting will take place and how to call you using NetMeeting. At the time the meeting is scheduled to begin, choose Call | Host Meeting, and choose the options you want from the Host A Meeting dialog box, shown in Figure 25-8. When you click OK, you return to the NetMeeting window, with only you listed as a caller. When the other callers connect, you see a dialog box asking whether they can join; click Accept or Ignore.

Because you are the host of the meeting, the meeting ends when you hang up. Other participants can come and go without ending the meeting. As the host, you can also throw people out of your meeting: right-click the person's name on the list of callers and choose Remove from the menu that appears.

To join an existing meeting, call someone who is in the meeting. You see a message that the person is currently in a meeting, asking whether you want to try to join the meeting; click Yes. When the person you called leaves the meeting, you leave too, so it's best to call the person who is hosting the meeting.

If you don't want anyone else to join the meeting (or any NetMeeting call), choose Call | Do Not Disturb. Remember to choose the same command again when you want to re-enable receiving calls.

Typing Messages in a Call

During a call, you can use written words, as well as a voice (especially useful if you don't have a microphone and speakers on your computer). Click the Chat button at the bottom of the NetMeeting window; NetMeeting displays a Chat window, as in Figure 25-9. To send a message to everyone in the call, type the message in the Message box and press ENTER. To send a message to one caller, click that person's name in the Send To box, type the message in the Message box, and press ENTER.

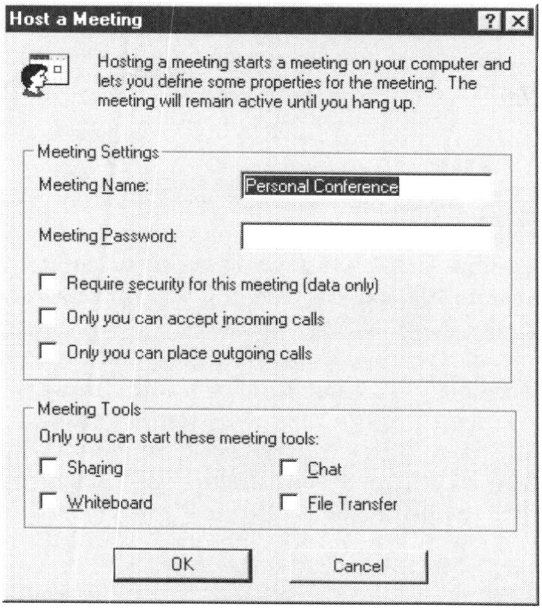

Figure 25-8.   *The Host A Meeting dialog box*

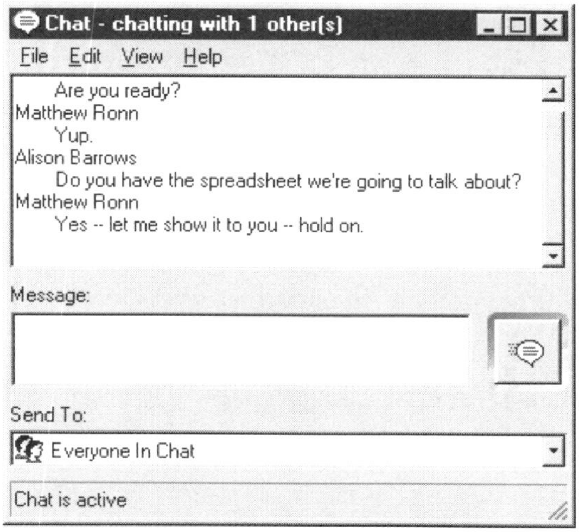

Figure 25-9.   *The Chat window in NetMeeting*

The Chat window is a good place to take notes on the call. You can save a transcript of the meeting (the typed chat part, anyway) by choosing File | Save from the Chat window's menu bar. NetMeeting saves the messages in a text file with the filename you specify. Then you can e-mail your notes to the others in your call.

Seeing Callers on Video

If other people in your call have video cameras (even if you don't have one), you can see video from one of their cameras (one at a time) in your NetMeeting window. The video appears in the Remote Video window, a small box on the right side of the window when the Current Call icon is selected. If you don't see the video, click the button at the bottom of the Remote Video window.

To set your video options, choose Tools | Options and click the Video tab. You can tell NetMeeting to enable your video camera automatically when you make a call, set the size of the video image, choose between faster low-quality video and slower high-quality video, and specify the properties of your camera. If you have a camera, be sure to light your face (or whatever the camera points at) from the front.

You can't see more than one person at a time; to switch the person in the call you can see, choose Tools | Switch Audio And Video and choose the name of the person whom you want to see.

Sharing a Whiteboard

If you and the other participants in your call want to draw diagrams or pictures that are visible by everyone in the call, use the Whiteboard feature. When you click the Whiteboard button near the bottom of the NetMeeting window, you see the Whiteboard window (shown in Figure 25-10), which works similarly to Microsoft Paint (see Chapter 5, section "Drawing Pictures Using Microsoft Paint"). When anyone in the call makes a change to the Whiteboard window, everyone in the call sees the change.

Unlike real whiteboards, the Whiteboard window can have as many pages as you want. (It's actually more like a flip chart.) To create a new page, click the Insert New Page button in the lower-right corner of the Whiteboard window. You can use the buttons to its left to switch from page to page.

If you want to take control of the whiteboard for a while, choose Tools | Lock Controls from the menu bar in the Whiteboard window. Only you can make changes to the whiteboard until you choose the command again.

When you have produced a useful drawing or diagram, you can save or print the contents of the whiteboard by choosing File | Save (or Print).

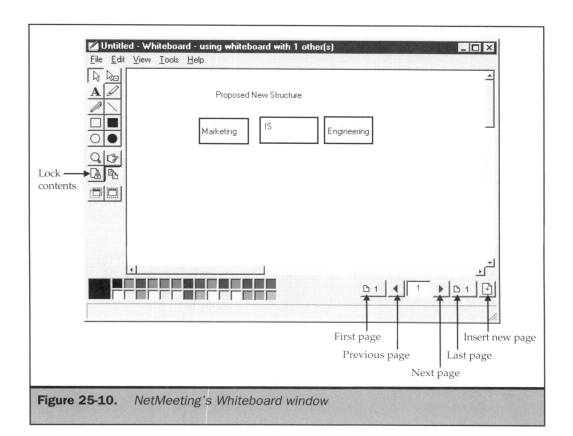

Figure 25-10. *NetMeeting's Whiteboard window*

Sending and Receiving Files

You can send files to anyone else in your call. Choose Tools | File Transfer or click the File Transfer button at the bottom of the NetMeeting window to open the File Transfer window, shown in Figure 25-11. Click the Add Files button and specify which file you want to send. Alternatively, drag the name of the file from Windows Explorer onto the File Transfer window. Click the Send All button to send the files. To send a file to one caller, rather than to everyone in the call, select the person from the drop-down list at the top right of the File Transfer window.

If someone sends you a file, NetMeeting automatically receives the file, storing it in the C:\Program Files\NetMeeting\Received Files folder. You see a window telling

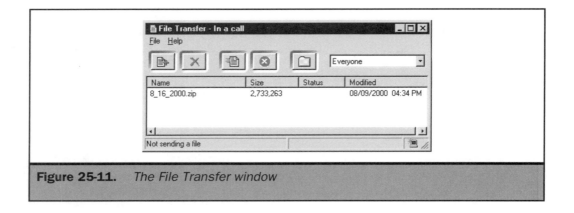

Figure 25-11.   *The File Transfer window*

you about the arrival of the file. To open the file with the default application for the type of file you received, click the Open button.

 Beware of viruses in executable files and of generally offensive material when receiving files from people you don't know.

Sharing Programs

You and the other people in your meeting can share the windows of a running program that one member has on his or her screens. For example, you could show a group around your Web site by running a browser on your machine and sharing the browser window so that the other callers can see the contents of the browser window on their screens, too.

You can also allow the other callers to control the program on your machine. For example, if you are working on a document in WordPerfect, all callers can edit the document together. Even if the other people in the call don't have the program you are using to create the file, you can give them control of your WordPerfect window to edit the file.

Letting Everyone Else See Your Program

To share a program with others in your call, run the program, click the Share button on the toolbar, and choose the program from the list that appears. Now everyone in the call can see the program, even if they don't have the program on their computers. Only you can give commands to the program.

Here are a few pointers when sharing a program:

■ Before you start to share an application, be sure to agree on a screen resolution for everyone to use. Using the same resolution as the rest of the people in the call prevents the screen from jumping around as the cursor and mouse pointer move in the shared application.

■ Others in the call can see only as much of the program's window as you can see on your screen; when you click another window that overlaps the window that is editing the file, the obscured part of the window disappears on everyone else's screen, too.

■ Unless you and everyone else in the call have fast Internet connections (faster than dial-up), displaying windows with a shared program can take a long time—a minute or two. Everyone in the call needs to wait for the shared window to appear, or everyone's screens will get hopelessly confusing. This feature works best for users connected by a high-speed LAN.

Letting Others Control a Shared Program

If you want the other callers to be able to control the shared program, you can let them. First, share the file by using the Share button; and then click the Collaborate button on the Sharing dialog box. Then, in the main NetMeeting window, right-click the name of a person you want to work in the program and click Grant Control.

A person can request control, too, by choosing Control | Request Control from the toolbar of the shared window. While another caller is controlling the shared program, the program's owner loses use of the cursor. The owner of the program can press ESC at any time to get control (and get the cursor back). Everyone else can still see the shared program's window. To stop sharing the program, so that the other callers can no longer see the program's window, click the Share button on the toolbar again, and then choose the application to stop sharing.

Here are some tips about sharing control of a program:

■ If you share Windows Explorer, all Explorer windows are shared with the other callers, including windows that you open after clicking the Share button.

■ If you are going to edit a file collaboratively, make a backup copy of the file first, just in case. When you have finished editing the file collaboratively, only the person who originally shared the file can save or print the file. If other callers want copies of the finished file, the owner of the file can send the file to the other callers.

■ Each person in the call does not need to have the program that the call is sharing; mouse clicks and keystrokes are transmitted to the program owner's computer.

Adding a NetMeeting Link to a Web Page

You can make it easy for other NetMeeting users to call you by adding a NetMeeting-compatible *callto* link on your Web page. On the Web page, create a link with the URL callto:*servername*/*emailaddress*. For example, a callto link might look like this:

```
<ahref="callto:ils.devx.com/winmetcr@gurus.com>Call me!</a>
```

Other Things NetMeeting Can Do

Here are other things that you can do with NetMeeting:

■ **See a history of calls**   Choose History from the drop-down list in the Find Someone dialog box.

■ **Omit your name from the directory server listing**   Choose Tools | Options, click the General tab, and select the Do Not List My Name In The Directory option. People can still call you by using the New Call dialog box, but they have to know your e-mail address and to which directory server you are connected.

Chapter 26

Other Internet Programs That Come with Windows Me

W orking better with the Internet was one of Microsoft's main goals in creating Windows Me, so Windows Me comes with lots of Internet-related programs. In addition to the automated sign-up software, the Internet Connection Wizard, and Dial-Up Networking (all described in Chapter 21), you get lots of Internet applications—which are described in the other chapters in this part of the book.
Windows also comes with these other useful Internet programs:

- HyperTerminal acts as a terminal emulator and lets you log in to text-based systems, either over the Internet (like telnet) or by dialing directly.

- Telnet can also do terminal emulation over the Internet, faster but not as nicely as HyperTerminal.

- FTP lets you transfer files to or from FTP servers.

This chapter describes how to use these programs. You can download other Internet programs from the Internet itself; we recommend some programs that complement those that come with Windows and suggest where to find the programs on the Web. In fact, you can use almost any Internet program that is Winsock compatible (see Chapter 21, section "What Is Winsock?").

Logging in to Text-Based Systems with HyperTerminal

HyperTerminal is Windows's built-in terminal-emulation program. It lets your powerful Windows computer—loaded with RAM, hard disk space, and other hardware—pretend to be a dumb terminal. HyperTerminal is useful for connecting to computers that are designed to talk to terminals, including UNIX shell accounts and bulletin board systems (see Chapter 21, section "UNIX Shell Accounts and Bulletin Board Systems"). The computer you connect to by using HyperTerminal is called the *remote computer* (as opposed to your own *local computer*).

Note *HyperTerminal is not automatically installed when you install Windows Me; you may need to open the Control Panel, open the Add/Remove Programs icon, click the Windows Setup tab, choose Communications from the list of components, click Details, and then select HyperTerminal from among the Communications options.*

You can use HyperTerminal in three ways:

- **Dial-up connections**   You can use HyperTerminal to call another computer over a modem and phone line. No other communications program or account is involved. You use this method when connecting directly to a bulletin board system, UNIX shell account, or other text-based system that works with terminals. You tell HyperTerminal the modem to use to make the connection, along with the country, area code, and phone number to dial.

- **Direct cable connections**   You can use HyperTerminal to connect to a computer to which your computer is connected by a cable. You tell HyperTerminal the communications port (COM1 or COM2) to which the cable is connected. Alternatively, you can use the Direct Cable Connection program (see Chapter 18, section "Connecting Two Computers with Direct Cable Connection").

- **Telnet connections**   If you have an Internet account (or other TCP/IP-based connection), you can use HyperTerminal as a Winsock-compatible *telnet* program, a terminal program that works over the Internet. First, you connect to the Internet by using Dial-Up Networking. Then, you connect to a computer over the Internet by using a HyperTerminal telnet connection—you "telnet in." For example, you can look up books at the U.S. Library of Congress by making a telnet connection to the library's mainframe system and using its text-only interface. You tell HyperTerminal to connect using TCP/IP (Winsock), along with the port number and host address of the computer to which you want to connect. The standard *port number* (a number that tells an Internet host computer whether you are connecting for e-mail, the Web, telnet, or another Internet service) is 23. The *host address* is the Internet host name of the computer you want to telnet in to; for example, the host address of the U.S. Library of Congress is **locis.loc.gov**.

To dial up and connect to a computer, HyperTerminal creates a *HyperTerminal connection*, a configuration file with the specifications for the connection. HyperTerminal connection files have the extension .ht.

Running HyperTerminal

To run HyperTerminal, choose Start | Programs | Accessories | Communications | HyperTerminal. The HyperTerminal window appears, and the Connection Description window also opens to help set up a new first HyperTerminal connection.

Configuring HyperTerminal for Your Account

The first time you run HyperTerminal, it displays the Connection Description dialog box, as shown in Figure 26-1. Or, choose File | New Connection or click the New

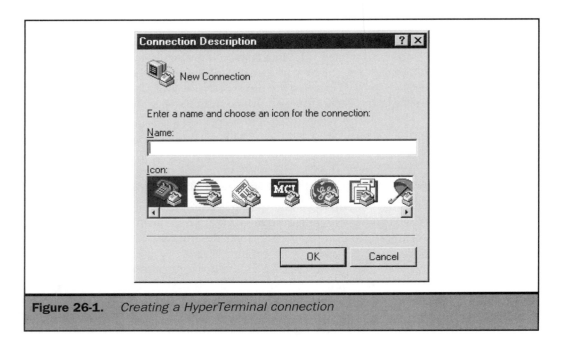

Figure 26-1.   *Creating a HyperTerminal connection*

button on the toolbar of the HyperTerminal window. When you see the Connection Description dialog box, follow these steps:

1. Type the name you want to use for the connection, choose an icon, and click OK. You see the Connect To dialog box, asking for information about how to dial the phone to connect to the computer:

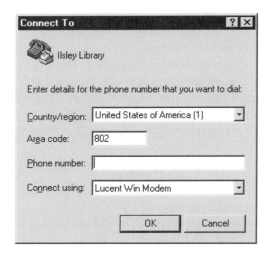

2. For a dial-up connection, set the Connect Using box to the modem to use for the connection, choose the country, type the area code, and type the phone number to dial. For a direct cable connection, set the Connect Using box to your modem or to COM1 or COM2 (the communications port to which the modem is connected). For a telnet connection, set the Connect Using box to TCP/IP (Winsock) and fill in the host address and port number.

3. Click OK. For dial-up connections, you see the Connect dialog box (for telnet connections, skip to step 6):

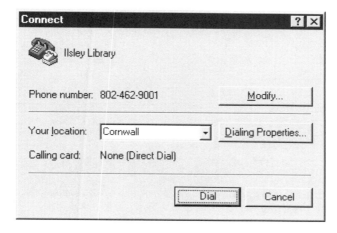

4. If you want to change your dialing location (where you are dialing from) or use a calling card, click the Dialing Properties button (see Chapter 20, section "Configuring Windows for Dialing Locations").

5. To connect, click Dial. (If you click Cancel, HyperTerminal remembers the connection information you entered, but doesn't make the connection.) For dial-up connections, HyperTerminal dials the phone. For telnet connections, if you're not already online, Dial-Up Networking displays its dialog box to get you connected to your Internet account; click Connect. When HyperTerminal has established a connection with the remote computer, you see the HyperTerminal window, shown in Figure 26-2.

6. Log in and use the remote computer, typing the commands that the remote computer requires. For example, if the remote computer displays a UNIX command line, you must type UNIX commands. You can use the scroll bar along the right side of the HyperTerminal window to see the *backscroll buffer*, which stores the last 500 lines of text that have scrolled up off the top of the terminal window (you can configure the buffer to be larger).

7. When you are done using the remote computer, log off by using the commands that it requires. HyperTerminal disconnects, too. If you have trouble getting

WINDOWS ME ON THE INTERNET

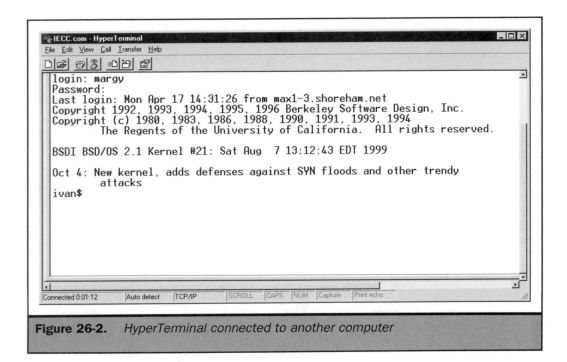

```
IECC.com - HyperTerminal                                          _ □ ×
File  Edit  View  Call  Transfer  Help

 □ ⏏  ☎ ⑧  ⏎ 🗂  ⚙

login: margy
Password:
Last login: Mon Apr 17 14:31:26 from max1-3.shoreham.net
Copyright 1992, 1993, 1994, 1995, 1996 Berkeley Software Design, Inc.
Copyright (c) 1980, 1983, 1986, 1988, 1990, 1991, 1993, 1994
         The Regents of the University of California.  All rights reserved.

BSDI BSD/OS 2.1 Kernel #21: Sat Aug  7 13:12:43 EDT 1999

Oct 4: New kernel, adds defenses against SYN floods and other trendy
        attacks
ivan$



Connected 0:01:12   Auto detect  TCP/IP     SCROLL  CAPS  NUM  Capture  Print echo
```

Figure 26-2.   *HyperTerminal connected to another computer*

disconnected, tell HyperTerminal to hang up by choosing Call | Disconnect
from the menu bar or by clicking the Disconnect icon on the toolbar.

8. When you exit HyperTerminal, it asks whether you want to save the session
(connection) you just created. Click Yes. (If you never plan to connect to this
remote computer again, click No to throw away the connection information
you entered.) HyperTerminal creates an icon for the connection in the
C:\Program Files\Accessories\HyperTerminal folder.

Connecting with HyperTerminal

You can connect to a computer for which you've already created a HyperTerminal
connection in two ways:

■ Open the C:\Program Files\Accessories\HyperTerminal folder. Then open the
icon for the connection (single-click or double-click, depending on how you
configured Windows).

■ Choose Start | Programs | Accessories | Communications | HyperTerminal.
When the HyperTerminal window appears, click Cancel to close the Connection
Description dialog box. Choose File | Open or click the Open button on the
toolbar and choose the connection.

HyperTerminal runs and displays the Connect dialog box; click Dial to make the connection. If you are using a telnet connection and you are not already connected to the Internet, Dial-Up Networking displays its window to prompt you to get online; click Connect.

When you are done using the remote computer, log off using whatever commands it requires; HyperTerminal should disconnect, too. If necessary, end the connection by choosing Call | Disconnect or by clicking the Disconnect icon on the toolbar.

Changing Information About a Connection

If the phone number for a remote computer changes or you need to change the modem (or other information about the connection), run HyperTerminal by using the connection, or choose File | Open to open the connection. Click the Properties button on the toolbar (the rightmost button) or choose File | Properties to display the connection Properties dialog box, shown in Figure 26-3. You can also display the Properties dialog box when you are using the connection. The settings on the

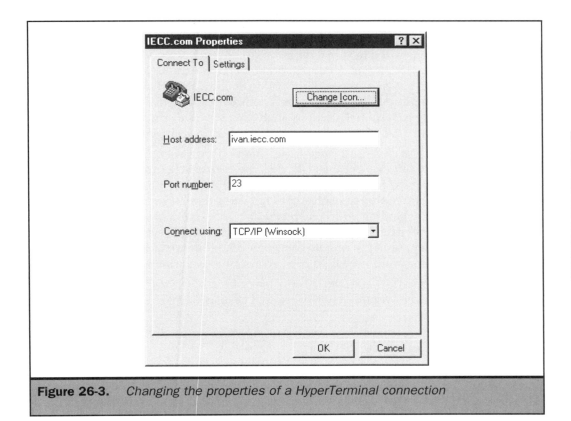

Figure 26-3.   *Changing the properties of a HyperTerminal connection*

Properties dialog box depend on the type of connection (dial-up, direct cable connection, or telnet).

In the Properties dialog box for the connection, you can set these types of options:

- **Connection method**   On the Connect To tab, you specify the icon and how to connect: via modem, via cable (connected to your modem, COM1, or COM2 port), or via TCP/IP (for a telnet connection). For dial-up connections, you also specify the phone number. For TCP/IP connections, you also specify the host address and port number (the default is 23, telnet's usual port). If you have Virtual Private Networking installed, VPN appears as an option (see Chapter 30, section "Connecting to Your Organization's LAN with Virtual Private Networking").

- **What keys do**   On the Settings tab, you specify whether the function keys, cursor motion keys, and CTRL key combinations are transmitted to the other computer or are interpreted by Windows. You can also control the actions of the BACKSPACE key.

- **Terminal emulation**   On the Settings tab, you tell HyperTerminal what type of terminal to emulate (act like). Most remote computers are configured to work with certain standard terminal types. HyperTerminal can emulate many of the most commonly used terminal types: ANSI, Minitel, TTY, Viewdata, VT100, VT100J, and VT52. If you set the Emulation box to Auto Detect, HyperTerminal tries to figure out what type of terminal to emulate, based on information from the remote computer. If you click the Terminal Setup button, you can further configure HyperTerminal's actions, including how the cursor looks, what keys on the keypad do, and whether the terminal window displays 80 or 132 columns.

- **Character set**   On the Settings tab, click the Terminal Setup button to control settings that are specific to the type of terminal that you are emulating. Click the ASCII Setup button to control the characters that HyperTerminal sends and receives, including which character(s) HyperTerminal sends at the end of each line, whether HyperTerminal displays the characters you type or waits to display them until the remote computer echoes them back, and whether HyperTerminal waits a fraction of a second after each character or line it sends.

- **Other settings**   You can specify how many lines of the text the backscroll buffer stores and whether HyperTerminal beeps when connecting and disconnecting.

Transferring Files

HyperTerminal can send files from your computer to the remote computer or receive files from the remote computer. A number of standard file transfer protocols exist;

HyperTerminal can send and receive files by using the Xmodem (regular or 1K), Kermit, Ymodem, Ymodem-G, Zmodem, and Zmodem With Crash Recovery protocols. Choose a protocol that the remote computer can also handle. If you have a choice, use Zmodem With Crash Recovery.

Sending a File to the Remote Computer

To send a file to the remote computer:

1. Connect to the remote computer. If applicable, move to the directory on the remote computer in which you want to store the file.

2. If the file transfer protocol you plan to use requires you to give a command on the remote computer to tell it to expect a file, do so. For example, when transferring a file to a UNIX system by using Xmodem, you type the command **rx** *filename* on the remote computer. When transferring a file by using Zmodem (with or without Crash Recovery), no command is required; the UNIX system can detect when the file begins to arrive, and stores it automatically.

3. Click the Send button on the toolbar or choose Transfer | Send File. You see the Send File dialog box, shown here:

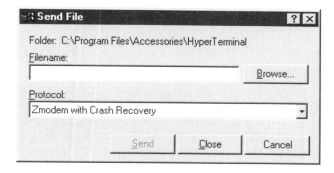

4. In the Filename box, type the name of the file you want to send or click the Browse button to select the file.

5. Set the Protocol box to a file transfer protocol that the remote computer can use when receiving files.

6. Click the Send button. You see a window displaying the status of the file transfer. How much information the window displays depends on which file transfer protocol you use. You can click the Cancel button to stop the file transfer. Click the cps/bps button to control whether you see the transfer speed in characters per second (cps) or bits per second (bps). When the window disappears, file transfer is complete.

WINDOWS ME
ON THE INTERNET

Receiving a File from the Remote Computer

To receive a file from the remote computer:

1. Connect to the remote computer. If applicable, move to the directory on the remote computer in which the file is stored.

2. Give the command on the remote computer to tell it to send the file. For example, to tell a UNIX system to transfer a file to your system by using Xmodem, you type the command **sx** *filename* on the remote computer.

3. If you are using Zmodem (with or without Crash Recovery), HyperTerminal detects that a file is arriving and begins receiving the file automatically (skip to step 8). Otherwise, click the Receive button on the toolbar or choose Transfer | Receive File. You see the Receive File dialog box:

4. In the Place Received File In The Following Folder box, type the path name of the folder into which you want to store the file or click the Browse button to change the pathname.

5. Set the Use Receiving Protocol setting to the file transfer protocol that the remote computer is using to send the file.

6. Click the Receive button.

7. For some protocols, HyperTerminal may need additional information. For example, when using Xmodem, the sending computer doesn't include the filename with the file, so HyperTerminal asks you what to name the file it receives. Type the additional information and click OK.

8. HyperTerminal displays a status window showing the progress of the file's transfer. You can click the Cancel button to stop the file transfer. Click the cps/bps button to control whether you see the transfer speed in characters per second (cps) or bits per second (bps). When the window disappears, the file transfer is complete.

Sending Text Files

You might want to send text to the other computer as though you were typing it. For example, if the remote computer asks a question to which you have an answer stored in a small text file, you can send the text file rather than retyping it—the remote computer doesn't realize that you are sending a file, and accepts the text as though you typed it. You can also send text that is displayed by some other program; for example, you might want to send a number that is displayed in your spreadsheet program.

You can send small amounts of text by using either of two methods:

- ■ **Copy-and-paste it** Display the text file in another program and copy it to the Windows Clipboard (see Chapter 7, section "What Is the Clipboard?"). In HyperTerminal, choose Edit | Paste To Host.

- ■ **Transfer it** Choose Transfer | Send Text File. When you see the Send Text File dialog box, choose the file to send. (Make sure that it's a small text file;

large files, or files that contain nontext information, rarely arrive intact.) HyperTerminal sends the contents of the file to the remote computer in the same way that it sends characters that you type.

> **Note** CTRL-C *and* CTRL-V *may not work for cut-and-paste in HyperTerminal, depending on whether these keystrokes are used by the terminal that HyperTerminal is emulating. Choose Edit | Paste To Host from the menu bar instead.*

Capturing Text from the HyperTerminal Window

If the remote computer displays interesting information in the HyperTerminal window, you may want to save it. You can use these three methods to save text:

- **Copy-and-paste it**   Select the text and choose Edit | Copy from the toolbar. You can use the scroll bar to see and select text that has already scrolled up off the top of the HyperTerminal window. HyperTerminal copies the text to the Windows Clipboard (see Chapter 7, section "What Is the Clipboard?"). You can paste this text into the Windows Notepad, WordPad, your word processing program, or any other program that accepts blocks of text.

- **Capture it**   Choose Transfer | Capture Text. When you see the Capture Text dialog box, type the folder and name of the file into which you want to store the text. (Click Browse to select the folder.) Then click Start. All the text that appears in the terminal window from this point forward is also stored in the file. To stop capturing text, choose Transfer | Capture Text | Stop. To stop temporarily, choose Transfer | Capture Text | Pause; to restart the text later and capture into the same file, choose Transfer | Capture Text | Resume. While HyperTerminal is capturing text to a file, the word Capture appears on the status bar along the bottom of the HyperTerminal window.

- **Print it**   To tell HyperTerminal to print the information as it arrives in the terminal window, choose Transfer | Capture To Printer from the menu bar. As the remote computer sends text to your computer and HyperTerminal displays it, the text is printed. To stop printing, choose Transfer | Capture To Printer again. While HyperTerminal is printing all incoming text, the message Print Echo appears on the status bar.

- **Print the whole session**   To print the entire session with the remote computer, starting at the beginning of the backscroll buffer, choose File | Print.

Other HyperTerminal Commands

Here are a few other things you can do with HyperTerminal:

- **To tell HyperTerminal to answer incoming calls**   If you are expecting a remote computer to dial into your computer, you can set your modem and HyperTerminal to answer the phone. Choose Call | Wait For A Call. The words Waiting For A Call appear on the status line. If an incoming call arrives on the phone line to which your modem is connected, your modem answers the phone, and HyperTerminal tries to connect to a computer on the other end of the phone line. To turn off auto-answer, choose Call | Stop Waiting.

- **To change the font that HyperTerminal displays in the terminal window**   Choose View | Font.
- **To set the size of the HyperTerminal window to fit the terminal window**   Choose View | Snap.

Logging in to Other Computers Using Telnet

Windows Me also comes with a Telnet program. Unlike HyperTerminal, it can connect only over the Internet; the Telnet program can't dial the phone (see "Logging in to Text-Based Systems with HyperTerminal"). If you do much telnetting, HyperTerminal is a much nicer program, because it can remember the settings for multiple host computers, transfer files, and emulate a wider variety of terminals. The only advantage of the Windows Me Telnet program is that it's faster over a LAN connection.

Running Telnet

To run Windows's built-in Telnet program:

1. Choose Start | Run, type **telnet**, and then click OK. You see the Telnet window, shown in Figure 26-4.

2. To connect to a remote computer over the Internet, choose Connect | Remote System. You see the Connect dialog box, shown next. If you want to connect to a computer that you've connected to before, the host name may appear on the File menu; if so, choose the host name from the File menu and skip to step 7.

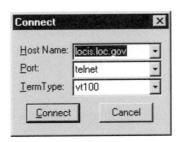

3. In the Host Name box, type the host name (host address) of the computer to which you want to connect. For example, the host name of the U.S. Library of Congress is **locis.loc.gov**. If you've connected to this host computer before, you can click the button at the right end of the Host Name box and choose the name from the drop-down list that appears.

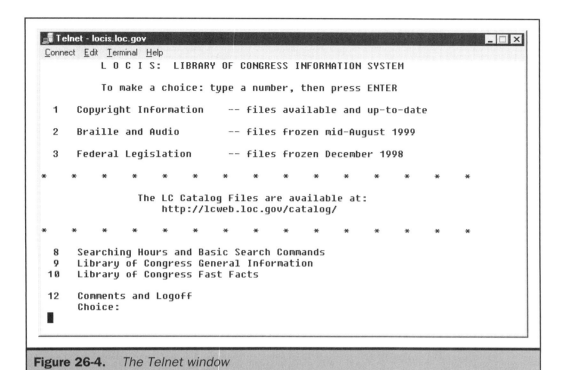

Figure 26-4.   *The Telnet window*

4. Leave the Port box set to telnet. The other options connect to the host computer using Internet services that are useful only for network debugging.

5. Set the TermType box to the string of characters to send to the remote computer, if it asks what type of terminal you are using. Note that this setting does not control the type of terminal that Telnet emulates (see "Configuring Telnet").

6. Click Connect. If your computer is not connected to the Internet, you see the Dial-Up Networking window, prompting you to connect; click the Connect button. Once you are online, Telnet connects to the remote computer. The Telnet window contains the terminal window, showing the text that you receive from the host computer, and your replies, as in Figure 26-4.

7. Log in and use the remote computer, typing the commands that the remote computer requires. You can use the scroll bar at the right side of the window to see lines of text that have scrolled up off the top edge of the window.

8. When you have finished using the remote computer, log out by using the commands that it requires. Telnet disconnects, too. If you have trouble disconnecting, choose Connect | Disconnect to tell Telnet to hang up.

WINDOWS ME
ON THE INTERNET

Configuring Telnet

You can configure the way the Telnet window looks by choosing Terminal | Preferences. You see the Terminal Preferences dialog box, shown here:

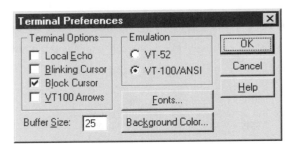

You can control the following settings:

■ **Local Echo** This option controls whether the Telnet program displays what you type or whether it waits and displays the text that the remote computer echoes back. This is turned off by default.

■ **Blinking Cursor, Block Cursor, Fonts, and Background Color** You can choose a blinking or block-style cursor (or both), and set the font and background color of the Telnet window.

■ **Emulation** You can control which terminal Telnet emulates (acts like). Telnet can emulate only two terminals: the DEC VT-100 and the DEC VT-52. (If the remote computer you want to use requires emulation of a different terminal, consider using the HyperTerminal program rather than Telnet.) If you choose to emulate a VT-100, you may also want to choose the VT100 Arrows options, so that the cursor motion keys send the same character sequences as would the same keys on a VT-100 terminal.

■ **Buffer Size** The Telnet program stores lines of text that have scrolled up off the top of the terminal window; you can choose how many lines are stored.

Other Telnet Commands

Here are other things that you can do with the Telnet program:

■ **Cut-and-paste** The Telnet program doesn't handle file transfer (if you can telnet somewhere, you may be able to use FTP), but you can cut-and-paste by using the Windows Clipboard (see Chapter 7, section "What Is the Clipboard?"). In addition to Edit | Copy (for copying selected text to the Clipboard) and Edit | Paste (for sending the Clipboard contents to the remote computer as if you had typed it), you can also use Edit | Select All to select the entire contents of the terminal window, and Edit | Copy All to copy the entire contents of the window to the Clipboard. See the next section for how to use FTP to transfer files.

- **Capturing text**   You can capture the text that appears in the Telnet window by choosing Terminal | Start Logging. Telnet asks you for the folder and name of the log file in which to store the text. If the log file already exists, Telnet deletes its previous contents and replaces them with the log of this terminal session. To stop storing the terminal text, choose Terminal | Stop Logging.

Note   CTRL-C *and* CTRL-V *don't work for cut-and-paste in Telnet. Choose Edit | Copy and Edit | Paste from the menu bar instead.*

Transferring Files Using FTP

FTP (File Transfer Protocol) is a system for transferring files over the Internet. An *FTP server* stores files, and *FTP clients* can log in to FTP servers either to upload (transfer) files to the FTP server or (more commonly) download files from the FTP server. To use FTP, you must have an FTP client program.

Most Web browsers, including Internet Explorer and Netscape Navigator, include an FTP client program that you can use to download files (see Chapter 23). Some Web browsers, including Netscape Navigator, can also let you upload files to an FTP server. However, you can also use a separate FTP client program to upload files to, or download files from, an FTP server.

Windows Me comes with a basic command-driven FTP client program called Ftp. If you plan to do much file transfer, especially uploading, you'll want a better FTP client program, such as WS_FTP (see "Downloading, Installing, and Running Other Internet Programs").

Basics of FTP

To connect to an FTP server, you specify the host name of the server (for example, **rtfm.mit.edu**), and then you log in. You have two choices:

- If you have an account on the FTP server, log in with your user name and password. You can access all the files that your user name gives you permission to use.

- If you don't have an account on the FTP server, the server may accept connections from guests. Connection without an account on the FTP server is called *anonymous FTP*. To use anonymous FTP, type **anonymous** for the user name and your own e-mail address as the password. Thousands of FTP servers on the Internet allow you to use anonymous FTP to download files, although some are so busy that it may be hard to get connected.

UNIX, the operating system of choice among Internet servers, is sensitive to the case of the names of files, unlike Windows. Be aware of capitalization in file names.

Once you are connected to an FTP server, it displays lots of messages to let you know what's going on. These messages start with three-digit numbers, which you can ignore. For example, when you have transferred a file, you see the message "226 Transfer Complete".

When you transfer a file—by either uploading or downloading—you must choose between two modes:

- **ASCII mode**   When transferring text files, use ASCII mode. Different computer systems use different characters to indicate the ends of lines. In ASCII mode, the Ftp program automatically adjusts line endings for the system to which the file is transferred.

- **Binary or Image mode**   When transferring files that consist of anything but unformatted text, use Binary mode. In Binary mode, the Ftp program does not make any changes to the contents of the file during transfer. Use Binary mode when transferring graphics files, audio files, video files, programs, or any kind of file other than plain text.

Running the Ftp Program

The Ftp program connects to an FTP server over the Internet, and then you type commands to move from directory to directory on the FTP server, upload or download files, and disconnect. Each command consists of a word that may be followed by additional information; press ENTER after typing the command line. For example, to download a file, you type **get** followed by a space and the name of the file you want to download and press ENTER. For example, to download a file named winzip80.zip, you type **get winzip80.exe** and press ENTER.

To run Windows's built-in Ftp program:

1. Choose Start | Run and type **ftp** *serverhost*, where *serverhost* is the host name of the FTP server, and click OK. If you are not connected to the Internet, you see the Dial-Up Networking window; click Connect. You see the Ftp window, shown in Figure 26-5.

2. You see a message confirming that you are connected. (Alternatively, you see a message saying that the host name is unknown or that the maximum number of connections to this host is already in use.) Then the FTP server asks for a user name and password. If you have an account on the server, type your user name, press ENTER, type your password, and press ENTER again. If you don't have an account on the server, type **anonymous**, press ENTER, type your e-mail address as the password, and press ENTER again.

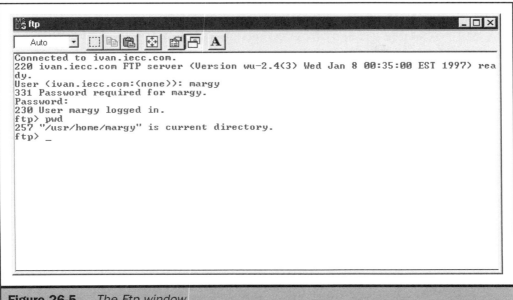

Figure 26-5.   *The Ftp window*

3. If you connect successfully to the FTP server, you see a welcome message. Some FTP servers display a long welcome message (dozens of lines long) detailing the contents of and the rules for using the FTP server. Scroll up to read the welcome message if it scrolls up off the top of the Ftp window. The program displays the prompt ftp> to ask you to type a command.

4. Once you are connected, type commands to move to the directory that contains the file you want to download or to which you want to upload a file. Then give commands to upload or download files. These commands are described in the following sections.

5. When you have finished transferring files, type **quit** or **bye** to disconnect from the FTP server. A message confirms that you have left the FTP server.

Tip   *If you want to disconnect from the FTP server and connect to a different server, you don't have to exit the Ftp program. Instead, type **close** or **disconnect** and press ENTER to disconnect from the FTP server. Next, type **open**, followed by a space and then the host name of another FTP server; then press ENTER to connect to the other server.*

Changing Directories on the FTP Server

Once you are connected to an FTP server, you must move to the directory (folder) to which you want to upload a file or from which you want to download a file. To change directories, type **cd** (for "change directory"), followed by the name of the directory to which you want to move. To find out the name of the current directory, type **pwd** (for "print working directory"). For example, you might see the following (what you type appears in boldface; what the FTP server types appears in regular type):

ftp> **pwd**
257 "/usr/home/ivan" is current directory

Each FTP server has its own directory structure. On many publicly accessible FTP servers, all the downloadable files are in a directory called pub. Here are a few tips for moving to the directory you want:

- To move to the parent directory of the current directory, type **cd ..** (that is, the cd command followed by a space and two dots).

- To move to the top-level directory on the FTP server, also called the root directory, type **cd /** (that is, the **cd** command followed by a forward slash). Most FTP servers run the UNIX operating system, which uses forward slashes in place of the backslashes used in Windows.

- You can move directly to a directory by typing its full path name, starting at the root; the full path name starts with a / to represent the root directory.

- If the FTP server runs the UNIX operating system, capitalization is important. When typing directory or filenames, be sure to use the correct capitalization—most names use lowercase letters.

Seeing What's in the FTP Server's Current Directory

To see a list of files and subdirectories in the current directory on the FTP server, type **dir**. The exact format of the listing depends on the FTP server's operating system. Figure 26-6 shows a typical listing.

If **dir** produces a long listing, you can use wildcards to limit the files and directories that are included. The wildcard character * matches any number of characters. For example, type **dir c*** to list the file and directory names that begin with C. In listings from UNIX systems, the very first character on the line indicates whether the item is a file (indicated by a -) or a directory (*d*).

You can also tell the Ftp program to store the file listing in a file on your computer. Type this command:

dir . *filename*

Mark

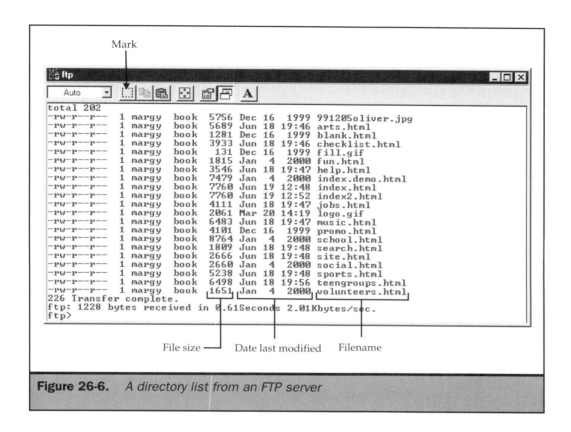

```
MS ftp                                                                    _ □ ×
  Auto        ▼   [:] 🗎 🗎  🔲  🗗🗗  A
total 202
-rw-r--r--   1 margy   book   5756 Dec 16   1999 991205oliver.jpg
-rw-r--r--   1 margy   book   5689 Jun 18 19:46 arts.html
-rw-r--r--   1 margy   book   1281 Dec 16   1999 blank.html
-rw-r--r--   1 margy   book   3933 Jun 18 19:46 checklist.html
-rw-r--r--   1 margy   book    131 Dec 16   1999 fill.gif
-rw-r--r--   1 margy   book   1815 Jan  4   2000 fun.html
-rw-r--r--   1 margy   book   3546 Jun 18 19:47 help.html
-rw-r--r--   1 margy   book   7479 Jan  4   2000 index.demo.html
-rw-r--r--   1 margy   book   7760 Jun 19 12:48 index.html
-rw-r--r--   1 margy   book   7760 Jun 19 12:52 index2.html
-rw-r--r--   1 margy   book   4111 Jun 18 19:47 jobs.html
-rw-r--r--   1 margy   book   2061 Mar 20 14:19 logo.gif
-rw-r--r--   1 margy   book   6483 Jun 18 19:47 music.html
-rw-r--r--   1 margy   book   4101 Dec 16   1999 promo.html
-rw-r--r--   1 margy   book   8764 Jan  4   2000 school.html
-rw-r--r--   1 margy   book   1809 Jun 18 19:48 search.html
-rw-r--r--   1 margy   book   2666 Jun 18 19:48 site.html
-rw-r--r--   1 margy   book   2660 Jan  4   2000 social.html
-rw-r--r--   1 margy   book   5238 Jun 18 19:48 sports.html
-rw-r--r--   1 margy   book   6498 Jun 18 19:56 teengroups.html
-rw-r--r--   1 margy   book   1651 Jan  4   2000 volunteers.html
226 Transfer complete.
ftp: 1228 bytes received in 0.61Seconds 2.01Kbytes/sec.
ftp>
```

File size ——   Date last modified   Filename

Figure 26-6.   *A directory list from an FTP server*

The dot specifies that you want a listing of the current directory. Replace *filename* with the name of the file on your own computer to which you want to store the file listing (you can type a full path name to specify which folder in which to store the file). FTP stores the file in your C:\Windows folder.

    If you want to see filenames only, with no other information, you can use the ls (list) command.

Selecting the Current Folder on Your Computer

Before you upload or download files, set the *current local directory*, the currently selected folder on your computer. This is the folder from which FTP can upload files and to which it can download files.

To change the current local directory, type **lcd** (local directory), followed by the name of the folder on your computer. If the path name of the folder contains spaces, enclose the path name in quotes. To move to the parent folder of the current folder, type **lcd ..** (the lcd command followed by a space and two dots).

For example, this command changes the current local directory to C:\My Documents:

ftp> **lcd "C:\My Documents"**
Local directory now C:\My Documents

To see what's in the current local directory, use Windows Explorer.

Uploading Files

You use the put command to upload the files. To upload a group of files, you can use the mput command.

You can upload files only if you have write permission in the directory on the FTP server. Most anonymous FTP servers don't accept uploads, or they accept them into only one specific directory. Read the welcome message to find out the rules for the FTP server you are using.

To upload a file, follow these steps:

1. Connect to the FTP server, move to the directory on the FTP server in which you want to store the file, and set the current local directory to the folder on your computer that contains the files you want to upload.

2. If the file or files you want to upload contain anything but unformatted ASCII text, type **binary** to select Binary mode (see "Basics of FTP"). To switch back to ASCII mode to transfer text files, type **ascii**. Type **put**, a space, the filename on your computer, a space, and the filename to use on the FTP server. Then press ENTER. For example, to upload a file named draft13.doc and call the uploaded version report.doc, you would type **put draft13.doc report.doc**.

3. You see a series of messages; the message Transfer Complete appears when the file transfer is done.

If a file with the name that you specify already exists on the FTP server, the put command may overwrite the existing file with the uploaded file.

4. If you want to check that the file is really on the FTP server, type **dir** to see a listing of files in the current directory.

You can copy a group of files to the FTP server by typing **mput** (multiple put). Type **mput**, followed by a wildcard pattern that matches the names of the files you want to upload. The pattern * indicates that all files in the current directory on your computer should be copied. For example, to upload all the files with the extension .html, you would type **mput *.html**. As it copies the files, mput asks you about each file. Type **y** to upload the file or **n** to skip it.

 If you don't want mput to ask you about each file before uploading it, type the prompt command first before giving the mput command. The prompt command turns off filename prompting.

Downloading Files

To download files from the FTP server to your computer, follow these steps:

1. Connect to the FTP server, move to the directory on the FTP server that contains the file that you want to download, and set the current local directory to the folder on your computer in which you want to store the files you download (see "Changing Directories on the FTP Server," earlier in the chapter).

2. If the file or files you want to download contain anything but unformatted ASCII text, type **binary** to select Binary mode (see "Basics of FTP"). To switch back to ASCII mode to transfer text files, type **ascii**.

3. Type **get**, a space, the filename on the FTP server, a space, and the filename to use on your computer. Then press ENTER. (You can't use filenames with spaces.) For example, to download a file named bud9812.doc and call the downloaded version budget.dec1998.doc, the command is **get bud9812.doc budget.dec1998.doc**.

4. You see a series of messages; the message Transfer Complete appears when the file transfer is done. To interrupt the file transfer, press CTRL-C. Sometimes that doesn't work, and the only way to interrupt the transfer is to close the FTP window.

5. If you want to check whether the file is really downloaded, use Windows Explorer to see a listing of files on your computer.

You can copy a group of files to the FTP server by typing **mget**, followed by a wildcard pattern that matches the names of the files that you want to download. The pattern * means that all files in the current directory on your computer should be copied. For example, to download all the files whose names start with *d*, you would type **mget d***. As it copies the files, mget asks you about each file. Type **y** to download the files or **n** to skip it.

 If you download a nontext file that is unusable, you probably forgot to issue the binary command before downloading the file.

Listing of Ftp Commands

Table 26-1 lists all the commands you can use with the Ftp program.

Command	Description
!	Runs a DOS command shell and displays a DOS prompt. You can type DOS commands, such as **dir**, which displays the contents of a folder (see Chapter 38). To exit from DOS and see the ftp> prompt again, type **exit**.
?	Displays a list of the commands that Ftp can perform (that is, the commands in this table).
Append	Uploads a file and appends it to an existing file. Type **append**, the name of the file on your computer that you want to upload, and then the name of the file on the FTP server to which you want to append the file.
Ascii	Transfers files in ASCII mode (used for text files).
Bell	Turns *bell mode* on or off; when bell mode is on, Ftp beeps whenever it completes a command.
Binary	Transfers files in Binary or Image mode (used for all files except text files).
Bye	Disconnects from the FTP server and exits the Ftp program.
cd *dir*	Changes to the *dir* directory on the FTP server. If you omit the *dir*, Ftp says Remote Directory and waits for you to type the directory name and press ENTER.
Close	Disconnects from the FTP server, without exiting the Ftp program.
Debug	Turns on and off debugging mode (which displays more information about what Ftp is doing).
delete *name*	Deletes the file *name* on the FTP server. If you omit the *name*, Ftp says Remote File and waits for you to type the filename and press ENTER. Most publicly accessible FTP servers don't let you delete files.

Table 26-1. *Listing of Ftp Commands*

Command	Description
dir *pat*	Lists the files in the current directory on the FTP server that match the wildcard pattern *pat*, with full information about the files. Omit *pat* to list all the files.
Disconnect	Disconnects from the FTP server, without exiting the Ftp program.
get *old new*	Downloads the file *old* to your computer and names it *new*. Omit *new* to use the same name.
Glob	Turns on and off metacharacter expansion of local filenames. When on, the Ftp program replaces wildcard patterns with the list of filenames they match. When off, Ftp passes wildcard patterns along to the FTP server.
Hash	Turns on and off hash mode (in which Ftp displays a # for each block transferred).
Help	Displays a list of the commands that Ftp can perform (that is, the commands in this table). Type the **help** *command* to get a short description of that *command*.
lcd *dir*	Changes to the folder *dir* on your computer.
literal *command*	Sends a command to the FTP server that the Windows Ftp program doesn't support. Type **literal**, followed by a space and the command you want to send.
ls *pat*	Lists only the filenames of the files in the current directory on the FTP server that match the wildcard pattern *pat*. Omit *pat* to list all the files.
mdelete *pat*	Deletes the files that match the wildcard pattern *pat* on the FTP server.
mget *pat*	Downloads the files to your computer that match the wildcard pattern *pat*.
mkdir *dir*	Creates a directory named *dir* on the FTP server (assuming that you have permission to do so).
mls *dir filename*	Stores a listing of the contents of the *dir* directory on the FTP server, and all of its subdirectories, in the file *filename* on your computer. Type * as *dir* to list all files.

Table 26-1.   *Listing of Ftp Commands* (continued)

Command	Description
mput *pat*	Uploads the files to the FTP server that match the wildcard pattern *pat*.
open *hostname*	Connects to the FTP server named *hostname*.
Prompt	Turns on or off filename prompting for mput and mget commands. When prompting is on, Ftp asks before transferring each file.
put *old new*	Uploads the file *old* to the FTP server and names it *new*. Omit *new* to use the same name.
Pwd	Displays the current directory on the FTP server.
Quit	Disconnects from the FTP server and exits the Ftp program.
quote *command*	Sends a command to the FTP server that the Windows Me Ftp program doesn't support. Type **quote**, followed by a space and the command you want to send.
recv *old new*	Downloads the file *old* to your computer and names it *new*. Omit *new* to use the same name.
remotehelp *command*	Displays the help information provided by the FTP server. Omit *command* to see a list of the commands the FTP server supports.
rename *old new*	Renames the file named *old* on the FTP server, using the filename *new* (assuming that you have permission to do so).
rmdir *dir*	Deletes the directory *dir* on the FTP server (assuming that you have permission to do so).
send *old new*	Uploads the file *old* to the FTP server and names it *new*. Omit *new* to use the same name.
Status	Displays the status of the Ftp program, including the name of the FTP server to which you are connected, the file transfer mode (ASCII or Binary), and the bell mode.
Trace	Turns packet tracing on and off.

Table 26-1.   *Listing of Ftp Commands* (continued)

Command	Description
type *transfertype*	Sets the transfer type (see "Basics of FTP"). *Transfertype* must be ascii, binary, or image.
user *name password*	Logs in to the FTP server using a different user name. If you omit *name* and *password*, Ftp prompts you for them.
Verbose	Turns verbose mode on and off. When verbose mode is off, Ftp displays fewer messages.

Table 26-1.   *Listing of Ftp Commands* (continued)

Other Ftp Tips

Here are other things you can do with the Ftp program:

- You can select a block of text and copy it to the Windows Clipboard (see Chapter 7, section "What Is the Clipboard?"). Click the Mark button on the toolbar (the dotted box button), select the block of text to copy, and then click the Copy button (to the right of the Mark button). These commands are also available by clicking the System Menu button (the MS-DOS icon in the upper-left corner of the Ftp window) and choosing Edit | Mark or Edit | Copy from the drop-down menu.

- You can paste text from the Clipboard into the Ftp window; if the text isn't an Ftp command or filename, Ftp will probably get confused. Click the Paste button on the toolbar (the button showing a clipboard), or click the System Menu button and choose Edit | Paste from the system menu.

- You can change the size of the Ftp window and the font it displays. To maximize the Ftp window, click the Full Screen button on the toolbar (the button with four red arrows). To return to running Ftp in a window, press ALT-ENTER. To choose a font size, click the Font box (the leftmost item on the toolbar) and choose the size you want; sizes are shown in pixels. Alternatively, you can click the Font button (the rightmost button on the toolbar) to choose the font size and style.

- You can change other properties of the Ftp program by clicking the Properties button on the toolbar (the third button from the right). See Chapter 38 for a description of the properties of DOS programs.

WINDOWS ME
ON THE INTERNET

Downloading, Installing, and Running Other Internet Programs

Once you have established a Dial-Up Networking connection to the Internet, you can run any Winsock-compatible program (see Chapter 21, section "What Is Winsock?"). Although Windows comes with some good Internet applications, you can supplement (or replace) them with other programs. For example, the Ftp program that comes with Windows is not particularly powerful or easy to use; we vastly prefer the excellent shareware WS_FTP program, which shows you the contents of the local and remote directories, and lets you transfer files by clicking buttons rather than typing commands. (Read on to find out how to get it.)

Where to Get Internet Programs

Lots of Winsock-compatible Internet programs are available for downloading from the Internet itself. Some are *freeware* programs that are entirely free to use; some are *shareware* programs that require you to register the program if you decide that you like it; some are demo programs that let you try a partially disabled version of the program before you decide whether to buy the real program; and some are commercial programs that ask you to pay before downloading.

Many Web-based libraries offer all types of programs. Here are our favorites:

- **The Ultimate Collection of Windows Software (TUCOWS)** at **http://www.tucows.com**   Classifies programs by operating system and type. It has lots of mirror sites (identical Web sites) all over the globe, so it's rarely a problem to begin downloading even very popular programs. It's particularly easy to browse a long list of programs of a given type (browsers, or e-mail programs, for example) and compare reviews.

- **The CWApps List** at **http://cws.internet.com**   The original Winsock library, and it is still excellent. Forrest Stroud set up this site when shareware and freeware Internet software were just starting to become available.

- **Shareware.com** at **http://www.shareware.com**   Offers lots of non-Internet-related programs.

- **Download.com** at **http://download.cnet.com**   Has thousands of downloadable programs organized by category.

Installing and Running Internet Programs

Once you've downloaded a program from the Internet, it's a good idea to check it for *viruses*, self-replicating programs that may infect other programs on your computer. Windows doesn't come with a virus checker, but you can download a good one from any of the software libraries in the preceding section (see Chapter 31, section

"Preventing Infection by Viruses"). We like McAfee's and Symantec's Norton antivirus programs, too (commercial software downloadable from McAfee's Web site at **http://www.mcafee.com** and Symantec's Web site at **http://www.symantec.com/nav/**).

Most downloaded programs arrive as self-installing files; in Windows Explorer, run the file you downloaded. The program usually installs itself, asking you configuration questions along the way. Most programs either add themselves to the Start | Programs menu or add an icon to the desktop (or both). Other downloaded programs arrive in ZIP (compressed) files, which the Windows compressed folders feature can uncompress (see Chapter 9, section "Working with Compressed Folders").

The first time you run a program, you might need to configure it further; check any documentation files that are installed along with the program. Look for a Tools | Options command or an Edit | Preferences command; these usually display configuration or preference dialog boxes.

WINDOWS ME
ON THE INTERNET

The Complete Reference

Windows
Me

Part V

Networking with Windows Me

Chapter 27

Designing a Windows-Based Local Area Network

653

I f you have more than one computer, you should consider connecting them with a *local area network (LAN)*. Windows Me provides all the features needed to connect your computer to a LAN—no other software is needed.

This chapter introduces the basic concepts of LANs, including what a network is and why you might want one and the two major kinds of networks. When designing a LAN, you must choose a networking technology (Token Ring or Ethernet), and then a cabling topology (star or bus). These choices dictate your choice of hardware, including network interface cards and cabling, which you have to install.

This chapter provides the background for the specifics covered in the rest of the chapters in Part V, which cover configuring Windows for a LAN (Chapter 28), sharing disks and printers (Chapter 29), sharing an Internet connection (Chapter 30), and LAN security (Chapter 31).

> **Note** *This chapter covers setting up your network from scratch. However, if you are adding a Windows Me computer to an existing Windows-based peer-to-peer network or upgrading a computer on a network from an earlier version of Windows to Windows Me, the steps you need to follow are also found in this chapter (see the sidebars on "Adding to an Existing Network" and "Upgrading a Computer on an Existing Network").*

What Is a Network and Why Would You Need One?

A *network* provides a connection between computing resources, a way to share hardware and files, and a paperless way to communicate. A local area network (LAN) is a network limited to one building or group of buildings, in which the computers are usually connected by cables. A LAN can be as useful in a small office of two or three computers as it is in a large office. Each computer attached to a network is called a *node*.

Larger networks also exist. *Wide area networks (WANs)* connect computers that are geographically dispersed, and the *Internet* (see Chapter 21)—the biggest network of them all—is a worldwide network of interconnected networks.

Sharing Hardware

Without a network, each *resource* (hard disk, CD-ROM drive, printer, or other device) is connected to only one computer (printers may be an exception if you have a switch box). Examples of resources in your office may include a hard drive on which the company's main database is stored, the color printer everyone wants to use, and the tape drive on which nightly backups are made. Without a network, you can use a resource only from the computer to which the resource is attached. With a network, anyone using a computer attached to the network can print to the color printer or open the database, and the computer with the tape drive can access all the hard disks on various machines that need to be backed up. You might also want to share more specialized devices, such as CD-ROM writers, Zip drives, and tape drives.

The cheapest way to share resources is what some techie types call *sneakernet*—take a floppy disk, copy the file you need to print or share, and walk over (hence, *sneaker*) to the computer with the printer or the person who needs to use the file. But sneakernet isn't very efficient—in the long run you save time and hassle (which of those 12 floppies has the current version of that file?) with a network. If you have a small office, using a network and only one printer—to which everyone can print—is more cost effective.

Sharing Files

If you want to share files without the danger of creating multiple versions, you need a network, so every person who accesses the file uses the same copy. Some software (notably database software) enables multiple users to use one file at the same time. Other software warns you when a file is being used by someone else on the network and may even notify you when the file is available for your use.

When you work with large files that are too large to fit on a floppy disk, moving them to other computers is cumbersome without a network.

Communicating on the Network

A network enables you to communicate electronically. Applications like e-mail and WinPopup provide a way to disseminate information around the office without wasting paper (see Chapter 29, section "Communicating over the LAN by Using WinPopup"). In addition, if you travel, you can use Dial-Up Networking to dial in to your network and use the resources there, even when you are out of town.

Sharing an Internet Connection

If everyone on the network needs to access the Internet—to send and receive e-mail, browse the Web, or other Internet applications—it's silly for each computer to have its own modem, phone line, and Internet account. Instead, one computer on the LAN can have a fast modem (perhaps a DSL or cable modem, or an even faster phone line). This computer can serve as the gateway to the Internet. Or, you can use a specialized device called a *router*, which connects a LAN to the Internet over one or more phone lines.

Chapter 30 describes how to use Windows Me's Internet Connection Sharing (or third-party programs) to connect a LAN to the Internet.

What Types of Networks Exist?

Networks are either peer-to-peer and client-server. We describe these two types in the next two sections.

Understanding either kind of network requires having at least a passing familiarity with two terms: client and server. A *client* is a computer that uses resources on the network. A *printer client*, for instance, is a computer that uses a network printer. A *server* is a computer (or a device with a computer hidden inside) that has resources used by other devices on the network. For instance, a *file server* is a computer that stores files used by other computers; a *print server* is a computer with a printer attached to it—the print server lets other computers on the network send print jobs to the printer. The server makes a resource available to the network, and a client uses the resource.

Peer-to-Peer Networks

In a *peer-to-peer network*, as the term implies, all computers start out equal. All computers can function as both clients and servers. Security and permissions are administered from each computer in the network. Each computer in a peer-to-peer network can both request resources from other computers and share its own resources with other computers in the network. You can also configure the network so that some computers only share their resources and others only use resources. Even in this situation, however, the network is still a peer-to-peer network because each computer on the network is administered individually.

A peer-to-peer network is relatively easy to set up—any small office with more than one computer can create a small peer-to-peer network by using Windows to share printers and files and exchange e-mail. Only a small amount of hardware is required. The rest of this explains how to choose, install, and configure the hardware to create a peer-to-peer network, and Chapter 28 describes how to connect to a peer-to-peer LAN using Windows.

Client-Server Networks

In a *client-server network*, server computers provide resources for the rest of the network, and client computers (also called *workstations*) only use these resources. No one uses the server computers as workstations; they are *dedicated servers*. For instance, a file server is used to store files shared on the network. Client computers use the files on this file server by running, opening, changing, saving, or deleting these files.

Client-server networks typically are more difficult and expensive to set up and administer than peer-to-peer networks, but they also have many advantages: they can handle more computers, they provide more-sophisticated administration and security options, and all resources are managed centrally on dedicated servers. Client-server networks require a *network operating system* (NOS)—Windows 2000 Server, Windows NT, Novell Netware, Linux, and UNIX are common NOSs—as well as a greater initial outlay of time and money for setup and equipment and a network administrator to create and maintain user IDs and permissions.

Table 27-1 lists differences between peer-to-peer and client-server networks. To set up your Windows computer on an already-existing Novell or Windows NT network, contact your LAN administrator.

	Peer-to-Peer	**Client/Server**
Size	Good for small networks (under 12 computers, depending on the uses for the network). Keeping track of available resources and passwords for each resource becomes difficult on a large peer-to-peer network.	Good for medium-to-large networks. Because administration of network resources is central, the user can use all available resources with only one password (more passwords may be necessary if the network has more than one server).
Hardware	No dedicated file server is needed.	At least one computer must be a dedicated file server.
Operating system	Windows Me, 98, or 95 will do.	Requires a network operating system (NOS).
Administrator training	Little training for users to administer their own computers' resources for all users on the network.	System administrator must be trained.
Resource control	Each computer's user has full control of that computer's resources.	The system administrator is in control of shared resources.
Resource administration	Administered by the owner of each workstation.	Administered by network administrator.
Resource security	Password is assigned to each resource.	Password is assigned to each user of a server. Each user is given permission to use certain resources by the network administrator.

Table 27-1.   *Differences Between Peer-to-Peer and Client-Server Networks*

	Peer-to-Peer	**Client/Server**
Security administration	Permissions are granted by the owner of each computer.	Only one password per user is required for the use of the resources associated with one server. Security is administered by a network administrator.

Table 27-1. *Differences Between Peer-to-Peer and Client-Server Networks* (continued)

What Do You Need to Do?

Setting up a network consists of four major tasks:

- Choosing the network technology (the type of cabling, cable connections, and adapter cards for your computers). These choices are described in the next few sections of this chapter.

- Choosing and buying the hardware (see "Buying Network Hardware").

- Installing the hardware (see "Installing Your Network Hardware").

- Configuring Windows to use the network (see Chapter 28).

While you needn't be a network engineer to set up a small peer-to-peer network, you do need to have some knowledge about your computer. Ideally, you:

- **Have some experience installing hardware**   You need to install a *network interface card* (NIC) in each computer that will be on the LAN (unless the NIC has already been installed).

- **Are comfortable using Windows Explorer to browse more than one disk**   You need to find the other computers on the LAN using Windows Explorer (see Chapter 8, section "What Is Windows Explorer?")

- **Are comfortable with dialog boxes with multiple tabs and options in dialog boxes**   You plan to use the Network dialog box extensively, which has a lot of different kinds of options.

If you feel the preceding statements don't describe you, you might want to hire someone to install your hardware and configure your network. Make sure you tell the installer what type of network you're expecting—a peer-to-peer network run by your Windows operating system. Otherwise—read on.

Adding to an Existing Network

If you're adding a computer to an existing network, you can skip the sections regarding choosing a network technology and a topology—someone has already made those choices for you. Find out what technology is in use on your network, and then buy the appropriate NIC for the computer you want to add to the network. Also, if no leftover cable is on hand, buy the correct kind of cable for your network. Once you've done these things, you can dive into the section "Installing Your Network Hardware" later in this chapter.

Upgrading a Computer on an Existing Network

If you are upgrading the operating system of a computer on an existing network from an earlier version of Windows to Windows Me, you may find your network works right away—open the My Network Places icon on the desktop to see whether other computers on the network appear. If the network doesn't appear to be working, skip ahead to Chapter 28.

Choosing a Cabling Technology for Your Network

Before you buy hardware for your network, you need to decide which standard you want to use to connect your network. The network interface cards and cabling you choose must support the standard you choose.

Two network standards are commonly used: Token Ring and Ethernet. Newer Ethernet- based wireless networking devices are coming on the market, too. These are still slower than cabled networks, though, and most are so new, the kinks have yet to be worked out.

Ethernet

Ethernet is a contention-based technology, which means you have no control over which computers are allowed to send information over the network. This results in data collisions when two computers try to send information over the cables at the same time (data *contends* with other data when it collides). When two devices talk at exactly the same time, none of the data gets to where it's supposed to go—both computers retransmit the data after a random interval, so the information gets through fine after this delay. Data contention can slow down a busy network, so Ethernet networks top out a little below their nominal fastest speed.

Using Ethernet technology is cheaper than Token Ring technology because Ethernet technology doesn't have a device controlling when a computer can begin to transmit. But when an Ethernet network has many users, lots of data collisions can lead to delays; overloaded Ethernet networks with many users can be slow. Ethernet is perfect for small or medium-sized offices and home offices. Ethernet network interface boards are relatively cheap and are also available as PC Cards that fit most laptops.

There are two speeds of Ethernet. Original Ethernet has a speed of 10 Mbps (megabits/second). "New" Ethernet, called *Fast Ethernet*, has a speed of 100 Mbps. An even faster version, *Gigabit Ethernet*, is on the horizon and is intended to transmit data at a maximum speed of 1 Gbps (gigabits/second), or ten times the Fast Ethernet standard.

Wireless network adapters are also available, allowing your computers to communicate using a slower Ethernet-based protocol over radio waves, so you don't need strong cables between your computers. Some wireless network adapters actually do use wires—they send data over the power or phone wires in the walls of your house.

Token Ring

With *Token Ring* technology, data transmission is controlled by means of a *token* (an electronic marker), which is passed around the ring of computers that make up the network. Only the machine with the token can transmit data. Once the data is transmitted and received, the token is passed to the next computer on the ring. There is no contention on a Token Ring network, because each computer has its turn to transmit, and no other computer is transmitting at that time.

Token Ring networks can operate at speeds of 4 Mbps (oldest standard) to 16 Mbps (current standard). A 100 Mbps standard is in the works. Token Ring networks don't slow down much as more computers are added to the network—the token takes longer to get around the ring, but actual transmission always occurs at the standard rate.

Buying the hardware needed for a Token Ring network is much more expensive than the equivalent Ethernet hardware, or even than faster Ethernet hardware. Currently, Token Ring network interface cards can be five to eight times more expensive than Ethernet cards, and an additional piece of hardware called a *MAU* (*multiple access unit*) is also needed. On the other hand, Token Ring is a reliable technology. It was developed by IBM and is found most often at companies that have (or had) IBM mainframe installations. Because switching from Token Ring to Ethernet usually requires new cabling, Token Ring hardware is still found in offices where it would be too expensive to rewire the building.

How to Choose

The standard you choose determines the hardware you buy. Each standard has advantages and disadvantages. However, if you are starting a network from scratch, you should choose the cheaper and more common Ethernet or Fast Ethernet. Most users choose Token Ring hardware only if they are adding to an existing Token Ring network.

From here on, this chapter assumes you are setting up an Ethernet network. Ethernet is the most common network standard, and the cheapest and easiest to set up in a small office. However, the steps outlined here don't differ much for setting up a Token Ring network. The major difference is you would need to buy network interface cards and cabling that work with the Token Ring standard.

Choosing a Network Topology

The *topology* of a network determines the pattern of cabling you use to connect the computers. The topology usually also determines the type of cable you use. Because NICs must provide the correct connection for the chosen type of cable, you must choose the topology before you buy NICs (although you can buy NICs that support both types of cable). So you must choose the network topology before shopping for hardware.

You can cable an Ethernet network in two traditional ways—bus and star topology—and one new way—wireless.

Bus Topology

In a *bus topology* network, the *bus* is the main cable to which all the other computers are attached. (Communication within a computer also happens along a bus.) A *coaxial cable* (or *coax*) cable is connected from one computer to the next, in a long line, until all computers are connected. Figure 27-1 shows a diagram of a network using bus topology.

The bus topology uses the least amount of cable and the least amount of hardware, because no hub is required. Another advantage of bus topology is this configuration makes keeping track of the cabling in the network relatively easy.

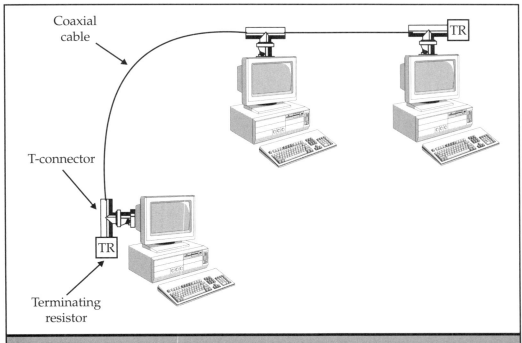

Figure 27-1.   *Bus topology (with coaxial cable)*

Bus topology does have disadvantages. It can be awkward to move computers—you might need new cables if the original cables aren't long enough. You may even have to reroute cables entirely to re-create the bus configuration. The bus topology is vulnerable—if the LAN cable is unhooked in the middle, all the computers lose their network connection (the network works fine if computers are turned off). Similarly, if one piece of cable in the network is bad, many computers on the network can be affected (depending on the position in the bus of the bad cable). Troubleshooting a hardware problem with a network that uses bus topology can be more difficult than troubleshooting a network that uses star topology. This is because the problem can be harder to pinpoint. Unless you're adding computers to an existing small bus topology network, we recommend you use a star topology.

Star Topology

In a *star topology* network, each computer is connected by a cable to a *hub*, the computer in the center of the star. One end of the cable plugs into a computer's network interface card, and the other end plugs into the hub, which provides a central connection point for the network cabling. Hubs come in different sizes (with different numbers of ports), and more advanced hubs can correct signal errors and amplify signals. The cable used in Ethernet star topology is *unshielded twisted-pair* (also called *Category-5* or *Cat-5*). Figure 27-2 shows a diagram of a network using star topology.

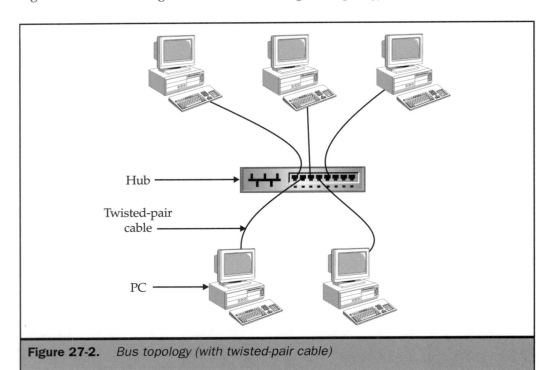

Figure 27-2.   *Bus topology (with twisted-pair cable)*

Medium and large networks often use a star topology. This configuration uses more cable and more hardware than a bus topology network, but it's easier to manage and less likely to fail. Star topology is easy to set up, and the network is easier to troubleshoot than a bus network because a damaged cable affects only one computer.

On the downside, twisted-pair cable is usually more expensive than coax. Star topology requires much more cable and a hub, all of which results in a bigger bill for the network, although NICs for star topology are less expensive than for bus topology or dual-mode. Generally, the difference in price is worth avoiding the inconvenience of trying to pinpoint a hardware problem in a large network.

You can also use hybrid networks, such as a set of hubs connected by a bus, which can minimize the amount of star cabling necessary.

Wireless LANs

In a *wireless LAN*, each computer has a wireless network adapter, allowing the computers to communicate via radio waves over the AC power wires in your walls, or over phone wires. Wireless LAN adapters enable you to put computers as far as 300 feet away from each other, depending on what walls and furniture are between them. The adapters include scrambling or encryption to prevent other computers from listening in on your data transmissions or adding themselves to your LAN.

A wireless LAN looks like a star topology LAN, but without the cable. The LAN includes one *access point* as the hub of the star. The access point connects to one computer on the LAN and contains a radio transceiver, hardware and software for communications and encryption, and a cable connection that lets you connect it to a cabled LAN, if you have one. The rest of the computers on the LAN have wireless LAN adapters that contain a radio transceiver, which communicates with the access point.

Two standards for wireless LANS—*IEEE 802.11b* and *Wi-Fi*—exist to ensure that wireless adapters from different manufacturers can communicate with each other. IEEE 802.11b networks can communicate at 11 Mbps, as fast as slower cabled networks. For more information about these standards, see **http://www.wirelessethernet.com**. *HomeRF* is another standard based on IEEE 802.11b, but it is limited to home rather than business networks (see **http://www.homerf.org**).

Buying Network Hardware

You need the following hardware to set up your Ethernet network:

- A NIC or *network adapter* for each computer in the network.

- A connection among all the computers, most commonly, copper wires, but can also be fiber-optic cable, infrared, radio waves, or a mixture. The amount and type of cable you need depends on the topology you choose for your network.

- A hub (if you choose star topology).

This hardware is not expensive to install—often less than $50 per PC on the network.

A client-server network is more expensive because it requires at least one computer to be a dedicated server.

 If you are creating a small network, you may be able to buy a network kit with all the hardware you need to set up a small network: network interface cards, cable, and a hub. Check at your local Staples or OfficeMax (or a similar store).

Buying Network Interface Cards

When you shop for your NICs, choose cards that:

- Match the type you've chosen for your network—Ethernet, Fast Ethernet, or Token Ring.
- Fit the cable you are using—coaxial cable, twisted-pair cable, or wireless.
- Fit the computer you buy it for—computers with PCI, ISA, PC Card, or other slots. If a computer doesn't have any available slots, consider a USB or parallel-port based network adapter, if either of those ports is free. Contact your computer's manufacturer if you're not sure.
- Match the speed you chose for your LAN—the two most common speeds for network adapters are 10 Mbps and 100 Mbps.

All the network interface cards in each computer in the network must support the same standard—in an Ethernet network, for instance, all network interface cards must be Ethernet cards. Decide whether you want a speed of 10 Mbps or 100 Mbps (or a newer standard) and buy cards that are all the same speed (most people base their decision on price).

Check that each card you chose fits the cable you are using. If you are using star topology and twisted-pair cable, choose a card that has an *RJ-45 connector*, which looks like a large phone jack. If you have chosen bus topology and coaxial cable, choose a card that has a *BNC connector*, which looks like a sturdier version of a cable TV connector. Some cards have more than one type of connector. If you are planning a wireless LAN, all the computers on the LAN must use the same time of wireless LAN adapter—don't mix different wireless LAN adapters (yet—standards are emerging that allow adapters from different manufacturers to communicate). A wireless LAN needs one access point (base station) as its hub.

Take inventory of every computer that will be on the LAN and make a note of the type of slot each has available. You have to buy a network interface card that fits a slot in each computer. The easiest way to determine slot types is to check the documentation for each computer. ISA and PCI slots are all common, with EISA, VESA, and MCA also present on older computers. Laptops usually have PC Card slots (also called PCMCIA) that look like they fit a credit card. You may be able to tell what kind of slot your computer has by taking the cover off and looking, and then describing the slot to your local computer store expert. However, it's safer to check your documentation for the type of architecture the motherboard has for each computer that will be on the LAN. You can and probably will mix cards of different slot types so long as the network type is consistent. For example, one of our networks has ISA, PCI, MCA, and PCMCIA interface cards all connected to a 10 Mbps coaxial Ethernet.

Look for cards that are Windows Plug-and-Play compatible, which includes cards made by most major manufacturers. Using a plug-and-play card makes configuring the card much easier because Windows can identify it automatically.

Newer computers may come with a network interface card preinstalled. Check your system's documentation before you shop for your NICs.

Buying Cable

The type and amount of cable you choose depends on the topology you use in your network. We assume the computers you are connecting are relatively near to each other. A general rule is not to run a cable more than 150 meters between computers (although the actual specifications for different types of cable in different types of networks may be greater). If you are connecting computers that are not close to each other, you need to do some research on how to create a network over medium distances.

When you buy your cable, remember you will string it so people don't trip over the cable. Measure carefully and allow extra—you can hide cable that's too long. If your cable is too short, you'll have to go shopping again.

Coaxial Cable

If you've chosen bus topology, you need to use coaxial cable. Coax cannot be plugged directly into a NIC. Instead, a *T-connector* is attached to the BNC connector on the NIC, and a cable is attached to either side of the T-connector. A diagram of the cable and T-connectors in a bus network is shown in Figure 27-1. The computer in the middle of the bus has a T-connector with cable attached to each side. Computers at each end of the bus have cable on one side of the T-connector and a *terminating resistor* on the other side. You cannot have any cable between the T-connector and the computer.

When you shop for hardware for your Ethernet bus network using coax cable, you need to buy a T-connector for each computer and a terminating resistor for each end of the bus (two terminating resistors for the whole network).

You cannot *just plug the coax cable directly into the computers on either end of your network. You must use a T-connector with the coax cable plugged in on one side, and a coax cable or a 50-ohm terminating resistor on the other side. Also remember that Ethernet 50-ohm cable is not interchangeable with cable TV 75-ohm cable, even though the two look nearly identical.*

When determining how much cable you need, remember computers are connected in an approximate line. Choose computers to be at the ends, and then measure the distance between each computer in the bus, allocating extra cable to go around furniture and out of the way of office traffic.

Twisted-Pair Cable

If you've chosen star topology, you need twisted-pair or Category-5 cable (as shown in Figure 27-2). The ends of these cables have RJ-45 connectors, which look like telephone cord connectors (the ones that plug into a telephone wall jack), but are about twice as big. When using twisted-pair cable, plug one end of each cable into a network interface card installed in a PC and plug the other end into the hub that's at the center of the star topology.

To determine how much cable you need, decide where you are going to place the hub, and then measure from each computer to the hub's location. Remember to allocate extra cable to go around furniture and out of the way of office traffic.

Although it's tempting, you cannot take a twisted-pair cable and connect two computers directly, unless you have a specially manufactured crossover cable. You need to connect the cable into a hub because the hub manages which pairs of wires inside your cable are used for transmitting and receiving data. If you try to connect two computers directly with a standard cable, the transmit and receive wires will be incorrect on one end, and your connection won't work. Even if you only have two computers, an inexpensive hub is a good investment to ease network debugging and future upgrades.

Buying a Hub

If you've chosen star topology with twisted-pair cable, you need a *hub*, a small box with lots of cable connectors. Buy a hub with enough connections for all the computers on your network. You may want a few extra connections, so you can add additional computers to the network later. Hubs are widely available with 4, 8, 16, or 24 ports. Instead of a hub, you can use a *switch*, which distributes information faster than a hub.

Installing Your Network Hardware

Now that you have all your parts—a NIC for each computer, enough cabling, and a hub (for star topology) or T-connectors and terminators (for bus topology), you're ready to put it all together to create the physical network. This procedure is best done when the computers aren't in use and when you have a good chunk of time to devote to it—on a weekend.

Installing Network Interface Cards

The first step to installing your network hardware is to install your network interface cards (NIC) in each computer that will be on the network. Turning off each computer, take the cover off, install the NIC, and put the cover on again. For a laptop, this is usually as easy as sliding the card into the PC slot. For a desktop computer, this requires installing the card in a slot on the motherboard according to the manufacturer's installation instructions.

Once the NIC is installed, start the computer. Windows should detect the new hardware and ask you to install the adapter drivers for it. (The driver tells the operating system how to talk to the hardware.) In the next chapter, the section on installing your adapter walks you through the process of checking whether the NIC (adapter) drivers have been automatically installed and, if they haven't, installing them (see Chapter 14).

Stringing Cable

Once the NIC and its driver are installed, you can connect the cabling. The computers can be turned on when you connect the cables.

Cabling can be a simple job or an extravagant one, depending on your needs and how much time, effort, and money you're willing to invest. A home office network that consists of two computers close together probably means cables running on the floor around the edge of the room and behind furniture. Cabling for an office probably means cables hidden by conduit, running inside walls, and running above dropped ceilings. You may want to hire someone if you have many computers to connect and want it done neatly. If you put cable inside ceilings or walls, be sure the installation conforms to fire and electrical codes.

When planning your wiring job, plan for the future. If you're wiring your office, add extra cables while the walls and ceiling are open. Put network jacks in the walls of any room that you think might have a computer in it some day. Plan your network cabling in the same manner that you would plan phone extensions. Doing all the wiring now can make adding a computer to your network much easier in the future.

Coaxial Cable

If you're wiring coaxial cable, remember to use a T-connector on each network interface card. Each T-connector has cable attached to one side; the other side has either another cable or a terminating resistor.

Begin cabling at one end of the network—connect cable and a terminating resistor to the T-connector. Run the cable to the next computer and then attach it to the

T-connector. If this computer is in the middle of the bus, attach cable to the other side of the T-connector, and then run the cable to the next computer in the bus. When you reach the last computer, attach the cable to one side of the T-connector and a terminating resistor to the other.

Twisted-Pair Cable

If you're using twisted-pair cable and star topology, run cable from each computer to the hub. The RJ-45 jacks are easy to use—just plug the cable into the network interface card as you would plug a phone wire into a phone jack.

Don't run twisted-pair cable in a bundle with electrical power cable because the electromagnetic interference can adversely affect the network—a short circuit between power and network cables could cause injury or fire.

Once you complete the construction phase, you need to sit at each computer and configure Windows so it knows about the network, as described in the next chapter.

Chapter 28

Configuring Windows
for a LAN

If you have a small number of computers (say, 15 or less), and they all run some version of Windows (Me, 98, 95, 3.11, NT, or 2000), you can set up a peer-to-peer local area network (LAN) using Windows as your network operating system. Read the previous chapter for how to choose a cabling technology, cabling topology, and network interface cards, and how to install the hardware you need.

Once the network adapter cards are installed and the cable is strung, you still have to work the software side of the problem. You need to make sure Windows's networking components are installed and then configure the components. The easiest way to configure your computer to communicate over the LAN is usually to run the Home Networking Wizard. Once your system in configured, you log in to the network each time you start Windows. Windows comes with some network troubleshooting tools described at the end of this chapter.

What Windows Components Are Needed for a Network?

No matter what kind of network you're attaching your Windows machine to, you must take some steps to configure it for the network. Specifically, you have to identify the client, the adapter, and the protocol the network uses. If you want to share your local resources (your hard drive or the printer attached to your computer, for instance), you also have to install a service. You work with these four types of network components:

- **Adapter**   Identifies the specific network interface card you have installed and the driver needed to make it work. The adapter should be configured automatically when you install the network interface card—Windows should install the proper device driver automatically.

- **Client**   Specifies the type of network to which you are attaching: a Windows-compatible peer-to-peer network, a Microsoft Windows 2000 or NT network, or a Novell NetWare network, for example.

- **Protocol**   Identifies the way information is passed between computers on the network. TCP/IP is the protocol used by the Internet, for example.

- **Service**   Enables you to share resources on the computer (for example, file or printer sharing).

Before you start working with Windows's networking components, shutting down all applications is a good idea. When you finish using the Network dialog box, Windows reboots your computer, which is quicker if applications are already closed.

The Network Dialog Box

To configure the network, you use the Network dialog box, shown in Figure 28-1. You can display the Network dialog box in two ways:

- Choose Start | Settings | Control Panel. Then click or double-click the Network icon, depending on whether your desktop uses single- or double-click (see Chapter 1, section "Choosing Between Single-Click and Double-Click").

- Right-click the My Network Places icon (described in the next section) on the desktop and choose Properties from the shortcut menu.

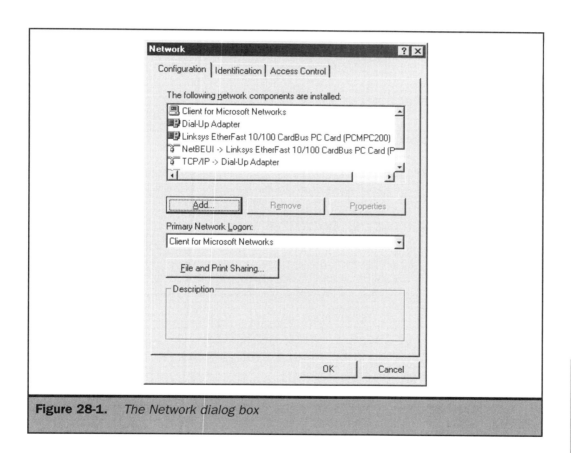

Figure 28-1.   *The Network dialog box*

The Network dialog box displays all the installed components used for networking. Because using a PPP or SLIP connection to the Internet is also considered networking, you may see the TCP/IP protocol listed, even though you don't (yet) have a LAN installed. The installed components can be one of three types—client, protocol, or service. (Adapters also appear in this dialog box, although you add and configure them as described in the section "Configuring Windows for New Hardware" in Chapter 14.) Different icons identify the different types of components:

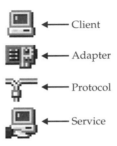

You use the Network dialog box throughout this chapter. The tabs on the Network dialog box depend on what network software you have installed and configured.

 You also use the Network dialog box to configure Windows to communicate with an Internet account via a DSL phone line or cable modem: see Chapter 30 for the details.

The My Network Places Window

My Network Places is an icon that appears on your desktop after your network adapter is installed, which may happen when Windows finds your network interface card. When you open the My Network Places icon, you see an Explorer window with icons for each of the computers on your LAN, as shown in Figure 28-2. Three other icons also appear.

- **Add Network Place**   This adds a shared network resource to this window.

- **Home Networking Wizard**   This helps you configure your computer to connect to a LAN.

- **Entire Network**   This displays additional shared printers or disks, or computers on other LANs to which you have access.

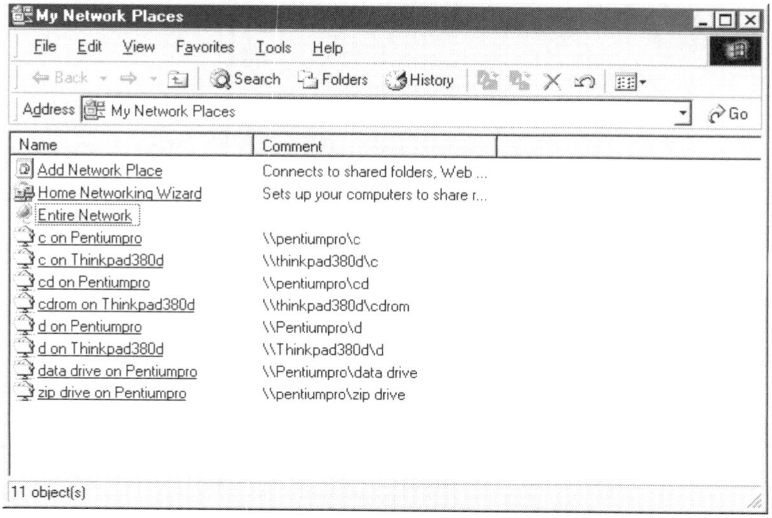

Figure 28-2.   *My Network Places lists shared disks and printers.*

Configuring Your LAN Connection by Using the Home Networking Wizard

Microsoft has identified home LANs as a big growth area and has tried to make setting up Windows-based LANs easier. Windows Me installs many networking components automatically, either when you install Windows or when it detects a network interface card among your computer's hardware. The Home Networking Wizard can step you thought the rest of the process of configuring your computer to communicate on your LAN, including setting up Internet Connection Sharing (described in Chapter 30). The Wizard can also create a floppy disk containing a configuration program that you can use to configure a Windows 98 or 95 system to work with your network (to use this creature, you need a blank floppy disk).

Running the Wizard

After closing all your other programs (because the Wizard must restart your computer), follow these steps:

1. Start the Home Networking Wizard by choosing Start | Programs | Accessories | Communications | Home Networking Wizard. Or, open the My Network Places icon on your desktop and run the Home Networking Wizard icon that appears there. Either way, you see the Home Networking Wizard window.

2. Follow the instructions the Wizard displays, clicking Next to move to the next set window (see Figure 28-3). You tell it whether you dial into the Internet directly from this computer, you want to connect to the Internet over the LAN, or you don't connect to the Internet.

3. Provide a computer name and workgroup name for your computer (see "Identifying the Computer").

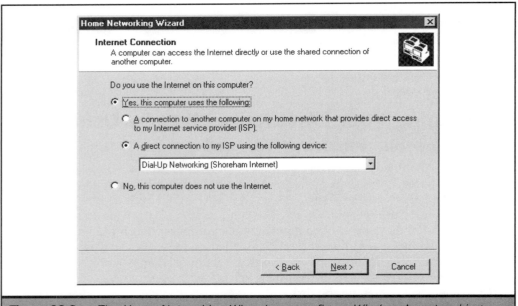

Figure 28-3. *The Home Networking Wizard can configure Windows's networking along with Internet Connection Sharing.*

4. Tell the Wizard which folders on your computer's disk you want to be available to other people on the network. Also tell it whether you want other people to be able to use printers connected to your computer. If you share any folders, the Wizard requires you to enter a password other people must type to use your folders. See Chapter 29 for more about sharing folders and printers.

5. If you want the Wizard to create a floppy disk with a LAN configuration program that you can run on Windows 98 and 95 computers on your LAN, insert a blank floppy disk into the drive when the Wizard prompts you.

After the Wizard restarts your computer, your computer is on the LAN.

After the Wizard Runs

If you tell the Home Networking Wizard that you connect to the Internet over the LAN, you don't want to share your Internet dial-up connection, or you don't connect to the Internet, it installs File And Printer Sharing For Microsoft Networks (a service) and configures all your adapters (Dial-Up Adapter and any network interface cards you have installed) to use this service. This configuration is actually a bad idea: you don't want File And Printer Sharing For Microsoft Networks available over your Dial-Up Adapter if you plan to dial in to the Internet. If you connect to the Internet over a connection for which file and printer sharing is enabled, Windows offers to turn off the service for that connection. To turn sharing off yourself, follow the steps in "Configuring the Protocol" to deselect file and printer sharing from the TCP/IP protocol bound to both the Dial-Up Adapter and your network interface cards. If you are using NetBEUI as the protocol for your LAN, also deselect Client For Microsoft Networks.

If you tell the Home Networking Wizard that you dial directly in to the Internet and you want to share your Internet connection with other computers on the LAN, the Wizard installs Internet Connection Sharing: see Chapter 30 for more information.

If you created a configuration floppy disk, you can run the Home Networking Wizard on Windows 98 or 95 computers on your LAN by putting the floppy disk in the drive, choosing Start | Run, typing **a:setup** in the Open box, and clicking OK. The Wizard needs to restart each computer after it runs.

Installing Network Components

You start network component installation on the Configuration tab of the Network dialog box to install clients, protocols, and services. (Adapters should already be installed.) In many cases, you won't have to install all four components manually—Windows does some of the work for you. If you see Windows has already installed a component for you, skip to the next section.

Installing the Adapter

The adapter is the software driver that allows your PC to communicate with the network interface card in your PC. Every brand and model of network interface card has its own adapter that must be installed so the client software knows how to package information and send it to the network interface card. If Windows detects a Plug and Play network interface card, or if you upgraded to Windows Me on a machine that was already connected to a network, you see the My Network Places icon on your desktop, and the adapter appears in the Network dialog box.

You will probably see the Dial-Up Adapter listed in the list of installed network components in the Network dialog box, too. Unlike other adapters, the Dial-Up Adapter is not a driver for a network interface card. Instead, it's the driver Windows uses for Dial-Up Networking (see Chapter 21, section "What Is the Dial-Up Adapter?").

To check whether an adapter is installed or the installed adapter is the correct one, look at the Network dialog box. Here's how to check if an adapter is installed:

1. Display the Network dialog box, shown in Figure 28-1. Click the Configuration tab (if it's not already selected).

2. In the list at the top of the dialog box, look for a description of your network interface card with the adapter icon next to it.

If you see the icon, an adapter is already installed. (Check to see that the description shown matches your brand of network adapter—if not, install the correct adapter.) If you don't, give Windows another chance to find the network interface card by using the Hardware Wizard (see Chapter 14, the section "Using the Add New Hardware Wizard").

   In some cases, you may need to install more than one adapter. For instance, if you have two different network interface cards because your computer is a node on two different networks, then you need to install two adapters. If you need more than one adapter installed, install them all now.

Installing the Client

The next step is to install the client component, which identifies the type of network on which your computer will be. When you installed the adapter (or when Windows found your Plug and Play network interface card), Windows also installed a client, the Client For Microsoft Networks. If a client is installed, you can recognize it in the Network dialog box by its client icon (which looks like a little computer with a blue screen).

Because you are installing a peer-to-peer Windows network, the Client For Microsoft Networks is the one you need. If you mistakenly deleted your Client For Microsoft Networks, follow these steps (you should also follow these steps to install a client for a different kind of network):

1. Display the Network dialog box. Click the Configuration tab (if it's not already selected).

2. Click the Add button. You see the Select Network Component Type dialog box, shown in Figure 28-4.

3. Select Client as the type of network component you want to install and click the Add button. You see the Select Network Client dialog box, shown in Figure 28-5. Unless you installed additional network software, the only entry in the Manufacturers list is Microsoft.

4. Choose the manufacturer you want to use to see the available network clients. For a Windows peer-to-peer network, choose Microsoft as the manufacturer and Client For Microsoft Networks as the network client.

5. Click OK. You see the Network dialog box, with the client you just defined listed.

Installing the Protocol

Without a protocol, the computers on your network won't know how to talk to each other. The protocol is the language your computer uses on the network. More than one protocol may be installed on a single computer because computers can speak more than one language. Networks that use Microsoft software (such as the peer-to-peer network you're creating now using Windows) support the three most common protocols—TCP/IP, IPX/SPX, and NetBEUI—as well as other less-common protocols.

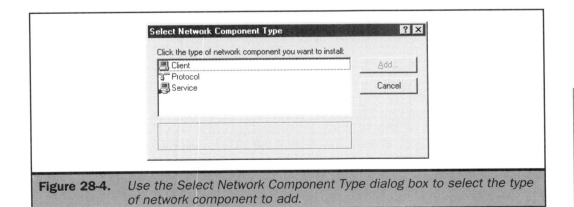

Figure 28-4.   *Use the Select Network Component Type dialog box to select the type of network component to add.*

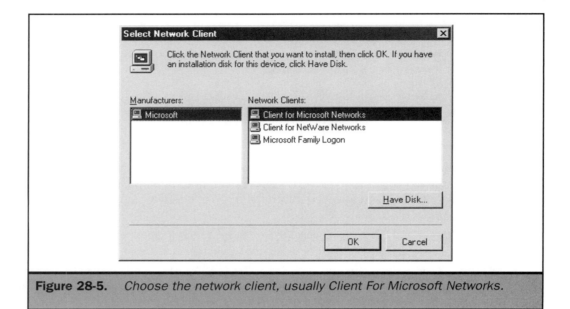

Figure 28-5.   *Choose the network client, usually Client For Microsoft Networks.*

- **TCP/IP (Transmission Control Protocol/Internet Protocol)**   This is the language spoken by computers on the Internet. Any computer using the Internet through a direct connection needs to have TCP/IP installed.

- **IPX/SPX (Internetwork Packet eXchange/Sequenced Packet eXchange)**   This is a protocol used primarily by Novell in its NetWare operating system. It is still widely used because of its ease of setup.

- **NetBEUI (NetBIOS Extended User Interface)**   This is used primarily by Microsoft in its networking products. It's fast and requires almost no configuration.

NetBEUI is by far the simplest protocol to use and configure. That simplicity has a drawback, however—NetBEUI is *nonroutable*, which means it can be used only on simple networks where routing devices aren't used. Routers are devices used to connect multiple segments of networks; they can't transmit the NetBEUI protocol from one segment to another. Simple office and home-office networks usually don't require the use of routers (other than for connecting to the Internet), so NetBEUI is a good choice.

When you install an adapter, Windows automatically installs the TCP/IP protocol, in case you want to use TCP/IP for Internet communication. If you are setting up a simple peer-to-peer network, however, NetBEUI is an easier protocol to use—TCP/IP requires additional configuration that NetBEUI doesn't require.

You can delete the TCP/IP protocol if you're sure you won't use it, but wait until you've installed the new protocol, NetBEUI, so Windows doesn't also delete the client. If you're not sure whether the computer uses TCP/IP, don't delete it. If you plan to connect to the Internet over the LAN, you'll need TCP/IP.

Installing a protocol is similar to installing other network components. Follow these steps to install NetBEUI or another protocol:

1. Display the Network dialog box. Click the Configuration tab (if it's not already selected). The installed protocols appear with a little cabling icon to their left.

2. Click the Add button to display the Select Network Component Type dialog box, shown in Figure 28-4.

3. Select Protocol and click the Add button. You see the Select Network Protocol dialog box, shown in Figure 28-6. Again, Microsoft appears as the only manufacturer unless you installed other software.

4. If you are installing NetBEUI, select Microsoft as the manufacturer. Otherwise, select the manufacturer of the protocol you want to install.

5. Select NetBEUI (or the protocol you chose) as the Protocol and click OK. You return the Network dialog box.

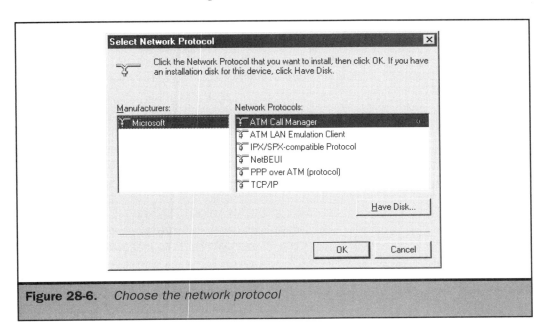

Figure 28-6. *Choose the network protocol*

When you install any protocol, Windows also installs the Client For Microsoft Networks, if it isn't already installed.

Deleting Unneeded Protocol Bindings

Windows "binds" the new protocol to all the adapters you have available—usually the Dial-Up Adapter (the adapter Windows uses for Dial-Up Networking) and each network interface card you have installed. A *binding* means Windows can use a specific protocol with a specific adapter. For example, Figure 28-1 shows these bindings:

- **NetBEUI -> Linksys EtherFast 10/100 CardBus PC Card**   This enables file and printer sharing (which use Microsoft's NetBEUI protocol) over the LAN to which the Linksys Ethernet network interface card is connected.

- **TCP/IP -> Dial-Up Adapter**   This enables TCP/IP (the Internet protocol) over the phone, for use by Windows Dial-Up Networking/link].

You might not want to use all your installed protocols to work with all your installed adapters. For example, binding NetBEUI to your Dial-Up Adapter is a terrible idea because it's unlikely you'll want to allow people on the Internet access to your files and printers. If you want to share your files and printers over the Internet, consider using VPN instead (see Chapter 30, section "Connecting to Your Organization's LAN with Virtual Private Networking").

To delete a binding, click it on the list on the Network dialog box, and then click the Remove button.

Delete the NetBEUI -> Dial-Up Adapter binding to avoid exposing your LAN file and printing sharing to the Internet.

Installing the Service

A service is the last network component you install—it also is the only optional component. Your network can work fine without a service, but no one on the network will be able to share resources, such as hard disks, CD-ROM drives, files, or printers. If you don't want to share resources, don't install any services.

Even when a service has been defined, you can add some security measures to ensure the resources on your computer are not abused (see Chapter 29, section "Using Shared Drives and Folders with Passwords").

If you are creating a peer-to-peer network of Windows computers, you should install the File And Printer Sharing For Microsoft Networks service. Install a service in the same way you installed the other network components:

1. Display the Network dialog box. Click the Configuration tab (if it's not already selected).

2. Click the Add button to display the Select Network Component Type dialog box, shown in Figure 28-4.

3. Select Service and click the Add button. You see the Select Network Service dialog box, shown in Figure 28-7.

4. Select File And Printer Sharing For Microsoft Networks and click OK. You see the Network dialog box, with the service you just added listed.

The Configuration tab of the Network dialog box should now look like Figure 28-1 (additional components may also appear). If it doesn't look like this, install any additional components that are needed.

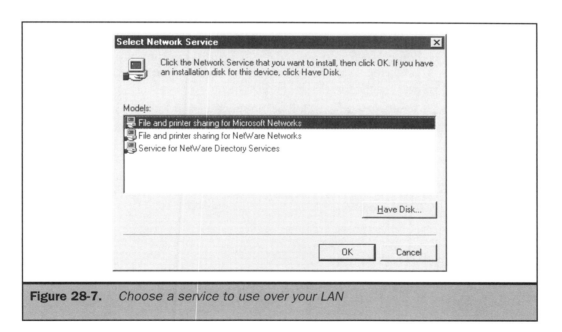

Figure 28-7.   *Choose a service to use over your LAN*

Configuring Your Network Components

To configure an installed network component, display its properties by selecting the component on the Network dialog box and clicking the Properties button. In some cases, the default setting may be exactly what you need.

 Install all the network components before setting the properties of each component because the components are interrelated. When components are installed before they are configured, Windows provides many of the correct configuration settings, thereby reducing the amount of work you have to do.

Configuring the Adapter

Follow these steps on each computer in the network to configure the properties for each adapter, along with the protocols to which it is bound:

1. Display the Network dialog box. Click the Configuration tab (if it's not already selected, as shown in Figure 28-1).

2. Select the network adapter in the list of installed components.

3. Click the Properties button. You see the Properties dialog box for the adapter. (Double-clicking the component on the list produces the same result.) Figure 28-8 shows the Bindings tab of the Properties dialog box for one network adapter, but the exact contents depend on the adapter driver.

4. Click the Driver Type tab. Check that the Enhanced Mode NDIS Driver radio button is selected (if it's available).

5. Click the Bindings tab, which lists the protocols to which the card is bound. If your network uses the NetBEUI protocol, only NetBEUI should be selected, so the computer doesn't have to do extra work—click any other protocols to deselect them, if necessary. If you plan to communicate with the Internet over this adapter, select the TCP/IP protocol.

6. Close the Properties dialog box.

Configuring the Protocol

If you use the NetBEUI protocol, follow these steps (if you use another protocol, follow steps 1 and 2, and then determine what settings to change, if any):

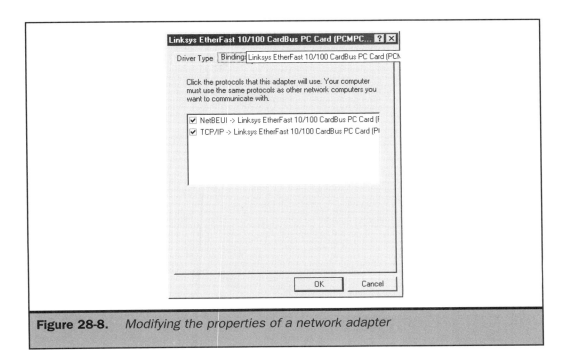

Figure 28-8.   *Modifying the properties of a network adapter*

1. Display the Network dialog box. Click the Configuration tab (if it's not already selected).

2. In the list of installed network components, select the binding of NetBEUI to the adapter that is connected to the LAN (for example, NetBEUI -> DLink Ethernet Adapter).

3. Click the Properties button. You see the NetBEUI Properties dialog box, shown in Figure 28-9.

4. On the Bindings tab, check that the NetBEUI protocol is bound to Client For Microsoft Networks and File And Printer Sharing For Microsoft Networks (check marks should be in both boxes).

5. Close the NetBEUI Properties dialog box.

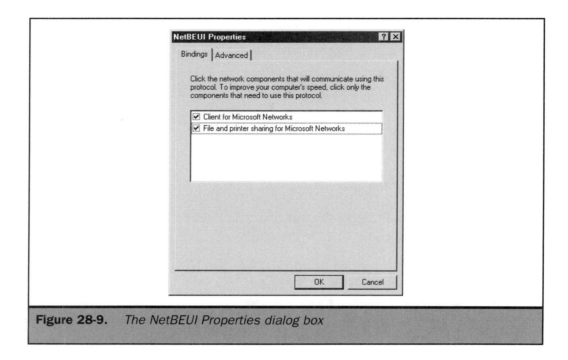

Figure 28-9.   *The NetBEUI Properties dialog box*

See the section "Configuring Windows to Use TCP/IP" in Chapter 30 for how to configure the TCP/IP protocol if you plan to use the LAN to connect to the Internet. You can also consult your LAN administrator for the necessary settings.

Configuring File and Print Sharing

If you plan to share resources on the computer, complete these additional steps:

1. Display the Network dialog box. Click the Configuration tab (if it's not already selected).

2. Click the File And Print Sharing button. You see the File And Print Sharing dialog box, shown here:

3. Select the check box(es) for the resources you want to share: files on any drives and/or printers attached to the computer.

4. Click OK to return to the Network dialog box.

Enabling file and printer sharing only makes it possible for you to share resources—it doesn't automatically share resources, which might compromise security. In other words, your computer has the capability to enable others to print to your printer or to access files on your drives, but until you actually give others that permission, the resources remain unusable to others. The procedure for sharing resources is covered in Chapter 29.

Identifying the Computer

Once you have added and configured all the network components, you need to name the computer with a unique name, identify the workgroup, and provide an options description:

- **Computer Name**   Naming your computer lets the users of other computers to refer to your computer by name. Some LAN administrators pick a convention to use to name all their computers: cartoon characters, planets, friends, grade-school teachers, or the first or last name of the person using the computer. You may want to name your computers according to their primary function.

- **Workgroup**   The *workgroup* is a group of computers on your network. The computers in a workgroup don't need to be physically close to each other, but they should be used by people who work together. The workgroup is a way to organize your peer-to-peer network's computers, similar to the way folders and subfolders organize the files on your PC.

- **Computer Description**   This optional entry provides a space to enter a longer description that Windows doesn't use during logon, but displays in the My Network Places window (if you select a view that includes a Comment column).

For example, a small network of five computers may all belong to the same workgroup called Office. There's probably no reason to complicate things beyond that. Within the workgroup, the computers might be named Pluto, Neptune, Jupiter, Saturn, and Mars, or Accounting, Sales, Marketing, Administration, and Shipping.

A larger organization with a larger network might need many workgroups to categorize its computers. Workgroups might be named Admin, Accounting, Shipping, and Maintenance. The computers within these workgroups each have their own names. However, a peer-to-peer network is not the best way to network many computers. Because you're probably creating a small peer-to-peer network, you should stick with one workgroup.

Here's how to give each PC a name and assign it to a workgroup:

1. Display the Network dialog box (if it isn't already displayed).

2. Click the Identification tab to see the identification settings, shown in Figure 28-10.

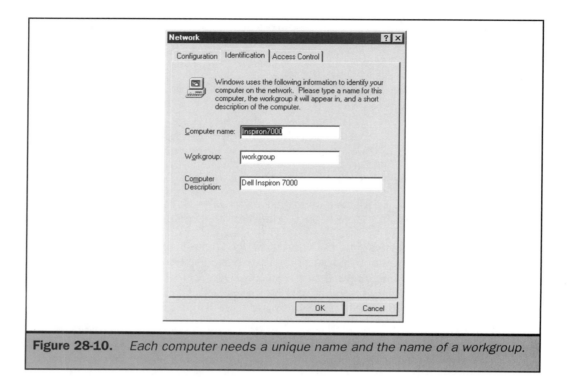

Figure 28-10. *Each computer needs a unique name and the name of a workgroup.*

3. Type a name for the computer in the Computer Name box. Each computer in a workgroup needs a unique name.

4. Type a name for the workgroup in the Workgroup box.

5. Optionally, type the type of computer, the name of the user, or other information into the Computer Description box. Click OK.

Note *If your computer is connected to a Windows 2000 or NT network, you might need to specify the domain (workgroup name) on the network you belong to (ask your LAN administrator). If so, select Client For Microsoft Networks from the list of installed network components on the Network dialog box and click Properties. On the Client For Microsoft Networks Properties dialog box that appears, click the Log On To Windows NT Domain check box, and type the Windows NT domain (workgroup) name.*

Restarting the Computer

After you install and configure the adapter, client, protocol, and services for each computer, you're finished with the Network dialog box. Close the dialog box by clicking OK. Restart the computer when prompted to do so. You may be asked to insert your Windows Me CD-ROM, so keep it on hand.

Checking Whether the Network Works

Once you've installed and configured the network components for a computer, you need to see whether your network works. Sit down at any of the computers on the network and follow these steps:

1. Open the My Network Places icon on the desktop. You see the My Network Places window (Figure 28-2), listing all the computers on the network.

2. If you don't see the names of all the computers on the network, open the Entire Network icon and then the Workgroup icon. Wait a minute or two. Your computer needs time to chat with the other computers on your network to find out who's out there and to build a list.

3. If you still don't see icons for the other computers on the network, read through the section "Troubleshooting Your Network" to find and fix the problem. If you see only your own computer in the list, or the Entire Network window is blank, communication has broken down with the other computers. It could be physical, like a bad cable, or it could be software configuration, like the wrong protocol being used. Check the configuration of computers that are working (make sure you've followed all the steps in this chapter). It's a good way to see whether you've missed something.

Once your network is working, the next step is to use it by sharing resources (see Chapter 29).

Logging In and Out

Each time you start Windows after you have configured Windows to connect to a LAN, you see the Enter Network Password dialog box. Type your user name in the User Name box (the name you used the last time already appears in the box). Type your password in the Password box and click OK. If you use Windows user profiles and your network user name is different from your user profile name, you may have to log in again with your Windows user profile name and password. Then the desktop and Taskbar appear. You now have access to the shared resources on the LAN and can share your own computer's resources with others, as described in Chapter 29. Click the My Network Places to see what disk drives and printers your computer can find on the LAN.

Note   *If you don't see the Enter Network Password dialog box, choose Start | Log Off to log in with your user name.*

When you finish working, you can log off the network to prevent anyone else from using your computer with your user name. Choose Start | Log Off. When Windows asks if you really want to log off, click Yes. Windows closes all applications and displays the Enter Network Password dialog box.

NETWORKING
WITH WINDOWS ME

What Is the Primary Network Logon?

If your computer uses user profiles and isn't on a LAN, the Welcome To Windows dialog box appears when you start Windows, asking for your user name and password (see Chapter 31, section "What Is a User Profile?"). Once you hook your computer to a LAN, Windows logs on to the LAN when it starts up, and you see the Enter Network Password dialog box on startup. If there's a problem connecting to the LAN, Windows lets you know when it logs on.

If you don't want Windows to verify its connection to the LAN each time it starts, you can configure Windows to display the Welcome To Windows dialog box rather than the Enter Network Password dialog box. Open the Network dialog box and set the Primary Network Logon to Windows Logon. To switch back to logging in to the LAN on startup, set the Primary Network Logon box back to Client For Microsoft Networks.

Troubleshooting Your Network

Although Windows networking generally works well, you may have trouble with one computer or all the computers on the network, especially when you first set up the network. This section recommends some steps to take to solve your problems.

The Windows online help system has a useful Troubleshooter (see Chapter 34, section "Diagnosing Problems Using Troubleshooters"). Find it by choosing Start | Help, clicking the Troubleshooting link, and clicking the Home Networking & Network Problems link.

The most common problems and solutions follow.

Some Computers Don't Appear in My Network Places

If you see some, but not all, computers in the network in My Network Places, one of these problems may be the culprit:

- The computers that don't appear in My Network Places may not be turned on or logged into the network. Restarting Windows on your computer or on the missing computer may help.

- One of the other computers may have a loose cable connection, or a network interface card that isn't working properly. Open My Network Places on that computer to see whether the network can be seen from there.

- The Browse Master for the LAN may not be working properly (see "What Is the Browse Master?").

What Is the Browse Master?

When you use Microsoft's File And Printer Sharing For Microsoft Networks service, the *Browse Master* is a computer on the LAN that keeps track of which computers are on the LAN and what resources (disks and printers) they have to share. When you start up a computer on the LAN, it asks the Browse Master computer for shared resources and displays this list when you open your My Network Places window. One computer can be the Browse Master at a time. The Browse Master stays in touch with each computer on the LAN every 10 or 15 minutes to update its list of available shared resources. If a Windows 2000 or NT computer is on the LAN, it automatically becomes Browse Master.

What determines which computer is the Browse Master? When a computer starts up and looks for a Browse Master, if it doesn't find out, it decides to become the Browse Master itself. If the Browse Master disappears (that is, gets turned off or is rebooted), the other computers eventually notice it's gone and hold an election among themselves to choose which computer becomes Browse Master, based on connection speed, processor speed, and Windows version.

If there's a problem with the Browse Master, not all the computers on the LAN appear in the My Network Places window. Shared resources may vanish and reappear from the window. If this happens, you need to make a different machine the Browse Master. Strangely, you can't find out directly which computer is the Browse Master but, in our experience, the problem is usually that a laptop has become the Browse Master.

You can configure your computer never to become the Browse Master. This is a good idea if you use a laptop because having a laptop as the Browse Master doesn't seem to work. To turn off your computer's capability to be the Browse Master, open the Network dialog box, click File And Printer Sharing For Microsoft Networks in the list of installed network components, click Properties, click the Browse Master, and set the Value box to Disabled.

Only Your Computer Appears in My Network Places

If no other computers on the network appear in My Network Places, you may have one of these problems:

■ You need to log in. Sometimes Windows doesn't display the Enter Network Password dialog box. If you don't see the Enter Network Password dialog box, choose Start | Log Off. Windows shuts all open windows and displays the Enter Network Password dialog box.

- A cable may be loose or bad. Check all the connections of the cables. Occasionally, cables become damaged, so you might want to try replacing a suspect length of cable with one you know is good.

- A protocol may be missing or incorrectly configured. Check to see that your computer is speaking the same language as all the others. If the other computers are using TCP/IP and you are trying to use NetBEUI, then you can't communicate with them. The protocol must be an installed network component, and the network interface card must be bound to the protocol (display the Bindings tab of the network interface card's Properties dialog box to make sure the card is bound to the right protocol).

- You may have a hardware conflict. Your PC may have a problem using the network interface card. Open Control Panel and then open the System icon. Click the Device Manager tab. If the network interface card appears with a yellow exclamation point, the card isn't working properly. Check the installation instructions for your card.

- The Browse Master for the LAN may not be working properly (see "What Is the Browse Master?").

No My Network Places Icon Appears on the Desktop

My Network Places doesn't appear unless a network interface card has been recognized. Install the network interface card and its driver (adapter) to see My Network Places.

You Can't Use Resources on Another Computer

You may not have set the resources to be shared yet. See Chapter 29 for more information on sharing resources.

The Complete Reference

Windows Me

Chapter 29

Sharing Drives and Printers on a LAN

If you have a LAN, you probably set it up because you have resources that you want to share. Perhaps you have three computers and only one printer. Perhaps several people use a database from different computers, and you want to make sure that they're always working with updated information. Whatever the reason, your LAN isn't much good if you don't know how to share your hardware and files.

This chapter tells you how to enable sharing the disks or printers on your own computer, use shared disks or folders on other computers, and choose which of your own disk drives to make available to other people on your LAN. We also describe how to share the printers on your system, and how to use printers on other people's systems.

When sharing resources, it's important to control who can do what, limiting the use of shared resources through passwords and monitoring who is using the resources on your computer. You can use Net Watcher, a Windows utility, to see who is using what shared resource on the LAN. The last section of this chapter explains how to use WinPopup to exchange messages with people over the LAN.

This chapter assumes that you have connected your computer to a LAN and have installed file-sharing and printer-sharing services (see Chapters 27 and 28).

Enabling Hardware Sharing

In order to share your hardware—disk drives and printers—with others on the LAN, you need to make sure that sharing is enabled. For a Windows peer-to-peer network, see "Installing the Service" in Chapter 28 to install File And Printer Sharing For Microsoft Networks, then see "Configuring File and Print Sharing" in Chapter 28 to configure sharing on your computer. For a NetWare, Windows 2000 or NT, or other type of network, ask your LAN administrator what you need to do.

To see whether you have allowed your computer's resources to be shared by others on the LAN (which you must do before you can make specific drives, folders, or printers sharable), follow these steps on your computer:

1. Right-click the My Network Places icon on the desktop and choose Properties to display the Network dialog box or display the Control Panel and open the Network icon. Click the Configuration tab if it's not already selected.

2. Check to see whether File And Printer Sharing For Microsoft Networks is listed in the box that shows all installed network components. (It usually appears last on the list of installed network components.)

3. If it is not listed, click the File And Print Sharing button to display the File And Print Sharing dialog box.

4. Select both check boxes: I Want To Be Able To Give Others Access To My Files and I Want To Be Able To Allow Others To Print To My Printer(s).

5. Click OK on both open dialog boxes. Windows may prompt you to insert your Windows Me CD-ROM. You need to reboot for file and printer sharing to take effect.

Installing file and printer sharing does not automatically share your printer and disk drives—that could compromise security. Instead, this feature allows you to choose exactly which of resources to share on your computer, by using the techniques covered in this chapter.

You can monitor the use of shared resources by using Net Watcher (see "Monitoring Shared Resources by Using Net Watcher").

Sharing Disk Drives and Folders on a LAN

Network drives (also called *shared drives*) are disk drives that have been configured to be available for use from other computers on the LAN. Similarly, *shared folders* are folders that have been configured to be usable by other computers on the LAN. For a disk drive or folder to be shared by other people on a LAN, it must be configured as sharable. Once a drive is sharable, other people can read and write files on the disk drive or in the folder.

This section describes how to use disk drives that are attached to other computers on the LAN and how to share your disk drives with other computers.

Using Shared Drives from Other Computers

You can access a shared drive or shared folder in one of two ways:

- If you use the drive or folder only occasionally, you can use My Network Places to access the drive.

- If you use the drive or folder frequently, you can *map* the drive or folder, which means that you assign the drive or folder a letter so that it appears on the drop-down list of drives in Open and Save As dialog boxes.

Using Network Drives with My Network Places

You can see a list of the shared drives and folders to which you have access. The My Network Places window, shown in Figure 29-1, lists all the shared drives and folders available to you on the LAN.

The name of each shared drive or folder appears, along with its UNC (Universal Naming Convention) address—the path name you use when referring to that shared drive or folder. The UNC address consists of two backslashes, the name of the

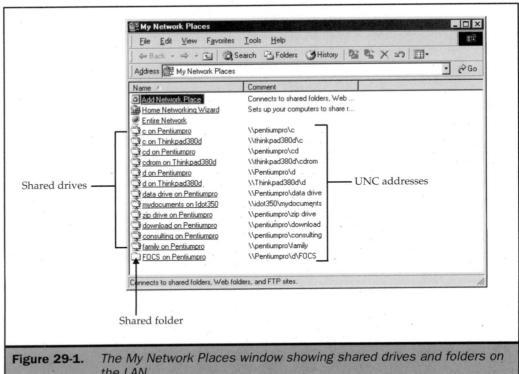

Figure 29-1.   *The My Network Places window showing shared drives and folders on the LAN*

computer, another backslash, and the share name of the drive or folder (see Chapter 8, section "What Are Addresses?").

To display the My Network Places window, open the My Network Places icon on the desktop; click or double-click the icon, depending on whether your desktop uses single-clicking or double-clicking (see Chapter 1, section "Choosing Between Single-Click and Double-Click") or move to My Network Places in Windows Explorer (click the downward-pointing arrow at the right end of the Address box and choose My Network Places from the list that appears). If you don't see a list of computer names, consider troubleshooting your network (see Chapter 28, section "Troubleshooting Your Network").

If your Explorer window doesn't display the Folders Explorer Bar, click Folders on the toolbar to display it. My Network Places appears near the bottom of the folder tree, as shown in Figure 29-2. Click the plus box to the left of My Network Places to see a list of available shared drives and folders.

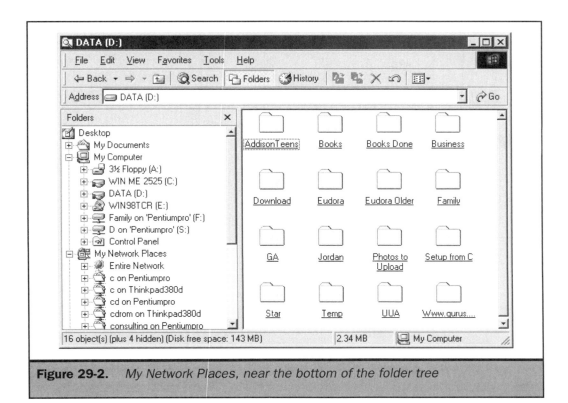

Figure 29-2.   *My Network Places, near the bottom of the folder tree*

You can change the name of a shared drive or folder as it appears on your computer. For example, if a drive appears as "data drive on iDot" and you'd rather see the name "Accounting Data," you can rename it by right-clicking the shared drive or folder in an Explorer window, choosing Properties from the shortcut menu that appears, and editing the contents of the box at the top of Properties dialog box. Renaming a shared drive or folder on your computer doesn't change its real name on the computer on which it's stored, just how it appears in your Explorer windows.

Opening and Saving Files on Shared Drives and Folders
You can see the folders and files on a shared drive by clicking or double-clicking the drive or folder in the My Network Places window. Once you see the drive, you can work with it as you do any drive on your own computer (see Chapter 8, section "Working with Windows Explorer").

NETWORKING WITH WINDOWS ME

My Network Places is also available from dialog boxes of any applications you use. Figure 29-3 shows Microsoft Word 2000's Open dialog box with the contents of My Network Places displayed. Use the Look In drop-down list to choose My Network Places (it appears near the bottom of the list). Once you have opened My Network Places, move to the folder and file you want. A few programs don't allow saving to a network drive unless you assign it a drive letter.

Mapping a Drive

If you use a shared drive or folder frequently, you can map the drive to a drive letter. The process is easy, and when you want to find or save a file to the shared drive, you don't have to spend so much time navigating through My Network Places to find it.

For example, if you frequently use files on drive D of your department's server, you can map drive letter S to that drive. Drive S appears as a disk drive on your computer, even though it's actually on the server.

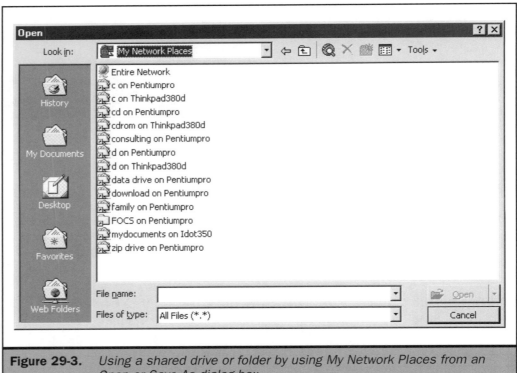

Figure 29-3. *Using a shared drive or folder by using My Network Places from an Open or Save As dialog box*

Here's the easiest way to map a drive to a drive letter:

1. Find the drive by using My Network Places in Windows Explorer.

2. Choose Tools | Map Network Drive from the menu bar. You see the Map Network Drive dialog box, shown here:

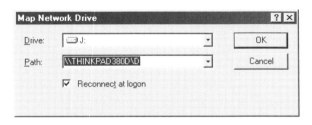

3. Choose a drive letter for the drive. Use the drop-down list to see the available letters. Letters that are mapped to drives on your own computer don't appear. Letters that are already mapped to shared drives or folders appear with the name of the resource they are mapped to.

4. In the Path box, type the UNC address of the shared drive or folder you want to Map. Better yet, click the downward-pointing arrow at the right end of the Path box and choose from the UNC addresses that appear. The list includes all the drives and folders on the LAN that have been configured to be sharable.

5. If you want to continue to map this drive or folder to this drive letter each time you restart Windows, click the Reconnect At Logon check box so that a check mark appears in it.

6. Click OK to close the dialog box. If the shared drive requires a password, Windows prompts you to type it.

Note   *In Windows 98, you could right-click a drive in Windows Explorer and choose Map Network Drive from the shortcut menu that appears, but Windows Me doesn't include this feature. To display a Map Network Drive button on the Windows Explorer toolbar, right-click the toolbar, choose Customize from the shortcut menu that appears, click Map Drive from the Available Toolbar Buttons list, click Add, and click Close.*

Once you have mapped a drive, it appears in the folder tree with your local drives, and in Windows Explorer you see it when you open My Computer. In Figure 29-2, the folder tree includes two mapped items—drive F is mapped to a folder named Family on a computer named Pentiumpro, and drive S is mapped to drive D on the same computer. You can access a mapped network drive in the same way that you access a local drive from any dialog box.

NETWORKING WITH WINDOWS ME

To map a drive to a folder, the folder itself must be defined as shared. It is not enough to share the drive on which the folder resides.

Tips for Mapping

When you map a drive, you only map it for only one computer at a time. If you want the drive mapped for other computers in the LAN, you need to sit down at each of them and repeat the steps in the preceding section. That is, if you want all the computers in your office to be able to use the drive letter F to refer to the Consulting folder on the Pentiumpro computer, you must map the Consulting folder to the F drive on each computer in the LAN.

If you use a shared drive or folder from more than one computer, you might want to spend a moment considering which drive letter to use. You will find it more convenient if the shared network drive has the same drive letter on each computer in the LAN—that way you won't have to refer to "the C drive on the computer in the corner near the door—the one called Bambi." Instead, you can just call it the F drive (the exception, of course, is the person who uses the computer called Bambi, for whom it's just the C drive). Choose a letter that people can remember—for example, map the main disk drive on the server to drive S, or the drive that everyone in the Purchasing department uses to drive P. Before you assign the drive letter, make sure that letter is available on the other computers on the LAN (letters up to about G are frequently already occupied by hard disks, CD-ROM drives, Zip drives, and other devices).

You may have noticed the Reconnect At Logon check box on the Map Network Drive dialog box. When this option is selected, your computer checks that the shared resource is available each time you log on. Reconnecting at logon slows down the log on process slightly, but means that using the drive the first time is quicker, because the drive is already connected. If you are mapping a drive only temporarily (you need it only for the next twenty minutes, for example), or if the computer that drive is on gets rebooted or turned off often, turn off the Reconnect At Logon option.

Unmapping a Drive

If you want to "unmap" a drive, you can do so by disconnecting it: right-click the drive in Windows Explorer and choose Disconnect from the shortcut menu. The drive remains accessible through My Network Places, but a drive letter is no longer mapped to it. (To make a drive inaccessible even through My Network Places, you must disable sharing from the computer that owns the resource.)

Using Shared Drives and Folders with Passwords

If you try to open a shared drive or folder in My Network Places or another Explorer window, you may see an Enter Network Password dialog box like this one:

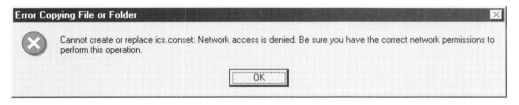

This dialog box tells you that this shared drive or folder requires a password. Depending on which password you type, you may have read-only or full access to the files on the drive or in the folder (see "Choosing an Access Type"). Get the password from the owner of the computer on which the drive or folder is stored or ask your LAN administrator.

The Save This Password In Your Password List check box is usually selected so that you don't have to type this password again (even if you restart Windows). If you don't want the password stored in a file on your computer, click the check box to clear it; when you restart Windows, you'll need to type the password again.

If the password you typed gives you only read-only access, you can't save, delete, or edit files on the shared drive or folder. If you try, you see an error message like this:

If the owner of the shared drive or folder specified that there be a password, but left the password blank, then you see the Enter Network Password dialog box anyway. Leave the Password box blank and click OK.

Sharing Your Disk Drives and Folders with Others

You might want to share the files stored on your computer's disk drives in a number of ways. You might want to permit all the computers on the LAN to access a Zip drive, Jaz drive, or CD-ROM writer, so that you don't have to buy a drive for each computer. You can even permit other users of the LAN to read files in a certain folder on a particular hard drive. Give read-only access to the folder that contains the company personnel policies, so that you don't waste space on each computer saving the same files (and time updating numerous copies of the files). You can allow some users to be able to read and write to one file, perhaps the one containing the database in which orders are entered, so that the information each user sees is always the most up-to-date information available. Maybe there is one shared folder on your hard drive that you want other people to be able to use—maybe you just want to share everything—you want to allow everyone on the LAN to read and write to your hard drive.

Before anyone else can read or write files on your disk drives, you must configure either the entire drive or specific folders as sharable. You choose a *share name* for the drive or folder—the name that you want to appear in Windows Explorer as *name* on *computer name*. For example, if your computer is named Laptop, and you share your CD-ROM (which is drive D on your computer) with the share name CD-ROM Drive, it appears as CD-ROM Drive on Laptop in Windows Explorer on other people's computers. You can provide a comment to further identify a shared drive or folder. The comment is visible only when the properties are displayed, however.

When you make a drive or folder sharable, you also decide what access to specify. There are alternatives to sharing a whole drive with full read and write access:

- You can share just a folder.
- You can specify read-only rights.
- You can password-protect the drive.
- For NetWare and Windows 2000 and NT networks, you can choose the users who can access the drive.

Choosing an Access Type

When you allow others to access your drive, you choose what kind of access to give them. You have the choice of three different *access types*:

- **Read-Only**   Allows other users to open and copy files, but not alter a file, save a new file, or delete a file, all of which require full access. If you are sharing a read-only drive, like a CD-ROM drive, it is a good idea to specify that the drive is read-only.

- **Full**   Allows anyone with access to the drive to read from the drive and write to the drive.

- **Depends On Password**   Allows users access, depending on which password they provide. You can define two different passwords—one for read-only access and one for full access. If you use different passwords, you can determine who has read-only access and who has full access by limiting who knows which password. Specify a read-only password to allow read-only access only to those who know the password; leave the read-only password blank to give anyone on the LAN read-only access. Specify a full access password to allow full access only to those who know the password; leave the full access password blank to give anyone on the LAN full access to the drive.

Access Control on Windows 2000 or NT LANs

When you specify passwords for shared resources, each resource has its own password. This is called *share-level access control*, which means that each resource has one password, and each user who wants access to that resource must use that resource's password. This can result in having to remember many passwords. In a peer-to-peer Windows network, this is the only option for using passwords to protect resources.

An alternative to this type of security is to give each user one password and then define the resources that each user has access to. This is called *user-level access control*. In most client-server networks, such as a Novell NetWare or Windows 2000 or NT network, user-level access control is the norm, and a network administrator is needed to define the permissions for each user.

If you use a Windows 2000 or NT network, you can specify which users can have access to your shared drive or folder. Follow the steps in section "Making a Drive Sharable," next. When you have displayed the Properties dialog box for the driver or folder to share, click the Add button to display the Add Users dialog box, from which you can choose users who may use your shared disk drive. Select users who may use your drive and click OK to return to the drive's Properties dialog box. The Add button doesn't appear if you use a Windows peer-to-peer network.

Making a Drive Sharable

Follow these steps to share a drive or folder:

1. Open Windows Explorer and display the name of the drive or folder you want to share with others.

2. Right-click the drive or folder you want to share and choose Sharing from the shortcut menu. (If you don't see Sharing, you need to install File And Printer Sharing For Microsoft Networks from the Network dialog box.) You see the Sharing tab of the Properties dialog box for the drive (shown in Figure 29-4).

3. Click the Shared As radio button.

4. Type the share name into the Share Name box. A share name can be up to 12 characters long, including spaces.

5. If you want anyone on the LAN to be able to read files from the drive, but not to write on the drive, choose Read-Only as the Access Type.

6. If you want anyone on the LAN to be able to read from and write to the drive, including editing and deleting your files, choose Full as the Access Type.

7. If you'd like some people to have read-only address, some to have full access, and some to have no access, choose Depends On Password for the Access Type.

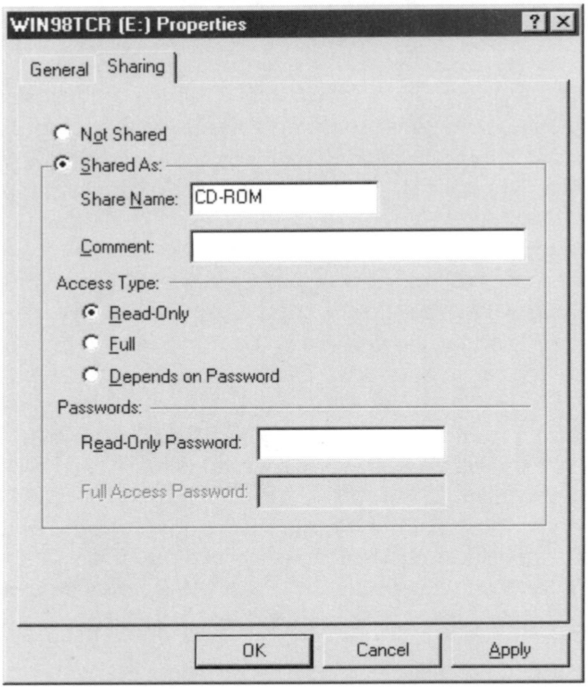

Figure 29-4. *Sharing a disk drive*

Then type passwords into the Read-Only Password and Full Access Password boxes. Don't leave a password blank unless you want anyone on the LAN to have that access.

8. Close the Properties dialog box. If you specified passwords, Windows prompts you to type them again.

You now see a hand as part of the drive or folder icon, signifying that the resource is shared. Other users can use your files by navigating to them through My Network Places. If they use the drive or folder often, they have the option of mapping the drive. If you decide to turn off sharing of the drive, open the Properties dialog box for the drive and select the Not Shared radio button on the Sharing tab.

If you make a folder sharable, then from another computer on the LAN, the shared folder looks like a whole drive, but other people can see and use only the shared folder.

Sharing Printers on a LAN

Sharing a printer on a LAN has two steps. First you sit at the computer that is directly attached to the printer and configure the printer to be a *network printer* (so that other computers on the network can print to it). Then you configure the other computers on the LAN so that they know about the network printer—with luck, Windows on each computer automatically detects the existence of the newly sharable printer and installs the new printer driver itself. Not all printers come with printer drivers that work for sharing the printer on a LAN.

Printing to a Network Printer from Another Computer

 When Windows detects a shared printer on another computer on the LAN, it tries to install the printer's driver automatically. When you print from an application, check the list of available printers—the list may already include shared printers on other computers. To see the list of printers you can use, choose Start | Settings | Printers to display the Printers window. The icon for a shared printer has a cable running beneath it.

If the printer doesn't appear on the list, you need to install a driver for the printer. Here's how:

1. Choose Start | Settings | Printers to see the Printers folder.
2. Open the Add Printer icon. You see the Add Printer Wizard. The Wizard asks the following:

   ■ **Whether you're installing a local or network printer**   You're installing a network printer.

   ■ **The network path for the printer**   Unless you can type the path for the printer from memory, use the Browse button to find it. To find the printer, first find the computer to which it is attached by expanding the My Network Places hierarchy; click My Network Places, then Entire Network, then the computer to which the printer is attached, then the name of the printer.

   ■ **Whether you print from MS-DOS-based programs**   Usually the answer is No. Printing from DOS-based programs requires that Windows captures the output that the DOS program sends to a printer port (see Chapter 15, section "Adding a New Network Printer").

   ■ **Which driver to install**   If you already have a driver installed for this type of printer, the Wizard asks whether you want to keep the existing driver or install a new one (one of these options will be recommended). If you don't have a driver installed, the Wizard prompts you to install one—you'll probably need your Windows CD-ROM or a printer driver from another source (many can be found on the Internet).

- **What name you want to call the printer** This should be a name that enables you to identify the printer. If you have six LaserJets on your network, you probably don't want to call it just "LaserJet"—instead, you might want to call it "Cindy's LaserJet" since it's attached to Cindy's machine. That way, when you print to this printer, you'll know where to go to pick up your printout.

- **Whether you want this printer to be your default printer** If you want to print automatically to this printer every time you print, then the answer is Yes. If you usually want to print to another printer, choose No.

- **Whether you want to print a test page** Choose Yes or No.

Once you've completed these steps, you can print to the shared printer from this computer any time you want. If you defined the shared printer as your default printer, then anything you print automatically goes to that printer. If you didn't define the network printer as the default printer, then you have to choose it from the list of defined printers before you print. This is usually done on the Print dialog box of the application you are using.

If a password is required for the shared printer, a dialog box appears asking you to provide the password after you give the print command. If the Save Password In Password List check box is selected, you will not have to provide the password again when printing from the same computer and using the same user name.

If the network printer is unavailable, any print jobs will be held on your computer until the printer is again available.

For more information about printing, installing and configuring a printer, and changing the default printer, refer to Chapter 15.

Making Your Printer Sharable

If you want other people on the LAN to be able to print on your printer, the first step is to install the printer on your own computer and make sure that you can print to it from that computer (see Chapter 15, section "Adding a New Local Printer"). Once the printer is correctly installed, you can share it so that other computers on the network can print to it.

The computer that the printer is attached to is called a *print server*. The print server can also be someone's PC, the usual arrangement on a small network, or a computer that does nothing else. You give the printer a share name, the name that other people will see when they connect to the printer. The share name can be the type of printer (for example, HP1100A), the group that uses the printer (for example, Accounting), or some other name. A straightforward name makes it easier for others on the network to figure out which printer they are using.

To share the printer so that other computers on the LAN can print to it, follow these steps:

1. Choose Start | Settings | Printers to see the Printers folder.

2. Right-click the printer you want to share and choose Sharing from the Shortcut menu (or select the printer and choose File | Properties from the menu bar).

You see the Properties dialog box for the printer, with the Sharing tab displayed, as shown in Figure 29-5 properties. (Depending on what type of network you use, you may see different settings.)

3. Click the Shared As radio button.

4. Give your printer a share name. You can enter a comment, too.

5. If you want other people to enter a password in order to print on your printer, type a password in the Password box.

6. Close the printer's Properties dialog box. The icon for the printer you just shared now has a hand under it, indicating the printer is shared.

If you type a password into the Password box on the Sharing tab of the printer's Properties dialog box, anyone on the LAN wanting to print to your printer must supply that password in order to print. Windows asks you to confirm the password

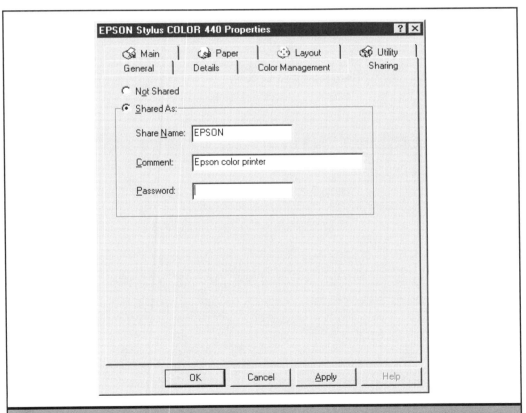

Figure 29-5.   *Giving the printer a name and description when you share it*

when you close the Properties dialog box. It is a good idea to make a note of the password, since you might not be using it yourself (when printing from the computer attached to the printer, no password is required).

To turn sharing off, open the Properties dialog box for the printer and select the Not Shared radio button on the Sharing tab. To remove the password, delete the contents of the Password box.

Monitoring Shared Resources by Using Net Watcher

Net Watcher is a Windows utility that shows you who is using the resources on your computer. Before you can run Net Watcher, you have to install the Client For Microsoft Networks, as described in "Installing a Service" and "Configuring File and Printer Sharing" in Chapter 28.

The Net Watcher program doesn't automatically install as part of Windows. To install Net Watcher from the Windows Me CD-ROM, open Control Panel, open Add/Remove Programs, click the Windows Setup tab, choose System Tools from the Components list, click Details, and choose Net Watcher.

To run Net Watcher, choose Start | Programs | Accessories | System Tools | Net Watcher. You see the Net Watcher window shown in Figure 29-6.

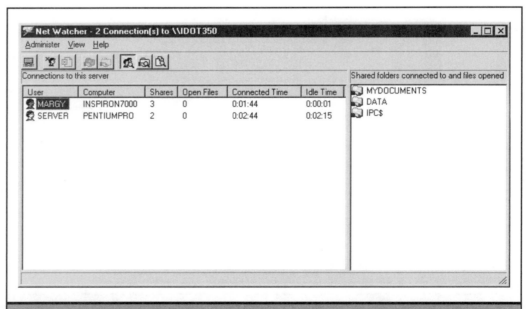

Figure 29-6.   *Net Watcher shows whether other people are using resources on your computer.*

If you use Windows' remote administration feature, you can see resource usage on other computers on the LAN, too (see Chapter 31, section "Managing Remote Administration").

Seeing Who Is Using Resources on Your Computer

To see what resources other people are using on your computer, choose one of these commands:

- **View | By Connections**   Lists the people on your LAN who are connected to your computer. When you select a user from the list at the left (for example, MARGY on Figure 29-6), the right pane of the Net Watcher window shows the files that person is using.

- **View | By Shared Folders**   Lists the resources on your computer to which other people are connected, including the folders for shared printers, shared drives, and shared folders (see Figure 29-7). When you select a resource from the list at the left, the right pane shows the people who are connected to that folder, along with the access type.

- **View | By Open Files**   Lists the files on your computer that are open by other people. The Accessed By column shows who has opened the file.

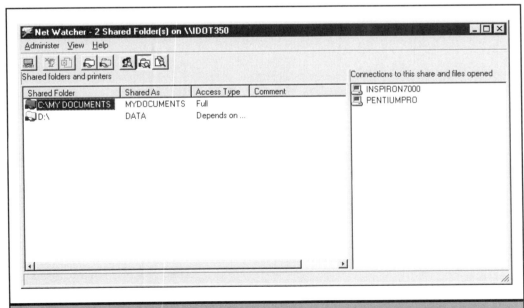

Figure 29-7.   *Listing the shared resources on your computer and who is using them*

Administering Your Shared Resources

Here are additional things you can do in Net Watcher:

- **Disconnect other users from the resources on your computer** Choose View | By Connections to see the list of users and then choose Administer | Disconnect User.

- **Close a specific file that someone else has opened** Choose View | By Open Files to list the files that other people have opened and then choose Administer | Close File.

- **Stop sharing a shared drive, folder, or printer** Choose View | By Shared Folder, select the item you want to stop sharing, and choose Administer | Stop Sharing Folder. Windows asks you confirm that you want to stop sharing the folder.

- **Look at the sharing properties of a shared folder** Choose View | By Shared Folder and select the shared item. Then choose Administer | Shared Folder Properties (or press ALT-ENTER). You see a dialog box that contains the same settings as the Sharing tab of the Properties dialog box for the shared item. Click OK when you are done working with the dialog box.

- **Share an additional drive or folder** Choose View | By Shared Folder and then choose Administer | Add Shared Folder. In the Enter Path dialog box that appears, type the path (address) of the item you want to share or click the Browse button to find the drive or folder. Then click OK.

Caution *Before disconnecting someone or closing a file, be sure to warn the user first, so that the person can save any open files.*

Communicating over the LAN by Using WinPopup

WinPopup is a cute little program that allows you to receive messages from other people and devices on your LAN. WinPopup is not sophisticated—if you want reliable interoffice communication, you need to use e-mail. It can, however, be useful for sending short, urgent messages. For WinPopup to work, everyone who wants to send or receive messages has to be running the program. WinPopup is also available with Windows 98 and 95, and the versions are completely compatible.

 Note *WinPopup doesn't automatically install as part of Windows. To install WinPopup from the Windows Me CD-ROM, open the Control Panel, open Add/Remove Programs, click the Windows Setup tab, choose System Tools from the Components list, click Details, and choose WinPopup.*

For some reason WinPopup does not appear in the Start or Programs menu (you can put it there, of course—see Chapter 11 for details).

Running WinPopup

The WinPopup program file is stored in C:\Windows. The easiest way to run it is to look in C:\Windows using Windows Explorer. Once you see the WinPopup.exe file, you can open the icon to run WinPopup, create a shortcut on the desktop or add a shortcut to the Start menu. Or, choose Start | Run, type **winpopup**, and click OK. The WinPopup window looks like this:

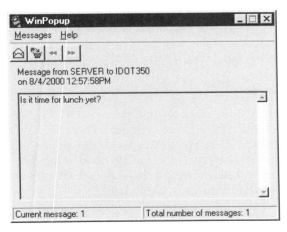

 If you plan to use WinPopup for office communication, add a shortcut it to the C:\Windows\Start Menu\Programs\StartUp folder on every computer in the office so that it runs each time Windows starts up (see Chapter 2, section "Running Programs When Windows Starts").

Sending a Message

To send a message to another user, computer, or workgroup on your LAN, choose Messages | Send, press CTRL-S, or click the Send button on the WinPopup toolbar (the leftmost button). You see the Send Message dialog box, shown here:

Use the To radio buttons to choose to send the message to a user or computer or a whole workgroup. If you choose User Or Computer, you need to fill in the name of the user or computer where you want the message to show up. (Hint: the names of the computers are available in My Network Places.) If you choose workgroup, WinPopup fills in the name of the workgroup you belong to; if you want to send the message to a different workgroup on the LAN, you need to know the name of the workgroup and fill it in. Type the message in the Message box and click OK to send it. A dialog box appears telling you that the message was successfully sent—this, however, does not mean that the message was actually received or read. WinPopup must be running for the message to be received, and the user must notice the beep that WinPopup makes when a message is received and display the WinPopup window to read the message.

Receiving a Message

When you receive a WinPopup message, it appears in the WinPopup window. If that window is minimized, however, you may not even know that a message has been received. You can change WinPopup's options so that you are more likely to read a received message. Choose Messages | Options to display the three options: you can play a sound when a new message arrives, have the WinPopup window always on top, or display a dialog box when a message is received.

Messages are stored in WinPopup for as long as the program is running. You can see how many messages you have by looking at the status bar, and you can read different messages by using the Previous and Next buttons on the toolbar. Get rid of the displayed message by clicking the Delete button on the toolbar.

The
Complete
Reference

Windows
Me

Chapter 30

Connecting Your LAN
to the Internet

If you have a LAN, connecting the whole LAN to the Internet makes more sense than connecting each individual computer on the LAN. By connecting the LAN to the Internet, all of the PCs on the LAN can share one Internet account and one phone line or cable connection.

For the PCs on a LAN to use the Internet, you must configure each PC to communicate using TCP/IP, the Internet's communication protocol. Then a program or device must *route* (send) the TCP/IP information between the LAN and the Internet; you can use a dedicated device (a *router*) or a gateway program running on a PC. You can use the IP Configuration program (Winipcfg) program to check the TCP/IP settings on your computer.

When many people share one Internet connection, you usually want a fast connection—a DSL phone line or cable Internet account. To configure a PC to connect to a one of these high-speed lines, you use a network interface card and the Network dialog box—the same type of card and program you used for connecting to a LAN (see Chapter 28). This chapter describes the general steps for configuring Windows to the Internet using an ISDN, DSL, or cable connection, although you must contact your ISP or cable company for the specifics.

Windows Me comes with Internet Connection Sharing (ICS), a gateway program that can route information between a LAN and the Internet. This chapter describes how to configure the ICS server program on the computer connected to the Internet and the ICS client program on the other computers on the LAN. Once ICS (or another gateway) is installed, everyone on the LAN can send and receive e-mail, browse the Web, and use other Internet programs at the same time. If your LAN already uses another gateway, you might need to configure your PC to connect to the Internet via that server.

Virtual Private Networking (VPN) is a system that lets your organization create a private LAN over the Internet. Windows Me comes with a VPN program that enables your computer to connect to a virtual private network, as described in the last section of this chapter.

How Does TCP/IP Work on a LAN?

When a computer communicates with other computers on the Internet, it sends messages addressed to the other computers using their numeric IP (Internet Protocol) addresses. To share an Internet connection, the computers on your LAN must be able to communicate with TCP/IP (see Chapter 28, section "Installing the Protocol"). The computers can also communicate with another protocol (for example, a LAN might use NetBEUI for file and printer sharing on the LAN and TCP/IP for Internet Connection Sharing.)

When you use TCP/IP, the network interface card in each computer on the LAN has an IP address on the LAN. IP addresses are in the format *xxx.xxx.xxx.xxx*, where each *xxx* is a number from 0 to 254. IP addresses are used on the Internet to identify Internet host computers and on LANs to identify the computers on the LAN.

On a TCP/IP LAN, computers usually use "private" IP addresses that are not used on the Internet. Several ranges of IP addresses have been set aside for private use. The most commonly used set of private IP addresses are in the format 192.168.0.*xxx*, where *xxx* is a number from 1 to 253. If one computer on the LAN connects to the Internet, that computer has the address 192.168.0.1, and the rest of the computers have addresses from 192.168.0.2 up to 192.168.0.253. Figure 30-1 shows a LAN with an IP address assigned to each computer.

How are IP addresses assigned? You can use one of three methods:

■ **Static IP addressing**   You can assign the IP addresses yourself, using addresses in the format 192.168.0.*xxx*. You need to keep track of which addresses you've assigned, so that you don't give two computers the same address. (Windows' ICS program doesn't work with static IP addressing.)

■ **Automatic private IP addressing**   This system, part of Windows Me and 98, assigns IP addresses to the computers on a LAN automatically (called *dynamic addressing*. The addresses are in the format 169.254.*xxx.xxx*, where each *xxx* can be a number from 1 to 253. (Microsoft calls this range *LINKLOCAL network addresses*. You can't use LINKLOCAL addresses with ICS, or on LANs that use DHCP addressing.

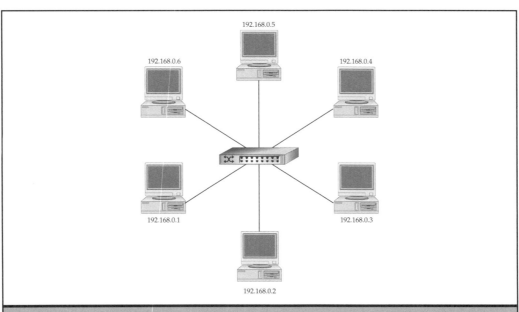

Figure 30-1.   *Assigning IP addresses to computers on a LAN*

■ **DHCP addressing**   A *DHCP server* (Dynamic Host Configuration Protocol) is a server such as Windows 2000 or NT running software that assigns IP addresses for the LAN. Like automatic private IP addressing, DHCP assigns an IP address to your computer automatically, but it is designed to work with much larger LANs. ICS includes a simplified DHCP server. Microsoft's TCP/IP networking systems generally use DHCP addressing.

When setting up a LAN that uses TCP/IP, you must choose among these IP addressing methods. Use static addressing only for very small LANs (with fewer than 10 computers) that don't use ICS. If your network includes Windows 2000 or NT computers or Linux or Unix servers, it probably already uses DHCP.

 If your computer has more than one TCP/IP connection, it needs more than one IP address. For example, your computer might have a network interface card that connects it to the LAN and a modem it uses when dialing the Internet. The network interface card has one TCP/IP address (assigned as described earlier in this section), and the Dial-Up Adapter has one TCP/IP address (assigned by your ISP).

The section "Configuring Windows to Use TCP/IP" later in this chapter describes how to configure Windows to communicate using TCP/IP.

How Can You Connect a LAN to the Internet?

The device or program that connects your LAN to the Internet acts as a *gateway*, passing messages between the computers on the LAN and computers on the Internet, and possibly controlling what types of information can pass.

What Does a Gateway Do?

An Internet gateway can perform the following tasks:

■ **Translating between the IP address on the LAN and the IP addresses on the Internet**   The gateway accepts packets (messages) on the LAN, strips off private IP address, substitutes its own IP address, and passes the packet along to the Internet. When replies return, the gateway passes the replies back to the computer that made the request. To the rest of the Internet, all packets from the LAN appear to be from the gateway, so no information leaks out about the individual systems on your LAN. This service is called *Network Address Translation (NAT)*. All gateways to networks that use private addresses must perform this task.

■ **Controlling the types of information that can flow between the Internet and your LAN**   The gateway, for example, can prevent telnet sessions (remote terminal sessions, described in section "Logging in to Other Computers Using Telnet" in Chapter 28) from coming in from the Internet or prevent chat sessions from going in either direction between the LAN and the Internet. Firewall software provides this type of control; not all gateways do.

- **Caching**   The gateway can store information that has been requested from the Internet, so that if a user requests the same information, the gateway can provide it without having to get it from the Internet again.

- **Logging usage of the Internet**   The gateway can log all packets that pass between the LAN and the Internet, so you can have a record of who has access to your LAN from the Internet, and what Internet services your LAN users have used.

Some gateway software (like ICS) provides only address translation. Other gateway programs, called *proxy servers*, provide address translation, caching, and logging. If the proxy server also provides security, controlling what information can pass between the LAN and the Internet, it's called a *firewall*.

Devices That Can Act as Gateways

Three kinds devices are commonly used as gateways, connecting LANs to the Internet:

- **Routers**   A "black box" that connects to your LAN hub or switch and to a phone line (dial-up, ISDN line, DSL line, or cable modem connection). Firewall software is built into the router. All you have to do is cable it to your LAN, plug it into power, and your LAN is on the Internet. Routers can be the simplest and most effective way to connect your LAN to the Internet. You connect your Internet connection (phone line or cable Internet cable) to the router, and run a LAN cable from the router to the LAN's hub or switch.

- **UNIX or Linux systems**   Because the Internet was built on UNIX systems, lots of excellent TCP/IP communication software comes with most UNIX and Linux systems. Many "black box" routers are actually computers running UNIX or Linux, but you can set up your own for less money. You can run a wide variety of firewall software, as well as Web server, POP (e-mail) server, or other Internet server software on the UNIX orLinux system. The UNIX or Linux system needs two connections: an Internet connection (phone line or cable Internet cable) and a LAN connection (cable to the LAN's hub or switch).

- **Windows systems running proxy server software**   A Windows Me, 98, 2000, or NT system can act as a router, running a gateway program. The Windows system connects to the Internet over a phone line or cable connection, and the gateway program provides the IP address translation. If you run proxy server or firewall programs, the Windows system also provides security.

Software and Hardware for a Windows-Based Gateway

If you use a Windows system running NAT (Network Address Translation), proxy server, or firewall software, the system has two connections: one to the LAN (using a network interface card) and the other to the Internet (using a modem for dial-up or another network interface card for DSL or cable Internet connection).

Even though DSL and cable Internet connections use the same cabling as a LAN (RJ45 Category-5 cable), don't plug the DSL or cable Internet cable into your LAN's hub or switch. The DSL or cable Internet must connect to a PC or router, so that you have a gateway between the Internet and the LAN. (Connecting the modem to the hub is possible, but tricky and prone to error.)

Several Windows-based proxy server programs have been available for years, including Sybergen SyGate (at **http://www.sygate.com**), WinGate (at **http://wingate.deerfield.com**), and WinProxy (at **http://www.winproxy.com**). All three of these programs have downloadable versions that you can try before buying. You install the proxy server program on the computer that is connected to the Internet and a matching client program on each of the other computers on the LAN. When the user of any computer on the LAN wants to check e-mail or browse the Web, the computer running the proxy server program connects to the Internet (if it's not already connected) and passes data from the user's computer to and from the Internet.

*Test the security of your LAN's Internet connection by going to the Gibson Research Corporation's Web site at **http://grc.com**. Follow the links to their Shields UP! service, which can check how vulnerable your computer is to attack or data theft from the Internet.*

What Is Internet Connection Sharing?

Windows Me comes with its own gateway program, called Internet Connection Sharing (or ICS). ICS is a NAT program, and doesn't provide any other proxy server or firewall services. ICS allows one computer—the *ICS server*—to provide an Internet connection for all the computers on a LAN. The ICS host runs the ICS server program. The other computers—the ICS *clients*—on the LAN can run Windows Me, Windows 98, Windows 95, Windows 2000, Windows NT, older Windows versions, or other operating systems, as long as they support TCP/IP.

ICS uses private IP addresses in the format 192.168.0.*xxx*. You can't use static IP addressing (Microsoft claims that there's a way, but we haven't had any luck). Instead, Microsoft suggests that you use DHCP (Dynamic Host Configuration Protocol) to assign IP addresses to the ICS clients automatically. Figure 30-2 shows a LAN with five computers, including the ICS server computer, with private IP addresses from 192.168.0.1 to 192.168.0.5. The ICS server has a separate IP address for communicating with the Internet over a DSL line; this address is assigned by the ISP (in the figure, it has the address 245.62.168.33).

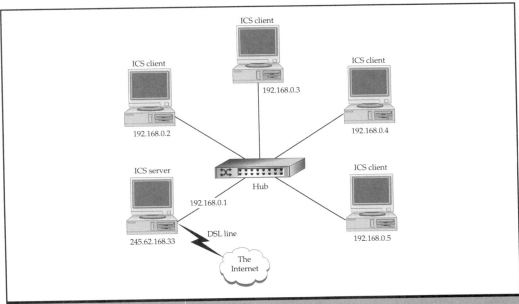

Figure 30-2.   *A LAN with Internet Connection Sharing*

ICS includes these components:

- **DHCP Allocator**   Assigns IP addresses to ICS client computers on the LAN
- **DNS Proxy**   Translates between IP addresses and Internet host names (like **www.yahoo.com**), using your ISP's DNS server
- **Network Address Translation (NAT)**   When passing packets of information between the LAN and the Internet, replaces the private IP address with the ICS server's IP address, and vice versa

The section "Configuring and Using Internet Connection Sharing" later in this chapter describes how to install ICS on the ICS server and how to configure the rest of the computers on the LAN to share the connection.

Configuring Windows to Use TCP/IP

For your computer to communicate using TCP/IP, it needs an IP address (see "How Does TCP/IP Work on a LAN?"). Here's how to configure Windows with a static (preassigned) IP address or with an automatically assigned address (the IP address is reassigned each time you start up Windows).

Assigning IP Addresses to Your Computer

If you use TCP/IP for communication on your LAN, you need to assign an IP address to your computer's network interface card, using static addressing, automatic private IP addressing, or DHCP. Follow these steps:

1. Open the Network dialog box by right-clicking the My Network Places icon on the desktop and choosing Properties from the shortcut menu. (The Network dialog box is shown in Figure 28-1.)

2. On the list of installed network components, select the binding of TCP/IP to your network interface card (for example, TCP/IP -> LinkSys EtherFast 10/100).

3. Click Properties. You see the TCP/IP Properties dialog box shown next. Click the IP Address tab if it's not already selected.

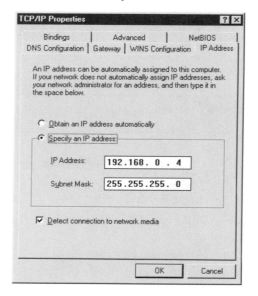

4. To assign a static IP address, click Specify An IP Address. In the IP Address box, type the IP address you've chosen. Windows supplies the dots that separate the four parts of the address. In the Subnet Mask box, type **255.255.255.0**.

5. To use automatic private IP addressing or DHCP, click Obtain An IP Address Automatically. If your LAN has a DHCP server, Windows will get IP addresses from the server. Otherwise, Windows will use its automatic private addressing feature to assign an address.

6. Click OK in each dialog box.

When you close the Network dialog box, Windows may prompt you to restart your computer.

Checking Your TCP/IP Settings with the IP Configuration Program (Winipcfg)

Windows comes with an IP Configuration program that can display your computer's IP address and other TCP/IP settings. To run IP Configuration, choose Start | Run, type **winipcfg** in the Open box, and click OK. You see the IP Configuration window:

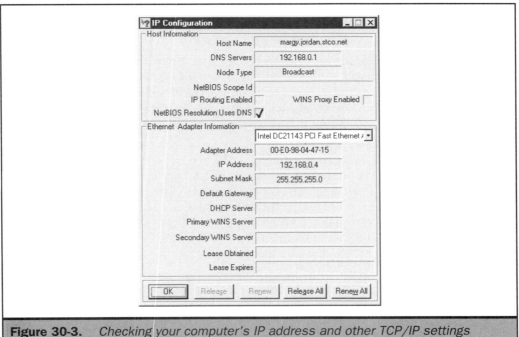

For details, click the More Info button. The IP Configuration window expands to look like Figure 30-3. If your computer has more than one network adapter configured to use TCP/IP, click the downward-pointing arrow at the right end of the box displaying

Figure 30-3. *Checking your computer's IP address and other TCP/IP settings*

the adapter name and choose another adapter. The settings in the lower part of the dialog box change to the settings you chose.

 If you have trouble with the IP addresses on the LAN, use the Networking (TCP/IP) Troubleshooter. Choose Start | Help, click Troubleshooting in the Help And Support window, click Home Networking & Network Problems, and click Networking (TCP/IP) Troubleshooter.

Connecting to a Broadband Internet Account

This section describes how to configure your Windows system to connect to the Internet using an ISDN phone line, a DSL phone line, or a cable Internet account.

Connecting with a DSL Line or Cable Internet Account

If you have a cable Internet connection or a high-speed DSL phone line, your computer connects to the Internet via a network interface card, with an RJ-45 jack (see Chapter 27, section "Buying Network Interface Cards"). Here are the general steps for configuring Windows to work with a your broadband account:

1. Install your network interface card as described in Chapter 14.

2. Your Internet connection communicates using TCP/IP, and you configure it in the Network dialog box (see Chapter 28, section "The Network Dialog Box"). Make sure that the TCP/IP protocol is installed and that it is bound to the network interface card to which your DSL or cable modem is connected (see Chapter 28, section "Installing the Protocol").

3. Delete the bindings for NetBEUI or IPX/SPX to that network interface card—you don't need them to communicate with the Internet, and they will just slow Windows down. Select the network interface card from the list of installed components, click Properties, click the Bindings tab, and make sure that TCP/IP is the only binding that is selected.

4. Your ISP, phone company, or cable Internet company should have supplied configuration instructions to set up TCP/IP to work with the DSL or cable modem, but here is information to supplement those instructions. Select the item on the list of installed network components that binds TCP/IP to the network interface card to which the DSL or cable modem is connected and click Properties. You see the TCP/IP Properties dialog box for your Internet connection that you saw in Figure 30-3.

5. Click the IP Address tab of the TCP/IP Properties dialog box. Although static IP addresses are rare among dial-up accounts, they are more common among high-speed accounts. Most ISPs run a DHCP server that assigns you an IP address when you log in: for these ISPs, you select the Obtain An IP Address Automatically on the IP Address tab. If your ISP assigns static IP addresses, click Specify An IP Address and ask your ISP what values to type into the IP Address and Subnet Mask boxes.

6. Click the DNS Configuration tab. When communicating with the Internet, your computer needs to use a DNS server, a computer that can do domain name service (translating between the numeric IP addresses that identify computers on the Internet and the names that are easier for people to use, like www.yahoo.com and net.gurus.com). Most ISPs assign a DNS server to you when you log in, and require that you select Disable DNS. Ask your ISP whether to enter static DNS server IP addresses, or whether they assign you a DNS server address when you connect.

7. Click the Bindings tab. Make sure that if File And Printer Sharing For Microsoft Networks appears as a possible binding, it isn't selected.

8. Click the Gateway tab. Most ISPs require that no IP addresses be listed on this tab. Ask your ISP.

9. Click the WINS Configuration tab. Make sure that Disable WINS Resolution is selected (ISPs don't usually use WINS).

10. When you exit from the TCP/IP Properties and Network dialog boxes, Windows may require you to restart your computer.

If you run into trouble getting your broadband connection to work, contact your ISP or cable company for the correct settings.

 If your ISP didn't give you a paper or e-mail message with the correct settings, ask for one and keep it handy.

Connecting with an ISDN Line

Before you configure Windows, install your ISDN line and terminal adapter (see Chapter 20, section "What Is ISDN?"). Then run the ISDN Configuration Wizard to set up your connection. Choose Start | Programs | Accessories | Communications | ISDN Configuration Wizard. The Wizard steps you through the procedure for configuring an ISDN connection.

 Microsoft's Web site about ISDN is at **http://www.microsoft.com/windows/getisdn**.

Configuring and Using Internet Connection Sharing (ICS)

The easiest way to install and configure ICS is by running the Home Networking Wizard, as described in the section "Configuring Your LAN Connection by Using the Home Networking Wizard" in Chapter 28. The Wizard can create a floppy disk with a version of the Wizard that you can use to configure the other Windows Me, 98, and 95 computers on the LAN.

Installing ICS on the ICS Server

One computer on your LAN, the ICS server, runs the ICS program. This computer must connect to the Internet with a dial-up account, ISDN line, DSL line, cable modem, or other Internet connection. Choose Start | Programs | Accessories | Communications | Home Networking Wizard to install ICS on the ICS server. As the Wizard asks you questions, make these choices:

- **Internet Connection**   Choose A Direct Connection To My ISP Using The Following Device. Specify the Dial-Up Networking connection (or for DSL or cable Internet connections, the network interface card to which the DSL or cable modem is attached).

- **Internet Connection Sharing**   Choose Yes to configure this computer as an ICS server.

- **Establishing Internet Connection**   If you want the ICS server to connect to the Internet automatically whenever anyone on the LAN requests an Internet connection, choose Yes and type your Internet user name and password. If you'd rather enter your user name and password each time the ICS server tries to connect to the Internet, choose No.

- **Computer and Workgroup Names**   Type a unique name for your computer and a name for your workgroup (see Chapter 28, section "Identifying the Computer"). If you've already got your LAN working, use the same workgroup name you've been using (we use **workgroup** for small LANs).

- **Sharing Files and Printers**   Select the folders and printers to share with other people on the LAN (see Chapter 29).

- **Home Networking Setup Disk**   Choose Yes to create a floppy disk containing a version of the Wizard that you can run on all the Windows Me, 98, and 95 computers on the LAN to configure them as ICS clients.

The Home Networking Wizard restarts your computer after it finishes installing and configuring your computer as the ICS server. Try connecting to the Internet from the ICS server—you should connect as if ICS weren't installed. Browsing, e-mail, and other Internet services should be unaffected.

ICS Server Configuration Details

Here are ways you can check the configuration of your ICS server.

Make sure that the Dial-Up Networking connection (or other Internet connection) works. To test it, connect to the Internet and browse the Web or send and receive e-mail.

Make sure that the ICS server is set to connect to the Internet whenever it receives a request to connect. To set your Internet options to dial the Internet on demand, choose Start | Settings | Control Panel, and run the Internet Options program to display the Internet Properties dialog box (shown in Figure 21-7). Click the Connections tab and choose Always Dial My Default Connection so that Windows can connect to the Internet on demand (see Chapter 21, section "Setting Additional Dial-Up Networking Options"). Click the default connection and click the Settings button to display the Settings dialog box for the connection, as shown in Figure 30-4. The name of the connection is part of the dialog box's title.

On the Settings dialog box for your Internet connection, the user name and password should appear (you supplied these when you ran the Home Networking Wizard to install ICS). Edit them if they have changed, or might be wrong. The Automatic Configuration and Proxy Server settings are used if your computer is a on a LAN with another computer running a proxy server other than ICS. None of these settings should be selected. Click the OK button to dismiss this dialog box.

On the Internet Properties dialog box, click the Sharing button to see the Internet Connection Sharing dialog box, shown in Figure 30-5. You can also see this dialog box by right-clicking the ICS icon in the system tray and choosing Options from the shortcut menu. The settings are as follows:

- **Enable Internet Connection Sharing**   Clear this check box if you want to turn ICS off temporarily.

- **Show Icon In Taskbar**   Select this check box if you want the ICS icon to appear on the system tray section of the Taskbar. See "Using Internet Connection Sharing" for how to use the ICS icon to monitor ICS activities on the LAN.

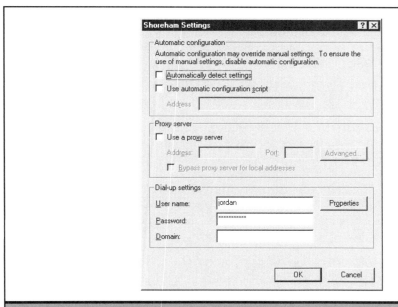

Figure 30-4.   *Connection settings for your ISP*

NETWORKING
WITH WINDOWS ME

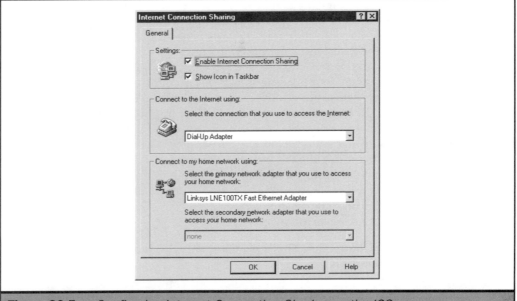

Figure 30-5.   *Configuring Internet Connection Sharing on the ICS server*

- **Connect To The Internet Using**   Select the network adapter with which you connect to the Internet. For dial-up Internet accounts, choose Dial-Up Adapter. For DSL or cable Internet accounts, choose the network interface card that connects to your DSL or cable modem.

- **Connect To My Home Network Using**   Select the network interface card that attaches your computer to the LAN.

Click the LAN Settings button on the Internet Properties dialog box to see the Local Area Network (LAN) Settings dialog box, shown in Figure 30-6. These are settings you might need to use if you connect to the Internet using a proxy server other than ICS. For ICS, select Automatically Detect Settings and leave the rest of the settings deselected.

Make sure that the ICS networking components are installed. In the Control Panel, run the Network icon. You should see installed components that look like this (items in italics don't appear exactly as shown on your list of installed components; substitute the name of the appropriate network interface card):

- Client For Microsoft Networks
- Dial-Up Adapter or *<network interface card for connection to a DSL or cable Internet>* account
- Internet Connection Sharing adapter

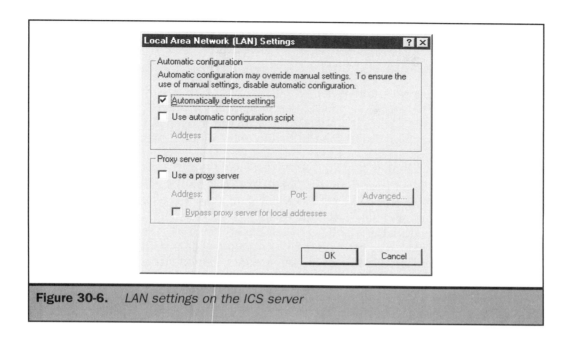

Figure 30-6.   *LAN settings on the ICS server*

- *<Network interface card for connection to the LAN>*
- Internet Connection Sharing (protocol) -> Dial-Up Adapter or *<network card for Internet>*
- Internet Connection Sharing (protocol) -> Internet Connection Sharing
- Internet Connection Sharing (protocol) -> *<network card for LAN>*
- TCP/IP (Home) -> *<network card for LAN>*
- TCP/IP (Shared) -> Dial-Up Adapter or *<network card for Internet>*
- TCP/IP -> Internet Connection Sharing

You may also see File And Printer Sharing For Microsoft Networks entries for file sharing on the LAN.

If other network protocols are installed (like NetBEUI or IPX/SPX), you may see additional protocols bound to Internet Connection Sharing, like NetBEUI -> Internet Connection Sharing or IPX/SPX -> Internet Connection Sharing. Delete those protocols, since Internet Connection Sharing works only with TCP/IP. If NetBEUI or IPX/SPX are bound to the Dial-Up Adapter, delete those entries, too.

If the TCP/IP entries don't appear, or don't include "(Home)" for the LAN network adapter and "(Shared)" for the connection to the Internet, ICS isn't installed properly, and you need to uninstall and reinstall it.

NETWORKING
WITH WINDOWS ME

Make sure that the network interface card to which the LAN is attached is ready to communicate using TCP/IP. Select your network card from the list of installed components on the Network dialog box, click the Properties button, click the Bindings tab, make sure that a check mark appears by the TCP/IP (Home) and Internet Connection Sharing entries, and click OK.

Check the TCP/IP settings on the ICS server by running the IP Configuration program (see "Checking Your TCP/IP Settings with the IP Configuration Program"). Click the More Info button. Set the box at the top of the Ethernet Adapter Information section to the network interface card to which your LAN is connected. Make a note of the IP address, because the ICS clients on the LAN need this IP address as part of their configuration—this IP address is always 192.168.0.1. The DNS Servers, Default Gateway, and DHCP Server boxes should all be blank (see "How Does TCP/IP Work on a LAN?"). IP Routing Enabled should be selected.

Take a look at the Icssetup.log file, which is stored in your C:\Windows folder. It lists the actions that the Home Networking Wizard took when installing and configuring ICS, including searching your system for networking components and deciding which to use.

Configuring the ICS Clients

You must configure each of the ICS clients—the other computers that share the ICS connection to the Internet. When you installed the ICS server, the Home Networking Wizard created a floppy disk that contains a version of the Wizard with which you can configure the ICS clients. The Wizard configures only computers running Windows Me, 98, or 95.

To configure your computer as an ICS client, insert the floppy disk that the Home Networking Wizard created, choose Start | Run, type **a:setup**, and click Open. As the Wizard asks you questions, make these choices:

- **Internet Connection**   Select A Connection To Another Computer On My Home Network That Provides Direct Access To My Internet Service Provider (ISP).

- **Computer and Workgroup Names**   Type a unique name for your computer and a name for your workgroup (see Chapter 28, section "Identifying the Computer"). Use the same workgroup name you entered for the ICS server.

- **Sharing Files and Printers**   Select the folders and printers to share with other people on the LAN (see Chapter 29).

- **Home Networking Setup Disk**   Choose No, since you already have a disk.

The Home Networking Wizard may restart your computer after it finishes installing and configuring your computer as an ICS client. If it doesn't restart your system automatically, remove the floppy disk from the drive and restart it yourself.

When you ask a browser or other Internet program to display a Web page or sent or received e-mail, the ICS server should connect to the Internet, rather than your own ICS client computer. If the ICS server was already logged into the Internet, you should see your Web page or e-mail right away; if the ICS server has to connect, there's the usual delay in logging in. Once the ICS server and clients are configured correctly, users on all ICS servers and clients can use the Internet connection simultaneously.

ICS Client Configuration Details

Here are ways you can check the configuration of your ICS client.

Check that your computer is configured to communicate over the LAN using TCP/IP. Choose Start | Settings | Control Panel and run the Network icon. Check that TCP/IP -> *<your network card>* appears in the list of installed components in the Network dialog box. You may also see TCP/IP -> Dial-Up Adapter, which you can use to dial into the Internet when you're not on the LAN (this is especially useful if your computer is a laptop).

If the TCP/IP entries don't appear, install TCP/IP by clicking the Add button, choosing Protocol, clicking the Add button, choosing Microsoft from the list of manufacturers, choosing TCP/IP from the list of network protocols, and clicking OK (see Chapter 28, section "Installing the Protocol"). Configure your network card to communicate with TCP/IP by selecting your network card from the list of installed components on the Network dialog box, clicking the Properties button, clicking the Bindings tab, and making sure that the TCP/IP entry on the list is selected.

Configure Windows to assign your computer a private IP address automatically. In the list of installed components in the Network dialog box, click the TCP/IP -> *<your network card>* component, and click the Properties button to display the TCP/IP Properties dialog box that you saw above. On the IP Address tab, select Obtain An IP Address Automatically, which uses DHCP to assign a private IP address to this computer.

On the Gateway tab of the TCP/IP Properties dialog box, if any gateways appear on the Installed Gateways list, select each one and click Remove. On the DNS Configuration tab, choose Disable DNS. On the WINS Configuration tab, choose Use DHCP for WINS Resolution (it's at the bottom of the dialog box). Click OK to dismiss the TCP/IP Properties dialog box. Click OK to dismiss the Network dialog box. (If you changed your network settings, Windows asks you to restart the computer. Do so.)

Check to see that your computer is not configured to connect to the Internet directly. Choose Start | Settings | Control Panel and run the Internet Options program. On the Connections tab of the Internet Properties dialog box (shown in Figure 21-7), select either Never Dial A Connection or Dial Whenever A Network Connection Is Not Present. (If no connections appear in the Dial-Up Settings box, the Never Dial A Connection setting is gray, but it's still selected.)

Click the LAN Settings button on the Connections tab of the Internet Properties dialog box to display the Local Area Network (LAN) Settings dialog box (shown in Figure 30-6). None of the check boxes should be selected.

Check the TCP/IP settings on the ICS client by running the IP Configuration program (see "Checking Your TCP/IP Settings with the IP Configuration Program"). Click the More Info button. Set the box at the top of the Ethernet Adapter Information section to the network interface card to which your LAN is connected. The IP Address should be in the format 192.168.0.*xxx*, where *xxx* is a number other than 1 (because the ICS server is always 192.168.0.1). The DNS Servers, Default Gateway, and DHCP Server boxes should all be 192.168.0.1—the ICS server performs all those functions. IP Routing Enabled should not be selected.

Using Internet Connection Sharing

Once you've configured the ICS server and the ICS clients, ICS is easy to use. From either the server or a client, run a Web browser, e-mail program, or other program that works with the Internet. When the program sends information to or requests information from the Internet, the ICS server connects to the Internet to provide the Internet connection.

To see how many people are sharing the Internet connection on the ICS server, double-click the ICS icon on the system tray (or click it and choose Status from the menu that appears). A small dialog box pops up, telling you how many computers are sharing the connection, including the ICS server itself.

Troubleshooting ICS

If you can't get connected to the Internet from an ICS client computer, here are some things to try.

■ Give the ICS server time to connect to the Internet. The program on the ICS client may time out before the ICS server gets connected to your Internet account and ICS passes your request along.

■ If you have restarted the ICS server since you restarted the ICS client, restart the client.

■ Check the settings on the ICS server and client as described in the preceding sections.

■ Run the Internet Connection Sharing Troubleshooter on the ICS server and at least one ICS client. Choose Start | Help, click Troubleshooting, click Home Networking & Network Problems, and click Internet Connection Sharing Troubleshooter.

■ Run the Network Diagnostics program. Choose Start | Programs | Accessories | System Tools | System Information. Then choose Tools | Network Diagnostics from the Help And Support window that appears.

Using Gateway Programs Other Than ICS

ICS isn't the only (or the best) program that allows computers on a LAN to share an Internet account. Your LAN may share an Internet connection using another NAT, a proxy server, or firewall system. WinGate, WinProxy, Sygate, and other proxy servers have been around since before Microsoft added ICS to Windows 98 Second Edition, and these products have many more options and capabilities than ICS. Or, your LAN may connect to the Internet via a router, which contains a built-in proxy server.

To connect to the Internet via another gateway, you need to configure Windows to find the gateway. Choose Start | Settings | Control Panel, open the Internet Options icon, and click the Connections tab of the Internet Properties dialog box that appears. Click LAN Settings to display the Local Area Network (LAN) Settings dialog box shown in Figure 30-6. The dialog box contains these settings:

- **Automatically Detect Settings**   Configure this connection by detecting settings stored in a configuration file created by your LAN administrator.

- **Use Automatic Configuration Script**   Configure this connection by running a script created by your LAN administrator. Type the address of the script in the Address box.

- **Use A Proxy Server**   Connect to the Internet via a proxy server. Enter the IP address of the proxy server (frequently **192.168.0.1**) and the port number on the proxy server (usually left blank, to use the default port).

- **Bypass Proxy Server For Local Addresses**   Do not use the proxy server when connecting to computers on your LAN.

The Advanced button displays the Proxy Settings dialog box shown in Figure 30-7, in which you specify addresses for use with your proxy server. On small LANs, one gateway handles all the traffic between the LAN and the Internet. Larger LANs may have several proxy servers, with different proxy servers handling different types of Internet traffic. Your LAN administrator can tell you whether you need to fill in different addresses in this dialog box. For small LANs, select the Use The Same Proxy Server For All Protocols check box.

Connecting to Your Organization's LAN with Virtual Private Networking

Many large organizations have LANs that are accessible to computers within the organization (see Chapter 27). Although the LAN is connected to the Internet, users on the Internet can't access information on computers on the LAN, because a firewall connects the LAN to the Internet and controls what information can pass through.

What if you work for such an organization and you are on a business trip? You can connect to the Internet through an Internet provider, but how can you access your organization's LAN? *Virtual Private Networking* (*VPN*) provides a way for an authorized computer on the Internet to *tunnel* through the firewall and connect to a LAN.

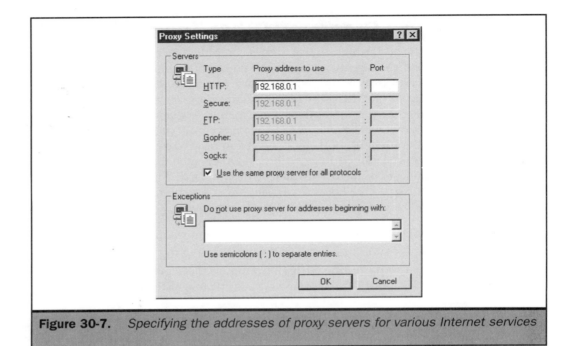

Figure 30-7. *Specifying the addresses of proxy servers for various Internet services*

To work, your organization's firewall must support *Point-to-Point Tunneling Protocol* (*PPTP*). PPTP lets VPN connect you through the firewall. Your organization's LAN administrator must have set up the firewall and a *VPN server*, the program that provides PPTP. You'll need to contact your organization's system administrator to find out the host name of the virtual private networking server.

To connect to your organization's LAN, you use two Internet connections from your computer. One connection—a Dial-Up Networking connection for a dial-up account or network connection for a DSL or cable Internet account—connects your computer to the Internet. A second connection, which is always a Dial-Up Networking connection, "tunnels" through the Internet and your organization's firewall to connect to your LAN.

Note *VPN is not automatically installed when you install Windows. If it is not, open the Control Panel, open the Add/Remove Programs icon, click the Windows Setup tab, choose Communications from the list of components, click Details, and select Virtual Private Networking from among the Communications options. You might need to insert your Windows Me CD-ROM.*

Follow these steps for using VPN to connect to a LAN through a firewall:

1. Sign up with an ISP so that you can connect to the Internet from where you plan to be located. Configure Dial-Up Networking to connect to your dial-up Internet account (or configure your computer for your ISDN, DSL, or cable Internet account). Test your Internet connection.

2. Create another Dial-Up Networking connection for your VPN connection. Choose Start | Settings | Control Panel and open the Dial-Up Networking icon to display the Dial-Up Networking window (shown in Figure 21-1). Run the Make New Connection icon.

3. In the Make New Connection window, type a name for the connection (like VPN or the name of your organization) in the top box. Set the Select A Device box to Microsoft VPN Adapter. Click the Next button.

4. In the Host Name Or IP Address box, type the host name of your organization's VPN server (for example, **pptp.microsoft.com**. If your system administrator gives you the IP Address of the server, you can type that instead (see Chapter 21, section "Configuring a TCP/IP Connection"). Click Next.

5. You see a window confirming that you have created a Dial-Up Networking connection. Click Finish.

Now when you want to connect to your private network, connect to the Internet through the Dial-Up Networking connection for your ISP, and then connect to the private network through the connection you just created.

Tip   *Some ISPs offer PPTP services that let you connect to your private network by using one Dial-Up Networking connection. If your Internet provider does offer these services, ask your ISP what to type in the User Name box in the Dial-Up Networking Connect To dialog box. You may need to type an entry in the* format name@companyname.com, *rather than your usual user name. When you use this special user name, you connect both to the Internet and to your private network.*

NETWORKING
WITH WINDOWS ME

Windows Me

Chapter 31

Computer and Network Security

Windows Me is designed for use by one person at a time, so it offers only limited security features compared to UNIX, Linux, Windows 2000, or Windows NT. This chapter examines the Windows security features, including password protection, user profiles, remote administration, and the security features in Internet Explorer and Netscape Navigator. Outlook Express and other e-mail programs also offer e-mail security features. If you download files from the Web or receive attached files by e-mail (or any other way), you also need to install an antivirus program to protect your system from viruses.

What Password Protection Does Windows Offer?

Windows has many different resources that can be password protected. The major passwords are the following:

- **Windows password**   A largely cosmetic password that you enter when you enter a user name as you start up Windows or switch from one user to another. Your Windows password controls whether your user profile is active. If you do not enter a password, Windows starts anyway. If you have a laptop or other computer with advanced power management that enters standby or hibernate modes to save power, you can set Windows to ask for your Windows password when it resumes from power saving mode. You can change your Windows password at any time (see "Setting the Windows Password").

- **Network password**   The password used to validate your user name to other host computers on the network. If your network password is missing or invalid, you can't gain access to remote disks or printers. The network password you use has to match the password required by the remote servers to which you connect. To change your network password, you have to ask the manager who controls the server(s) you use to change your password on the server. (The network password doesn't affect your use of Internet resources.)

- **Screen saver password**   A password used to leave screen saver mode. Without the password, the Windows screen savers won't resume what the computer was doing previously, although you can regain control by rebooting the computer. Screen saver passwords are useful on unattended print and file servers to prevent casual or accidental misuse of the server (see "Setting the Screen Saver Password"). They can also be useful on your desktop computer if you're working on private or confidential materials to prevent casual snooping when you're away from your desk and in homes with inquisitive children who like to emulate Mother or Father and do "some work."

What Is a User Profile?

When two or more users share a computer, they don't have to argue about what color the background should be, what programs should be on the Start menu, or whether to use single-click or double-click style. Instead, each user can have a *user profile*, a folder in the directory C:\Windows\Profiles that contains files that describe each user's preferences. Each time a user logs in, Windows finds the appropriate user profile and makes the appropriate changes. If you change any of your preferences, for example, by choosing a new wallpaper, that information is stored in your user profile, so that the change will still be there the next time you log on, but not the next time someone else logs on. Whenever your computer acquires a new user, you should establish a new user profile (see "Sharing a Computer").

Table 31-1 lists the settings that are stored separately for each user. These items are stored in the C:\Windows\Profiles*username* folder, where *username* is replaced by the name of the user profile (see "Understanding a User Profile").

Profile Item	Contents
User.dat file (hidden)	This user's configuration settings for the desktop, Windows Explorer, accessibility options, and other information
Application Data folder	This user's application program configuration settings
Cookies folder	The cookies stored by this user's Web browser (see Chapter 24, section "What Are Cookies?")
Desktop folder	The items that appear on this user's desktop
Favorites folder	Items this user has added to the Favorites folder
History folder	Shortcuts to Web sites this user has viewed recently
My Documents folder	The files and folders that appear in this user's My Documents folder
NetHood folder (hidden)	This user's network settings
Recent folder (hidden)	Shortcuts to files this user has opened recently for display on the Start	Documents menu
Start Menu folder	The shortcuts and folders that Windows uses to display the Start and Programs menus for this user

Table 31-1. *Information Stored in User Profiles*

What Security Does Windows Me Provide for Resources Shared with Other Computers?

When you share disks or printers with other computers on a LAN, you can use either share-level access control (in which you assign a password to each shared resource) or user-level access control (in which you create a list of people who are allowed access to each shared resource). Share-level access control is available only on NetWare, Windows NT/2000, and other client/server networks. If your computer is on a Windows Me/98/95 peer-to-peer network, only share-level access control is available (see Chapter 27 for definitions of these types of LANs). Share-level passwords also apply when you use the Dial-Up Server to allow other computers to connect to your computer by using Dial-Up Networking (see Chapter 18, section "Connecting Two Computers by Using Dial-Up Networking").

What Security Do Web Browsers Offer?

Internet Explorer and Netscape Navigator have complex security systems that control two completely separate aspects of Web use: communication security and downloaded object security.

Communication Security

Communication security ensures that the data you transmit and receive through the Internet or an intranet is sent to and received from the actual systems with which you intend to communicate, as opposed to another system impersonating the desired system. It also ensures that messages are sent and received without being intercepted or spied upon.

No Remote Administration in Windows Me

Remote administration permits someone on one computer to manage the resources of another computer elsewhere on the network. In corporate LANs, remote administration permits system managers to fix many networking and setup problems without physically visiting your computer.

Windows 98, NT, and 2000 include remote administration features, but because Windows Me is intended for home and small business users, Microsoft has removed this feature. The Remote Administration tab still appears on the Passwords dialog box in early versions of Windows Me (choose Start | Settings | Control Panel and run the Passwords program to see it), but Microsoft has indicated that the feature is not supported in Windows Me—they may just have forgotten to remove the tab from the dialog box.

Browsers store *certificates*, cryptographic data that can identify your computer to remote computers or vice versa. Certificates are issued by *certificate authorities*, each of which has its own certificate. Internet Explorer and Netscape Navigator are each delivered with about 30 *authority certificates* that they can use to check that the certificates presented to your computer by other sites are, in fact, issued by known certificate authorities. To provide secure communication with a remote Web site, Internet Explorer and Navigator use *SSL* (*Secure Sockets Layer*) to provide a variation of the standard HTTP Web protocol, called *HTTPS*. Web servers that use HTTPS are called *secure servers*.

You can also acquire a *personal certificate* to use to identify yourself when your Internet Explorer or Navigator contacts a Web site. The most widely used authorities for personal certificates are VeriSign, at **http://www.verisign.com** and Thawte (which is owned by VeriSign) at **http://www.thawte.com**. See RSA Data Security's list of questions and answers at their Web site at **http://www.rsasecurity.com/rsalabs/faq**, for more information about certificates.

Downloaded Object Security

Internet Explorer and Netscape Navigator use two different types of *downloaded object security*—security for information you download.

Internet Explorer's Downloaded Object Security

Internet Explorer can retrieve a wide variety of files and objects, ranging from innocuous plain text files and images to potentially destructive ActiveX controls and other executable programs. Internet Explorer's downloaded object security allows you to decide, based on both the Web site where an object came from and the type of object, whether to retrieve an object, and once it's retrieved, what to do with it (see "Managing the Security of Files Downloaded by Internet Explorer"). Internet Explorer defines three levels of object access (low, medium, and high) to give varying amounts of access to your computer. You can also define custom access permissions, if the three standard settings don't meet your needs.

Internet Explorer divides the world into four *zones*:

- **Local Intranet**   Contains computers on your local network. They're usually considered fairly trustworthy, and objects are given a medium level of access to your computer.

- **Trusted Sites**   Includes the sites that you or Microsoft have listed as trustworthy. Objects from this zone generally are given the high level of access to your computer.

- **Restricted Sites**   Includes the sites that you have listed as untrustworthy. Objects from this zone are given the low level of access to your computer.

- **Internet**   Includes all sites that are not in one of the other three zones. Objects from this zone generally are given the medium level of access to your computer.

Downloaded ActiveX controls and other executable objects can and should be signed by their authors using a certificate scheme similar to that used for validating remote servers.

Netscape Navigator's Downloaded Object Security

Since Netscape Navigator supports only Java and JavaScript and doesn't support the intrinsically insecure ActiveX, it has a much simpler downloaded security system. It runs all Java and JavaScript programs in a *virtual machine* or "sandbox" that is designed to prevent deliberate or accidental damage to your system. The virtual machine doesn't include the files and hardware on your system—only a limited amount of disk space, your keyboard, mouse, and screen. For example, a Java or JavaScript program can display a stock ticker on your screen, but it can't change or delete the files on your hard disk.

What Security Features Do Mail Programs Provide?

E-mail programs offer two kinds of security: signatures and encryption. Both depend on certificates that serve as electronic identity keys. The security system that Microsoft provides with Outlook Express, *S/MIME*, uses certificates issued by third parties, such as VeriSign and Thawte. Another popular security system, *Pretty Good Privacy* (or *PGP*), lets each user generate his or her own keys (Eudora can work with PGP keys). Both are forms of *public-key cryptography*. Each certificate consists of a *public key* (or *digital ID*), a *private key*, and a *digital signature*. You keep your private key and digital signature secret, while you provide your public key to anyone with whom you exchange secure mail, either directly or via a generally available key server.

Signatures allow you to add to your mail a *signature block*, generated with your private key, that verifies the author is indeed you, and that the message was not modified in transit. Anyone who wants to validate your signature can check it by using your public key. The signature is added as an extra block at the end of the message, without modifying the other contents, so that the recipient can read your message, whether he or she validates your signature or not.

Encryption scrambles a message so that only the recipient can decode it. A message encrypted with someone's public key can be decrypted only with that person's private key. You encrypt a message with the recipient's public key, and the recipient uses his or her private key to decode it. Anyone else looking at the message would see only unreadable gibberish. It's possible both to sign and encrypt the same message, so that only the designated recipient can decode the message, and the designated recipient can then verify that the message is really from you.

Mail security depends on a *key-ring* of keys. On your key ring, you need your own private key and digital signature and the public key of everyone with whom you plan to exchange secure mail. Outlook Express security keeps your private key and digital signature as one of the properties of your Mail account and keeps other people's public keys in the Address Book (see "Sending and Receiving Secure Mail").

For more information about encryption and signature, see RSA Data Security's Web site at **http://www.rsasecurity.com** and Network Associates' Pretty Good Privacy Web site at **http://www.pgp.com**. These sites describe how to use encryption with various e-mail programs.

What Is a Virus or Worm?

One of the less appealing aspects of the Internet has been security and the potential for becoming the victim of a *virus* (a program that reproduce by infecting—or copying itself into—other files or computers). More properly, a *virus* is a self-reproducing program that can infect files on one computer but needs help in order to find other systems to infect (like people sharing programs), while a *worm* is a self-reproducing program that can send itself to other systems (e-mail viruses are actually worms). Some viruses and worms are just annoying; they take up space on your system or displaying an annoying message. But many others are destructive, deleting or altering files or clogging up Internet e-mail systems with thousands of unwanted messages (see the sidebar "How Do Viruses Spread?" for more information).

John M. Goodman, author of many computer books, says, "If your computer is in good health (with regular backups), a virus is annoying and can waste several days work. If your computer's health is shaky (with irregular or no backups), a virus can kill you."

Viruses and worms can be stored in several types of files:

- **.exe or .com (program files)**   These viruses and worms run when they are opened (clicked or double-clicked in Windows Explorer or your e-mail program, for example).

- **.doc (Word documents), .xls (Excel spreadsheets), or .mdb (Access databases)**   These files may contain viruses and worms written in Microsoft Word, Excel, or Access macro languages. The macros (customized automation instructions) usually run when you open the file. Because Word and Excel are the most popular programs that run macros, Word documents and Excel spreadsheets are the most common macro virus carriers.

- **.vbs (Visual Basic Script files)**   These viruses and worms are written in Visual Basic, and run when you click or double-click them. Visual Basic is a programming language used, among other things, to write macros for the Office suite of applications, including Outlook 2000.

The section "Preventing Infection by Viruses" describes ways to avoid receiving or running virus-infected files.

 Scraps, a Windows file type created by cut-and-paste operations, can contain executable files (including viruses and worms) that appear to be other types of (harmless) files. An article on this issue is at **http://pc-help.org/security/scrap.htm**.

How Do Viruses Spread?

The commonly cited psychological reasons for individuals to open suspicious e-mails are fear, greed, and sex. Greed is the least enticing of the dastardly trio. While fear can cause people to open an e-mail to find out how to stop something bad from happening, sex is the most effective motivator. The notorious Melissa worm by David Smith was started by simply being posted to the **alt.sex** newsgroup. Smith asked that the file not be circulated, so of course, it was. That single posting to a newsgroup was the only action that Smith performed to spread his worm throughout the world, causing millions of dollars in damages and, in some cases, days of mail server downtime for some major companies.

So, the moral of the story is: If you receive a message from someone you don't know, or from someone you know but didn't expect to hear from, approach it with caution. If it has an attachment, just delete it. If you're not sure, let it sit unopened in your inbox for a few days, while you check the anti-virus and e-mail hoax Web sites. A six or eight hour delay in opening the ILOVEYOU virus would have been enough for most people to have heard about the danger of the virus.

Sharing a Computer

When several users share a computer, user profiles allow each user to personalize the user interface, without inconveniencing the other users (see "What Is a User Profile?"). Profiles don't offer any security among users, since each user still has full access to every file on the computer, but profiles do offer a way for different users to share a computer more conveniently.

Setting Up for Multiple Users

By default, Windows treats all users the same, even if they have different user names. The system has one set of preferences for everyone, and they are stored in subfolders of the C:\Windows folder. Anyone who changes a preference changes it for everyone else.

To give each user an independent profile, open the Passwords Properties dialog box by choosing Start | Setting | Control Panel and running the Users program. Click or double-click the Users icon, depending on whether your desktop is configured for single-clicking or double-clicking (see Chapter 1, section "Choosing Between Single-Click and Double-Click"). If you haven't set up user profiles before, Windows prompts to you create a user profile now by running the Add User Wizard. If you have already created users, you see the User Settings dialog box (shown in Figure 31-1). Click the New User button to create a user profile. The Add User Wizard asks you for the user's name and password and then displays the Personalized Items Settings dialog box, shown in Figure 31-2. Choose the items that you want to store as part of the user profile.

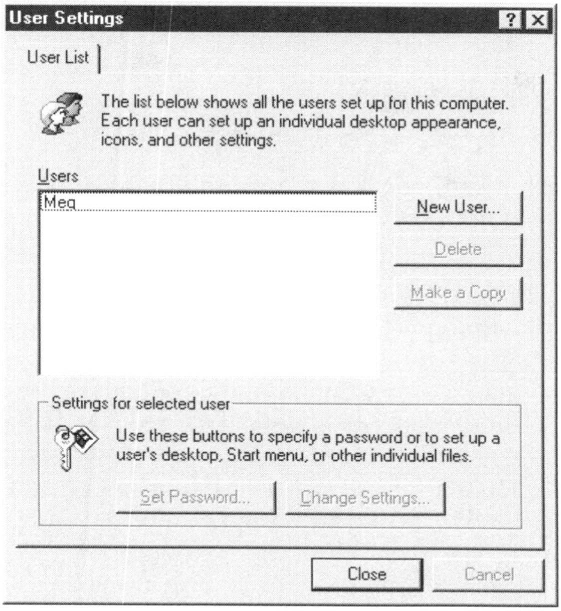

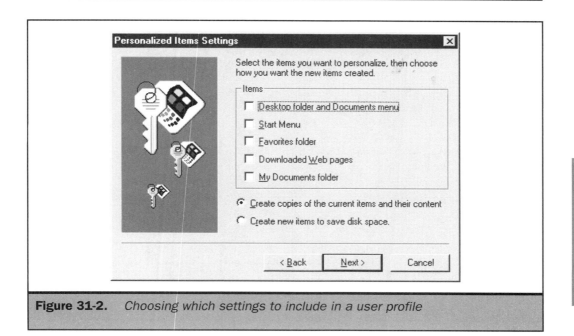

Figure 31-1.   *The User Settings dialog box*

Figure 31-2.   *Choosing which settings to include in a user profile*

You can also control whether user profiles are enabled by running the Passwords icon in the Control Panel. In the Passwords Properties dialog box, click the User Profiles tab, as shown in Figure 31-3.

At the top of the dialog box are two choices:

■ All Users Of This PC Use The Same Preferences And Desktop Settings

■ Users Can Customize Their Preferences And Desktop Settings. Windows Switches To Your Personal Settings Whenever You Log In

The first choice is the default, and provides no independence among the users. The second choice allows different users to have different backgrounds, colors, fonts, and display resolutions. The differences even go down to the application level—one user can, for example, configure the toolbars in Word differently than another user. However, not all applications store separate configurations for separate users.

The User Profile Settings check boxes at the bottom of the dialog box extend the independence of users even further. The first check box allows each user to have a different collection of shortcuts and other icons on the desktop and to have different network settings, a different preferred server, for example, or access to a different collection of shared resources.

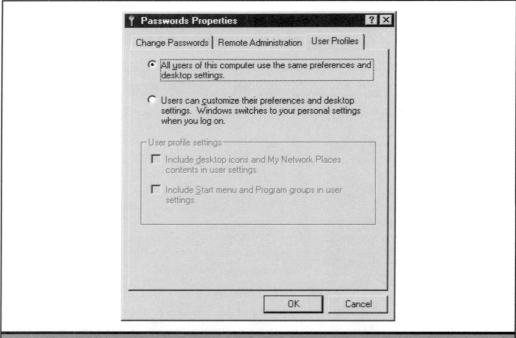

Figure 31-3.   *The User Profiles tab of the Passwords Properties dialog box*

The second check box lets each user arrange his or her own Start menu and Programs menu. This option is handy if the different users use very different collections of software. An accountant might want to have a spreadsheet program at the top of the Start menu, while a graphics designer might want a drawing program there.

 If you choose maximum independence of users, be careful that the users don't inadvertently hide resources from each other. For example, when new software is installed, the installation program typically adds it to the Programs menu or makes a desktop shortcut for it automatically—for the user doing the installation. If the other users have their own Programs menu and desktop icons, they might not realize that the new software exists. We recommend that you install your application software and other resources before setting up user profiles.

Logging On as a New User

Whenever your computer powers up, or one user logs on, the Welcome To Windows dialog box appears. If your computer is on a LAN, you see the Enter Network Password dialog box instead. The User Name box may be blank, or Windows may suggest the name of the previous user.

To establish a new user profile, follow these steps:

1. Type a new user name. If you want to have a password for this user profile, type a password. (If you leave the password line blank, you have a blank password, so you won't need to enter one in the future.)

2. Windows requests that you type your password again (if you typed a password in step 1) to ensure that you typed it correctly. Take your time with this. If you misspell it both the first *and* second time you probably won't be able to remember it when you need it.

3. Click OK. If Windows is configured to store separate settings for each user (see the previous section), Windows asks whether you want to store settings for this new user. Click Yes.

4. Windows sets up personalized settings for the desktop, Outlook Express, and other programs. Then you see the usual Windows desktop.

Modifying a User Profile

To modify the information in your user profile, change your Windows settings while you are logged in with your user name. The changes you make are stored as part of your user profile.

You can change the types of settings that are stored as part of your profile. Open the Control Panel and run the Users program to display the User Settings dialog box you saw in Figure 31-1. Select your name from the list of users and click the Change Settings button. You see the Personalized Items Settings dialog box (shown in Figure 31-2). Select the types of information you want in your user profile, click OK, and click Close to dismiss the User Settings dialog box.

NETWORKING
WITH WINDOWS ME

Displaying a List of Users When Windows Starts

You can tell Windows to display a list of user profiles when Windows starts up, so that family members don't have to type their name in the sign-in dialog box. Instead, they can choose their names from a list. To display this list, you install the Microsoft Family Logon network client that comes with Windows. Close all your programs first, because you will need to restart Windows, and then follow these steps:

1. Display the Network dialog box by right-clicking the My Network Places icon on the desktop and choosing Properties from the shortcut menu that appears, or choose Start | Settings | Control Panel and run the Network program.

2. Click Add, choose Client from the list of available network components, and then click Add. You see a list of the network clients.

3. In the Manufacturers list, click Microsoft (usually the only entry).

4. In the Network Clients list, click Microsoft Family Logon. Click OK. You return to the Network dialog box.

5. Set the Primary Network Logon box to Microsoft Family Logon. Close the network dialog box.

6. When Windows asks you if you want to restart, click Yes.

You can also delete and copy user profiles from the User Settings dialog box. If you want to create a new user with the same settings as an existing user, you can copy the existing user's profile for the new user.

Understanding a User Profile

Information about the various users of your computer is contained in the folder C:\Windows\Profiles, with one subfolder for each user name (see Table 31-1 earlier in this chapter). Once you tell Windows to maintain user profiles for each user, Windows asks, whenever someone without a profile logs in, whether the user would like to create one.

If you want to know what user names have been defined on your computer, look at the folders inside C:\Windows\Profiles.

You can get a good idea of what a user profile entails by looking at the subfolders that are created automatically inside each user profile folder (see Figure 31-4). The folder Desktop, for example, contains the shortcuts, files, and folders that appear on that

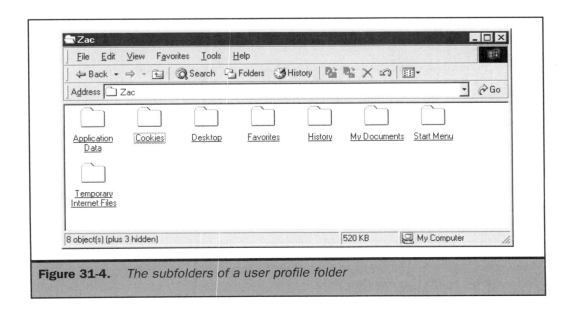

Figure 31-4. *The subfolders of a user profile folder*

particular user's desktop. The folders Cookies, Favorites, History, and Temporary Internet Files contain the information necessary to customize the user's Internet browsing (see Chapter 23). Favorites chosen by one user, for example, remain in his or her Favorites folder and are not noticed by other users (see Chapter 11, section "Adding and Editing Favorites"). The Start Menu folder gives each user a separate Start menu, and the My Documents folder contains the files that are stored in the user's My Documents folder on the desktop. The Application Data folder remembers the settings that they establish in Microsoft applications.

When a user profile is established, these folders are not empty. Instead, they are given the contents of the corresponding folders inside C:\Windows. So, for example, when Bob's user profile was established, the contents of C:\Windows\Favorites was copied into the new folder C:\Windows\Profiles\Bob\Favorites. As Bob adds or subtracts from his list of favorites, C:\Windows\Profiles\Bob\Favorites changes, but C:\Windows\Favorites does not. The other folders containing Bob's preferences behave similarly.

Note *When user profiles are in effect, changing the contents of the C:\Windows\Desktop and C:\Windows\Start Menu folders don't affect your desktop or Start menu. These folders don't belong to any user, so they are never in effect. However, when you create a new user, the contents of these folders are copied to the new user's folders. If you create many new users, edit these folders to create a default Start menu and desktop for new users or create new users by copying the user profile of an existing user.*

NETWORKING
WITH WINDOWS ME

Switching Users

When Windows starts up, you choose which user to log on as by typing the user name in the Welcome To Windows or Enter Network Password dialog box. If Windows is already running, you can switch users by choosing Start | Log Off. (Actually, the command is named Log Off, followed by the name of the current user; for example, if Margy is currently logged on, the command appears as Log Off Margy.) All programs shut down, and you see the Welcome To Windows or Enter Network Password dialog box.

If you are logged on to a local area network, the Start | Log Off command logs you off of the network, too. When you log on, you might only see the Enter Network Password dialog box, rather than the Welcome to Windows dialog box.

Undoing User Profiles

You can make your computer treat all users equally again by returning to the User Profiles tab of the Passwords Properties box and selecting All Users Of This PC Use The Same Preferences And Desktop Settings.

After you do this, it may seem as if the system has "forgotten" your recent preferences. For example, anything you added to the Favorites menu during the period when your user profile was in use is no longer there. Any icons that you added to the desktop have disappeared. You can recover any or all of this information, since it is still in the C:\Windows\Profiles*YourUserName* folder. To recover the Favorites, for example, simply open the folder C:\Windows\Profiles*YourUserName*\Favorites and copy whatever shortcuts you want into the folder C:\Windows\Favorites.

Setting the Windows Password

You can change your Windows password at any time. Open the Passwords Properties dialog box from the Control Panel, click the Change Passwords tab if it's not already selected, and click the Change Windows Password button. In the window that opens, enter your existing password as the Old Password; then enter the new password as the New Password and again as Confirm New Password for verification and click OK.

If you haven't assigned a password before, leave the Old Password blank. To remove a password, leave the two New Password fields blank.

Tip

If your Windows password and the network password are the same, Windows prompts only for the network user name and password at startup time or when changing users. If the passwords are different, Windows prompts you first for your network user name and password and then Windows user name and password. Microsoft recommends that you use the same password for both, which is more convenient although less secure than separate passwords.

Setting the Screen Saver Password

To change the screen saver password, run the Display program from the Control Panel and click the Screen Saver tab. In the middle of the Display Properties dialog box is the Password Protected check box. Check it to enable the screen saver password. To change that password, click the Change button next to the check box and type a new password into both boxes on the Change Password dialog box that appears.

Keeping Your Web Communication Secure

Internet Explorer and Netscape Navigator handle communication security by using SSL (Secure Sockets Layer) to encrypt messages sent to and from remote servers, and certificates to verify who the party is at the other end of a connection (see "Communication Security," earlier in this chapter). For example, you use this type of security when you place a credit card order with a Web-based retailer that uses a secure Web server. For the most part, SSL works invisibly, with all the security validation happening automatically. Internet Explorer and Netscape Navigator, by default, warn you when you switch between secure and normal pages. (We find these warnings annoying and turn them off.) You can tell whether the current page is secure in the following ways:

- Look at the URL for the page in the browser's Address or Location box to see whether the page's address starts with **https://** rather than **http://**.
- Look at the status bar at the bottom of the browser window to see whether a little lock icon appears. Netscape Navigator shows a padlock that is open (insecure) or closed (secure) in the lower-left corner of its window. Internet Explorer shows a lock icon on the status bar when the connection is secure.

Whenever your browser opens an HTTPS connection to a server that supports SSL, the server presents a certificate to your computer. If the certificate is validated by one of the authority certificates known to your browser, and the name on the certificate matches the name of the Web site, the browser uses the connection and displays Web pages as usual. If either of those checks fail, the Web browser warns you and gives you the option to continue. You see a Security Alert or similar dialog box when your browser can't validate a remote site's certificate. Although it's possible to continue and use the connection despite the warning, this error usually means that there is a software failure on the server.

Managing the Security of Files Downloaded by Internet Explorer

Internet Explorer has a complex security scheme for downloaded objects. For each of the four zones into which a Web page can fall, you can set the security to high, medium, or low (see "Downloaded Object Security"). For each zone, you can set exactly which remote operations you're willing to perform. To prevent downloading and running software that might infect your system with a virus, see the section "Preventing Infection by Viruses" later in this chapter.

Your Download Security Settings

To check or set your download security settings, open the Internet Options dialog box. You can open it either from the Control Panel or, in Internet Explorer, by selecting Tools | Internet Options. Click the Security tab, as shown in Figure 31-5.

Displaying and Changing Settings for Zones

To see the current settings for a zone, select that zone in the Zone box. The rest of the information on the Security tab changes to show the settings for that zone.

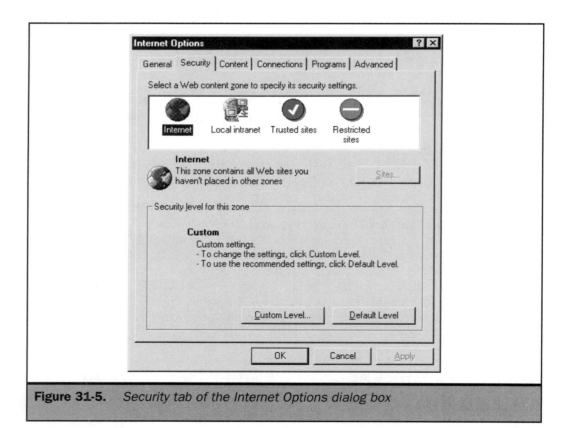

Figure 31-5.   *Security tab of the Internet Options dialog box*

To add or delete a Web site from the Local Intranet, Trusted Sites, or Restricted Sites Zones, click the Add Sites button. (There's no button for the Internet Zone, since it contains all the Web sites that are not contained in the other three zones.)

Controlling Which Web Sites Are in the Local Intranet Zone

The Local Intranet Zone normally contains sites on your own local area network, and is set up that way by your network administrator when he or she sets up the network. When you click Add Sites on the Security tab, Windows displays the Local Intranet Zone dialog box, with these three check boxes:

- **Include All Local (Intranet) Sites Not Listed In Other Zones**   Select this check box to include all other sites on the same local area network in the Local Intranet Zone. This check box is usually checked.

- **Include All Sites That Bypass The Proxy Server**   Many organizations have a *proxy server* that mediates access to sites outside the organization. Select this check box to include sites outside your organization to which your organization lets you connect directly in the Local Intranet zone. You can see a list of the sites that bypass the proxy server by displaying the Internet Properties or Internet Options dialog box, clicking the Connections tab, and clicking the Advanced button.

- **Include All Network Paths (UNCs)**   Select this check box to include all the sites with UNC addresses (Universal Naming Convention addresses), which apply only to computers on your LAN.

You can also click the Advanced button to add sites individually, as for Trusted and Restricted sites. See Chapter 30 for more information on how networks connect to the Internet.

Controlling Which Web Sites Are in the Trusted and Restricted Sites Zones

The Trusted and Restricted Sites zones start with no Web sites listed; you must specify the Web sites to include in these zones. To specify sites, select the zone to which you want to add sites, and then click Sites on the Security tab of the Internet Options dialog box. You see the Trusted Sites or the Restricted Sites dialog box, the first of which is shown in Figure 31-6. To add a new site, type its full address, starting with **https://** or **http://**, into the Add This Web Site To The Zone box and then click Add. The Web site appears in the Web Sites list. To remove a site, select it in the Web Sites list and click Remove. You can require a verified secure connection to all sites in this zone by clicking the Require Server Verification (https:) For All Sites In This Zone check box at the bottom of the dialog box; when selected, this setting prevents you from adding any sites that don't support HTTPS (see "Communication Security").

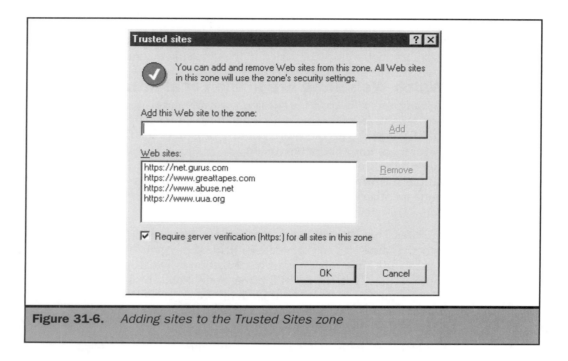

Figure 31-6. *Adding sites to the Trusted Sites zone*

Using Object Certificates When Downloading Files

Whenever Internet Explorer retrieves a Web page that uses a hitherto unknown ActiveX or Java applet, Internet Explorer checks to see whether your settings permit you to download it. If your settings don't permit the download, Internet Explorer warns you and doesn't download the file. You see the dialog box shown here:

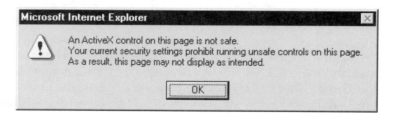

New applets usually are signed digitally by their authors, that is, each applet includes certificate information that identifies the applet's author and verifies that the applet wasn't tampered with since the author signed it (see "Communication Security"). Unless a site is in the Trusted Zone (in which case Internet Explorer accepts the applet without question), Internet Explorer displays information about the certificate, as in Figure 31-7. You see who the signer is and who verified the signature. If the signer is someone you're

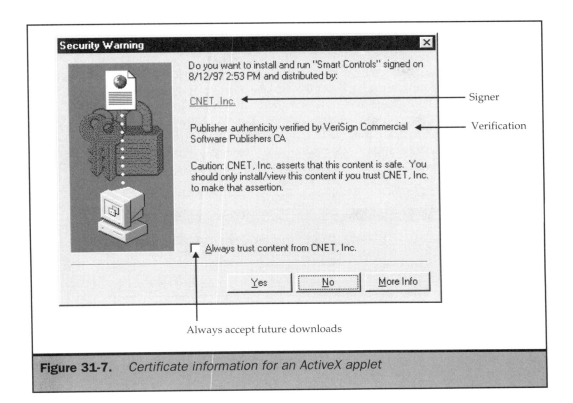

Signer

Verification

Always accept future downloads

Figure 31-7. *Certificate information for an ActiveX applet*

inclined to trust, such as a large reputable organization or someone you know personally, click Yes to accept the applet. If you expect always to accept applets from this signer, click the Always Trust Content From *ThisSigner'sName* check box at the bottom of the dialog box to tell Internet Explorer not to ask about signatures from this signer in the future. (If you check the box and later change your mind, the list of signers you've checked is in the Internet Properties dialog box; click the Content tab and then click Publishers to examine and change the list.)

Managing Your Certificates

If you expect to download many programs (or display Web pages that contain applets), you will end up with a collection of certificates with which Internet Explorer can verify the sources of the programs. You can also get your own certificate to identify yourself to secure remote Web servers that demand user certificates for identification. (There are almost no such servers now, but there probably will be in the future. As of mid-2000, only Thawte (at **http://www.thawte.com**) offers free personal certificates.) You can see lists of the certificates that you have received. Click the Content tab on the Internet Options dialog box. Click the buttons in the Certificates section of the dialog box.

NETWORKING WITH WINDOWS ME

Managing Your Personal Certificates

Clicking the Certificates button in the Certificates section of the Content tab displays the Certificates dialog box, shown in Figure 31-8. You see a list of the certificates you have installed on your computer that you can use to identify yourself.

If you receive a certificate and store it on your disk, click Import to read the certificate and include it on the list in this dialog box. Windows can read certificates stored in personal certificate files (with the extension .pfx). You can export a certificate and its associated information to a personal certificate file; select the certificate from the list on the Certificates dialog box and click Export. See "Getting a Certificate," later in

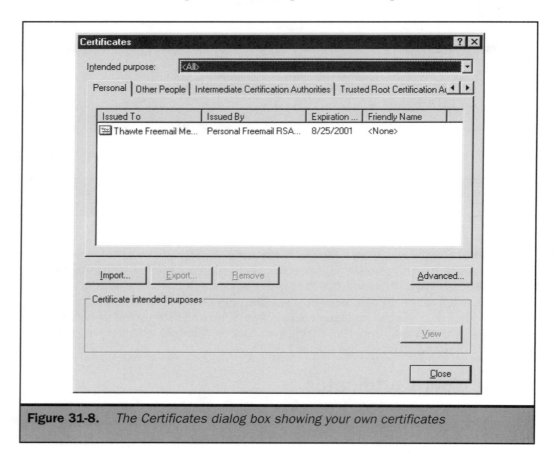

Figure 31-8.   *The Certificates dialog box showing your own certificates*

this chapter, for how to get your own certificate. If you get a certificate in Internet Explorer, you can export it to a file and then import the certificate from that file into Netscape Navigator or vice versa.

Managing Certificates from Certificate Publishers

Clicking the Publishers button on the Content tab displays the Authenticode Security Technology dialog box, shown in Figure 31-9. The dialog box lists certificates for software publishers that you have told your browsers to trust (by clicking the Always Trust Content From check box in the Security Warning dialog box, shown in Figure 31-7). New certificates are added when you download authenticated software from the Internet. You can delete a certificate from this list by selecting it and clicking Remove.

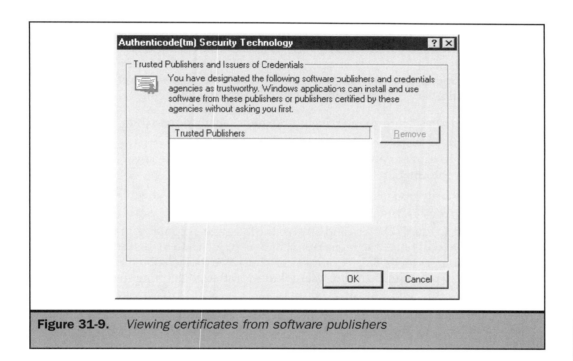

Figure 31-9.   *Viewing certificates from software publishers*

Sending and Receiving Secure Mail

Outlook Express and other Microsoft e-mail programs provide a certificate-based system (called S/MIME) for signing and encrypting mail (see "What Security Features Do Mail Programs Provide?"). *Signed* mail uses your own certificate to prove to the recipient that the author of the message is you, and that the message arrived without tampering (these are the same type of certificates described in the preceding sections for authenticating material you download from the Web). *Encrypted* mail uses the recipient's certificate to protect the message's contents, so that only the intended recipient can read the messages. A single message can be both signed and encrypted.

Getting a Certificate

The only source of certificates is a certificate authority, and for a certificate to be useful, the authority has to be one that is widely accepted. The best-known certificate authority is VeriSign, at **http://www.verisign.com**, who also owns Thawte at **http://www.thawte.com**. It provides a variety of certificates at various prices, usually including a free two-month trial of a personal certificate suitable for signing e-mail. The certificate authority's Web site walks you through the process of getting a certificate. Details vary, but generally the steps include the following:

- You enter basic information, including your e-mail address, into a form on the authority's Web site.

- Your Web browser automatically downloads your private key, part of the security information from the authority.

- The authority e-mails a confirmation code to the address you give. This ensures that the address you provide is really yours.

- You run Outlook Express and receive the message. It contains the URL of a page that will finish the registration, and a unique code to identify yourself when you get there. Use Windows cut-and-paste tool to copy the code from your mail program to the browser window, rather than trying to retype it.

- The authority generates the public key that matches your private key and downloads it as well.

 This process of obtaining a certificate only verifies your e-mail address, not any other aspect of your identity. VeriSign offers more secure certificates with more careful identity checks, but the vast majority of certificates in use are the simplest kind.

Sending Signed Mail

Once you have a certificate, sending signed mail is simple. While you're composing a message in Outlook Express, click the Digitally Sign Message button (the one with the little orange seal) to tell Outlook Express to sign the message as it's sent. Signed messages appear with the orange seal in the list of messages, as shown here:

Sending Encrypted Mail

Sending encrypted mail is only slightly harder than sending signed mail. The difference is that before you can send signed mail to someone, you have to have that recipient's digital ID (public key) in your Windows Address Book (see Chapter 5, section "Storing Addresses in the Address Book"). Once you have the digital ID, create the message as usual in Outlook Express and click the Encrypt Message button (the envelope with the little blue lock) before sending the message. The encrypted mail icon looks like this:

There are three common ways to obtain someone's digital ID: from a signed message he or she sent, from an online directory, or from a file obtained elsewhere, such as a Web-based lookup system.

Getting a Digital ID from Incoming Mail

Any time someone sends you a digitally signed message, you can get that person's digital ID from the message and add it to your Address Book. (Note that the digital ID is the equivalent of the sender's public key; the corresponding private key is not disclosed.) Open the message, select File | Properties and then click the Security tab; you see the dialog box shown in Figure 31-10 (the title bar reflects the subject line of the message). Assuming that the signature is valid, click Add Digital ID To Address Book. The Address Book opens, creating a new entry for your correspondent (if one does not already exist). Click the Digital IDs tab and observe that a digital ID is listed; then click OK to update the Address Book.

Getting a Digital ID Through LDAP Search

If you know that your correspondent has a digital ID, and you know which certificate authority issued it, you can look it up in that authority's directory.

In Outlook Express, open the Address Book and then click the Find button to open the search window, shown in Figure 31-11. In the Look In box, select the directory to search, which is most likely VeriSign for personal digital IDs. Enter the person's name or e-mail address and click Find Now.

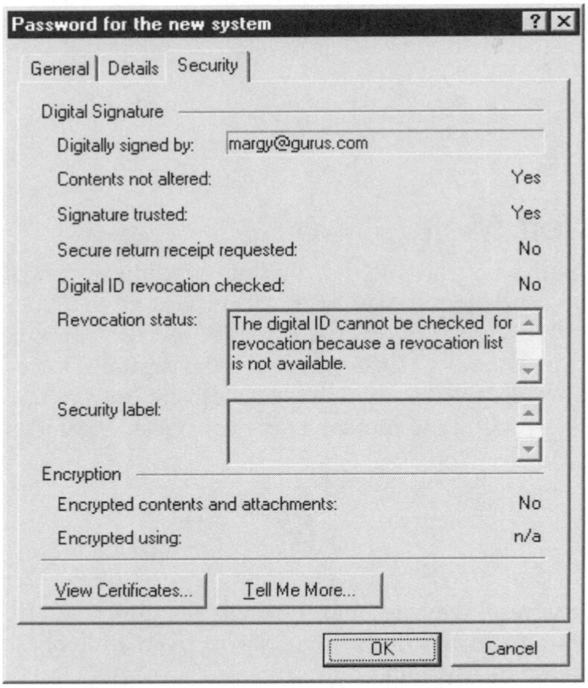

Figure 31-10.   *Getting a digital ID from a mail message*

The directory returns a list of entries that match your request. Double-click any entry in the list to see the details, which are arranged like an address book entry, to be sure it's the person you want. If it is, click Add To Address Book to turn it into an Address Book entry, edit as desired (adding more personal info, usually), and click OK to update the Address Book.

Getting a Digital ID from a File

Digital IDs can be stored in certificate files, usually with the extension .cer. Someone can mail you a third party's ID as a file, or you might download the file from a Web-based search system.

To add the digital ID to your Address Book, open the Address Book and create an entry for the person, including his or her e-mail address. (The e-mail address has to match the one to which the certificate is assigned.) Then click the Address Book's Digital IDs tab, shown in Figure 31-12. Click the Import button and select the file

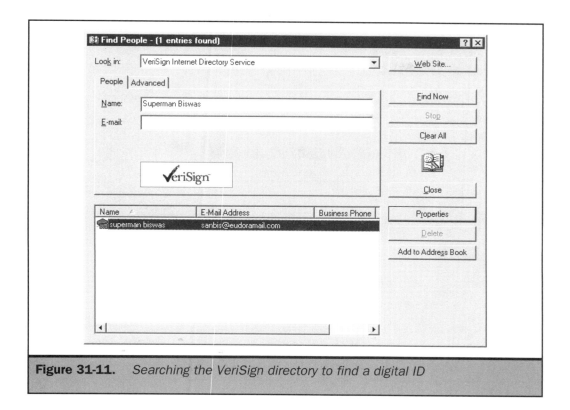

Figure 31-11. *Searching the VeriSign directory to find a digital ID*

containing the ID. The Address Book reads the digital ID and adds it to the Address Book entry.

If you want to store someone's digital ID in a file to transfer it to another computer or send it to a third person, open the Address Book entry for that person, click the Digital IDs tab, click Export, and then specify the file to create.

 Don't try to export your own digital ID this way; bugs in Windows keep it from working. Remember, you can send anyone your digital ID by sending a signed e-mail message.

Receiving Encrypted or Signed Mail

Outlook Express automatically handles incoming encrypted or signed mail. Signed messages have a little orange seal at the right end of the Security line of the message headers; encrypted messages have a little blue lock. When you open the message, Outlook Express automatically validates the signature or decrypts the message. The

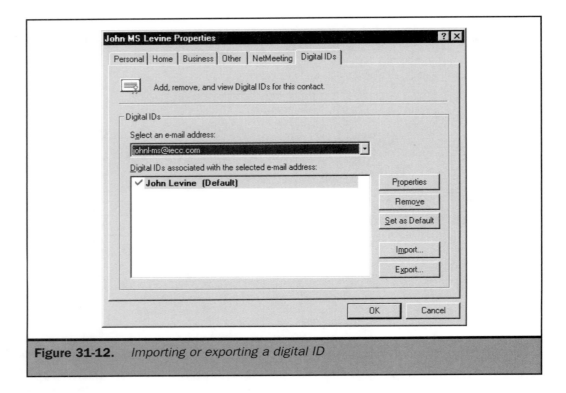

Figure 31-12.   *Importing or exporting a digital ID*

first time it does so, it displays a special window in place of the actual message, telling you what it did. Scroll down and click Continue to see the actual message. If you'd rather not see the special window in the future, a box above the Continue button lets you avoid the window in the future.

Preventing Infection by Viruses

The best prevention for viruses is to avoid getting infected in the first place (practice safe computing). If you do get infected, tools are available to clean your system.

Avoiding Getting Infected

The generally accepted method of preventing viruses (described in section the "What Is a Virus or Worm?" earlier in this chapter) from successfully attacking your computer is the use of *antivirus software*—programs that detect known viruses before they run and infect your computer. Of course, there is the tried and true method of not downloading or opening anything that you cannot verify, validate, or otherwise determine the source.

Note   *The Internet isn't the only way to catch viruses. If you commonly move files from one place to another using removable media (for example, floppy disks, writable CD-ROMs, Zip disks, or Jaz disks) then you need to be careful with these as well. The data on a disk, whether it be from school, office, or library, likely came from the Internet. This simple fact makes it possible for the disk to contain a virus. Office networks are typically more secure, because your LAN administrator has probably installed antivirus software, but don't take that for granted. School networks can be less secure because of insufficient staffing resources. Public access points like ones in libraries, copy shops, or cyber cafés are a mixed bag. Your best bet is to be wary of any data coming to your computer from the outside. Even commercial software has been known to be a transmission source for viruses. Trust no one. When in doubt, wait at least 24 hours before opening attachments, and check an anti-virus Web site in the meantime.*

Antivirus Programs

Take our word for it and do *not* wait until you have contracted a virus to install an antivirus program. An antivirus program can't prevent infection if it's not running. Buying and installing an antivirus application is a small price to pay, compared to losing all of your work for a week, all of your carefully collected bookmarks, the hours that you spent making all of your CDs into MP3 files, your family pictures from last year's picnic in Hawaii—whatever your most treasured files include. Here are some of the most popular and effective antivirus programs:

- **Symantec Norton AntiVirus, at (http://www.symantec.com/nav)**   Norton AntiVirus is a complete solution. You can go with the simple Norton AntiVirus or pop for the complete Internet Security Family Edition suite of security applications—the Family Edition is a particularly good deal, including a personal *firewall* application that is particularly well suited to protecting broadband (cable and DSL) users.

- **McAfee VirusScan, at http://www.mcafee.com**   McAfee has lately turned many of their programs into online applications—online information services that are updated 24 hours a day. They also offer an application update service that tracks what you have and sends you updates as they become available.

- **Dr. Solomon's Virex, at http://www.drsolomon.com**   The Doctor offers a simple, straight-forward approach to virus protection: research. They maintain a solid database of information on viruses that have plagued computer-kind for years.

Note   *McAfee and Dr. Solomon's are owned by Network Associates, Inc. (NAI), so they share some resources. Two in particular are the online storefront and the virus information knowledge base.*

After you install an antivirus program, make sure that you arrange to get regular updates. Some antivirus programs can update themselves by downloading lists of viruses from the manufacturer's Web site automatically. You also can visit the manufacturer's Web site and download new virus lists yourself. An antivirus program won't protect you from the latest virus if your virus lists are months old.

Once you have an antivirus program installed, configured, and running according to the documentation that came with the program, the antivirus program scans all incoming files (via e-mail and Web) for viruses. Some antivirus programs also scan your hard disk regularly to look for viruses that might have sneaked through. If the program sees a virus, it displays a message telling you what to do. For example, the antivirus might display a dialog box while you are retrieving your e-mail, reporting that a message contains the Happy99 virus and offering to delete it for you.

Practicing Safe Computing Online

Here's a brief list of ways to protect yourself when you're online:

- Do not open an attachment that you either did not specifically request or that would not normally be unexpected. If a colleague sends you a file that you asked for, it's likely to be safe. But if someone named GaToR | RoTaG or something similar sends you a file, don't touch it. Similarly, if someone you know (whose address book you are likely to be in) sends a file you aren't expecting, write back and ask about it *before* opening the file.

- Before opening an attachment, wait a few hours or days. In the meantime, check an antivirus Web site for news of new viruses and worms.

- Do not download files from sources you are not familiar with. Stick to known, reputable Web sites like ZDNet (**http://www.zdnet.com**), Tucows (**http://www.tucows.com**), and C I Net (**http://www.cnet.com**), or the Web sites of well-known hardware and software manufacturers, as sources for downloadable software. Many pornographic sites require you to download a viewer program: think twice, since these programs have been known to contain dangerous viruses.

- Do not accept any file that is offered unsolicited. If you receive an e-mail notifying you that you have won a contest and you can click a URL in the message to download your prize, think again. Did you sign up for a contest? Legitimate sources invariably draw from an existing customer base and rely on word of mouth and advertising campaigns to get new customers, not random free give-aways.

- Ask friends and family not to forward too many jokes to you (or choose *one* friend to be your Internet joke source). This reduces your potential for infection, as well as cutting down on your e-mail volume.

Avoiding Outlook and Outlook Express

Many people believe that your computer can't get infected by a virus simply by opening a e-mail message that has no attachments. This used to be true, but is no longer. Formatted e-mail messages can carry viruses, too.

Due to a known security hole in the version of Outlook Express that shipped with Windows 98, scripts can be executed when a message is opened by simply placing the scripting code into the message body. The Wscript.Kakworm.B worm discovered on July 27, 2000 performs exactly this action by placing a 4Kb "signature" into every e-mail message sent by Outlook Express on the infected computer. Once the message is opened, Outlook Express scans the file and executes any code of a specific type. If the worm is not removed properly, its *payload* (infecting code) runs on the eleventh of each month at 4 P.M. and subsequently shuts down your computer. More on this worm can be found at the Symantec AntiVirus Research Center (SARC) at **http://www.symantec.com/avcenter/venc/data/wscript.kakworm.b.html**. Microsoft has a patch that fixes this security bug; follow the link from the SARC page to download it.

*One simple solution to this and many other worms is not to use Outlook or Outlook Express. If you use Eudora, an excellent and widely used e-mail program from Qualcomm, Inc. (at **http://www.eudora.com**), you can avoid most viruses by not opening attached files.*

Knowing When You're Infected

You may find out that your system is infected when you see a strange message, telling you that you're a victim. Some other ways of telling are as follows (although all but the last can be signs of other Windows problems):

- Your system slows down (especially programs loading).
- Files disappear.
- Programs crash unexpectedly.
- For e-mail based viruses, people e-mail you to say that they received a virus from you.

Dealing with an Infected Windows System

If you have already been infected with a virus, follow these steps:

1. If an unfamiliar dialog box, error message, or something else unfamiliar appears, make a note of the message or other symptom. Then shut down the computer. Continuing to use an infected computer is a bad idea for several reasons. Depending on what type of virus or worm you have, additional damage can be done. With the speed of today's systems, a virus or worm can

delete or write over gigabytes of data in a matter of minutes. Also, some viruses exploit functions in Microsoft Outlook and Outlook Express that can cause your computer to forward a copy of the virus to all entries in your address book.

2. Do not try to repair or otherwise contain the damage or effects of a virus or worm using software that was not specifically designed to do so. In other words, don't run Norton Speed Disk to try and solve the problem.

3. Do not install antivirus software *after* you discover a virus or worm. Unless you are sure that the virus is nondestructive, leave the computer turned off until you find out how to get rid of the specific virus that your system has contracted.

4. Locate a computer that is not infected. Go to a virus resource Web site and find out how to fix it. Try the Web site of one of the most popular antivirus programs (listed in a previous section), or one of the virus information sites listed in the next section. Look for step-by-step instructions for removing the virus. Companies like Symantec and McAfee often develop scripts that aid in the removal of recently discovered viruses and publish of the details about what that virus has done or can do, so that they can be safely removed.

5. Once you know which virus you have, follow the steps to disinfect your system (that is, remove the virus). If the virus has deleted or overwritten files, it might not be possible to get the files back, but you can at least prevent further damage to your system and infection of other systems.

6. If you can't find identify the virus or find a procedure for getting rid of it, call technical support for your computer (or your local technical support person). Explain to them what happened and that you would like some assistance in removing the virus, or at least to take steps to minimize the damage.

7. Once you are sure that the virus is gone, buy and install an antivirus program. Don't make the same mistake twice!

Another approach is to back up all your data files (but none of your programs), reformat your hard disk, reinstall Windows and your applications, restore your data files, and buy and install an antivirus program to prevent reinfection. However, leaving your computer running while you make the backups may give the virus time to delete more files.

If you make regular backups, check the backups that you made within at least 72 hours of discovering the infection. Your system may have been infected for days (or longer) before you realized it. See Appendix B for how to use Microsoft Backup.

Sources of Antivirus Information

Here is a quick list of applications and sites that you should investigate long before you need them:

- **Doug Muth's Anti-Virus Help Page, at http://www.claws-and-paws.com/virus**   A fantastically deep collection of information regarding computer viruses with lots of helpful papers, reports, and links to additional resources. One thing that makes this site great is that it's not tied to any commercial concern.

- **Symantec AntiVirus Research Center (SARC), at http://www.sarc.com**   An easy enough domain name to remember, especially when you need fast access to the latest virus alerts. Muth's page is great, but the SARC team is fast, which is one of the benefits of commercial relations.

- **McAfee AVERT, at http://www.mcafeeb2b.com/asp_set/anti_virus/avert**   The aptly named AntiVirus Emergency Response Team is particularly well equipped to deal with viruses encountered in the wild. One of the first places you should look to get help or find out what's going on.

- **Vmyths (formerly the Computer Virus Myths page), at http://www.vmyths.com**   Myths and news about viruses and hoaxes.

Please take our advice and make sure you're covered.

The Story of the ILOVEYOU Worm

At about 3 A.M. on May 4, 2000, someone in the Philippines released the ILOVEYOU worm (or more correctly, the VBS.LoveLetter.A worm). Within hours, people began notifying the SARC (Symantec Antivirus Research Center). Within days, millions of computers were infected when users opened the ILOVEYOU e-mail attachment, and millions more were affected by the peripheral effect of the attack. Many businesses that rely on Microsoft's Outlook and Outlook Express client programs and Microsoft Exchange servers for internal and external mail, scheduling, project management, and other communications usage simply turned everything off to avoid being infected.

A massive search for the perpetrators was launched in Manila. The search turned up a man and woman believed to have authored the worm, but they were later released on lack of evidence. There are no additional leads at the time of this writing and a suspect was never located. All known tracking methods have been tried and have yielded nothing.

Unfortunately, the structure of such viruses is designed to completely bypass established network blocking methods like firewalls and proxy servers, and perform additional damage from the inside out. The ILOVEYOU worm arrived via e-mail with a Visual Basic script contained in an attached file. The file had a harmless-sounding name, like *Love-Letter-For-You.txt.vbs* or *Very Funny.vbs*. The whimsical filename prompted recipients to believe that it was a harmless message and open it. On the contrary, the file was a Visual Basic script that executed on the target computer, replacing files and taking other actions without the user knowing it. When the Visual Basic script ran, it read the user's Outlook Address Book and sent copies of itself to every e-mail address in the address list. Each of these people who opened the attachment became infected and likely infected others as well.

Here's how the Visual Basic script works. If you executed (opened) the attachment on your system, the script would do the following:

- Place the worm's core file, Win32dll.vbs, in the C:\Windows folder and the files Mskernel32.vbs and Love-Letter-For-You.txt.vbs into the C:\Windows\System folder.

- Send copies of itself to all addresses listed in your Outlook Address book

- Try to run an Internet Relay Chat program called mIRC and send copies of itself to all individuals that are in connected channels.

- Locate and destroy all files on the infected computer and connected computers (whose drives are mapped to the infected machine) that have filename extensions of .jpg, .jpeg, .vbe, .js, .jse, .css, .wsh, .sct, .hts, .mp2, .mp3, and .vbs, replacing them with copies of itself using the destroyed file's name with an added .vbs extension. Any attempt to open these files reinfects your system.

- Collect and send passwords stored on your system to an e-mail address in the Philippines.

- Attempt to download a program called Win-bugsfix.exe from an ISP's Web site.

- Make several entries into your system's Registry file that affect the viability of any user's names and passwords stored on the system.

As for the possible death of the ILOVEYOU worm, the worm has not been killed off. Instead it has been contained and the latest versions of all the major antivirus programs contain a vaccine. Unfortunately, like a real virus, it is not dead and probably won't be for as long as Visual Basic scripts still run. We still have some time to go before ILOVEYOU and its 28 known variants become obsolete. In the meantime, we have the potential for any number of mutations from any corner of the globe where some individual who saved a copy of the code is brewing up a new generation of ILOVEYOU viruses for release.

The
Complete
Reference

Windows
Me

Part VI

Windows Housekeeping

The Complete Reference

Windows Me

Chapter 32

Keeping Your Disk Safe

Your disk contains an incredible amount of information; the hard disks on most Windows Me machines hold at least 4GB (4 gigabytes, or 4 billion bytes). Chapter 10 describes how information is stored on a hard disk and how to set up a hard disk for use with Windows. Some of the space on each disk is used to store the structure of the disk, including a table of the parts of the disk that are free (available for storing new information), a table of the files and folders on the disk, and a list of which blocks on the disk store the information in which file.

If this structural information gets garbled, you can lose some of the information on the disk. It's wise to check the structure of the information on each hard disk regularly by using a Windows program called ScanDisk—which not only checks the disk structure, but can also fix some of the errors that it finds.

Another disk problem arises when you create and delete many files over a long period of time. Files are stored in a series of sectors on your disk, and the sectors are not necessarily next to each other. The more you create and delete files, the more scattered, or *fragmented*, the available disk space becomes, and the more fragmented newly created files are. Scattered sectors are slower to find and read than sectors that are adjacent, so your disk access slows down.

To fix this problem, you can run the Disk Defragmenter utility that comes with Windows. Disk Defragmenter moves the information on your disk around to speed up access.

Many programs create temporary or backup files, which are not always deleted when they are no longer needed. The Disk Cleanup program can delete stale temporary files for you.

Does it sound like you have a lot to worry about to keep your Windows system tidy? Fortunately, you can schedule Windows to run these housekeeping programs for you. In fact, you can tell the Scheduled Tasks program to run any program on a regular basis. Easier yet, run the Maintenance Wizard to schedule all the necessary housekeeping programs for your system. Be sure to make regular backups of your hard disk, too. See Appendix B for how to use the Microsoft Backup program that comes on the Windows Me CD-ROM.

Note *If you need to restore your Windows system files to the way they were before you installed an upgrade or before your system started having problems, try the System Restore program (see Chapter 34, section "Returning Your System to a Predefined State with System Restore"). For information about your system, try the System Information program (see Chapter 34, section "System Configuration Information").*

Testing Your Disk Structure with ScanDisk

ScanDisk can both diagnose and repair errors on a wide variety of devices, including hard disks, floppy disks, RAM drives, removable disks, and laptop memory cards. ScanDisk can check the physical surface of disk drivers for bad sectors, and checks the file allocation table (FAT), the directory structure, and the long filenames associated with many files.

Windows System File Protection

Windows Me comes with a new feature called *System File Protection*, or *SFP*. SFP is running whenever Windows is running, monitoring the files that make up Windows itself. Whenever a program replaces one of the Windows system files, SFP checks whether the new file was accompanied by a "signed" (verified and encrypted) file from Microsoft. If not, or if an earlier version of a file has replaced a later version, SFP moves the offending file to an archive folder (C:\Windows\System\Sfp\Archive), replaces the file with its own copy (from the SFP database at C:\Windows\System\Sfp\Sfpdb.sfp), and makes a note in its log (C:\Windows\System\Sfp\Sfplog.txt).

You don't have to turn SFP on, and there's no way to turn it off. SFP doesn't display any messages when it decides to replace a system file with its own version.

Note   *If Windows crashes or you turn off the computer without shutting down, when you restart Windows, it automatically runs ScanDisk to check your hard disk for errors resulting from Windows' unexpected termination.*

Running ScanDisk

Follow these steps to run ScanDisk:

1. Choose Start | Programs | Accessories | System Tools | ScanDisk. You see the ScanDisk window, shown in Figure 32-1.

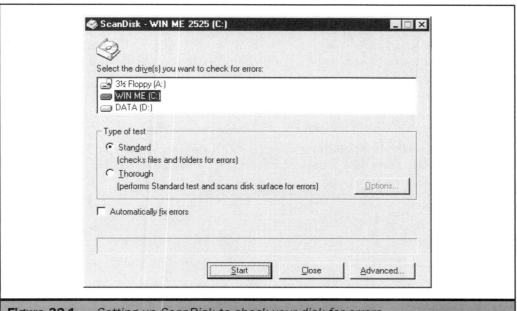

Figure 32-1.   *Setting up ScanDisk to check your disk for errors*

2. In the list of disk drives, click the disk you want to check. You can scan hard disks, floppy disks, and removable disks.

3. Click the type of test you want to run: Standard or Thorough. The Thorough test checks the physical surface of the disk for errors, while the Standard test does not.

4. If you chose to run a Thorough test, click the Options button to display the Surface Scan Options dialog box, shown next. If you chose to run a Standard test, skip to step 6.

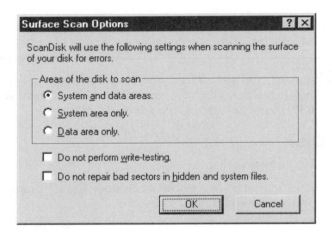

5. In the Surface Scan Options dialog box, choose which areas of the disk to scan, whether to perform write-testing (that is, writing information on the disk), and whether to repair bad sectors in which hidden or system files are stored (if any). Then click OK.

6. If you do not want ScanDisk to ask your permission before it repairs each error it finds, make sure that an X appears in the Automatically Fix Errors check box (click the box if no X appears).

7. Click the Advanced button to see your other options, shown next. Click OK when you have selected the options you prefer or click Cancel to leave the options as they were.

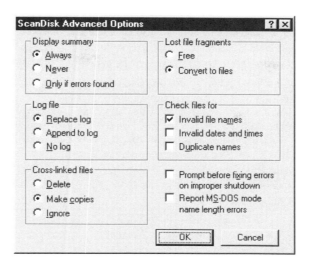

8. Click the Start button in the ScanDisk window to begin scanning your disk for errors. As the program runs, it indicates what it is checking and how far it has gotten. When ScanDisk is done, you see the ScanDisk Results window:

9. Click the Close button to dismiss the ScanDisk Results window and click Close again to close the ScanDisk program.

Running ScanDisk Each Time You Start Your Computer

If you restart your computer every day, or every few days, you can check your disks regularly by running the ScanDisk program automatically when Windows starts. You can use the Maintenance Wizard to schedule when ScanDisk runs. If you'd like to choose ScanDisk's settings, follow these steps:

1. Using Windows Explorer, copy the ScanDisk shortcut to your C:\Windows\ Start Menu\Programs\StartUp folder. (If Windows is installed in a folder other than C:\Windows, adjust the folder name accordingly.) You can copy the shortcut from the C:\Windows\Start Menu\Programs\Accessories\System Tools folder (select the ScanDisk shortcut and press CTRL-C), and then paste it in the StartUp folder (press CTRL-V).

2. Right-click the ScanDisk icon in your C:\Windows\Start Menu\Programs\ StartUp folder and choose Properties from the menu that appears. You see the ScanDisk Properties window.

3. Click the Shortcut tab if it's not already selected. The Target box shows the command that runs ScanDisk, as shown in Figure 32-2. The command is usually C:\WINDOWS\SCANDSKW.EXE.

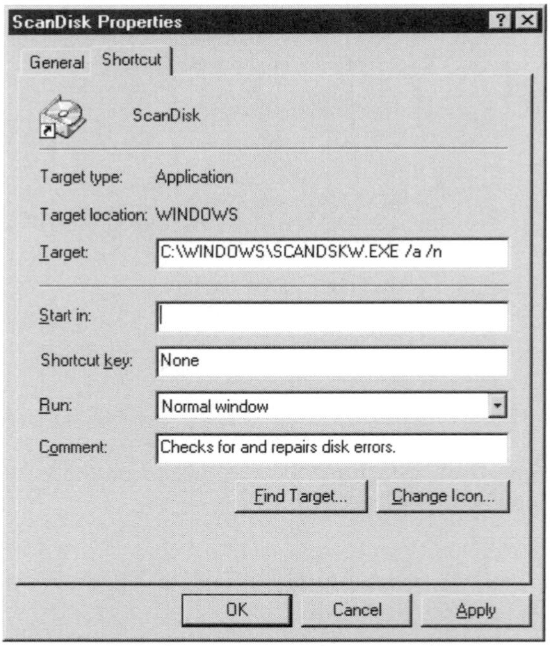

Figure 32-2.   *Configuring the way ScanDisk runs when you start Windows*

4. Click in the Target box and press END to move your cursor to the end of the command that appears in the box. You are ready to type command-line options to control which drives ScanDisk checks each time you start Windows.

5. To tell ScanDisk to scan all the hard disks that are installed on your machine (skipping removable disks, such as floppy disks and Zip disks, which might not be in the drive), type a space and type **/a** in the Target box, adding to the text already in the box; or, to specify one or more drives to check, type a space, the letter of the drive you want to check, and a colon (for example, to test drive D, type **d:**). To specify another drive, repeat this step with another drive letter.

6. To tell ScanDisk to start, run, and close automatically, without asking you for input, type a space and type **/n** in the box.

7. Click OK to save your settings.

The next time you start Windows, ScanDisk checks the hard disk(s) you specified.

Tip *If you want ScanDisk to check your disk without correcting any errors, add the /p option to the end of the command in step 6.*

Defragmenting Your Disk

As you create and delete files, Windows may have to split up the information into many chunks when it stores a file on disk. The more chunks a file is split into, the slower Windows accesses the file, because the disk drive heads have to move all over the disk to find pieces of the file. To move the contents of files around on your hard disk so that each file is stored as one big chunk, run the Disk Defragmenter. It runs in the background—you can go on working while the program defragments your disk; your system may just be a little slow.

When Disk Defragmenter is done, nothing will appear to have changed. Your folders and files won't look any different in Windows Explorer. But your system will act a little perkier when you open large files.

Note *If you use new hard disks, fragmentation doesn't affect speed as much as it does on older hard disks. One reason is that newer disks read an entire track (concentric circle of information) at a time from the disk into memory, so it doesn't matter if the sectors of the track contain information in the wrong order. Another reason is that newer disks have much faster access times, so that disk reads don't cause long delays.*

Running Disk Defragmenter

Follow these steps to run Disk Defragmenter.

1. Choose Start | Programs | Accessories | System Tools | Disk Defragmenter. You see the Select Drive dialog box, shown here:

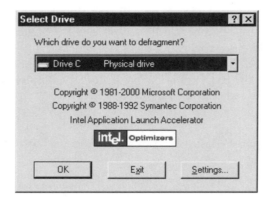

2. Choose the drive you want to defragment by clicking the box and choosing from the list that appears. The list of drives includes physical drives (actual disk drives or partitions of drives) and removable drives. The list does not include networked drives on other systems (see Chapter 29).

3. Click OK. Disk Defragmenter starts to work and displays the Defragmenting Drive progress window, shown here:

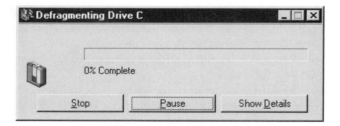

4. If any running program makes a change to a file on disk, Disk Defragmenter notices that the contents of the hard disk have changed and may opt to start over. You can stop or pause anytime by clicking the Stop or Pause button. It's safe to stop and resume later. Pause lets you do some work and then continue where you left off. If the program keeps stopping and starting mysteriously,

some program is accessing the disk drive, and you need to figure out what program it is and exit from that program.

5. When Disk Defragmenter is done, a message asks whether you want to exit the program; click Yes.

Tips for Defragmenting

When Disk Defragmenter is running, you can see a map of the sectors on your hard disk. Click the Show Details button on the Defragmenting Drive window. The screen fills with a grid of rectangles, each representing one sector of your hard disk, as in Figure 32-3. The amount of information stored in each sector is the same for your entire hard disk; the sector size of your disk depends on its format (see Chapter 10, section "What Are Partitions, File Systems, FAT32, and Drive Letters?"). For an explanation of what the colors of the rectangles mean, click the Legend button. When you are done looking at the map, click the Hide Details button.

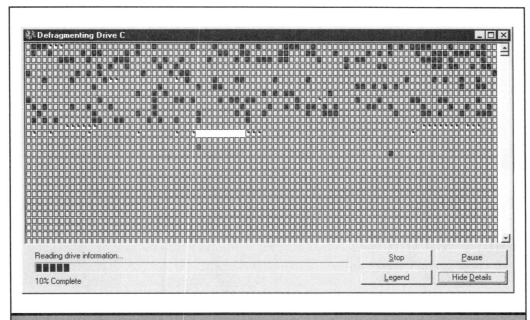

Figure 32-3. *Disk Defragmenter's map of the sectors on your disk*

On the Select Drive dialog box, you can click the Settings button to change settings that control defragmentation:

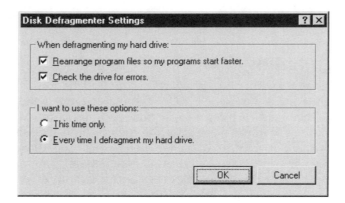

Deleting Temporary Files with Disk Cleanup

Disk Cleanup is a program that can delete unneeded temporary files from your hard disk. Some programs create temporary files and then forget to delete the files when they are through with them. If a program, or Windows itself, exits unexpectedly (or "crashes"), temporary files can be left on your hard disk. Deleting these files from time to time is a good idea, not only because they take up space, but also because their presence can confuse the programs that created them.

 Disk Cleanup may recommend deleting files that haven't been used in months, without regard to type. Take a look at the names of the files it recommends deleting to make sure that they don't include important documents that you haven't used in months but want to keep.

Deleting Files Once

Here's how to run Disk Cleanup:

1. Choose Start | Programs | Accessories | System Tools | Disk Cleanup.

2. The Disk Cleanup program runs and asks which disk you want to clean up. Choose a disk drive and click OK. The Disk Cleanup window, shown in Figure 32-4, tells you how much disk space you can reclaim by deleting temporary files right now. Of course, this may include temporary files that your programs are currently using!

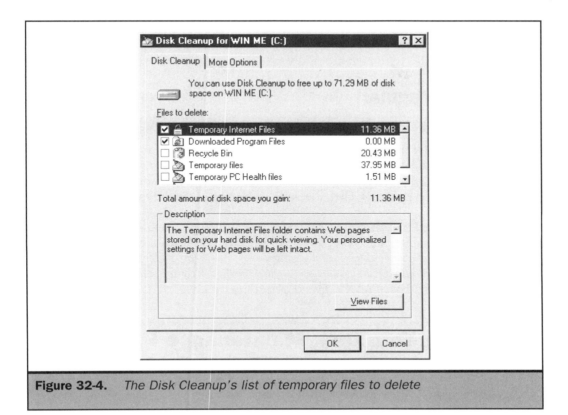

Figure 32-4.   *The Disk Cleanup's list of temporary files to delete*

3. Click the box for each type of temporary file you want Disk Cleanup to delete. For more information on a type of temporary file, click the description; the program displays an explanation of what the files are and what folders Disk Cleanup will delete them from.

4. For additional options, click the More Options tab. Three buttons provide other ways to free up disk space, including deleting Windows components you don't use, uninstalling programs, and reducing the amount of space used by the System Restore program (see Chapter 34, section "Returning Your System to a Predefined State with System Restore"). Click the corresponding button to try any of these methods.

5. If you want to see the names of the files that will be deleted (in a separate Explorer window), select the type of files to be deleted and click the View Files button.

6. To begin deleting files, click OK. The program asks whether you are sure you want to delete files. Click Yes.

The programs shown on the More Options tab that can free up disk space are one-time operations. If you schedule the Disk Cleanup program to run on a regular basis (using the Task Scheduler or Maintenance Wizard), these other programs do not run.

Deleting Files Regularly

Run the Maintenance Wizard or Task Scheduler to tell Windows to run the Disk Cleanup program regularly (see Chapter 2, section "Running Programs on a Schedule Using Task Scheduler"). If you use Task Scheduler to schedule running the program, be sure to run Disk Cleanup once following the steps in the preceding section so that you can choose the types of files to delete. If you use the Maintenance Wizard to schedule running the program, click the Settings button to choose the files to delete.

 When you run Disk Cleanup, be sure to include the Temporary Files in the Files To Delete list. Windows stores temporary files in the C:\Windows\Temp folder (if you installed Windows in a different folder, they are in the Temp folder wherever Windows is installed). Windows can become confused if this folder contains lots of temporary files that should have been deleted automatically but weren't.

Scheduling Your Disk Maintenance Programs

Windows comes with the Maintenance Wizard, which can schedule Windows' disk housekeeping programs to run automatically.

To run the Maintenance Wizard, follow these steps:

1. Choose Start | Programs | Accessories | System Tools | Maintenance Wizard.

2. Follow the instructions in the Maintenance Wizard window to speed up your favorite programs by using Disk Defragmenter, scan your hard disk for errors by using ScanDisk, and delete unneeded temporary files by using Disk Cleanup. Choose a Custom installation to choose settings for these programs or choose Express to let Windows choose your settings. If you choose to delete your unnecessary temporary files, click the Settings button to tell the Wizard which files you'd like to delete.

3. When you click Finish, the Wizard schedules your selected programs to run at the times you specified.

If you want to check, change, or stop any of the programs that the Maintenance Wizard scheduled, double-click the Task Scheduler icon in the system tray on the Taskbar or choose Start | Programs | Accessories | System Tools | Scheduled Tasks (see Chapter 2, section "Running Programs on a Schedule Using Task Scheduler").

Chapter 33

Tuning Windows Me for Maximum Performance

W indows Me automatically sets itself up to give you adequate performance. That performance is greatly improved over Windows 98, but it can still be improved. Several tools enable you to tune your configuration to improve performance, primarily disk performance. The System Properties dialog box shows you hardware settings, including tuning settings. You may also want to track the system resources of your computer by using the Resource Meter program or monitor system usage by using the System Monitor program.

In our experience, few of the tuning techniques make a noticeable difference on a balanced system with adequate memory and disk, although they do make some difference on small systems with slow disks. The best ways to improve system performance remain to add more memory and a faster disk, in that order. Microsoft says Windows Me can run in only 32MB of memory (RAM), but we recommend at least 64MB. You need up to 635 MB of free disk space when installing Windows Me, but we recommend having at least 2GB.

What Are System Resources and How Can You Monitor Them?

To keep Windows running smoothly, it helps to know when your system resources are running low.

What Are System Resources?

System resources or *resource pools* are fixed-size areas of memory used by Windows applications. Windows has three resource pools:

- **System pool**   Used for communication between applications and the system
- **User pool**   Used to manage windows, menus, and other parts of the Windows user interface
- **GDI (graphic device interface) pool**   Used to manage fonts, colors, and other tools used to create screen and printer images

The primary reason you need to care about these resources is that if any of the pools runs out of space, applications—and sometimes Windows itself—fail in unpredictable ways. The Resource Meter program lets you trace how much space is left in each of these pools, so you can see whether you're in danger of running out of space. A distressingly common error in Windows applications is *resource leakage*, applications allocate resource memory, but fail to release it when done (see "Using Resource Meter to Track System Resources"). If you suspect an application is leaking, you can use Resource Meter to compare available resources before and after you run the application. Assuming the system is otherwise quiet, after you run an application, the resources should return to the level they were before the application started.

 If you do run out of system resources, the only reliable way to recover is to restart Windows.

How Can You Monitor System Use?

Windows, like any computer system, can monitor many aspects of its own operation, including CPU use, the software disk cache, disk operations, serial port operations, and network operations. Sometimes, when system performance is unacceptable, you can monitor key aspects and determine where the bottleneck is occurring. This helps determine whether the most effective improvements would be through software reconfiguration or a hardware upgrade, such as adding more memory. The System Monitor program displays and, optionally, logs performance data (see "Using System Monitor to Display Performance Data").

Tuning Your Computer's Performance with the System Properties Performance Tab

The System Properties dialog box includes all the hardware settings you can change and offers several tuning features that can improve performance or at least make the system crash less often. Open the System icon in the Control Panel to display the System Properties dialog box. Click or double-click the System icon depending on how your desktop is configured (see Chapter 1, section "Choosing Between Single-Click and Double-Click"). You also can press WINDOWS-BREAK if your keyboard has a WINDOWS key (with the Windows logo on it) or right-click the My Computer icon on the desktop and select Properties from the shortcut menu that appears.

The System Properties dialog box has the following tabs:

- **General**   Showing the Windows version and registration information.
- **Device Manager**   See Chapter 14, section "Using the Device Manager".
- **Hardware Profiles**   See Chapter 18, section "Creating and Using Hardware Profiles".
- **Performance**   Enables you to tune features related to disks, virtual memory, and the screen (see Figure 33-1, although the dialog box may look different, depending on your installed file systems).

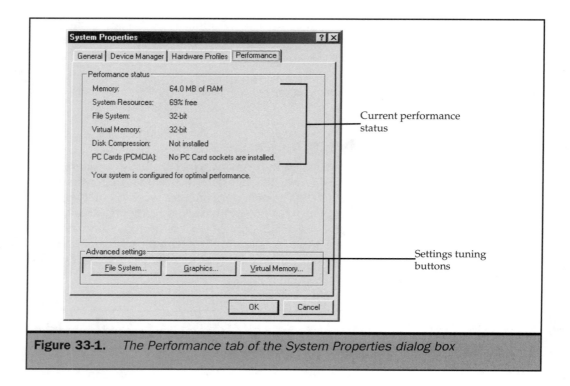

Figure 33-1.   *The Performance tab of the System Properties dialog box*

The Files System button enables you to tune performance if your disks—hard disks, floppy disks, and other types disks, as described in the next section. The Graphics button displays the Advanced Graphics Settings dialog box, which is discussed in "Diagnosing Display Problems" in the next chapter. The Virtual Memory button enables you to control how Windows uses temporary disk space to store information normally stored in RAM (see "Virtual Memory").

Tuning the File System

Click the File System button on the Performance tab of the System Properties dialog box to see the File System Properties dialog box. We cover each of its five tabs in turn.

Hard Disk Tuning

The Hard Disk tab of the File System Properties dialog box, shown in Figure 33-2, lets you choose from three settings that describe the way you use your computer: Desktop Computer, Mobile Or Docking System, or Network Server. Choose the one that most closely describes your computer. The System Restore Disk Space Use slider enables

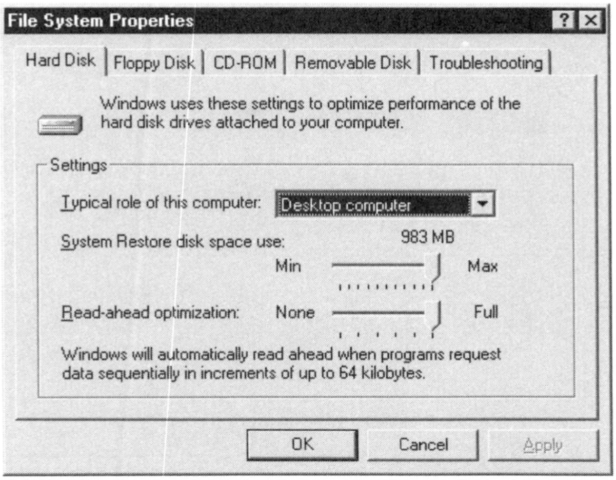

WINDOWS
HOUSEKEEPING

Figure 33-2. *Hard disk drive performance settings*

you to adjust the amount of hard disk space allocated to System Restore—leave the setting alone, unless you have a specific reason to change it. The Read-Ahead Optimization slider lets you adjust the amount of disk *read-ahead* the system uses— the amount of extra information Windows reads from the disk and stores in memory. Unless your system is extraordinarily short on memory (less than 8MB), use Full read-ahead.

Floppy Disk Tuning

The only setting on the Floppy Disk tab of the File System Properties dialog box, shown in Figure 33-3, tells Windows whether to search for new floppy disk drives as it boots. Unless you have an unusual setup in which Windows finds "phantom" drives that don't actually exist, leave it checked. (On the other hand, Microsoft points out that your system starts a few seconds faster if the box is not checked.)

CD-ROM Tuning

The settings on the CD-ROM tab of the File System Properties dialog box, shown in Figure 33-4, enable you to set the CD-ROM cache size and the speed of your drive. Unless you have a very slow drive and very little memory, use the largest cache and the Quad-Speed Or Higher setting.

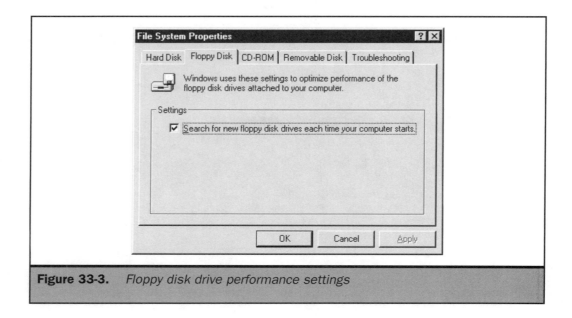

Figure 33-3.   *Floppy disk drive performance settings*

Removable Disk Tuning

The Removable Disk tab of the File System Properties dialog box, shown in Figure 33-5, offers a single setting that turns on or off *write-behind caching* on removable disk drives

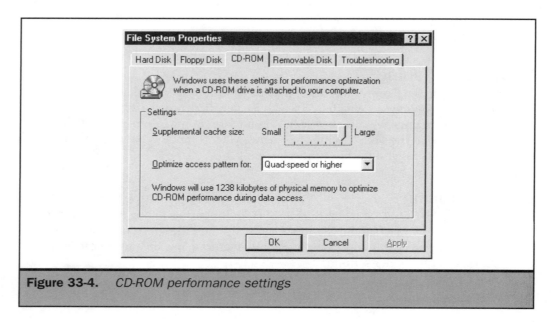

Figure 33-4.   *CD-ROM performance settings*

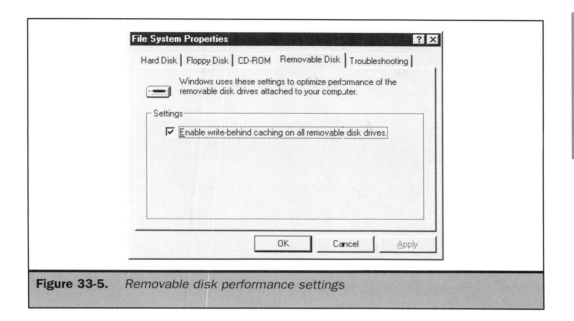

Figure 33-5.   *Removable disk performance settings*

(floppy disks, Zip disks, Jaz disks, and other drives from which the disk can be removed). This setting entails a trade-off between performance and safety. With write-behind caching turned off (the default setting), whenever a program writes data to a file on a removable disk, Windows writes the data to the disk immediately. With write-behind caching turned on, Windows collects the data into larger chunks, which it can write faster. The disadvantage of write-behind caching is that if you remove a disk while a file is open for writing (or if the power should go out), the file may not be written to the disk, and the file and file system may be damaged slightly, although the ScanDisk program can fix them.

Unless you have trouble telling when a program has finished writing a file to a removable disk, we recommend you leave write-behind caching enabled.

Troubleshooting File System Problems

The Troubleshooting tab of the File System Properties dialog box, which is shown in Figure 33-6, lists settings that advanced users can use to diagnose and work around disk problems. Unless you have disk problems, don't use these settings.

Each of the first two settings turns off a specific performance feature that occasionally causes trouble with old and badly designed applications. The rest of the settings turn off features that occasionally cause trouble with old or badly designed disk controllers. If you have inexplicable disk errors, select all the troubleshooting setting check boxes and see whether the trouble goes away. If it goes away, clear the check boxes one at a time until the problem reappears, at which point you know the setting you just turned off has

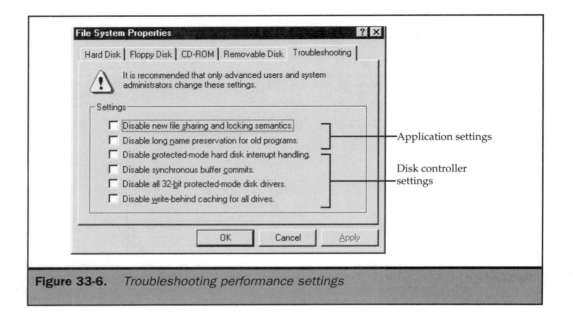

Figure 33-6.   *Troubleshooting performance settings*

triggered the problem. If it's one of the application settings (the first two settings), get an updated version of the application that causes the problem. If it's one of the disk controller settings, get a new disk controller. The last item, which is new for Windows Me, enables you to turn off System Restore (see Chapter 34, section "Returning Your System to a Predefined State with System Restore").

Virtual Memory

Windows automatically manages program storage by using *virtual memory*, which moves chunks of program and data storage between disk and memory automatically, so individual programs don't have to do all their own memory management. Normally, Windows manages virtual memory automatically but in a few cases, you may want to change its parameters. Click the Virtual Memory button on the Performance tab of System Properties dialog box to see the Virtual Memory dialog box, shown in Figure 33-7. You can specify the disk drive on which Windows stores its *swap file* (the file to which virtual memory is copied), along with the minimum and maximum sizes of the swap file.

You might want to set your own virtual memory settings in two cases:

■ If you have more than one disk, Windows normally puts the swap file on the boot drive (the drive from which Windows loads). If you have another drive

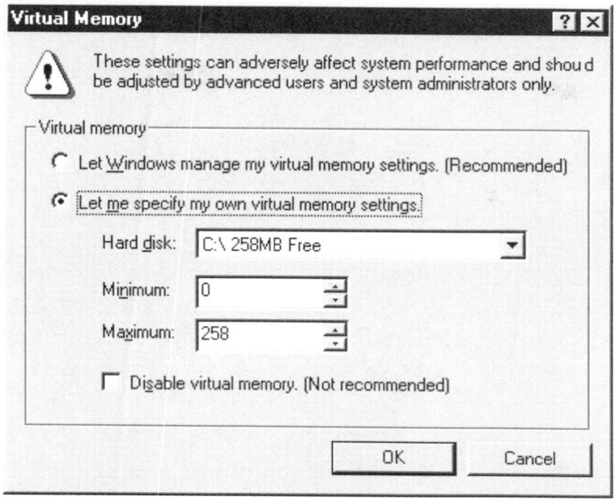

WINDOWS
HOUSEKEEPING

Figure 33-7.   *Virtual Memory settings*

that is larger or faster, you might want to tell Windows to swap to that other drive, instead (that is, store the swap file on that drive).

■ If you are extremely short of disk space, you can decrease the amount of virtual memory and, hence, the disk space Windows allocates. If you decrease virtual memory too far, programs may fail as they run out of memory. Generally, there's no advantage to increasing the amount of virtual memory beyond the default because extra virtual memory doesn't make the system run any faster.

You can also disable virtual memory altogether, which is usually a bad idea unless you have an enormous amount of RAM.

Using Resource Meter to Track System Resources

Resource Meter is a small application that displays the amount of each of the three system resource pools currently in use (see "What Are System Resources?"). You can run Resource Meter by choosing Start | Programs | Accessories | System Tools |

Resource Meter. The first time Resource Meter runs it displays a warning that it, too, uses some resources, and then appears as a small icon in the system tray, with bars that indicate how much resource space remains in each resource pool.

 Resource Meter is not usually installed with Windows Me. To install it, open the Control Panel, open Add/Remove Programs, click the Windows Setup tab, choose System Tools from the list of categories, click Details, and click System Resource Meter. You may need to insert the Windows Me CD-ROM.

If you double-click that icon, you see the Resource Meter window, shown here, which displays each resource pool as a bar.

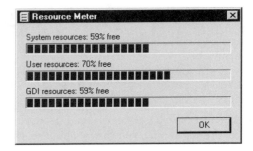

To close the Resource Meter window, click OK. To exit the program, right-click the icon in the system tray and select Exit from the shortcut menu that appears.

Using System Monitor to Display Performance Data

System Monitor displays and logs information about the way your Windows system is operating. System Monitor can display information in a variety of formats and log the information to a file for later analysis.

System Monitor is not usually installed with Windows Me. To install it, go to the Control Panel, open Add/Remove Programs, click the Windows Setup tab, choose System Tools from the list of categories, click Details, and click System Monitor. You may need to insert the Windows Me CD-ROM.

To start System Monitor, choose Start | Programs | Accessories | System Tools | System Monitor. The program starts by displaying one item (Kernel Processor Usage, a measure of CPU load) as a line chart, as shown in Figure 33-8.

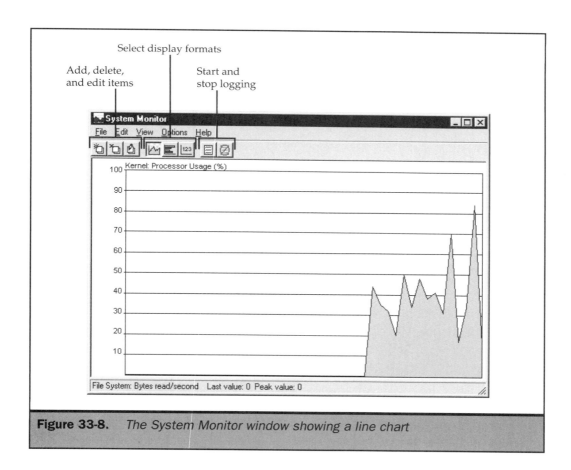

Figure 33-8. *The System Monitor window showing a line chart*

WINDOWS HOUSEKEEPING

Customizing the Display

System Monitor offers extensive customization of the displayed data.

Selecting Data to Display

You can add, edit, and delete displayed items. To add an item, follow these steps:

1. Click the Add button on the toolbar (the leftmost button). System Monitor displays the Add Item dialog box with a list of categories:

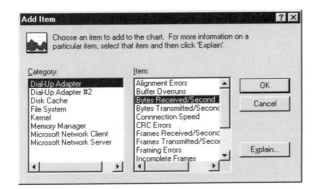

2. Click a category of interest (in the left-hand box), and System Monitor displays a list of items in that category (in the right-hand box). (To see a description of an item, click a category and an item, and then click the Explain button.)

3. Select the item(s) of interest, and then click OK. The newly selected items appear in the System Monitor window. You may want to expand the window to make the display easier to read.

The categories and useful items in each category include the following:

- **Dial-Up Adapter**   Usually the COM1 serial port. Frames Received/Second and Frames Transmitted/Second provide an estimate of network throughput.

- **Dial-Up Adapter #2**   Usually the COM2 serial port (if your system has one).

- **Disk Cache**   Software component that manages disk data. Cache Hits and Cache Misses give an estimate of how effectively the cache is managing data.

- **File System**   Software component that transfers data between disk and memory. Reads/Second and Writes/Second provide an estimate of disk throughput. (Note: this interacts with the cache—in many cases, data read previously can be reread from the cache, avoiding a second read from the disk.)

- **Kernel**   Fundamental Windows functions. Processor Usage (%) tells how CPU-bound your system is (that is, to what extent delays are due to your CPU speed).

- **Memory Manager**   Virtual memory functions. Page-Ins and Page-Outs (per second) provide an estimate of how much disk activity is related to virtual memory.

- **Microsoft Network Client**   Network client functions, such as use of disks on other computers on the LAN (see Chapter 27). Bytes Read/Second, Bytes Written/Second, and Transactions/Second estimate how much use is being made of remote disks.

- **Microsoft Network Server**   Network server functions, such as providing shared disks to other computers on a LAN. Bytes Read/Sec and Bytes Written/Second estimate the amount of disk activity requested by other systems on the LAN.

To remove an item from the display, click the Remove button on the System Monitor toolbar (the second button from the left), select the desired item from the menu, and then click OK.

Selecting the Display Format

The default scales and colors that System Monitor uses are usually acceptable, but you can customize them if you want. To change the displayed color or scale of an item, click the Edit button on the toolbar (the third button from the left), select the item you want to change from the menu, and then click OK. You see the Chart Options dialog box, shown here:

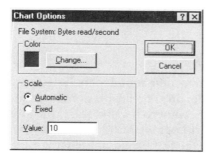

To change the color, click the Change button, select a color from the Color dialog box that appears, and click OK. Choose either automatic scaling (which asks Windows to set the scale based on the actual values of the item) or manually set a maximum displayed value. Then click OK.

System Monitor offers three formats:

- **Line charts**   Display how values of each item have changed over time (shown in Figure 33-8).

- **Bar charts**   Show the current value of each item graphically (shown in Figure 33-9). In each bar chart, the bar shows the current reading, and a narrow stripe shows the maximum reading since the program was started.

- **Numeric charts**   Show the current value of each items as numbers. Numeric chart are useful when displaying a lot of items.

To switch among the three views, click the Line Charts, Bar Charts, and Numeric Charts buttons on the toolbar.

System Monitor rearranges the displayed items as you resize its window, and inserts or deletes captions, depending on the layout. Try changing the size and shape of the window until you get a layout you like.

Other Customizations

To display the maximum amount of data, select View | Hide Title Bar to remove all borders and titles around the System Monitor window. Press ESC to restore the display.

System Monitor normally updates its display every three seconds. To change the interval at which it updates and logs data, select Options | Chart. You can select an interval as short as one second or as long as one hour.

Logging to a File

System Monitor can log data to a file for later analysis. System Monitor writes a comma-delimited text file that any spreadsheet or database package can read directly.

First, select the items you want to log and select the interval at which you want to log them. Then click the Start Logging button on the toolbar and choose the file to which the data should be logged (the default filename is Sysmon.log). System Monitor logs performance data until you either stop logging (by clicking the Stop Logging button on the toolbar) or exit the program.

Each time you start logging, System Monitor overwrites any existing log file with the same name. A good plan is to create a daily log file, putting the date into the name of the file, such as Sysmon-20010704.log.

Tuning Your Hard Disk's Performance

The most effective way to speed up most Windows systems, short of adding extra memory or a new disk, is to optimize your hard disk. After you use the settings on the Performance tab of the System Properties dialog box to tune performance (see "Tuning the File System"), try these two Windows utilities:

- **Disk Defragmenter**   The most important Windows tuning program is the Disk Defragmenter (see Chapter 32, section "Defragmenting Your Disk"). As it defragments your disk, this program can also rearrange your executable programs so they can start and run faster.

- **Disk Cleanup**   As time passes, your computer's hard disk gathers junk in the form of unneeded files. Windows slows down and may act strangely if too many of these unneeded files have accumulated, especially if they are in the Windows temporary storage folder (usually C:\Windows\Temp). The Disk Cleanup utility deletes these troublesome files (see Chapter 32, section "Deleting Temporary Files with Disk Cleanup").

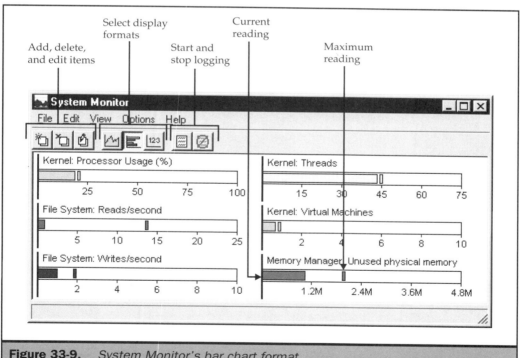

Figure 33-9.   *System Monitor's bar chart format*

The
Complete
Reference

Chapter 34

Troubleshooting
Windows Me

795

Usually Windows Me works quite well, and even though it is more stable than its predecessor, it still hangs and crashes on occasion. Fortunately, Windows Me comes with a number of diagnostic tools that can help. Microsoft has also added two new tools, Auto Update and System Restore; modified two old ones, Help and System Information; and integrated them into a single interface—to bring them more in line with today's technologies and make them more useful.

This chapter describes techniques for dealing with programs that hang or crash, stopping programs from running automatically, diagnosing other problems, using the built-in Troubleshooters, using System Restore to return to a more reliable configuration, and if all else fails, reporting problems to Microsoft for resolution. Be sure to follow the instructions in Appendix B to set up a system of regular backups for your most important files.

 Microsoft has invented a new term—PC Health—for three features that help your Windows system run more smoothly: System Restore, Auto Update, and System File Protection (see Chapter 32, section "Windows System File Protection").

What Diagnostic Tools Does Windows Me Provide?

Windows provides a wide range of diagnostic tools that you can use for different kinds of problems. In addition to the tools listed here, see "Configuring Windows Using the System Configuration Utility" in Chapter 36.

Startup Modes

The worst problems prevent Windows from starting up at all. If the data on your hard disk are intact, you can start Windows in one of several special *startup modes* that provide limited function and help diagnose problems. The startup modes are the following:

- **Normal**   Windows starts normally.
- **Logged**   Windows starts normally, but logs all the drivers it loads in the file Bootlog.txt.
- **Step-By-Step Confirmation**   Windows processes its initialization files one line at a time, stopping and telling you each driver it's about to load.
- **Safe Mode**   Windows starts by using the simplest possible set of drivers and hardware devices.

Windows Me no longer directly supports DOS, with the exception of a DOS Virtual Machine to run legacy applications. Because of this, Windows can no longer start up in DOS mode. Of course, you can still start up DOS from a floppy disk, Zip drive (if your BIOS supports it), or bootable CD-ROM.

See the section "Starting in a Special Mode" for how to use startup modes.

Startup Floppy Disk

If you installed Windows from a CD-ROM, one of the steps in the installation process created a startup floppy disk, or emergency boot disk (EBD). If the file system on your hard disk is damaged, you can often start your computer from the startup floppy disk and repair the damage enough to make the hard disk bootable (that is, the startup files usable) again.

If you don't have a startup floppy disk, you can easily make one while Windows is running. You need a single 1.44MB floppy disk. Follow these steps:

1. Write-enable the disk and put it in the disk drive.

2. Choose Start | Settings | Control Panel and open the Add/Remove Programs icon (single- or double-click, depending on how you have your desktop configured).

3. Click the Startup Disk tab.

4. Click the Create Disk button and follow the instructions that Windows displays. Windows creates a bootable startup disk.

5. Remove the disk from the drive, write-protect it, label it, and put it in a safe place.

Be sure you have a startup floppy disk available at all times, and be sure to create one if you don't have one. If your computer breaks, you won't be able to create one when you need it.

Safe Mode

Safe mode is a limited operating mode used to diagnose problems. All of Windows' basic functions are available, but the screen runs in basic VGA mode (640 × 480, 16 colors) and no devices are available beyond the screen, keyboard, and disks (see "Booting in Safe Mode" in Chapter 14 for more information).

System Configuration Information

The System Properties dialog box, started by opening the System icon in the Control Panel or by pressing WINDOWS-BREAK (if your computer has a WINDOWS key), includes information about all the devices and hardware drivers configured into your copy of Windows. This dialog box is the place to resolve hardware and driver problems, and it includes the Device Manager (see Chapter 14, section "Using the Device Manager").

Another way to see information about your system configuration is to run the System Information program. Choose Start | Programs | Accessories | System Tools | System Information. The program collects information about your Windows system and displays it in the Help And Support window shown in Figure 34-1. Click the plus boxes in the left pane to see all the categories of information the program can display. When you choose an item in the left pane, the right pane displays information about that item.

When it displays system information, the Help And Support window includes a menu bar with commands that can display additional configuration information. You can print the displayed information by choosing File | Print or save the information in

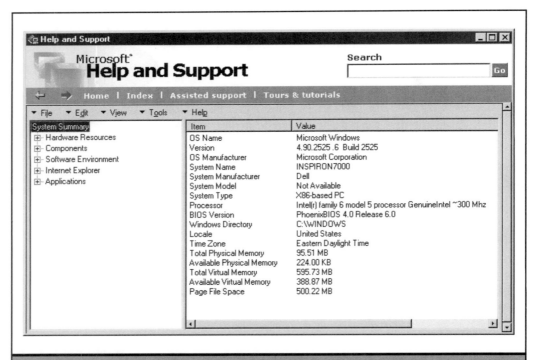

Figure 34-1. *The Help And Support window displays a summary of the results of the System Information program.*

a text file by choosing File | Export. The Tools menu lists a number of other useful diagnostic programs you can run.

Windows Troubleshooters

For many problems, Microsoft provides a Troubleshooter that steps through some of the most common problems and offers suggestions on how to fix them (see "Diagnosing Problems Using Troubleshooters").

Debugging Tools

For hard-to-reproduce software problems, Microsoft includes Dr. Watson, a testing tool primarily used by software developers, which can be useful to report software errors (see "Reporting Problems Using Dr. Watson").

Dealing with Hung or Crashed Programs

Despite all the testing that software vendors do, Windows and the applications you run under it have bugs and sometimes *hang* (stop responding) or *crash* (fail altogether). When an application crashes, Windows displays a box telling you about it. There's not much you can do at that point other than click OK. You may want to restart Windows if you're concerned that the program may have damaged files or Window's internal operations. When Internet Explorer crashes and you use the Active Desktop, Windows goes into a special recovery mode, with a white screen and explanatory messages. Click the link to restore the Active Desktop and get back to where you were.

If a program hangs, you generally can force Windows to stop the hung program. Press CTRL-ALT-DEL to open the Close Program dialog box, shown here:

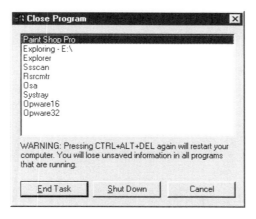

In the Close Program dialog box, a hung program usually has the notation "Not responding" after its name. Select the name of the program and click End Task. Normally the program then exits. If the program is hung badly, then after a few seconds, Windows reports that the program is not responding and asks whether you really want to terminate it. You do.

If all else fails, press CTRL-ALT-DEL twice and Windows should restart. Windows runs ScanDisk if you didn't exit Windows properly, so that disk errors can be repaired (see Chapter 32, section "Testing Your Disk Structure with ScanDisk").

Tip   *We recommend leaving your computer on all the time, so that Windows can run housekeeping and backup programs in the middle of the night. However, we find that we need to restart Windows every day or two to prevent Windows from eventually crashing. If programs you run leak resources (lose track of the memory they use), Windows finally runs out of memory (see Chapter 33, section "What Are System Resources?"). Run the Resource Meter so you can see when Windows is running low on memory (see Chapter 33, section "Using Resource Meter to Track System Resources").*

Stopping Programs from Running at Startup

When you start Windows, other programs may start up automatically, which can be very convenient (see Chapter 2, section "Running Programs When Windows Starts"). It's not always easy, however, to *stop* a program from running automatically when you start Windows. Here are three places to look for the entry that causes Windows to run the program:

- Make sure that a shortcut for the program isn't in the C:\Windows\Start Menu\ Programs\StartUp folder. If a shortcut for the program is there, delete it.

- Look for a line in your Win.ini file that runs the program (see Chapter 36, section "The Win.ini File"). You can use the System Configuration Utility to display and edit the Win.ini file (but make a backup first, see Chapter 36, section "Configuring Windows Using the System Configuration Utility"). The line would start with "run=" or "load=" in the windows section.

- Examine the Registry for an entry that runs the program (see Chapter 37, section "What Is the Registry?"). You can use the Registry Editor to remove the offending entry, after making a backup of the Registry (see Chapter 37, section "Editing the Registry"). Look in the HKEY_LOCAL_MACHINE\SOFTWARE \ Microsoft\Windows\CurrentVersion\RUN "hive" (group of Registry keys), which lists programs that are run automatically. Alternatively, choose Start | Run, type **msconfig**, and press ENTER to see the System Configuration Utility. Click the Startup tab to see a list of the programs that run at startup.

Diagnosing Problems

If Windows doesn't start, or a piece of hardware is operating strangely, you may have either a hardware configuration problem or broken hardware. The most likely culprit is the last piece of software you installed.

Starting in a Special Mode

Starting Windows in one of the special startup modes is easy in principle, but can be tricky in practice. You have to press F8 the moment that your computer's hardware boot process transfers control to the Windows startup program. This usually is about one second after the last screen display from BIOS startup (such as screen and disk configuration messages). Usually, Windows displays a message like "Starting Windows Me…" at the moment you need to press F8, but often it flashes by too quickly to see. You can try holding down the F8 key during startup, until the keyboard beeps.

If you press F8 at the right time, Windows shows the Microsoft Windows Millennium Startup Menu, with the following choices:

```
Microsoft Windows Millennium Startup Menu

    1. Normal
    2. Logged (\BOOTLOG.TXT)
    3. Safe mode
    4. Step-by-step confirmation

Enter a choice: 1
```

Type the number of the choice you need, and then press ENTER.

Diagnosing Hardware Problems

If Windows doesn't start up properly, start the system in Step-By-Step Confirmation mode. Windows prompts you to press Y or N at each stage of system startup. Press Y to each question until the system fails—whatever it just did caused the problem.

Restart Windows in Step-By-Step Confirmation mode again, but press N when it asks for the step that failed last time. With luck, you can get Windows running and then remove or reinstall the component that is causing trouble.

Another possibility, once you know which driver or component is causing trouble, is to restart Windows in Safe mode and then remove or reinstall the troublesome component. After you start Windows in Safe mode, reconfigure or disable the offending driver by using the Device Manager (see Chapter 14, section "Using the Device Manager").

Diagnosing Display Problems

If your display is acting strangely, Windows offers several possible ways to fix the problem. This section describes the most common ways; also see the next section for how to use Windows' Troubleshooters.

If the screen is utterly unreadable, restart Windows in Safe mode. After the Windows is running in Safe or normal mode, open the Display Properties dialog box from the Control Panel and click the Settings tab (see Chapter 12, section "Changing Display Settings").

Your screen might not be able to handle the display resolution your adapter is using. Try setting the Screen Area, which controls the resolution (number of pixels displayed), to a smaller value to see whether the screen clears. (The number of colors doesn't matter—all modern screens can display an unlimited number of colors. What you actually get, however, depends on your video card's capabilities.)

Your screen might be able to handle the display resolution but might not be able to handle the adapter's *refresh rate*, the number of times per second the adapter sends the image to the monitor. Click the Advanced button to display the Properties dialog box for your display adapter and then click the Adapter tab. There may be a Refresh Rate box; if there is, try setting it to the slowest available refresh rate, usually 60 Hz. If that works, try faster rates until you find the fastest one that works reliably.

One final possibility is that the accelerator features in your display adapter aren't compatible with your computer. Symptoms typically are that the display is clear, but wrong, with lines or areas of the wrong color or pattern on the screen. Click the Advanced button on the Settings tab in the Display Properties dialog box (as previously described) to display the Properties dialog box for your display adapter. Click the Performance tab; depending on your display adapter, there may be a hardware acceleration slider ranging from None to Full. Try setting it to None; if this improves the display, try increasing the acceleration setting one notch at a time. (Another way to display this dialog box is to open the System icon on the Control Panel, click the Performance tab, and click the Graphics button.)

Diagnosing Problems Using Troubleshooters

Windows Me includes seven *Troubleshooters*, step-by-step diagnostics that look for some of the most common problems and suggest solutions. The Troubleshooters start at a basic level and walk you through the details of system configuration changes.

All of the Troubleshooters are part of the Help system (see Chapter 6). Follow these steps to run a Troubleshooter:

1. Choose Start | Help to display the Help And Support window.

2. Click the Troubleshooting topic and then select the topic that most closely matches the problems you're experiencing, as shown in Figure 34-2.

3. Follow its advice. Windows asks whether its suggestion solved the problem.

4. Click Yes or No and then click Next to try the rest of the Troubleshooter's suggestions.

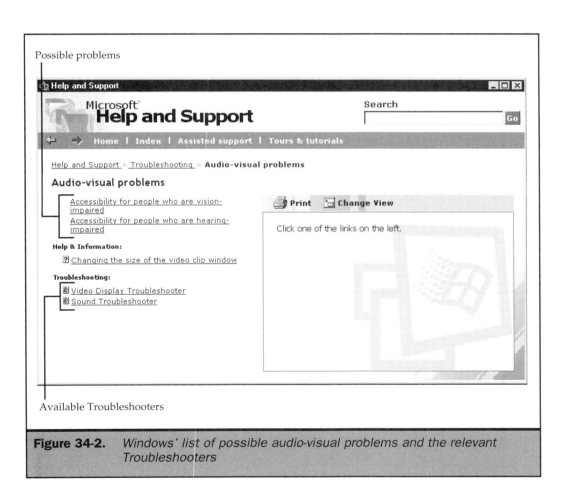

Figure 34-2. *Windows' list of possible audio-visual problems and the relevant Troubleshooters*

Reporting Problems Using Dr. Watson

Dr. Watson is a program that takes a "snapshot" of the system's state, including RAM usage, what tasks were running, and what programs loaded at startup. After a troublesome program fails (crashes or hangs), you can take a snapshot that the program's support department can use to figure out what went wrong. If you are having trouble with a program (including Windows itself), start Dr. Watson, and then run the troublesome program. When the program fails, immediately take a snapshot to document the current state of Windows and your programs, to aid in diagnosing the problem.

To use Dr. Watson, choose Start | Run, type **drwatson**, and then press ENTER. The program doesn't open a window, but adds a small icon to the system tray:

When a program fails, immediately double-click the Dr. Watson icon in the system tray, or click it and choose Dr. Watson from the menu that appears. (If Dr. Watson detected the crash, it may appear onscreen automatically.) Dr. Watson creates a snapshot of the state of your system, reporting its progress as it does so. It then opens a report window in which it lists any possible trouble spots it noted and lets you enter a sentence or two describing what you were doing when the program crashed, as shown in Figure 34-3. If you want to make a note of what you were doing when the problem occurred, click in the lower box and type a description.

To save the information you've gathered, choose File | Save and save the report to a file. Dr. Watson creates a log file with the extension .wlg. When you contact your software vendor about the problem, they may ask you either to open the saved report and read them some of the saved information or, more likely, e-mail or upload the entire log file to them.

You can open a saved log file later by running Dr. Watson and choosing File | Open Log File from the menu (or open the .wlg file—Windows runs Dr. Watson automatically).

If you want all the information possible about what your system was doing when the program failed, choose View | Advanced from the menu. Tabs appear along the top of the Dr. Watson window—so many that you need to click the right-arrow button at the right side of the window to see the rest of the tabs. (You can drag the right side of the Dr. Watson window toward the right to make the window wider.)

You can change how Dr. Watson works by choosing View | Options from the Dr. Watson menu bar, or by clicking the Dr. Watson icon on the system tray and choosing Options from the menu that appears. You can specify how many log files to save, where to store them, and whether Dr. Watson opens in standard or advanced view.

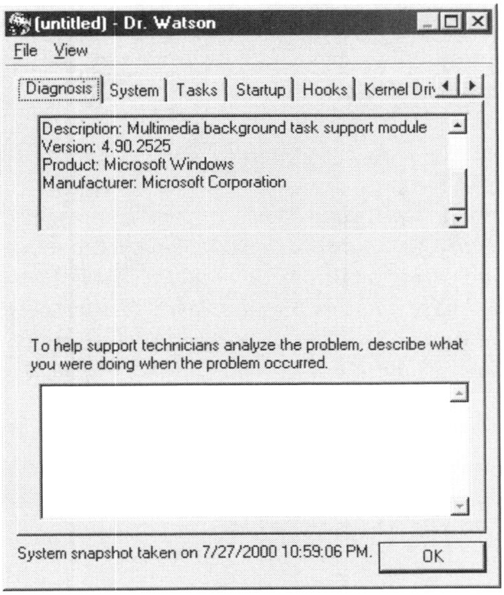

Figure 34-3.   *Dr. Watson's report dialog box in advanced view*

Returning Your System to a Predefined State with System Restore

Many people run into trouble with Windows, especially after they install a new program, upgrade to a program, or upgrade Windows. When new program files interfere with the operation of other programs, you may wish that you could undo the installation and put your system back the way it was. Another common occurrence is that Windows' operation and performance degrades over time, and you may wish that you could return it to the way it ran a few weeks or months ago.

Windows Me contains a new utility called System Restore. This program watches your system as you work, noting when program files are installed, changed, or deleted. It keeps a log of these changes for the last one to three weeks (depending on how many changes you make). You can also tell it to take a "snapshot"—a *restore point*—of the state of the system and store it away. For example, you might want to take a snapshot right after you have installed Windows from scratch, along with all the applications you rely on. Later, if you decide that an installation or some other fault has irreparably damaged your computer's stability, you can tell System Restore that you'd rather return your system to the way it was when you took the restore point snapshot.

When you tell System Restore to create a restore point, it makes copies of the critical files that define how the system works and what applications it is registered to use. It stores these copies, which are used later to restore the system to that state, to another location on your hard drive.

*Not all files are copied—only program files. Your documents aren't stored—System Restore does not take the place of regular backups of the files you create and edit. System Restore does not take your computer back in time, as a product called GoBack from Adaptec (**http://www.adaptec.com**) claims to do. Under System Restore, all of the nonsystem changes and additions you make will still be there. Even an offending application will still have all of its files available. The important thing is that the system files, including the Registry, the central repository for all configuration settings in Windows, are returned to a state prior to the bad change.*

System Restore restores programs, not documents. It doesn't restore Word documents, Excel spreadsheets, Access databases, text files, Web pages, or files in the My Documents folder. If you want to make sure that restoring from a restore point won't affect a file, move it to the My Documents folder.

Restore Points That Happen Automatically

System Restore creates a number of restore points automatically:

- **Initial system checkpoint**   Created the first time you start your computer after installing Windows Me.
- **System checkpoints**   Created every 10 hours that Windows is running, or every 24 hours (or as soon thereafter as you run Windows again).
- **Program installation checkpoints**   Created when you install a new program, it records the state of the system just *before* the installation.
- **Windows automatic update restore points**   Created when you install an update to Windows, it records the state of the system just *before* the installation.

In addition, you can create a restore point whenever you like, as described in the next two sections.

Running System Restore

System Restore is installed and running behind the scenes by default all the time that Windows is running. You can do only two things with it directly:

- Create a restore point for the current state of your system
- Return your system to a previously recorded restore point

To run the System Restore program, choose Start | Programs | Accessories | Systems Tools | System Restore. If you happen to have the System Information window open (as shown in Figure 34-1), you can choose Tools | System Restore. You see the System Restore window, with two options: Restore My Computer To An Earlier Time, and Create A Restore Point. If you've restored your system to a restore point recently, a third option also appears: Undo My Last Restoration.

Configuring System Restore

Although System Restore is running all the time by default, you can turn it off. To do so, to make sure that it's turned on, or to change its configuration, follow these steps:

1. Choose Start | Settings | Control Panel and open the System icon to display the System Properties dialog box.

2. Click the Performance tab and the File System button to display the File System Properties dialog box (see Chapter 33).

3. Click the Troubleshooting tab. The last setting is the Disable System Restore check box.

4. Click the check box until it contains a check mark if you *don't* want to be able to use System Restore. Click it until it is empty so that System Restore runs in the background all the time, creating restore points to which you can return.

5. Click the Hard Disk tab to display the System Restore Disk Space Use slider. Move the slider to specify how much of your hard disk (the disk on which the Windows program file is stored, if you have more than one) may be used to store restore points.

6. Click OK on both dialog boxes.

Note   *System Restore won't run if you have less than 200MB free on your hard disk (the hard disk that contains the Windows system folder, if you have more than one hard disk).*

Creating a Restore Point

You can create a restore point any time you think you are about to make a change to the system that might be risky. It's a good idea to create a restore point when everything is working fine, so you can get your Windows system back to that state again later. A restore point you create is called a *manual checkpoint*. To create a restore point of your own, follow these steps:

1. Choose Start | Programs | Accessories | Systems Tools | System Restore.

2. Select Create A Restore Point and click Next.

3. Enter a description of the save point for future reference (as shown in Figure 34-4). If you are installing software immediately after creating the save point, make note of it.

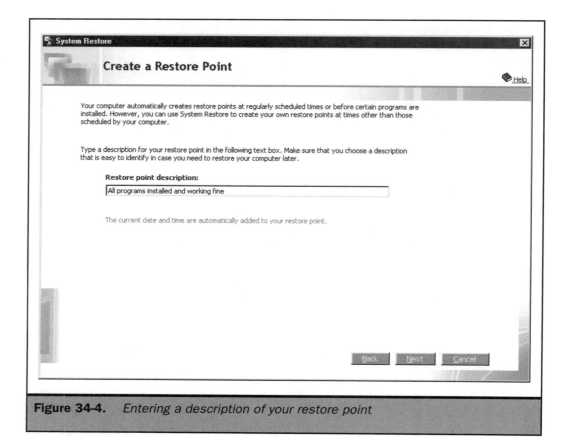

Figure 34-4. *Entering a description of your restore point*

4. Click Next. System Restore creates the restore point and asks you to confirm the information about it.

5. Read the description to make sure you haven't missed anything. Click Back if you want to change the description you entered. Click OK.

That's it. You've finished. If you need to access System Restore when there's a serious problem that prevents you from restarting your computer normally, reboot into Safe mode (see the section "Booting in Safe Mode" in Chapter 14).

Restoring Your System to a Restore Point

If your system starts acting strangely, if you get a virus, or if you delete a program file by accident, you can return the program files on your system to the way they were when System Restore created a restore point. Follow these steps:

1. Choose Start | Programs | Accessories | Systems Tools | System Restore.

2. Select Restore My Computer To An Earlier Time and click Next.

3. You see a calendar of the month. Days for which there is a restore point appear highlighted. Click a date to see a list of the restore points created on that day (as shown in Figure 34-5).

4. Click the restore point to which you want to return your system and click Next.

5. System Restore reminds you to close all other programs before continuing. Do so and click OK.

6. System Restore shows the date, time, and description of the restore point you chose, for your confirmation. Click Next. The restoration may take a few minutes, and includes restarting Windows. When Windows is running again, you see the System Restore window, reporting whether the restore was successful.

7. Click OK.

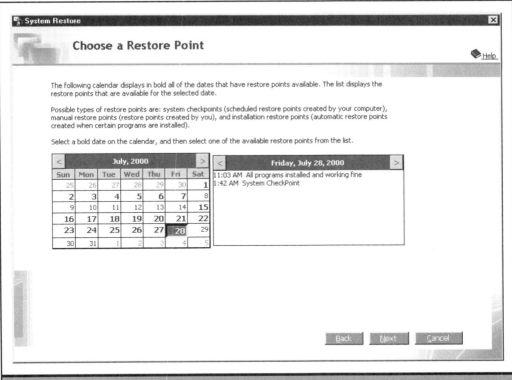

Figure 34-5. *System Restore shows the restore points you can choose from.*

Undoing a Restoration

If you return your system to a restore point, and it doesn't solve the problem you were facing, you can undo the restoration by following these steps:

1. Choose Start | Programs | Accessories | Systems Tools | System Restore.

2. Choose Undo My Last Restoration and click Next.

3. System Restore prompts you to close all other programs and confirm the operation that you want to undo. In the process of undoing the restoration, it restarts Windows.

Chapter 35

Other Windows Me Resources

Microsoft updates Windows constantly to accommodate new hardware and software and to enhance features already found in the system. To stay up to date with these changes, you can run the Windows Update program to scan your system and look for outdated drivers and programs. You can configure the Auto Update program to download and install updates automatically. You can also check the information that Microsoft provides on the Internet and do your own sleuthing by using resources and information available there.

This chapter explains how to update your computer by using the Windows Update and AutoUpdate programs, and how to locate information about Windows from Microsoft and other sources.

Before searching the Internet for information about Windows, take a look at the documentation that comes with the program. The Windows program folder (usually C:\Windows) contains a number of helpful text files (with the extension .txt). The easiest way to read these files is by opening the file C:\Windows\Readme.htm in your Web browser—this Web page contains links to the text files.

Updating Your Computer with Windows Update

Windows Update is a program that is available from Microsoft's Windows Update Web site at **http://windowsupdate.microsoft.com** (the address **http://windowsupdate.com** works, too). Windows Update examines your computer and gives you a list of device drivers and other files that can be updated. When the scan is complete, a list of available updates is presented, and you can choose which update(s) you want to install. In case you install an update that is not what you expected or does not work properly, Windows Update includes a Restore option that returns your computer to its condition prior to the update.

You can run Windows Update at any time to see whether new updates are available. It is especially important to run Windows Update after you install a new piece of hardware or a new software program to be sure you have the drivers and files that you need on your system.

Windows Update uses a wizard that guides you through the screens to complete the setup information. The first time you run Windows Update, you may be asked to register as a Windows user and supply some personal information, such as your name, location, and e-mail address. Windows Update uses Internet Explorer and your Internet settings to connect you to the Microsoft site on the Web. *Before you start Windows Update, be sure your computer is connected or is ready to connect to the Internet.*

To run Windows Update, choose Start | Windows Update. The Internet Explorer window opens. If you see the Dial-Up Connection dialog box, enter your user name

and password and click Connect. When you are connected to the Internet, the
Windows Update page appears, as shown in Figure 35-1.

The Windows Update page shows options that you can use to update Windows,
get answers to technical support questions, or send your feedback about the Update
page to Microsoft. (Since this page is on the Web, Microsoft may change its design at
any time, but similar options will probably be available.) You see a catalog of available
updates from which you can choose those appropriate for your system. Be sure to
download all the Critical Update items. When you've chosen the updates you want,
click the Download button

You can uninstall most updates later, if you don't want them. Go to the Product
Updates page on the Windows Update Web site. Click the Show Installed Updates
button to see a list of the updates you've installed on your system. You can choose
updates to uninstall.

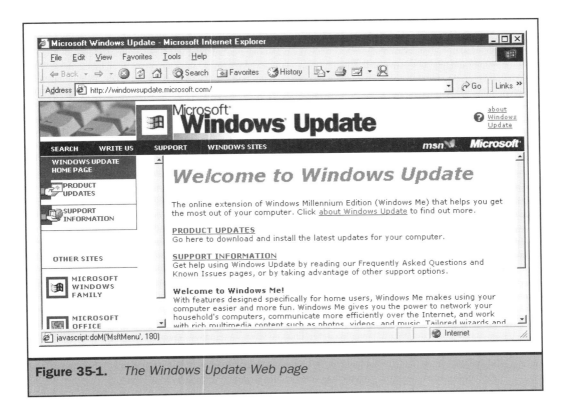

Figure 35-1.   *The Windows Update Web page*

Updating Your Computer Automatically with Auto Update

If you've used your Windows Me for more than a few days, you may have seen a little Update Reminder box appear above the system tray on the Taskbar, asking you to configure Windows to update itself automatically over the Internet:

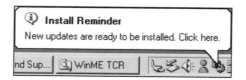

Auto Updates is a new Windows feature that contacts Microsoft over the Internet, checks for Windows updates, downloads them, and installs them. You can configure Auto Update to ask you before downloading or installing updates.

To configure Auto Update, either click the Auto Updates icon in the system tray (if it appears) or choose Start | Settings | Control Panel and run the Automatic Updates program. If you click the icon in the system tray, you see the Updates dialog box. Click Settings to configure Auto Updates, Remind Me Later if you want the Update Reminder Box to appear later, or Next to view the license for Windows Updates and to turn the feature on.

If you run the Automatic Updates program from the Control Panel, you see the Automatic Updates window shown in Figure 35-2. The window gives you three options:

- **Automatically Download Updates And Notify Me When They Are Ready To Be Installed**   Enables Auto Update. When Auto Update downloads a group of updates, you can choose which ones to install. An icon appears in the system tray on the Taskbar, and an Update dialog box (shown in Figure 35-3) asks whether you want to install them. Double-click the icon in the system tray to see a list of the downloaded updates. Follow the instructions in the dialog box to install the updates you choose.

- **Notify Me Before Downloading Any Updates And Notify Me Again When They Are Ready To Be Installed**   Enables Auto Update. Windows checks to see whether updates are available. If they are, an icon appears in the system tray, and a reminder box asks whether you want to download and install them. Double-click the icon to see the list of updates, and click the check boxes so that a check mark appears next to each update you want to download.

- **Turn Off Automatic Updating**   Windows doesn't do automatic updating.

If you decide not to install an update you've downloaded, Windows deletes it from your hard disk. However, you can decide to install it later. From the Automatic Updates window, click the Restore Hidden Items button to display a list of the updates

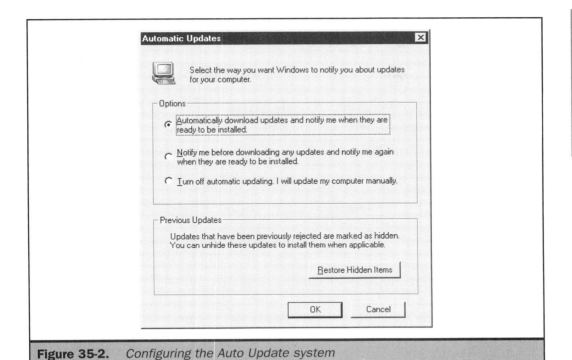

Figure 35-2.   *Configuring the Auto Update system*

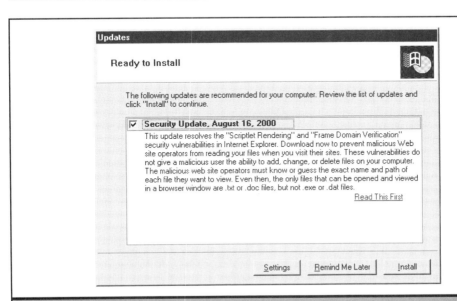

Figure 35-3.   *Auto Update has downloaded an update to Windows and asks whether you want to install it.*

that you declined to install. You can choose which items you want to install after all. The next time Automatic Update checks the Microsoft site for updates, it includes the item you specified.

What Materials Are Available from Microsoft?

In addition to using Windows Update to install updates on your computer, you can also use it to gather information and learn more about Windows. The Support link on the Windows Update page gives you access to reference materials that are available from Microsoft, including articles dealing with program changes, work solutions, and better ways to use Microsoft products.

To access materials about Windows from Windows Update, choose Start | Windows Update and then click Support. You see the Support Web page.

Other materials about windows, in addition to those listed on the Technical Support page and the Help And Support window, are available from Microsoft:

- **Microsoft Support addresses and phone numbers**   Open the file C:\Windows\ Support.txt on your hard disk.

- **Windows Me home page at http://www.microsoft.com/windowsme**   A good resource for general announcements and information about Windows Me. You can also check the general Windows site at **http://www.microsoft.com/windows**.

- **Internet Explorer home page at http://www.microsoft.com/windows/ie**   Each component included with Windows has its own page at the Microsoft Web site. From the Internet Explorer page, click Features to see an overview of the new features incorporated as part of Internet Explorer.

- **Outlook Express home page at http://www.microsoft.com/windows/oe**   Click the Features button to see details about Outlook Express.

- **Support Web site at http://support.microsoft.com**   Site with support information for all Microsoft products. Use the searchable Knowledge Base to find articles about problems and solutions, known bugs, and overviews of how products work.

- **Computing Central at http://computingcentral.msn.com**   Microsoft's MSN-hosted Web site about computers. Click the Operating Systems link for information about Windows. The Windows 95/98/Me forum is at **http://computingcentral.msn.com/topics/windows95**.

- **Microsoft's Usenet newsgroups**   Discussion groups about Microsoft products (see Chapter 22, section "What Are Newsgroups?"). Microsoft hosts over a thousand discussions on its news server, with newsgroups about its major products in a variety of languages (two-letter country codes appear in the newsgroup names, like *br* for Brazil or *fr* for France). To add a Microsoft news server to your list of servers in Outlook Express, click Launch Outlook

Express on the Taskbar. Select Tools | Accounts, and click the News tab. Click Add, choose News, and follow the prompts as the wizard walks you through the steps to add the news server. The public Microsoft news server is named **msnews.microsoft.com**. After you add the server, download all the newsgroups so that you can see a list of what's available on the server. Many newsgroups discuss Windows and its components.

What Other Materials Are Available on the Internet?

Windows is a popular topic on the Internet. A number of Web sites and newsgroups cover Windows and are not connected to or sponsored by Microsoft.

Web Sites

These Web sites provide information on a variety of computer-related issues, including Windows:

- **Absolute WinInfo at http://www.barkers.org/windows**   News and information about all versions of Windows.

- **Annoyances.org at http://www.annoyances.org**   When this book went to press, there wasn't a Windows Me section, but we imagine that it'll be at **http://www.annoyances.org/winme**.

- **CNET.com at http://www.cnet.com**   Current news on all things related to computers. If you don't see an article on Windows on the home page, click Search.Com and search for Windows Me. CNET searches resources around the Web to locate pages. Click a link to visit the site and view the information.

- **Internet Gurus at http://net.gurus.com/winmetcr**   Our own Web site for readers of the book. As we find useful information about Windows, we'll post it on this Web site.

- **Paul Thurrott's SuperSite for Windows at http://www.winsupersite.com**   FAQs (frequently asked questions and their answers), reviews, and news.

- *PC Magazine* **at http://www.zdnet.com/pcmag**   Prints articles on a variety of computer topics, including Windows. To search for an article from the magazine, click Search and type **Windows Me** in the Search box. The most recent articles are listed first.

- **The Trouble with Windows at http://www.windowstrouble.com**   Troubleshooting strategies, bug fixes, and lots of other useful information.

- *Windows Magazine* **at http://www.winmag.com** Contains articles on all facets of Windows. Type **Windows Me** in the search box and click Search. Articles are rated and listed in order according to the best match. When you see an article you want to read, click the link to see the full article.

Information on the Internet changes quickly. To search the Web for other
Windows-related information, see "Finding What You Want on the Web"
in Chapter 24.

Usenet Newsgroups

Newsgroups are discussion arenas on the Internet (see Chapter 22, section "What Are Newsgroups?"). In addition to the newsgroups hosted by Microsoft, many other newsgroups, unaffiliated with Microsoft, discuss Windows topics.

To find newsgroups about Windows, run Outlook Express or your favorite newsreader and search for newsgroups with **win** in the newsgroup name. Most should be in the *comp* (computing) hierarchy, but you may find them in the *alt* or other hierarchies as well.

When you are searching for newsgroups, you can enter as few or as many characters as
you like. The more characters you enter, the narrower the search. For example, a search
for "Windows" will not show newsgroups with "WinMe" in the title.

If you can't find the type of discussion you want in the newsgroups listed on your ISP's news server, use the Web site **http://www.deja.com/usenet** as a resource for newsgroup information. The Deja.com Usenet Web site lets you search past newsgroup articles. You can search for newsgroup messages containing a word or phrase, or you can read messages from newsgroups that do not appear on your news server.

As of August 2000, no newsgroups are dedicated to Windows Me; but by the time you read this, new newsgroups may have formed. You might want to start at **alt.windows98** (or see if a newsgroup named **alt.windowsme** exists). Or try **comp.os.ms-windows.win95.misc**, **comp.os.ms-windows.win95.moderated**, and **comp.os.ms-windows.win95.setup**—these three newsgroups are for Windows 95, 98, and Me.

Mailing Lists

Many mailing lists discuss various versions and aspects of Windows, and Windows Me–specific lists will pop up as people upgrade to the product. To find mailing lists that discuss Windows Me, or e-mail-based "tip-a-day" newsletters with Windows Me tips, go to the Liszt Web site at **http://www.liszt.com** and search for "Windows" or "Windows Me." For more information about how to subscribe to and participate in mailing lists, go to the List Gurus Web site at **http://lists.gurus.com**.

The Complete Reference

Windows Me

Part VII

Behind the Scenes:
Windows Me Internals

Chapter 36

Windows Me
Configuration and
Control Files

Windows stores its control and configuration information in a variety of files of different formats, including files for configuring both DOS and Windows. Windows comes with a program called System Configuration Utility (or Msconfig, for short) to help make controlled changes to some of its configuration files. This chapter explains the configuration files used by Windows Me, as well as how to run the System Configuration Utility program. The last section, "Disk Formats and Coexisting with Other Operating Systems," offers some pointers for running both Windows and another operating system (such as UNIX) on the same computer.

What Kinds of Control Files Does Windows Me Use?

Other than the Registry (described in Chapter 37), most of Windows' control information is stored in text files that you can open with Notepad or any other text editor. Although changing these files is usually a bad idea unless you're quite sure you know what you're doing, opening them and looking at their contents is entirely safe.

Hidden and Read-Only Files

Most of the control information is stored in hidden, system, and read-only files (see Chapter 9, section "What Are Attributes?"). Hidden and system files are like any other files, except that they don't normally appear in file listings when you use Windows Explorer to display a folder that contains them. (Any file can be hidden, but only a couple of required files in the root folder of the boot drive are system files.) Read-only files can't be changed or deleted.

You can tell Windows to show you all the hidden files on your computer. In an Explorer window, select Tools | Folder Options and click the View tab. The list of Advanced Settings includes a Hidden Files And Folders category. Click Show Hidden Files And Folders so a check appears in the check box. This setting reveals hidden files in all folders, not just the current folder. Hidden files appear listed with regular files, but their icons are paler than regular files. To reveal the hidden files that Windows considers "special," return to the View tab of the Folder Options dialog box and uncheck the Hide Protected Operating System Files (Recommended) check box. Click Yes in the warning dialog to make the change active.

You can change a file's hidden or system status by right-clicking the file and selecting Properties. Click the Hidden and Read-only check boxes at the bottom of the Properties dialog box to select or deselect these attributes.

DOS Initialization Files

Previous versions of Windows ran "on top" of DOS—that is, DOS loaded first, and then Windows loaded, continuing to run DOS for basic operating system functions. Windows Me doesn't load DOS; it performs these operating system functions itself.

Windows Me comes with a *DOS Virtual Machine*, which you can use to run DOS programs or commands. The DOS Virtual Machine is a program that simulates DOS, displaying the DOS prompt and running DOS programs.

Several DOS configuration files control the DOS Virtual Machine *boot* (startup) process. All of them reside in the root folder of the *boot disk*, usually C:\.

The Msdos.sys File

In versions of MS-DOS through 6.2, Msdos.sys was an executable program file that was run as part of the initial boot process. In Windows 95, 98, and Me, it is a text file with commands to control the startup process. A typical Msdos.sys starts like this:

```
WinDir=C:\WINDOWS
WinBootDir=C:\WINDOWS
HostWinBootDrv=C
UninstallDir=C:\

[Options]
BootMulti=1
BootGUI=1
DoubleBuffer=1
AutoScan=1
```

Rather than editing Msdos.sys directly, use the System Configuration Utility to make changes in a controlled fashion (see "Changing Your Startup Settings").

The Config.sys File

MS-DOS gives you considerable control over its configuration. Config.sys contains commands that control the way DOS sets itself up and also contains commands to load

---

Special Setup for MS-DOS Programs

Although Windows provides backward-compatible support for MS-DOS drivers, it's a good idea to avoid DOS drivers, if at all possible, since they run with full system privileges (meaning that any bugs can corrupt or crash the system) and can slow down the system.

If you have a DOS program that requires special setup or drivers, you can configure that program so it runs in the DOS Virtual Machine using its own Config.sys and Autoexec.bat files. If you have a DOS program that you run in a DOS window, put startup commands into a batch file and configure the DOS program so that the batch file runs just before the program starts (see Chapter 38, section "Controlling Startup and Basic Operation"). In most cases, these techniques let you avoid loading DOS drivers into Windows.

real-mode device drivers. On most Windows systems, this file is empty, but it's available in case you have a device that has a DOS driver but no Windows driver, or an old MS-DOS application that requires special DOS drivers to work.

To make changes to Config.sys, you can use Notepad or any text editor, but it's safer to use the System Configuration Utility (see "Configuring Windows Using the System Configuration Utility").

The Autoexec.bat File

Autoexec.bat complements Config.sys. While Config.sys is read during the DOS startup process, Autoexec.bat contains regular DOS commands to be run as soon as DOS has finished starting up. Although any DOS command is valid, the only command commonly used is SET, which defines environment variables used by some programs and drivers.

You can use Notepad or any text editor to make changes to Autoexec.bat, but it's safer to use the System Configuration Utility (see "Configuring Windows Using the System Configuration Utility").

Windows Initialization Files

Windows uses a combination of initialization files and the Registry to control its operations. The initialization files are, for the most part, a holdover from Windows 3.1, with newer control information placed in the Registry. Some Windows 3.1 applications stored their setup information in individual *INI files* (initialization files), such as Progman.ini for the Windows 3.1 Program Manager, while others used sections in the general-purpose Win.ini file.

All INI files have the file extension .ini, and nearly all reside in the C:\Windows folder. All INI files have a common format, of which the following is a typical example:

```
[Desktop]
Wallpaper=C:\WINDOWS\BLACKT~1.BMP
TileWallpaper=1
WallpaperStyle=0
Pattern=(None)

;; International settings
[intl]
iCountry=1
ICurrDigits=2
iCurrency=0
```

An INI file is divided into sections, with each section starting with a section name in square brackets. Within a section, each line is of the form *parameter=value*, where the value may be a filename, number, or other string. Blank lines and lines that start with a semicolon are ignored.

In general, editing the Win.ini or System.ini file is a bad idea, but if you need to do so, use the System Configuration Utility (see "Configuring Windows Using the System Configuration Utility").

The Win.ini File

In Windows 3.1, nearly every scrap of setup information in the entire system ended up in the Win.ini file in C:\Windows, meaning that if any program messed up Win.ini, the system could be nearly unusable. Windows Me, 98, and 95 alleviate this situation by moving much of the information into the Registry, but Win.ini still contains a great deal of setup information, primarily from components that haven't changed much since the days of Windows 3.1. You'll typically find sections for many of your application programs in Win.ini, plus a little setup information for Windows itself.

Use the System Configuration Utility to edit the Win.ini file (see "Configuring Windows Using the System Configuration Utility").

The System.ini File

In Windows 3.1, the System.ini file in C:\Windows listed all the Windows device and subsystem drivers to be loaded at startup. In Windows Me, 98, and 95, some of the driver information is in the Registry, but System.ini still contains a lot of driver configuration information. Use the System Configuration Utility to edit the System.ini file (see "Configuring Windows Using the System Configuration Utility").

The Registry

The Windows Registry contains all of the configuration information not in an INI file, including the vast majority of the actual information used to control Windows and its applications. Use the Registry Editor to examine and manage the Registry (see Chapter 37).

Configuring Windows Using the System Configuration Utility

Microsoft provides the System Configuration Utility to help you make controlled changes to the various configuration files described earlier in this chapter. To run the System Configuration Utility, choose Start | Run, type **msconfig** in the Open box, and click OK. (Alternatively, click or double-click the Msconfig.exe filename in your C:\Windows\System folder using Windows Explorer.) You see the System Configuration Utility window, shown in Figure 36-1.

Some of the tabs in this window display information that disappears off the right side of the System Configuration Utility window. Drag the right edge of the window toward the right to make it wide enough to display some of the longer settings.

BEHIND THE SCENES: WINDOWS ME INTERNALS

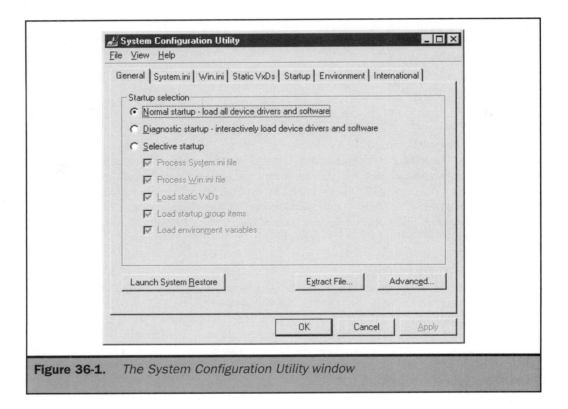

Figure 36-1.   *The System Configuration Utility window*

The System Configuration Utility includes a tab for each configuration file, along with the Startup tab, which lists information from the Registry about programs to be run at startup time. Changes you make don't take effect until the next time Windows restarts, so when you close the System Configuration Utility, it asks whether you want to save the changes you've made; if you click Yes, it offers to reboot Windows for you.

In the System Configuration Utility window, you can choose View from the menu bar to see a list of dialog boxes and windows that you might want to refer to when editing your system configuration (a nice convenience!).

Restarting Windows with Various Startup Options

The General tab of the System Configuration Utility window can help you restart Windows in one of its startup modes that help diagnose problems (see Chapter 34, section "Startup Modes"). To restart Windows in Step-By-Step Confirmation Mode, follow these steps:

1. Click the General tab, click the Diagnostic Startup setting, and then click OK. Windows asks whether you want to reboot your computer.

2. Click Yes. Windows shuts down and then restarts. You see the Windows Me Startup menu.

3. Choose Step-By-Step Confirmation from the menu. Windows prompts you to press Y or N at each stage of system startup.

If you want to restart Windows and tell it to process only specific configuration files, click the Selective Startup setting on the General tab of the System Configuration Utility window, and then choose the files to process. When you click OK, Windows asks whether you want to reboot your computer. Click Yes. Windows restarts and processes only the files you specified. To save your changes without restarting Windows, click Apply (the changes to the files are saved, but still don't go into effect until you reboot).

Changing Advanced Settings

A number of settings can be changed using the System Configuration Utility, but Microsoft doesn't recommend changing them unless you know exactly what you are doing. To see and change these settings, click the Advanced button on the General tab of the System Configuration Utility window. You see the Advanced Troubleshooting Settings dialog box:

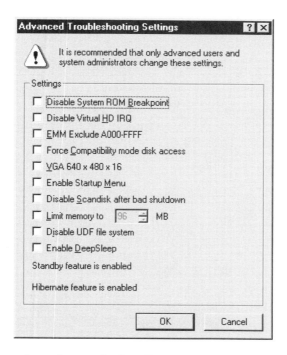

Table 36-1 describes each setting on the list. Be sure to click Cancel when exiting this dialog box unless you are absolutely sure you want to make changes.

Setting	Description
Disable System ROM Breakpoint	Specifies that Windows cannot use addresses in the ROM (read-only memory) address space for a breakpoint.
Disable Virtual HD IRQ	Specifies that program routines in your computer's ROM handle interrupts from the hard disk controller, rather than Windows handling them.
EMM Exclude A000-FFFF	Specifies that the upper memory area (address A000-FFFF), often used by the system's BIOS and by screen controllers, be excluded from Windows' memory space. This setting is usually selected.
Force Compatibility mode disk access	Specifies that disk input and output (I/O) occur using your computer CPU's Real mode.
VGA 640 x 480 x 16	Specifies that Windows use the low-resolution VGA display driver.
Enable Startup Menu	Specifies that every time your computer starts up, you see the Windows Me Startup Menu rather than Windows starting.
Disable ScanDisk after bad shutdown	Specifies that when you restart your computer after shutting down abnormally (for example, turning off the computer without shutting down Windows), Windows does not automatically run ScanDisk.
Limit Memory To *xx* MB	Specifies the maximum amount of memory that Windows uses. Use this setting when you suspect that bad memory locations are causing errors. Windows requires at least 16MB to load, so don't enter a number less than 16.

Table 36-1.   *Advanced Windows Configuration Settings*

BEHIND THE SCENES:
WINDOWS ME INTERNALS

Setting	Description
Disable UDF file system	Specifies that Universal Disk Format file system support not be loaded. This is suggested when using a non-UDF standards–compliant DVD player.
Enable DeepSleep	DeepSleep is a hibernation mode supported by very few computers (yet).

Table 36-1.   *Advanced Windows Configuration Settings* (continued)

Changing Your System.ini and Win.ini Files

The System Configuration Utility window's Win.ini and System.ini tabs, shown in Figure 36-2, show a list of the sections in the System.ini and Win.ini files. To see the individual lines within a section, click the plus box to the left of the section name. To disable an entire section, click the check box to the left of the section name. To disable

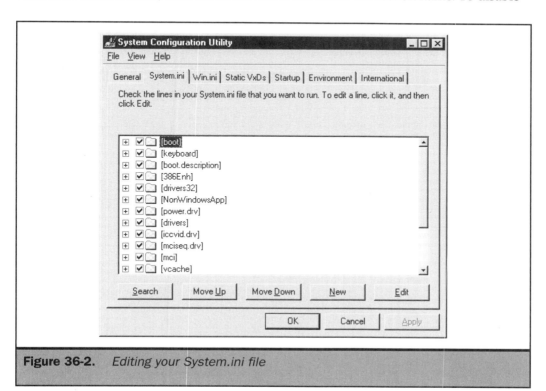

Figure 36-2.   *Editing your System.ini file*

an individual line, click the check box to its left. You can also edit or change the order of the lines or insert new lines as described in the preceding section.

Managing Static VxD files

The Static VxDs tab shows which *static Virtual Device Drivers (VxDs)* are loaded at boot time. These special drivers are critical to the operation of certain aspects of your system, mainly networking, SCSI devices, and Java. Though you will not likely need to modify which VxDs get loaded during boot time, these options may come in handy when troubleshooting problems that relate to networking, Internet access, SCSI, or CD-R/RW problems, and Java Virtual Machine failures.

Changing Your StartUp Settings

The Startup tab in the System Configuration Utility window (Figure 36-3) shows the programs that run when Windows starts up, including the startup programs listed in the Registry, the programs in your StartUp folder (usually stored in the C:\Windows\Start Menu\Programs\StartUp folder), and files mentioned in your Msdos.sys file. You can disable loading a program at startUp by clicking its check box to remove the check mark. Unlike editing your Config.sys and Autoexec.bat files, you can't change the order in which the programs load.

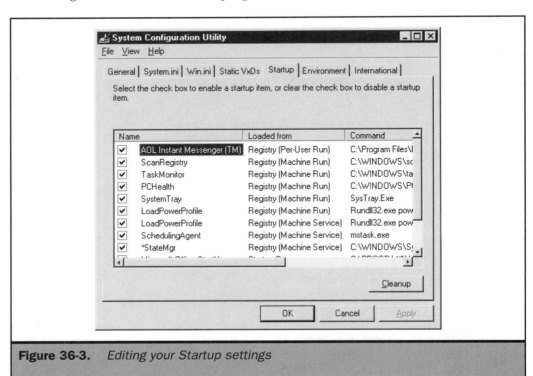

Figure 36-3.   *Editing your Startup settings*

Changing Your Environment Settings

The Environment tab of the System Configuration Utility (shown in Figure 36-4) gives you simplified access to environment startup variables. The four default variables define the following:

- **PATH**   Where Windows looks for executable programs for launching applications from the DOS prompt
- **PROMPT**   How the DOS prompt appears
- **TEMP**   Where to store temporary files
- **TMP**   Where to store temporary files

These variables should not be removed or modified.

Changing Your International Settings

Most of the Windows international and regional settings appear in the Regional Settings dialog box (see Chapter 13, section "Windows' Regional Settings"). The International tab of the System Configuration Utility (shown in Figure 36-5) enables you to set your keyboard driver to a language other than English. Set the Language box

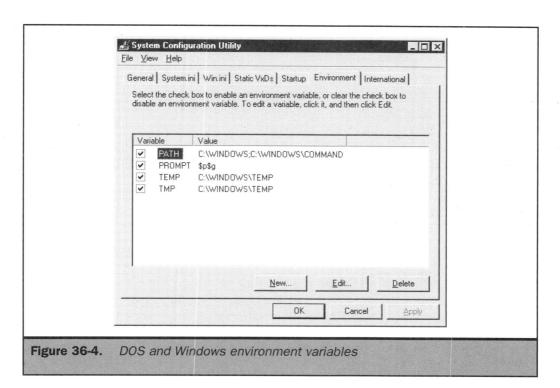

Figure 36-4.   *DOS and Windows environment variables*

BEHIND THE SCENES:
WINDOWS ME INTERNALS

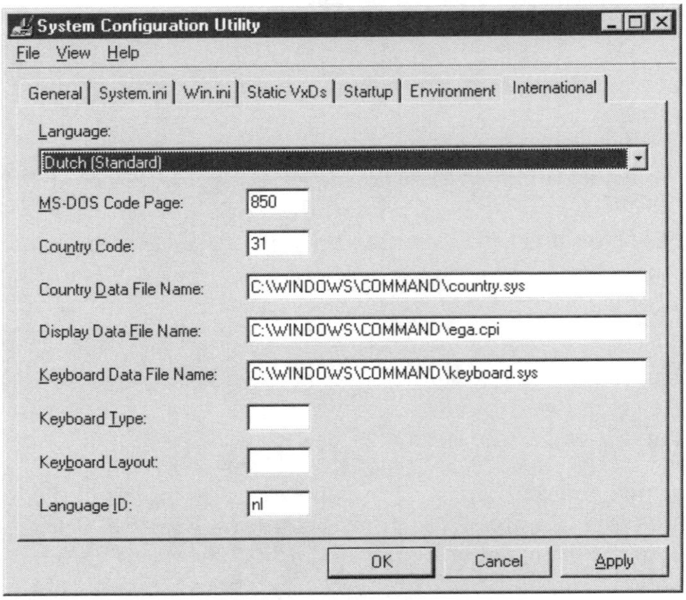

Figure 36-5. *International settings enable Windows to work with other alphabets*

to the language of your choice—Windows updates the rest of the settings on the tab to match. Don't edit the individual settings unless you know what you are doing.

Disk Formats and Coexisting with Other Operating Systems

Windows can share a hard disk with some other operating systems. Because different operating systems format the disk differently, sharing a disk requires splitting it up into partitions.

Fdisk and the Disk Partition Table

One way for multiple operating systems to be installed on a single hard disk is for each system to be assigned one or more partitions on the disk and use its partition(s) when running. Windows can share a disk with OS/2 or UNIX this way. Windows uses a Primary DOS partition and, optionally, a Secondary DOS partition. Most other operating systems use a single partition. The Windows Fdisk utility creates Windows partitions and respects partitions created by other systems, but cannot itself create a partition for any other system (see Chapter 10, section "Partitioning a Disk with the Fdisk Program").

Here are ways to partition a disk between Windows and another system:

- **Install Windows first.**   When running Fdisk, tell it to use only as much of the disk as you want to assign to Windows, and leave the rest of the disk unassigned. Once Windows is installed, shut Windows down and install the other system, which generally creates its own partition using the rest of the disk.

- **Install the other system first.**   The equivalent of Fdisk provided with most other operating systems can usually create a Primary DOS partition at the same time it creates its own partition. Once the other system is installed, shut the system down and install Windows, which automatically uses the existing Primary DOS partition.

- **Use a partitioning program like Partition Magic to create the partitions.**   There are utility programs designed for creating, modifying, and copying partitions of all types (see Chapter 10, section "Installing Multiple Versions of Windows with Partition Magic").

A few systems offer other ways to coexist with Windows or DOS. For example, some versions of Linux (a popular version of UNIX) can create a large file in a DOS partition and use that file as the Linux partition. This makes it possible to install Linux, even on a system that has Windows preinstalled and assigns the entire disk to the DOS partition.

Note   *When installing more than one operating system to a computer with one or more drives, it's important to know that if you install Windows last, it will only boot the computer to Windows and will ignore the existence of another operating system. The easiest way around this is to install Windows first, followed by whatever your second selection might be. CalderaSystems OpenLinux eDesktop 2.4 uses a utility called GRUB to give you a graphical choice between Linux and Windows. Other Linux versions use a similar utility called LILO. If you want to install Windows Me on the same computer as Windows 2000, install Windows 2000 last, so that its boot loader program works to create a dual-boot installation (see Appendix A, section "Creating Dual-Boot Installations").*

Other Operating Systems and Windows Files

Windows can't read or write files in anything other than a FAT16 or FAT32 DOS partition. It can't even read files in an NFTS formatted partition, the file system used by Windows NT and Windows 2000.

BEHIND THE SCENES: WINDOWS ME INTERNALS

Fortunately, nearly every other operating system that runs on a PC can deal with DOS and Windows files. Most UNIX and Linux systems, for example, can logically mount a FAT16 DOS partition so that it appears to be part of the UNIX file system. Consult the documentation for your other operating system to find out how to give it access to your Windows files.

Note   *You cannot create a system that can run both Windows Me and Windows 98 or 95, except by using a utility like Partition Magic (see Chapter 10, section "Installing Multiple Versions of Windows with Partition Magic"). Windows 2000 includes a boot loader that can create a dual-boot installation with Windows Me.*

The Complete Reference

Windows
Me

Chapter 37

Registering Programs and File Types

The Windows Registry stores configuration information about the programs you run, including which program is used to open, create, and edit each type of data file. You can use the Registry Editor program to edit the Registry, but do so with caution!

What Is the Registry?

Early versions of Windows scattered configuration settings among dozens of different files. Many settings were stored in C:\Windows\Win.ini and C:\Windows\System.ini, but programs were as likely to use their own INI files as the standard ones, and there was no consistency in the way that INI files were created and maintained (see Chapter 36, section "Windows Initialization Files"). In Windows 95, Microsoft created the *Registry*, a single centralized database in which programs keep their setup information. It contains all of the information that the INI files contained, as well as other settings from around the system.

Most of the time, the Registry works automatically in the background, but in a few circumstances, you may want to change it yourself.

The Registry is stored in two hidden files, System.dat and User.dat, which are stored in your C:\Windows folder. Windows automatically makes backups of these files each time you start Windows, in cabinet files with names like C:\Windows\Sysbckup\rb002.cab. (It can keep several backups in several cabinet files, usually storing up to five backups, one for each of the last five days Windows started up.) The System.dat file stores information about the software on your computer system, and User.dat stores information about your usage of the software; if your computer is set up for several users, user-specific information about all users is stored in User.dat.

Associating File Types with Programs

In Windows, every file has a *file type*, determined by the three-letter file extension after the dot (see Chapter 8, section "What Are Extensions and File Types?"). For example, My Proposal.doc has type DOC, so one usually calls it a DOC file. Every file type can be associated with a program or group of programs, so when you open a file of that type in an Explorer window (by clicking or double-clicking the file), the associated program runs automatically to process the file. Most programs associate themselves with the appropriate file types when you install the program, but in a few circumstances, as described next, you may want to set your own associations:

- **Dueling programs** When two or more programs can handle the same type of file, whichever one you installed most recently wins, unless you intervene. This is particularly common with graphics formats such as GIF and JPG, because any graphics editing program and most Web browsers can display them. You can change the association to whichever program you prefer. Another common pair of dueling programs are Microsoft Word and the Word Viewer. When you click a DOC file, depending on how you prefer to work, you may want Word to run as the default action, so that you can edit the file, or you may want Word Viewer to run, so that you can quickly look at the file.

■ **Nonstandard file extensions**   Many files with unknown types are, in fact, known types in disguise, or close enough to known types that a program you have installed can handle them. For example, most .log files are actually text files that Notepad, WordPad, or any other text editor can read. Word processors can almost all read each other's files; for example, if you use WordPerfect rather than Word, you can associate DOC files with WordPerfect.

The Windows file association facility is extremely complex and flexible. A file type can have several programs associated with it to do different actions, such as viewing and editing a file. The usual way to process a file is to open an application, but file associations can also use DDE (Dynamic Data Exchange), a Windows facility that enables one running program to send a message to another program (see Chapter 7, section "What Is DDE?").

For each registered file extension, there's a MIME type and an application to handle that type of file. The MIME type is a description used in e-mail and Web pages; it's useful if you send and receive mail with attached files, but it's not essential (see Chapter 22, section "Attaching a File to a Message").

To see or change the details of a file association or to create a new association, open any disk drive or folder in Windows Explorer and choose Tools | Folder Options. In the Folder Options window, click File Types. Highlight a file type in the list of types and click Edit to see the Edit File Type dialog box, which contains a description of the type, the MIME type (if any), the usual extension for the type, and a list of actions (see Chapter 3, section "Creating or Editing an Association").

Tip *When you select a file whose extension isn't associated with any program, Windows opens an Open With window listing most, but not all, applications that you have on your computer. If you do not see the application you want to use, click the Other button at the bottom of the dialog box and find the file that contains the program. If the application does not have any Registry entries, the Open With dialog box disables the Always Use This Program To Open This File option, but you can add the association to the Folder Options dialog box at any time. You can also create a file association by entering a short description of the file type and selecting the appropriate application from the list. Unless you uncheck the Always Use This Program To Open This File box, Windows Explorer saves the association.*

Editing the Registry

The Windows Registry contains a great deal of information beyond the file associations discussed in the previous section. For the most part, you won't need to do any editing yourself, but occasionally, a bug fix or parameter change requires a change to the Registry, so you need to be prepared to do a little editing now and then. If you're interested in how Windows works, you can also spend as much time as you want nosing around the Registry to see what's stored in it. You use Windows Registry Checker to make sure that the Registry is not corrupted and Registry Editor to look at or edit the Registry.

Checking the Registry for Consistency

Windows Registry Checker (also called Scanreg) checks the Registry for internal consistency. Use it before and after you do any Registry editing. To run Windows Registry Checker, follow these steps:

1. Choose Start | Run.
2. In the Run window, type **scanreg**, and press ENTER.
3. Windows Registry Checker checks the Registry. Then it offers to back up the Registry.
4. Click Yes to make a backup copy of the Registry.

Making a Backup of the Registry Before Editing and Restoring from a Backup

Before you make any changes to the Registry, it's a good idea to make a backup of the two files in which the Registry is stored: C:\Windows\System.dat and C:\Windows\User.dat. To make backup copies, run Windows Registry Checker as just described. To skip the consistency check, type **scanreg /backup** in the Run window to force a backup.

If you corrupt the Registry while editing it, you can restore it to its state before the backup (see "In Case of Registry Disaster").

Running Registry Editor

Registry Editor (Regedit for short) lets you edit anything in the Registry. To run Registry Editor, select Start | Run, type **regedit**, and press ENTER.

Registry Editor has almost no built-in checks or validation, so be very sure that you make any changes correctly. Incorrect Registry entries can lead to anything from occasional flaky behavior to complete system failure.

The Registry is organized much like the Windows file system. The Registry contains a set of six *hives*, which are like folders, inside of which are stored *keys*. Additional keys can be stored within keys. Each key defines a setting or behavior for Windows or an installed application. Key path names are written with reverse slashes between them, much like filenames, so a typical key name is

```
HKEY_LOCAL_MACHINE\System\CurrentControlSet\Services\VxD\VNETSUP
```

Each key is shown as a folder in the left pane of the Registry Editor window. Each key can have one or more *values*, each of which consists of a name and some data. The data can be a *string* (text), a *DWORD* (a numeric value), or a *binary string* (a sequence of binary or hexadecimal digits). A key at any level can contain any number of values, so in the example here, values can be associated with HKEY_LOCAL_MACHINE\System\ CurrentControlSet\Services or HKEY_LOCAL_MACHINE\System. (In practice, most of the values are stored at the lowest level or next lowest level.) When you select a key in the left pane, the name and data of each of its values appear in the right pane.

As you edit Registry entries, Registry Editor makes the changes right away. There's no Save, Cancel, or Undo command. You can edit the Registry and leave the Registry Editor window open while you see whether the changes had the desired effect. Some programs aren't affected by Registry changes until they are restarted; others see the changes immediately.

Finding Registry Entries

If you know the name of the key you want, navigating through the key names is very similar to navigating through files in Windows Explorer. Registry Editor has a two-part window, shown in Figure 37-1, much like Windows Explorer. You can expand and contract parts of the name tree by clicking the + and – icons in the key area. Select any key to see the names and data of the values, if any, associated with that key.

If you don't know the name of the key, you can search for it by choosing Edit | Find. You can search for any combination of keys, value names, and value data. For example, if you mistyped your name at the time you set up Windows Me and want to correct it, search for the mistyped name as value data. Use F3 to step from one match to the next.

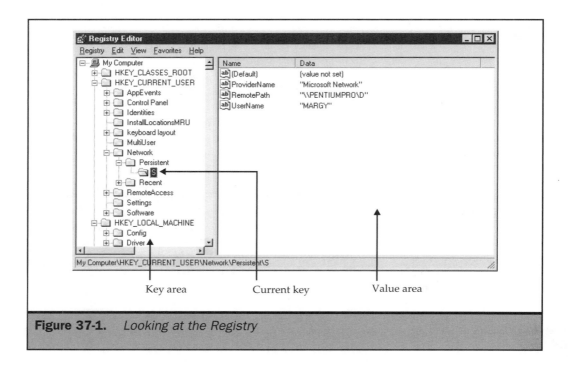

Figure 37-1. *Looking at the Registry*

Adding and Changing Registry Entries

You can add, edit, and delete Registry entries (but be sure you backed up the Registry first):

- **Changing the data of a value** Double-click the name of the value (in the Name column of the right pane of the Registry Editor window). Registry Editor displays a dialog box in which you can enter the new data for the value. You can't change the type of a value, so you have to enter a text string, a numeric value, or a string of hexadecimal digits, depending on the type of the data.

- **Renaming a key or a value** Right-click its name and choose Rename from the menu that appears.

- **Creating a new key** Right-click the folder (key) into which you want to add the new key and choose New | Key from the menu that appears. As in Windows Explorer, the new key is created with a dummy name. Type the name you actually want and press ENTER.

- **Creating a new value** Right-click the key in which you want store the new value, choose New from the menu that appears and choose the type of value

(String Value, Binary Value, or DWORD). Once you've created a value, double-click the value's name to enter its data.

■ **Deleting a value or key**   Select the value or key and press DELETE.

If you're not absolutely sure about deleting a key, rename it. Add an underscore or number to the end, so that the Registry doesn't recognize it, but you will if you need to change it back later.

You can also rename and delete keys and values by using the Edit menu.

Editing the Registry as a Text File

Another way to edit the Registry is to export all or part of the Registry to a text file, edit the text file, and then import the changed values back into the Registry. You can export and import the entire Registry or just one "branch" of the Registry's tree of keys. Registry Editor stores the exported Registry entries in a *registration file* with the extension .reg.

A registration file consists of a series of lines that look like this:

```
[HKEY_CLASSES_ROOT\.bfc\ShellNew\Config]
"NoExtension"="Temp"
```

The first line is the name of the key (enclosed in square brackets) and the lines that follow are the values in the key, in the format *"name"="value"*.

Follow these steps to edit the Registry by using a text editor:

1. Select a hive (folder) in the left pane, choosing one that contains all the keys that you want to edit. To export the entire Registry, select the My Computer item at the root of the Registry tree.

2. Choose Registry | Export to write the text file. Registry Editor asks you for the folder and filename to use for the registration file.

3. Edit the registration file in any text editor. Notepad works if you export only a section of the Registry. Right-click the .reg file in Windows Explorer and choose Edit from the shortcut menu that appears. Notepad runs (or WordPad, if the file is too large for Notepad). Make as few changes as possible to the file and save the file.

4. In Registry Editor, choose Registry | Import to read the edited file back into the Registry. The keys and values in the imported file replace the corresponding keys and values in the Registry.

The Registry is quite large—an exported version of the whole thing can be 3MB or more. If you do plan to edit it, just export the branch you plan to work on.

In Case of Registry Disaster

Each time you start Windows, it makes a backup of the entire Registry, and you can make additional backups whenever you want. Windows keeps the last five backups (one from each day that you started Windows), just in case of disaster. If the Registry becomes seriously damaged, either due to an editing mistake or program failure, you can restore the Registry to its state as of the last time it was automatically backed up.

To restore your Registry if Windows won't start, you can start your computer using a DOS boot disk. If you have a retail version of Windows 98, 98 Second Edition, or Me (not the upgrade versions) then you can use the supplied DOS boot disk that comes with CD-ROM support (and skip to "Restoring Your Registry" later in this chapter). Otherwise you can create a DOS boot disk from within Windows Me as described in the next section.

Creating a DOS Boot Disk

You need one blank floppy disk, or a disk whose contents you no longer need. If your computer can still run Windows, use your computer. Otherwise, find another computer running Windows Me or 98. Follow these steps:

1. Place a blank floppy disk (or one that you no longer need the contents from) into drive A.
2. Run My Computer from the desktop to display an Explorer window.
3. Right-click 3½ Floppy (A:) and select Format form the shortcut menu that appears.
4. Make sure Capacity is set to 1.44 Mb (3.5") and the Format type is Full.
5. Click Start and wait while Windows formats the floppy disk.
6. When Windows finishes, click the entry for the floppy disk in the Explorer window so you can see its contents (it should be blank).

7. Run My Computer again to open another Explorer window displaying the contents of the root folder (\) on drive C.

8. Reveal the names of the files you need to copy to the floppy disk by choosing Tools | Folder Options in the Explorer window that displays C:\. Click the View tab and uncheck the Hide Protected Operating System Files check box. Also click the Show Hidden Files And Folders radio button. Click OK. Now you can see the hidden system files you need to copy.

9. Drag the following files from C:\ to drive A by dragging them from one Explorer window to the other:

   - Command.com
   - Io.sys
   - Msdos.sys
   - Autoexec.bat
   - Config.sys

10. Examine the files listed on the floppy disk to verify that the files are there. Restart Windows with the floppy disk in the floppy drive.

Restoring Your Registry

Once you have started your computer from a DOS boot disk, you are ready to restore the Registry from a backup. Follow these steps:

1. When you see the A:\> prompt, type the following command and press ENTER:

   ```
   c:\windows\command\scanreg /restore
   ```

2. Windows gives you a choice of the backup files available and their dates. Restore the Registry from the most recent backup file or the most recent one you trust.

3. Remove the DOS boot disk from the floppy drive and put it in a safe place.

4. Restart Windows normally. Windows should start.

BEHIND THE SCENES:
WINDOWS ME INTERNALS

The Complete Reference

Windows Me

Chapter 38

Running DOS Programs and Commands

Y   ou might need to install and run older DOS programs on your Windows Me
        system. Windows provides ways to run DOS programs and commands,
        cut-and-paste between DOS and Windows programs, and configure how DOS
programs work with the screen, mouse, and keyboard. If you're an old hand at DOS,
you may also wonder what's happened to two files that were crucial to DOS:
Autoexec.bat and Config.sys. This chapter covers all of these topics.

Windows 95, 98, and 98 Second Edition (SE) all had a special version of DOS
(version 7.0) to run DOS applications and games. Those predecessors could also be
rebooted into a DOS mode, where the machine became a DOS-only computer until
it was rebooted. In Windows Me, Microsoft has finally removed all vestiges of DOS
as it is traditionally known and has replaced it with the *DOS Virtual Machine* (*DOS
VM*). The only real difference is the absence of a DOS mode on startup, but the vast
majority of DOS programs can still run successfully in the new DOS VM, and you'd
be hard pressed to tell the difference when using it.

What Is DOS?

MS-DOS (or *DOS*, Disk Operating System, for short) is a simple operating system that
was the predecessor to Windows. DOS version 1.0 was created in about 1981, at the
same time as (but not originally for) the original IBM PC, and later versions—through
DOS 6.22—added features and supported more recent hardware. Early versions of
Windows (through 3.11) were add-ons for DOS—first you installed DOS on your
computer and then Windows, and then you started Windows from the DOS command
prompt. Windows 95, 98, 98SE, and Windows Me still have a version of DOS buried
inside them, although Microsoft's engineers have integrated almost all of the DOS
functions into Windows.

DOS provides only disk file management and the most rudimentary support for
the screen, keyboard, mouse, timer, and other peripherals. As a result, interactive *DOS
programs* (programs written to work with DOS rather than Windows) have to create their
own user interfaces, usually by directly operating the hardware controllers for the screen
and sometimes other devices. DOS supports only 640K of memory. Subsequently,
Microsoft and other companies developed a variety of add-on drivers to handle larger
amounts of memory.

DOS doesn't have a graphical user interface (GUI) and usually doesn't display
windows or work with a mouse. Instead, you type commands at the *DOS prompt*,
a symbol that indicates DOS is waiting for you to type a *command line* (command,
optionally followed by additional information). The default DOS prompt is C:\>.

Windows, on the other hand, provides extensive facilities to handle the screen and
keyboard and sophisticated memory management, which all Windows applications
use. These facilities made it difficult to run some DOS programs in Windows, because
the DOS programs and Windows can't both control the same hardware at the same

time. Fortunately, the new DOS VM eliminates most of those hurdles and makes it easier to run pesky DOS programs.

How Does Windows Handle DOS Programs?

Previous versions of Windows could run DOS programs in two different ways: as an application running in Windows or as a stand-alone program in a bare DOS environment. In Windows Me, the MS-DOS mode is no longer available, although you are welcome to boot your computer using a floppy disk that has DOS on it. (But if you do so, most extended DOS services will not be available unless you have taken the time to prepare a bootable DOS floppy with all the necessary DOS programs or have a fully configured DOS hard disk and partition management software).

If you have an Emergency Boot Disk for Windows 98, hold on to it. You might want to use it to start your computer in DOS mode.

The DOS Window

The most convenient way to run most DOS programs is in a DOS window while Windows is running. Windows creates a *virtual machine* for the DOS program—a special hardware and software environment that emulates enough of the features of a stand-alone environment, to allow most DOS programs to run correctly. DOS programs that don't use extensive graphics can usually run within a DOS window, sharing the screen with Windows applications. Programs that require full access to the screen hardware can also take over the screen while Windows continues to run in the background.

Since Windows doesn't give the DOS program full control of the system, DOS programs running in a DOS window can run side by side with Windows applications, and even with other DOS applications. You can cut-and-paste material between DOS programs and other programs.

Some DOS programs are *Windows aware*, so that even though they don't run as Windows applications, they can check whether they're running under Windows and handle their screen and keyboard in a way that lets them run efficiently in Windows.

Stand-Alone DOS Mode

Some DOS programs, particularly some highly interactive games, require complete control of the computer. These applications expect access to hardware and system services that are not normally just handed over by Windows, so Windows creates a special, extended DOS Virtual Machine environment.

For those programs, Windows can run in *stand-alone DOS mode*, in which Windows shuts itself down leaving only a small DOS system, starts the DOS application, and then restarts when the DOS application finishes. Although this procedure lets you run practically any DOS program, it's extremely slow, since it restarts Windows twice, once before the program starts and once after it runs. While the stand-alone DOS program is running, Windows isn't active, so no other programs can run.

What Are the Config.sys and Autoexec.bat Files?

When DOS starts up, it reads configuration instructions from these two files in the root folder of the boot disk drive (usually C:\). In Windows these files are obsolete because Windows has its own configuration management system; however, they remain in place for backward compatibility with older programs. The Config.sys file contains configuration commands that DOS reads during the boot process, most notably DEVICE commands that load device drivers (see Chapter 36, section "DOS Initialization Files"). The Autoexec.bat file contains DOS commands to be run as soon as DOS starts.

When you run DOS programs under Windows, Windows can provide Autoexec.bat and Config.sys files for programs that need them. For each program that runs in stand-alone DOS mode, Windows can create customized Config.sys and Autoexec.bat files with commands to be run before that program starts (see "Controlling Startup and Basic Operation").

Running DOS Programs

Once you run a DOS program, you can adjust the way it looks on the screen, copy-and-paste material to and from the Windows Clipboard, and finally exit.

 If you have trouble running a DOS program, use the MS-DOS Troubleshooter (see Chapter 34, section "Diagnosing Problems Using Troubleshooters").

Starting DOS Programs

You run a DOS program the same way you run a Windows program, by clicking or double-clicking its icon or filename in the Windows Explorer window or the Start menu, or by choosing Start | Run and typing its name into the Run window.

You can also type DOS commands at a DOS prompt by selecting Start | Programs | Accessories | MS-DOS Prompt (or by choosing Start | Run and typing **command**). You see the MS-DOS Prompt window, in which you can type DOS commands, such as DIR, CHDIR, MKDIR, and DELETE, as well as run programs.

When you start either a DOS program or an MS-DOS Prompt window, you see a *DOS window*, shown in Figure 38-1. If you run a specific program to open the window, the program name appears in the title bar, if you choose the Start | Programs | Accessories | MS-DOS Prompt command, the window is named MS-DOS Prompt.

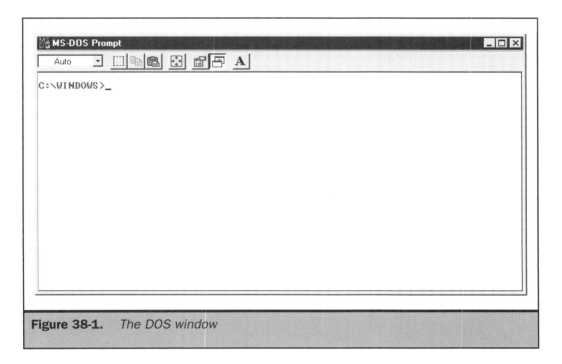

Figure 38-1.   *The DOS window*

To get help with a particular DOS command, type the command followed by /? (for example, type **copy /?** to get help with the DOS COPY command). To stop the help text from scrolling off the top of the DOS window, add | **more** to the end of the command line, like this:

```
copy /? | more
```

*If you can open a file by clicking or double-clicking it in Windows Explorer, you can open the file from the DOS prompt. Type **start** followed by a space and the path name (address) of the file. If the path name contains spaces, enclose it in double-quotes. The Start program opens the file (or folder) using the Windows file association.*

Exiting DOS Programs

Every DOS program has its own idiosyncratic command to exit. Some use a function key, some use a text command, and some use a menu command started with a slash or other character. Once the program exits, Windows changes the DOS window's title bar to Finished. The window remains open to give you a chance to read any final output from the program. When you're done, click the Close button or press ALT-F4 to close the DOS window.

You can also force Windows to close a DOS window by clicking the Close button while the program is running. Windows warns you that closing the program will lose unsaved information, but if you click Yes, Windows stops the program and closes the window anyway.

Adjusting the Screen

Windows normally starts each DOS window as a 25 × 80 character window, choosing a font to make the window fit your screen. You can select a different font from the Font box (the leftmost item on the toolbar) or by clicking the Font button (the rightmost button on the toolbar) to see the Font tab of the MS-DOS Prompt Properties window.

To switch between running in a window and using the full screen, click the Full screen button on the toolbar or press ALT-ENTER. Once in a full screen, ALT-ENTER is the only way short of exiting the program to return the program to running in a window.

To turn on and off the toolbar at the top of the DOS window, click the MS-DOS icon on the window's title bar (the System menu button) and select Toolbar from the System menu.

Using the Mouse and Clipboard

Early versions of DOS provided no mouse support at all, and even in later versions, DOS provided only the low-level support, leaving it entirely up to each application which (if any) mouse features to provide. As a result, most DOS programs provide no mouse support, so the primary use of the mouse is to cut-and-paste material to the Windows Clipboard (see Chapter 7, section "What Is the Clipboard?").

Using the Windows Clipboard

You can copy material from a DOS window to the Clipboard. To do so, first click the Mark button on the toolbar or click the MS-DOS icon in the upper-left corner of the window and select Edit | Mark from the System menu that appears. Then use the mouse to highlight the area to copy, and click the Copy button on the toolbar or press ENTER to copy the selected area to the Clipboard.

DOS programs can place the screen (or the virtual screen emulated in a DOS window) into either text mode (which can display only text) or graphics mode (which can display any pattern of dots, including text). Windows copies the marked area as text if the screen is in text mode and as a bitmap if the screen is in graphics mode. Some programs, such as word processors, often use graphics mode to display text so that they can show font changes. Tell the DOS program to switch back to text mode before copying, to get text on the Clipboard.

Windows lets you paste text from the Clipboard into DOS applications, too. The text is entered as though you had typed it on the keyboard. To paste, click the Paste button on the toolbar or select Edit | Paste from the System menu.

Using the Mouse in DOS Programs

In those DOS programs that do provide mouse support, using the mouse in a DOS window can be difficult. Since DOS provides no high-level mouse support, each application displays its own mouse pointer. In some Windows- aware applications, the DOS mouse pointer is synchronized with the Windows mouse pointer, but more often than not it isn't. In the latter case the best solution is usually to press ALT-ENTER to switch to full screen mode, so there's no Windows mouse pointer at all.

Printing from DOS Programs

Windows provides very limited support for printing from DOS programs. It offers a pass-through scheme that receives output from DOS programs and sends it directly to the printer. DOS programs have no access to the Windows printing subsystem, so each DOS application must have its own driver for any printer that it prints to.

DOS programs can print to a printer that is directly connected to your computer. Normally, Windows provides direct access to the printer, so DOS applications print directly to the printer port. In most cases it's preferable to configure your printer so that Windows intercepts the DOS output and *spools* the output as it does printer output from Windows applications (that is, Windows stores the output and then sends it to the printer). This provides more flexibility in printer management and avoids the possibility that a DOS program will interfere with an active print job from another program.

To spool DOS printer output to a local printer:

1. Select Start | Settings | Printers to open the Printers window right-click the desired printer, and select Properties to open the printer's Properties dialog box (see Chapter 15, section "Managing Printer Activity").

2. Click the Details tab and then the Port Settings button to get the Configure LPT Port dialog box (see Chapter 15, section "Configuring Printers").

3. Check the Spool MS-DOS Print Jobs check box.

4. Click OK in the Configure LPT Port dialog box and then in the printer Properties dialog box.

DOS programs can also print to network printers. Windows captures the output from a simulated printer port and then spools the printer output through the network in the same way that printer output is spooled from Windows programs.

To spool DOS printer output to a network printer:

1. Open the Properties dialog box for the printer you want to use, as previously described.

2. Click the Details tab and then click Capture Printer Port to open the Capture Printer Port dialog box.

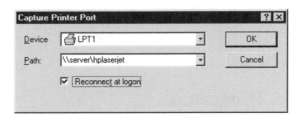

3. Set the Device box to a device (such as LPT1 or LPT2) that does *not* correspond to a locally attached printer. (If you capture a port with a locally attached printer, you lose all access to that local printer.)

4. In the Path box, type the network path to the printer (for example, \\server\hplaserjet.

5. If you want this captured port to be available whenever you use Windows (most people do), check the Reconnect At Logon check box.

6. Click OK in the Capture Printer Port dialog box and then in the printer Properties dialog box.

To remove the connection between a captured printer port and a network printer, use the End Capture button on the Details tab of the printer Properties dialog box.

When you print from a DOS program to a spooled printer, either local or networked, Windows has no reliable way to tell when the DOS program is done printing. If your program doesn't print anything for several seconds, Windows assumes that it's finished. This occasionally causes problems when an application prints part of a report, computes for a while, and then resumes printing, because Windows can interpret the pause in printing as the end of the print job. If this is a problem, use a locally connected printer and do *not* configure the printer to spool DOS print jobs.

Running Batch Files

DOS provides *batch files*, text files that contain a sequence of commands to be run as though typed at the DOS prompt. DOS batch files have the filename extension .bat.

Windows treats a batch file as a DOS program and opens a DOS window to run the batch file and any programs that the batch file runs. Since the Windows version of DOS lets you run any DOS or Windows program from the DOS prompt, you can use batch files as a poor man's script, listing a sequence of programs you want to run.

Coexisting with Other Programs

Windows normally assumes that a DOS program is interactive and can do no useful work when the DOS window is not active. Therefore, Windows suspends the program when you activate any other window. In a few cases, you do want the DOS program to continue running when its window is not active; for example, a long-running spreadsheet recalculation, or an application printing a long report. Click the Background button on the DOS window's toolbar to tell Windows to let the program continue to run *in the background* (in an inactive window).

Configuring the DOS Environment

Windows provides a long list of settings for customizing the DOS environment. Nearly all the settings are parameters you can tweak to help a recalcitrant DOS program run in the Windows environment. More often than not, you can leave the settings alone and your program runs adequately, but if you need to tweak something, there are plenty of settings to tweak.

Earlier versions of Windows put the settings for DOS programs into separate *PIF files* (program information files). Windows Me associates the settings directly with the executable file or a shortcut. (Nearly all settings can be associated with the executable file, except that if you change the icon that Windows displays for a program, Windows makes a shortcut, if you don't already have one.)

To see the properties for a DOS program, either click the Properties button on the toolbar while the program is running or right-click the program's icon in Windows Explorer and select Properties. If you open a DOS window by using the Start | Programs | Accessories | MS-DOS Prompt command, changing the properties for that window affects all DOS windows, not just whatever program happens to be running when you click the Properties button.

Tip   *You can tell whether you are setting properties for all DOS windows or for a specific DOS program by looking at the title of the Properties dialog box. If the dialog box is entitled MS-DOS Prompt Properties, you are setting properties for the default DOS window. If the title bar includes the name of a program file, you are setting properties for a specific DOS program. Some DOS programs have Properties dialog boxes that display different settings from those described here.*

Although you can edit a program's properties while the program is running, most changes do not take effect until you close the program and run it again. (The main exception is changing fonts.) The following sections describe the settings on all the tabs of the MS-DOS Prompt Properties dialog box or the Properties dialog box for a DOS program.

Controlling Startup and Basic Operation

The settings on the Program tab of the MS-DOS Prompt Properties dialog box, shown in Figure 38-2, control the startup and basic operation of a DOS program. At the top of the dialog box are the icon and name that appear on shortcuts or the Start menu item for the program. The other settings are listed next.

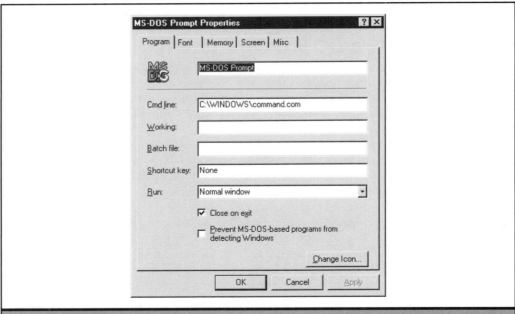

Figure 38-2. *Choosing basic default program properties for DOS programs*

■ **Cmd Line**   The command line to pass to the DOS program. The first thing on the command line must be the filename of the program. Many programs let you put parameters, switches, and filenames in the command line as well. If you type a space followed by a question mark in the command line, Windows prompts you for command line data when you start the program and replaces the question mark with the data you enter.

■ **Working**   The name of the folder to use as the program's *working folder*. The program reads and writes its files from this folder unless the program specifically names a different folder.

■ **Batch File**   The name of a DOS batch file to run before the program starts. This is rarely used.

■ **Shortcut Key**   You can choose a key combination to use to start or activate the program (see Chapter 2, section "Starting Programs Using Shortcut Keys"). You can specify a CTRL- or ALT- key in combination with another key, or a plain function key. Any combination you specify as a shortcut can no longer be used as input by any other program running on your computer, so choose a combination that isn't commonly used.

■ **Run**   This parameter controls whether to start the program in a normal, minimized, or maximized window (see Chapter 2, section "What Sizes Can Windows Be?") Most DOS programs can't handle a maximized window.

■ **Close On Exit**   You can choose whether to close the window in which the program appears when the program exits.

■ **Prevent MS-DOS-Based Programs From Detecting Windows**   Some DOS programs try to detect whether Windows is running and refuse to run if Windows is there. Select this check box if you don't want Windows to respond when the DOS program asks whether Windows is running.

The Change Icon button that appears at the bottom of the dialog box enables you to select an icon to use for the program; the selection provided is rather nice. If you want to use an icon from another program, DLL file, or icon file (with extension .ico), click the Browse button on the Change Icon dialog box.

Controlling Fonts

The Font tab of the MS-DOS Prompt Properties dialog box lets you select the font to use in a DOS window:

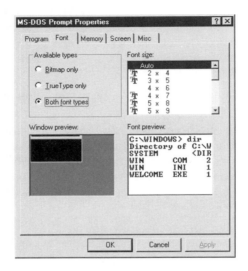

The Font tab doesn't let you do anything you can't do on the DOS window toolbar, but it is marginally more convenient.

You can choose among just bitmap fonts, just TrueType fonts, or both font types. Normally, you choose to display both.

The Window Preview box shows you how big your window will be relative to the Windows screen, and the Font Preview box shows what the text in the window will look like. Refer to the two boxes to select a font that makes the window fit on the screen and still be legible.

Controlling Memory Allocation

The Memory tab of the MS-DOS Prompt Properties dialog box controls how much memory is available to a program using each of the DOS addressing schemes:

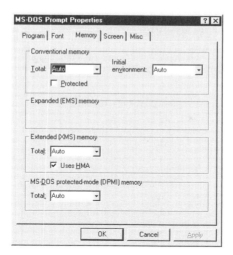

In nearly all cases, Windows automatically allocates an appropriate amount of each kind of memory to the program when it runs the program. A few programs fail if given as much memory as Windows makes available (at the time many DOS programs were written, most people never imagined that anyone would ever put as much as 4MB in a single PC). If this is a problem, determine the kind of memory that the program uses, EMS, XMS, or DPMI, and try limiting it to 8192K.

Select the Protected check box in the Conventional Memory section of the Memory tab. This setting tells Windows to protect Windows' system memory from accidental modification by the DOS program and can keep a DOS program failure from crashing Windows.

Controlling Screen Properties

The Screen tab of the MS-DOS Prompt Properties dialog box sets the initial size and resolution of the DOS application's window:

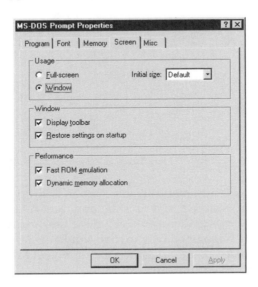

The settings on the Screen tab are

- **Usage** You can choose between starting full screen or in a window and can select 25, 43, or 50 text lines on the screen by clicking the Initial Size box and choosing a number from the drop-down menu. (If you select more than 25, be sure that the program can handle the size you select.)

- **Window** You can control whether to display the DOS window toolbar when the program starts, and whether to remember changes that the program makes to the screen setup from one run of the program to another. Check Restore Settings On Startup to tell Windows always to start the program with the initial settings.

- **Performance** The two Performance settings make DOS emulation a little faster. Leave them checked unless you observe errors in the screen display.

Controlling Other Properties

The Misc tab of the MS-DOS Prompt Properties dialog box controls a grab bag of other DOS settings:

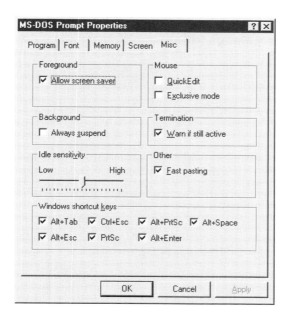

The settings on the Misc tab are

- **Allow Screen Saver**   If checked, Windows can use its screen saver, even when this program is in the foreground.

- **QuickEdit**   If checked, any use of the mouse marks text as though you'd pressed the Mark button first. Check this box if your program makes no use of the mouse.

- **Exclusive Mode**   Dedicate the mouse to this program. Not recommended, since it makes the mouse unusable as the Windows pointer until the program exits. Switch the DOS window to full-screen mode instead (by pressing ALT-ENTER), which makes the Windows mouse pointer vanish.

- **Always Suspend**   Suspend this program whenever it's not the active window. Leave this box checked, unless the program does useful background activity.

- **Warn If Still Active**   If checked, Windows pops up a warning box if you try to close this program before it exits.

- **Idle Sensitivity**   Windows attempts to detect when an active DOS program is idle and waiting for keyboard input, so that Windows can give more processor time to other applications. High sensitivity makes Windows give more time to other applications. Leave this alone unless keyboard response to the program is sluggish, in which case make the sensitivity lower.

- **Fast Pasting**   Windows uses an optimized technique for pasting text into a DOS window that fails with a few programs. If pasting doesn't work, turn this off.

- **Windows Shortcut Keys**   The key combinations listed in this box normally perform Windows functions, even when Windows is running a DOS program. If your DOS application needs to use any of these combinations itself, uncheck the ones it needs.

Installing DOS Programs

DOS provides no standard way to install programs. Most DOS programs include a simple installation batch file that copies the program's files from the installation disks to your hard disk. Once a program's files are installed, you can create shortcuts to the executable file and put those shortcuts in the Start menu or on the desktop, or both, just like native Windows applications.

Some DOS programs require that you install DOS drivers, which are loaded when Windows starts via lines in the Config.sys or Autoexec.bat files. Although Windows provides surprisingly good backward-compatible support for DOS drivers, if you have an application that requires its own drivers, we recommend that you run it in a DOS window and use the Program settings on the Properties dialog box for the program to create customized Config.sys and Autoexec.bat files for that application. These files let you run your application with its drivers when you need to do so, but won't leave the drivers installed when running other Windows applications.

The Complete Reference

Windows
Me

Chapter 39

Automating Tasks with the Windows Scripting Host

If you've used computers long, you may remember *DOS batch files*, files containing lists of commands. Using batch files, you could store up a series of commands and run the whole series by giving just one command. When Windows supplanted DOS, many advanced users complained about the lack of a similar *scripting* capability in Windows. The Windows Scripting Host fills this lack by letting you create and run scripts. You can run scripts from Windows by using the Wscript program or from the DOS prompt by using the Cscript program. This chapter describes how to create script files, run them, configure the Wscript program, and store script settings.

 Windows Scripting Host can run scripts that are more powerful than batch files, and can do a lot of damage. The ILOVEYOU virus used Windows Scripting Host as part of its system of infection and propagation.

What Is the Windows Scripting Host?

Windows Me, like Windows 98 Second Edition and Windows 98 before it, comes with the Windows Scripting Host (WSH), a program that can run scripts from either DOS or Windows. A *script* is a file containing a series of commands, like a batch file that you can use to automate tasks that you repeat often. Administrators of large Windows installations will find scripts invaluable for creating and maintaining standard Windows configurations. For example, if you administer a large Windows installation, you can write a script that logs on to your organization's LAN, connects to various servers, and runs other housekeeping programs. You can use the Windows Task Scheduler and WSH to run the script on a schedule, or you can configure Windows to run WSH and the script automatically when Windows starts up (see Chapter 2, sections "Running Programs on a Schedule Using Task Scheduler" and "Running Programs When Windows Starts").

The Windows Scripting Host can run scripts written in a variety of languages, including VBScript (the scripting language used by Internet Explorer), and JavaScript (what Microsoft calls JScript). The makers of other scripting languages may also provide programs that will allow WSH to run scripts in their languages (Microsoft hopes that they do).

This chapter doesn't describe the VBScript or JavaScript languages; we suggest that you buy a book about the programming language you choose. Instead, this chapter describes how to use the Windows Scripting Host to run scripts after you've written them.

For more information about the Windows Scripting Host, visit its Web sites at **http://www.microsoft.com/management** and **http://msdn.microsoft.com/scripting**.

What Is a WSH File?

If you plan to run a script frequently, you can store the configuration settings for the script in a text file with the extension .wsh (see "Creating WSH Files to Store Script Settings"). You can make more than one WSH file for a script, and each WSH file runs the script using different settings.

Running Scripts from Windows

To run a script, just open the script's icon or filename in Windows Explorer or the desktop. Click or double-click, depending on whether your desktop is configured for single-clicking or double-clicking (see Chapter 1, section "Choosing Between Single-Click and Double-Click"). The Wscript program, which is part of WSH and is stored in the C:\Windows folder, runs the script. Alternatively, you can choose Start | Run, type the full path name of the script you want to run into the Run dialog box, and click OK.

Caution *Running scripts can adversely affect your computer's health! Because certain types of viruses are scripts, they use Windows Scripting Host to run. Checking the source and trustworthiness of the scripts you run is vitally important.*

Wscript is registered to run VBScript (with the extension .vbs), JavaScript (with the extension .js) scripts, and WSH files (with the extension .wsh). If you want to use Wscript to run scripts with other extensions, run the script's icon or filename or type its filename into the Run dialog box as previously described. If Windows displays an Open With dialog box, you can tell Windows to run all scripts of this type using Wscript. Choose C:\Windows\Wscript.exe in the Open With dialog box and select the Always Use This Program To Open This File check box. In addition to running the script you specified, Windows registers Wscript to be the program used to open all files with this extension.

Tip *To try out WSH, you can run one of the sample scripts that come with WSH. In Windows Explorer, look in your C:\Windows\Samples\WSH folder and run one of the scripts listed. If you want to take a look at the text of a script, right-click the script file and select Edit to open the script in NotePad.*

Configuring the Wscript Program

Wscript has two properties that you can set, which are described in the following table:

Option	Description
Stop scripts after specified number of seconds	Specifies a maximum number of seconds that a script can run, to prevent scripts that never terminate. This setting is the equivalent of Cscript's //T:*nn* option or the WSH file Timeout setting, which are described in the next two sections.
Display logo when scripts executed in MS-DOS prompt	Displays the version number for WSH each time Wscript runs a script. This setting is the equivalent of Cscript's //logo or //nologo option or the WSH file DisplayLogo setting.

To see or set properties for Wscript, run Wscript with no script by running its filename (Wscript.exe) in the C:\Windows folder. You can also choose Start | Run, type **wscript** in the Run dialog box, and then click OK. Either way, you see the Windows Scripting Host window, shown here:

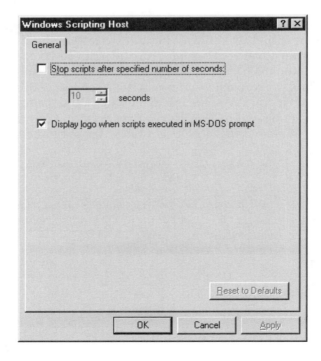

Running Scripts from the DOS Command Line

Despite the replacement of DOS with the DOS Virtual Machine, you can still run scripts from the DOS command line by using the Cscript program (see Chapter 38, section "What Is DOS?"). The Cscript.exe file is part of WSH and is installed in the C:\Windows\Command folder.

To run a script using Cscript, follow these steps:

1. Open a DOS window by choosing Start | Programs | Accessories | MS-DOS Prompt. You see the DOS prompt, which is usually C:\Windows>. You can also open the prompt by pressing WINDOWS-R (if your keyboard has a WINDOWS key) to display the Run dialog box, typing **command** in the Open box, and pressing ENTER.

2. Type **cscript** followed by a space and the full path name (file address) of the script you want to run. You can also type the command-line options listed in Table 39-2.

3. Press ENTER. The script runs.

You can run one of the sample scripts that come with WSH. For the script name, type the name of one of the files in the C:\Windows\Samples\WSH folder.

You can use two kinds of command-line options with Cscript:

- **Host options**   Options that control WSH features. These options always start with two slashes (//).

- **Script options**   Information that is passed to the script itself. These options always start with one slash (/).

The command-line options you can use with Cscript are as follows:

Option	Description
//?	Displays information about the Cscript command.
//B	Runs the script in batch mode, so that all user prompts and script errors are suppressed. This is the opposite of the //I option and is the equivalent of the BatchMode=1 setting in a WSH file (described in the next section).
//H:*name*	Registers the program *name* (which must be either Cscript or Wscript) as the application for running this type of script. The default program for running scripts is Wscript.

Option	Description
//I	Runs the script in interactive mode, displaying all user prompts and script errors. (This is the default setting.) This is the opposite of the //B option and is the equivalent of the BatchMode=0 setting in a WSH file.
//logo	Displays a banner when the script starts. (This is the default setting.) This is the opposite of the //nologo option and is the equivalent of the DisplayLogo=1 setting in a WSH file.
//nologo	Does not display the WSH banner. This is the opposite of the //logo setting and is the equivalent of the DisplayLogo=0 setting in a WSH file.
//S	Saves the command-line options you use this time so that they become the default.
//T:*nn*	Specifies the maximum number of seconds that the script can run before Cscript cancels the script. This is the equivalent of the Timeout=*nn* setting in a WSH file.

Creating WSH Files to Store Script Settings

To create a WSH file to store the settings for a script, follow these steps:

1. Right-click the filename of the script in Windows Explorer and choose Properties from the menu that appears. You see a Properties dialog box for the script. The General tab shows the name, size, and dates for the file. The Script tab shows the same settings that are shown in the first illustration in this chapter.

2. Click the Script tab and choose the settings you want to use when you run the script with the WSH file.

3. Click OK. Windows creates a text file with the extension .wsh. The WSH file has the same name (except for the extension) as the script file and is stored in the same folder.

4. Run the WSH file the same way you run VBScript, JavaScript, and other script files, using Wscript or Cscript.

A WSH file is a text file that looks like the following:

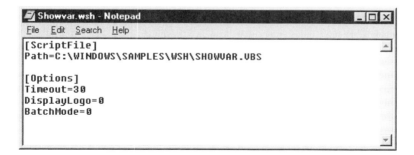

To look at the contents of a WSH file, open it in Notepad (see Chapter 4, section "Reading Text Files with Notepad"). The file has two sections, ScriptFile and Options. Each section starts with the section name on a line by itself enclosed in square brackets. In each section, each setting appears on a line by itself in the following format:

```
settingname=value
```

The single line in the ScriptFile section of a WSH file contains a line like the following, specifying the name of the script to run:

```
Path=C:\WINDOWS\SAMPLES\WSH\SHOWVAR.VBS
```

The settings in a WSH file are shown in the following table.

Section	Setting Name	Description
ScriptFile	Path	Specifies the full path name of the script file to run.
Options	Timeout	Specifies the maximum number of seconds the script can run. If this value is 0, there is no maximum. This is the equivalent of the Stop Scripts After Specified Number Of Seconds setting on the Script Properties dialog box or the //T:*nn* Cscript command-line option.

Section	Setting Name	Description
Options	DisplayLogo	Specifies whether to display (if the value is 1) or not display (if the value is 0) the WSH banner when the script runs. This is the equivalent of the Display Logo When Scripts Executed In MS-DOS Prompt setting in the Script Properties dialog box or the //logo and //nologo Cscript command-line options.
Options	BatchMode	Specifies whether to run the script in batch mode (if the value is 1), suppressing user input and error messages, or in interactive mode (if the value is 0). This setting doesn't appear in the Script Properties dialog box; the only way to set it to 1 is to edit the WSH file. This setting is equivalent to the //B and //I Cscript command-line options.

Scripts can access any object present on a Windows system, including applications, networks, and the Windows Registry. See the sample scripts provided with Windows for some examples of how this works.

The
Complete
Reference

Appendix A

Installing or Upgrading to Windows Me

If you don't buy a computer with Windows Me already installed, you face the task of installing Windows—either installing it on a blank hard disk or upgrading your existing operating system. This chapter explains your installation options and details how to run the Windows Me Setup Wizard to install, upgrade to, and uninstall Windows. You'll also find out how to check your installation, how to create a dual-boot installation, and other installation tips.

To install Windows Me, you need the following:

- A Windows Me CD-ROM and a CD-ROM drive. If you have the upgrade version of Windows Me, You'll need the CD-ROM or all the floppy disks from a previous version of Windows, too.

- A Pentium, Pentium Pro, Pentium II, or compatible CPU running at a speed of at least 150 Mhz

- At least 32MB of RAM memory (although your system will run slowly with less than 64MB)

- A hard disk with at least 500MB free, depending on which options you choose to install (perhaps more for temporary files) (see "How Much Disk Space Does Windows Me Require?")

- A blank floppy disk to use when creating an emergency boot disk

- CD-ROMs or floppy disks with hardware drivers for devices needing drivers that don't come with Windows Me

The Windows Me CD-ROM contains an installation program called Setup, or the Windows Me Setup Wizard. Windows itself is stored in compressed format in a group of *cabinet files* (*CAB* files) with the extension .cab—Setup copies and decompresses the Windows programs during installation.

 Earlier versions of Windows were available on floppy disks, but Windows Me comes only on CD-ROM—the system would require hundreds of floppy disks.

What Are Your Installation Options?

You can install Windows Me in one of the following ways:

- **From scratch** Install Windows on a blank formatted hard disk.

- **Upgrade** Install it over Windows 95, Windows 98, or Windows 98 Second Edition , replacing your previously installed operating system. Systems running DOS or Windows 3.1 are unlikely to be capable of running Windows Me, because hardware requirements have increased dramatically since those versions were popular.

■ **Dual-boot**   Create a dual-boot installation with Windows 3.1, Windows 98, Windows 95, Windows 2000, Windows NT, Linux, UNIX, or DOS so that you can choose to start your computer in either Windows or your previously installed operating system.

Each of these methods is described in detail later in this appendix.

Once you begin the installation, the Windows Me Setup Wizard gives you the following additional options:

■ **Windows program folder**   The Setup Wizard installs Windows in your *Windows program folder*. The default location for this folder is C:\Windows. During installation, Setup asks what folder to install Windows in; you can specify a different folder to be your Windows program folder. Microsoft recommends that you use the default location of C:\Windows, unless you have a good reason to choose another folder.

■ **Optional programs**   The Setup Wizard offers to let you choose which optional programs to install. Your options are: Typical (all the most useful programs for a desktop computer), Portable (all the most useful programs for a laptop computer), Compact (the minimum number of programs), or Custom (you choose the programs).

■ **Uninstallation**   The Setup Wizard asks whether you want to save the system files from your old operating system, so you will be able to uninstall Windows later and return to the operating system you used before. If you choose this option, the Setup Wizard stores your existing operating system in a backup file which you can restore later (see "Uninstalling Windows Me"). You don't see this option if you are installing Windows to a new Windows program folder (to create a dual-boot system), if you are installing on a blank hard disk partition, or if you are upgrading from DOS.

How Much Disk Space Does Windows Me Require?

How much space Windows requires depends on what operating system is already installed on your hard disk and what options you select. During the installation process, the Setup Wizard tells you how much disk space it will need. The amount of space required depends on the following:

■ What operating system, if any, is already installed.

■ Whether you specify that the Setup Wizard save the previous operating system (if any) to enable you to uninstall Windows Me later. This optional uninstall file (a hidden file called C:\Winundo.dat) can be up to 150MB. You can tell the Setup Wizard to store this file on another partition or disk drive.

■ The cluster size of the disk on which you are installing Windows (see Chapter 10, section "What Are the FAT16 and FAT32 File Systems?"). If your disk uses FAT32 (most do), even small files take up 32K each, bloating the space that Windows occupies.

■ How many optional programs you install along with Windows. Windows comes with dozens of utilities and applications that aren't needed to run Windows, but that may come in handy.

Depending on these factors, Windows can require anywhere from 455MB to 635MB during installation.

If you don't have enough space to install Windows, try emptying your Recycle Bin (if you are upgrading from Windows 95 or 98), deleting your Web browser's cache (or the temporary file caches of other application programs), and deleting all .tmp and .bak files. If you run Windows 98 or 95, exit all programs and delete all the files in C:\Windows\Temp except those dated within the last few days. If you still don't have enough space, you can uninstall programs and reinstall them later when Windows is running. However, Windows requires lots of elbow room; if your disk space is tight, consider buying a larger hard disk.

If your system has more than one hard disk, the free space Windows requires must be on the drive that contains your Windows program folder (usually C:\Windows).

The Windows installation program creates a folder called C:\Windows\Options\Install with the CAB files that you need when adding or deleting Windows components. The files in this folder take up almost 150MB of disk space. If you don't mind inserting the Windows Me CD-ROM when installing new Windows options, and you need the disk space, you can delete the C:\Windows\Options\Install folder.

What Is a Dual-Boot Installation?

A *dual-boot installation* is an installation of Windows that leaves the installation of another operating system intact. When you start your computer, you can decide which operating system to run.

You can install Windows Me in the same partition as Windows 3.1, Windows NT, or Windows 2000, but this is not a great idea. Instead, use a third-party partitioning program to create a separate partition for each operating system you want to install and to switch between them. Chapter 10 describes how to partition your hard disk. For how to create a dual-boot installation, see "Creating Dual-Boot Installations" later in this chapter.

What Is an Emergency Boot Disk?

The *Emergency Boot Disk* (or *EBD*) is a floppy disk that you create during the Windows installation or upgrade process. Be sure to make an emergency boot disk when the Windows Me Setup Wizard suggests it. You can use this floppy disk to restart your computer if you have a problem starting from your usual hard disk; put the floppy disk into the disk drive before you turn on your computer (see Chapter 34, section "Startup Floppy Disk"). You can also use the Emergency Boot Disk to run Windows if you reformat your hard disk.

If you are upgrading from Windows 98 or 95, keep your old Emergency Boot Disk in case you ever want to start your machine up in DOS. The Windows Me Emergency Boot Disk doesn't provide this capability.

The EBD contains generic CD-ROM drivers, so that if you need to start your computer from the diskette, your CD-ROM drive should work. The drivers provided don't work with all CD-ROM drives, though; if your CD-ROM drive came with a floppy disk containing drivers, make sure that you know where that disk is.

If you use a laptop computer that has one shared bay for both a CD-ROM and floppy disk drive, you cannot make an Emergency Boot Disk if your computer requires rebooting to switch from the CD-ROM drive to the floppy disk drive. Click the Cancel button when Setup asks you to insert a floppy disk into the drive.

You can create an EBD any time you are running Windows. Choose Start | Settings | Control Panel, open (single- or double-click) the Add/Remove Programs icon, and click the Startup Disk tab.

Preparing to Install Windows Me

Here are some tips, including suggestions from Microsoft, for a smoother installation:

- **Virus-checking**   Run a virus-checker on your system before installing Windows, so that no viruses interfere with the installation. You can download several good virus-checkers from the Internet, including those from McAfee (at **http://www.mcafee.com**) and Symantec (at **http://www.symantec.com**). Then disable your virus checker before installing Windows. Some computers have antivirus programs stored in the computer's BIOS; if your computer does, Setup won't run. If you see an error message reporting an antivirus program, check your system's documentation for instructions on how to disable virus checking.

■ **Disk errors**   Run ScanDisk (if you use Windows 95 or 98) or Chkdsk (if you use DOS or Windows 3.1) to clean up any formatting errors on your hard disk. Windows runs ScanDisk again during installation, and it can't continue if it finds any errors.

■ **Backups**   Make a complete backup of your system. If that's not possible, make a backup of all of your data files. See Appendix B for how to use the Microsoft Backup program that comes on the Windows Me CD-ROM.

■ **Disk space**   Make sure that you have enough free space on the hard disk on which your Windows program folder is (or will be) stored (see "How Much Disk Space Does Windows Me Require?") You need at least 500MB, and more if you plan to install lots of optional programs.

■ **Hardware problems**   If you have problems with hardware or software on your system, fix the problems first or uninstall the hardware or software.

■ **Other utilities**   Disable any non-Microsoft disk-caching programs, such as the caching programs that come with the Norton Utilities and PC Tools. Turn off other utilities that might interfere with installation, such as programs like CleanSweep that monitor software installations. Exit from all programs.

When you install Windows, the Setup Wizard will ask for the following information:

■ **Windows Me serial number**   The 25-character serial number is printed on the CD-ROM cover. We suggest that you write this serial number right on the CD-ROM, using a fine-point permanent marker, on the same side that the printing appears on the disk. *Don't write on (or touch) the other (bottom) side of the disk.*

■ **Name**   name can appear as you want it in applications that get your name from Windows (for example, Outlook Express's e-mail program). You can change your name in most applications, but getting it right the first time is more convenient.

■ **Company**   Your company's name can appear as you want it in applications that get your company name from Windows (for example, Word's document summary information feature).

■ **Computer name**   This is the name you want to use for your computer. If your computer is connected to a local area network, the LAN administrator might want to issue your computer a name. Be sure to check with your LAN administrator before installing Windows Me.

■ **Workgroup**   This is the name of the workgroup your computer is part of, if your computer is on a LAN. Ask your LAN administrator for the workgroup name.

- **User name**   This is the user name you'll type when you log onto Windows (see Chapter 31, section "What Password Protection Does Windows Offer?")
- **Password**   This is the password you'll type when you log onto Windows.

Installing Windows on a Blank Hard Disk

If your hard disk has gotten full of junk, or your Windows installation is unreliable, you may want to start from scratch, rather than installing Windows on top of what you already have on the hard disk. You can save the data files you want to keep, reformat the hard disk, install Windows, install the programs you want to use, and restore your data files.

To install Windows from scratch, you must be able to create a floppy disk with enough of your existing operating system on it to let you start your computer and access the CD-ROM drive. You can use this floppy disk while you are repartitioning and reformatting the hard disk and running the Windows Me Setup program. If you don't have an existing operating system—if your hard disk is truly blank—you need a Windows Me, 98, or 95 startup floppy disk with which to partition and format the hard disk before you can install Windows Me. Many new computers come with a Windows Startup disk for this purpose.

 Caution   *Formatting your hard disk deletes everything on it. You can't use the Recycle Bin or other unerase programs to get files back. Be sure to make and verify a backup copy of all the files you want to save (see Appendix B for how to install and use the Microsoft Backup program).*

If you want to erase your existing Windows or DOS system, follow these steps to completely erase one or more partitions on your hard disk and install Windows Me:

1. Back up all the data files that you want to save, so that you can restore them on your hard disk after you install Windows.

2. Make sure that you have the program disks for all the programs you want to install with Windows Me.

3. Using your old operating system, create a boot disk—a floppy disk from which you can start your computer, including drivers your CD-ROM drive requires. You will need at least one blank floppy disk.

   - If you run Windows 95 or 98, create a boot disk. Choose Start | Settings | Control Panel, open the Add/Remove Programs icon, click the Startup Disk tab, and click the Create Disk button (you may have to insert your Windows 95 or 98 CD-ROM or installation floppy disks, so have them handy).

■ If you run Windows 3.1, use your DOS boot disk (or make one by using the DOS **FORMAT A: /S** command).

4. Look at the contents of the boot disk. If it doesn't contain the Format.com and Fdisk.exe files (which you will need to partition and format your hard disk), copy them from your hard disk. If you run Windows 95 or 98, these files are usually in the C:\Windows\Command folder. If you run Windows 3.1, these files are usually in your DOS folder.

5. Test the floppy disk and CD-ROM to make sure that they work. You may need to install CD-ROM drivers from a floppy disk that came with your CD-ROM drive. Insert the boot disk in the floppy disk drive, exit from Windows, and restart the computer from the floppy disk. The computer should restart and display a DOS prompt. It might ask first whether you want Windows with or without CD-ROM support—you'll need CD-ROM support to read the Windows ME CD-ROM.

6. If you want to repartition the hard disk, run the Fdisk program to delete any partitions you no longer need and to create a new Primary DOS partition on your hard disk (see Chapter 10, section "What Are Partitions, File Systems, FAT32, and Drive Letters?"). If you would rather reformat your existing Windows partition, skip to step 9.

7. Type **fdisk** and press ENTER. When you see the Fdisk menu, delete all the unneeded partitions from your hard disk (for example, if you have a partition for Windows 98 and a partition for your data, delete only the Windows 98 partition). Then create a new Primary DOS partition (Windows uses DOS partitions). Choose to make this partition active (that is, this partition is the one that the computer uses when starting up).

8. Restart the computer as directed by the Fdisk program. Leave the boot disk in the drive so that the computer can start up from its files. Again, you see the DOS prompt. You can't use the DOS DIR command to list the contents of the hard disk, because you have not yet formatted it.

9. Run the Format command to reformat your hard disk, using the /s command-line option to make the hard disk bootable. Assuming that your hard disk is drive C, type **format c:\ /s** and press ENTER.

10. Formatting takes a few minutes, depending on the size of your hard disk. When formatting is complete, type a volume label for the hard disk (any name for the disk or the computer, up to 11 characters, with no punctuation). Press ENTER.

11. When you see the DOS prompt again, run the Setup.exe program from the Windows Me CD-ROM to install Windows. Assuming that your CD-ROM drive is drive D, type **d:\setup** and press ENTER. (If your CD-ROM drive isn't drive D, substitute the correct letter.) Follow the prompts on the screen.

12. The Setup Wizard installs Windows Me. The Wizard runs ScanDisk to check your hard disk for errors. When it finishes, press X to exit from ScanDisk and continue with the installation.

13. Follow the instructions to complete the installation, which can take up to an hour.

Dealing with Disk Errors

Before installing Windows, the Setup Wizard runs a version of ScanDisk to check your hard disk for errors. If it finds any errors, it can't proceed. If you see a message that ScanDisk has found an error, follow the steps appropriate to your situation, provided next, to fix the problem.

If you are upgrading from Windows 3.1, Windows 95, Windows 98, or MS-DOS:

1. Exit Windows so that you see the DOS prompt.

2. Put the Windows Me CD in the CD-ROM drive and type this command (replace the *d* with the drive letter of your CD-ROM drive if it differs):

   d:\win9x\scandisk

3. ScanDisk runs and checks your hard disk. Follow the instructions on the screen to fix the problems that it finds.

4. Run the Windows Me Setup Wizard again.

If you are reinstalling Windows Me, follow these steps:

1. Exit the Setup Wizard.

2. Choose Start | Programs | Accessories | System Tools | ScanDisk. The ScanDisk program runs.

3. Follow the instructions on the screen to fix the problems that it finds.

4. Run the Windows Me Setup Wizard again.

Upgrading to Windows Me

You can upgrade to Windows Me if your computer has Windows 98, Windows 95, Windows 3.1, Windows for Workgroups 3.11, or MS-DOS. However, it's unlikely that a system running Windows 3.1 or DOS has enough processing power, memory, and disk space to run Windows Me. It's also unlikely that you'd want to install Windows Me over Windows 2000 or NT (if you do, follow the instructions in the preceding section to delete the Windows 2000 partition and install Windows Me from scratch).

 If you want to be able to run either another version of Windows or Windows Me when you start the computer, you can set up a dual-boot configuration (see "Creating Dual-Boot Installations").

Upgrading from Windows 98 or 95

Windows Me can use many Windows 98 and 95 configuration settings, so the process of upgrading from Windows 98 or 95 is quicker than upgrading from other operating systems. To upgrade from Windows 98 or 95 to Windows Me, follow these steps:

1. Start Windows 98 or 95.
2. Put the Windows Me CD-ROM in the CD-ROM drive. You may see a message asking whether you want to upgrade to Windows Me. If you don't see this message, you should see the Windows Me CD-ROM window; click the Browse This CD icon and double-click the Setup icon. If no window appears, run the Setup.exe program in the root folder of the CD-ROM drive (choose Start | Run, type **d:\setup**, and press ENTER, if your CD-ROM drive is drive D).
3. Follow the instructions that the Setup Wizard displays, clicking the Next button to move to the next step. The process takes almost an hour.

 The Setup Wizard asks in which folder to install Windows Me (usually C:\Windows). If you choose a different folder than the one in which Windows 98 or 95 was installed, you must reinstall all of your application programs, and possibly all of your hardware drivers.

Installing over Windows 2000 or NT

Installing Windows Me over Windows 2000 or Windows NT isn't exactly an upgrade, but it can be done. Start your computer from a floppy disk and then run the Setup.exe program in the root folder of the Windows Me CD-ROM. If you want to continue to be able to run Windows 2000 or NT, though, consider creating a dual-boot installation (see the next section).

Creating Dual-Boot Installations

You can create a dual-boot installation with Windows 3.1, Windows 2000, or Windows NT, installing both operating systems in the same partition. This type of installation gets confusing, though, because the two operating systems can change each other's files by accident. A better method is to use Partition Magic (from PowerQuest Corp., at **http://www.powerquest.com/partitionmagic**) or another third-party partitioning program.

Fdisk, the partitioning program that comes with Windows, creates only one Primary DOS partition, the type of partition from which you can start and run Windows. Partition Magic and similar programs can create up to three Primary DOS partitions, although only one can be active at a time. For your data, you can create as many Extended DOS partitions as you like (although one is usually enough). To create a dual-boot system with Windows Me and another version of Windows, follow these steps:

1. Make a backup copy of all your data files. See Appendix B for how to install and use the Microsoft Backup program.

2. Use Partition Magic (or a similar program) to create three partitions:

   ■ A Primary DOS partition for the other version of Windows. If this version is already installed, you can leave it in its existing partition.

   ■ A Primary DOS partition for Windows Me.

   ■ An Extended DOS partition for your data.

3. Use Partition Magic to set your existing Windows partition to be the *active partition*—the one from which programs load when you start or restart the computer. At this point, your system looks like this:

   ■ Drive C is the active Primary DOS partition containing your existing version of Windows.

   ■ Drive D is the Extended DOS partition for your data.

   ■ The inactive Primary DOS partition for Windows Me is hidden.

4. Copy your data files to drive D so that they will be visible to both the existing version of Windows and Windows Me.

5. Use Partition Magic to set your Windows Me partition to be the active partition and restart your system. Now, your system looks like this:

   ■ Drive C is the active Primary DOS partition to which you will install Windows Me.

   ■ Drive D is the Extended DOS partition for your data.

APPENDIXES

- The inactive Primary DOS partition, in which the other version of Windows resides, is hidden.

6. Format the active partition of your C drive and install Windows Me in this partition, as described in the section "Installing Windows on a Blank Hard Disk" earlier in this chapter.

Once you have both versions of Windows installed in separate Primary DOS partitions, you can switch back and forth by using Partition Magic and restarting Windows. From either version of Windows, the files on drive D are accessible, and the files on the other (inactive) Primary DOS partition are hidden.

You can use Partition Magic or a similar program to create a third Primary DOS partition for a third version of Windows or for a Linux Ext2 partition.

Note	*On a dual-boot system with Windows NT or Windows 3.1, you can't use FAT32 (see Chapter 10, section "What Are the FAT16 and FAT32 File Systems?") for your data partition because Windows NT and Windows 3.1 don't support FAT32 (as Windows 2000 does). On a dual-boot system with Windows 2000, you can't use an NTFS partition for your data partition, since Windows Me can't read it.*

To create a dual-boot system with Windows 2000, install Windows Me and then install Windows 2000. Windows 2000's boot manager can create a dual-boot system without a third-party program like Partition Magic.

Checking Your System After Installing Windows Me

If you didn't reformat your hard disk to install Windows Me from scratch, and if you installed Windows Me in the same folder as your previous version of Windows (that is, you didn't create a dual-boot installation), you shouldn't have to reinstall any of the application programs that were installed on your hard disk. The Setup Wizard looks for installed programs and installs them in Windows Me, too.

The Windows Me Setup Wizard tries to detect all the hardware components of your computer and configure itself to use them. Check that all of your hardware was correctly detected by Windows Me, including your modem, network cards, and printer. If they don't work right, refer to Chapter 14 to reinstall them.

If your computer is connected to a LAN, check that network communication is functioning normally. If it's not, see "Troubleshooting Your Network" in Chapter 27, or talk to your LAN administrator.

You can print a summary of your Windows configuration. Choose Start | Programs | Accessories | System Tools | System Information. Then choose File | Print.

Uninstalling Windows Me

When you installed Windows Me, you may have chosen to back up your current operating system. You don't have this option if you installed Windows Me to a new folder or partition (to create a dual-boot system, for example) or if you were running a version of MS-DOS older than 5.0.

If you backed up your previous operating system, you can probably uninstall Windows Me and return to that operating system. Follow these steps to determine whether you can uninstall Windows Me:

1. Choose Start | Settings | Control Panel.

2. Run the Add/Remove Programs program (single- or double-click the icon, depending on how Windows is configured). When you see the Add/Remove Programs Properties window, click the Install/Uninstall tab (it's probably already selected).

3. Look at the contents of the large box in the lower half of the window, which contains a list of the programs you can uninstall. If Uninstall Windows Millennium is listed, you can uninstall it; select it and click the Add/Remove button.

APPENDIXES

The Complete Reference

Appendix B

Backing Up Your Files with Microsoft Backup

The most important thing to say about backing up your files is this: Back up your files.You can back up your files onto floppies, tapes, network servers, extra hard drives, writable CDs, Zip drives, Jaz drives, or whatever you happen to have. How you back up your files is much less important than that you do it. If you have only a few files or folders to back up, you can use Windows Explorer to make the copies.

A backup program (written by Seagate Software, and called simply Microsoft Backup) is included on the Windows Me CD-ROM, although it doesn't install as part of Windows. Microsoft Backup makes backing up large numbers of files and folders reasonably painless. Your tape drive, Zip drive, Jaz drive, or CD-RW may come with its own backup program. You use Microsoft Backup to create backup jobs (descriptions of what and how to back up) and then back them up. If a file is deleted or corrupted, you use Backup to restore the file from your backup tape or disk. Note: You might hope that Microsoft Backup would work with Task Scheduler to do backups automatically, but unfortunately it does not.

What Is Backing Up?

Backing up means making copies of your files so that you can get the information back should anything happen to the originals.

Many unfortunate things can happen to files:

- A physical disaster like fire, flood, or cat hair could destroy your computer.

- A hardware failure could make your disk unreadable.

- A software problem could erase some of your files. For example, installing an upgrade to an application program might accidentally write over the folders in which you stored the previous documents that were created with that application.

- On a business computer system, a disgruntled employee might steal, erase, or corrupt important files.

- A well-meaning roommate, spouse, child, or coworker might delete or alter files without realizing it.

- You might get confused and get rid of files you meant to keep.

Any one of these possibilities might seem remote to you. (We used to think so, until we learned better.) But when you put them all together, it's amazing how often having a recent backup copy of your files turns out to be handy.

What Should You Back Up?

Ideally, you would back up everything; but (depending on the speed of your machine, the size of your hard drive, and the type of backup medium you use) a complete backup can take a considerable length of time. Once you have a complete backup to work from, updating that backup takes considerably less time.

A backup of only files that are new or have changed is called an *incremental backup*. A complete backup of all files and folders is called a *full backup* or *baseline backup*.

Backing up files is a little like flossing your teeth: we all know it's good for us, but few of us do it as often as we know we should. If it takes you a month or two to get around to doing a complete backup, you should consider backing up the following parts of your system more often:

- **Documents you are working on**   Many applications put new documents in the folder C:\My Documents by default. You may choose to put your documents anywhere you like, but for backup purposes, it is convenient to have them organized in subfolders of one easy-to-find folder.

- **Databases to which you regularly add data**   For example, if you use Quicken to balance your checkbook once a month, back up the file in which Quicken stores your checkbook data.

- **Correspondence, especially your e-mail files**   Letters and memos that you write are probably already in your documents folder(s). E-mail files, however, are usually stored in whatever folder you set up when you installed your e-mail program. If you use Outlook Express, the default folder is C:\Windows\Application Data\Microsoft\Outlook Express. The Windows Address Book is in the folder C:\Windows\Application Data\Microsoft\Address Book (see Chapter 5).

- **Your Favorites menu**   The World Wide Web would be much less useful if you suddenly lost your list of favorite sites (see Chapter 23). For Internet Explorer, that list is a set of shortcuts in the folder C:\Windows\Favorites. Back up the whole folder. If you use Netscape Navigator, use Start | Search | For Files Or Folders to look for the file Bookmark.htm.

If you back up these files frequently, a hard drive disaster is much less of an ordeal. Still, nothing beats the security of knowing that you have backups of *everything*.

Programs are not on the list of important items to back up. We assume that you (or the person who maintains your machine) still have the disks that you used to install the programs in the first place. Make sure you know where they are, and that they are in a safe place. Be sure to store the CD serial numbers with them. If you lose your hard disk, reinstalling all of your software is a nuisance, but not a disaster. You would, however, lose all the special settings that you have made to personalize the software for yourself. If reselecting all of those settings would be an ordeal, then you need to either back up the program's entire folder, or find out which specific files contain those settings.

How Often Should You Back Up?

Different sources will tell you to back up your files daily or weekly or monthly, but the real answer is that you should back up your files as soon as you have created or changed something that you don't want to lose. You need to balance the regular nuisance of backing up your files against the possible ordeal of regenerating your creative work.

A document that you are working on changes daily, and a single day's work can be a lot to lose. System files change when you reconfigure the settings of your system or when you install new hardware or software. Only you know how frequently your databases change or how much e-mail you are willing to lose in an accident. Backing up these frequently updated files need not be as involved as a full system backup (see the earlier section "What Should You Back Up?").

If your machine is part of a larger network, such as an office-wide local area network, check with the network administrator to see whether your hard drive is backed up automatically, and if so, how often. If it isn't, you might consider nagging an appropriate person. Programs exist that allow a network administrator to back up all the hard drives on the network automatically. Many offices do this every night, relieving individuals of the need to worry about backups at all.

What Should You Do with Your Backup Disks or Tapes?

Put your backup disks or tapes in a safe place, preferably as far from your computer as practical. Backups that sit right next to your computer may be handy in a hardware or software crash—but they don't protect you at all in case of fire, theft, or sabotage. If your backups are magnetically stored (tapes, removable disks, or hard drives—anything but CD-ROMs), keep them away from strong electromagnetic fields.

What Is Microsoft Backup?

Microsoft Backup is a program that is included on the Windows Me CD-ROM, although it doesn't install as part of Windows Me. Its purpose is to allow you to back up and recover files quickly and efficiently. Microsoft Backup uses file compression techniques to use as little disk space as possible in storing your backups. It can also spread your backup files across many floppy disks or other removable media without confusing itself. This appendix describes how to install and run the program, which requires 5.1MB of free space on your hard disk.

*Microsoft Backup was written by Seagate Software, which sold it to Veritas Software. Veritas Software sells a more full-featured backup program (see **http://www. veritas.com/us/products/backupexec**). The version of Microsoft Backup that comes with Windows Me appears to be the same program that shipped with Windows 98.*

What Is a Backup Job?

Backing up files requires you to make a series of decisions: what files to back up, what device to store the backup files on, and a number of more technical decisions, like whether to use compression. Ideally, you would make these decisions once for each type of backup that you regularly do (complete backup, document backup, mail backup, system backup, and so on), and then have the computer remember those decisions so that you don't have to go through them again every time you back up.

Microsoft Backup handles this situation by maintaining a list of *backup jobs*. Its Backup Wizard helps you define a backup job by leading you through all the necessary decisions. In the course of that process, you give the job a name. The next time you want to back up those same files and/or folders, you need only tell Microsoft Backup the name of the job. When you perform a backup job, the set of files that it creates is called a *backup set*.

Backing Up a Few Files or Folders

Even if you can't get around to a complete backup, you can protect yourself against the worst without too much effort by backing up your most valuable files and folders each day that you work on them.

Copying Files onto a Floppy Disk

Even on a slow system, it usually takes only a minute or two at the end of each day to pop in a floppy and copy the files you worked on that day. It's a good habit to develop.

If you typically work on only a few files each day, just find them in the right pane of an Explorer window and drag-and-drop them onto the floppy drive icon in the left pane (see Chapter 8, section "Dragging and Dropping Files and Folders"). You can save yourself some clicks and drags by using the Send To menu (see Chapter 8, section "Using the Send To Menu"). When you find a file you want to back up, select it in

Windows Explorer and choose File | Send To (or right-click the file and choose Send To from the menu that appears). Your floppy drive should appear on the list of Send To destinations—choose it, and the file is copied to the floppy.

If you work on a larger number of files, look at the Start | Documents menu to make sure you remember them all. If you want to make sure you don't miss any, use Start Search | For Files Or Folders to search for all files modified in the last day (see Chapter 9, section "Searching by Date"). You can drag-and-drop files directly out of the Search Results window onto a floppy disk icon in Windows Explorer. Or you can right-click any file in the Search Results window and choose Send To from the menu.

> **Tip**   *If you use Search to list the files you've worked on today, construct your search in such a way as to avoid finding all the temporary files that Windows creates in the course of a day. (If you do a lot of Web browsing, there can be hundreds of them.) These files are contained in subfolders of the C:\Windows folder. Either use the Look In box of Start | Search | For Files Or Folders to constrain your search within a folder that doesn't contain C:\Windows or specify a file type.*

Copying Files onto Larger Drives

Anything you can copy onto a floppy, you can copy onto a writable CD, a Zip drive or other removable disk, a second hard drive, or another machine on your LAN. The drag-and-drop techniques work in exactly the same way. If the drive (or folder) that you use for storing backup copies isn't already available on the Send To menu, you can add it (see Chapter 8, section "Using the Send To Menu").

A larger backup drive makes it less important to be selective about what you copy. A Zip disk is approximately 70 times larger than a floppy, and a backup hard drive may be dozens of times larger yet. You probably can copy, without too much time or trouble, your entire documents folder (whether it is C:\My Documents or some other folder that you have chosen) at the end of each day. You probably can copy your entire e-mail folder, as well (see the earlier section "What Should You Back Up?").

Using Microsoft Backup

Microsoft Backup has several advantages over a more informal system of copying key files onto floppies or other storage media:

- Backup copies files in a compressed form, so that they take up less disk space.
- Backup can spread a single backup job over several floppies or removable disks. This feature makes it possible to back up larger jobs.

- When you define a backup job, you decide once and for all what folders you want the job to back up. You don't have to go through the decision process again every time you do a backup.

- Backup is thorough. It doesn't lose its place when the phone rings.

- Backup is automated. Once the job starts, all you need to do is feed it a new disk if it asks for one. If you are backing up onto a tape drive or some other medium with sufficient size, you don't need to do anything at all.

Installing Microsoft Backup

If you don't find Backup on the Start | Programs | Accessories | System Tools menu, follow these steps:

1. With the Windows Me CD-ROM in your CD-ROM drive, display the folder D:\Add-ons\MSBackup in an Explorer window (substitute your CD-ROM drive letter for D if it's not drive D).

2. Run the Msbexp.exe file, the Backup Iexpress Installation program. After installing the Microsoft Backup program files in your C:\Program Files\Accessories\Backup folder, the installation program prompts you to restart Windows.

A text file with documentation about the program is on the Windows Me CD-ROM in \Add-ons\MSBackup\Backup.txt file.

If you upgraded Windows Me from Windows 98 or 95 and installed Backup in your previous version of Windows, the Backup Iexpress Installation program doesn't install anything—it leaves the existing version of Backup. To find out whether you have installed the version of Backup that comes with Windows Me, choose Start | Settings | Control Panel, run the Add/Remove Programs program, click the Install/Uninstall tab if it's not already selected, and see whether Microsoft Backup appears in the list of installed programs. To uninstall Microsoft Backup, choose it from the list of programs and click the Add/Remove button.

Running Microsoft Backup

You run Microsoft Backup by selecting Start | Programs | Accessories | System Tools | Backup. The first time you run Microsoft Backup, it checks whether you have a backup device installed—it's hoping to find a tape drive or similar drive. If it doesn't find a backup device, it asks you to install one or continue without one. (If you install a tape drive or other backup device later, choose Tools | Media from the menu to tell Backup about it.) Backup doesn't consider removable disks (like Zip and Jaz disks) to be backup devices, but you can back up to them, anyway.

When you start Backup, the startup dialog box, shown next, asks whether you want to create a new backup job, run an existing job, or restore files from a previous backup job. Click the appropriate radio button and click OK.

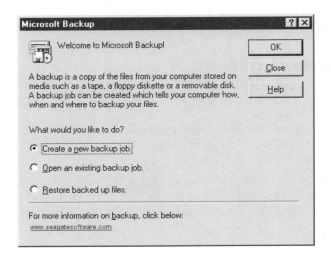

 Note *If someone has configured Backup not to display the startup dialog box, you see the main backup window instead.*

Creating a Backup Job with the Backup Wizard

Selecting Create A New Backup Job from Backup's startup dialog box starts the Backup Wizard, which takes you through the following decisions that you need to make to create a new backup job:

- Which files to back up
- Whether to back up all the selected files, or just the ones that have changed since the previous backup
- Where to store the backup data
- Whether to verify the backup
- Whether to use compression to make the backup file smaller
- What name to give the backup job

You can also start the Backup Wizard by clicking the Backup Wizard button on the toolbar in the main Backup window (the sixth from the left) to start the Backup Wizard.

Selecting Files to Back Up

The first decision you need to make is whether this backup job should be a complete backup or a backup only of selected files. Selecting the Back Up My Computer radio button defines this job as a complete backup—it backs up everything under My Computer on the folder tree. If this is your choice, click Next, and you are ready to move on to the next section.

Selecting the Back Up Selected Files, Folders, And Drives radio button defines this job as a partial backup. Click Next to move to the screen shown in Figure B-1, where you select the specific files, folders, and drives to back up.

This window works much like an Explorer window: Each of your computer's disk drives (other than the floppy drive) are listed in the left pane (see Chapter 8, section "What Is Windows Explorer?"). When a folder in the left pane is selected, its contents

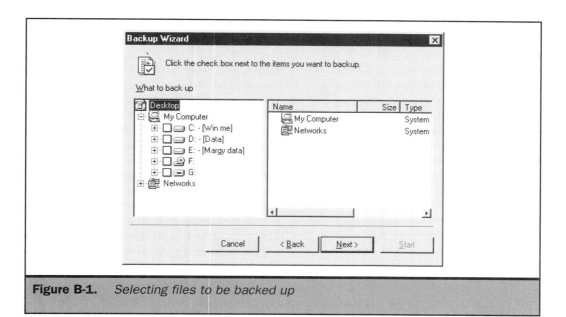

Figure B-1. *Selecting files to be backed up*

appear in the right pane. The boxes with plus or minus signs denote whether a folder is expanded. Click a plus sign to see the next level of the folder tree under a given folder.

The difference between this window and an Explorer window is that each folder has a second check box next to it. Clicking this second check box puts a blue check mark in the box, indicating that the entire folder (and all its subfolders) have been added to the list of files and folders to be backed up. For example, clicking the check box next to the C drive icon adds the entire contents of the C drive to the backup job.

If you want to back up some of the files on a drive, but not all of them, click the plus box to expand the folder tree underneath that drive. This gives you an opportunity to decide to back up some of its subfolders but not others. Continue this process until you have selected only those files and folders that you want to be part of this backup job. A gray check mark appears in the box next to a folder from which you have chosen to back up some, but not all, of its contents.

Documents on your desktop are stored in the folder C:\Windows\Desktop. That's where they show up on Backup's folder tree.

Choosing a Baseline or an Incremental Backup

After you have chosen which files to back up, whether you have chosen all or only a few, the next screen of the Backup Wizard asks whether to back up all the files you selected, or only files that are new or changed since the previous backup. If this is the first time you have backed up these files, choose All Selected Files. Otherwise, you have a judgment call: if you choose New And Changed Files, the job runs faster, but you have to keep both the original full backup and the incremental backup. Click one of the two radio buttons and click Next.

Choosing a Destination for the Backup File

The next screen of the Backup Wizard allows you to tell the Wizard where to store the backup files. The Where To Back Up box asks you to choose the backup medium: either a file on one of your computer's disk drives or a backup medium such as a cartridge tape drive. If you have no backup media on your system, File is the only choice on the pull-down menu.

Backup doesn't consider removable drives (like Zip and Jaz drives) to be backup media. You can back up onto them, however, by choosing to back up to a file, and storing the file on a removable disk.

If you choose File in the Where to Back Up box, a second box appears, asking for an address for the backup file. The Wizard may suggest a location (its default filename is MyBackup), or the box may be blank. In either case, you can either type an address into the box or click the button next to it—the Backup Wizard's version of a Browse button. Clicking the button opens a Browse window. Find a folder for the backup file and type a name for the file into the File Name box. Click Open to return to the Backup Wizard. The address of the backup file should be in the second box. Click Next.

If you choose a tape drive in the Where To Back Up box, no second box appears, because tapes don't allow you to select locations on the tape. Just click Next.

Choosing How to Back Up

The Backup Wizard's next screen consists of two check boxes:

- Compare Original And Backup Files To Verify Data Was Successfully Backed Up
- Compress The Backup Data To Save Space

Both of these options cost you a little time, but they're worth it. Verifying that the backup was successful takes only a little less time than the backup itself and may seem unnecessary, but remember: Paranoia is what backing up is all about. If you had faith that things would always work properly, you wouldn't be backing up at all.

Compression makes the backup file roughly half the size of the original files (unless the files you're backing up are already compressed). When you're talking gigabytes, that's space worth saving. And for smaller jobs, compression can make the difference between being able to back up onto a single removable disk.

Naming and Starting a Backup Job

The final screen of the Backup Wizard asks for a name for the backup job. Give the job a name and check over the summary of the choices you have made. Since this is the last screen, the Next button is grayed out. You can click Cancel to throw away the information you've entered about the job, Back to change some of your choices, or Start to start backing up.

Choosing a Media Name

Unless you are backing up to a file, one more question pops up after you click Start: Backup asks you to provide a unique media name and also suggests one—the job name followed by a number. This is intended to be the label that you put on the disks, tapes, or other media on which you store the backup. It allows you to tell the difference between this week's backup and last week's, as well as the difference between the second disk in the backup set and the fourth.

If you are reusing disks or tapes that you have used on this job before, replace Backup's suggested name with the media name on the disk label. Otherwise, accept Backup's suggestion (by clicking OK) and copy the new media name onto the disk or tape label.

Modifying an Existing Backup Job

Choosing Open An Existing Backup Job in Backup's startup dialog box (Figure B-1) takes you to the Open Backup Job dialog box. You can also see this dialog box by choosing Job | Open from the Backup menu bar.

The Open Backup Job dialog box contains a list of your previously defined backup jobs. Click one of the jobs and click Open. You see Backup's main window, shown in Figure B-2. The main Backup window has two tabs: Backup and Restore. When modifying an existing backup job, you see the Backup tab.

 If you are already looking at the main Backup window, just click the Backup Job box and choose from the list which backup job you want to modify.

Revising Your Choices

The parts of the Backup tab of the main Backup window should be familiar if you have created a backup job with the Backup Wizard: the Wizard's questions correspond to the parts of this window (see "Creating a Backup Job with the Backup Wizard"). From here, you can change any of the decisions you made when you created the job: the name of the job, the files to back up, whether to do a baseline or incremental backup, and where to store the backup file. When you finish your editing, you can either save the changes to this job, save the revised job under a new name, or not save at all.

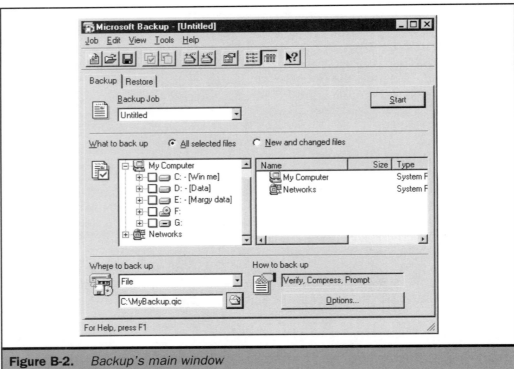

Figure B-2. *Backup's main window*

You can change your decisions about verification and compression by clicking the Options button. The Backup Job Options dialog box appears with the General tab selected, as in Figure B-3. The check box corresponds to the verify/don't verify decision made during the creation of the job (see "Choosing How to Back Up," earlier in the chapter). The When Backing Up To Media set of radio buttons gives the same no-compression/maximum- compression options as the Backup Wizard, but adds a third option, Compress Data To Save Time. This option means exactly what it says: the resulting backup file is larger than if you choose maximum compression, but running the backup job takes less time. Table B-1 shows all the options available when backing up files.

Overwriting Backup Files

When you run a backup job that has been run before, Backup creates a file of the same name as a file that already exists. The bottom set of radio buttons on the General tab of the Options dialog box addresses this situation. You have three options: Append This Backup To My Media (available only if the destination is a backup device, such as a tape drive), Overwrite The Media With This Backup, and Let Me Choose This Option During The Backup.

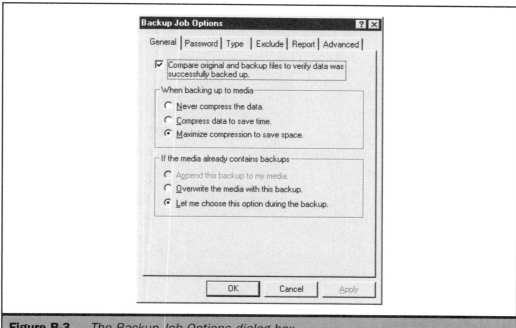

Figure B-3.   *The Backup Job Options dialog box*

Tab	Setting	Description
General	Compare original and backup files to verify data was successfully backed up	Specifies that after backing up the files, Backup compares the backup copies to the original files.
General	Never compress the data	Turns off compression during backups.
General	Compress data to save time	Compresses the backup copies of the files without sacrificing speed.
General	Maximize compression to save space	Compresses the backup copies of the files as much as possible, even if doing so slows down the backup operation.
General	Append this backup to my media	Specifies that Backup store this backup set after any existing information on the backup media.
General	Overwrite the media with this backup	Specifies that Backup delete the current contents of the backup media and replace them with the new backup set.
General	Let me choose this option during the backup	Specifies that when you perform a backup, Backup displays a dialog box that lets you choose whether to append the new backup set to the media or overwrite the existing data.
Password	Protect this backup with a password	Specifies that a password be necessary to restore files from backups. Type the same password in the Password and Confirm password boxes.
Type	All selected files	Specifies that Backup include all the files you select in the backup.
Type	New and changed files only	Specifies that Backup include only files that are either new or that have changed since the last backup.

Table B-1. *Backup Job Options*

Tab	Setting	Description
Type	Differential backup type	Specifies that Backup include only the files that have changed since the last backup for which the All Selected Files setting was selected.
Type	Incremental backup type	Specifies that Backup include only the files that have changed since the last backup for which the All Selected Files setting or the Incremental backup Type setting was selected.
Exclude	Do not back up these file types	Specifies the list of file types to skip when backing up (for example, temporary and backup files, with extensions .tmp and .bak). Click Add to add a file type to the list.
Report	List all files that were backed up	Specifies that the backup report include filenames of all files that were backed up.
Report	List files that were not backed up	Specifies that the backup report include files that were not backed up.
Report	List errors reported while backing up files	Specifies that the backup report include error messages.
Report	List warnings reported while backing up files	Specifies that the restore report include warning messages.
Report	List unattended messages and prompts	Specifies that the backup report include all the messages that were responded to on your behalf during an unattended backup.
Report	Show report summary	Specifies that the backup report include a summary of the numbers of files backed up and other statistics.

Table B-1.   *Backup Job Options* (continued)

APPENDIXES

Tab	Setting	Description
Report	Perform an unattended backup	Specifies that Backup not prompt for any information during the backup operation.
Advanced	Back up Windows Registry	Specifies that when you back up the Windows program folder (usually C:\Windows), you back up the Windows Registry, too (see Chapter 37).

Table B-1.   *Backup Job Options* (continued)

Each of the three choices has its advantages. Overwriting takes the least space. Appending means that the old backup is still there, in case the new backup is deficient in some way. Choosing during the backup preserves your options; but because Backup will wait for you to make the decision before continuing, you must be present and paying attention during the backup.

Establishing a Password

Stealing a backup tape or disk is an easy way to get all of a person's important files. Moreover, since backups are needed in case of emergency only, you might not notice a stolen backup tape for some time. For these reasons, you might want to protect your backup with a password.

 If you forget the password on a backup job, no one can get it back for you. Make sure you have a record of your password—somewhere other than in one of the files you are backing up.

From Backup's main window, you can establish a password for a backup job as follows:

1. Select the job name from the Backup Job drop-down list.
2. Click the Options button. The Options dialog box appears, as in Figure B-4.
3. Click the Password tab.
4. Click the Protect This Backup With A Password check box.
5. Enter a password into the Password box.
6. Enter the same password into the Confirm Password box.
7. Click OK.

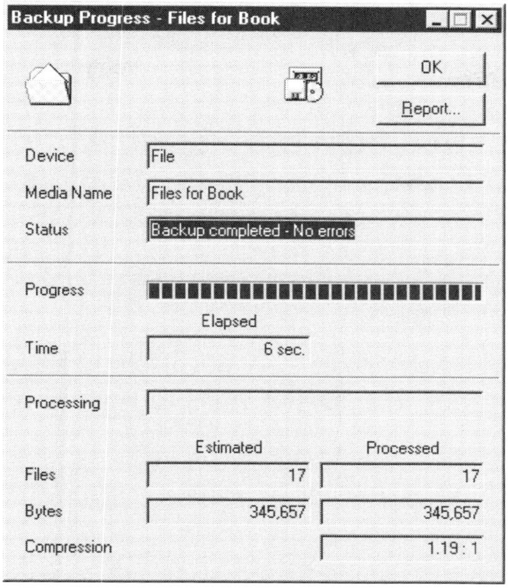

Backup Progress - Files for Book

			OK
			Report...

Device	File
Media Name	Files for Book
Status	Backup completed - No errors

Progress	████████████████████████████████
	Elapsed
Time	6 sec.

Processing	

	Estimated	Processed
Files	17	17
Bytes	345,657	345,657
Compression		1.19 : 1

Figure B-4.   *The Backup Progress box*

APPENDIXES

To remove a password from a backup job, repeat these steps, but uncheck the check box in step 4. Then click OK.

Eliminating the Startup Dialog Box

You can set up Backup so that it opens directly into its main window (Figure B-2), skipping the startup dialog box:

1. Start Backup. The Backup Wizard starts.
2. Click Close to get out of the Backup Wizard, revealing Backup's main window.
3. Select Tools | Preferences.
4. Uncheck the Show Startup Dialog When Microsoft Backup Is Started check box.
5. Click OK.

You can still access the Backup Wizard and the Restore Wizard from the toolbar or from the Tools menu.

 Note   *Leave the Back Up Or Restore The Registry When Backing Up Or Restoring The Windows Directory check box selected.*

Running a Backup Job

Once you have created and named a backup job, you can run it without going through the Backup Wizard.

Running a Backup Job from the Startup Dialog Box

To run an existing backup job from the startup dialog box (Figure B-1), select Open An Existing Backup Job. Backup presents you with a list of existing backup jobs—choose one by clicking its name and click Open. The main window appears, with the job already selected. Follow the instructions for running a backup job from the main window in the next section.

Running a Backup Job from the Main Backup Window

To run an existing backup job from the main Backup window (Figure B-3):

1. Select the name of the job from the Backup Job drop-down menu.

2. Check over the information about the job presented in the rest of the main window.

3. Click the Start button.

4. Answer any questions Backup asks (such as whether to overwrite previous Backup files). The Backup Progress box appears, as shown in Figure B-4.

5. If you are backing up onto floppies or other removable media, Backup may ask for additional disks from time to time. Insert the disks and deal with Backup's questions about media names (see "Choosing a Media Name").

6. At some point, the status line of this box announces that the job is complete, and tells you (if verification is part of the job) whether or not there were errors. If you want to look at the report on this job—which is worth doing if the verification showed errors—click the Report button. A text box appears. Close it when you have finished reading it. The report is stored in the folder C:\Program Files\Accessories\Backup\Reports, with the same name as the backup job.

7. Click OK in the Backup Progress box.

No Way To Run a Backup Job Automatically

The most convenient way to arrange backups is for them to run automatically in the middle of the night. For reasons we can't fathom, Windows' Task Scheduler can't run Backup unattended (see Chapter 2, section "Running Programs on a Schedule Using Task Scheduler"). When Backup opens, it waits for someone to tell it what job to run. There appears to be no way to tell it to just go ahead and run Job X if Task Scheduler wakes it up in the middle of the night. If you want the capability to have your files backed up automatically on a schedule, you'll have to find a different backup program.

Restoring Files with Backup

To restore files that you have backed up with Microsoft Backup, you can use the Restore Wizard or you can select options yourself.

Restoring Files Using the Restore Wizard

To run the Restore Wizard to step you through restoring one or more files, follow these steps:

1. Start Backup.

2. Select Restore Backed Up Files from Backup's startup dialog box, or if Backup opens with the main Backup window, click the Restore Wizard button on the toolbar (the seventh button from the left). A list of backup jobs appears.

3. Choose a backup job, and then click Open to start the Restore Wizard, whose opening screen is shown next. (You can exit the Restore Wizard at any point by clicking Cancel, returning you to the main Backup window, shown in Figure B-1.)

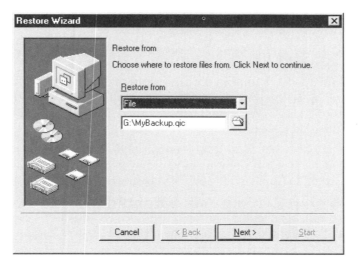

4. The two boxes in this illustration show where the Restore Wizard thinks the backup data is stored: the Restore From (upper) box shows whether it is on a backup medium or in a file on a disk, and the lower box shows the address of the file. Unless you have moved the backup file since you backed up, this information should be correct. If it is correct, click Next. If it isn't correct, click

the Browse button (the one with the folder icon on it) and find the backup file's current location. Then click Next. The Select Backup Sets box appears:

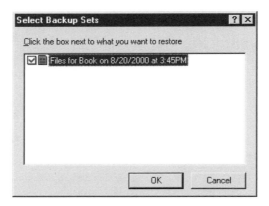

5. If more than one backup set is in the box, select the sets you want to restore by clicking the check boxes next to their names. Selected sets have blue check marks in the boxes next to their names. Click OK.

6. The Restore Wizard then asks you to select which files to restore. This dialog box works just like the box in the Backup Wizard in which you selected files to back up (see "Selecting Files to Back Up," earlier in the chapter). When you have chosen the files you want to restore, click Next.

7. The Wizard asks where to restore the files to, giving the choices Original Location and Alternate Location. If you choose Alternate Location, a second box appears in which you can type the address of a folder in which to put the restored files. You can click the Browse button next to this line and browse for a location instead. When you have finished choosing a location for the restored files, click Next.

8. The Wizard asks what to do if the destination folder already contains a file of the same name. Your options are never to overwrite, to choose whichever version of the file is newer, or always to overwrite. Pick one and click Start.

9. The Media Required dialog box asks whether the appropriate media is available. Make sure appropriate disks or tapes are inserted and click Yes. If the job has a password, Backup asks for it now. The restoring process begins.

10. A Restore Progress box appears, resembling the Backup Progress box shown earlier. It asks for additional disks or tapes as needed and announces when the job is complete.

11. If you want to read a report on the job (as you should if errors are reported), click the Report button. When you have finished with the report, close it, returning to the Backup Progress box.

12. Click OK to end the restoration.

Restoring Files Using the Restore Tab

Alternatively, you can use the Restore tab on the main Backup window to select what to restore. Follow these steps:

1. Click the Restore tab in the main Backup window. If Backup asks whether you'd like to refresh the current view (that is, update the Backup window to display the information from your backup device), click Yes. You see the Restore tab shown in Figure B-5.

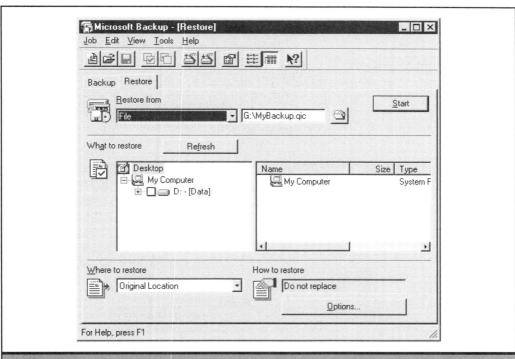

Figure B-5.   *The Restore tab of the main Backup window*

2. Set the Restore From drop-down menu to the device from which you want to restore the backups. Backup displays a list of backup sets on the current backup device (each backup set is the result of running a backup job). The list shows the time and date that each backup set was made.

3. In the What To Restore part of the Backup window, Backup displays the folders and files in that backup set. If you are restoring from a tape, this can take a few minutes. Backup isn't restoring any files yet; it's just displaying filenames so you can choose what to restore. Choose which files to restore. Click the plus box to the left of drives or folders to see their contents or click the folder icon. Click the check box to the left of drives, folders, or files to select them for restoration.

4. The Where To Restore box is normally set to Original Location to restore the file to the location from which it was backed up. You can change this setting to Alternate Location if you want to specify a different folder to store the restored copy of the file. A box appears below the Where To Restore box in which you can specify the folder (click the little yellow folder button to the right of the box to choose a folder from the folder tree).

5. Click the Options button to choose other options for restoring files. Table B-2 shows the options available when restoring files.

6. When you have selected the file(s) to restore, click the Start button on the Restore tab of the Backup window. If you are restoring from a tape or other removable media, Backup prompts you to put in the necessary tape or disk; do so and click OK. Then Backup restores the file or files.

Tab	Setting	Description
General	Do not replace the file on my computer	Specifies that if a file with the same name in the same location already exists, Backup doesn't overwrite the existing file with the backup file.
General	Replace the file on my computer only if the file is older	Specifies that if a file with the same name in the same location already exists, Backup overwrites the existing file only if it is older than the backup file.

Table B-2. *Restore Options*

Tab	Setting	Description
General	Always replace the file on my computer	Specifies that if a file with the same name in the same location already exists, Backup always overwrites the existing file.
Report	List all files that were restored	Specifies that the restore report include filenames of all files that were restored.
Report	List files that were not restored	Specifies that the restore report include files that were not restored.
Report	List errors reported while restoring files	Specifies that the restore report include error messages.
Report	List warnings reported while restoring files	Specifies that the restore report include warning messages.
Report	List unattended messages and prompts	Specifies that the restore report include all the messages that were responded to on your behalf during an unattended restore.
Report	Show report summary	Specifies that the restore report include a summary of the numbers of files restored and other statistics.
Report	Perform an unattended restore	Specifies that Backup not prompt for any information during the restore operation.
Advanced	Restore Windows Registry	Specifies that when Backup restores files, it restores the Windows Registry, too.

Table B-3. *Restore Options* (continued)

APPENDIXES

The Complete Reference

Windows Me

Glossary

10Base-T   *See* unshielded twisted pair cable.

16-bit application   Program designed to run with DOS and Windows 3.1. Windows Me, 98, and 95 can run both 16-bit and 32-bit applications.

32-bit application   Program designed to run with Windows 95, Windows 98, Windows Me, Windows NT, or Windows 2000.

access control   Security feature that controls who has access to shared resources (hardware or files).

access point   Hub of a wireless LAN, a "base station" for the radio transmitters on the LAN adapters of the other computers.

access type   Security feature that controls what people can do with a shared resource.

Accessibility   Features that allow people with disabilities to use Windows or other programs.

ACPI   Advanced Configuration and Power Interface, a standard for saving power by automatically turning off computer hardware when it is not in use.

action   Part of the definition of a file type, specifying what Windows does with files of that type.

Active Desktop   Desktop configuration in which your desktop can display Web pages. Rarely used.

active partition   Disk partition from which your computer starts, usually the Primary DOS partition.

Active Streaming Format   Streaming audio or video file format used by NetShow.

active window   Window that appears "on top" of other windows, obscuring parts of other windows that overlap. The active window is the window that is currently accepting input from the keyboard and mouse.

ActiveX controls   Small programs embedded in Web pages that can automatically be downloaded and run on your computer to add features to Web browsers.

adapter   Setting that identifies both the network interface card in a computer and the driver needed to make that card work.

adapter card   Printed circuit board that you can plug into an expansion slot inside your computer.

address   Information that tells you and Windows where to find a piece of information. *See* **e-mail address**; **file address**; **I/O address**; **memory address**; **UNC address**; **URL**.

Address Bar toolbar   Toolbar that can appear in Explorer windows and includes only the Address box.

Address Book   Windows utility that stores names and addresses.

Address box   Box appearing on the Address Bar toolbar in an Explorer window in which the name of the open folder appears.

Address toolbar   Toolbar that can appear on the Taskbar, containing a box in which you can type a URL to view a Web page.

Advanced Configuration and Power Interface   *See* **ACPI**.

Advanced Power Management   *See* **APM**.

anonymous FTP   Connecting to a publicly available FTP server by using *anonymous* as the user name and your e-mail address as the password. *See* **FTP**.

antivirus software   Program that detects viruses and worms and may also delete them from your system.

APM   Advanced Power Management, a standard for saving power by automatically turning off computer hardware when it is not in use.

applet   Small application program, frequently received as part of a Web page.

application or application program   Program for getting real-world work done. Applications include word processing, database, and spreadsheet programs.

Archive attribute   Setting for a file or folder that is used by backup programs. Many backup programs use the Archive attribute to indicate whether the file has been changed since the last time it was backed up.

area code rules   Rules that describe when to dial 1 and/or the area code when dialing the phone.

article   Message posted to a newsgroup.

ASCII file   *See* **text file**.

ASCII mode   In FTP, a setting used to transfer files that contain only plain, unformatted text. *See* **binary mode**.

ASF or ASX   File extension for Active Streaming Format files, a streaming audio or video file format used by NetShow.

attached file or attachment   File that is sent as part of an e-mail message or newsgroup article.

attribute   Setting for a file or folder. The four attributes are **Archive**, **Hidden**, **Read-Only**, and **System**.

audio CD   Compact disk containing audio information (rather than a Windows-compatible file system).

authenticode   Microsoft's technique for digitally signing ActiveX and Java applets to identify the applet's author and verify that the applet was received without tampering or modification.

authority certificate   Certificate authority's own certificate, used to check that other certificates it issued are valid.

Auto Hide   Feature that hides the Taskbar when you are not using it.

Autoexec.bat   DOS batch file that runs automatically when the computer is started; Autoexec.bat must be stored in the root folder of the active partition.

Automatic private IP addressing   Feature of Windows Me and 98 that automatically assigns IP addresses to computers on a TCP/IP-based LAN.

Autorun   Program on a CD-ROM that tells Windows to run a program on the CD-ROM whenever the CD-ROM is inserted into the drive.

AVI file   Video file with extension .avi.

background   Program running while its window is not active.

backscroll buffer   Temporary storage for the last 500 lines of text that have scrolled up off the top of the HyperTerminal window.

backup   Duplicate copy of information, stored separately in case something happens to the original copy.

backup job   Specification of the information to be backed up by the Microsoft Backup program and the location to store the duplicate copy.

backup set   Set of backup files, the result of running a backup job.

baseline backup   *See* **full backup**.

batch file   List of DOS commands to execute, stored in a text file with the extension .bat.

BBS   *See* **bulletin board system**.

Bcc   Blind Carbon Copy; e-mail addresses to which to send a copy of an e-mail message without the other recipients seeing the addresses.

Bell mode   In Ftp, whether the program beeps whenever it completes a command.

Binary mode   In Ftp, a setting used to transfer files that contain information in a format other than plain unformatted text. *See* **ASCII mode**.

binary string   Sequence of binary or hexadecimal digits used as the data portion of a value in the **Registry**.

binding   Specification of which network protocols work with your network interface card.

BIOS setup   Computer's low-level configuration information, including how much memory and what types of disks are installed.

bit   Binary digit, which can be either 0 or 1.

bitmap   Graphics format in which a picture or character is stored as a grid of dots. Standard Windows bitmap files have the extension .bmp. Older fonts are stored as bitmaps.

BMP file   Graphics file in bitmap format (a Windows standard format for graphics files) with the extension .bmp.

BNC connector   Connector used to connect network interface cards to coaxial cable in a bus topology network.

body   Text of an e-mail message, not including the header lines at the top of the message.

bookmark   Information about a Web page that you might want to come back to, as stored by Netscape Navigator in its Bookmark.htm file.

boot   Start up or turn on your computer.

boot disk or boot drive   Disk drive from which Windows loads on startup. *See also* **emergency boot disk**.

bps   Bits per second, a measure of data transmission speed. Sometimes confused with "baud."

Briefcase   Folder containing files and subfolders to move between two computers.

broadband   High-speed communications, including ISDN, DSL, and cable Internet connections.

BrowseMaster   Computer on a LAN that keeps track of which computers are on the LAN and what resources (disks and printers) they have to share.

browser   Program that your computer runs to communicate with Web servers on the Internet and display Web pages.

buffer   Temporary storage area.

bulletin board system (BBS)   Text-based account that runs on a small computer (such as a PC), usually predating the widespread use of the Internet. Some bulletin board systems are also connected to the Internet, and most have been superceded by Internet sites.

bus topology   Network topology in which each computer connects to a main cable (the *bus*).

byte   Eight bits, enough to hold one alphanumeric character.

CAB or cabinet file   File containing a group of files for installation with the file extension .cab. The Windows Me CD-ROM contains many cabinet files.

cable   Wire that connects the computers in a LAN, or type of Internet account provided by a cable television company.

cable Internet account   Internet account provided by a cable television company.

cable modem or cable television modem   Device that connects your computer (through its network interface card) to a cable Internet account.

cache   Area on disk (usually a folder) for the temporary storage of information. Browsers store recently viewed Web pages in a cache, in case you want to see them again. Windows also maintains caches for CD-ROMs and removable disks.

call log   List of calls you made by using Phone Dialer.

call waiting   Telephone line feature that beeps when another call is coming in on the line.

calling card   Telephone credit card, which you can configure Windows to use when dialing long-distance calls.

callto link   Link on a Web page that provides the information required to contact you by using an Internet-based conferencing system, such as NetMeeting.

Cascade Windows   Overlapping arrangement of windows

Category-5 or Cat-5 cable   Unshielded twisted-pair cable used for star-topology LANs.

Cc   Carbon Copy; e-mail addresses to which to send a copy of an e-mail message.

CD-ROM   Compact Disk/Read-Only Memory; compact disk containing digital (rather than audio) information.

central processing unit   *See* **CPU**.

certificate   Cryptographic data that can identify one computer or user to another. *See also* **digital ID**.

certificate authority   Organization that issues certificates.

certificate file   File containing a certificate (digital ID), usually with the extension .cer.

chat   Online communication in real time (minimal delay between when you send a message and when the recipient receives it). The oldest chat system is Internet Relay Chat (IRC). Windows comes with NetMeeting, an Internet conferencing program that includes chat.

check box   Box onscreen that can either be blank or contain a check mark (or X), usually appearing in a dialog box.

checkpoint   *See* **restore point**.

Classic style   *See* **double-click style**.

client   Program or computer that uses resources on a network. In Windows, a setting that identifies the type of network to which you are attaching the computer.

client-server network   Network on which server computers provide resources for the rest of the network, and client computers use only these resources.

clip   Video, audio, or graphics file that is part of a **collection** in Windows Movie Maker.

Clipboard   Temporary storage space in memory for storing cut-and-paste information.

clipboard file   File saved by Clipboard Viewer, with the extension .clp.

clock   *See* **system clock**.

Close button   Button in the upper-right corner of a window; click this button to close the window and possibly exit the program.

CMOS setup   *See* **BIOS setup**.

coaxial cable or coax   Type of cable used to connect computers in a bus topology LAN.

codec   System for audio or video compression and decompression.

collaboration   NetMeeting feature that allows everyone in a meeting to control a program running one person's computer.

collection   Group of video, graphic, and audio files to include in a movie in Windows Movie Maker.

color profile   System for precisely representing colors on your monitor and printer.

COM1, COM2, COM3, COM4, or com port   *See* **serial port**.

command button   Button you can click to perform a command.

command line   Command that you type at the DOS prompt, optionally followed by additional information.

communication security   Security that protects the data you transmit over the Internet or LAN.

Compact mode   Windows Media Player mode in which the program two small windows instead of one larger one.

compiled help module   File displayed by the Windows HTML Help program (Hh), stored with the extension .chm.

compressed folder   ZIP (compressed) file containing other files. If you have the Compressed Folders feature installed, ZIP files appear as folders in Windows Explorer.

connection   *See* **Dial-Up Networking connection**.

contact list   List of names and addresses in the Address Book.

container file   In OLE, a file that contains a link to an object in another file or that contains an embedded object from another file.

Content Advisor   Microsoft's program for limiting the content that Internet Explorer displays.

control character   Character you type by holding down the CTRL key while pressing another key.

control files   Files that Windows uses to store parts of its own programs and configuration information.

Control Panel   Window that displays icons for a number of programs that let you control your computer, Windows, and the software you have installed.

cookie   Small (at most 4KB) file that a Web server can cause your browser to store on your machine and return to the server.

copying   As part of cut-and-paste, copying selected information from its current location and storing it (temporarily) on the Clipboard.

CPU   Central processing unit, a computer chip that executes the instructions in programs. CPUs that can run Windows and compatible programs include Pentium, Pentium Pro, and Pentium II, as well as AMD and Cyrix chips.

crash   Failure in which a program stops running.

CSLIP   Compressed Serial Line Internet Protocol, a communications protocol for computers connected to the Internet. CSLIP has been superceded by PPP.

current local directory   Current directory (folder) on your computer to which FTP transfers files from a remote server and vice versa.

cursor   Screen element (usually a blinking vertical bar) that indicates where the text you type will be inserted. Not to be confused with the *mouse pointer*.

cursor blink rate   How fast the cursor blinks.

cut-and-paste   Feature of Windows that lets you select information from one file and move or copy it to another file (or another location in the same file).

cutting   Removing selected information from its current location and storing it (temporarily) on the Clipboard.

CWApps List Web site from which you can download a wide variety of freeware and shareware programs.

data bits How many bits of information are included in each byte sent (usually eight).

DB-15 Standard screen display connector.

DB-25 Standard parallel or serial connector. *See* **parallel port** or **serial port**.

DB-9 Standard nine-pin serial connector. *See* **serial port**.

DCC *See* **direct cable connection**.

DHCP Dynamic Host Configuration Protocol, Industry-standard software that assigns IP addresses for the LAN.

DHCP server Unix, Linux, Windows 2000, or NT system running DHCP software.

DDE Dynamic Data Exchange, a way for programs to exchange information.

DDE action DDE command that defines how data moves to or from files of a specified type.

dedicated server Computer used only as a server on a client-server network; not used to run user applications.

default The information or mode that a program uses unless you specify otherwise.

default printer Printer to which print jobs are sent unless you specify otherwise.

default Web browser Browser that Windows runs when you open a Web page by clicking a shortcut to a Web page or the filename of an HTML file.

deferred printing Queuing print jobs on a computer without a printer to be printed when you connect a printer to your computer later.

defragmenting Moving the contents of files around on your hard disk so that each file is stored as one big chunk, speeding up access to the file.

desktop Work area on your screen on which you see your programs. The desktop can contain windows, icons, and the Taskbar.

desktop scheme Group of desktop settings, including colors and fonts, saved with a name. Not the same as a **desktop theme**.

desktop theme   Set of desktop background, cursor, font, and color settings to dress up your desktop. Like a **desktop scheme**, but with a wider range of elements, including a screen saver, desktop background, mouse pointer, sounds, and icons.

Desktop toolbar   Toolbar that can appear on the Taskbar, containing a button for each icon on the desktop.

Details view   Way of representing the contents of a folder, in which items are listed with a tiny icon, the filename, the file's size, the file's type, when it was last modified, and its attributes.

device driver   *See* **driver**.

Device Manager   Windows program that lists all the devices that make up your computer and lets you see and modify their configuration.

dialing location   Location from which you place phone calls. You can tell Windows the area code and other information about the phone line at that location.

dialog box   Special kind of window that allows you to change settings or give commands in a program. Most dialog boxes include OK and Cancel buttons.

Dial-Up Adapter   Windows network driver that enables Dial-Up Networking to connect to PPP, CSLIP, and SLIP accounts.

dial-up client   Computer that calls another computer via Dial-Up Networking.

Dial-Up Networking   Windows facility that lets your computer connect to the Internet and some other accounts.

Dial-Up Networking connection   Icon with all the settings required to connect to an Internet account or other computer.

Dial-Up Server   Program used to allow other computers to connect to a local area network using Dial-Up Networking.

digital camera   Device that digitizes video input (through the lens of the camera) for use by your computer.

digital ID   File containing encryption and digital identification information that you can use to digitally sign or encrypt e-mail and newsgroup messages in Outlook Express. *See also* **certificate**.

digital signature   Information added to the end of an e-mail message to prove who sent it.

digitize   Convert information into a digital format so that it can be processed by your computer.

DIN connector   Standard, round keyboard or mouse connector.

Direct Cable Connection (DCC)   Connecting two computers with a serial cable to allow file or printing sharing. Also the name of the Windows program that allows two computers to communicate over a direct cable connection.

Direct Memory Access   *See* **DMA**.

directory   *See* **folder**.

directory server   Computer that stores the addresses of people who use NetMeeting.

directory service   Searchable listing of names, e-mail addresses, and other information about people.

DirectX   Enhanced video system built into Windows.

Disk Defragmenter   Disk cleanup program that stores files more efficiently on your disk.

display properties   Properties of your display and your Windows desktop.

distribution file   *See* **installation file**.

DLL file   Dynamic Link Library file, an executable file with the file extension .dll invoked from a running program.

DMA   Direct Memory Access, a system board facility used by a few medium-speed devices to communicate with the **CPU**.

DNS or DNS server   *See* **domain name server**.

DOC file   Document file, with the file extension .doc. DOC files are usually (but not always) created by Microsoft Word or a compatible program.

docking station   Hardware device into which you plug a laptop to provide connections to a monitor, keyboard, mouse, local area network, and/or additional PC Card slots.

Documents menu   Menu of recently used files. Choose Start | Documents.

domain name   Alphanumeric name of a computer or group of computers on the Internet; for example, **gurus.com**.

domain name server (DNS)   Computer on the Internet that translates between domain names and numeric IP addresses. You can specify two DNSs in Dial-Up Networking: a primary server and a secondary server.

DOS   Disk Operating System, the operating system on which Windows runs. Sometimes called **MS-DOS**.

DOS initialization file   One of the files that DOS reads when starting up: Autoexec.bat, Config.sys, and Msdos.sys.

DOS program   Program written to work with the DOS operating system.

DOS prompt   Prompt that DOS displays when it is waiting for you to type a command.

DOS Virtual Machine   Program that simulates DOS, displaying a DOS prompt and running DOS programs and commands.

DOS window   Window in which a DOS program is running.

double-click style   Desktop mode in which clicking an icon or filename twice runs the program or opens the file. To select the icon or filename without running or opening it, click it once. Formerly called *Classic style*.

download   Transfer a file from the Internet, other network, or mainframe to a PC.

downloaded object security   Security for information you download from the Internet.

Dr. Watson   Windows utility that takes a snapshot of the system's state when a program fails.

drag-and-drop   Method of moving or copying information from one file to another, or to another location in the same file.

drive letter   Letter that identifies a disk drive, other storage device, or a partition of a drive.

driver   Software that allows Windows to communicate with a device, such as a display or printer.

drop-down menu   Menu that appears when you click a command on a menu bar.

DSL   Digital Subscriber Line, an all-digital telephone line that uses the "last mile" of copper line between your computer and the central phone company offices. Actually a family of types of lines, including ADSL, HDSL, SDSL, and others.

DSL modem   Device that connects a computer (usually via a network interface card) to a DSL phone line.

dual-boot installation   Computer that can be started in either of two operating systems; for example, Windows Me and Windows NT, or Windows Me and Linux.

DVD   Digital Versatile Disk or Digital Video Disk, a digital disk that can contain video material.

DWORD   Type of Registry entry that contains a numeric value.

dynamic addressing   System that assigns an address to a computer when the computer connects to the network. Each time the computer connects, it may get a different address.

EBD   *See* **emergency boot disk**.

echo   Whether a communications program displays what you type or waits and displays the text that the remote computer sends back.

ECMAScript   *See* **JavaScript**.

EIDE   *See* IDE.

EISA   Enhanced Industry Standard Architecture, an improved version of ISA now superceded by PCI.

electronic mail   Messages sent over a local area network, the Internet, or other network.

e-mail address   Address that identifies the recipient of an e-mail message. The e-mail address for comments or suggestions about this book is **winmetcr@gurus.com**.

embedding   In OLE, storing an object of one type file a file of another type, optionally maintaining linkage from the second file to the file that originally contained the object, for example, an Excel spreadsheet embedded in a Word Perfect document.

emergency boot disk   Floppy disk from which you can restart Windows in the event of trouble. Also called *startup floppy disk* or *EBD*.

EML   File extension, used for e-mail messages, that is used by Outlook Express's Inbox Assistant to reply to messages automatically.

encrypted mail   E-mail that has been encoded so that only the intended recipient can read it.

encryption   Scrambling a message so that it can be read only by someone with a secret decryption key.

Enhanced ISA   *See* **EISA**.

error control   Feature of some modems that checks transmitted data for errors.

Ethernet   Type of local area network communication.

event   Windows operation that can trigger a sound. For example, exiting a program is an event.

executable or EXE file   Executable file, with the file extension .exe.

expansion slot   Slot inside a computer into which you can insert an adapter card.

Explorer   One of two programs that come with Windows: Internet Explorer (a Web browser) or Windows Explorer (a file management utility).

Explorer bar   Left pane of a Windows Explorer window, usually displaying a folder tree.

Explorer window   Window displayed by the Windows Explorer program.

Extended DOS partition   Section of a hard disk that stores an additional DOS or Windows file system.

extension   Last part of a filename, attached to the rest of the filename by a period (.). Extensions are usually three letters long and indicate the **file type**. For example, a file named Example.txt has the extension .txt.

external modem   Modem that connects to your computer's serial port by a serial cable.

extracting   Copying a file from a compressed folder or ZIP file and decompressing it as you copy it.

FAQ   Frequently Asked Questions (and their answers).

FAT   *See* **file allocation table**.

FAT16   File system used in all versions of DOS since DOS 2.0, as well as Windows. FAT 16 is also supported in Windows for disks up to 2GB.

FAT32   New file system supported by Windows 95, 98 and Windows Me, in which data is stored more efficiently on disks larger than 500MB.

Favorites   Files, folders, Web pages, and programs to which you want easy access. Windows stores shortcuts to Favorites in your Favorites folder and displays them on the Favorites menu.

Favorites menu   Menu displayed by choosing Start | Favorites listing files, shortcuts, and Web sites that you have added.

file   Collection of information that has a name and stored on a disk—for example, a document, spreadsheet, or program component.

file address   Address of a file on your computer or on a network to which your computer is attached. Also called a *path name*.

file allocation table   Table that stores information about each sector on a disk.

file association   Which program you use to open, edit, or print a specified type of file.

file attachment   *See* **attached file.**

file icon   Icon that represents a file; it looks like a piece of paper with the design of the program that created the file or that can open the file.

filename   Name given to a file. The last part of a filename, after the last period, is the **extension.**

file server   Computer that stores files that are used by other computers on a network.

file system   Information that keeps track of which files are stored where on the disk. Its properties are displayed on the File System Properties dialog box.

File Transfer Protocol   *See* FTP.

file type   Type of information contained in a file, indicated by the extension portion of the filename.

filter   Feature of Outlook Express and other mail clients that can automatically sort (or take other actions in response to) your incoming e-mail messages. Outlook Express and other newsreaders can also filter newsgroup articles for newsgroups to which you have subscribed.

FilterKeys   Accessibility feature that "filters out" repeated keystrokes.

firewall   Gateway program that provides security features when translating between a LAN and the Internet. A firewall includes or works with a **proxy server**.

FireWire   New standard type of connector introduced on Macintosh computers, and also available on many PCs. Also known as *IEEE 1394* or Sony *i.Link*.

fixed spacing   Typeface design in which all letters in the typeface are the same width.

floppy disk   Also called a *diskette*, a removable disk that stores up to 2.8MB, depending on the capacity of the disk drive.

flow control   System that controls the flow of data between your modem and your computer.

folder   Special kind of file that contains a list of other files. Folders can contain other folders.

folder hierarchy   *See* **folder tree**.

folder icon   Icon that represents a folder; it looks like a manila folder.

folder tree   Diagram showing which folders are contained in which other folders. Also called a *folder hierarchy* or *folder list*.

Folder window   *See* **Explorer window.**

Folders Explorer bar   In a Windows Explorer window, when the Explorer bar displays a folder tree.

font   All the characters in a typeface of a given size and style. Commonly but incorrectly used to mean **typeface**.

font substitution   To speed up printing, using built-in printer fonts where possible for similar TrueType fonts.

formatting   Writing the file system onto a disk.

fragmentation   Storage of files in discontinuous groups of sectors on your disk. When too many files are split up into too many groups of sectors, disk performance slows down, and you should defragment the disk.

freeware   Programs that are entirely free to use and frequently downloadable from the Internet.

FTP   File Transfer Protocol, a method for transferring files over the Internet. The built-in Windows program that transfers files by using FTP is called Ftp.

FTP client   Program that lets you upload files to, or download files from, an FTP server. Windows comes with the Ftp program. Internet Explorer and Netscape can also act as FTP clients.

FTP server   Internet host computer that acts as a file archive, allowing other computers to upload or download files by using FTP.

full access   Access type that allows other people to read from or write to a shared resource.

full backup   Complete backup of all files and folders; also called a *baseline backup*.

Full mode   Windows Media Player mode in which the program appears using its default interface—one large window.

game controller   Device that allows you to play arcade-style games on your computer.

gateway   Device or program that connects your LAN to the Internet (or one network to another network), passing messages between the computers on the LAN and computers on the Internet. A gateway usually includes a **proxy server** or a **NAT**.

GDI   Graphic Device Interface, the part of Windows that formats program output for screens and printers.

GDI pool   Fixed-size area of memory used to manage fonts, colors, and other tools that are used to create screen and printer images.

GIF file   File in Graphics Information Format, a popular format for graphics files that is widely used in Web pages. GIF files have the extension .gif.

Graphical User Interface (GUI)   Software design that allows you to control your computer by using a mouse, windows, and icons.

graphics mode   In a DOS window, the mode that displays any pattern of dots on the screen, including text.

guest computer   Computer that uses shared resources from other computers over a network or direct cable connection.

GUI   *See* **Graphical User Interface**.

hang   When a program or the Windows system stops responding to input from the keyboard or mouse.

hard disk   Disk that is sealed into its disk drive.

hard disk controller   Adapter card that connects a hard disk to your computer.

hardware profile   Description of your computer's hardware resources.

header   Lines at the top of an e-mail message that contain the address, return address, date, and other information about the message, not including the **body** (text) of the message.

Hh   Program that displays HTML Help files in compiled help module format.

hibernation and Hibernate Mode   *See* **Standby Mode**.

hidden file   File whose Hidden attribute is selected so that the file doesn't appear in Windows Explorer.

hierarchical file system   System of storing files on disks, in which files are stored in folders and folders can contain other folders.

High Contrast   Accessibility option that uses a high contrast color scheme, and increases legibility wherever possible.

History   List of recently displayed Web pages, maintained by a browser.

hive   Group of Registry entries (like a folder).

home page   Main (or starting) page of a Web site. Also used to refer to a browser's **start page**.

HomeRF   Standard, with **IEEE 802.11b**, for wireless LAN communications.

hop   Stage of the route that a packet of information takes to get from its starting point to its destination.

host address   On the Internet, address of a host computer.

host computer   Computer that has the resources to be shared over a network or direct cable connection.

hot docking   Docking or undocking a laptop without turning it off.

hot swapping   Installing or uninstalling a piece of hardware while the computer is turned on.

hover color   Color a Web page link turns when the mouse pointer is on it.

HSV   Numerical way of describing a color by its hue, saturation, and luminescence value.

HT file   HyperTerminal connection file, with extension .ht.

HTML   Hypertext Markup Language, the language in which Web pages are written. You can create files in HTML by using a Web page editor.

HTML mail or HTML messages   E-mail messages formatted using HTML.

HTTP   Hypertext Transfer Protocol, the language that Web browsers and Web servers use to communicate with each other.

HTTPS   Secure version of HTTP, the protocol with which Web browsers communicate with Web servers.

hub   Device to which all other computers connect in a star topology LAN.

hyperlink   *See* link.

HyperTerminal connection   Configuration file (with extension .ht) containing the specifications HyperTerminal needs for connecting to another computer.

hypertext   Interlinked text.

Hypertext Markup Language   *See* HTML.

Hypertext Transfer Protocol   *See* HTTP.

I/O   Input and output.

I/O address   Hexadecimal number that the CPU uses to identify a device.

icon   Little picture on your screen that responds with an action when you point to it with the mouse, single-click it, or double-click it.

ICS client   Computer on a LAN that uses an ICS server to share a connection to the Internet.

ICS server   Computer running the Internet Connection Sharing (ICS) proxy server software and serving as a gateway from a LAN to the Internet.

IDE   Integrated Drive Electronics, a standard type of disk connection, used for hard disks and CD-ROM drives.

identity   In Address Book, user name that enables each user of the computer to maintain a separate list of address.

IE   *See* **Internet Explorer**.

IEEE 1394   *See* **FireWire**.

IEEE 802.11b   Standard for wireless LAN communications. *Wi-Fi* and *HomeRF* are both based on the IEEE 802.11b standard.

i.Link   *See* **FireWire**.

Image mode   *See* **Binary mode**.

IMAP   Internet Message Access Protocol, used for storing and delivering Internet e-mail.

incremental backup   Backup of only those files that are new or have changed since the last backup.

Industry Standard Architecture   *See* **ISA**.

INI file   Initialization file with the extension .ini.

initialization file   File that contains configuration information used when a program loads. *See* **DOS initialization file**; **Windows initialization file**.

input device   Hardware device used to digitize information so that it can be stored in your computer. Microphones, scanners, keyboards, and mice are input devices.

installation file   File that contains all the files required for a program to run, along with an installation program.

internal modem   Modem on an adapter board inside your computer.

Internet   Worldwide network of networks.

Internet account   Account with an Internet service provider (**ISP**) that allows you to connect your computer to the Internet.

Internet address   *See* **URL**.

Internet Service Provider   *See* **ISP**.

Internet shortcut File that acts as a placeholder for a Web page, stored with the extension .url.

Internet zone Security zone that includes the computers that don't fall into any other zone.

interrupt Channel that a device can use to alert the CPU that the device needs attention.

intranet Network installed within an organization, with a Web server that allows only people within the organization to view Web pages from that server.

IP address Internet protocol address, the numerical address of a computer connected to the Internet.

IPX/SPX Internetwork Packet eXchange/Sequenced Packet eXchange, a protocol used primarily in Novell's NetWare operating system.

ISA Industry Standard Architecture, a standard type of expansion slot or card.

ISDN Integrated Services Digital Network, a phone line that enables your computer to connect to another computer digitally.

ISDN terminal adapter, ISDN TA, or ISDN modem Device that connects your computer to an ISDN line (instead of a modem).

ISP Internet Service Provider, an organization that provides dial-in Internet accounts, usually PPP, CSLIP, or SLIP accounts, but sometimes UNIX shell accounts.

Java Language for writing applets that can be sent over the Web so that they can be executed by your computer.

JavaScript Language often used for extending HTML by embedding scripts in Web pages. Microsoft's version is called *JScript*. The international standard version is called *ECMAscript*. JavaScript scripts are also stored in files with the extension .js.

Jaz disk Removable disk that stores about 1GB.

joystick Device that enables you to play arcade-style games on your computer.

JPEG or JPG file File in the Joint Photographic Experts Group graphics format, a format well suited for storing scanned photographs and widely used in Web pages. JPEG files have the extension .jpg or .jpeg.

JS file File containing a JavaScript script.

JScript   *See* **JavaScript**.

kernel   Fundamental part of Windows (or of any operating system) that loads first and controls disk, process, and memory management.

key   Component in the Registry. For information about encryption, *see* **private key**; **public key**.

key ring   Collection of cryptography data that you need for sending secure e-mail.

keyboard layout   Physical arrangement of keys on the keyboard.

LAN   *See* **local area network**.

landscape   Print orientation in which lines of print are parallel to the long side of the paper.

Large Icons view   Way of representing the contents of a folder, in which each item in the folder appears as a large icon with the file or folder name below it.

LDAP   Lightweight Directory Access Protocol, a standard way for programs to search a directory service. The Windows Address Book uses LDAP.

link   Word, phrase, or picture that you can click to display another related Web page (or another page of the same Web page). Also called *hyperlink*.

linking   In OLE, storing a link in one file that links to an object in another file.

LINKLOCAL network address   Range of IP addresses used by Microsoft's **Automatic private IP addressing** system.

Links toolbar   Toolbar that can appear on the Taskbar, containing the same buttons that appear on the Links toolbar in Internet Explorer. This toolbar can also appear in Explorer windows.

list box   Box that contains a list of options, one of which is selected, usually appearing on a dialog box.

List view   Way of representing the contents of a folder, in which items are listed with a tiny icon and the filename.

local   File or device that is stored on or attached to the computer you are using (the **local computer**), rather than being stored on or attached to a computer connected to your computer by a network.

local area network (LAN)   Network that connects computers that are in the same building or campus, usually with cables.

local computer   Your own computer, rather than a **remote computer** connected to your computer over a network.

local disk   Disk drive connected to your own computer (as opposed to a **network disk**).

Local Intranet zone   Security zone that includes the computers on your own LAN.

local printer   Printer attached to your own computer.

Logged mode   Startup option similar to the usual Windows way of running, except that Windows logs all the drivers it loads in the file Bootlog.txt.

logon script   File that specifies what prompts to wait for and what to type in response when logging in to an Internet account or LAN.

lurking   Reading the messages in a newsgroup or mailing list without posting messages of your own. Entirely respectable.

magnification   Size at which Windows displays text onscreen.

mail client   Program for sending and receiving e-mail messages. Windows comes with Outlook Express. Informally called an *e-mail program*.

mail gateway   Computer that handles outgoing e-mail messages, sending them out to the Internet.

mail   *See* **e-mail**.

mail rules   *See* **message rules**.

mail server   Computer that handles incoming e-mail, storing it in mailboxes.

mailbox   Location on your mail server where your e-mail is stored until you retrieve it using your mail client (such as Outlook Express).

mailing list   E-mail-based discussion group.

manual checkpoint   "Snapshot" of your Windows and program files created by the System Restore program at your command.

mapping   Assigning a drive letter to a network drive on another computer.

Maximize button   Button in the upper-right corner of a window that is clicked to maximize the window.

maximized window   Window that takes up the entire screen or is running at its maximum window size.

MCA   *See* **Microchannel**.

meeting   NetMeeting call that is scheduled in advance.

memory   Temporary storage your computer uses for the programs you are running and the files you currently have open. Also called **RAM**.

memory address   Number that uniquely identifies one piece of memory storage.

Memory Manager   Part of Windows that handles virtual memory.

menu   List of commands from which you can choose. *See* **drop-down menu**; **menu bar**; **pull-down menu**; **shortcut menu**.

menu bar   Row of one-word commands that appears along the top of a window, just below the title bar.

Microsoft Exchange Personal Address Book Format   Format for storing name and address information. Address Book can export files in this format.

MIDI   Musical Instrument Digital Interface, a standard for digital musical instruments and the computer hardware and software that works with them.

MIDI channel   Input from a MIDI device, containing one musical line. One MIDI input device can produce up to 16 channels; for example, one channel for each musical part or one channel for each instrument being simulated.

MIDI scheme   Definition that indicates which MIDI instrument plays each MIDI channel.

MIME   Multipurpose Internet Mail Extensions, the most widely used method of including nontext information, such as attached files, in e-mail messages. *See also* **S/MIME**.

Minimize button   Button in the upper-right corner of a window that is clicked to minimize the window.

minimized window   Window that is not displayed, so that only the window's button on the Taskbar appears on the screen.

minus box   Small minus sign in a box that appears to the left of an item in a list. Click the minus box to hide its subitems.

modem driver   Modem control program.

modifier keys   Keys that you hold down while pressing another key: SHIFT, CTRL, and ALT.

modulation   Conversion of digital information from your computer into analog "sound" information for transmission over the phone.

motherboard   *See* **system board**.

mouse   Device for moving the mouse pointer on the screen and selecting the item the pointer points to.

mouse pointer   Indicator on the screen that shows where the mouse is pointing. Also called the *pointer* or (incorrectly) the **cursor**.

MouseKeys   Accessibility option that enables you to use the numeric keypad to control the pointer.

MPEG or MPG   Video file format based on the **JPEG** graphics file format.

MS-DOS   Microsoft Disk Operating System, also called **DOS**.

MS-DOS name   Eight-or-fewer-character name that resembles a file's real name, but is legal under the pre-Windows 95 file-naming rules.

multilink   System that allows a single Dial-Up Networking to use multiple modems and phone lines for greater speed.

multimedia   Information in a format other than plain text. Multimedia information can include pictures, movies, and sound.

multitasking   Running multiple tasks at the same time. Windows is a multitasking operating system, because it can run many tasks (programs) simultaneously.

My Computer   Folder that contains items for each disk drive on your computer, along with a few other special subfolders.

My Network Places   Folder that contains entries for all the computers to which your computer is connected on a local area network or direct cable connection. Called *Network Neighborhood* in previous versions of Windows.

named meeting   NetMeeting meeting hosted by a teleconferencing company or some other meeting server.

NAT   *See* **Network Address Translation.**

navigating   Displaying the contents of one folder after another, usually when looking for a folder or file. In your browser, moving from one Web page to another.

net   *See* **Network; Internet; local area network.**

NetBEUI   NetBIOS Extended User Interface, the network protocol used primarily by Microsoft in its LAN networking products.

netiquette   Net etiquette, etiquette on the Internet, conventions for what is appropriate in newsgroup and e-mail messages.

network   Group of computers that are connected together. *See also* **Internet; local area network**.

Network Address Translation (NAT)   Program that translates between the IP addresses on a LAN and those on the Internet. Can be part of a **proxy server** or **firewall.** Internet Connection Sharing includes a NAT program.

network adapter   *See* **network interface card.**

Network dialog box   Dialog box for configuring the software components for a connection to a local area network or the Internet.

network disk or network drive   Disk drive connected to a computer that your computer can access over a network (as opposed to a **local disk**). Also called a **shared disk** or **shared drive**.

network interface card   Adapter that connects a computer to a local area network.

network operating system (NOS)   Operating system that includes support for a client-server local area network.

network password   Password you use when logging into a LAN.

network printer   Printer that is attached to a computer on a local area network and can be used by other computers on the network.

news account   Name of the news server to use when reading and posting to Usenet newsgroups.

newsgroup   Discussion group that is part of Usenet. Windows comes with Outlook Express, which lets you read and post to newsgroups.

newsreader or newsreading program   Program for reading and posting to newsgroups. Windows comes with Outlook Express, which is both a mail client and a newsreader.

NIC   *See* **network interface card**.

NNTP   Net News Transfer Protocol, the protocol used by Usenet for distributing newsgroup articles.

node   Computer attached to a network.

non-routable protocol   Network protocol that can be used only on a simple network where routing devices are not used.

Normal mode   Usual way of running Windows.

NOS   *See* **network operating system**.

Notepad   Text editor that comes with Windows.

NTFS   File system used by Windows 2000 and NT; not supported by Windows Me.

null-modem cable   Serial cable used to connect two computers in a direct cable connection (not to connect a computer to a modem).

object   In OLE, a piece of information from a file; you can link or embed an object in a different file.

Object Linking and Embedding   *See* **OLE**.

offline mode   When your printer is not available (turned off or not connected to your computer).

offline   Not connected to any network or computer.

OLE   Object Linking and Embedding, a method of linking and combining information from files created by different applications.

on top   Window that appears "above" other windows on the desktop, obscuring other windows where they overlap. The active window appears on top.

online   Connected to a computer or a network (a **local area network**, the **Internet**, or another network).

online help   Helpful information stored on your computer that you can look at by using the Help And Support window.

online service   Commercial service that allows you to connect to and access their proprietary information system (for example, America Online).

OnNow   Feature that allows Windows to power down the computer when nothing is happening and power back up when the computer is needed again, if the computer's hardware permits.

opening   Displaying the contents of a file or folder, or running a program.

operating system (OS)   Program that manages your entire computer system, including its screen, keyboard, disk drives, memory, and central processor. Windows Me is an operating system.

output device   Hardware device that can display, play, print, or otherwise use information from your computer. Printers, displays, and speakers are output devices.

packaged object   In OLE, a piece of information from a file that you have linked or embedded in a different file.

packet   Chunk of information transmitted on a network or other communications line.

pane   Section of a window.

parallel port   Connector on your computer used for parallel communications. You connect most printers to the parallel port.

parity   Simple method of error detection in which the value of one bit is calculated from the values of a group of bits.

partition   Logical section of a hard disk.

pasting   Copying the information on the Clipboard to the location of the cursor in the active application.

path or path name   *See* **file address**.

payload   Infectious part of a virus or worm program.

PC Card   Credit-card-sized adapter cards used mainly in laptops. They fit in PC Card slots. Formerly called PCMCIA.

PC file transfer cable   *See* **null-modem cable**.

PC Health   Windows Me features that try to solve many system failures. PC Health includes System Restore, Auto Update, and System File Protection.

PCI   Personal Computer Interface, a standard type of expansion slot or card that fits into a PCI slot.

PCMCIA   *See* **PC Card**.

PCX file   Graphics file with extension .pcx.

peer-to-peer network   Network on which all computers can function as both clients and servers.

peripheral   Hardware device that is attached to your computer, such as a printer or modem.

personal certificate   Cryptographic information that identifies you when viewing Web sites or sending e-mail. Stored in files with the extension .pfx.

Personal Computer Interface   *See* **PCI**.

PGP   Pretty Good Privacy, a method of sending secure e-mail.

Personalized Menus   Start menu, Program menu, and their submenus, with less frequently used commands omitted. Click the double arrow at the bottom of the menu to see the rest of the available commands.

PICS   Platform for Internet Content Selection, a method of labeling Web site content developed by the World Wide Web Consortium.

PIF file   Program Information File with the extension .pif, containing configuration information for a DOS program.

ping   Test message sent to find out whether another system will respond. Ping is also the name of a program that sends pings on the Internet; Windows comes with a Ping program.

pixel   Single dot that can take on any color on the screen.

playlist   List of audio or video tracks in the order in which you want to play them.

Plug and Play   Type of device that can communicate with Windows to provide its own configuration information.

plug-in   Program that "plugs in" to your browser program, adding new features to the browser.

plus box   Small plus sign in a box that appears to the left of an item in a list, to show that the item contains subitems.

point   In printing measurement, $\frac{1}{72}$ of an inch.

pointer scheme   Set of shapes that the mouse pointer assumes.

pointer   *See* **mouse pointer**.

pointer trail   Shadowy trail left behind the moving mouse pointer.

Point-to-Point Protocol (PPP)   Communications protocol for computers connected to the Internet by telephone (or telephone-like) lines.

Point-to-Point Tunneling Protocol (PPTP)   Communications protocol used by Virtual Private Networking.

POP or POP 3   Post Office Protocol 3, a program on a mail server that stores your incoming e-mail until you retrieve it by using Outlook Express or another mail client.

port   Connector on your computer to which you can connect a cable. *See* **parallel port**; **serial port**.

port number   On the Internet, a number that tells an Internet host computer whether you are connecting for e-mail, the Web, telnet, or another Internet service.

port replicator   Docking station that contains only additional ports.

portal   Web site that displays a directory, search engine, and other free services and resources in hopes that you will visit the site frequently.

portrait   Print orientation in which lines of print are parallel to the short side of the paper.

power management   Settings that automatically turn off computer components to save electricity.

Power Meter   Icon in the system tray that shows whether the computer is connected to AC power or running on batteries.

power scheme   Group of settings that define when and if Windows should turn off the power to parts of your computer.

PPP   *See* **Point-to-Point Protocol**.

PPP account   Internet account that uses the PPP communications protocol; the most popular kind of Internet account.

PPTP   *See* **Point-to-Point Tunneling Protocol**.

preference   Setting or option that controls the way you want a program to work.

Pretty Good Privacy   *See* **PGP**.

preview   In Windows Explorer, the small copy of the first page of the selected file that appears in the Web panel.

primary DNS   *See* **domain name server**.

Primary DOS partition   Section of a hard disk that stores the main DOS or Windows file system.

print job   Document sent to a printer.

print server   Computer to which a printer is attached that is used by other computers on a network.

printer driver   Printer control program.

printer port   *See* **parallel port**.

printer window   Window that displays the status of print jobs for one printer.

private key   One of a pair of cryptographic keys: you use your private key to decode messages you receive that were encoded with your **public key** and to encode messages you want to sign.

process   *See* **task**.

profile   Group of settings stored with a name (also called a **scheme**). *See* **color profile**; **hardware profile**; **user profile**.

program   Sequence of computer instructions that performs a task.

program file   File containing a program, usually with the extension .exe or .com.

Programs menu   Menu displayed when you choose Start | Programs, showing a list of programs you can run.

property   Setting that affects how an object works. You can set the properties of many objects by right-clicking the object, choosing Properties from the menu that appears, and changing the settings on the resulting Properties dialog box.

proportional spacing   Typeface design in which letters in the typeface are different widths.

protocol   Setting that identifies the way information is passed between computers on the network.

proxy server   Gateway program that provides caching, logging, and other service when translating between a LAN and the Internet.

PS/2 port   Standard keyboard or mouse connector.

public key   One of a pair of cryptographic keys: you use a person's public key to encode a message so that it can be decoded only with the person's **private key** and to verify signed messages.

public-key cryptography   Cryptography system that uses pairs of keys, one public and one private to the key's owner. Two forms are commonly used: PGP and S/MIME.

pull-down menu   Box onscreen with a downward-pointing triangle button at its right end, usually appearing in a dialog box.

push technology   Web-based Internet facility in which your Web browser automatically downloads Web pages to your computer.

QT file   QuickTime video file, with the extension .qt.

queue   List of tasks waiting to be done. For example, a print queue is a list of print jobs waiting to be printed.

Quick Launch toolbar   Toolbar on the Taskbar (usually at the left end, next to the Start button) with small icons for programs you run frequently.

QuickTime   Video file format with file extension .qt.

RA   File extension (.ra) used for RealAudio, a streaming audio file format.

radio button   One of a group of round buttons that can either be blank or contain a dot, usually appearing in a dialog box.

RAM   Random Access Memory, the memory chips used for the short-term memory of a computer. Also a file extension (.ram) used for RealAudio files.

RAM drive   Memory that simulates a disk drive.

read-ahead   Extra information Windows reads from the disk and stores in memory so that the information will be instantly available if Windows needs it.

read-only file   File or folder whose Read-Only attribute is selected, so that the file cannot be accidentally deleted or modified. Shared disks and folders can be designated read-only.

real-time chat   *See* **chat**.

Recycle Bin   Special folder in which Windows stores files and folders you have recently deleted.

refresh   Redisplay a window using updated information.

REG file   *See* **registration file**.

regional settings   Windows settings that control how numbers, dates, times, and currency amounts appear.

registered file types   *See* **file association**.

registration file   File with the extension .reg, created by exporting part or all of the Registry.

Registry   Files in which Windows stores a database of program and system setup information.

remote administration   Facility in Windows 2000 and NT (but not Me) that allows someone (usually a network administrator) at one computer to change the Windows settings on another computer.

remote control   Program that allows one computer to take control of another computer over a local area network, dial-up connection, the Internet, or other network.

remote node   Computer that is attached to a local area network via Dial-Up Networking.

remote computer   Computer attached to the computer you are using over a local area network, Internet, or other network.

removable disk   Disk that can be removed from its disk drive (unlike a hard disk). Floppy disks and Zip disks are removable.

repartitioning   Change the layout of partitions on a hard disk.

repeat delay   Delay between starting to hold down a key and when the key begins repeating.

repeat rate   How fast a key repeats once it starts repeating.

RepeatKeys   Accessibility setting that enables you to change the way keys are repeated.

resolution   Number of pixels (dots) your screen can display, expressed by a vertical and horizontal count. Standard screen resolutions include 640x480 (640 dots across and 480 dots high), 800x600, 1024x768, 1152x864, and 1600x1200.

resource   Hardware, software, or data that can be shared by users of a network. *See also* **system resources**.

resource leakage   Loss of system resources when applications allocate memory but fail to release it when done.

Resource Meter   Windows utility that monitors system resources.

resource pool   *See* **system resources.**

Restore button   Button in the upper-right corner of a window that is clicked to restore the window (display the window within window borders).

restore point   "Snapshot" of your Windows and program files, stored by the System Restore program.

restored window   Window that appears within window borders—not maximized or minimized.

Restricted Sites zone   Security zone that includes the computers you have told Windows not to trust.

RGB   Numerical way of describing a color by its red, green, and blue components.

Rich Text Format   *See* **RTF file.**

right-clicking   Clicking with the right mouse button (unless you have configured your mouse to swap the functions of the buttons).

RJ-11 jack   U.S. standard telephone connector.

RJ-45 connector   Connector used to connect network interface cards to twisted pair cable in a star topology network.

RMI   File extension (.rmi) used for MIDI-format music files.

root, root folder, or root directory   Main or top-level folder (or directory) in a hierarchical file system.

router   Specialized computer used to connect multiple segments of networks; for example, to connect a local area network to the Internet.

RSACi   Recreational Software Advisory Council for the Internet, an organization that rates Web sites regarding topics that people might find offensive so that your browser can screen out possibly offensive sites.

RTF file   Rich Text Format, a portable format for storing formatted documents, defined by Microsoft. WordPad can read and write RTF files, which have the extension .rtf.

RTS/CTS   Request To Send/Clear To Send, a method of flow control used by some modems. Also known as hardware flow control.

RV   File extension (.rv) for RealVideo, a streaming video file format.

S/MIME   Standard security system used by Outlook Express and other mail programs to send e-mail securely. *See* **MIME**.

Safe Mode   Windows startup mode that provides minimal Windows functions by disabling all devices except the keyboard, screen, and disk.

sandbox   Limited set of computer resources with which Netscape Navigator or Internet Explorer runs downloaded Java programs.

saved search   Search criteria saved in a file with extension .fnd. You use the Start | Find | Files Or Folders command to rerun the search.

scanner   Device that digitizes pictures (or anything on paper) for use by your computer.

scheme   Group of settings, stored with a name so that you can easily switch from one group of settings to another (similar to a **profile**). *See* **desktop scheme**; **MIDI scheme**; **pointer scheme**; **power scheme**.

scrap   OLE object that has been left on the desktop or in a folder.

screen saver   Program that displays an image, frequently one that moves, on your desktop when you are not using the computer.

screen shot   Picture of what is on the screen.

script   Program written using a scripting language such as JavaScript or VBScript. *See also* **batch file**; **logon script**; **Windows Scripting Host**; **WSH file**.

scroll bar   Vertical or horizontal bar running along the right side or bottom of a window allowing you to scroll the information displayed in the window.

SCSI   Small Computer Systems Interface, a standard for connecting peripherals to computers. SCSI devices include hard disks, CD-ROMs, tapes, and scanners.

SCSI controller   Adapter board for connecting SCSI devices to a computer.

SCSI device number   Unique number of the SCSI device connected to one SCSI controller.

search engine   Web site that helps you find information on the Web by searching the full text of the World Wide Web for the words or phrases you type.

secondary DNS   *See* **domain name server**.

sector   Physical block of storage on a disk.

secure e-mail   E-mail that has been encoded so that only the intended recipient can read it.

Secure Sockets Layer   *See* **SSL**.

secure server   Web server that supports SSL (Secure Sockets Layer) to encrypt data sent between the server and your computer. Pages loaded from a secure server have URLs beginning with https://.

security   Control over your computer system, who uses it, what programs run on it, and who reads or changes the information stored on your disks.

selecting   Indicating the items you plan to work with. How you select files and folders on the desktop or in Windows Explorer depends on your desktop style (single- or double-click).

selective startup   Windows startup in which you choose which initialization files to process.

Send To menu   Menu found on the File menu of Explorer windows that allows you to copy files to preselected locations.

separator page   Blank page between print jobs on a network printer.

serial port   Connector on your computer that is used for serial communication. You connect serial mice, external modems, and serial printers to a serial port.

SerialKey   Accessibility option that turns on support for alternative input devices attached to the serial port.

server   Program or computer that provides resources that others can use on a network.

service   Setting that allows you to share a computer's resources on a network.

setup program   Installation program, such as the Setup program that comes with Windows.

SFP   *See* **System File Protection**.

share name   Name by which a shared drive, folder, or printer can be referred to by other users on a LAN.

share-level access control   Method of controlling who can use shared network resource, in which anyone who knows the resource's password can use the resource.

shared disk or shared drive   Disk that is shared with other users on a LAN. Also called a **network disk**. May be a hard disk, CD-ROM drive, or removable disk drive (for floppy disks or Zip disks).

shared folder   Folder that has been configured to be usable by other computers on a LAN.

shared printer   Printer that is shared with other users on a LAN. Also called a **network printer**.

shared resources   Hardware or files that are shared with other users on a LAN.

shareware   Programs that require you to register and pay for the program if you decide that you like it. They are frequently downloadable from the Internet.

shell account   *See* **UNIX shell account**.

shortcut   File with a .lnk extension, used as a placeholder in your file system. *See also* **shortcut key; shortcut menu**.

shortcut icon   Icon that represents a shortcut, usually on the desktop or in Windows Explorer. Shortcut icons always include a little white curving arrow in the lower-left corner.

shortcut key   Combination of the CTRL key, the ALT key, and one other key; pressing these keys at the same time runs a specified shortcut.

shortcut menu   Menu that appears when you right-click an object. A shortcut menu contains commands that pertain to the object you right-clicked.

ShowSounds   Accessibility feature that displays a caption when the computer makes a sound.

shutdown   Exiting Windows.

signature   Lines that an e-mail program added to the end of each message you send, usually containing your e-mail address, name, and a witty tag line. For encrypted e-mail, *see* **digital signature**; **signature block**.

signature block   Encryption-related text that is automatically added to the end of your outgoing e-mail messages.

signed file   Audio or video file for which you have a digital license, usually a file you copied from an audio CD (which you presumably own).

signed mail   E-mail that has been encoded using your private key to prove that you sent it.

single-click style   Desktop mode in which clicking an icon or filename once runs the program or opens the file. To select the icon or filename without running or opening it, position the mouse pointer over it without clicking. Also known as *Web style*.

skin   User interface, or the arrangement of buttons, menus, and other items on the windows and dialog boxes displayed by a program. Windows Media Play comes with several skins.

Skin mode   Windows Media Player mode in which the program appears using a **skin**, or alternate user interface.

SLIP   Serial Line Internet Protocol, a communications protocol for computers connected to the Internet. SLIP has been superceded by PPP.

slot   *See* **expansion slot**; **PC Card**.

SlowKeys   Accessibility setting that enables you to filter out keys that are pressed only briefly.

Small Icons view   Way of representing the contents of a folder, in which each item in the folder appears as a small icon with a file or folder name below it.

SMTP   Simple Mail Transfer Protocol, the method used by mail gateways on the Internet to send outgoing messages.

software   Sequence of computer instructions that performs a task; program.

sound board   Adapter board that lets you connect speakers or headphones (and possibly a microphone) to your computer.

sound scheme   Set of associations between Windows events and the sounds that Windows plays when that event occurs.

SoundSentry   Accessibility feature that displays a visual warning when the computer makes a sound.

special characters   Characters that do not appear on the standard U.S. 101-key keyboard, such as fractions and accented letters.

splash screen   Screen Windows displays during startup, before you see the desktop. Many programs display splash screens while they are loading, before their windows appear.

spooling   Multitasking system that allows a program to send information to a printer while performing other tasks.

SSL   Secure Sockets Layer, the method that Web browsers use to provide secure encrypted communication.

Standard Buttons toolbar   Toolbar that can appear in Explorer windows and displays standard buttons for switching folders, cut-and-paste, displaying properties, and controlling which view appears in the window.

Standby mode   When power is off to most of the components of your computer (usually a laptop), but the state of the computer, including running programs, is preserved.

star topology   Network topology in which each computer connects to a central hub.

Start command   DOS program that switches to Windows to open a program or file.

Start menu   Menu displayed by clicking the Start button on the Taskbar. It contains commands and additional menus listing most of the programs that you can run on your computer.

start page   Web page that the browser loads when you open the browser without asking for a specific page. Also referred to as **home page**.

startup floppy disk   *See* **emergency boot disk**.

StartUp folder   Folder that contains programs that Windows runs automatically when you start Windows. Usually C:\Windows\Start Menu\Programs\StartUp.

startup menu   Menu that appears if you press F8 while Windows is loading.

startup modes   Modes in which you can run Windows if you are having trouble starting Windows in the normal manner.

static IP addressing   Manually assigned IP.

static Virtual Device Drivers   *See* **Virtual Device Drivers**

stationery   HTML-based e-mail formats that you can use when composing e-mail to send to recipients whose e-mail programs can handle HTML messages.

status bar   Section of a window that displays information about the program. The status bar is usually a gray bar running along the bottom of the window.

Step-By-Step Confirmation mode   Way of starting Windows in which Windows processes its initialization files one line at a time, stopping and telling you each driver it's about to load.

StickyKeys   Accessibility option that lets you avoid pressing multiple keys by making keys such as CTRL, SHIFT, and ALT stay in effect after they have been released.

stop bits   How many extra bits of information are included after each byte sent through a serial port (usually one).

Storyboard   Windows Movie Maker view that shows a series of video clips and still pictures in the order in which they appear in a movie.

streaming audio   Audio (sound) data stored in a format that allows the beginning of the file to be played, even before later parts of the file are read.

streaming video   Video (movie) data stored in a format that allows the beginning of the file to be played, even before later parts of the file are read.

string   Series of text characters, including letters, numbers, spaces, and punctuation.

styles of desktop   How desktop icons (and filenames in Windows Explorer) appear and react to clicks. The styles are **single-click** and **double-click**.

subfolder   Folder contained in another folder.

submenu   Menu displayed by a command from another menu.

SUBST   DOS command that comes with Windows, used to assign a drive letter to a folder. Not recommended.

supervisor password   Password needed to make changes to Content Advisor settings.

surface scan   Scan of the physical surface of a disk to detect bad sectors.

Suspend Mode   *See* **Standby Mode**.

Super-VGA (SVGA)   Type of display with higher resolution than a VGA monitor.

swap file   File to which Windows copies data in virtual memory.

switching programs   Choosing another window as the active window. Pressing ALT-TAB switches windows.

system board   Printed circuit board that carries the CPU and memory inside your computer.

system clock   Digital clock that can appear on the system tray part of the Taskbar.

system file   File or folder whose System attribute is selected, indicating that the file or folder stores part of the actual Windows operating system.

System File Protection   Windows Me feature that monitors the files that make up Windows itself.

System menu   Menu displayed by clicking the **System Menu button**, pressing ALT-SPACEBAR, or right-clicking the title bar of the window. This menu was called the Control menu in Windows 3.1 and Windows 95.

System Menu button   Tiny icon in the upper-left corner of each window, at the left end of the window's title bar. Click this button to display the **System menu**. This button was called the Control menu button in Windows 3.1 and Windows 95.

system pool   Fixed-size area of memory used for communication between applications and Windows.

system resources   Fixed-size areas of memory used by Windows applications.

system tray or systray   Section of the Taskbar (usually the right end) that displays a group of tiny icons, along with the system clock.

systems program   Program that performs a computer-oriented task, such as a printer driver or hard disk housekeeping program.

tab   Page of settings on a dialog box selected by a manila-folder-tab-shaped tab along the top of the dialog box.

task   Series of instructions that your computer is executing. A program can create one or more tasks. For example, a word processing program might run one task that displays the program window and accepts your input to edit a file, and a second task that prints a file at the same time.

Task Manager   Part of the Taskbar that shows a button for each program that is running.

Taskbar   Row of buttons and icons that usually appears along the bottom of the screen.

T-connector   Connector used with network interface cards and coaxial cable in a bus topology Ethernet network.

TCP/IP   Transmission Control Protocol/Internet Protocol, the system that computers use to communicate with each other on the Internet or some local area networks.

TCP/IP stack   Communications program that Windows programs use for communicating via TCP/IP.

telephony driver   Configuration file containing information that will eventually be used for making phone calls over the Internet.

telnet   Program that emulates a terminal over the Internet. Windows comes with two: Telnet and HyperTerminal.

terminal-emulation program   Program that makes your computer act like a terminal, for communicating with computers that are designed to attach to terminals. You use a terminal-emulation program, such as HyperTerminal, to connect to a UNIX shell account.

terminal window   Window that allows you to see a communications session and type commands to the remote computer.

terminating resistor   Terminator used with network interface cards and T-connectors in a bus topology network.

text box   Box onscreen in which you can type information, usually appearing on a dialog box.

text file   File that contains only letters, numbers, and special characters that appear on the keyboard. Text files frequently have the extension .txt.

text mode   In a DOS window, mode that displays only text.

thumbnail   Tiny version of a picture.

Thumbnail view   Way of representing the contents of a folder, in which items are listed with a small icon followed by the filename. The icon is a miniature version of the first page of the file.

TIF or TIFF file   File in Tagged-Image Format, a graphics file format. TIF files have the extension .tif.

Tile Windows   Command that arranges windows on the screen so that they touch but don't overlap, covering the screen.

tiling   Repeating a graphic to fill up a space (such as the desktop).

Timeline   Windows Movie Maker view that shows the timing of the series of video clips and still pictures that appear in a movie.

title bar   The colored bar that runs along the top of a window.

ToggleKeys   Accessibility feature that sounds a tone when the CAPS LOCK, SCROLL LOCK, and NUM LOCK keys are activated.

Token Ring   Type of local area network hardware.

tool tip   Little informational box that appears when you leave the mouse pointer on something for a few seconds, usually used for buttons on toolbars.

toolbar   Row of small buttons with icons on them. Toolbars appear just below the menu bar in many windows, as well as on the **Taskbar**.

toolbar handle   Raised vertical bar on the left end of a toolbar on the **Taskbar**, used for dragging the toolbar to a different location.

topology   Pattern of cabling that is used to connect computers together into a network.

track   Concentric circle on which information is stored on a disk. Tracks are divided into **sectors**. In Windows Media Player, an audio or video file.

transceiver   Transmitter and receiver. For example, wireless LANs use radio transceivers to communicate between PCs and the access point (hub).

transfer protocol   Method that a computer needs to use to access a file over the Internet: the first part of a URL.

Troubleshooter   Part of the Windows Help system that asks a series of questions to help you track down and solve hardware or software problems.

TrueType   Method of storing typefaces as a set of formulas for drawing the characters at almost any size.

Trusted Sites zone   Security zone that includes the computers you or Microsoft have told Windows to trust.

TTL   Time To Live, how many times a packet can be passed from one computer to another while in transit on the Internet.

tunneling   Connecting to a private network over the Internet using **Virtual Private Networking**.

TV tuner card   Adapter board you can install in your computer that allows you to connect your computer to a television antenna or cable and watch television programs on your computer screen.

TWAIN   Standard for communications between scanners and computer software.

twisted pair   *See* **unshielded twisted pair cable**.

TXT file   Text file, with the file extension .txt.

typeface   Set of shapes for letters, numbers, and punctuation (for example, Times Roman). A **font** is a typeface at a specific size and weight (for example, 12-point Times Roman Bold).

UART   Universal Asynchronous Receiver/Transmitter, a chip used in serial communication ports.

UNC address   Universal Naming Convention addresses, used when referring to files on some local area networks.

undeleting   Reversing the action of deleting something.

Unicode   Character codes that allow you to use characters from practically every language on Earth.

Uniform Resource Locator   *See* URL.

uninstall program   Program that uninstalls another program.

Universal Plug and Play   Configuration system that allows Windows to detect new hardware and automatically install the necessary drivers.

Universal Serial Bus (USB)   New standard type of connector introduced on Windows computers.

UNIX   Operating system widely used on Internet host computers.

UNIX shell account   Type of Internet account that gives you access to a computer running the UNIX operating system, which you control by typing UNIX commands.

unshielded twisted pair cable   Type of cable used to connect computers in a star topology.

unsigned file   File for which you do not have a digital license. If you copy an audio file from an audio CD (which you presumably own), the file is **signed**.

upload   Transfer a file from a PC to the Internet, other network, or mainframe.

URL   Uniform Resource Locator, the address of a piece of information on the Internet, usually a Web page.

USB   *See* **Universal Serial Bus**.

USB hub   Device that lets you connect several USB devices to one USB port on your computer.

Usenet   Internet-based system of tens of thousands of newsgroups (discussion groups). Windows comes with Outlook Express, which lets you read and post to Usenet newsgroups.

user pool   Fixed-size area of memory that is used to manage windows, menus, and other parts of the Windows user interface.

user profile   Windows settings that are stored for use when you log into the computer. Each user's user profile can contain different settings.

user-level access control   Method of controlling who can use shared network resources, in which each resource has a list of users who can use the resource.

utility   Small program that performs a housekeeping or other useful task. Windows Me comes with many utilities.

value   Element stored in a key in the Registry. Each value consists of a name and some data.

VBS file   File containing a VBScript script, with extension .vbs.

VBScript   Language resembling Microsoft's Visual Basic that can be used to add scripts to Web pages or other applications.

vCard   Virtual business card format, exportable from Address Book.

VCF file   Virtual business card file, with extension .vcf.

VGA   Type of display. *See also* **Super-VGA**.

video capture device   Hardware device that digitizes video information for use by your computer; for example, a digital video camera.

view settings   Settings that control how folders appear in Folder and Windows Explorer windows.

virtual business card file   File with extension .vcf that contains information about a person.

Virtual Device Driver   Software that communicates with devices that include DVDs and SCSI devices.

virtual machine   Hardware and software environment that emulates the features of one computer on another computer. For example, the **DOS virtual machine** within Windows Me emulates a stand-alone DOS environment well enough to allow most DOS programs to run correctly. Sometimes called a *sandbox*.

virtual memory   System that moves chunks of program and data storage between disk and memory automatically, so that individual programs don't have to do all of their own memory management.

Virtual Private Networking (VPN)   Program that allows an authorized computer on the Internet to tunnel through the firewall and connect to a private network.

virus   Self-replicating program, frequently with destructive side-effects.

visualization   Graphical representation of a sound, displayed by Windows Media Player.

VPN   *See* **Virtual Private Networking**.

VPN server   Computer that supports Point-to-Point Tunneling to allow computers to connect from the Internet to a LAN using VPN.

VxDs   *See* **Virtual Device Drivers.**

wait time   Length of time that your system is inactive before the screen saver starts up.

wallpaper   The background pattern behind all the windows, icons, and menus on your desktop.

WAN   *See* **wide area network**.

WAV file   Audio file with extension .wav.

Web   *See* **World Wide Web**.

Web address   *See* **URL**.

Web browser   *See* **browser**.

Web directory   *See* **Web guide**.

Web editor   *See* **Web page editor**.

Web guide   Web site that helps you find information on the Web by categorizing Web pages by subject.

Web page   HTML file stored on a Web server.

Web page editor   Program for creating and editing files in HTML format for use as Web pages. Windows 98 came with FrontPage Express, but Windows Me doesn't come with a Web page Editor. If you know HTML, you can use Notepad to edit the HTML source code of Web pages.

Web panel   Left-hand part of the working area of a Windows Explorer window, displaying information about the selected folder and file.

Web server   Computer that stores Web pages and responds to requests from Web browsers.

Web site   Collection of Web pages belonging to a particular person or organization.

Web style   *See* **single-click style**.

WebTV For Windows   Program bundled with Windows that allow your computer, when equipped with a television-tuner adapter card, to display broadcast television. Not to be confused with WebTV, the box that you can connect to a television and phone line in order to browse the Web and send and receive e-mail, without a separate computer.

whiteboard   Feature of NetMeeting that allows callers to draw a shared picture that all can edit and see.

wide area network (WAN)   Network that connects computers that are not all in the same building or campus.

WiFi   Standard, with **IEEE 802.11b**, for wireless LAN communications.

wildcard   Special character (* or ?) used when specifying a group of filenames or folder names.

Win.ini file   Windows 3.1 initialization file, which is still used by Windows.

window   Rectangular area on the screen that displays information from a running program.

window borders   Gray border running around the sides of a restored window.

Windows Me   Latest desktop version of Microsoft's Windows series of operating systems, successor to Windows 98.

Windows 2000   Windows version targeted at corporate and high-end users, successor to Windows NT.

Windows-aware DOS program   Type of DOS program that handles its screen and keyboard in a way that lets it run efficiently under Windows.

Windows Clipboard   *See* **Clipboard**.

Windows initialization file   One of the configuration files that Windows reads during startup. These files have the extension .ini. *See also* **Registry**.

WINDOWS key   On some keyboards, the key with the Microsoft Windows logo: pressing the WINDOWS key displays the Taskbar and Start menu. Equivalent to pressing CTRL-ESC.

Windows password   Password you use when starting Windows or switching from one user to another.

Windows program folder   Folder that contains the Windows program files (along with many subfolders with Windows-related files), usually C:\Windows.

winmetcr@gurus.com   E-mail address for comments or corrections about this book.

WINS   Microsoft's Windows Internet Naming Service, which automatically manages network parameters.

Winsock   Standard way for Windows programs to work with Internet connection software. Most popular Internet programs are Winsock-compatible, including Internet Explorer, Netscape Navigator, and Outlook Express.

wireless LAN   Star-topology LAN that communicates by radio transmissions in the 2.4 GHz frequency band.

wizard   Program that steps you through the process of creating or configuring something. Wizards come with Windows and other Microsoft products.

word wrap   Feature of text editors and word processors that allows the program to insert line endings automatically.

workgroup   Group of computers on a local area network.

working folder   Folder in which a program reads and writes files unless another folder is specified.

workstation   Computer used by a person, rather than one used only as a server for people at other computers.

World Wide Web   Collection of millions of files stored on thousands of Web server computers all over the world.

worm   Self-replicating program that can infect other computers (by e-mail or over a LAN or the Internet), frequently with destructive side-effects.

write-behind caching   Storing information in memory to be written to a removable disk and saving the information to the removable disk in large chunks.

WSH file   Text file with the extension .wsh that contains configuration settings for a script to be run by Windows Scripting Host.

XON/XOFF   Method of flow control used by some modems.

Zip disk   Removable disk that stores either 100MB or 250MB.

ZIP file   File that contains compressed versions of one or more files, compressed by WinZip, PKZIP, ZipMagic, or a compatible compression program. ZIP files have the extension .zip.

zone   Categorization of the sources of downloaded information, for security purposes.

Index

Z

About the CD-ROM

The *Windows Millennium Edition: The Complete Reference* CD-ROM

In the back cover of this book is a CD-ROM containing a Web version of the entire text of this book. Using Internet Explorer, Netscape Navigator, or any other Web browser, you can read the text of this book on your computer screen. What's the advantage of reading about Windows Me on your screen? The Web version contains thousands of links throughout the book: if you see a reference to a topic you need more information about it, click the link to see the chapter about that topic. Your computer doesn't have to be online with the Internet to read this book on the screen, because the book's Web pages are stored on your CD-ROM.

Using the CD

The *Windows Millennium Edition: The Complete Reference* CD-ROM doesn't contain software—it doesn't have to because Windows comes with a Web browser. Follow these steps to read the Web version of the book:

1. Put the CD-ROM into your CD-ROM drive. If your drive's autorun feature works, your Web browser runs and you see the title page for the book. Skip to step 3.
2. If the Web page for the book doesn't appear, run Windows Explorer and display the contents of the root folder of the CD-ROM. Click or double-click the filename Winmetcr.htm (single- or double-click depending on how your desktop is configured (see Chapter 1, section "Choosing Between Single-Click and Double-Click"). Your browser runs and displays the title Web page for the book.
3. Click links as usual to browse the contents of the book.

 If you want to read the CD-ROM Web pages in the same order in which they appear in the printed book, click the Next link at the top of each Web page to move to the next Web page in the chapter. The Previous link takes you to the previous Web page in the chapter.

Searching for Information in the Book

The Web version of the book includes a complete Glossary with links to the places that the terms appear. From the title Web page (or from the bottom of any of the book's Web pages), click the Glossary link, click the first letter of the term you are looking for, and find and click the term.

To search for information on the Web page you are looking at:

- In Internet Explorer, choose Edit | Find (On This Page) from the menu (or press CTRL-F), type the word or phrase to search for, and click the Find Next button.
- In Netscape Navigator, choose Edit | Find In Page from the menu (or press CTRL-F), type the word or phrase to search for, and click the Find Next button.

What if the word or phrase you are looking for doesn't appear in the Glossary? Here's the beauty of reading the book on-screen: you can search all the pages for all appearances of the word or phrase you need:

1. Choose Start | Search | For Files Or Folders to display the Search Results window.
2. Type a word or phrase into the Containing Text box.
3. Set the Look In box to your CD-ROM drive (which is drive D on most computers). Click Find Now.

Windows displays a list of the CD-ROM Web pages that contain the word or phrase you typed. Single- or double-click the name of a Web page to display that page.

If You Run into Trouble

If you run into trouble, write to the authors of this book at **winmetcr@gurus.com**. We'd also be interested in your comments about the book. Don't write to us with Windows questions, though—we're not equipped to replace Microsoft's Technical Support department! *See* Chapters 6 and 35 for how to get Windows technical support.

WARNING: BEFORE OPENING THE DISC PACKAGE, CAREFULLY READ THE TERMS AND CONDITIONS OF THE FOLLOWING COPYRIGHT STATEMENT AND LIMITED CD-ROM WARRANTY.

Copyright Statement
This software is protected by both United States copyright law and international copyright treaty provision. Except as noted in the contents of the CD-ROM, you must treat this software just like a book. However, you may copy it into a computer to be used and you may make archival copies of the software for the sole purpose of backing up the software and protecting your investment from loss. By saying, "just like a book," The McGraw-Hill Companies, Inc. ("Osborne/McGraw-Hill") means, for example, that this software may be used by any number of people and may be freely moved from one computer location to another, so long as there is no possibility of its being used at one location or on one computer while it is being used at another. Just as a book cannot be read by two different people in two different places at the same time, neither can the software be used by two different people in two different places at the same time.

Limited Warranty
Osborne/McGraw-Hill warrants the physical compact disc enclosed herein to be free of defects in materials and workmanship for a period of sixty days from the purchase date. If the CD included in your book has defects in materials or workmanship, please call McGraw-Hill at 1-800-217-0059, 9am to 5pm, Monday through Friday, Eastern Standard Time, and McGraw-Hill will replace the defective disc.

   The entire and exclusive liability and remedy for breach of this Limited Warranty shall be limited to replacement of the defective disc, and shall not include or extend to any claim for or right to cover any other damages, including but not limited to, loss of profit, data, or use of the software, or special incidental, or consequential damages or other similar claims, even if Osborne/McGraw-Hill has been specifically advised of the possibility of such damages. In no event will Osborne/McGraw-Hill's liability for any damages to you or any other person ever exceed the lower of the suggested list price or actual price paid for the license to use the software, regardless of any form of the claim.

OSBORNE/McGRAW-HILL SPECIFICALLY DISCLAIMS ALL OTHER WARRANTIES, EXPRESS OR IMPLIED, INCLUDING BUT NOT LIMITED TO, ANY IMPLIED WARRANTY OF MERCHANTABILITY OR FITNESS FOR A PARTICULAR PURPOSE. Specifically, Osborne/McGraw-Hill makes no representation or warranty that the software is fit for any particular purpose, and any implied warranty of merchantability is limited to the sixty-day duration of the Limited Warranty covering the physical disc only (and not the software), and is otherwise expressly and specifically disclaimed.

   This limited warranty gives you specific legal rights; you may have others which may vary from state to state. Some states do not allow the exclusion of incidental or consequential damages, or the limitation on how long an implied warranty lasts, so some of the above may not apply to you.

   This agreement constitutes the entire agreement between the parties relating to use of the Product. The terms of any purchase order shall have no effect on the terms of this Agreement. Failure of Osborne/McGraw-Hill to insist at any time on strict compliance with this Agreement shall not constitute a waiver of any rights under this Agreement. This Agreement shall be construed and governed in accordance with the laws of New York. If any provision of this Agreement is held to be contrary to law, that provision will be enforced to the maximum extent permissible, and the remaining provisions will remain in force and effect.

   NO TECHNICAL SUPPORT IS PROVIDED WITH THIS CD-ROM.